P9-BBQ-094

DATA
NETWORKS

DIMITRI BERTSEKAS

DIMITRI P. BERTSEKAS received a B.S. in Mechanical and Electrical Engineering from the National Technical University of Athens, Greece in 1965, and a Ph.D. in system science from the Massachusetts Institute of Technology in 1971. He has held faculty positions with the Engineering-Economic Systems Department, Stanford University, and the Electrical Engineering Department of the University of Illinois, Urbana. In 1979 he joined the faculty of the Massachusetts Institute of Technology where he is currently Professor of Electrical Engineering and Computer Science. He consults regularly with private industry, and has held editorial positions in several journals. He has been elected Fellow of the IEEE.

Professor Bertsekas has done research in control of stochastic systems, and in linear, nonlinear, and dynamic programming. He has written numerous papers in each of these areas. His current interests are primarily in data networks and distributed computation. He is the author of *Dynamic Programming and Stochastic Control*, Academic Press, 1976, *Constrained Optimization and Lagrange Multiplier Methods*, Academic Press, 1982, *Dynamic Programming: Deterministic and Stochastic Models*, Prentice-Hall, 1987, and the co-author of *Stochastic Optimal Control: The Discrete-Time Case*, Academic Press, 1978.

ROBERT GALLAGER

ROBERT G. GALLAGER received the S.B. degree in electrical engineering from the University of Pennsylvania, Philadelphia, PA, in 1953, and the S.M. and Sc.D. degrees in electrical engineering from the Massachusetts Institute of Technology, Cambridge, MA, in 1957 and 1960, respectively.

Following several years as a member of the Technical Staff at Bell Telephone Laboratories and service in the U.S. Army Signal Corps, he has been with the Massachusetts Institute of Technology since 1956. He is currently a Professor in the Department of Electrical Engineering and Computer Science, Co-Director of the Laboratory for Information and Decision Systems, and Co-Chairman of the Department Area I (Control, Communication, and Operations Research). He is a consultant to Codex Corporation and CNR. He is the author of the textbook, *Information Theory and Reliable Communication* (New York: Wiley, 1968). His major research interests are data communication networks, information theory, and communication theory.

Dr. Gallager was awarded the IEEE Baker Prize Paper Award in 1966 for the paper "A simple derivation of the coding theory and some applications." He has been a member of the Administrative Committee of the IEEE Group on Information Theory from 1965 to 1970 and from 1979 to the present, and was Chairman of the Group in 1971. He was elected a member of the National Academy of Engineering in 1979.

DATA
NETWORKS

Dimitri Bertsekas

Massachusetts Institute of Technology

Robert Gallager

Massachusetts Institute of Technology

PRENTICE-HALL, INC., Englewood Cliffs, New Jersey 07632

To Joanna and Marie

Editorial/production supervision by Margaret Rizzi
Cover design by Wanda Lubelska
Manufacturing buyer: Rhett Conklin

© 1987 by Prentice-Hall, Inc.
A Division of Simon & Schuster
Englewood Cliffs, New Jersey 07632

All rights reserved. No part of this book may be
reproduced, in any form or by any means,
without permission in writing from the publisher.

Printed in the United States of America

10 9 8 7 6 5 4 3 2 1

ISBN 0-13-196825-4   025

PRENTICE-HALL INTERNATIONAL (UK) LIMITED, London
PRENTICE-HALL OF AUSTRALIA PTY. LIMITED, Sydney
PRENTICE-HALL CANADA INC., Toronto
PRENTICE-HALL HISPANOAMERICANA, S.A., Mexico
PRENTICE-HALL OF INDIA PRIVATE LIMITED, New Delhi
PRENTICE-HALL OF JAPAN, INC., Tokyo
PRENTICE-HALL OF SOUTHEAST ASIA PTE. LTD., Singapore
EDITORA PRENTICE-HALL DO BRASIL, LTD., Rio de Janeiro

Contents

Chapter 2
DATA LINK CONTROL AND COMMUNICATION CHANNELS   31

Chapter 4
MULTIACCESS COMMUNICATION   **205**

Chapter 5
ROUTING IN DATA NETWORKS   297

Chapter 6
FLOW CONTROL   423

Preface

The field of data networks has evolved over the last fifteen years from a stage where networks were designed in a very ad hoc and technology-dependent manner to a stage where some broad conceptual understanding of many underlying issues now exists. The major purpose of this book is to convey that conceptual understanding to the reader.

Previous books in this field broadly separate into two major categories. The first, exemplified by Tannenbaum [Tan81] and Stallings [Sta85], are primarily descriptive in nature, focusing on current practice and selected details of the operation of various existing networks. The second, exemplified by Kleinrock [Kle76], Hayes [Hay84], and Stuck and Arthurs [StA85], deal primarily with performance analysis. This book, in contrast, is balanced between description and analysis. The descriptive material, however, is used to illustrate the underlying concepts, and the analytical material is used to provide a deeper and more precise understanding of the concepts. We feel that a continuing separation between description and analysis is unwise in a field after the underlying concepts have been developed; understanding is then best enhanced by focusing on the concepts.

The book is designed to be used at a number of levels, varying from a senior undergraduate elective, to a first year graduate course, to a more advanced graduate course, to a reference work for designers and researchers in the field. The material has been tested in a number of graduate courses at M.I.T. and in a number of short courses at varying levels. The book assumes some background in elementary probability and some background in either electrical engineering or computer science, but aside from this, the material is self-contained.

Throughout the book, major concepts and principles are first explained in a simple non-mathematical way. This is followed by careful descriptions of modelling issues and then by mathematical analysis. Finally, the insights to be gained from the analysis are explained and examples are given to clarify the more subtle issues. Figures are liberally used throughout to illustrate the ideas. For lower-level courses, the analysis can be glossed over; this allows the beginning and intermediate-level to grasp the basic ideas, while enabling the more advanced student to acquire deeper understanding and the ability to do research in the field.

Chapter 1 provides a broad introduction to the subject and also develops the layering concept. This layering allows the various issues of data networks to be developed in a largely independent fashion, thus making it possible to read the subsequent chapters in any desired depth (including omission) without seriously hindering the ability to understand other chapters.

Chapter 2 treats the two lowest layers of the above layering. The lowest, or physical, layer is concerned with transmitting a sequence of bits over a physical communication medium. We provide a brief introduction to the subject which will be helpful but not necessary in understanding the rest of the text. The next layer, data link control, deals with transmitting packets reliably over a communication link. Section 2.4, treating retransmission strategies, should probably be covered in any course, since it brings out the subtleties, in the simplest context, of understanding distributed algorithms, or protocols.

Chapter 3 develops the queueing theory used for performance analysis of multiaccess schemes (Chapter 4) and, to a lesser extent, routing algorithms (Chapter 5). Less analytical courses will probably omit most of this chapter, simply adopting the results on faith. Little's theorem and the Poisson process should be covered however, since they are simple and greatly enhance understanding of the subsequent chapters. This chapter is rich in results, often developed in a far simpler way than found in the queueing literature. This simplicity is achieved by considering only steady-state behavior and by sometimes sacrificing rigor for clarity and insight. Mathematically sophisticated readers will be able to supply the extra details for rigor by themselves, while for most readers the extra details would obscure the line of argument.

Chapter 4 develops the topic of multiaccess communication, including local area networks, satellite networks, and radio networks. Less theoretical courses will probably skip the last half of section 4.2, all of section 4.3, and most of section 4.4, getting quickly to local area networks and satellite networks in section 4.5. Conceptually, one gains a great deal of insight into the nature of distributed algorithms in this chapter.

Chapter 5 develops the subject of routing. The material is graduated in order of increasing difficulty and depth, so readers can go as far as they are comfortable. Along with routing itself, which is treated in greater depth than elsewhere in the literature, further insights are gained into distributed algorithms. There is also a treatment of topological design and a section on recovery from link failures.

Chapter 6 deals with flow control (or congestion control as it is sometimes called). The first three sections are primarily descriptive, describing first the objectives and the problems in achieving these objectives, second, some general approaches, and finally, the ways that flow control is handled in several existing networks. The last section is more advanced and analytical, treating recent work in the area.

A topic that is not treated in any depth in the book is that of higher-layer protocols, namely the various processes required in the computers and devices using the network to communicate meaningfully with each other given the capability of reliable transport of packets through the network provided by the lower layers. This topic is different in nature than the other topics covered and would have doubled the size of the book if treated in depth.

We apologize in advance for the amount of acronyms and jargon in the book. We felt it was necessary to include at least the most commonly used acronyms in the field, both to allow readers to converse with other workers in the field and also for the reference value of being able to find out what these acronyms mean.

An extensive set of problems are given at the end of each chapter except the first. They range from simple exercises to gain familiarity with the basic concepts and techniques to advanced problems extending the results in the text. Solutions of the problems are given in a manual available to instructors from Prentice-Hall.

Each chapter contains also a brief section of sources and suggestions for further reading. Again, we apologize in advance to the many authors whose contributions have not been mentioned. The literature in the data network field is vast, and we limited ourselves to references that we found most useful, or that contain material supplementing the text.

The stimulating teaching and research environment at M.I.T. has been an ideal setting for the development of this book. In particular we are indebted to the many students who have used this material in courses. Their comments have helped greatly in clarifying the topics. We are equally indebted to the many colleagues and advanced graduate students who have provided detailed critiques of the various chapters. Special thanks go to our colleague Pierre Humblet whose advice, knowledge, and deep insight have been invaluable. In addition, Erdal Arikan, David Castanon, Robert Cooper, Tony Ephremides, Eli Gafni, Marianne Gardner, Paul Green, Ellen Hahne, Bruce Hajek, Robert Kennedy, John Spinelli, and John Tsitsiklis have all been very helpful. We are also grateful to Nancy Young for typing the many revisions and to Amy Hendrikson for computer typesetting the book using the T_EX system. Our editors at Prentice-

Hall have also been very helpful and cooperative in producing the final text under a very tight schedule. Finally we wish to acknowledge the research support of DARPA under grant ONR-N00014-84-K-0357, NSF under grants ECS-8310698, and ECS-8217668, and ARO under grant DAAG 29-84-K-000.

Dimitri Bertsekas

Robert Gallager

DATA
NETWORKS

1

Introduction
and Layered Network
Architecture

1.1 HISTORICAL OVERVIEW

Primitive forms of data networks have a long history, including the smoke signals used by primitive societies, and certainly including nineteenth century telegraphy. The messages in these systems were first manually encoded into strings of essentially binary symbols, and then manually transmitted and received. Where necessary, the messages were manually relayed at intermediate points.

A major development, in the early 1950s, was the use of communication links to connect central computers to remote terminals and other peripheral devices, such as printers and remote job entry points (RJE) (see Fig. 1.1). The number of such peripheral devices expanded rapidly in the 1960s with the development of time-shared computer systems and with the increasing power of central computers. With the proliferation of remote peripheral devices, it became uneconomical to provide a separate long-distance communication link to each peripheral. Remote multiplexers or concentrators were developed to collect all the traffic from a set of peripherals in the same area and to send it on a single link to the central processor. Finally, to free the central processor from handling all this communication, special processors called *front ends* were developed to control the communication to and from all the peripherals. This led to the more complex structure shown in Fig. 1.2. The communication is automated in such systems, in contrast to telegraphy, for example, but the control of the communication is centrally exercised at the computer. While it is perfectly appropriate and widely accepted to refer to such a system as a data network, or computer communication network, it is simpler to view it as a computer

1

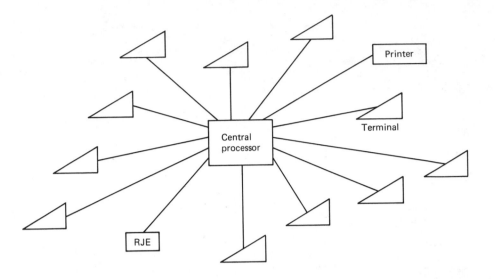

Figure 1.1   A network with one central processor and a separate communication link to each device.

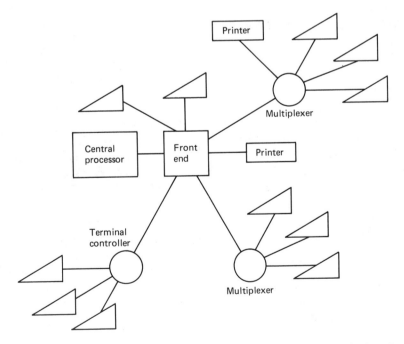

Figure 1.2   A network with one central processor but with shared communication links to devices.

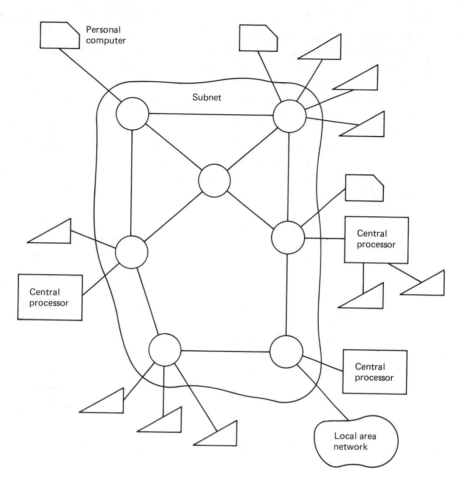

Figure 1.3   A general network with a subnet of communication links and nodes. External devices are connected to the subnet via links to the subnet nodes.

with remote peripherals. Many of the interesting problems associated with data networks, such as the distributed control of the system, the relaying of messages over multiple communication links, and the sharing of communication links between many users and processes, do not arise in these centralized systems.

The ARPANET and TYMNET, introduced around 1970, were the first large-scale, general-purpose data networks connecting geographically distributed computer systems, users, and peripherals. Figure 1.3 shows such networks. Inside the "subnet" are a set of nodes, various pairs of which are connected by communication links. Outside the subnet are the various computers, data bases, terminals, etc. that are connected via the subnet. Messages originate at these external devices, pass into the subnet, pass from node to node on the communication links, and finally pass out to the external recipient. The nodes of the subnet, usually computers in their own right, serve primarily to route the messages through the subnet. These nodes are sometimes called IMPs (interface message processors) and sometimes called switches. In some networks (e.g., DECNET), some of the subnet nodes can be implemented within the computers using the network. It is helpful, however, to view the subnet nodes as being logically distinct from the computers outside the subnet.

It is important to observe that in Figs. 1.1 and 1.2 the computer system is the center of the network, whereas in Fig. 1.3 the subnet (*i.e.*, the communication part of the network) is central. Keeping this picture of external devices around a communication subnet in mind will make it easier both to understand network layering later in this chapter and to understand the issues of distributed network control throughout the text.

Since 1970 there has been an explosive growth in the number of data networks. These networks will be discussed later, including the seminal ARPANET and TYMNET networks, but for the moment Fig. 1.3 provides a generic model for data networks.

1.1.1 Technological and Economic Background

Before data networks are examined, a brief overview will be given, first, of the technological and economic factors that have led to network development, and, second, of the applications that require networks. The major driving force in the rapid advances in computers, communication, and data networks has been solid state technology and in particular the development of Very Large Scale Integration (VLSI).

In computers, this has led to faster, less expensive processors; faster, larger, less expensive primary memory; and faster, larger, less expensive bulk storage. The result has been the lowering of the cost of computation by roughly a factor of two every two years.

On the other hand, with the development of more and more powerful microprocessor chips, there has been a shift in cost effectiveness from large time-shared computer facilities to small, but increasingly powerful, personal computers and work stations. Thus, on the one hand, an increasing number of applications can be computerized at reasonable cost, and on the other hand, the primary growth is in the number of computer systems rather than in the increasing power of a small number of very large computer systems.

The above discussion of computational costs neglects the cost of software. While the art of software design has been improving, the improvement is partly counterbalanced by the increasing cost of good software engineers. When software can be replicated, however, the cost per unit goes down inversely with the number of replicas. Thus, even though software is a major cost of a new computer system, the increasing market decreases its unit cost. Each advance in solid state technology decreases cost and increases the performance of computer systems; this leads to an increase in market, thus generating decreased unit software costs, leading, in a feedback loop, to further increases in market. Each new application, however, requires new specialized software which is initially expensive (until a market develops) and which requires a user learning curve. Thus, it is difficult to forecast the details of the growth of the computer market and similarly of the data network market.

1.1.2 Communication Technology

The cost of transmitting data on a communication link from one point to another has also been dropping, but at a much slower rate than computational costs. The cost of a data link increases with the available data rate, but the increase is much less than linear in the data rate. Thus, the cost per transmitted binary symbol decreases with the data rate of the link. It is often economically advantageous for many users to share one high-rate data link rather than having separate data links for each (this effect is seen in Fig. 1.2 with the use of multiplexers or concentrators to share communication costs).

One result of sharing high-speed (*i.e.*, high data rate) communication links is that the cost of sending data from one point to another increases less than linearly with the geographic separation of the points. This occurs because the communication path could include a short link to a shared long-distance, high-speed link and then another short link to the destination.

Estimating the cost of transmission facilities is highly specialized and complex. The cost of a communication link depends on whether one owns the facility or leases it; with leasing, the cost depends on the current competitive and regulatory situation. The details of communication cost will be ignored in what follows, but there are two overall effects of these costs that are important.

First, for wide area networks (*i.e.*, networks covering more than a metropolitan area), the cost of a network is presently dominated by transmission costs. Thus, it is desirable to use the communication links efficiently, perhaps at added computational costs. As will be shown in section 1.3, the sporadic nature of most data communication, along with the high cost of idle communication links, have led to the development of packet data networks which can increase utilization of the links.

Second, for local area networks, the cost of a network is not dominated by transmission costs. Coaxial cable and even a twisted pair of wires can achieve relatively high-speed communication at modest cost in a small geographic area. The use of such media and the desire to avoid relatively expensive switching have led to a local area network technology in which many nodes share a common high speed communication medium on a shared multiaccess basis. This type of network structure is discussed in Chapter 4.

There are two important pending developments that could radically change the importance of using transmission facilities efficiently in wide area data networks. The first is the installation of high-speed optical fibers. One finds it difficult to worry too much about the efficient use of a transmission facility which can carry a gigabit per second of data. In this case, accessing, processing, and switching at the ends of such a facility become the important problems.

The second is the development of standards for integrated service digital networks (ISDNs). Current voice telephone networks will eventually be replaced with all-digital networks, providing both telephone service and high-data-rate digital service wherever telephones now exist. When such networks will become available and at what cost are unknown, but they could significantly reduce the cost of data transmission, making efficient use of transmission facilities less important.

1.1.3 Applications of Data Networks

With the proliferation of computers referred to above, it is not difficult to imagine a growing need for data communication. A brief description of several applications requiring communication will help to understand the basic problems that arise with data networks.

First, there are many applications centered on remote accessing of data bases. Simple examples are the information services and financial services available to personal computer users. More sophisticated examples, requiring many interactions between the remote site and the data base and its associated programs, include remote, computerized, medical diagnoses and remote computer-aided education. In some of these examples, there is a cost trade-off between maintaining the data base wherever it might be required and the communication cost of remotely accessing it as required. In other examples, in which the data base is rapidly changing, there is no alternative to communication between the remote sites and the central data base.

Next, there are many applications involving the remote updating of data bases, perhaps in addition to accessing the data. Airline reservation systems, automatic teller machines, inventory control systems, automated order entry systems, and word processing with a set of geographically distributed authors provide a number of examples. In general, for applications of this type, there are many geographically separated points at which data enter the system and often many geographically separated points at which outputs are required. Whether the inputs are processed and stored at one point (as in Figs. 1.1 and 1.2) or processed and stored at many points (as in Fig. 1.3), there is a need for a network to collect the inputs and disseminate the outputs. There is also a need for considerable care to ensure that delays within the system do not give rise to faulty outputs.

Another popular application is electronic mail between the human users of a network. Such mail can be read, filed, forwarded to other individuals, perhaps with added comments, or read by the addressee at different locations. It is clear that such a service has many advantages over postal mail in terms of delivery speed and flexibility. It also has advantages over voice telephone service in terms of providing a record, reducing cost (for long-distance calls), and eliminating the need for both users to communicate at the same time. Voice service with answering machines can, in principle, have the flexibility of electronic mail, but it is more expensive for long-distance calls. Also, many people have an aversion to leaving voice messages on machines.

As a final application, one might want to use a remote computer system for some computational task. This could happen as a means of load sharing if the local computer is overutilized. It could also arise if there is no local computer, if the local computer is inoperational, or the remote computer is better suited to the given task. There are also "real time" computational tasks in which the computer system must respond to inputs within some maximum delay. If such a task is too large for any one computer, it might be shared between remote computer systems.

It will be noted that all the applications above could be satisfied by a network with centralized computer facilities as in Figs. 1.1 or 1.2. To see this, simply visualize moving all of the computers in a network, such as Fig. 1.3 to one centralized location. The computers would then be connected by short communication lines rather than long, but aside from some changes in communication delays, the overall network would be unchanged. Such a structure would both allow for shared memory between the computers and for centralized repair. Why, then, are data networks with geographically distributed computational facilities growing so quickly in importance? One major reason is the cost of communication. With distributed computers, many computational tasks can be handled locally. Even for the applications above, the communication costs can often be reduced significantly by local processing. Another reason is that organizations often acquire computers for local automation tasks, and only after this local automation takes place does the need for remote interactions arise. Finally, organizations often wish to have control of their own computer systems rather than be overly dependent on the pricing policies, software changes, and potential security violations of a computer utility shared with many organizations.

Another advantage often claimed for a network with distributed computational facilities is increased reliability. For the centralized system in Fig. 1.2 there is some truth to this claim, since the failure of a communication link could isolate a set of sites from all access to computation. For the network in Fig. 1.3, especially if there are several disjoint paths between each pair of sites, the failure of a communication link is less critical and the question of reliability becomes more complex. If all the computers in a network were centralized, then the network could be destroyed by a catastrophe at the central site. Aside from this possibility, however, a central site can be more carefully protected and repairs can be made more quickly and easily than with distributed computational sites. Other than these effects, there appears to be no reason why geographically distributed computational facilities are inherently more or less reliable than geogaphically centralized (but logically distributed) facilities. At any rate, the main focus in what follows will be on networks as in Fig. 1.3 where the communication subnet is properly viewed as the center of the entire network.

1.2 MESSAGES AND SWITCHING

1.2.1 Messages and Packets

A message in a data network corresponds roughly to the everyday English usage of the word. For example, in an airline reservation system, we would regard a request for a reservation, including date, flight number, passenger names, etc., as a message. In an electronic mail system, a message would be a single document from one user to another. If that same document is then forwarded to several other users, we would sometimes want to regard this forwarding as several new messages and sometimes as forwarding of the same message, depending on the context. In a file transfer system, a message would usually be regarded as a file. In an image transmission system (*i.e.*, pictures, figures, diagrams, etc.), we would regard a message as an image. In an application requiring interactive communication between two or more users, a message would be one unit of communication from one user to another. Thus, in an interactive transaction, user 1 might send a message to user 2, user 2 might reply with a message to 1, who might then send another message to 2, and so forth until the completion of the overall transaction.

The important characteristic of a message is that, from the standpoint of the network users, it is a single unit of communication. If a recipient receives only part of a message, it is usually worthless.

It is sometimes necessary to make a distinction between a message and the representation of the message. Both in a subnet and in a computer, a message is usually represented as a string of binary symbols, 0 or 1. For brevity, a binary symbol will be referred to as a *bit*. When a message goes from sender to recipient, there are frequently a number of transformations on the string of bits used to represent the message. Such a transformation is sometimes desirable for the sake of data compression and sometimes for the sake of facilitating the communication of the message through the network. A brief description of these two purposes follows.

The purpose of data compression is to reduce the length of the bit string representing the message. From the standpoint of information theory, a message is regarded as one of a collection of possible messages, with a probability distribution on the likelihood of different messages. Such probabilities can only be crudely estimated either a priori or adaptively. The idea, then, is to assign shorter bit strings to more probable messages and longer bit strings to less probable messages, thus reducing the expected length of the representation. For example, with text, one can represent common letters in the alphabet (or common words in the dictionary) with a small number of bits and represent unusual letters or words with more bits. As another example, in an airline reservation system, the common messages have a very tightly constrained format (date, flight number, names, etc.) and thus can be very compactly represented, with longer strings for unusual types of situations. Data compression will be discussed more in Chapter 2 in the context of compressing control overhead. Data compression will not be treated in general here, since this topic is separable from that of data networks, and is properly studied in its own right, with applications both to storage and point- to-point communication.

Transforming message representations to facilitate communication, on the other hand, is a central topic for data networks. In subsequent chapters, there are many examples in which various kinds of control overhead must be added to messages to ensure reliable communication, to route the message to the correct destination, to control congestion, etc. It will also be shown that transmitting very long messages as units in a subnet is harmful in several ways including delay, buffer management, and congestion control. Thus, messages represented by long strings of bits are usually broken into shorter bit strings called *packets*. These packets can then be transmitted through the subnet as individual entities and reassembled into messages at the destination.

The purpose of a subnet, then, is to receive packets at the nodes from sites outside the subnet, then transmit these packets over some path of communication links and other nodes, and finally deliver them to the destination sites. The subnet must somehow obtain information about where the packet is going, but the meaning of the corresponding message is of no concern within the subnet. To the subnet, a packet is simply a string of bits that must be reliably and quickly sent through the subnet.

1.2.2 Sessions

When two users of a data network wish to send messages to each other, they first set up a session, much like a call in a telephone network. Why special arrangements should be made for two users to start exchanging messages is a topic for later discussion. For now, simply consider the sessions in a network at a given time as the current set of user pairs that are occasionally sending messages to each other. Thus, for a given session between user 1 and 2, for example, there is some sequence of messages that go from 1 to 2 and some sequence of messages that go from 2 to 1. From the standpoint of the users, these messages are typically triggered by particular events. From the standpoint of the subnet, however, these message initiation times are somewhat arbitrary and unpredictable.

It is reasonable, for subnet purposes, to model the sequence of times at which messages or packets arrive for a given session as a random process. For simplicity, these arrivals will usually be modeled as occuring at random points in time, independently of each other and of the arrivals for other sessions. This type of arrival process is called a *Poisson* process and will be defined and discussed in section 3.3. This model is not entirely realistic for many types of sessions and ignores the interaction between the messages flowing in the two directions for a session. However, such simple models provide insight into the major trade-offs involved in network design, and these trade-offs are often obscured in more realistic and complex models.

To put this question of modeling message arrivals for a session in a more pragmatic way, note that networks, and particularly networks of the type in Fig. 1.3, generally handle multiple applications. Since the design and implementation of a subnet is a time-consuming process, and since applications are rapidly changing and expanding, subnets must be designed to handle a wide variety of applications, some of which are unknown and most of which are subject to change. Any complex model of message arrivals for sessions is likely to be invalid by the time the network is used. This point of view, that subnets must be designed to work independently of the fine details of applications, will be discussed further in section 1.3 on layering.

At this point, we have a conceptual view, or model, of the function of a subnet. It will provide communication for a slowly varying set of sessions; within each session, messages of some random length distribution arrive at random times according to some random process. Since we will largely ignore the interaction between the two directions of message flow for a session, we shall usually model a two-way session as two one-way sessions, one corresponding to the message flow in one direction and the other in the opposite direction. In what follows, we use the word *session* for such one-way sessions. In matters such as session initiation and end-to-end acknowledgement, distinctions are made between two-way and one-way sessions.

Although the detailed characteristics of different kinds of applications will not be examined, there are some gross characteristics of sessions that must be kept in mind. The most important are listed:

1. *Message arrival rate and variability of arrivals.* Typical arrival rates for sessions vary from one hundred arrivals per second to one arrival per many minutes. Simple models for the variability of arrivals include Poisson arrivals, deterministic arrivals (*i.e.*, a fixed time interval from each message to the next message), and uniformly distributed arrivals (*i.e.*, the time interval between successive messages is uniformly distributed between some minimum and maximum).

2. *Session holding time.* Sometimes (as with electronic mail) a session is initiated for a single message. Other sessions last for a working day or even permanently.

3. *Expected message length and length distribution.* Typical message lengths vary roughly from a few bits to 10^8 bits, with file transfer applications at the high end and interactive sessions from a terminal to a computer at the low end. Simple models for length distribution include an exponentially decaying probability density, a uniform probability between some minimum and maximum, and fixed length.

4. *Allowable delay.* The allowable expected delay varies from about 10 milliseconds for some real-time control applications to 1 second or less for interactive terminal to computer applications, to several minutes or more for some file transfer applications. In other applications, there is a maximum allowable delay (in contrast to expected delay). For example, with packetized voice, fixed-length segments of the incoming voice waveform are encoded into packets at the source. At the destination, these packets must be reconverted into

waveform segments with some fixed overall delay; any packet not received by this time is simply discarded.

5. *Reliability.* For some applications, all messages must be delivered error free. For example, in banking applications, in transmission of computer programs, or in file transfers, a single bit error in a message can have serious consequences. In other applications, such as electronic mail, all messages must be delivered, but an occasional bit error in a message can usually be visually corrected by the reader. Finally, in other applications, both occasional bit errors and occasional loss of entire packets or messages are allowable. For example, in distributed sensor systems, messages are sometimes noisy when transmitted, and occasional lost messages are soon replaced with more up-to-date messages. For packetized voice, the occasional loss (or late delivery) of a packet or an occasional bit error simply increase the noisiness of the received voice signal. It should be noted, however, that the use of data compression for packetized voice and other applications greatly increases the need for error-free communication.

6. *Message and packet ordering.* The packets within a message must either be maintained in the correct order going through the network or restored to the correct order at some point. For many applications (such as updating data bases), messages must also be delivered in the correct order, whereas for other applications, message order is unimportant. The question of where to handle reliability and message ordering (*i.e.*, at the external sites or within the subnet or both) is an important design issue. This will be discussed in section 2.8.

In keeping all these characteristics in mind, it is often helpful to focus on three types of applications which lie somewhat at the extreme points and which do not interact very well together in subnets. One is interactive terminal to computer sessions in which messages are short, message rate is low, the delay requirement is moderately stringent, and the need for reliability is high. Another is file transfer sessions in which the messages are very long, the message arrival rate is typically low, the delay requirement is very relaxed, and the need for reliability is very high. The third is packetized voice. Here the concept of a message is not very useful, but the packets are short, the packet arrival rate is high, the maximum delay requirement is stringent, and the need for reliability is rather low. A network that can handle all these applications together will probably not have too much difficulty with all the other applications of interest.

1.2.3 Circuit Switching and Store and Forward Switching

There are two general approaches, known as circuit switching and store-and-forward switching, that can be used within a subnet to transmit the traffic for the various sessions. A brief overview will be given of the circuit switching approach, followed by the reason why this approach leads to inefficient utilization of the communication channels for many types of sessions. Next, an overview of the store-and-forward

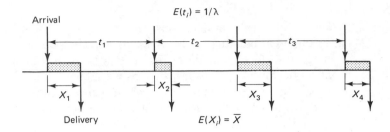

Figure 1.4   Link utilization. The expected transmission time of a message is $\overline{X}$. The expected interarrival period is $1/\lambda$. Thus, the link is used at most $\lambda\overline{X}$ of the time.

approach will be given, showing how it overcomes the above inefficiency.

For the circuit switching approach, when a session s is initiated, it is allocated a given transmission rate r_s in bits per second (this could be different in the two directions of a two-way session, but we focus on a one-way session here). A path is then created from the transmitting site through the subnet and to the destination site. Each communication link on this path then allocates a portion r_s of its total transmission capability in the given direction for that session. This allocation of transmission rates to different sessions on a communication link is usually done by time-division multiplexing (TDM) or frequency-division multiplexing (FDM), but the details of that will be explained later. What is important is that the sum of the transmission rates for all the sessions using a link cannot exceed the total transmission rate of the link. Thus, if a communication link is fully allocated to existing sessions, a new session cannot use that link. If no path can be found using links with at least r_s bits per second of unused rate, then the new session must be rejected (*i.e.*, given a busy signal). The other important point is that once the session has been successfully initiated, then it has a guaranteed transmission rate of r_s through the network. The nodes then simply take the incoming bit stream for a given session off the incoming link and switch it to the allocated portion of the outgoing link. This is not quite as simple as it appears, but the technology for doing this is old and well established.

Circuit switching is almost universally used for telephone networks but is rarely used for data networks. Given the simplicity and well-developed technology for circuit switching, we must ask why it is inappropriate for data networks. Let λ be the message arrival rate for a given session s. More precisely, $1/\lambda$ is the expected interarrival time between messages of s. Let $\overline{X}$ be the expected transmission time of a message over a given link in the path; that is, if $\overline{L}$ is the expected length of messages from s in bits, and r_s is the bit rate allocated to s, then $\overline{X} = \overline{L}/r_s$. Figure 1.4 illustrates these arrivals and transmission times.

Note from the figure that the fraction of time in which session s's portion of the link is actually transmitting messages is rather small; that portion of the link is otherwise idle. It is intuitively plausible, since $1/\lambda$ is the expected interarrival time, and $\overline{X}$ is the expected busy time between arrivals, that the ratio of $\overline{X}$ to $1/\lambda$, *i.e.*, $\lambda \overline{X}$, is the fraction of time in which the portion of the link allocated to s is busy. This argument is made precise in Chapter 3. Our conclusion then is that if $\lambda X \ll 1$, then session s's portion of the link is idle most of the time (*i.e.*, inefficiently utilized).

To complete our argument about the inefficiency of circuit switching for data networks, we must relate $\overline{X}$ to the allowable expected delay T in transmitting a message from source to destination. Since $\overline{X}$ is the expected transmission delay on a single link, it is clear that $\overline{X}$ must satisfy $\overline{X} < T$ to meet the overall delay requirement; since $\overline{X} = \overline{L}/r_s$, this means that r_s must be chosen large enough to satisfy $\overline{X} \leq T$. Thus, if $\lambda T \ll 1$ (*i.e.*, message arrivals are infrequent and required delay is small), then $\lambda \overline{X} \ll 1$ and the links are inefficiently utilized for the given session.

For many of the sessions carried by data networks, λT is on the order of 0.01 or less. This means that the portions of links allocated to those sessions are utilized at most 1% of the time. In summary, the bit rate r_s allocated to a session must be large enough to transmit messages within the required delay, and when λT is small, this forces the links to be inefficiently utilized. Since communication costs are a major factor in the cost of a network, circuit switching is an unattractive choice for data networks in which λT is small for many sessions. The argument above has ignored propagation delays, switching delays in the nodes, and queueing delays. (Queueing delay arises when a message from session s arrives while another message from s is in transmission). Since these delays must be added to the link transmission time $\overline{X}$ in meeting the delay requirement T, $\overline{X}$ must often be substantially smaller than T, making circuit switching even more inefficient. While propagation and switching delays are often negligible, queueing delay is not, as shown in Chapter 3, particularly when λT exceeds 1.

In the store-and-forward approach to subnet design, each session is initiated without making any reserved allocation of transmission rate for the session. Similarly, there is no conventional multiplexing of the communication links. Rather, one packet or message at a time is transmitted on a communication link, using the full transmission rate of the link. The link is shared between the different sessions using that link, but the sharing is done on an as needed basis (*i.e.*, demand basis) rather than a fixed allocation basis. Thus, when a packet or message arrives at a switching node on its path to the destination site, it waits in a queue for its turn to be transmitted on the next link in its path.

Store-and-forward switching has the advantage over circuit switching that each communication link is fully utilized whenever it has any traffic to send. In Chapter 3, when queueing is studied, it will be shown that using communication links on a demand basis markedly decreases the delay in the network relative to the circuit switching approach. Store-and-forward switching, however, has the disadvantage that the queueing delays in the nodes are hard to control. The packets queued at a node come from inputs at many different sites, and thus there is a need for control mechanisms to slow down those inputs when the queueing delay is excessive, or even worse, when the buffering capacity at the node is about to be exceeded. There is a feedback delay associated with any such control mechanism. First, the overloaded node must somehow send the offending inputs some control information (through the links of the network) telling them to slow down. Second, a considerable number of packets might already be in the subnet heading for the given node. This is the general topic of flow control and is discussed in Chapter 6. The reader should be aware, however, that this problem is caused by the store-and-forward approach and is largely nonexistent in the circuit switching approach.

There is a considerable taxonomy associated with store-and-forward switching. *Message switching* is store-and-forward switching in which messages are sent as unit entities rather than being segmented into packets. If message switching were to be used, there would have to be a maximum message size, which essentially would mean that the user would have to packetize messages rather than having packetization done elsewhere. *Packet switching* is store-and-forward switching when messages are broken into packets, and from the above discussion, we see that store-and-forward switching and packet switching are essentially synonymous. *Virtual circuit routing* is store-and-forward switching in which a particular path is set up when a session is initiated and maintained during the life of the session. This is like circuit switching in the sense of using a fixed path, but it is virtual in the sense that transmission capability is only used as needed. *Dynamic routing* (or *datagram routing*) is store-and-forward switching in which each packet finds its own path through the network according to the current information available at the nodes visited. Virtual circuit routing is generally used in practice, although there are many interesting intermediate positions between virtual circuit routing and dynamic routing. The general issue of routing is treated in Chapter 5.

1.3 LAYERING

Layering, or layered architecture, is a form of functional modularity that is central to data network design. The concept of functional modularity (although perhaps not the name) is as old as engineering. In what follows, the word *module* is used to refer either to a device or to a process within some computer system. What is important is that the module performs some given function. The designers of a module will be intensely aware of the internal details and operation of that module. Someone who uses that module as a component in a larger system, however, will treat the module as a "black box." That is, the user will be uninterested in the internal workings of the module, and will be concerned only with the inputs, the outputs, and, most important, the functional relation of outputs to inputs. Thus, a black box is a module viewed in terms of its input-output description. It can be used with other black boxes to construct a more complex module, which again will be viewed at higher levels as a bigger black box.

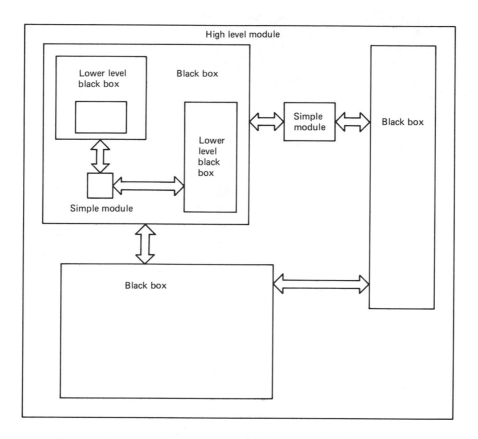

Figure 1.5   A hierarchy of nested black boxes. Each black box (except that at the lowest level) contains black boxes at a lower level, plus perhaps other modules.

This approach to design leads naturally to a hierarchy of nested modules. A complex system will be implemented as an interconnected set of high level modules, perhaps with some additional simple modules to implement the interconnections and to provide additional simple functions. At the overall system level, each of these modules is viewed as a black box, but at the next level down, each high level module is viewed as an interconnected set of next lower level modules, perhaps again with additional simple modules. (A simple module is one that is not further subdivided into lower level modules.) Each module at the next lower level is again subdivided into yet lower level modules, and so forth down to the lowest level of the hierarchical chain (see Fig. 1.5).

As an example of this hierarchical viewpoint, a computer system could be viewed as a set of processor modules, a set of memory modules, and a bus module. A processor module could, in turn, be viewed as a control unit, an arithmetic unit, an instruction fetching unit, and an input-output unit. Similarly, the arithmetic unit could be broken into adders, accumulators, etc.

In most cases, a user of a black box does not need to know the detailed response of outputs to inputs. For example, precisely when an output changes in response to an input change is not important as long as the output has changed by the time it is to be used. Thus, modules (*i.e.*, black boxes) can be specified in terms of tolerances rather than exact descriptions. This leads to standardized modules, which leads, in turn, to the possibility of using many identical, previously designed (*i.e.*, off-the-shelf) modules in the same system. In addition, such standardized modules can easily be replaced with new, functionally equivalent modules that are cheaper or more reliable.

All of these advantages of functional modularity (*i.e.*, simplicity of design; understandability; and standard, interchangeable, widely available modules) provide the motivation for a layered architecture in data networks. A layered architecture can be regarded as a hierarchy of nested modules or black boxes, as described above. Each given layer in the hierarchy regards the next lower layer as one or more black boxes with some given functional specification to be used by the given higher layer.

What is unusual about the layered architecture for data networks is that the communication links constitute the black boxes at the bottom layer of the hierarchy. The consequence of this is that the black boxes at each higher layer are in fact distributed black boxes. Thus, at each higher layer, a black box consists of a set of simple modules (typically one per switching node or external site involved) plus one or more lower layer black boxes. The simple modules associated with a black box at a given layer are called *peer processes* or *peer modules.*

In the simplest case, a black box consists of two peer processes, one at each of two nodes, and a lower layer black box communication system connecting the two peer processes. One process communicates with its peer at the other node by placing a message into the lower layer, black box communication system. This lower layer black box, as illustrated in Fig. 1.6, might in fact consist of two lower layer peer processes, one at each of the two nodes, connected by a yet lower layer, black box communication system. As a familiar example, consider two heads of state who have no common language for communication. One head of state can then send a message to the peer head of state by a local translator, who communicates in a common language to a peer translator, who then delivers the message in the language of the peer head of state.

Note that there are two quite separate aspects to the communication between a module, say at layer n, and its layer n peer at another node. The first is the protocol (or distributed algorithm) that the peer modules use in exchanging messages or bit strings so as to provide the required services to the next higher layer. The second is the specification of the precise interface between the layer n module at one node and the layer $n - 1$ module at the same node through which the above messages are actually exchanged between layer n and the lower layer black box communication system. The first aspect above is the more important (and the more interesting) for a conceptual understanding of the operation of a layered

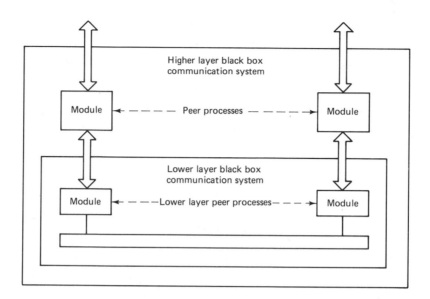

Figure 1.6   Peer processes within a black box communication system. The peer processes communicate through a lower layer, black box communication system that itself contains lower layer peer processes.

architecture, but the second is also vital in the actual design and standardization of the system. In terms of the previous example of communication between heads of state, the first aspect has to do with the negotiation between the heads of state, whereas the second has to do with each head of state insuring that the translator can actually translate the messages faithfully.

Figure 1.7 illustrates such a layered architecture. The layers are those of the reference model of open systems interconnection (OSI) proposed as an international standard for data networks by the International Standards Organization (ISO). Many existing networks, including SNA, DECNET, ARPANET, and TYM-NET, have slightly different layers than this proposed standard. However, the OSI layers have a particularly clean structure that helps in understanding the concept of layering. Some of the variations used by these other networks will be discussed later.

1.3.1 The Physical Layer

The function of the *physical layer* is to provide a virtual link for transmitting a sequence of bits between any pair of nodes (or any node and external site) joined by a physical communication channel. Such a virtual link is called a *virtual bit pipe*. To achieve this function, there is a physical interface module on each side of the communication channel whose function is to map the incoming bits from the next higher layer (*i.e.*, the data link control (DLC) layer) into signals appropriate for the

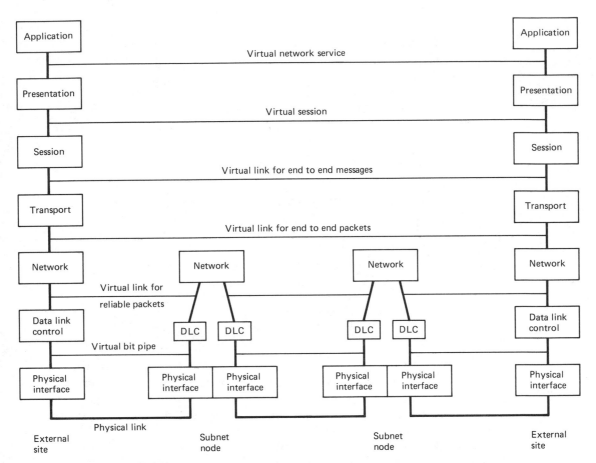

Figure 1.7   Seven-layer OSI network architecture. Each layer presents a virtual communication link with given properties to the next higher layer.

channel, and, at the receiving end, to map the signals back into bits. The physical interface module that performs these mapping functions is often called a *modem* (digital data *mo*dulator and *dem*odulator). The term modem is used broadly here to refer to any module that performs the above function, whether or not modulation is involved.

Modems and communication channels are discussed in section 2 of Chapter 2. The modem designer must be aware of the detailed characteristics of the communication channel (and different modems must be designed for different types of channels). To the higher layers, however, the black box formed by the modem-channel-modem combination appears as a bit pipe with the complexities of the physical channel hidden. Even viewed as a bit pipe, however, there are a few issues that must be discussed.

The first issue has to do with the timing of the bit sequence entering the bit pipe. There are three common situations. The first is that of a *synchronous* bit pipe where bits are transmitted and received at regular intervals, *i.e.*, 1 bit per t second interval for some t. The higher layer DLC module must supply bits at this synchronous rate whether or not it has any real data to send. The second situation is that of an *intermittent synchronous* bit pipe where the DLC module supplies bits at a synchronous rate when it has data to send and stops sending bits when there is no data to send. The third situation is that of *asynchronous characters*, usually used with personal computers and low-speed terminals. Here, keyboard characters and various control characters are mapped into fixed-length bit strings (usually 8-bit strings according to ASCII code) and the individual character bit strings are transmitted asynchronously as they are generated.

The next issue is that of the interface between the DLC module and the modem. One would think that not many problems should exist in delivering a string of bits from one module to another, especially if they are physically close. Unfortunately, there are a number of annoying details about such an interface. For example, the module on one end of the interface might be temporarily inoperable, and when both become operable, some initialization is required to start the flow of bits. Also, for synchronous operation, one side or the other must provide timing. To make matters worse, many manufacturers provide the modules on either end, so there is a need for standardizing the interface. In fact, there is a large set of such standards, so large that one applauds the effort but questions the success. Two of the better known are RS-232-C and the physical layer of X21.

The RS-232-C interface approaches the problem by providing a separate wire between the two modules for each type of control signal that might be required. These wires from the modules are joined in a standard 21-pin connector (although usually many fewer wires are required). In communication jargon, the interface is between a DCE (data communication equipment), which is the modem in this case, and a DTE (data terminal equipment), which is the DLC layer and higher layers in this case.

As an example of the interface use, suppose the DTE wants to start sending data (either on initialization or with a new data sequence in intermittant synchronous transmission). The DTE then sends a signal to the DCE on a "request-to-send" wire. The DCE replies with a signal on the "clear-to-send" wire. The DCE also sends a signal on the "DCE-ready" wire whenever it is operational and a signal in the "carrier detect" wire whenever it appears that the opposite modem and channel are operational. If the DTE receives all these sigals (which are just level voltages), then it starts to send data over the interface on the DTE to DCE data wire.

This interchange is a very simple example of a *protocol* or *distributed algorithm*. Each module performs operations based both on its own state and on the information received from the other module. Many less trivial protocols are developed in subsequent chapters. There are many other details in RS-232-C operation but no other new concepts.

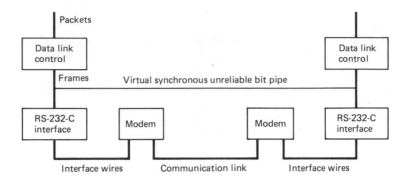

Figure 1.8   Layering with the interface between the DLC and the modem viewed as an interface over a physical medium consisting of a set of wires.

It is helpful when focusing on the interface between the DLC module and the modem to view the wires between the modules as a physical channel and to view the DLC and modem as peer processes executing the interface protocol. To avoid confusion between the DLC module's major function as a peer process with the opposite DLC module and its lower level function of interfacing with the modem, an extra module is created (see Fig. 1.8) which exercises the interface protocol with the modem.

The X21 physical layer protocol is similar in function to RS-232-C, but it uses a smaller set of wires (eight wires are used, although there is a 15-pin connector). The idea is to avoid using a separate wire for each possible signal and rather to double up on the use of wires by digital logic in the modules. The X21 physical layer is used as the physical layer for the X25 protocol, which is discussed in Chapter 2.

It should be clear from the above that there is a great conceptual advantage in removing the question of modem and modem interfaces from the higher level aspects of networks. Note that this has already been done, in essence, in previous sections in referring to the number of bits per second that could be transmitted over communication links. It should also be noted, however, that modems cannot be totally segregated from network issues. For example, is it better to have a modem that transmits R bits per second with an error rate of 10^{-6} or a modem that transmits $2R$ bits per second with an error rate of 10^{-4}? This cannot be answered without some knowledge of how errors are eliminated at higher layers of the architecture.

1.3.2 The Data Link Control (DLC) Layer

The second layer in Fig. 1.7 is the *data link control (DLC) layer*. Each point-to-point communication link (*i.e.*, the two-way virtual bit pipe provided by layer 1) has data link control modules (as peer processes) at each end of the link. The purpose of data link control is to convert the unreliable bit pipe at layer 1 into a higher level, virtual communication link for sending packets asynchronously but error free in both directions over the link. From the standpoint of the DLC layer, a packet is simply a string of bits that comes from the next higher layer.

The communication at this layer is asynchronous in two ways. First, there is a variable delay between the entrance of a packet into the DLC module at one end of the link and its exit from the other end. This variability is due both to the need to correct the errors that occur at the physical layer and to the variable length of the packets. Second, the time between subsequent entries of packets into the DLC module at one end of the link is also variable. This latter variability is caused both because higher layers might have no packets to send at a given time and also because the DLC is unable to accept new packets when too many old packets are being retransmitted due to transmission errors.

Data link control will be discussed in detail in Chapter 2. In essence, the sending DLC module places some overhead control bits at the beginning and end of each packet, resulting in a longer string of bits called a *frame*. Some of these control bits determine if errors occur in the transmitted frames, some request retransmissions when errors occur, and some delineate the beginning and ending of frames. The algorithms (or protocols) for accomplishing these tasks are distributed between the peer DLC modules at the two ends of each link and are somewhat complex because the control bits themselves are subject to transmission errors. Typically, the DLC layer ensures that packets leave the receiving DLC in the same order in which they enter the transmitting DLC, but not all data link control strategies ensure this feature; the relative merits of ordering are discussed in Chapter 2.

Our previous description of the physical layer and DLC was based on point-to-point communication links for which the received waveform at one end of the link is a noisy replica of the waveform transmitted at the other end. In some networks, some or all of the communication takes place over multiaccess links. For these links, the waveform received at one node is the sum of waveforms resulting from a multiplicity of transmitting nodes, and the waveform transmitted from one node might be heard at a multiplicity of nodes. This situation arises in satellite communication, radio communication, and communication over cables, optical fibers, and telephone lines with multiple taps. Multiaccess communication will be treated in Chapter 4.

The appropriate layers for multiaccess communication are somewhat different from those in networks of point-to-point links. There is still the need for a DLC layer to provide a virtual error-free packet link to higher layers, and there is still the need for a physical layer to provide a bit pipe. However, there is also a need for an intermediate layer to manage the multiaccess link so that frames can be sent by each node without constant interference from the other nodes. This is called *media access control* (MAC). It is usually considered as a sublayer of layer 2 with the conventional DLC considered as another sublayer. Figure 1.9 illustrates the relationship between these layers.

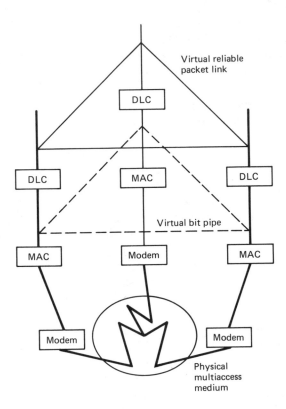

Figure 1.9   Layering for a multiaccess channel. The physical medium is accessed by all three users, each of whom hears the transmitted signals of the others. The DLC sublayer sees virtual point-to-point bit pipes below it. The MAC sublayer sees a multiaccess bit pipe, and the modems access the actual channel.

1.3.3 THE NETWORK LAYER

The third layer in Fig. 1.7 is the network layer. There is one network layer process associated with each node and with each external site of the network. All these processes are peer processes and all work together in implementing routing and flow control for the network. When a packet enters a node or site on one of the incoming communication links, that packet passes through the physical layer to the DLC layer and, if accepted by the DLC layer, it is passed up to the network layer at that node (see Fig. 1.10). Newly generated packets at external sites enter the network layer at that site from the transport layer. Similarly, higher level control packets enter the network layer at a site from the transport layer. Finally, as discussed later, control packets for routing and flow control functions can be generated within the network layer at a node.

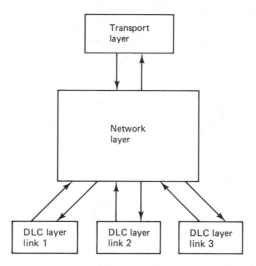

Figure 1.10   The network layer at a node or site can receive packets from a DLC layer for each incoming link and (in the case of a site) from the transport layer. It can send these packets out to the same set of modules.

The network layer process at a node performs a routing or switching function in deciding where to send all these arriving packets. Packets destined for some other node or site are sent out on the appropriate link via the DLC layer for that link whereas control packets for routing or flow control are processed directly within the module. Packets arriving at a given site are passed up to the transport layer.

The network layer process also determines when to accept packets from the higher layer and when to transmit packets on to other nodes or sites. These latter decisions exercise flow control, which controls congestion in the network. Because of these delays and also because of delays by the DLC layer in accepting packets, the network layer must provide buffering for packets.

The peer processes at the network layer must interchange information to accomplish routing and flow control. Part of this interchange occurs through control bits added to the data packets traveling between nodes. These control bits identify the packet's source and destination and help control the flow of packets for the given session. The other part of this interchange occurs through packets that carry only control bits. These latter packets set up new sessions and exchange the information required to set up routing tables.

The network layer is conceptually the most complex of the layered hierarchy since *all* the peer processes at this layer must work together. For the lower layers (except for the MAC sublayer for multiaccess), the peer processes are paired, one at each side of a communication link. For the higher layers, the peer processes are again paired, one at each end of a session. Thus, the network layer (and the MAC sublayer) are the only layers in which the overall algorithms are distributed between many geographically separated processes.

Acquiring the ability to design and understand such distributed algorithms is one of the basic objectives of this text. Chapter 2 covers the simpler forms of distributed algorithms involving just two peer processes at opposite ends of a link. Chapter 4 treats the MAC sublayer involving many peer processes, and Chapters 5 and 6, in the context of routing and flow control, deal with the distributed algorithms of the network layer involving many peer processes.

When the network layer and lower layers at all nodes and sites are regarded as one black box, a packet entering the network layer from the next higher layer at a site reappears at some later time at the interface between the network layer and the next higher layer at the destination site. Thus, the network layer appears as a virtual, packet carrying, end-to-end link from origin site to destination site. Depending on the design of the network layer, this virtual link might be reliable, delivering every packet, once and only once, without errors, or might be unreliable, failing to deliver some packets and delivering some packets with errors. The higher layers then have to recover from these errors. The network layer might also deliver all packets for each session in order or might deliver them out of order. The relative merits of these alternatives are discussed further in section 2.8.

1.3.4 The Transport Layer

The fourth layer in Fig. 1.7 is the *transport layer*. Here, for each virtual end-to-end link provided by the network layer, there is a pair of peer processes, one at each end of the virtual network layer link. The transport layer has a number of functions, not all of which are necessarily required in any given network.

First, the transport layer breaks messages into packets at the transmitting end and reassembles packets into messages at the receiving end. This reassembly function is relatively simple if the transport layer process has plenty of buffer space available, but can be quite tricky if there is limited buffer space that must be shared between many virtual end-to-end links. If the network layer delivers packets out of order, this reassembly problem becomes even more difficult.

Second, the transport layer might multiplex several low rate sessions, all from the same source site and all going to the same destination site, into one session at the network layer. Since the subnet sees only one session in this case, the number of sessions in the subnet and the attendant overhead is reduced. Somewhat similarly, the transport layer might split one high rate session into multiple sessions at the network layer. This might be desirable if the flow control at the network layer is incapable of providing higher rate service to some sessions than others, but clearly a better solution to this problem would be for the network layer to adjust the rate to the session requirement.

Third, if the network layer is unreliable, the transport layer might be required to achieve reliable end-to-end communication for those sessions requiring it. Even when the network layer is designed to provide reliable communication, the transport layer has to be involved when one or the other end site fails or when the network becomes disconnected due to communication link failures. These failure issues are discussed further in section 2.8 and in Chapters 5 and 6.

Finally, data networks are often joined, with communication paths passing through more than one subnet (this is known as *internetworking*). Typically, networks are connected by special nodes called *gateways*. These networks often have incompatible network layers, and thus a transport layer is required at the gateway to accept packets from the network layer of one network and convert them into a form suitable for the other network. If the networks have different maximum packet sizes, the transport layer must sometimes break larger packets into two or more smaller packets.

A particularly important example of interworking is that in which a number of local area networks (discussed in Chapter 4) are connected through a wide-area network. Since communication is relatively inexpensive in local area networks and since very small delays can be easily achieved, the design of the lowest three layers in a local area network is usually very different from what is appropriate in a wide-area network. Thus, it is not surprising that the network layers are incompatible.

1.3.5 The Session Layer

The session layer is the next layer above the transport layer in the OSI hierarchy of Fig. 1.7. One function of the session layer is akin to the directory assistance service in the telephone network. That is, if a user wants an available service in the network but doesn't know where to access that service, this layer provides the transport layer with the information needed to establish the session. For example, this layer would be an appropriate place to achieve load sharing between many processors that are sharing computational tasks within a network.

The session layer also deals with *access rights* in setting up sessions. For example, if a corporation uses a public network to exchange records between branch offices, then those records should not be accessible to unauthorized users. Similarly, when a user accesses a service, the session layer helps deal with the question of who pays for the service.

In essence, the session layer handles the interactions between the two end points in setting up a session, whereas the network layer handles the subnet aspects of setting up a session. The way that session initiation is divided between session layer, transport layer, and network layer varies from network to network, and many networks do not have these three layers as separate entities.

1.3.6 The Presentation Layer

The major functions of the *presentation layer* are data encryption, data compression, and code conversion. The need for encryption in military organizations is obvious, but in addition, corporations and individual users often must send messages that should only be read by the intended recipient. Although data networks should be designed to prevent messages from getting to the wrong recipients, one must expect occasional malfunctions both at the external sites and within the subnet; this leads to the need for encryption of critical messages.

The desirability of data compression in reducing the number of bits to be communicated has already been mentioned. This function could be performed at any of the layers, but there is some advantage in compressing the data for each session separately, in the sense that different sessions have different types of redundancy in their messages. In particular, data compression must be done (if at all) before encryption, since encrypted data will not have any easily detectable redundancy.

Finally, code conversion is sometimes necessary because of incompatible terminals, printers, graphics terminals, file systems, etc. For example, some terminals use the ASCII code to represent characters as 8-bit bytes, whereas other terminals use the EBCDIC code. Messages using one code must be converted to the other code to be readable by a terminal using the other code.

1.3.7 The Application Layer

The *application layer* is simply what is left over after the other layers have performed their functions. Each application requires its own software (*i.e.*, peer processes) to perform the desired application. The lower layers perform those parts of the overall task that are required for many different applications, while the application layer does that part of the task specific to the particular application.

At this point, the merits of a layered approach should be clear, but one may wonder whether the layers should have the exact division discussed here (particularly for the higher layers) and whether seven layers is slightly excessive. On the one hand, there is a strong desire for standardization of the interfaces and functions provided by each layer, even if the standard is slightly inappropriate. This desire is particularly strong for international networks and particularly strong among smaller equipment manufacturers who must design equipment to operate correctly with other manufacturers' equipment. On the other hand, standardization is an impediment to innovation, and this impediment is particularly important in a new field, such as data networks, that is not yet well understood.

One particular difficulty with the seven layers is that each message must pass through seven processes before even entering the subnet, and all of this might generate considerable delay. This text neither argues for this particular set of layers nor proposes another set. Rather, the objective is to create an increased level of understanding of the functions that must be accomplished, with the hope that this will contribute to standardization. The existing networks examined in subsequent chapters do not, in fact, have layers that quite correspond to the OSI layers.

1.4 A SIMPLE DISTRIBUTED ALGORITHM PROBLEM

All of the layers discussed in the last section have much in common. All contain peer processes, one at each of two or more geographically separated points, and the peer processes communicate via the communication facility provided by the next lower layer. The peer processes in a given layer have a common objective (*i.e.*, task or function) to be performed jointly, and that objective is achieved by some combination of processing and interchanging information. The algorithm to achieve the objective is a *distributed algorithm* or a *protocol*. The distributed algorithm is broken down into a set of *local algorithms*, one of which is performed by each peer process. The local algorithm performed by one process in a set of peers consists of carrying out various operations on the available data, and at various points in the algorithm, either sending data to one or more other peer processes or reading (or waiting for) data sent by another peer process.

In the simplest distributed algorithm, the order in which operations are carried out by the various local algorithms is completely determined. For example, one local algorithm might perform several operations and then reliably send some data to the other local algorithm, which then carries out some operations and returns some data. Only one local algorithm operates at a time and the distributed algorithm is similar to a centralized algorithm that performs all operations sequentially at one location.

In more complex cases, several local algorithms might operate concurrently, but each still waits at predetermined points in the local algorithm for predetermined messages from specific other local algorithms. In this case, the overall distributed algorithm still operates in a deterministic fashion (given the input data to the peer processes), but the lock step ordering of operations between different local algorithms is removed.

In the most complex case (which is of most interest), the order in which a local algorithm performs its operations depends on the order in which data arrives (either from the next higher layer or from a peer process). Also, if the underlying communication facility is unreliable, data sent by a peer process might never arrive or might arrive with errors.

Most people are very familiar with the above situation, since people must often perform tasks requiring interacting with others, often with unreliable communication. In these situations, however, people deal with problems as they arise rather than thinking through all possible eventualities ahead of time, as must be done with a distributed algorithm.

To gain some familiarity with distributed algorithms, a very simple problem is presented, involving unreliable communication, which in fact has no solution. Analogous situations arise frequently in the study of data networks, so it is well to understand such a problem in its simplest context.

There are three armies, two colored magenta and one lavender. The lavender army separates the two magenta armies, and if the magenta armies can attack simultaneously, they win, but if they attack separately, the lavender army wins. The only communication between the magenta armies is by sending messengers through the lavender army lines, but there is a possibility that any such messenger will be captured, causing the message to go undelivered (see Fig. 1.11). The magenta armies would like to synchronize their attack at some given time, but each

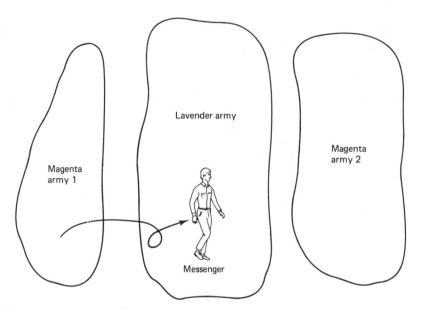

Figure 1.11   A messenger carries a message through enemy lines from
magenta army 1 to magenta army 2. If the messenger is caught, the message
is undelivered. Magenta army 1 is unaware of capture and magenta army 2 is
unaware of existence of message.

is unwilling to attack unless assured with certainty that the other will also attack.
Thus, the first army might send a message saying, "Let's attack on Saturday at
noon; please acknowledge if you agree."

The second army, hearing such a message, might send a return message saying,
"We agree; send an acknowledgement if you receive our message." It is not hard to
see that this strategy leads to an infinite sequence of messages, with the last army
to send a message being unwilling to attack until obtaining a commitment from the
other side.

What is more surprising is that no strategy exists for allowing the two armies
to synchronize. To see this, assume that each army is initially in state 0 and stays
in this state if it receives no messages. If an army commits itself to attack, it goes
to state 1, but it will not go to state 1 unless it is certain that the other army will
go to state 1. We also assume that an army can change state only at the time that
it receives a message (this assumption in essence prevents side information other
than messages from synchronizing the armies). Now consider any ordering in which
the two armies receive messages. The first army to receive a message cannot go to
state 1, since it has no assurance that any message will be received by the other
army. The second army to receive a message also cannot go to state 1 since it
is not assured that the other side will receive subsequent messages, and even if it
knows that the other side received a first message, it knows that the other side is

not currently in state 1. Proceeding in this way (or more formally by induction), neither army can ever go to state 1.

What is surprising about this argument is the difficulty in convincing oneself that it is correct. The difficulty does not lie with the induction argument, but rather with the question of whether the model fairly represents the situation described. It appears that the problem is that we are not used to dealing with distributed questions in a precise way; classical engineering problems do not deal with situations in which distributed decisions based on distributed information must be made.

If the conditions above are relaxed somewhat so as to only require a high probability of simultaneous attack, then the problem can be solved. The first army simply decides to attack at a certain time and sends many messengers simultaneously to the other side. The first army is then assured with high probability that the second army will get the message, and the second army is assured that the first army will attack.

Fortunately, most of the problems of communication between peer processes that are experienced in data networks do not require this simultaneous agreement. Typically, what is required is for one process to enter a given state with the assurance that the peer process will *eventually* enter a corresponding state. The first process might be required to wait for a confirmation of this eventuality, but the deadlock situation of the three-army problem, in which neither process can act until after the other has acted, is avoided.

1.5 NOTES AND SUGGESTED READING

The introductory textbooks by Tanenbaum [Tan81] and Stallings [Sta85] provide alternative treatments of the material in this chapter. Tanenbaum's text, although slightly dated, is highly readable and contains several chapters on the higher levels of the OSI architecture. Stalling's text contains a wealth of practical detail on current network practice. Some perspectives on the historical evolution of data networks is given in [Gre84].

New developments in technology are critically important both in network design and use. There are frequent articles in the IEEE Spectrum, IEEE Communications Magazine, and IEEE Computer that monitor these new developments.

A good reference on layered architecture is [Gre82], and some interesting commentary on future standardization of layers is given in [Gre86].

2

Data Link Control
and Communication
Channels

2.1 OVERVIEW

This chapter explores the lowest two layers of the architecture described in Fig. 1.7, *i.e.*, the physical layer and data link control layer. The physical layer refers to the actual communication channels used by the network plus whatever interface modules are required at the ends of the channels to transmit and receive digital data (see Fig. 2.1). We refer to these modules as modems (digital data *mo*dulator and *dem*odulator), although in many cases no modulation or demodulation is required. In sending data, the modem converts the incoming binary data into a signal suitable for the channel. In receiving, the modem converts the received signal back into binary data.

Section 2.2 briefly introduces communication channels and the way in which modems accomplish their functions for a given channel. The reason for the brevity is not that the subject lacks importance or inherent interest, but that a thorough understanding requires a background in linear system theory, random processes, and modern communication theory. The section will provide an overview to those lacking this background, and will provide a review and perspective to those with more background. To an extent, one can ignore the physical layer, simply recognizing that it provides a virtual bit pipe for use by the data link control (DLC) layer.

There are several different types of virtual bit pipes that might be implemented by the physical layer. One is the *synchronous* bit pipe, where the sending

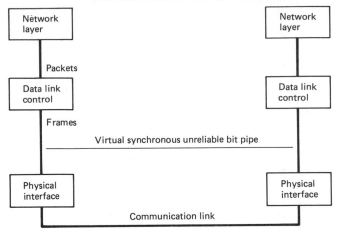

Figure 2.1   Data link control layer with interfaces to adjacent layers.

side of the DLC module supplies bits to the sending side of the modem at a synchronous rate, *i.e.*, one bit each T seconds for some fixed T. If the DLC module temporarily has no data to send, it must continue to send dummy bits, called *idle fill*, until it again has data. The receiving modem recovers these bits synchronously (with delay and occasional errors) and releases the bits, including idle fill, to the corresponding DLC module.

The *intermittent synchronous* bit pipe is another form of bit pipe in which the sending DLC module supplies bits synchronously to the modem when it has data to send, but supplies nothing when it has no data. The sending modem sends no signal during these idle intervals, and the receiving modem detects the idle intervals and releases nothing to the receiving DLC module. This somewhat complicates the receiving modem, since it must distinguish between 0, 1, and idle in each time interval, and it must also regain synchronization at the end of an idle period. In Chapter 4, it will be seen that the capability to transmit nothing is very important for multiaccess channels.

A final form of virtual bit pipe is the *asynchronous character* pipe, where the bits within a character are sent at a fixed rate, but successive characters can be separated by variable delays, subject to a given minimum. As will be seen in the next section, this is only used when high data rates are not an important consideration.

Sections 2.3 to 2.6 treat the DLC layer, which is the primary focus of this chapter. For each point-to-point link, there are two DLC peer modules, one module at each end of the link. For traffic in a given direction, the sending DLC module receives packets from the network layer module at that node. The peer DLC modules employ a distributed algorithm, or protocol, to transfer these packets to the receiving DLC and thence to the network layer module at that node. In most cases, the objective is to deliver the packets in the order of arrival, with no repetitions and with no errors. In accomplishing this task, the DLC modules make use of the virtual bit pipe (with errors) provided by the physical layer.

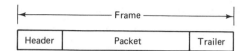

Figure 2.2   Frame Structure. A packet from the network layer is extended in the DLC layer with control bits in front and in back of the packet.

The major problem in accomplishing the above objective is that of correcting the bit errors that occur on the virtual bit pipe. This objective is generally accomplished by a technique called ARQ (*automatic repeat request*). In this technique, errors are first detected at the receiving DLC module and then repetitions are requested from the transmitting DLC module. Both the detection of errors and the requests for retransmission require a certain amount of control overhead to be communicated on the bit pipe. This overhead is provided by adding a given number of bits (called a *header*) to the front of each packet and adding an additional number of bits (called a *trailer*) to the rear (see Fig. 2.2). A packet, extended by this header and trailer, is called a *frame*. From the standpoint of the DLC, a packet is simply a string of bits provided as a unit by the network layer; examples arise later where single "packets" in this sense from the network layer contain pieces of information from many different sessions, but this makes no difference to the DLC layer.

Section 2.3 treats the problem of error detection and shows how a set of redundant bits can be used as part of the trailer for error detection. Section 2.4 then deals with retransmission requests. This is not as easy as it appears, first because the requests must be imbedded into the data traveling in the opposite direction, and second because the opposite direction is also subject to errors. This provides our first exposure to a real distributed algorithm, which is of particular conceptual interest since it must operate in the presence of errors.

Section 2.5 then discusses framing. The issue here is for the receiving DLC module to detect the beginning and end of each successive frame. For a synchronous bit pipe, the bits within a frame must contain the information to distinguish the end of the frame; also the idle fill between frames must be uniquely recognizable. This problem becomes even more interesting in the presence of errors.

A widely accepted standard of data link control is the HDLC protocol. This is discussed in section 2.6. This section also discusses some additional functions that must be handled by the DLC layer, such as initialization and termination of links.

Section 2.7 treats the topic of addressing. Each packet within a network must contain information indicating its destination, and there are many ways of representing that information. This is really a network layer isssue, but the representation of addresses is closely related to the representation of frame lengths.

Finally, section 2.8 provides a brief discussion of error recovery both at the network and transport layer. There are situations (especially where very small delay is required) in which it is undesirable to use ARQ at the DLC layer. There is also the possibility (although somewhat remote) of errors occurring within the nodes of a subnet; the use of ARQ on the links will not correct these errors. Finally, there is the possibility of links or nodes failing altogether, in which case packets might become lost. In all these cases, the network layer or transport layer may take responsibility for error recovery, and the advantages and disadvantages of each are discussed.

2.2 THE PHYSICAL LAYER: CHANNELS AND MODEMS

As discussed in the last section, the virtual channel seen by the data link control (DLC) layer has the function of transporting bits or characters from the DLC module at one end of the link to the module at the other end (see Fig. 2.1). This section will survey how communication channels can be used to accomplish this function. We focus on point-to-point channels (*i.e.*, channels that connect just two nodes), and postpone consideration of multiaccess channels (*i.e.*, channels connecting more than two nodes) to Chapter 4. We also focus on communication in one direction, thus ignoring any potential interference between simultaneous transmisson in both directions.

There are two broad classes of point-to-point channels: digital channels and analog channels. From a black box point of view, a digital channel is simply a bit pipe, with a bit stream as input and as output. An analog channel, on the other hand, accepts a waveform (*i.e.*, an arbitrary function of time), as input and produces a waveform as output. Analog channels are emphasized here; digital channels are equally important in practice, but are best understood in terms of analog channels.

A module is required at the input of an analog channel to map the digital data from the DLC module into the waveform sent over the channel. Similarly, a module is required at the receiver to map the received waveform back into digital data. These modules will be referred to as modems (digital data *mo*dulator and *dem*odulator). The term modem is used broadly here, not necessarily implying any modulation but simply referring to the required mapping operations.

Let $s(t)$ denote the analog channel input as a function of time; $s(t)$ could represent a voltage or current waveform. Similarly, let $r(t)$ represent the voltage or current waveform at the output of the analog channel. The output $r(t)$ is a distorted, delayed, and attenuated version of $s(t)$, and our objective is to gain some intuitive appreciation of how to map the digital data into $s(t)$ so as to minimize the deleterious effects of this distortion. Note that a black box viewpoint of the physical channel is taken here, considering the input-output relation rather than the internal details of the analog channel. For example, if an ordinary voice telephone circuit (usually called a voice-grade circuit) is used as the analog channel, the physical path of the channel will typically pass through multiple switches, multiplexers, demultiplexers, modulators, and demodulators. For dial-up lines, this path will change on each subsequent call, although the specification of tolerances on the input-output characterization remain unchanged.

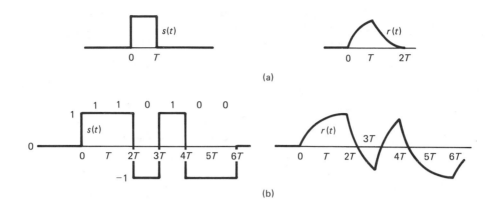

(a)

(b)

Figure 2.3   The relation of input and output waveforms for a communication channel with filtering. Part (a) shows the response $r(t)$ to an input $s(t)$ consisting of a rectangular pulse and part (b) shows the response to a sequence of pulses. Part (b) also illustrates the NRZ code in which a sequence of binary inputs (1 1 0 1 0 0) is mapped into rectangular pulses. The duration of each pulse is equal to the time between binary inputs.

2.2.1 Filtering

One of the most important distorting effects on most analog channels is linear time-invariant filtering. Filtering occurs not only from filters inserted by the channel designer but also from the inherent behavior of the propation medium. One effect of filtering is to "smooth out" the transmitted signal $s(t)$. Figure 2.3 shows two examples in which $s(t)$ is first a single rectangular pulse and then a sequence of rectangular pulses. The defining properties of linear time-invariant filters are as follows: (1) if input $s(t)$ yields output $r(t)$, then for any τ, input $s(t - \tau)$ yields output $r(t - \tau)$; (2) if $s(t)$ yields $r(t)$, then for any real number α, $\alpha s(t)$ yields $\alpha r(t)$; and (3) if $s_1(t)$ yields $r_1(t)$ and $s_2(t)$ yields $r_2(t)$, then $s_1(t) + s_2(t)$ yields $r_1(t) + r_2(t)$.

The first property above expresses the time invariance; namely, if an input is delayed by τ, then the corresponding output remains the same except for the delay of τ. The second and third properties express the linearity. That is, if an input is scaled by α, then the corresponding output remains the same except for being scaled by α. Also, the output due to the sum of two inputs is simply the sum of the corresponding outputs. As an example of these properties, the output for Fig. 2.3(b) can be calculated from the output in Fig. 2.3(a). In particular, the response to a negative-amplitude rectangular pulse is the negative of that from a positive-amplitude pulse (property 2), the output from a delayed pulse is delayed from the original output (property 1), and the output from the sum of the pulses is the sum of the outputs for the original pulses (property 3).

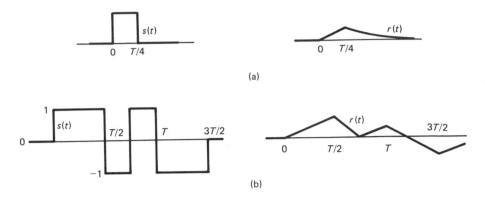

Figure 2.4   The relation of input and output waveforms for the same channel as in Fig. 2.3. Here, the binary digits enter at four times the rate of Fig. 2.3, and the rectangular pulses last one fourth as long. Note that the output $r(t)$ is more distorted and more attenuated than that in Fig. 2.3

Figure 2.3 also illustrates a simple way to map incoming bits into an analog waveform $s(t)$. The virtual channel accepts a new bit from the DLC module each T seconds; the bit value 1 is mapped into a rectangular pulse of amplitude $+1$, and the value 0 into amplitude -1. Thus, Fig. 2.3(b) represents $s(t)$ for the data sequence 110100. This mapping scheme is often referred to as a nonreturn to zero (NRZ) code. The notation NRZ arises because of an alternate scheme in which the pulses in $s(t)$ have a shorter duration than the bit time T, resulting in $s(t)$ returning to 0 level for some interval between each pulse. The merits of these schemes will become clearer later.

Next, consider changing the rate at which bits enter the virtual channel. Figure 2.4 shows the effect of increasing the rate by a factor of four (*i.e.*, the signaling interval is reduced from T to $T/4$). It can be seen that output $r(t)$ is more distorted than before. The problem is that the response to a single pulse lasts much longer than a pulse time, so that the output at a given t depends significantly on the polarity of several input pulses; this phenomenon is called *intersymbol interference*.

From a more general viewpoint, suppose that $h(t)$ is the channel output corresponding to an infinitesimally narrow pulse of unit area at time 0. We call $h(t)$ the impulse response of the channel. Think of an arbitrary input waveform $s(t)$ as a superposition of very narrow pulses as shown in Fig. 2.5. The pulse from $s(\tau)$ to $s(\tau + \delta)$ can be viewed as a small impulse of area $\delta s(\tau)$ at time τ; this gives rise to the output $\delta s(\tau)h(t - \tau)$ at time t. Adding the responses at time t from each of these input pulses and going to the limit $\delta \to 0$ shows that

$$r(t) = \int_{-\infty}^{+\infty} s(\tau)h(t - \tau)d\tau \qquad (2.1)$$

This formula is called the *convolution integral*, and $r(t)$ is referred to as the convolution of $s(t)$ and $h(t)$. Note that this formula asserts that the filtering aspects

coiling or
twisting together

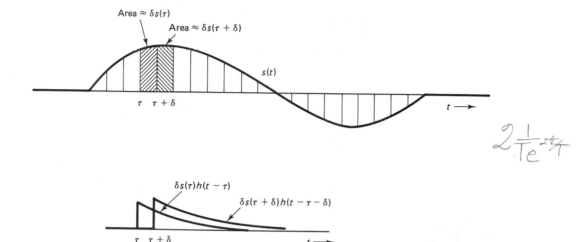

Figure 2.5   A graphical interpretation of the convolution equation. Input $s(t)$ is viewed as the superposition of narrow pulses of width δ. Each such pulse yields an output $\delta s(\tau)h(t - \tau)$. The overall output is the sum of these pulse respones.

of a channel are completely characterized by the impulse response $h(t)$; given $h(t)$, the output $r(t)$ for any input $s(t)$ can be determined. For the example in Fig. 2.3, it has been assumed that $h(t)$ is 0 for $t < 0$ and $\alpha e^{-\alpha t}$ for $t \geq 0$, where $\alpha = 2/T$. Given this, it is easy to calculate the responses in the figure.

From Eq. (2.1), note that the output at a given time t depends significantly on the input $s(\tau)$ over the interval where $h(t - \tau)$ is significantly nonzero. This means that if this interval is much larger than the signaling interval T between successive input pulses, then significant amounts of intersymbol interference will occur.

Physically, a channel cannot respond to an input before the input occurs, and therefore $h(t)$ should be 0 for $t < 0$; thus, the upper limit of integration in Eq. (2.1) could be taken as t. It is often useful, however, to employ a different time reference at the receiver than at the transmitter, thus eliminating the effect of propagation delay. In this case, $h(t)$ could be nonzero for $t < 0$, which is the reason for the infinite upper limit of integration.

2.2.2 Frequency Response

To gain more insight into the effects of filtering, it is necessary to look at the frequency domain as well as the time domain; that is, one wants to find the effect of filtering on sinusoids of different frequencies. It is convenient analytically to take a broader viewpoint here and allow the channel input $s(t)$ to be a complex function of t; that is, $s(t) = \text{Re}[s(t)] + j\text{Im}[s(t)]$, where $j = \sqrt{-1}$. The actual input to a channel is always real, of course. However, if $s(t)$ is allowed to be complex in

Eq. (2.1), then $r(t)$ will also be complex, but the output corresponding to $\text{Re}[s(t)]$ is simply $\text{Re}[r(t)]$ (assuming that $h(t)$ is real), and the output corresponding to $\text{Im}[s(t)]$ is $\text{Im}[r(t)]$. For a given frequency f, let $s(\tau)$ in Eq. (2.1) be the complex sinusoid $e^{j2\pi f\tau} = \cos(2\pi f\tau) + j\sin(2\pi f\tau)$. Integrating Eq. (2.1) (see Prob. 2.3),

$$r(t) = H(f)e^{j2\pi ft} \tag{2.2}$$

where

$$H(f) = \int_{-\infty}^{\infty} h(\tau)e^{-j2\pi f\tau}d\tau \tag{2.3}$$

Thus, the response to a complex sinusoid of frequency f is a complex sinusoid of the same frequency, scaled by the factor $H(f)$. $H(f)$ is a complex function of the frequency f and is called the *frequency response* of the channel. It is defined for both positive and negative f. Let $|H(f)|$ be the magnitude and $\angle H(f)$ the phase of $H(f)$ (*i.e.*, $H(f) = |H(f)|e^{j\angle H(f)}$). The response $r_1(t)$ to the real sinusoid $\cos(2\pi ft)$ is given by the real part of Eq. (2.2), or

$$r_1(t) = |H(f)|\cos[2\pi ft + \angle H(f)] \tag{2.4}$$

Thus, a real sinusoidal input at frequency f gives rise to a real sinusoidal output at the same freqency; $|H(f)|$ gives the amplitude and $\angle H(f)$ the phase of that output relative to the phase of the input.

As an example of the frequency response, if $h(t) = \alpha e^{-\alpha t}$ for $t \geq 0$, then integrating Eq. (2.3) yields

$$H(f) = \alpha/(\alpha + j2\pi f) \tag{2.5}$$

Equation (2.2) maps an arbitrary time function $h(t)$ into a frequency function $H(f)$; mathematically, $H(f)$ is the *Fourier transform* of $h(t)$. It can be shown that the time function $h(t)$ can be recovered from $H(f)$ by the *inverse Fourier transform*

$$h(t) = \int_{-\infty}^{\infty} H(f)e^{j2\pi ft}df \tag{2.6}$$

Equation (2.6) has an interesting interpretation; it says that an (essentially) arbitrary function of time $h(t)$ can be represented as a superposition of an infinite set of infinitesimal complex sinusoids, where the amount of each sinusoid per unit frequency is $H(f)$ as given by Eq. (2.3). Thus, the channel input $s(t)$ (at least over any finite interval) can also be represented as a frequency function by

$$S(f) = \int_{-\infty}^{\infty} s(t)e^{-j2\pi ft}dt \tag{2.7}$$

$$s(t) = \int_{-\infty}^{\infty} S(f)e^{j2\pi ft}df \tag{2.8}$$

The channel output $r(t)$ and its frequency function $R(f)$ are related in the same way. Finally, since Eq. (2.2) expresses the output for a unit complex sinusoid at frequency f, and since $s(t)$ is a superposition of complex sinusoids as given by Eq. (2.8), it follows from the linearity of the channel that the response to $s(t)$ is

$$r(t) = \int_{-\infty}^{\infty} H(f)S(f)e^{j2\pi ft}df \tag{2.9}$$

Since $r(t)$ is also the inverse Fourier transform of $R(f)$, the input-output relation in terms of frequency is simply

$$R(f) = H(f)S(f) \tag{2.10}$$

Thus, the convolution of $h(t)$ and $s(t)$ in the time domain corresponds to the multiplication of $H(f)$ and $S(f)$ in the frequency domain. One sees from Eq. (2.10) why the frequency domain provides insight into filtering.

If $H(f) = 1$ over some range of frequencies and $S(f)$ is nonzero only over those frequencies, then $R(f) = S(f)$, so that $r(t) = s(t)$. One is not usually so fortunate as to have $H(f) = 1$ over a desired range of frequencies, but one could filter the received signal by an additional filter of frequency response $H^{-1}(f)$ over the desired range; this additional filtering would yield a final filtered output satisfying $r(t) = s(t)$. Such filters can be closely approximated in practice subject to additional delay, i.e., satisfying $r(t) = s(t-\tau)$, for some delay τ. Such filters can even be made to adapt automatically to the actual channel response $H(f)$; filters of this type are usually implemented digitally, operating on a sampled version of the channel output, and are called *adaptive equalizers*. These filters can and often are used to overcome the effects of intersymbol interference.

The question now arises as to what frequency range should be used by the signal $s(t)$; it appears at this point that any frequency range could be used so long as $H(f)$ is nonzero. The difficulty with this argument is that the additive noise that is always present on a channel has been ignored. Noise is added to the signal at various points along the propagation path, including at the receiver. Thus, the noise is not filtered in the channel in the same way as the signal. If $|H(f)|$ is very small in some interval of frequencies, the signal is greatly attenuated at those ~weakened~ frequencies, but typically the noise is not attenuated. Thus, if the received signal is filtered at the receiver by $H^{-1}(f)$, the signal is restored to its proper level, but the noise is greatly amplified.

The conclusion from this argument (assuming that the noise is uniformly distributed over the frequency band) is that the digital data should be mapped into $s(t)$ in such a way that $|S(f)|$ is large over those frequencies where $|H(f)|$ is large and $|S(f)|$ is small (ideally zero) elsewhere. The cutoff point between large and small depends on the noise level and signal level and is not of great relevance here, particularly since the above argument is qualitative and oversimplified. Coming back to the example where $h(t) = \alpha e^{-\alpha t}$ for $t \geq 0$, the frequency response was

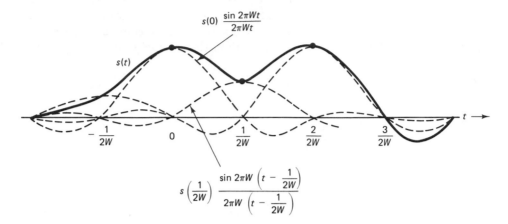

Figure 2.6   The sampling theorem, showing a function $s(t)$ that is low pass limited to frequencies at most W. The function is represented as a superposition of $\sin(x)/x$ functions. For each sample, there is one such function, centered at the sample and with a scale factor equal to the sample value.

given in Eq. (2.5) as $H(f) = \alpha/(\alpha + j2\pi f)$. It is seen that $|H(f)|$ is approximately 1 for small f and decreases as $1/f$ for large f. We shall not attempt to calculate $S(f)$ for the NRZ code of Fig. 2.3, partly because $s(t)$ and $S(f)$ depend on the particular data sequence being encoded, but the effect of changing the signaling interval T can easily be found. If T is decreased, then $s(t)$ is compressed in time, and this correspondingly expands $S(f)$ in frequency (see Prob. 2.5). The equalization at the receiver would then be required to either equalize $H(f)$ over a broader band of frequencies, thus increasing the noise, or to allow more intersymbol interference.

2.2.3 The Sampling Theorem

A more precise way of looking at the question of signaling rates comes from the sampling theorem. This theorem states that if a waveform $s(t)$ is low pass limited to frequencies at most W (*i.e.*, $S(f) = 0$, for $|f| > W$), then (assuming that $S(f)$ does not contain an impulse at $f = W$), $s(t)$ is completely determined by its values each $1/(2W)$ seconds; in particular,

$$s(t) = \sum_{i=-\infty}^{\infty} s[i/(2W)]\frac{\sin[2\pi W(t - i/(2W))]}{2\pi W[t - i/(2W)]} \qquad (2.11)$$

Also, for any choice of sample values at intervals 1/(2W), there is a low-pass waveform, given by Eq. (2.11), with those sample values. Figure 2.6 illustrates this result.

The impact of this result, for our purposes, is that incoming digital data can be mapped into sample values at a spacing of $1/(2W)$ and used to create a waveform

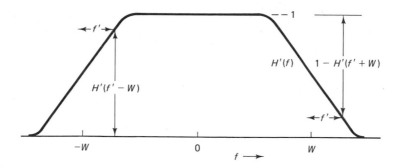

Figure 2.7   A frequency response $H'(f)$ that satisfies the Nyquist criterion for no intersymbol interference. Note that the response has odd symmetry around the point $f = W$.

of the given sample values that is limited to $|f| \leq W$. If this waveform is then passed through an ideal low-pass filter with $H(f) = 1$ for $|f| \leq W$ and $H(f) = 0$ elsewhere, then the received waveform will be identical to the transmitted waveform (in the absence of noise); thus, its samples can be used to recreate the original digital data.

The NRZ code can be viewed as mapping incoming bits into sample values of $s(t)$, but the samples are sent as rectangular pulses rather than the ideal $(\sin x)/x$ pulse shape of Eq. (2.11). In a sense, the pulse shape used at the transmitter is not critically important since the pulse shape can be viewed as arising from filtering sample impulses. If the combination of the pulse-shaping filter at the input with the channel filter and equalizer filter has the $(\sin x)/x$ shape of Eq. (2.11) (or, equivalently a combined frequency response equal to the ideal low-pass filter response), then the output samples will recreate the input samples.

The ideal low-pass filter and the $(\sin x)/x$ pulse shape suggested by the sampling theorem are nice theoretically but not very practical. What is required in practice is a more realistic filter for which the sample values at the output replicate those at the input (*i.e.*, no intersymbol interference) while the high-frequency noise is filtered out.

An elegant solution to this problem was found in a classic paper by Nyquist [Nyq28]. He showed that intersymbol interference is avoided by using a filter $H'(f)$ with odd symmetry at the band edge; *i.e.*, $H'(f+W) = 1 - H'(f-W)$ for $|f| \leq W$, and $H'(f) = 0$, for $|f| > 2W$ (see Fig. 2.7). The filter $H'(f)$ here is the composite of the pulse-shaping filter at the transmitter, the channel filter, and the equalizer filter. In practice, such a filter usually cuts off rather sharply around $f = W$ to avoid high-frequency noise, but ideal filtering is not required, thereby allowing considerable design flexibility.

It is important to recognize that the sampling theorem specifies the number of samples per second that can be utilized on a low-pass channel, but it does not specify how many bits can be mapped into one sample. For example, two bits per

Figure 2.8   An impulse response $h(t)$ for which $H(f) = 0$ for $f = 0$. Note that the area over which $h(t)$ is positive is equal to that over which it is negative.

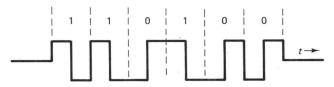

Figure 2.9   Manchester coding. A binary 1 is mapped into a positive pulse followed by a negative pulse, and a binary 0 is mapped into a negative pulse followed by positive pulse. Note the transition in the middle of each signal interval.

sample could be achieved by the mapping $11 \rightarrow 3, 10 \rightarrow 1, 00 \rightarrow -1$, and $01 \rightarrow -3$. As discussed later, it is the noise that limits the number of bits per sample.

2.2.4 Bandpass Channels

So far, only low-pass channels for which $|H(f)|$ is large for f small have been considered. Most physical channels do not fall into this category and instead have the property that $|(H(f)|$ is significantly nonzero only within some frequency band $f_1 \leq |f| \leq f_2$, where $f_1 > 0$. These channels are called bandpass channels and many of them have the property that $H(0) = 0$. A channel or waveform with $H(0) = 0$ is said to have no DC component. From Eq. (2.3), it can be seen that this implies that $\int_{-\infty}^{\infty} h(t)dt = 0$. The impulse response for these channels fluctuates around 0, as illustrated in Fig. 2.8; this phenomenon is often called ringing. This type of impulse response suggests that the NRZ code is not very promising for a bandpass channel.

To avoid the above problems, most modems for bandpass channels either directly encode digital data into signals with no DC component or else use modulation techniques. The best known direct encoding of this type is Manchester coding (see Fig. 2.9). As seen from the figure, the signals used to represent 0 and 1 each have no DC component and also have a transition (either 1 to -1 or -1 to 1) in the middle of each signaling interval. These transitions simplify the problem of timing recovery at the receiver (note that with NRZ code, timing recovery could be difficult for a long run of 0's or 1's even in the absence of filtering and noise). The price of eliminating DC components in this way is the use of a much broader band of frequencies than required. Manchester coding is widely used in practice, particularly in the Ethernet

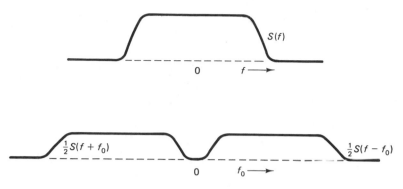

Figure 2.10   Amplitude modulation. The frequency characteristic of the waveform $s(t)$ is shifted up and down by f_0 in frequency.

system and the corresponding IEEE 802.4 standard to be described in Section 4.5 of Chapter 4. There are many other direct encodings, all of a somewhat ad hoc nature, with varying frequency characteristics and no DC component.

2.2.5 Modulation   *non return to zero code*

One of the simplest modulation techniques is amplitude modulation (AM). Here a signal waveform $s(t)$ (called a baseband signal) is generated from the digital data as before, say by the NRZ code. This is then multiplied by a sinusoidal carrier, say $\cos(2\pi f_0 t)$ to generate a modulated signal $s(t)\cos(2\pi f_0 t)$. It is shown in Prob. 2.6 that the frequency representation of this modulated signal is $[S(f - f_0) + S(f + f_0)]/2$ (see Fig. 2.10). At the receiver, the modulated signal is again multiplied by $\cos(2\pi f_0 t)$, yielding a received signal

$$
\begin{aligned}
r(t) &= s(t)\cos^2(2\pi f_0 t) \\
&= s(t)/2 + s(t)\cos(4\pi f_0 t)/2
\end{aligned}
\tag{2.12}
$$

The high-frequency component, at $2f_0$, is then filtered out at the receiver, leaving the demodulated signal $s(t)/2$, which is then converted back to digital data. In practice, the incoming bits are mapped into shorter pulses than those of NRZ and then filtered somewhat to remove high-frequency components. It is interesting to note that Manchester coding can be viewed as AM in which the NRZ code is multiplied by a square wave. Although a square wave is not a sinusoid, it can be represented as a sinusoid plus odd harmonics; the harmonics serve no useful function and are often partly filtered out by the channel.

AM is rather sensitive to the receiver knowing the correct phase of the carrier. For example, if the modulated signal $s(t)\cos(2\pi f_0 t)$ were multiplied by $\sin(2\pi f_0 t)$, then the low-frequency demodulated waveform would disappear. This suggests, however, the possibility of transmitting twice as much data by a technique known as quadrature amplitude modulation (QAM). Here, the incoming bits are mapped

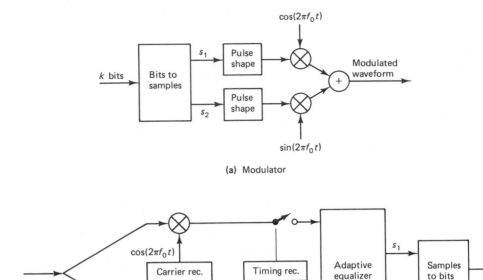

(a) Modulator

(b) Demodulator

Figure 2.11   Quadrature amplitude modulation. (a) Each sample period, k bits enter the modulator, are converted into quadrature amplitudes, are then modulated by sine and cosine functions, respectively, and are then added. (b) The reverse operations take place at the demodulator.

into two baseband signals, $s_1(t)$ and $s_2(t)$. Then $s_1(t)$ is multiplied by $\cos(2\pi f_0 t)$ and $s_2(t)$ by $\sin(2\pi f_0 t)$; the sum of these products forms the transmitted QAM signal (see Fig. 2.11). The received waveform is separately multiplied by $\cos(2\pi f_0 t)$ and $\sin(2\pi f_0 t)$ The first multiplication (after filtering out the high-frequency component), yields $s_1(t)/2$, and the second yields $s_2(t)/2$.

QAM is widely used in high-speed modems for voice-grade telephone channels. These channels have a useful bandwidth from about 500 to 2900 Hz (Hertz, *i.e.*, cycles per second), and the carrier frequency is typically about 1700 Hz. The signals $s_1(t)$ and $s_2(t)$ are usually low-pass limited to 1200 Hz, thus allowing 2400 sample inputs per second for each baseband waveform. Adaptive equalization is usually used at the receiver (either before or after demodulation) to compensate for variations in the channel frequency response.

The next question is how to map the incoming bits into the low-pass waveforms $s_1(t)$ and $s_2(t)$. The pulse shape used in the mapping is not of central importance; it will be filtered anyway, and the equalizer will compensate for its shape automatically in attempting to eliminate intersymbol interference. Thus,

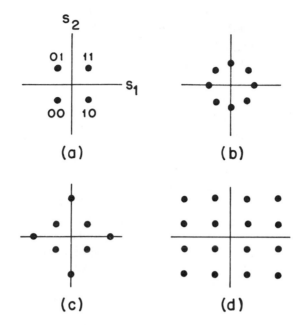

Figure 2.12   Signal constellations for QAM. Part (a) maps two binary digits into a quadrature amplitude sample. Parts (b) and (c) each map three binary digits and part (d) maps four binary digits. Parts (a) and (b) also can be regarded as phase-shift keying.

what is important is mapping the input bits into sample amplitudes of $s_1(t)$ and $s_2(t)$. One could map one bit into a sample of s_1, mapping 1 into $+1$ and 0 into -1, and similarly map a second bit into a sample of s_2. This is shown in Fig. 2.12(a), viewed as a mapping from two bits into two amplitudes.

Similarly, for any given integer k, one can map k bits into two amplitudes. Each of the 2^k combinations of k bits map into a different amplitude pair. This set of 2^k amplitude pairs in a mapping is called a signal constellation (see Fig. 2.12 for a number of examples). The first two constellations in Fig. 2.12 are also referred to as phase-shift keying (PSK), since they can be viewed as simply changing the phase of the carrier rather than changing its amplitude. For voice-grade modems, where $W = 2400$ Hz, $k = 2$ (as in Fig. 2.12(a)) yields 4800 bits per second (bps), whereas $k = 4$ (as in Fig. 2.12(d)) yields 9600 bps.

To reduce the likelihood of noise causing one constellation point to be mistaken for another, it is desirable to place the signal points as far from each other as possible subject to a constraint on signal power (*i.e.*, on the mean-squared distance from origin to constellation point, taken over all constellation points). It can be shown that the constellation in Fig. 2.12(c) is preferable in this sense to that in Fig. 2.12(b) for $k = 3$.

Modems for voice-grade circuits are also available at rates of 14,400 and 19,200 bps. These use correspondingly larger signal constellations and typically also use error-correction coding. It is reasonable to ask at this point what kind of limit is imposed on data rate by channels subject to bandwidth constraints and noise. Shannon [Sha48] has shown that the capacity (*i.e.*, the maximum reliable data rate in bps) of such a channel is given by

$$C = W \log_2[1 + S/(N_0 W)] \tag{2.13}$$

where W is the available bandwidth of the channel (essentially 2400 Hz for voice-grade telephone), S is the allowable signal power as seen by the receiver, and $N_0 W$ is the noise power within the bandwidth W seen by the receiver (*i.e.*, N_0 is the noise power per unit bandwidth, assumed uniformly distributed over W).

This is a deep and subtle result, and the machinery has not been developed here to even state it precisely, let alone to justify its validity. The description of QAM, however, at least provides some intuitive justification for the form of the result. The available sampling rate $1/T$ is equal to W by the sampling theorem (recall that W is twice the low-pass bandwidth of $s_1(t)$ and $s_2(t)$). Since k bits are transmitted per sample, Wk bps can be sent. Next note that some minimum area must be provided around each point in the signal constellation to allow for noise, and this area is proportional to $N_0 W$. Also, the total area occupied by the entire constellation is proportional to the signal power S. Thus, 2^k, the number of points in the constellation, should be proportional to $S/(N_0 W)$, making k proportional to $\log_2[S/(N_0 W)]$.

Communication engineers usually express the signal-to-noise ratio (*i.e.*, $S/(N_0 W)$) in terms of decibels (dB), where the number of dB is defined as $10 \log_{10}[S/(N_0 W)]$. Thus k, the number of bits per quadrature sample, is proportional to the signal-to-noise ratio in dB. The additional 1 in Eq. (2.13) is harder to explain; note, however, that it is required to keep the capacity positive when the signal-to-noise ratio is very small. The intuitive argument above would make it appear that the error probability depends on the spacing of points in the constellation and thus on k. The beauty of Shannon's Theorem, on the other hand, is that it asserts that with the use of error-correction coding, any rate less than C can be achieved with arbitrarily small error probability.

The capacity of voice-grade telephone channels is generally estimated to be about 25,000 bps, indicating that the data rates of voice-grade modems are remarkably close to the theoretical limit.

High-speed modems generally maintain signal timing, carrier phase, and adaptive equalization by slowly updating these quantities from the received signal. Thus, it is essential for these modems to operate synchronously; each T seconds, k bits must enter the modem, and the DLC unit must provide idle fill when there is no data to send. For low-speed modems, on the other hand, it is permissible for the physical channel to become idle in between frames or even between individual characters. For voice-grade modems, for example, data rates of 2400 bps or more are usually synchronous, whereas lower rates might be intermittent synchronous or character asynchronous. For a coaxial cable, on the other hand, the bandwidth is so large that intermittent synchronous data rates of 10 megabits per second (Mbps) or more can be used. As mentioned before, this is essential for multiaccess systems such as Ethernet.

2.2.6 Frequency- and Time-Division Multiplexing

In previous subsections, bandwidth constraints imposed by filtering on the physical channel and by noise have been discussed. Often, however, a physical channel is shared by multiple signals each constrained to a different portion of the available bandwidth; this is called frequency-division multiplexing. The most common examples of this are AM, FM, and TV broadcasting in which each station uses a different frequency band. As another common example, voice-grade channels are often frequency multiplexed together in the telephone network. In these examples, each multiplexed signal is constrained to its own allocated frequency band to avoid interference (sometimes called crosstalk) with the other signals. The modulation techniques of the previous subsection are equally applicable whether a bandwidth constraint is imposed by FDM or by channel filtering.

FDM can be viewed as a technique for splitting a big channel into many little channels. Suppose that a physical channel has a usable bandwidth of W Hz and we wish to split it into m equal FDM subchannels. Then, each subchannel has W/m Hz available, and thus W/m available quadrature samples per second for sending data (in practice, the bandwidth per subchannel must be somewhat smaller to provide guard bands between the subchannels, but that is ignored here for simplicity). In terms of Eq. (2.13), each subchannel is allotted $1/m$ of the overall available signal power and is subject to $1/m$ of the overall noise, so each subchannel has $1/m$ of the total channel capacity.

Time-division multiplexing (TDM) is an alternate technique for splitting a big channel into many little channels. Here, one modem would be used for the overall bandwidth W. Given m equal rate streams of binary data to be transmitted, the m bit streams would be multiplexed together into one bit stream. Typically, this is done by sending the data in successive frames. Each frame contains m slots, one for each bit stream to be multiplexed; a slot contains a fixed number of bits, sometimes 1, sometimes 8, and sometimes more. Typically each frame also contains extra bits to help the receiver maintain frame synchronization. For example, T1 carrier, which is in widespread telephone network use, multiplexes 24 data streams into slots of eight bits each with one extra bit per frame for synchronization. The overall data rate is 1.544 Mbps, with 64,000 bps for each of the multiplexed streams.

One way to look at FDM and TDM is that in each case one selects W quadrature samples per second (or more generally $2W$ individual samples) for transmission; in one case, the samples are distributed in frequency and in the other they are distributed in time.

2.2.7 Other Channel Impairments

The effects of filtering and noise have been discussed in preceding subsections. There are a number of other possible impairments on physical channels. Sometimes there are multiple stages of modulation and demodulation internal to the physical channel. These can cause small amounts of phase jitter and carrier frequency offset in the received waveform. Amplification of the signals, within the physical channel and in the modems, can cause non-negligible nonlinear distortion. Impulses of noise can occur due to lightning and switching effects. Repair personnel can short out or disconnect the channel for periods of time. Finally, there can be crosstalk from other frequency bands and from nearby wires.

To a certain extent, these effects can all be considered as extra noise sources. However, these noise sources have different statistical properties than the noise assumed by Shannon's Theorem (technically, that noise is known as additive white Gaussian noise). The principal difference is that the errors caused by these extra noise sources tend to occur in bursts of arbitrarily long length. As a result, one cannot, in practice, achieve the arbitrarily low error probabilities promised by Shannon's Theorem. One must also use error detection and retransmission at the DLC layer; this is treated in sections 2.3 and 2.4.

2.2.8 Digital Channels

In many cases, physical channels are designed to carry digital data directly, and the DLC unit can interface almost directly to the digital channel rather than to a modem mapping digital data into analog signals. To a certain extent, this is simply the question of whether the channel supplier or the channel user supplies the modem. This is an oversimplified view, however. A channel designed to carry digital data directly (such as the T1 carrier mentioned earlier) is often capable of achieving higher data rates at lower error probabilities than one carrying analog signals.

A major reason for this improved performance is the type of repeater used for digital channels. Repeaters are basically amplifiers inserted at various points in the propagation path to overcome attenuation. For a channel designed for analog signals, both the signal and the noise must be amplified at each repeater. Thus, the noise at the final receiver is an accumulation of noise over each stage of the path. For a digital channel, on the other hand, the digital signal can be recovered at each repeater. This means that the noise does not accumulate from stage to stage, and an error occurs only if the noise in a single stage is sufficient to cause an error. In effect, the noise is largely suppressed at each stage. Because of this noise suppression, and also because of the low cost of digital processing, it is increasingly common to use digital channels (such as the T1 carrier system) for the transmission of analog signals such as voice. Analog signals are sampled (typically at 8000 samples per second for voice) and then quantized (typically at 8 bits per sample) to provide a digital input for a digital channel. The increasing desirability of combining digital and analog data on digital channels provides some of the motivation for integrated services digital networks (ISDN).

2.2.9 Propagation Media for Physical Channels

The most common media for physical channels are twisted pair (*i.e.*, two wires twisted around each other so as to partially cancel out the effects of electromagnetic radiation from other sources), coaxial cable, optical fiber, radio, microwave, and satellite. For the first three, the propagated signal power decays exponentially with distance (*i.e.*, the attenuation in dB is linear with distance). Because of the attenuation, repeaters are used every few kilometers or so. The rate of attenuation varies with frequency, and thus as repeaters are spaced more closely, the useful frequency band increases, yielding a trade-off between data rate and the cost of repeaters. Despite this trade-off, it is helpful to have a ballpark estimate of typical data rates for channels using these media.

Twisted pair is widely used in the telephone network between subscribers and local stations and is increasingly used for data. One Mbps is a typical data rate for paths on the order of a kilometer or less. Coaxial cable is widely used for local area networks, cable TV, and high-speed point-to-point links. Typical data rates are from ten to several hundred Mbps. For optical fiber, data rates of 1000 Mbps or more are possible. Optical fiber is rapidly growing in importance, and the major problems lie in the generation, reception, amplification, and switching of such massive amounts of data.

Radio, microwave, and satellite channels use electromagnetic propagation in open space. The attenuation with distance is typically much slower than with wire channels, so repeaters can either be eliminated or spaced much further apart than for wire lines. Frequencies below 1000 MHz are usually referred to as radio frequencies, and higher frequencies are referred to as microwave.

Radio frequencies are further divided at 30 MHz. Above 30 MHz, the ionosphere is transparent to electromagnetic wave, whereas below 30 MHz, the waves can be reflected by the ionosphere. Thus, above 30 MHz, propagation is on line-of-sight paths. The antennas for such propagation are frequently placed on towers or hills to increase the length of these line-of-sight paths, but the length of a path is still somewhat limited and repeaters are often necessary. This frequency range, from 30 to 1000 MHz, is used for UHF and VHF TV broadcast, for FM broadcast, and many specialized applications. Packet radio networks, which will be discussed in section 4.6 of Chapter 4, use this frequency band. Typical data rates in this band are highly variable; the DARPA (U.S. Department of Defense Advanced Research Projects Agency) packet radio network, for example, uses 100,000 and 400,000 bps.

Below 30 MHz, long-distance propagation beyond line-of-sight is possible by reflection from the ionosphere. Ironically, the 3 to 30 MHz band is called the high-frequency (HF) band, the terminology coming from the early days of radio. This band is very noisy, heavily used (for example, by ham radio), and subject to fading. Fading can be viewed as a channel filtering phenomenon with the frequency response changing relatively rapidly in time; this is caused by time-varying multiple propagation paths from source to destination. Typical data rates in this band are 2400 bps and less.

Microwave links (above 1000 MHz) must use line-of-sight paths. The antennas (usually highly directional dishes) are generally placed on towers or hilltops, yielding typical path lengths of 10 to 200 kilometers. Longer paths than this can be achieved by the use of repeaters. These links can carry 1000 Mbps or so and are usually multiplexed between long-distance telephony, TV program distribution, and data.

Satellite links use microwave frequencies with a satellite as a repeater. They have similar data rates and uses as microwave links. One satellite repeater can receive signals from many ground stations and broadcast back in another frequency band to all those ground stations. The satellite can contain multiple antenna beams, allowing it to act as a switch for multiple microwave links. In Chapter 4, multiaccess techniques for sharing individual frequency bands between different ground stations are studied.

This section has provided a brief introduction to physical channels and their use in data transmission. A link in a subnet might use any of these physical channels, or might share such a channel on a TDM or FDM basis with many other uses. Despite the complexity of this subject (which we have barely touched), these links can be regarded simply as unreliable bit pipes by higher layers.

2.3 ERROR DETECTION

The subject of the next four sections is data link control. This section treats the detection of transmission errors, and the next section treats retransmission requests. Assume initially that the receiving data link control (DLC) module knows where frames begin and end. The problem then is to determine which of those frames contain errors. From the layering viewpoint, the packets entering the DLC are arbitrary bit strings (*i.e.*, the function of the DLC layer is to provide error-free packets to the next layer up, no matter what the packet bit strings are). Thus, at the receiving DLC, any bit string is acceptable as a packet and errors cannot be detected by analysis of the packet itself. Note that a transformation on packets of K bits into some other representation of length K cannot help; there are 2^K possible packets and all possible bit strings of length K must be used to represent all possible packets. The conclusion is that extra bits must be appended to a packet to detect errors.

2.3.1 SINGLE PARITY CHECKS

The simplest example of error detection is to append a single bit, called a *parity check*, to a string of data bits. This parity check bit has the value 1 if the number of 1's in the bit string is odd, and has the value 0 otherwise (see Fig. 2.13). In other words, the parity check bit is the sum, modulo 2, of the bit values in the

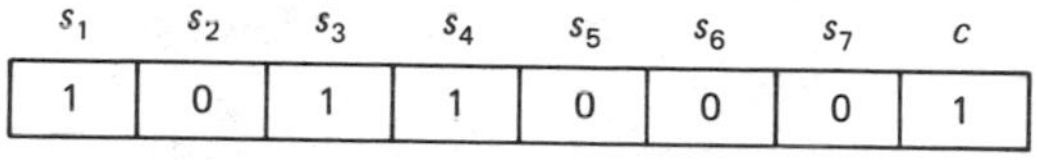

s_1	s_2	s_3	s_4	s_5	s_6	s_7	c
1	0	1	1	0	0	0	1

Figure 2.13   Single parity check. Final bit c is the modulo 2 sum of s_1 to s_k, where $k = 7$ here.

original bit string (k modulo j, for integer k and positive integer j, is the integer m, $0 \leq m < j$, such that $k - m$ is divisible by j).

In the ASCII character code, characters are mapped into strings of seven bits and then a parity check is appended as an eighth bit. One can also visualize appending a parity check to the end of a packet, but it will soon be apparent that this is not a sufficiently reliable way to detect errors.

Note that the total number of 1's in an encoded string (*i.e.*, the original bit string plus the appended parity check) is always even. If an encoded string is transmitted and a single error occurs in transmission, then, whether a 1 is changed to a 0 or a 0 to a 1, the resulting number of 1's in the string is odd and the error can be detected at the receiver. Note that the receiver cannot tell which bit is in error, nor how many errors occurred; it simply knows that errors occurred because of the odd number of 1's.

It is rather remarkable that for bit strings of any length, a single parity check enables the detection of any single error in the encoded string. Unfortunately, two errors in an encoded string always leave the number of 1's even so that the errors cannot be detected. In general, any odd number of errors are detected and any even number are undetected.

Despite the appealing simplicity of the single parity check, it is inadequate for reliable detection of errors; in many situations, it only detects errors in about half of the encoded strings where errors occur. There are two reasons for this poor behavior. The first is that many modems map several bits into a single sample of the physical channel input (see subsection 2.2.5), and an error in the reception of such a sample typically causes several bit errors. The second reason is that many kinds of noise, such as lightning and temporarily broken connections, cause long bursts of errors. For both these reasons, when one or more errors occur in an encoded string, an even number of errors is almost as likely as an odd number and a single parity check is ineffective.

2.3.2 Horizontal and Vertical Parity Checks

Another simple and intuitive approach to error detection is to arrange a string of data bits in a two-dimensional array (see Fig. 2.14) with one parity check for each row and one for each column. The parity check in the lower right corner can be viewed as a parity check on the row parity checks, or on the column parity checks, or on the data array. If an even number of errors are confined to a single row,

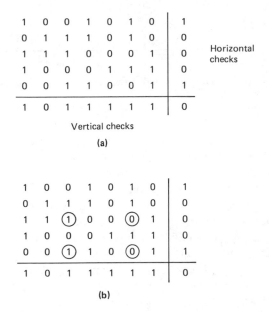

Figure 2.14   Horizontal and vertical parity checks. Each horizontal parity check checks its own row and each column parity check checks its own column. Note, in part (b), that if each circled bit is changed, all parity checks are still satisfied.

each of them can be detected by the corresponding column parity checks; similarly, errors in a single column can be detected by the row parity checks. Unfortunately, any pattern of four errors confined to two rows and two columns (*i.e.*, forming a rectangle as indicated in Fig. 2.14(b)) is undetectable.

    The most common use of this scheme is where the data is a string of ASCII encoded characters. Each encoded character can be visualized as a row in the array of Fig. 2.14; the row parity check is then simply the last bit of the encoded character. The column parity checks can be trivially computed by software or hardware. The major weakness of this scheme is that it can fail to detect rather short bursts of errors (*e.g.*, two adjacent bits in each of two adjacent rows). Since adjacent errors are quite likely in practice, the likelihood of such failures is undesirably high.

2.3.3 Parity Check Codes

The nicest feature about horizontal and vertical parity checks is that the underlying idea generalizes immediately to arbitrary parity check codes. The underlying idea is to start with a bit string (the array of data bits in Fig. 2.14) and to generate parity checks on various subsets of the bits (the rows and columns in Fig. 2.14). The transformation from the string of data bits to the string of data bits and parity checks is called a *parity check code* or *linear code* An example of a parity check code

s_1	s_2	s_3	c_1	c_2	c_3	c_4	
1	0	0	1	1	1	0	
0	1	0	0	1	1	1	$c_1 = s_1 + s_3$
0	0	1	1	1	0	1	$c_2 = s_1 + s_2 + s_3$
1	1	0	1	0	0	1	$c_3 = s_1 + s_2$
1	0	1	0	0	1	1	$c_4 = s_2 + s_3$
1	1	1	0	1	0	0	
0	0	0	0	0	0	0	

Figure 2.15   Example of a parity check code. Code words are listed on the left, and the rule for generating the parity checks is given on the right.

(other than the horizontal and vertical case) is given in Fig. 2.15. A parity check code is defined by the particular collection of subsets used to generate parity checks. Note that the word *code* refers to the transformation itself; we refer to an encoded bit string (data plus parity checks) as a *code word*.

Let K be the length of the data string for a given parity check code and let L be the number of parity checks. For the frame structure in Fig. 2.2, one can view the data string as the header and packet, and view the set of parity checks as the trailer. Note that it is important to detect errors in the control bits of the header as well as to detect errors in the packets themselves. Thus, $K + L$ is the frame length, which for the present is regarded as fixed. For a given code, each of the possible 2^K data strings of length K is mapped into a frame (*i.e.*, code word) of length $K + L$. In an error-detection system, the frame is transmitted and the receiving DLC module determines if each of the parity checks is still the modulo 2 sum of the corresponding subset of data bits. If so, the frame is regarded by the receiver as error free, and if not, the presence of errors is detected. If errors on the link convert one code word into another, then the frame is regarded by the receiver as error free, and undetectable errors are said to have occurred in the frame.

Given any particular code, one would like to be able to predict the probability of undetectable errors in a frame for a particular link. Unfortunately, this is very difficult. First, errors on links tend to be dependent and to occur in bursts; there are no good models for the length or intensity of these bursts, which vary widely among links of the same type. Second, for any reasonable code, the frequency of undetectable errors is very small and is thus both difficult to measure experimentally and dependent on rare, difficult to model events. The literature contains many calculations of the probability of undetectable errors, but these calculations are usually based on the assumption of independent errors; the results are usually orders of magnitude away from reality.

As a result of these difficulties, the effectiveness of a code for error detection is usually measured by three parameters: (1) the minimum distance of the code, (2) the burst detecting capability, and (3) the probability that a completely random string will be accepted as error free. The minimum distance of a code is defined as the smallest number of errors that can convert one code word into another. As we have seen, the minimum distance of a code using a single parity check is 2, and the minimum distance of a code with horizontal and vertical parity checks is 4.

The length of a burst of errors in a frame is the number of bits from the first error to the last, inclusive. The burst detecting capability of a code is defined as the largest integer B such that a code can detect all bursts of length B or less. The burst detecting capability of the single parity check code is 1, whereas the burst detecting capability of a code with horizontal and vertical parity checks is 1 plus the length of a row (assuming that rows are sent one after the other).

By a completely random string of length $K + L$ is meant that each such string is received with probability 2^{-K-L}. Since there are 2^K code words, the probability of an undetected error is the probability that the random string is one of the code words; this occurs with probability 2^{-L} (the possibility that the received random string happens to be the same as the transmitted frame is ignored). This is usually a good estimate of the probability of undetectable errors given a frame in which the errors greatly exceed both the minimum distance and the burst detecting capability of the code.

Parity check codes can be used for error correction rather than just for error detection. For example, with horizontal and vertical parity checks, any single error can be corrected simply by finding the row and column with odd parity. It is shown in Prob. 2.10 that a code with minimum distance d can be used to correct any combination of fewer than $d/2$ errors. Parity check codes (and convolutional codes, which are closely related but lack the frame structure) are widely used for error correction at the physical layer. The modern view of error correction is to view its use, along with signal design, as a way to create a high-rate virtual bit pipe with relatively low error rate.

Error correction is generally not used at the DLC layer, since the performance of an error correction code is heavily dependent on the physical characteristics of the channel. One needs error detection at the DLC layer, however, to detect rare residual errors from long noisy periods.

2.3.4 Cyclic Redundancy Checks

The parity check codes used for error detection in most DLCs today are cyclic redundancy check (CRC) codes. The parity check bits are called the CRC. Again, let L be the length of the CRC (*i.e.*, the number of check bits) and let K be the length of the string of data bits (*i.e.*, the header and packet of a frame). It is convenient to denote the data bits as $s_{K-1}, s_{K-2}, \ldots, s_1, s_0$, and to represent the string as a polynomial $s(D)$ with coefficients $s_{K-1}, \ldots, s_0$,

$$s(D) = s_{K-1}D^{K-1} + s_{K-2}D^{K-2} + \cdots + s_0 \qquad (2.14)$$

The powers of the indeterminate D can be thought of as keeping track of which bit is which; high-order terms are viewed as being transmitted first. The CRC is represented as another polynomial,

$$c(D) = c_{L-1}D^{L-1} + \cdots + c_1 D + c_0 \qquad (2.15)$$

The entire frame of transmitted information and CRC can then be represented as $x(D) = s(D)D^L + c(D)$, *i.e.*, as

$$x(D) = s_{K-1}D^{L+K-1} + \cdots + s_0 D^L + c_{L-1}D^{L-1} + \cdots + c_0 \qquad (2.16)$$

The CRC polynomial $c(D)$ is a function of the information polynomial $s(D)$, defined in terms of a *generator polynomial* $g(D)$; this is a polynomial of degree L with binary coefficients that specifies the particular CRC code to be used.

$$g(D) = D^L + g_{L-1}D^{L-1} + \cdots + g_1 D + 1 \qquad (2.17)$$

For a given $g(D)$, the mapping from the information polynomial to the CRC polynomial $c(D)$ is given by

$$c(D) = \text{Remainder } [s(D)D^L/g(D)] \qquad (2.18)$$

The polynomial division above is just ordinary long division of one polynomial by another, except that the coefficients are restricted to be binary and the arithmetic on coefficients is performed modulo 2. Thus, for example, $(1 + 1)$ modulo $2 = 0$ and $(0 - 1)$ modulo $2 = 1$. Note that subtraction, using modulo 2 arithmetic, is the same as addition. As an example of the operation in Eq. (2.18),

$$
\begin{array}{r}
D^2 + D \\
D^3 + D^2 + 1 \enclose{longdiv}{D^5 + D^3 } \\
\underline{D^5 + D^4 + D^2 } \\
D^4 + D^3 + D^2 \\
\underline{D^4 + D^3 + D } \\
D^2 + D = \text{Remainder}
\end{array}
$$

Since $g(D)$ is a polynomial of degree at most L, the remainder is of degree at most $L-1$. If the degree of $c(D)$ is less than $L-1$, the corresponding leading coefficients $c_{L-1}, \ldots$, in Eq. (2.18) are taken as zero.

This long division can be implemented easily in hardware by the feedback shift register circuit shown in Fig. 2.16. By comparing the circuit with the long division above, it can be seen that the successive contents of the shift register cells are just

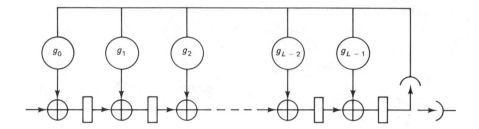

Figure 2.16   Shift register circuit for dividing polynomials and finding the remainder. Each rectangle indicates a storage cell for a single bit and the preceding circles denote modulo 2 adders. The large circles at the top indicate multiplication by the value of g_i. Initially, the register is loaded with the first L bits of $s(D)$ with s_{K-1} at the right. On each clock pulse, a new bit of $s(D)$ comes in at the left and the register reads in the corresponding modulo 2 sum of feedback plus the contents of the previous stage. After K shifts, the switch at the right moves to the horizontal position and the CRC is read out.

the coefficients of the partial remainders in the long division. In practice, CRCs are usually calculated by VLSI chips, which often perform the other functions of DLC as well.

Let $z(D)$ be the quotient resulting from dividing $s(D)D^L$ by $g(D)$. Then, $c(D)$ can be represented as

$$s(D)D^L = g(D)z(D) + c(D) \qquad (2.19)$$

Subtracting $c(D)$ (modulo 2) from both sides of this equation and recognizing that modulo 2 subtraction and addition are the same,

$$x(D) = s(D)D^L + c(D) = g(D)z(D) \qquad (2.20)$$

Thus, all code words are divisible by $g(D)$, and all polynomials divisible by $g(D)$ are code words. It has not yet been shown that the mapping from $s(D)$ to $x(D)$ corresponds to a parity check code. This is demonstrated in Prob. 2.15, but is not necessary for the subsequent development.

Now suppose that $x(D)$ is transmitted and that the received sequence is represented by a polynomial $y(D)$, where $x(D)$ and $y(D)$ differ because of the errors on the communication link. If the error sequence is represented as a polynomial $e(D)$, then $y(D) = x(D) + e(D)$, where $+$, as throughout this section, means modulo 2 addition; each error in the frame corresponds to a nonzero coefficient in $e(D)$, *i.e.*, a coefficient in which $y(D)$ and $x(D)$ differ. At the receiver, REM$[y(D)/g(D)]$ can be calculated by essentially the same circuit as that above. Since it has been shown that $x(D)$ is divisible by $g(D)$,

$$\text{REM}[y(D)/g(D)] = \text{REM}[e(D)/g(D)] \qquad (2.21)$$

If no errors occur, then $e(D) = 0$ and the remainder above will be 0. The rule followed by the receiver is to decide that the frame is error free if this remainder is 0 and to decide that there are errors otherwise. When errors actually occur (*i.e.*, $e(D) \neq 0$), the receiver fails to detect the errors only if this remainder is 0; this occurs only if $e(D)$ is itself some code word. In other words, $e(D) \neq 0$ is undetectable if and only if

$$e(D) = g(D)z(D) \tag{2.22}$$

for some nonzero polynomial $z(D)$. We now explore the conditions under which undetected errors can occur.

First, suppose that a single error occurs, say $e_i = 1$, so that $e(D) = D^i$. Since $g(D)$ has at least two nonzero terms (*i.e.*, D^L and 1), $g(D)z(D)$ must also have at least two nonzero terms for any nonzero $z(D)$ (see Prob. 2.13). Thus $g(D)z(D)$ cannot equal D^i; since this is true for all i, all single errors are detectable. By the same type of argument, since the highest order and lowest order terms in $g(D)$ (*i.e.*, D^L and 1, respectively) differ by L, the highest order and lowest order terms in $g(D)z(D)$ differ by at least L for all nonzero $z(D)$. Thus, if $e(D)$ is a code word, the burst length of the errors is at least $L + 1$ (the $+1$ arises from the definition of burst length as the number of positions from the first error to the last error *inclusive*).

Next, suppose a double error occurs, say in positions i and j so that

$$e(D) = D^i + D^j = D^j(D^{i-j} + 1), \quad i > j \tag{2.23}$$

From the argument above, D^j is not divisible by $g(D)$ or by any factor of $g(D)$; thus, $e(D)$ fails to be detected only if $D^{i-j} + 1$ is divisible by $g(D)$. For any binary polynomial $g(D)$ of degree L, there is some smallest n for which $D^n + 1$ is divisible by $g(D)$. It is known from the theory of finite fields that this smallest n can be no larger than $2^L - 1$; moreover, for all $L > 0$, there are special L degree polynomials, called *primitive polynomials*, such that this smallest n is equal to $2^L - 1$. Thus, if $g(D)$ is chosen to be such a primitive polynomial of degree L, and if the frame length is restricted to be at most $2^L - 1$, then $D^{i-j} + 1$ cannot be divisible by $g(D)$; thus, all double errors are detected.

Actually, the generator polynomial $g(D)$ usually used in practice to form a CRC is the product of a primitive polynomial of degree $L - 1$ times the polynomial $D + 1$. It is shown in Problem 2.14 that a polynomial $e(D)$ is divisible by $D + 1$ if and only if $e(D)$ contains an even number of nonzero coefficients. This ensures that all odd numbers of errors are detected, and the primitive polynomial ensures that all double errors are detected (as long as the block length is less than 2^{L-1}). Thus, any code of this form has a minimum distance of at least 4, a burst detecting capability of at least L, and a probability of failing to detect errors in completely random strings of 2^{-L}. There are two standard CRCs with $L = 16$, one called CRC-16 and the other called CRC-CCITT. Both have the form above (and thus the above properties). Their generator polynomials are

$$g(D) = D^{16} + D^{15} + D^2 + 1, \quad \text{for CRC-16}$$
$$g(D) = D^{16} + D^{12} + D^5 + 1, \quad \text{for CRC-CCITT}$$

2.4 ARQ—RETRANSMISSION STRATEGIES

The general concept of *automatic repeat request* (ARQ) is to detect frames with errors at the receiving DLC module and then to request the transmitting DLC module to repeat the information in those erroneous frames. Error detection was discussed in the last section, and the problem of requesting retransmissions is treated in this section. There are two quite different aspects of retransmission algorithms or protocols. The first is that of correctness; *i.e.*, does the protocol succeed in releasing each packet, once and only once, without errors, from the receiving DLC? The second is that of efficiency; *i.e.*, how much of the bit transmitting capability of the bit pipe is wasted by unnecessary waiting and by sending unnecessary retransmissions? First, several classes of protocols are developed and shown to be correct (in a sense to be defined more precisely later). Later, the effect that the various parameters in these classes have on efficiency is considered.

Recall from Fig. 2.2 that packets enter the DLC layer from the network layer; a header and trailer are appended to each packet in the DLC module to form a frame and the frames are transmitted on the virtual bit pipe (*i.e.*, are sent to the physical layer for transmission). When errors are detected in a frame, a new frame containing the old packet is transmitted. Thus, the first transmitted frame might contain the first packet, the next frame the second packet, the third frame a repetition of the first packet, and so forth. When a packet is repeated, the header and trailer might or might not be the same as in the earlier version.

Since framing will not be discussed until the next section, we continue to assume that the receiving DLC knows when frames start and end; thus a CRC (or any other technique) may be used for detecting errors. We also assume, somewhat unrealistically, that *all* frames with errors are detected. The reason for this is that we want to prove that ARQ works correctly except when errors are undetected. This is the best that can be hoped for, since error detection cannot work with perfect reliability and bounded delay; in particular, any code word can be changed into another code word by some string of transmission errors. This can cause erroneous data to leave the DLC or, perhaps worse, can cause some control bits to be changed.

Next, a number of assumptions are made about the bit pipes over which these frames are traveling. These assumptions are somewhat more general than before. The major reason for this generality will appear when framing is studied; in effect, these general conditions will allow us to relax the assumption that the receiving DLC has framing information.

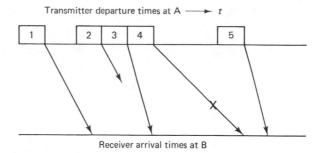

Figure 2.17   Model of frame transmissions: frame 2 is lost and never arrives; frame 4 contains errors; the frames have variable transmission delay, but those that arrive do so in the order transmitted.

Assume first that each transmitted frame is delayed by an arbitrary and variable time before arriving at the receiver, and assume that some frames might be "lost" and never arrive. Those frames that arrive, however, are assumed to arrive in the same order as transmitted, with or without errors. Figure 2.17 illustrates this behavior.

2.4.1 Stop-and-Wait ARQ

The simplest type of retransmission protocol is called *stop-and-wait*. The basic idea is to ensure that each packet has been correctly received before initiating transmission of the next packet. Thus, in transmitting packets from point A to B, the first packet is transmitted in the first frame, and then the sending DLC waits. If the frame is correctly received at B, B sends an acknowledgment (called an ack) back to A; if the frame is received with errors, B sends a negative acknowledgment (called a nak) back to A. Since errors can occur from B to A as well as from A to B, the ack or nak is protected with a CRC.

If a frame is received without errors at B, and the corresponding ack is received without errors at A, then A can start to send the next packet in a new frame. Alternatively, detected errors can occur either in the transmission of the frame or the return ack or nak, and in this case A resends the old packet in a new frame. Finally, if either the frame or the return ack or nak is lost, A must eventually time out and resend the old packet. Since frames can be arbitrarily delayed, it is possible for A to time out, to resend an old packet, and subsequently to get an ack or nak for the earlier transmission (see Fig. 2.18).

Note that because of the time outs, and also because of the potential errors in the B to A channel, it is possible that B receives the first packet correctly in the first frame and then receives it again in the second frame (see Fig. 2.18). By assumption, packets are arbitrary bit strings, and the first and second packet could be identical. Thus, if B receives the same packet twice, it cannot tell whether

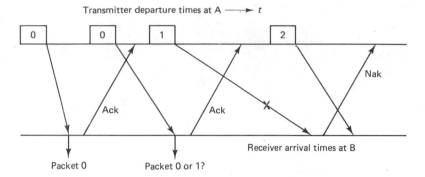

Figure 2.18   The trouble with unnumbered packets. If the transmitter at *A* times out and sends packet 0 twice, then the receiver at *B* cannot tell whether the second frame is a retransmission of packet 0 or the first transmission of packet 1.

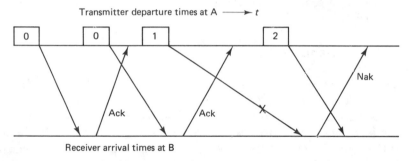

Figure 2.19   The trouble with unnumbered acks. If the transmitter at *A* times out and sends packet 0 twice, and then sends packet 1 after the first ack, node *A* cannot tell whether the second ack is for packet 0 or 1.

the second frame is repeating the first packet or sending the second packet (which happens to be the same bit string as the first packet).

The simplest solution to this problem is for the sending DLC module (at *A*) to add a sequence number to identify successive packets. Although this strategy seems simple and straightforward, it will not work as just described. The problem is that acks can get lost on the return channel, and thus when *B* gets the same packet correctly twice in a row, it has to send a new ack for the second reception (see Fig. 2.19). Node *A*, after transmitting the packet twice but receiving only one ack, could transmit the next packet in sequence, and then on receiving the second ack, could interpret that as an ack for the new packet, leading to a potential failure of the system.

To avoid this type of problem, the receiving DLC (at *B*), instead of returning ack or nak on the reverse link, returns the number of the next packet awaited. This provides all the information of the ack/nak, but avoids ambiguities about which frame is being acked. An equivalent convention would be to return the number of the packet just accepted, but this is not customary. Node B can request this next awaited packet on the receipt of each packet, at periodic intervals, or at an arbitrary selection of times. In many applications, there is another stream of data from B to A, and in this case, the requests for the next packet in one direction are usually "piggybacked" into the header of the frames in the opposite direction.

It should be evident that this stop-and-wait strategy, including the sender's sequence number (SN) on each transmitted packet and the receiver's request number (RN) in the feedback direction, works correctly (assuming no CRC failures). Node A never sends a new packet until B requests it, thus signifying acceptance of the previous packet, and B always knows which packet it is receiving if the CRC checks. The only trouble is that the numbers SN and RN can become arbitrarily large as transmission continues. The final modification to the stop-and-wait strategy, then, is to transmit SN and RN with some modulus; it turns out that a modulus of 2 is sufficient.

We now show why sending SN and RN modulo 2 works correctly for the given assumptions. Assume that the system starts initially with no frames in transit on the bit pipe, with A starting to send packet 0, and B looking for packet 0. Consider A as having two possible states, 0 and 1, corresponding to the number (modulo 2) of the packet currently being sent (or awaited from the higher layer if no packet currently exists). Thus, A starts in state 0; a transition to state 1 occurs upon receipt of an error-free request for packet 1 modulo 2. Note that A has to keep track of more information than just this state, such as the contents of the current packet and the time until time out, but the above binary state is all that is of concern here.

Node B similarly is regarded as having two possible states, 0 and 1, corresponding to the number modulo 2 of the packet currently awaited. When a packet of the desired number modulo 2 is received, the DLC at B releases that packet to the higher layer and changes state, awaiting the next packet. The combined state of A and B is then initially (0,0); when the first packet is received error free, the state of B changes to 1, yielding a combined state (0, 1). When A receives the new RN value (*i.e.*, 1), the state of A changes to 1 and the combined state becomes (1,1). Note that there is a fixed sequence for these combined states, (0,0), (0,1), (1,1), (1,0), (0,0), etc., and that A and B alternate in changing states. It is interesting that at the instant of the transition from (0,0) to (0,1), B knows the combined state, but subsequently, up until the transition later from (1,1) to (1,0), it does not know the combined state (*i.e.*, B never knows that A has received the ack information until the next packet is received). Similarly, A knows the combined state at the instant of the transition from (0,1) to (1,1) and of the transition from (1,0) to (0,0). The combined state is always unknown to either A or B, and is frequently unknown to both. The situation here is very similar to that in the three-army problem discussed in section 1.4. Here, however, information is transmitted even though the combined state information is never jointly known, whereas in the three-army problem, it is impossible to coordinate an attack because of the impossibility of obtaining this joint knowledge.

The stop-and-wait strategy is not very useful for modern data networks because of its highly inefficient use of communication links. The problem is that it should be possible to do something else while waiting for an ack. There are three common strategies for extending the basic idea of stop-and-wait so as to achieve higher efficiency: the ARPANET ARQ, go back n ARQ, and, finally, selective repeat ARQ.

2.4.2 ARPANET ARQ

The ARPANET achieves efficiency by using eight stop-and-wait strategies in parallel, multiplexing the bit pipe between the eight. That is, each incoming packet is assigned to one of eight virtual channels, assuming that one of the eight is idle; if all the virtual channels are busy, the incoming packet waits outside the DLC (see Fig. 2.20). The busy virtual channels are multiplexed on the bit pipe in the sense that frames for the different virtual channels are sent one after the other on the link. The particular order in which frames are sent is not very important, but a simple approach is to send them in round robin order. If a virtual channel's turn for transmission comes up before an ack has been received for that virtual channel, then the packet is sent again, so that the multiplexing removes the need for any time outs. (The actual ARPANET protocol, however, does use time outs.) When an ack is received for a frame on a given virtual channel, that virtual channel becomes idle and can accept a new packet from the higher layer.

Somewhat more overhead is required here than in the basic stop-and-wait protocol. In particular, each frame carries both the virtual channel number (requiring three bits), and the sequence number modulo 2 (*i.e.*, one bit) of the packet on that virtual channel. The acknowledgment information is piggybacked onto the frames going in the opposite direction. Each such frame in fact carries information for all eight virtual channels. In particular, an eight bit field in the header of each return frame gives the number modulo 2 of the awaited packet for each virtual channel.

One of the desirable features of this strategy is that the ack information is repeated so often (*i.e.*, for all virtual channels in each return frame), that relatively few retransmissions are required because of transmission errors in the reverse direction. Typically, only one retransmission is required for each frame in error in the forward direction. We shall see that the go back n protocol to be discussed next requires more retransmissions and thus has a somewhat lower link efficiency. The undesirable feature of the ARPANET protocol is that packets are released to the higher layer at the receiving DLC in a different order than that of arrival at the sending DLC. The DLC layer could, in principle, reorder the packets, but since a packet on one virtual channel could be arbitrarily delayed, an arbitrarily large number of later packets might have to be stored. The ARPANET makes no effort to reorder packets on individual links, so this protocol is not a problem for ARPANET. We shall see later that the lack of ordering on links generates a number

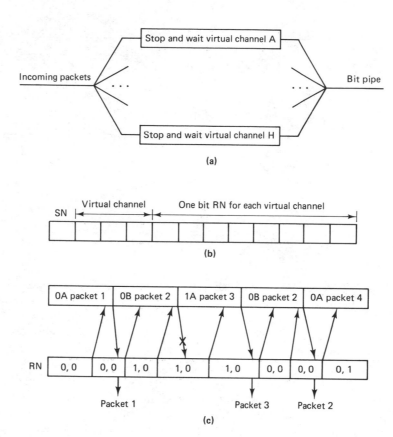

Figure 2.20   ARPANET ARQ. (a) Eight multiplexed, stop-and-wait virtual channels. (b) Bits in the header for ARQ control. (c) Operation of multiplexed stop and wait for two virtual channels. Top to bottom frames show *SN* and the channel number, and bottom to top frames show *RN* for both channels. The third frame from bottom to top acks packet 1 on the *A* channel.

of problems at higher layers. Most modern networks maintain packet ordering for this reason, and consequently do not use this protocol despite its high efficiency and low overhead. For very poor communication links, where efficiency and overhead are very important, it is a reasonable choice.

2.4.3 Go back n ARQ

Go back n ARQ is the most widely used type of ARQ protocol; it appears in the various standard DLC protocols, such as HDLC, SDLC, ADCCP, and LAPB. It is not elucidating to know the meaning of these acronyms, but, in fact, these standards are almost the same. They are discussed in section 2.6, and some of their differences are mentioned there.

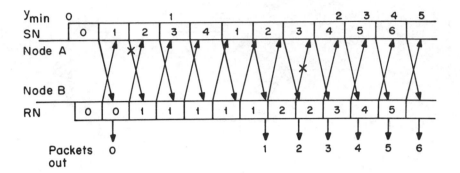

Figure 2.21   Go back 4 protocol. Send numbers SN are shown for frames going from A to B, and receive numbers RN are shown in frames from B to A. Note that an error in the second frame forces node A to retransmit packet 1 after packet 4. An error in the return frame carrying $RN = 2$ causes no problem.

The basic idea of go back n is very simple. Incoming packets to a transmitting DLC module for a link from A to B are numbered sequentially, and this sequence number SN is sent in the header of the frame containing the packet. In contrast to stop-and-wait, successive packets are sent without waiting for the next packet to be sent. The receiving DLC at B sends request numbers RN back to A requesting packet RN and acknowledging all packets prior to RN.

The go back number n in a go back n protocol is a parameter that determines how many successive packets can be sent in the absence of a request for a new packet. Specifically, node A is not allowed to send packet $i + n$ before i has been acknowledged (*i.e.*, before $i + 1$ has been requested). For any given time, let y_{min} denote the number of the last request number RN that A has received from B. Then, in a go back n system, A can send packets with numbers in the "window" from y_{min} to $y_{min} + n - 1$, but cannot send higher numbered packets. As successively higher numbered packets are requested, y_{min} increases and this window slides upward; thus, go back n protocols are often called *sliding window* ARQ protocols.

The operation of the receiving DLC (node B) in a go back n protocol is essentially the same as stop-and-wait. Packets are accepted in order, and the number of the next desired packet, RN, is sent in the header of each packet in the reverse direction. For the present, assume that RN and SN are integers that can be arbitrarily large; later it will be shown that they can be sent modulo m for a modulus $m > n$. Thus, when B receives a packet containing errors, it cannot accept any of the higher numbered packets until A goes back and retransmits the packet that was received in error.

Figure 2.21 illustrates this operation for the case of go back 4. We focus on the flow of packets from A to B. Thus, the sequence numbers SN are shown for the frames going from A to B, and the receive numbers RN, providing acks for the A to B traffic, are shown in the feedback frames from B to A. Assume that RN

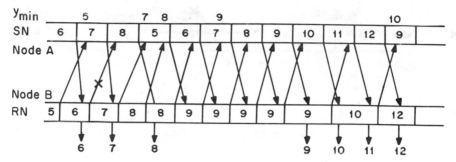

Figure 2.22   Continuation of Fig. 2.21 for go back 4 ARQ. Note that an error in the reverse frame carrying $RN = 6$ causes node A to go back to packet 5. Note also that long reverse frames cause node A to go back and retransmit packet 9.

is placed in the frame header, so that when a packet is correctly received at B, the new RN is sent back in the following reverse frame; this RN cannot be used at A until the CRC at the end of that reverse frame is checked. Note in particular the ack for packet number 0; the packet is received at B while B is sending its own second frame, and thus it is acked (by $RN = 1$) in B's third frame. Node A cannot "believe" the information until the end of the frame when the CRC is checked, and at this time y_{min} is changed as shown.

Note that when an error occurs in the second frame from A, A continues with new packets as far as possible, and then repeats packet 1 after packet 4 (strangely, this is regarded as going back 4 from packet 5, which would normally follow 4, to 1). Node A thus repeats four packets for the one error.

Next, consider the error in the first reverse frame carrying $RN = 2$; this causes no problem for the forward traffic since the next reverse frame arrives before A is required to go back. Figure 2.22 (which is a continuation of Fig. 2.21) shows another example of an error, in the first frame from B carrying $RN = 6$, in which A is required to go back.

While A is retransmitting packet 5 in this example, $RN = 7$ arrives from B. Some implementations of go back n (such as the one illustrated) will foolishly follow packet 5 by packet 6 in this type of situation, and others will jump ahead and send packet 7 next, as requested. Finally, at the end of the diagram, it is seen that node A goes back because some long frames from B delayed the ack information. All the retransmissions in Fig. 2.22 could have been avoided by a larger choice of n. These efficiency aspects of go back n are explored later, but first we define the protocol more carefully and show that it works correctly.

There are many variations of go back n protocols. One of these appeared in Fig. 2.22. Another more important variation is the use of time outs or extra feedback information to determine when to go back and retransmit. Thus, we want to demonstrate the correctness of an entire class of protocols. We continue to assume that frames may be lost or arbitrarily delayed, and that all frames detected

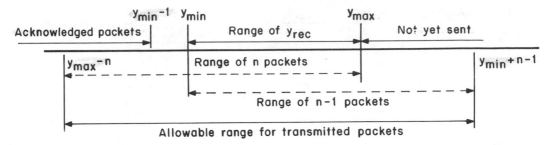

Figure 2.23   Allowable range for packets in a go back n ARQ system. y_{min} is the smallest packet number not yet acknowledged and $y_{max} - 1$ is the largest packet number yet sent. The awaited packet at the receiving DLC lies between y_{min} and y_{max}. The top dashed line indicates the range from the smallest allowable transmitted packet number to the largest possible awaited number. The bottom dashed line is the range from the smallest awaited number to the largest transmitted number.

as error free are in fact error free and arrive in the order sent. We also assume that SN and RN are arbitrary integers; the practical case in which SN and RN are sent within some modulus is considered later. The rules followed at a sending DLC, as a function of the go back number n, are now given and then followed by explanatory comments.

Rules Followed by the Sending DLC

The variable y_{min} initially has the value 0. Whenever an error-free frame is received on the reverse link by the sending DLC module, y_{min} is updated to equal the receive number RN in that frame. There is a variable y_{max} with initial value 0; after packet transmissions start, y_{max} is maintained to be 1 greater than the number of the largest numbered packet yet sent. When a new frame is prepared for transmission, the packet placed in the frame is constrained to have a number $z \geq 0$ in the range (see Fig. 2.23)

$$y_{max} - n \leq z \leq y_{min} + n - 1 \tag{2.24}$$

A sequence number $SN = z$ is sent in the header of the frame. New packets arrive, on request and as available, from the next higher layer and are sequentially numbered starting from 0. These packets, while in the range of Eq. (2.24), are buffered, conceptually within the DLC module. Finally, there is some $T > 0$ such that, if the packet numbered y_{min} is available, it will be transmitted at least once each T seconds until y_{min} changes (*i.e.*, y_{min} is acked).

      The significance of the notation y_{max} above is as follows: assume the sending DLC is sending from A to B; since packet y_{max} has never been sent, it is an upper bound on the packet awaited by B. Similarly, as noted before, y_{min} is a lower bound on the packet awaited by B. It will be seen shortly that y_{min} can never decrease, and therefore Eq. (2.24) asserts that the highest numbered packet yet transmitted can never exceed $y_{min} + n - 1$. Thus, y_{max} must satisfy

$$y_{max} \leq y_{min} + n \tag{2.25}$$

This means that the lower limit on z in Eq. (2.24) is always less than or equal to y_{min}, thus always allowing packet y_{min} to be sent. Note that in the example of Fig. 2.22, when A went back, it went back to $y_{max} - n$; thus, the lower limit in Eq. (2.24) allows A to keep sending packets in order after going back, even when y_{min} jumps to a larger value.

These rules permit A to send and resend packets in any order so long as they lie in the range of Eq. (2.24) (see Fig. 2.23). This provides the flexibility to use available timing information or subsidiary feedback information to increase the efficiency of the algorithm without worrying about correctness (after the class of protocols is shown to be correct).

The timing constraint that y_{min} is sent at least once each T seconds is somewhat artificial; its purpose is to exclude protocols that *never* go back and transmit the desired packet. Note, however, that the higher layer might have no new packets to send for an arbitrarily long time. Thus, if the last packet from the higher layer is y_{min}, then the timing rule (as well as common sense) forbids waiting until $y_{min} + n - 1$ comes from the higher layer. In other words, a "pure" go back n strategy, which only goes back to y_{min} after sending $y_{min} + n - 1$, will not function properly if the higher layer can run out of packets; such a strategy is ruled out by the timing assumption above. Some sort of time out feature is required in go back n protocols.

Finally, note that RN is compared with y_{min} for *each* error-free return frame. Problem 2.19 shows that the protocol can deadlock (*i.e.*, reach a point from which no further packets can be received) if RN is compared only for frames containing the awaited packet in the reverse direction.

Rules Followed by Receiving DLC

The receiving DLC has a variable y_{rec} initially set to 0. When an error-free frame arrives, the sequence number SN in the frame is compared to y_{rec}. If $SN = y_{rec}$, then the packet in the frame is accepted, it is passed to the higher layer, and the variable y_{rec} is incremented. The latest value of y_{rec} is used as the receive number RN in each frame on the reverse link. Finally, there is some $T > 0$ such that at least one such reverse frame is sent each T seconds. This implies that if a DLC module has no packets to send, it still must send receive numbers (at least each T seconds) to acknowledge the opposite traffic; this requires some type of "supervisory" frame carrying no packet data. The fact that y_{rec} is nondecreasing in time, coupled with the fact that the reverse frames carrying RN stay in order, insures that y_{min} is nondecreasing in time.

It will now be shown that this class of protocols is correct in the sense that if the receiving DLC is waiting for the packet numbered y_{rec}, and if that packet is available at the sending side, then that packet will eventually be delivered correctly to the higher layer at the receiving side. Assume that the probability of error in any frame transmitted in either direction is at most some constant p strictly less than 1.

While the receiving side is waiting for a frame with $SN = y_{\text{rec}}$, the frames in the reverse direction contain $RN = y_{\text{rec}}$ and are sent at least each T seconds. With probability 1, one of these frames is eventually received error free (given that y_{rec} doesn't change first). At this point, y_{min} at the sending side becomes equal to y_{rec} and this equality is maintained until y_{rec} changes (*i.e.*, until the packet is correctly received). The sending side must then send packet y_{rec} at least once each T seconds, so it will be correctly received eventually with probability 1. Thus, with the given assumptions, this class of protocols is correct.

Go back n with Modulus $m > n$

It will now be shown that if the sequence number SN and the receive number RN are sent modulo m, for some $m > n$, then the protocol continues to work correctly. An intuitive argument for this is illustrated by Fig. 2.23. One dashed line in the figure goes from the smallest possible packet number z to the largest possible y_{rec}, and the other dashed line from the smallest y_{rec} to the largest z. The magnitude $|z - y_{\text{rec}}|$ is at most n, which is less than m. Thus, if SN (which is z modulo m) equals y_{rec}, it must be that $z = y_{\text{rec}}$. To make this argument precise, one must be more careful about timing, *i.e.*, the fact that packet z might be arbitrarily delayed on the link.

First assume that only SN is sent modulo m, whereas RN is an unrestricted integer as before. Consider a link from node A to B and let $y_{\text{min}}, y_{\text{rec}}, y_{\text{max}}$, and the packet number z be unrestricted integers as before. The rules at the sending DLC (node A) are the same as before, except that $SN = z$ modulo m. The rules at the receiving DLC (node B) are also the same as before, except that $SN = y_{\text{rec}}$ modulo m is the new criterion for accepting a packet, passing it to the next higher layer, and incrementing y_{rec}. We shall show that packets are accepted at B for the system in which $SN = z$ modulo m if and only if (iff) they would have been accepted for the system with no modulus (*i.e.*, iff $z = y_{\text{rec}}$).

Let t be the time at which an error-free frame arrives at B and let $t' < t$ be the time at which that frame was prepared for transmission at A. Let y'_{min} and y'_{max} be the values of y_{min} and y_{max} at time t'. An important relation between these quantities for the system without the modulus is

$$y'_{\text{min}} \leq y_{\text{rec}} \leq y'_{\text{max}} \tag{2.26}$$

The first inequality above is true because y'_{min} is the last value of RN received at A before t'; that value of RN is a yet earlier value of y_{rec} at node B, which is less than or equal to y_{rec} at time t. The second inequality is true because y'_{max} has not been sent by A before t'; by the ordering of frames on the $A \rightarrow B$ link, y'_{max} cannot have reached B before z (*i.e.*, before time t).

To prove correctness when $SN = z$ modulo m, induction will be used on the successive times at which error-free frames arrive at B. We use Eq. (2.26) as the inductive hypothesis, and use this to show that y_{rec} modulo $m = SN$ iff $y_{\text{rec}} = z$. This will show that the system with a modulus performs the same update at time t as the modulus-free system; this will establish Eq. (2.26) until the next error-free arrival at B. Note that Eq. (2.26) holds before the first error-free arrival at B, providing a basis for the induction.

When the packet z is prepared for transmission at time t', Eq. (2.24) asserts that

$$y'_{\max} - n \le z \le y'_{\min} + n - 1 \tag{2.27}$$

Combining the first half of Eq. (2.27) with the last half of Eq. (2.26),

$$z \ge y'_{\max} - n \ge y_{\text{rec}} - n \tag{2.28}$$

Combining Eqs. (2.26) and (2.27) in the opposite way,

$$z \le y'_{\min} + n - 1 \le y_{\text{rec}} + n - 1 \tag{2.29}$$

The two dashed lines in Fig. 2.23 illustrate these relations; what has been added to the previous intuitive discussion is a precise interpretation of appropriate timing of events at sending and receiving DLCs. Combining these two relations,

$$|z - y_{\text{rec}}| \le n < m \tag{2.30}$$

This implies that $z - y_{\text{rec}}$ modulo $m = 0$ iff $z = y_{\text{rec}}$. Thus, the class of protocols for $n < m$ is correct with $SN = z$ modulo m.

Finally, assume that the receive numbers RN are also sent modulo m. Thus, the receiving DLC sets RN in each reverse frame to be y_{rec} modulo m, using the current value of y_{rec}. The rule for updating $y_{\min}$ at the sending DLC is changed as follows: whenever an error-free frame arrives in the reverse direction, the value of RN in the frame modifies $y_{\min}$ by the rule

$$\begin{aligned} &\text{until } y_{\min} \text{ modulo } m = RN \\ &\text{do } y_{\min} := y_{\min} + 1 \end{aligned} \tag{2.31}$$

To show that correctness is still maintained, we use induction on the times at which error-free reverse frames arrive at the sending DLC (node A). Let t be the time at which a given reverse frame with given RN arrives at A, and let t' be the time that the frame was prepared at B. Let y'_{rec} denote y_{rec} at B at that earlier time. The appropriate relation satisfied by the system without any modulus (and thus also by the system where only SN is sent with a modulus) is

$$y_{\min} \le y'_{\text{rec}} \le y_{\max} \le y_{\min} + n \tag{2.32}$$

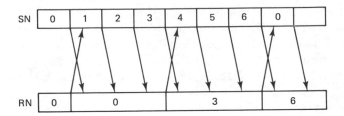

Figure 2.24   Go back 7 ARQ with long frames in the reverse direction. Note that the ack for packet 1 has not arrived at the sending side by the time packet 6 finishes transmission, thereby causing a retransmission of packet 0.

The first part of Eq. (2.32) follows from the ordering of frames on the $B \to A$ link; no frame sent by B after t' can arrive before t. The second part follows since y_{max} has not been sent from A before t, and certainly cannot have arrived at B before t'. The third part follows from Eq. (2.25).

We use Eq. (2.32) as an inductive hypothesis as before. The rule (2.31) updates y_{min} to a value y satisfying y modulo $m = RN = y'_{rec}$ modulo m and also satisfying $y_{min} \le y \le y_{min} + m - 1$. Since $n < m$, it is seen from Eq. (2.32) that $y = y'_{rec}$, completing the proof of correctness.

At this point, we can see that it is unnecessary for y_{min}, y_{rec}, and y_{max} to be saved as unrestricted integers; all values can be stored modulo m.

Efficiency of Go back n Implementations

Retransmissions, or delays waiting for time outs, occur in go back n ARQ for the following three reasons: first, errors in the forward direction, second, errors in the feedback direction, and third, longer frames in the feedback than the forward direction. These will be discussed in reverse order.

The likelihood of retransmissions caused by long reverse frames can be reduced by increasing the go back number n. Unfortunately, the normal value of modulus in the standard protocols is $m = 8$, which constrains n to be at most 7. Figure 2.24 illustrates that, even in the absence of propagation delay, reverse frames more than three times the length of forward frames can cause retransmissions for $n = 7$. Problem 2.23 also shows that if frames have lengths that are exponentially distributed, with the same distribution in each direction, then the probability q that a frame is not acked by the time the window is exhausted is given by

$$q = (1 + n)2^{-n} \tag{2.33}$$

For $n = 7, q = 1/16$. Frames normally have a maximum permissible length (and a minimum length because of the control overhead), so in practice q is somewhat smaller. However, links sometimes carry longer frames in one direction than in the other, and in this case, there might be considerable waste in link utilization for

$n = 7$. When propagation delay is large relative to frame length (as, for example, on satellite links), this loss of utilization can be quite serious. Fortunately, the standard protocols have an alternative choice of modulus as $m = 128$.

When errors occur in a reverse frame, the acknowledgement information is postponed for an additional reverse frame. This loss of line utilization in one direction due to errors in the other can also be avoided by choosing n sufficiently large.

Finally, consider the effect of errors in the forward direction. If n is large enough to avoid retransmissions or delays due to long frames and errors in the reverse direction, and if the sending DLC waits to exhaust its window of n packets before retransmitting, then a large number of packets are retransmitted for each forward error. The customary solution to this problem is the use of time outs. In its simplest version, if a packet is not acknowledged within a fixed time out period after transmission, then it is retransmitted. This time out should be chosen long enough to include round-trip propagation and processing delay plus transmission time for two maximum length packets in the reverse direction (one for the frame in transit when a packet is received, and one to carry the new RN).

In a more sophisticated version, the sending DLC, with knowledge of propagation and processing delays, can determine which reverse frame should carry the ack for a given packet; it can go back if that frame is error free and fails to deliver the ack.

In a more fundamental sense, increasing link utilization and decreasing delay is achieved by going back quickly when a forward error occurs, but avoiding retransmissions caused by long frames and errors in the reverse direction. One possibility here is for the receiving DLC to send back a short supervisory frame upon receiving a frame in error. This allows the sending side to go back much sooner than if RN were simply piggybacked on a longer reverse data frame. Another approach is to insert RN in the trailer of the reverse frame, inserting it before the CRC and inserting it at the last moment, after the packet part of the frame has been sent. This cannot be done in the standard DLC protocols, but would have the effect of reducing the feedback delay by almost one frame length.

It is not particularly difficult to invent new ways of reducing both feedback delay and control overhead in ARQ strategies. One should be aware, however, that it is not trivial to ensure the correctness of such strategies. Also, except in special applications, improvements must be substantial to outweigh the advantages of standardization.

2.4.4 Selective Repeat ARQ

Even if unnecessary retransmissions are avoided, go back n protocols must retransmit at least one round-trip delay worth of frames when a single error occurs in an awaited packet. In many situations, the probability of one or more errors in a frame is 10^{-4} or less, and in this case, retransmitting many packets for each frame in error has little effect on efficiency. There are some communication links, however, for which small error probabilities per frame are very difficult to achieve, even with error correction in the modems. For other links (*e.g.*, satellite links), the number of frames transmitted in a round trip delay time is very large. In both these cases, selective repeat ARQ can be used to increase efficiency.

The basic idea of selective repeat ARQ on a link (A, B) is for B, the receiving DLC, to accept out-of-order packets and to request retransmissions from A only for those packets that are not correctly received. There is still a go back number, or window size, n, specifying how far A can get ahead of y_{rec}, the lowest numbered packet not yet correctly received at B. The strategy is somewhat similar to the ARPANET ARQ in terms of typically requiring only one retransmission per forward frame in error. The major difference is that if B has to reorder the packets, at most n packets must be stored, whereas with ARPANET, there is no such bound.

Note that whatever ARQ protocol is used, only error-free frames can deliver packets to B, and thus, if p is the probability of frame error, the maximum expected number of packets delivered to B per frame from A to B is

$$\eta \le 1 - p \tag{2.34}$$

This limit can be approached in principle by selective repeat ARQ and is sometimes called the throughput of ideal selective repeat. Ideal go back n ARQ can be similarly defined as a protocol that retransmits the packets in one round-trip delay each time that a frame carrying the packet awaited by the receiving DLC is corrupted by errors. The throughput of this ideal is shown in Problem 2.26 to be

$$\eta \le (1 - p)/(1 + p\beta) \tag{2.35}$$

where β is the expected number of frames in a round-trip delay interval. This indicates that the increase in throughput available with selective repeat is only significant when $p\beta$ is appreciable relative to 1.

The constraints on node A for selective repeat ARQ are the same as for go back n. Node B maintains y_{rec} as before and sends $RN = y_{rec}$ modulo m back to A in each frame as before. Node B also accepts packets other than y_{rec}, using the rule that if $SN = (y_{rec} + i)$ modulo m for $0 \le i < n$, then the packet is accepted with the number $y_{rec} + i$. Equations (2.28) and (2.29) follow as before, bounding the packet number z of a received packet around y_{rec}. Since B is now accepting packets out of order, it must determine z from $SN = z$ modulo m for all received frames rather than just frames carrying packet y_{rec}. Since the range of z in Eqs. (2.28) and (2.29) is $2n$, we now require a modulus m satisfying

P 69

$$m \ge 2n, \quad \text{for selective repeat} \tag{2.36}$$

With this change, the correctness of this class of protocols follows as before. The real issue with selective repeat, however, is using it efficiently to achieve throughputs relatively close to the ideal $1 - p$. Note first that using RN alone to provide acknowledgment information is not very efficient, since if several frame errors occur in one round-trip delay period, node A doesn't find out about the second frame error until one-round trip delay after the first error is retransmitted. There are several ways of providing the additional acknowledgement information required by A. One is for B to send back the lowest j packet numbers that it has not yet received; j should be larger than $p\beta$ (the expected number of frame errors in a round-trip delay time), but is limited by the overhead required by the feedback. Another possibility is to send RN plus an additional k bits (for some constant k), one bit giving the ack/nak status of each of the k packets after y_{rec}.

Assume now that the return frames carry sufficient information for A to determine, after an expected delay of β frames, whether or not a packet was successfully received. The typical algorithm for A is then to repeat packets as soon as it is clear that the previous transmission contained errors; if A discovers multiple errors simultaneously, it retransmits them in the order of their packet numbers. When there are no requested retransmissions, A continues to send new packets, up to $y_{\text{min}} + n - 1$. At this limit, node A can wait for some time out or immediately go back to y_{min} to transmit successive unacknowledged packets.

Node A acts like an ideal selective repeat system until it is forced to wait or go back from $y_{\text{min}} + n - 1$. When this happens, however, the packet numbered y_{min} must have been transmitted unsuccessfully about n/β times. Thus, by making n large enough, the probability of such a go back can be reduced to negligible value. There are two difficulties with very large values of n (assuming that packets must be reordered at the receiving DLC). The first is that storage must be provided at B for all of the accepted packets beyond y_{rec}. The second is that the large number of stored packets are all delayed waiting for y_{rec}.

The amount of storage provided can be reduced to $n - \beta$ without much harm, since whenever a go back from $y_{\text{min}} + n - 1$ occurs, node A can send no new packets beyond $y_{\text{min}} + n - 1$ for a round-trip delay; thus, it might as well resend the yet unacknowledged packets from to $y_{\text{min}} + n - \beta$ to $y_{\text{min}} + n - 1$; this means that B need not save these packets. The value of n can also be reduced, without increasing the probability of go back, by retransmitting a packet several times in succession if the previous transmission contained errors. For example, Fig. 2.25 compares double retransmissions with single retransmissions for $n = 2\beta + 2$. Single retransmissions fail with probability p and cause β extra retransmissions; double retransmissions rarely fail, but always require one extra retransmission. Thus, double retransmissions can increase throughput if $pn > 1$, but might be desirable in other cases to reduce the variability of delay (see [Wel82] for further analysis).

2.5 FRAMING

The problem of framing is that of deciding, at the receiving DLC, where successive frames start and stop. In the case of a synchronous bit pipe, there is sometimes a

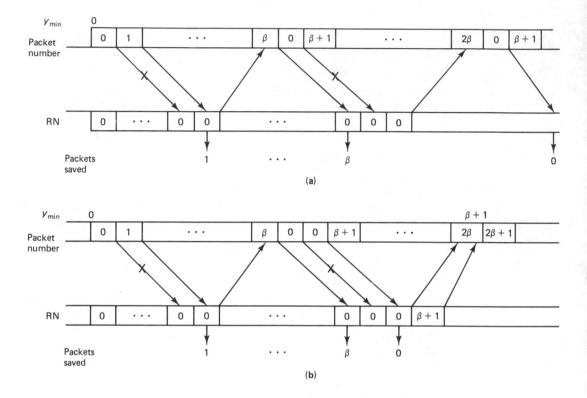

Figure 2.25   Selective repeat ARQ with $n = 2\beta + 2$ and receiver storage for $\beta + 1$ packets. (a) Note the wasted transmissions if a given packet (0) is transmitted twice with errors. (b) Note that this problem is cured, at the cost of one extra frame, if the second transmission of packet 0 is doubled. Feedback contains not only RN but additional information on accepted packets.

period of idle fill between successive frames, so that it is also necessary to separate the idle fill from the frames. For an intermittent synchronous bit pipe, the idle fill is replaced by dead periods when no bits at all arrive. This doesn't simplify the problem since, first, successive frames are often transmitted with no dead periods in between, and, second, after a dead period, the modems at the physical layer usually require some idle fill to reacquire synchronization.

There are three types of framing used in practice. The first, *character-based framing*, uses special communication control characters for idle fill and to indicate the beginning and ending of frames. The second, *bit-oriented framing* with flags, uses a special string of bits called a flag both for idle fill and to indicate the beginning and ending of frames. The third, *length counts*, gives the frame length in a field of the header. The following three subsections explain these three techniques, and the

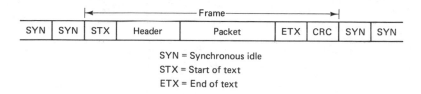

Figure 2.26   Simplified frame structure with character-based framing.

third also gives a more fundamental view of the problem. These subsections, except for a few comments, ignore the possibility of errors on the bit pipe. Subsection 2.5.4 then treats the joint problems of ARQ and framing in the presence of errors. Finally, subsection 2.5.5 explains the trade-offs involved in the choice of frame length.

2.5.1 Character-Based Framing

Character codes such as ASCII generally provide binary code words not only for keyboard characters and terminal control characters, but also for various communication control characters. In ASCII, all these code words are seven bits long, generally with an extra bit for parity which might or might not be stripped off in communication (since a cyclic redundancy check (CRC) can be used to detect errors in frames).

SYN (synchronous idle) is one of these communication control characters; a string of SYN characters can be used for idle fill between frames if a sending DLC has no data, but a synchronous modem requires bits. SYN can also be used within frames, sometimes for synchronization of older modems, and sometimes to bridge delays in supplying data characters. STX (start of text) and ETX (end of text) are two other communication control characters used to indicate the beginning and end of a frame as shown in Fig. 2.26.

The character-oriented communication protocols used in practice, such as the IBM binary synchronous communication system (known as Bisynch or BSC), are far more complex than this, but our purpose here is simply to illustrate that framing presents no insurmountable problems. There is a slight problem in the above example in that the header or CRC might, through chance, contain a communication control character. Since these always appear in known positions after STX or ETX, this causes no problem for the receiver. If the packet to be transmitted is an arbitrary binary string, however, rather than a string of ASCII keyboard characters, serious problems arise; the packet might contain the ETX character, for example, which could be interpreted as ending the frame. Character-oriented protocols use a special mode of transmission, called *transparent mode*, to send such data.

The transparent mode uses a special control character called DLE (data link escape). A DLE character is inserted before the STX character to indicate the start of a frame in transparent mode. It is also inserted before intentional uses of

data link escape

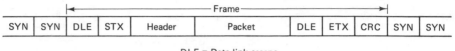

DLE = Data link escape

Figure 2.27   Character-based framing in a transparent mode as used in the ARPANET.

communication control characters within such a frame. The DLE is not inserted before the spurious appearances of these characters as part of the binary data. There is still a problem if the DLE character itself appears in the data, and this is solved by inserting an extra DLE before each spurious appearance of DLE in the data. The receiving DLC then strips off one DLE from each arriving pair of DLEs, and interprets each STX or ETX preceded by an unpaired DLE as an actual start or stop of a frame. Thus, for example, DLE ETX (preceded by something other than DLE) would be interpreted as an end of frame, whereas DLE DLE ETX (preceded by something other than DLE) would be interpreted as a spurious appearance of DLE ETX in the binary data.

With this type of protocol, the frame structure would appear as shown in Fig. 2.27. This frame structure is used in the ARPANET. It has two disadvantages, the first of which is the somewhat excessive use of framing overhead (*i.e.*, six characters, consisting of two SYN characters required between each pair of frames, DLE STX to start the frame, and DLE ETX to end it). The second disadvantage is that each frame must consist of an integral number of characters.

Let us briefly consider what happens in this protocol in the presence of errors. The CRC checks the header and packet of a frame, and thus will normally detect errors there. If an error occurs in the DLE ETX ending a frame, however, the receiver will not detect the end of the frame and thus will not check the CRC; this is why we assumed that frames could get lost in the last section. A similar problem is that errors can cause the appearance of DLE ETX in the data itself; the receiver would interpret this as the end of the frame and interpret the following bits as a CRC. Thus, we have an essentially random set of bits interpreted as a CRC, and the preceding data will be accepted as a packet with probability 2^{-L}, where L is the length of the CRC. These same problems will occur in the bit-oriented framing protocols to be studied next and will be discussed in greater detail in subsection 2.5.4.

2.5.2 Bit-Oriented Framing—Flags

In the transparent mode for character-based framing, the special character pair DLE ETX indicated the end of a frame and was avoided within the frame by doubling each DLE character. Here we look at another approach, using a *flag* at the end of

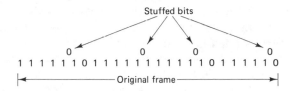

Figure 2.28   Bit stuffing. A 0 is stuffed after each consecutive five 1's in the original frame. A flag, 01111110, without stuffing, is sent at the end of the frame.

the frame. A flag is simply a known bit string, like DLE ETX, that indicates the end of a frame. Similar to the technique of doubling DLEs, a technique called *bit stuffing* is used to avoid confusion between spurious appearances of the flag within the frame and the actual flag indicating the end of the frame. One important difference is that with bit-oriented framing, a frame can have any length (subject to some minimum and maximum) rather than being restricted to an integral number of characters. Thus, we must guard against spurious appearances of the flag starting in any bit position rather than just on character boundaries.

In practice, the flag is the bit string 01^60, where the notation 1^j means a string of j 1's. The rule used for bit stuffing is to insert (stuff) a 0 into the data string of the frame proper after each successive appearance of five 1's (see Fig. 2.28). Thus, the frame, after stuffing, never contains more than five consecutive 1's, and the flag at the end of the frame is uniquely recognizable. At the receiving DLC, the first 0 after each string of five 1's is deleted; if instead a string of five 1's is followed by a 1, it indicates that the frame is over.

Bit stuffing has a number of purposes beyond eliminating flags within the frame. Standard DLCs have an abort capability in which a frame can be aborted by sending seven or more 1's in a row; in addition, a link is regarded as idle if 15 or more 1's in a row are received. What this means is that 01^6 is really the string denoting the end of a frame. If 01^6 is followed by a 0, it is the flag, indicating normal frame termination; if followed by a 1, it indicates abnormal termination. Bit stuffing is best viewed as preventing the appearance of 01^6 within the frame. One other minor purpose of bit stuffing is to break up long strings of 1's, which cause some older modems to lose synchronization.

It is easy to see that the bit stuffing rule above avoids the appearance of 01^6 within the frame, but it is less clear that so much bit stuffing is necessary. For example, consider the first stuffed bit in Fig. 2.28. Since the frame starts with six 1's (following a distinguishable flag), this could not be logically mistaken for 01^6. Thus, stuffing is not necessary after five 1's at the beginning of the frame (provided that the receiver's rule for deleting stuffed bits is changed accordingly).

The second stuffed bit in the figure is clearly necessary to avoid the appearance of 01^6. From a strictly logical standpoint, the third stuffed bit could be eliminated (except for the synchronization problem in older modems). Problem 2.31 shows how the receiver rule could be appropriately modified. Note that the reduction in overhead, by modifying the stuffing rules as above, is almost negligible; the purpose here is to understand the rules rather than to suggest changes.

The fourth stuffed bit in the figure is definitely required, although the reason is somewhat subtle. The original string 01^50 surrounding this stuffed bit could not be misinterpreted as 01^6, but the receiving DLC needs a rule to eliminate stuffed bits; it cannot distinguish a stuffed 0 following 01^5 from a data 0 following 01^5. Problem 2.32 develops this argument in detail.

There is nothing particularly magical about the string 01^6 as the bit string used to signal the termination of a frame (except for its use in preventing long strings of 1's on the link), and, in fact, any bit string could be used with bit stuffing after the next-to-last bit of the string (see Prob. 2.33). Such strings, with bit stuffing, are often useful in data communication to signal the occurrence of some rare event.

Consider the overhead incurred by using a flag to indicate the end of a frame. Assume that a frame (before bit stuffing and flag addition) consists of independent, identically distributed, random binary variables, with equal probability of 0 or 1. Assume for increased generality that the terminating signal for a frame is 01^j for some j (with 01^j0 being the flag and 01^{j+1} indicating abnormal termination); thus, $j = 6$ for the standard flag. An insertion will occur at (that is, immediately following) the ith bit of the original frame (for $i \geq j$) if the string from $i - j + 1$ to i is 01^{j-1}; the probability of this is 2^{-j}. An insertion will also occur (for $i \geq 2j - 1$) if the string from $i - 2j + 2$ to i is 01^{2j-2}; the probability of this is 2^{-2j+1}. We ignore this term and the probability of insertions due to yet longer strings of 1's, first, because these probabilities are practically negligible, and, second, because these insertions are used primarily to avoid long strings of 1's rather than to provide framing. Bit $j - 1$ in the frame is somewhat different than the other bits, since an insertion here occurs with probability 2^{-j+1} (that is, if the first $j - 1$ bits of the frame are all 1's).

Recall that the expected value of a sum of random variables is equal to the sum of the expected values (whether or not the variables are independent). Thus, the expected number of insertions in a frame of original length K is the sum, over i, of the expected number of insertions at each bit i of the frame. The expected number of insertions at a given bit, however, is just the probability of insertion there. Thus the expected number of insertions in a string of length $K \geq j - 1$ is

$$(K - j + 3)2^{-j}$$

Taking the expected value of this over frame lengths K (with the assumption that all frames are longer than $j - 1$), and adding the $j + 1$ bits in the termination string, the expected overhead for framing becomes

$$E\{OV\} = (E\{K\} - j + 3)2^{-j} + j + 1 \tag{2.37}$$

Since $E\{K\}$ is typically very much larger than j, we have the approximation and upper bound (for $j \geq 3$)

$$E\{OV\} \leq E\{K\}2^{-j} + j + 1 \tag{2.38}$$

One additional bit is needed to distinguish a normal from abnormal end of frame.

It will be interesting to find the integer value of j that minimizes this expression for a given value of expected frame length. As j increases from 1, the quantity on the right-hand side of Eq. (2.38) first decreases and then increases. Thus, the minimizing j is the smallest integer j for which the right-hand side is less than the same quantity with j increased by 1, that is,

$$E\{K\}2^{-j} + j + 1 < E\{K\}2^{-j-1} + j + 2 \qquad (2.39)$$

This inequality simplifies to $E\{K\}2^{-j-1} < 1$, and the smallest j that satisfies this is

$$j = \lfloor \log_2 E\{K\} \rfloor \qquad (2.40)$$

where $\lfloor x \rfloor$ means the integer part of x. It is shown in Problem 2.34 that for this optimal value of j,

$$E\{OV\} \leq \log_2 E\{K\} + 2 \qquad (2.41)$$

For example, with an expected frame length of 1000 bits, the optimal j is 9 and the expected framing overhead is less than 12 bits. For the standard flag, with $j = 6$, the expected overhead is about 23 bits (hardly cause for wanting to change the standard).

2.5.3 Length Fields

The basic problem in framing is to inform the receiving DLC where each idle fill string ends and where each frame ends. In principle, the problem of determining the end of an idle fill string is trivial; idle fill is represented by some fixed string (for example, repeated SYN characters or repeated flags) and idle fill stops whenever this fixed pattern is broken. In principle, one bit inverted from the pattern is sufficient, although, in practice, idle fill is usually stopped at a boundary between flags or SYN characters.

Since a frame consists of an arbitrary and unknown bit string, it is somewhat harder to indicate where it ends. A simple alternative to flags or special characters (used in DECNET, for example) is to include a length field in the frame header. Assuming no transmission errors, the receiving DLC simply reads this length and then knows where the frame ends. If the length is represented by ordinary binary numbers, the number of bits in the length field has to be at least $\lfloor \log_2 K_{\max} \rfloor + 1$, where $K_{\max}$ is the maximum frame size. This is the overhead required for framing in this technique; comparing it with Eq. (2.41) for flags, we see that the two techniques require similar overhead.

Could any other method of encoding frame lengths require a smaller expected number of bits? This question is answered by information theory. Given any probability assignment $P(K)$ on frame lengths, the source coding theorem of information theory states that the minimum expected number of bits that can encode such a length is at least the entropy of that distribution, given by

$$H = \sum_K P(K) \log_2[1/P(K)] \tag{2.42}$$

According to the theorem, at least this many bits of framing overhead, on the average, must be sent over the link per frame for the receiver to know where each frame ends. If $P(K) = 1/K_{\max}$, for $1 \le K \le K_{\max}$, then H is easily calculated to be $\log_2 K_{\max}$. Similarly, for a geometric distribution on lengths, with given $E\{K\}$, the entropy of the length distribution is approximately $\log_2 E\{K\} + \log_2 e$, for large $E\{K\}$. This is about $1/2$ bit below the expression in Eq. (2.41). Thus, for the geometric distribution on lengths, the overhead using flags for framing is essentially minimum. The geometric distribution has an interesting extremal property; it can be shown to have the largest entropy of any probability distribution over the positive integers with given $E\{K\}$ (that is, it requires more bits than any other distribution).

The general idea of source coding is to map the more likely values of K into short bit strings and less likely values into long bit strings; more precisely, one would like to map a given K into about $\log_2[1/P(K)]$ bits. If one does this for a geometric distribution, one gets an interesting encoding known as the unary- binary encoding. In particular, for a given j, the frame length K is represented as

$$K = i2^j + r; \quad 0 \le r < 2^j \tag{2.43}$$

The encoding for K is then i 0's followed by a 1 (this is known as a unary encoding of i) followed by the ordinary binary encoding of r (using j bits). For example, if $j = 2$ and $K = 7$, K is represented by $i = 1$, $r = 3$, which encodes into 0111 (where 01 is the unary encoding of $i = 1$ and 11 is the binary encoding of $r = 3$). Note that different values of K are encoded into different numbers of bits, but the end of the encoding can always be recognized as occurring j bits after the first 1.

In general with this encoding, a given K maps into a bit string of length $\lfloor K/2^j \rfloor + 1 + j$. If the integer value above is neglected, and the expected value over K is taken, then

$$E\{OV\} = E\{K\}2^{-j} + 1 + j \tag{2.44}$$

Note that this is the same as the flag overhead in Eq. (2.38). This is again minimized by choosing $j = \lfloor \log_2 E\{K\} \rfloor$. Thus, this unary-binary length encoding and flag framing both require essentially the minimum possible framing overhead for the geometric distribution, and no more overhead for any other distribution of given $E\{K\}$.

2.5.4 Framing with Errors

Several peculiar problems arise when errors corrupt the framing information on the communication link. First, consider the flag technique. If an error occurs in the flag at the end of a frame, then the receiver will not detect the end of frame and will not check the CRC. In this case, when the next flag is detected, the receiver assumes the CRC to be in the position preceding the flag. This perceived CRC might be the actual CRC for the following frame, but the receiver interprets it as checking what was transmitted as two frames. Alternatively, if some idle fill follows the frame in which the flag was lost, the perceived CRC could include the error-corrupted flag. In any case, the perceived CRC is essentially a random bit string in relation to the perceived preceding frame, and the receiver fails to detect the errors with a probability essentially 2^{-L}, where L is the length of the CRC.

An alternative scenario is for an error within the frame to change a bit string into the flag, as shown for the flag 01^60:

$$0\ 1\ 0\ 0\ 1\ 1\ 0\ 1\ 1\ 1\ 0\ 0\ 1\ \ldots \qquad \text{(sent)}$$
$$0\ 1\ 0\ 0\ 1\ 1\ 1\ 1\ 1\ 1\ 0\ 0\ 1\ \ldots \qquad \text{(received)}$$

It is shown in Problem 2.35 that the probability of this happening somewhere in a frame of length K is approximately $(1/32)Kp$, where p is the probability of a bit error. In this scenario, as before, the bits before the perceived flag are interpreted by the receiver as a CRC, and the probability of accepting a false frame, given this occurrence, is 2^{-L}. This problem is often called the data sensitivity problem of DLC, since even though the CRC is capable of detecting any combination of three or fewer errors, a single error that creates or destroys a flag, plus a special combination of data bits to satisfy the perceived preceding CRC, causes an undetectable error.

If a length field in the header provides framing, then an error in this length field again causes the receiver to look for the CRC in the wrong place, and again an incorrect frame is accepted with probability about 2^{-L}. The probability of such an error is smaller using a length count than using a flag (since errors can create false flags within the frame); however, after an error occurs in a length field, the receiver doesn't know where to look for any subsequent frames. Thus, if a length field is used for framing, some synchronizing string must be used at the beginning of a frame whenever the sending DLC goes back to retransmit. (Alternatively, the start of every frame could be marked, but this would make the length field almost redundant).

There are several partial solutions to these problems, but none are without disadvantages. DECNET uses a fixed-length header for each frame and places the length of the frame in that header; in addition, the header has its own CRC. Thus, if an error occurs in the length field of the header, the receiver can detect it by the header CRC which is in a known position. One difficulty with this strategy is that the transmitter must still resynchronize after such an error, since even though the error is detected, the receiver will not know when the next frame starts. The other difficulty is that two CRCs must be used in place of one, which is somewhat inefficient.

A similar approach is to put the length field of one frame into the trailer of the previous frame. This avoids the inefficiency of the DECNET approach, but still requires a special synchronizing sequence after each detected error. This also requires a special header frame to be sent whenever the length of the next frame is unknown when a given frame is transmitted.

Another approach, for any framing technique, is to use a longer CRC. This at least reduces the probability of falsely accepting a frame if framing errors occur. It appears that this is the most likely alternative to be adopted in practice; a standard 32 bit CRC exists as an option in standard DLCs.

A final approach is to regard framing as being at a higher layer than ARQ. In such a system, packets would be separated by flags, and the resulting sequence of packets and flags would be divided into fixed length segments. Thus, segment boundaries and packet boundaries would bear no relation. If a packet ended in the middle of a segment and no further packets were available, then the segment would be completed with idle fill. These segments would then enter the ARQ system and, because of the fixed length segments, the CRC would always be in a known place. One disadvantage of this strategy is delay; a packet could not be accepted until the entire segment containing the end of the packet was accepted. This extra delay would occur on each link of the packet's path.

2.5.5 Maximum Frame Size

The choice of a maximum frame length, or maximum packet length, in a data network depends on many factors. One of the most important is the overhead associated with each frame. Let V be the number of overhead bits per frame, including frame header, trailer, flag, and packet header, but not including fixed overhead associated with the message itself. Let K_{max} be the maximum packet length, not including the packet header. Let M be the length of a given message, including the fixed overhead associated with the message. Then, the total number of bits that must be transmitted for the message is

$$\text{Total bits } = M + \lceil M/K_{max}\rceil V \tag{2.45}$$

where $\lceil x\rceil$ denotes the smallest integer greater than or equal to x. In other words, as K_{max} is decreased, the required number of frames increases and the overhead V must be repeated for each frame. This factor then argues for a large maximum packet size. A closely related factor is that each station (node or external site) must do a certain amount of processing for each frame. It will be shown that all the other factors involved in maximum packet size argue for a small size.

The most important of these other factors is the pipelining effect illustrated in Fig. 2.29. The idea is that if a message is transmitted as one packet, then the entire message must be received over one link (assuming the use of ARQ) before starting transmission over the next link. If the message is broken into several packets, however, the earlier packets may proceed along the path while the later packets are still being transmitted on the first link, thus reducing overall message delay.

Now let us investigate the combined effect of overhead and pipelining. Suppose a message of length M is broken into maximum length packets, with a final packet

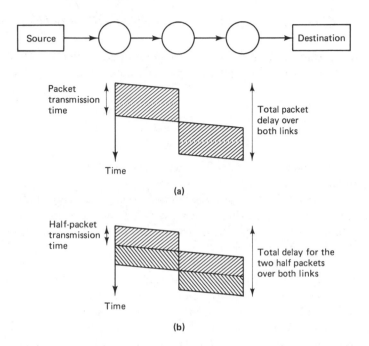

Figure 2.29   Decreasing delay by shortening packets to take advantage of pipelining. (a) The total packet delay over two empty links equals twice the packet transmission time on a link plus the overall propagation delay. (b) When each packet is split in two, a pipelining effect occurs. The total delay for the two half packets equals 1.5 times the original packet transmission time on a link plus the overall propagation delay.

of typically shorter length. Suppose that the message must be transmitted over j equal capacity links and that the network is lightly loaded, so that waiting at the nodes for other traffic can be ignored. Also, ignore errors on the links (which will be discussed later), and ignore propagation delays (which are independent of maximum packet length). Then the total time T required to transmit the message to the destination is the time it takes the first packet to travel over the first $j - 1$ links, plus the time it takes the entire message to travel over the final link (that is, when a nonfinal frame finishes traversing a link, the next frame is always ready to start traversing the link). Let C be the capacity of each link in bits per second, so that TC is the number of bit transmission times required for message delivery. Then,

$$TC = (K_{\max} + V)(j - 1) + M + \lceil M/K_{\max} \rceil V \qquad (2.46)$$

Now, take the expected value of this over message lengths M, making the approximation that $E\{\lceil M/K_{\max} \rceil\} = E\{M/K_{\max}\} + \frac{1}{2}$ (this is reasonable if the distribution of M is reasonably uniform over spans of $K_{\max}$ bits). Then,

$$E\{TC\} \approx (K_{\max} + V)(j - 1) + E\{M\} + E\{M\}V/K_{\max} + V/2 \qquad (2.47)$$

Ignoring that $K_{\max}$ must be an integer, we can differentiate this with respect to $K_{\max}$ to find the value of $K_{\max}$ that minimizes $E\{TC\}$. The result is

$$K_{\max} \approx \sqrt{\frac{E\{M\}V}{j - 1}} \qquad (2.48)$$

This shows the tradeoff between overhead and pipelining. As the overhead V increases, $K_{\max}$ should be increased, and as the path length j increases, $K_{\max}$ should be reduced. As a practical detail, recall that delay is often less important for file transfers than for other messages, so file transfers should probably be weighted less than other messages in the estimation of $E\{M\}$, thus arguing for a somewhat smaller $K_{\max}$ than otherwise.

As the loading in a network increases, the pipelining effect remains, although packets typically will have to queue up at the nodes before being forwarded. The effect of overhead becomes more important at heavier loads, however, because of the increased number of bits that must be transmitted with small packet sizes. On the other hand, there are several other effects at heavier loads that argue for small packet sizes. One is the "slow truck" effect. If many packets of widely varying lengths are traveling over the same path, then the short packets will pile up behind the long packets because of the high transmission delay of the long packets on each link; this is analogous to the pile up of cars behind a slow truck on a street with no passing. A similar effect on queueing delay, for packets on different paths, will be discussed in Chapter 3; a high variability in packet lengths (which occurs with a large maximum packet size) increases delay.

In subsection 2.4.3, the effect of high variability in frame lengths on go back n ARQ systems was shown. High variability either increases the number of packets that must be retransmitted or increases idle time. This again argues for small maximum packet size. Finally, there is the effect of transmission errors. Large frames have a somewhat higher probability of error than small frames. For most links in use (with the notable exception of radio links), the probability of error on reasonable size frames is on the order of 10^{-4} or less, so that this effect is typically less important than the other effects discussed. Unfortunately, there are many analyses of optimal maximum frame length in the literature focusing only on this effect. Thus, these analyses are valid only in those special cases where error probabilities are very high.

In practice, typical maximum packet lengths are on the order of several thousand bits. If the overhead could be reduced, then it would be reasonable to use even shorter maximum packet lengths, thus mitigating the effects of packet length variability discussed above.

2.6 STANDARD DLCs

There are a number of similar standards for data link control, namely HDLC, AD-CCP, LAPB, and SDLC. HDLC was developed by the International Standards Organization (ISO), ADCCP by the American National Standards Institute (ANSI), LAPB by the International Consultative Committee on Telegraphy and Telephony (CCITT), and SDLC by IBM. HDLC and ADCCP are virtually identical and are described here. They have a wide variety of different options and modes of operation. LAPB is the DLC layer for X-25, which is the primary standard for connecting an external site to a subnet; LAPB is, in essence, a restricted subset of the HDLC options and modes, as will be described later. Similarly, SDLC, which was the precursor of HDLC and ADCCP, is essentially another subset of options and modes.

HDLC and ADCCP are designed for a variety of link types, including either multiaccess or point-to-point links and either full duplex links (that is, both stations can transmit at once) or half duplex links (that is, only one station can transmit at a time). There are three possible *modes* of operation, one of which is selected when the link is initialized for use.

The first mode, the *normal response mode* (NRM), is for a master-slave type of link use such as is typical between a computer and one or more peripherals (the word "normal" is of historical significance only). There is a primary or master station (the computer) and one or more secondary or slave stations. The secondary stations can send frames only in response to polling commands from the primary station. This mode is reasonable in multiaccess situations where the polling commands ensure that only one station transmits at a time (see Chapter 4 for a general discussion of multiaccess communication). NRM is also reasonable for half duplex links or for communication with peripherals incapable of acting in other modes.

The second mode, the *asynchronous response mode* (ARM), is also a master-slave mode in which the secondary nodes are not so tightly restricted. It is not widely used and will not be discussed further.

The third mode, the *asynchronous balanced mode* (ABM), is for full duplex point-to-point links between stations that take equal responsibility for link control. This is the mode of greatest interest for point-to-point links in data networks. It is also used, in slightly modified form, for multiaccess communication in local area networks. LAPB uses only this mode, whereas SDLC uses only the first two modes.

We first describe the frame structure common to all three modes and all four standards. Then the operation of the normal response mode (NRM) and the asynchronous balanced mode (ABM) are described in more detail. Although ABM is our major interest, the peculiarities of ABM will be more easily understood once NRM is understood.

Figure 2.30 shows the frame structure. The flag, 01^60, is as described in subsection 2.5.2, with bit stuffing used within the frame (the flag is not considered as part of the frame proper). One or more flags must separate each pair of frames. The CRC uses the CRC-CCITT generator polynomial $g(D) = D^{16} + D^{12} + D^5 + 1$ as explained in subsection 2.3.4; it checks the entire frame (not including the flag).

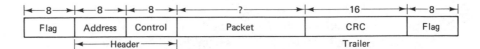

Figure 2.30   Frame structure of standard DLCs. The address, control and CRC fields can each be optionally extended in length.

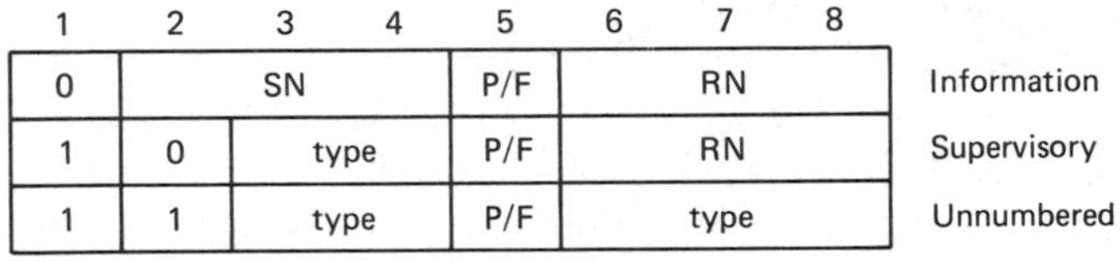

1	2	3	4	5	6	7	8	
0	SN			P/F	RN			Information
1	0	type		P/F	RN			Supervisory
1	1	type		P/F	type			Unnumbered

Figure 2.31   Structure of the control field for the information, supervisory, and unnumbered frame formats.

One modification is that the first 16 bits of the frame are inverted in the calculation of the CRC (although not inverted in transmission). Also, the remainder is inverted to form the CRC. At the receiving DLC, the first 16 bits of the frame are similarly inverted for recalculation of the remainder, which is then inverted for comparison with the received CRC. One reason for this is to avoid having an all-zero string (which is common if the link or modem is malfunctioning) satisfy the CRC. Another reason is to avoid satisfying the CRC if a few zeros are added or deleted from the beginning or end of the frame. As an option, a 32-bit CRC can be used; the coefficients of this generator polynomial have the value 1 in positions 32, 26, 23, 22, 16, 12, 11, 10, 8, 7, 5, 4, 2, 1, and 0. This optional 32-bit CRC is used in the IEEE 802 standard for local area networks.

The address field normally consists of one byte (eight bits). For NRM, the address is always that of the secondary station; *i.e.*, when the primary sends a frame to a secondary, it uses the secondary's address, and when the secondary responds, it uses its own address. Note that this address is not intended as a destination for a session, but simply to distinguish stations for multiaccess use. For point-to-point links, the address field has no natural function, although we shall see later that it has some rather peculiar uses in ABM. There is an option in which the address field is extendable to an arbitrary number of 1 or more bytes; the first bit in a byte is 1 if that byte is the last address byte, and otherwise it is 0.

The normal format of the control field is shown in Figure 2.31. There are three different frame formats: *information, supervisory*, and *unnumbered*. The information frames are the actual packet-carrying frames; they normally use go back n ARQ with a modulus of 8. As shown in the figure, the send and receive numbers SN and RN are part of the control field. The supervisory frames are used to return ARQ information (*i.e.*, RN) either when there are no data packets to send or when a speedy ack or nak is needed. Finally, the unnumbered frames are used for the initiation and termination of a link and for sending various kinds of supplementary control information.

There is an option under which the control field is two bytes long and in which SN and RN are each seven bits long each and use a modulus of 128. Aside from this lengthening of SN and RN, this option is essentially the same as the normal single byte control field which is assumed in the following description.

The first bit of the control field distinguishes the information format from the supervisory and unnumbered formats. Similarly, for noninformation formats, the second bit distinguishes supervisory from unnumbered formats. The fifth bit of the control field is the *poll final* (P/F) bit. For the normal response mode, the primary sends a 1 in this bit position to poll the secondary. The secondary must then respond with one or more frames, and sends a 1 in this bit position to denote the final frame of the response. This polling and response function of the P/F bit in NRM is used for supervisory and unnumbered frames as well as information frames. The P/F bit is used in a rather strange way for the balanced asynchronous mode, as will be described later.

There are four types of supervisory frames: *receive-ready* (RR), *receive-not-ready* (RNR), *reject* (REJ), and *selective-reject* (SREJ). The type is encoded in the third and fourth bits of the control field. All of these have the basic function of returning ARQ information (*i.e.*, all packets with numbers less than RN are acknowledged) and all of them omit the information field from the frame. RR is the normal response if there is no data packet on which to piggyback RN. RNR means in addition that the station is temporarily unable to accept further packets; this allows a rudimentary form of link flow control—that is, if the buffers at one end of the link are filling up with received packets, the other end of the link can be inhibited from further transmission.

The REJ supervisory frame is sent to indicate either a received frame in error or a received frame with other than the awaited sequence number. Its purpose is to improve the efficiency of go back n ARQ, as explained in subsection 2.4.3. Similarly, SREJ provides a primitive form of selective repeat. It acks all packets before RN, and requests retransmission of RN itself followed by new packets; one cannot provide supplementary information about multiple required retransmissions. This facility can be useful, however, on satellite links, where there is a very small probability of more than one frame error in a round-trip delay. The implementation of REJ and SREJ are optional, whereas RR and RNR are required.

The unnumbered frames carry no sequence numbers, and are used for setting up the link for communication, disconnecting the link, and special control purposes. There are five available bits in the control field available for distinguishing different types of unnumbered frames, but not all are used. Six of these types will be referred to generically as *set mode* commands. There is one such command for each mode (NRM, ARM, and ABM), and one for each mode using the extended control field. This command is sent by a primary (for NRM or ARM) and by either node (for ABM) to initiate communication on a link. Upon sending or receiving this command, a station sets its send and receive numbers to zero. The recipient of the command must acknowledge it with an unnumbered frame, either an *unnumbered ack* which agrees to start using the link, or a *disconnected-mode* which refuses to start using the link. Similarly, there is a disconnect command which is used to stop using the link; this also requires an unnumbered ack in response.

Figure 2.32 shows the operation of the NRM mode for a primary and two secondaries. Note that the primary initiates communication with each separately and disconnects from each separately. Note also that the P/F bit is set to 1 on each unnumbered frame that requires a response. The frames with $P = 1$ to a given secondary strictly alternate with the frames from that secondary with $F = 1$. The frames with $P = 1$ can be viewed as being sent via a stop-and-wait protocol, the $F = 1$ serving as the ack. This alternation has the same problem as a stop-and-wait protocol without sequence numbers; that is, with errors and with arbitrary delays, the acks cannot be uniquely matched to the polls.

It is difficult to determine how much damage this faulty stop-and-wait protocol causes. To start with, link delays are not arbitrary and are rather easily determined; thus, in practice, it is not hard to choose time outs long enough so that responses will not come back after the time out. Next, the underlying go back n ARQ is correct under all timing assumptions, and thus, even if the polls and acks for data get confused, the only effect is a loss of efficiency and occasionally having several secondaries transmitting at once. Third, the only way that confusion can arise on initiating the link is if there was confusion in the previous disconnect; such confusion might occur on link or station failures, but we already know that certain failures (such as CRC failures or stations losing track of sequence numbers) are going to cause loss of packets anyway. Despite all these rationalizations, however, it would have been preferable if the poll bits had been properly and reliably acked.

In the asynchronous balanced mode, the decision was made, in designing these protocols, to have each station act as both a primary and a secondary (thus replacing a simple problem with a more familiar but more difficult problem). When a station acts as a primary, it uses the other station's address in the address field, and the P/F bit is interpreted as a poll bit. When a station acts as a secondary, it uses its own address, and the P/F bit is interpreted as a final bit. In customary operation, all information frames and all unnumbered frames requiring acks are sent as primary stations; all unnumbered frames acting as acks or responses, and most supervisory frames (which ack primary data frames) are sent as secondary stations.

What this means in practice is that the P/F bit is either P or F, depending on the address field. This bit, in conjunction with the address field, has three possible values: $P = 1$, requiring a response from the other station acting in a secondary role; $F = 1$, providing the secondary response, and neither. Given the somewhat inadequate performance of this poll/final alternation, this modified use of the P/F bit was an unfortunate choice.

Figure 2.33 shows some typical operation of ABM. The most interesting part of this is the next-to-last frame sent by station A; this is a supervisory frame sent with $P = 1$, thus requiring an acknowledgment. Since A has signified unwillingness

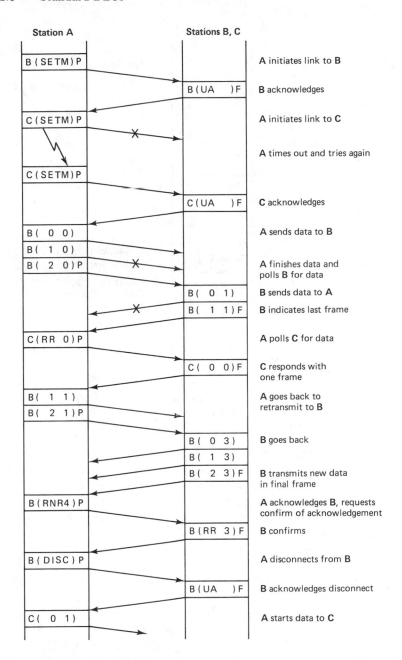

Figure 2.32   Normal mode operation of primary A with two secondaries B and C. SETM refers to the command setting the NRM mode with $SN = 0$ and $RN = 0$ at both stations. The address of each frame is given first, followed by (SN, RN) for information frames, (type,RN) for supervisory frames, and (type) for unnumbered frames; this is followed by a P/F bit if set to 1. Note that A uses different SN and RN values for B and C.

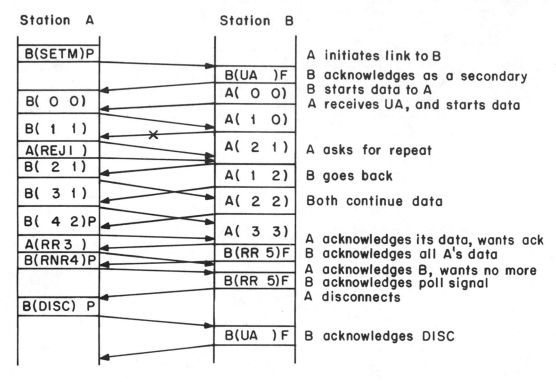

Figure 2.33   Asynchronous balanced mode (ABM) of operation. SETM refers to the set ABM command, which initiates the link with SN and RN at both sides equal to 0. Note the use of addresses in different types of frames.

to accept any more packets, a response from B signifies that B knows that packets up to 5 inclusive have been accepted and that no more will be accepted. Thus, upon receiving the acknowledgment of this, A can disconnect, knowing that B knows exactly which packets from B have been accepted; A also knows which of its packets have been accepted, so the disconnect leaves no uncertainty about the final condition of any packets at either A or B. Note that this "ideal" disconnect requires some previous agreement (not specified by the standard) between A and B; in particular, A must send RNR, with $P = 1$ and get an ack before disconnecting— this lets B know that A didn't go back to accepting packets again temporarily before the disconnect. This "ideal" disconnect doesn't work, of course, if the line is being disconnected because of a malfunction; in this case, the idea of an orderly sequence of RNR, ack, disconnect, and ack is unrealistic.

Another type of unnumbered frame is "frame-reject." This is sent in response to a received frame with a valid CRC but otherwise impossible value (such as exceeding the maximum frame length, being shorter than the minimum frame length, having an RN value not between $y_{\min}$ and $y_{\max}$, or having an impossible control field).

This means that either an undetectable error has occurred or one of the stations has malfunctioned. This is a serious error, outside of the realm of what the ARQ is designed for, and thus it should be reported at each station. The usual response to a "frame-reject" is for the opposite station to either reinitialize the link with a set mode command or to send an unnumbered "reset" command. The first resets RN and SN at each station to 0, and the second sets SN to 0 at the station that sent the faulty frame and RN to 0 at the receiving station. Both stations will again start to send packets (starting from the first packet not acked), but because of the resetting, some packets might arrive more than once and out of order. This is not a fault of the protocol, but a recognition that node malfunctions and undetectable errors cannot be dealt with.

2.7 SESSION IDENTIFICATION AND ADDRESSING

The issue of session identification is relevant at the network layer. A packet received by a node must contain enough information for the node to determine how to forward it toward its destination. This issue is discussed here since the encoding of this information is very similar to the issue of encoding framing information. The brute force approach to this problem is for the header of each packet to contain identification numbers for both the source and destination sites and additional identification numbers to identify the session within each site. This approach has great generality, since it allows different packets of the same session to travel over different paths in the subnet; it also requires considerable overhead.

If the network uses virtual circuits, then it turns out that far less overhead is required in the packet headers. With virtual circuits, each (one way) session using the network at a given time has a given path through the network, and thus there is a certain set of sessions using each link. It is helpful to visualize each link as being shared by a set of "virtual channels," distinguished by numbers. When a new session is set up, a path is established by assigning, on each link of the path, one unused virtual channel to that session. Each node then maintains a table mapping each busy incoming virtual channel on each link onto the corresponding outgoing virtual channel and link for the corresponding session (see Fig. 2.34). For example, if a given session has a path from node 3 to 5 to 8, using virtual channel 13 on link (3,5) and virtual channel 7 on link (5,8), then node 5 would map [link (3,5), virtual channel 13] to [link (5,8), virtual channel 7], and node 8 would map [link (5,8), virtual channel 7] to the access link to the appropriate destination site with a virtual channel number for that link. The nice thing about these virtual channels is that each link has its own set of virtual channels, so that no coordination is required between the links with respect to numbering.

With this virtual channel strategy, the only thing that must be transmitted in the packet header on a link is an encoding of the virtual channel number. The simplest way to do this, of course, is to represent the virtual channel number as a binary number in a fixed field of the header. Because of the limited capacity of

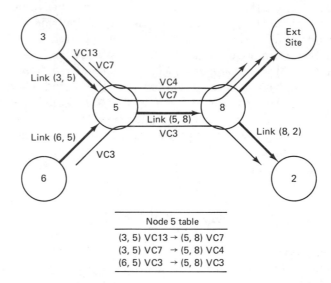

Figure 2.34   Use of virtual channel (VC) numbers to establish virtual circuits in a network. Each packet carries its VC number on each link and the node changes that number (by a table representing the virtual circuit) for the next link on the path.

the link, there is some natural upper bound on the number of sessions a link can handle, so there is no problem representing the virtual channel number by a fixed number of binary digits.

Later, other ways of representing virtual channel numbers will be discussed, but for now note that any method of distinguishing sessions must do something equivalent to representing virtual channel numbers. In other words, a given link carries data for a number of different sessions, and the transmitted bits themselves must distinguish which data belongs to which session. The packet header might supply a great deal of additional information, such as source and destination identities, but the bare minimum required is to distinguish the sessions of a given link. We now look at how this representation is handled in TYMNET.

2.7.1 Session Identification in TYMNET

TYMNET is a network developed in 1970 primarily to provide access for a time-sharing computer service, but rapidly expanded to allow users to communicate with their own computers. Since the terminals of that period usually transmitted only one character at a time and usually waited for an echo of that character to come back before transmitting the next character, the protocols were designed to work well with very short messages consisting of one or several characters. Although the network never received much academic publicity, many of the ideas first imple-

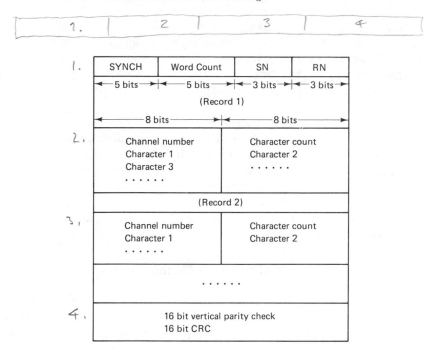

Figure 2.35   The frame structure in TYMNET. The first 16 bits is a frame header, and the last 32 bits is a frame trailer. Note that data from multiple sessions are included in a single frame.

mented there are now standard network practice. The frames are very short, with a maximum length of 66 bytes; the frames have the format shown in Fig. 2.35.

The two byte frame header uses five bits for a synchronization string, five bits for a word count, three bits for *SN*, and three bits for *RN*. The word count gives the number of 16 bit words in the frame, not counting the header and trailer. Since the nodes were implemented with 16 bit minicomputers, all the fields of the frame are organized in 16 bit (two byte) increments. Note that the 5 bit word count can represent up to 31 words of two bytes each, or 62 bytes. Thus, restricting the frames to be multiples of 16 bits serves to reduce (slightly) the overhead required for framing. The *SN* and *RN* fields provide conventional go back *n* ARQ with a modulus of m=8. The last four bytes (the frame trailer) provide error detection, using both a 16 bit CRC and 16 vertical parity checks. Thus, somewhat more error detection is provided than with the standard 16 bit CRC, but slightly less than with a 32 bit CRC.

Each record within a frame corresponds to data from a different session. A record starts with a byte giving the virtual channel number, which identifies the session. The next byte tells how many characters of data are contained in the record. If the number is odd, then the last byte of the record is just a fill character, so that the next record can start on a word boundary. A record here can be thought of as a very short packet, so that the channel number and character count correspond to the packet header. Thus, the packets are so short that a number of packets are normally grouped into one frame so as to avoid excessive frame overhead. These packets are somewhat different from the usual concept of a packet in that they do not necessarily contain the same number of characters from one link to the next on their path.

This type of strategy is usually referred to as *statistical multiplexing*. This means that the link is multiplexed between the virtual channels, but multiplexed on a demand basis. Conventional packet switching, in which there is just one packet per frame, is another form of statistical multiplexing, but, conventionally, one refers to that as packet switching and the type of strategy here as statistical multiplexing. When a frame is assembled for transmission at a node, the sessions are served in round robin order, taking some number of characters from each session that has characters waiting.

2.7.2 Session Identification in the Codex Networks

The Codex networks use quite a similar statistical multiplexing strategy, again with multiple sessions transmitting characters within the same frame. Here, however, a more efficient encoding is used to represent the virtual channel number and the amount of data for that session. In assembling a frame, the sessions are again served in sequential order, starting with virtual channel 1. Instead of sending the virtual channel number, however, an encoding is sent of the gap (*i.e.*, the number of idle virtual channels) between the number of the session being served and the previous session served (see Fig. 2.36). Thus, when all sessions have characters to send, these gaps are all zero, and if many but not all of the sessions have characters, most of the gaps are small. Thus, by encoding small gaps into a small number of bits, and large gaps into more bits, very high efficiency is maintained when large numbers of sessions are active. On the other hand, if only a small number of sessions are active, but have a large amount of data each, then only a small number of records will be in a frame, and again high efficiency is maintained.

Because of implementation issues, all of the fields in the Codex frames are multiples of 4 bit "nibbles". Thus, the smallest number of bits that can be used to represent a gap for identifying a session is one nibble. The method that identifies the number of characters in a record uses a special start record character, 0000, to start each new record. The characters for each session first go through a data compressor that maps highly probable characters into one nibble, less likely characters into two nibbles, and least likely characters into three nibbles. This is done adaptively, thus automatically using the current character statistics for the session. The 0000 nibble is reserved to indicate the start of a new record. Thus, the "packet header" consists of first a nibble to indicate a new packet (record), and next one or more nibbles representing the new session number. Under heavy loading, the packet header is typically just one byte long.

This strategy of encoding the difference between successive virtual channel

Unary-binary $0 \rightarrow 10$
gap encoding: $1 \rightarrow 11$
                        $2 \rightarrow 010$
                        $3 \rightarrow 011$
                        $4 \rightarrow 0110$
                        $\ldots \ldots$

Start record character: 0000

Sample Encoding of data:
(0000)(10)(Ch1)(Ch2)(Ch3)(Ch4)(0000)(10)(Ch1)(Ch2)
(0000)(11)(Ch1)(0000)(0010)(Ch1)(Ch2)(Ch3)...

Figure 2.36   Efficient encoding for virtual channels and lengths of records. In the example shown, there are four characters for VC1, two for VC2, one for VC4, and three for VC9. Each record starts with 0000 to indicate the start of new record (where 0000 cannot occur in data characters); this is followed by the encoding of the gap between virtual channels with data. The Codex protocols are similar, but gaps are encoded into multiples of four bits. Parentheses are for visual clarity.

numbers can also be used in conventional packet switched networks. There are two advantages in this. First, the packet overhead is reduced under heavy loading, and second, serving the sessions on a link in round robin order tends to promote fairness in the service that each session receives.

2.8 ERROR RECOVERY AT THE NETWORK AND TRANSPORT LAYER

The demonstration of the correctness of ARQ protocols in subsection 2.4.3 was based on a number of assumptions, namely that frames stayed in order on the links, that the CRC never experienced undetectable errors, that the link remained functional (recall that frames were correctly received with some nonzero probability), and, tacitly, that the DLC modules never failed or malfunctioned. In practice, undetectable errors will occur, links will fail, and nodes will fail (although presumably all of these events are rare). Thus, the question arises of what can and should be done about these failures at the network or transport layer?

One point of view is that the function of the network layer is to provide an error free packet pipe from source to destination site and that consequently error recovery should be done at the network layer. This point of view is popular among subnet designers who want to be sure that their subnet in fact works correctly. One of the advantages of this approach is that the error-recovery mechanism can take advantage of the mechanisms used in the network layer for routing and flow control. Also recovery can take place within the subnet, where implementation is simpler because of the similar nature of the nodes.

Another point of view is that packets must often travel through several subnets to reach their destination (this is particularly common where local area networks are used to access wide area networks). The individual subnets may not then be able to assure end-to-end recovery, making it necessary to provide a solution at the transport layer within the external sites. If packet sizes change on passing from one network to another, it becomes natural to provide an end-to-end acknowledgment on a message rather than packet basis, again making error recovery more appropriate at the transport layer.

Some sessions require a much higher degree of protection against errors than others. For example, financial transactions and some file transfers require very reliable transmission, whereas digitized speech requires very little protection (and should probably bypass the ARQ at the DLC layer). Error recovery at the network, transport, or higher layers can provide different degrees of added protection to different sessions. This does not remove the need for ARQ at the DLC layer, since, as will be seen, error recovery at the higher layers is more difficult and subject to greater delay than at the DLC layer.

2.8.1 End-to-End acks, Flow Control, and Permits

From a conceptual standpoint, error recovery at either the network or transport layer is quite similar to ARQ at the DLC layer. One general approach is to sequentially number the successive packets or messages for a given session at the source, then to provide an end-to-end acknowledgment by sequence number from the destination, and finally to retransmit those packets or messages for which no acknowledgment arrives back at the source. These retransmissions can be done either on a go back n basis or a selective repeat basis.

At the network layer, this approach is often tied in with flow control. The source sends a sequence number SN in each packet and the destination sends back receive numbers RN denoting the next awaited packet at the destination. RN is piggybacked into the packet header of return packets or sent in special control packets if there is no return traffic. With a given window size n, the source is then allowed to send packets from number RN up to $RN + n - 1$, inclusive.

This means that at most n packets for the given session can be outstanding in the network at a time, thus providing some restraint on congestion in the network. As congestion builds up and delay increases, acknowledgments are delayed and the source is slowed down. This effect will be described in more depth in Chapter 6. If the destination wishes to receive packets less rapidly, it can simply delay sending RN; thus, this type of flow control can be effective both in reducing congestion in the subnet and at the destination site. The main point here, however, is that this type of flow control also serves to provide end-to-end acknowledgments that can be used in error recovery.

Note that although this strategy is very similar to the ARQ strategies in data link control, the two are not the same. SN and RN in ARQ refer to successive packets traversing the link and have nothing to do with sessions; they appear in frame headers and are not seen at the network or higher layers. The SN and RN here appear in packet headers (or in transport layer headers) and are specific to individual sessions; they maintain their identity as they travel through successive links and are simply regarded as part of the packet (that is, part of a stream of arbitrary bits) at the DLC layer.

Another difference between ARQ and the window strategy here is that ARQ normally does not exercise flow control on a link. A link simply carries a fixed number of bits per second and there is no reason to limit this flow (other than the ability of the receiving node to handle the incoming data). Recall that the standard DLCs provide a receive-not-ready supervisory packet as a way to protect the receiving node from too many incoming packets. This mechanism allows speedy acknowledgments, thus preventing unnecessary retransmissions due to time outs, but also permits the receiving node to exert some flow control over the sending node.

Combining end-to-end acknowledgements with flow control has some limitations. If an acknowledgement doesn't arrive because of an error event, then the packet should be retransmitted, whereas if the ack is delayed due to network congestion, then the packet should not be retransmitted, since it would only add to the congestion. Since delays in the subnet are highly variable, it is difficult for time outs to distinguish between these cases. To make matters worse, the destination might be overloaded and postpone sending acks as a way of preventing further transmissions from the source; this again might cause unnecessary retransmissions due to time outs.

One partial solution to these problems is to provide the destination with a way to slow down the source without delaying acknowledgments. One way of doing this is by a technique like the receive-not-ready supervisory frames in the standard data link controls. Such a frame both provides a speedy ack and also prevents further transmission. This same technique can be used at the network layer (and is used in the X.25 network layer standard to be discussed shortly). A *permit* scheme is a more refined technique for the same objective. The destination sends two feedback numbers back to the source rather than one. The first, the usual RN, provides the ack function, and the second, a permit, tells the source how many additional packets the destination is prepared to receive. Thus if the permit number is j, the source is permitted to send packets from number RN to $RN + j - 1$ inclusive. In effect this allows the destination to change the window size with each acknowledgement to the source at will. It allows the destination to send permits for only as many packets as will fit in the available buffers. This permit scheme could be provided in DLCs as well, but it is less useful there because the buffering requirements at a node are relatively modest because of the fixed number of links at a node.

2.8.2 Using End-to-End acks for Error Recovery

Now comes the question: how can end-to-end acks be used for error recovery? One common reason for packets or messages not being received is link or node failure. In this case, assuming the use of virtual circuits, all the sessions using the failed link or node require new virtual circuits. How the nodes and external sites find out about such failures is an interesting question treated in Chapter 5, but assume such notification takes place. When the old virtual circuits are removed and the new ones set up, then the source for a session can start transmitting packets from its last received RN value; alternatively, as part of the process of setting up the new virtual circuit, the destination can return its current RN value to the source.

If error recovery is being handled at the network layer, it is usually the subnet source or destination node that establishes the new virtual circuit; this is somewhat easier than having the transport layer set up the new virtual circuit, since fewer layers are involved.

Another common source of unreceived packets is that many subnets and external sites will surreptitiously throw away packets if there is no readily available buffer for storing them. The viewpoint behind this is that if end-to-end error recovery is provided at either the network or transport layer, then these packets will eventually be retransmitted after some time out at the source and it thus doesn't do any harm to throw them away.

This is a flawed viewpoint, since packets start to be thrown away when the network is congested, which is precisely the time when retransmissions are undesirable. To make matters worse, if unreceived packets are relatively common events, retransmission time outs will tend to be relatively small, whereas if unreceived packets are truly rare, retransmission time outs can afford to be very large. Thus, when packets are commonly thrown away, one can expect many unnecessary retransmissions.

Whether networks should be designed to *never* throw away packets is a debatable issue. However, in today's technology, the cost of buffer storage is small relative to communication costs, and therefore enough buffer space should be provided so that packets are very rarely thrown away because of lack of buffer space. This, of course, also requires effective flow control, discussed in Chapter 6.

If errors occur due to an undetectable error pattern at the CRC or due to a temporary malfunction at a node, then the situation is much more complicated. The errors might remain undetected and simply proceed to the user with errors. Errors might occur in the packet address field, causing a packet to be delivered to the wrong destination. Some impossible frame header might occur at a receiving DLC, and this might cause the DLC to reinitialize, losing or repeating several packets. Finally, errors in the headers at higher layers might be detected by consistency checks at the destination site, perhaps leading to a session disconnect.

Some of these problems can be solved by using a supplementary end-to-end CRC within a packet (or message). This CRC would be ignored by the subnet and only checked at the destination site. This is helpful in detecting errors made inside the nodes of the subnet, and also in catching undetectable errors for the ordinary frame CRC. There is some question, however, of whether these errors are common enough to justify an end-to-end CRC. One possibility, of course, is to use an end-to-end CRC only for those sessions requiring extreme reliability.

There is one major deficiency in the use of end-to-end CRCs. They cannot check on the parts of the packet header that are changed from link to link. In particular, if the address information is carried as a virtual channel number, as discussed in the last section, then an error in this number made by a subnet node would be undetectable and the packet would arrive at the wrong destination (one of the worst kinds of errors). This problem could be cured by placing a unique identification number for the session in the packet header along with the virtual channel number; the end-to-end CRC would then check on that identification. The ARPANET is an example where an end-to-end set of check bits (similar to a CRC) is used. In that network, the address does not change from link to link and thus the above problem does not occur.

For datagram networks, in which each packet can take a different path to the destination, error recovery is more difficult, since packets can arrive at the destination out of order. For example, a given packet could take a very poor route, and the source could time out and retransmit that packet and many other packets, which could all be received before the given packet arrived at the destination. Assuming that sequence numbers are sent with some modulus, the sequence numbers could wrap around, and the given packet would be accepted in place of some later packet. Note that the proof of ARQ correctness in section 2.4 assumes that frames stay in order on the link; that assumption remains valid for virtual circuits, but is violated in datagram networks. One solution to this problem is to use a large modulus for sequence numbers, and also to use a time stamp in each packet; when a packet in the subnet becomes too old, it is thrown away. The modulus is chosen large enough that wraparound cannot occur while the given packet is still alive. The awkwardness of this solution is one of the reasons that most networks use virtual circuits.

2.8.3 The X.25 Network Layer Standard

The X.25 standard was developed by CCITT to provide a standard interface between external sites and subnet nodes. Recall that the physical layer, X.21, of this standard was briefly discussed in section 2.2, and the DLC layer, LAPB, was discussed in section 2.6. In X.25 terminology, the external site is referred to as DTE (Data Terminal Equipment) and the subnet node as DCE (Data Communication Equipment), but we shall continue to refer to them as sites and nodes.

The structure of an X.25 data packet is shown in Fig. 2.37. Recall that the DLC layer adds a frame header and trailer to this packet structure before transmission on the link. The third byte of the packet header is very similar to the control byte of the standard DLCs (except that SN and RN here refer to sequence numbers within the session as discussed above). The control bit, C, is 0 for data

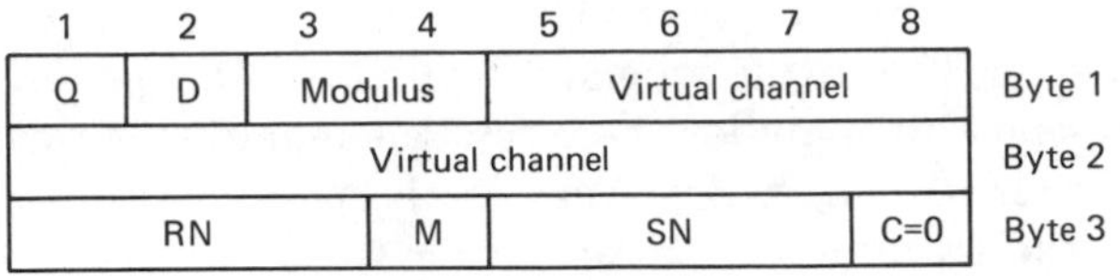

1	2	3	4	5	6	7	8	
Q	D	Modulus		Virtual channel				Byte 1
Virtual channel								Byte 2
RN			M	SN			C=0	Byte 3

Figure 2.37   Packet header for data in X.25. For a control packet the
C bit is 1.

packets and 1 for control packets (to be discussed later). This control bit is different
from the control bit in the frame header; at the DLC layer, all packets, data and
control, are treated indistinguishably, using 0 as the DLC layer control bit. Finally,
the "more" bit, M, in the packet header is 1 for nonfinal packets in a message and
0 for the final packet.

The last half of the first byte and the second byte of the packet header is
a 12-bit virtual channel number as discussed in section 2.7. This number can be
different at the two ends of the virtual circuit for a given session. Many subnets
use this same packet structure within the subnet, and the virtual channel number
can then change from link to link, as described in section 2.7.

The first bit, Q, in the packet header (if used at all) has the value 1 for control
packets at the transport and higher layers and has the value 0 for control packets
at the network layer and for data packets. The next bit, D, indicates whether
the acknowledgment (RN) has end-to-end significance or just link significance. If
$D = 1$, then RN signifies that the destination site has received all packets for the
session previous to RN, that RN is awaited, and that the source is free to send
a window of packets from RN on. If $D = 0$, RN signifies that the local subnet
node or site has received packets previous to RN, that RN is awaited, and the
other site or node is free to send a window of packets from RN on. It is possible
for some sessions to use end-to-end significance and others single-link significance.
As discussed above, end-to-end acks are very helpful in providing error recovery.
Some sessions, however, do not require error recovery, and some provide it at a
higher layer, for example, by using a query-response interaction between the sites.
For single-link significance, the acknowledgment function of RN is redundant (the
DLC layer guarantees that the packet is received). Thus, RN is used strictly for
flow control, and the receiving node delays sending RN until it is prepared to accept
a window of packets beyond RN.

The third and fourth bits of the header indicate whether the modulus is 8 or
128. If the modulus is 128, then the third byte is extended to two bytes to provide
seven bits for SN and seven for RN.

The control packets in X.25 are quite similar to the supervisory frames and
unnumbered frames in the standard DLCs. The third byte of the packet header
indicates the type of control packet, with the final bit (control bit) always 1 to

distinguish it from a data packet. The virtual channel number is the same as in a data packet, so that these control packets always refer to a particular session. There are receive-ready, receive-not-ready, and reject control packets, each of which carry RN; these are used for acknowledgments in the same way as in DLCs. The receive-not-ready packet provides some ability to acknowledge while asking for no more packets, but there is no ready made facility for permits.

One interesting type of control packet is the call-request packet. After the three-byte header, this packet contains an address field, containing the length of the calling address and called address in the first byte, followed by the addresses themselves. This is used to set up a virtual circuit for a new session in the network. Note that the virtual channel number is of no help in finding the destination; it simply specifies the virtual channel number to be used after the virtual circuit is established. The subnet node, on receiving a call-request packet, sets up a path to the destination and forwards the packet to the destination site. If the recipient at the destination site is willing and able to take part in the session, it sends back a call-accepted packet; when this reaches the originating site, the session is established.

Both the call-request and call-accepted packet contain a facilities field; this contains data such as the maximum packet length for the session, the window size, who is going to pay for the session, etc. The default maximum packet length is 128 bytes, and the default window size is 2. If the call-request packet specifies different values for maximum packet length or window size, the recipient can specify values closer to the default values, which must then be used. This is a sensible procedure for the external sites, but it is somewhat awkward for the subnet. The subnet can specify a maximum packet length and maximum window size to be used by the sessions using the subnet, but it is also desirable to have the ability to reduce window sizes under heavy loading, and this cannot be done naturally with X.25.

If the subnet is unable to set up the virtual circuit (because of heavy loading, for example), or if the recipient is unwilling to accept the call, then a clear-request control packet goes back to the initiating site, explaining why the session could not be established.

2.9 SUMMARY

In this chapter, an introductory survey of the physical layer, a fairly complete treatment of the data link control layer, and a few closely related topics at the network layer were presented. From a conceptual standpoint, one important issue has been distributed algorithms between two stations in the presence of errors and arbitrary delays. This has been developed in the context of ARQ, framing, and error recovery at higher layers. The correctness proof of the go back n class of protocols is important here since it shows how to reason carefully about such algorithms. There are many ad hoc algorithms used in data networks that contain subtle bugs, and it is important for designers to learn how to think about such algorithms in a more fundamental and structured way.

Another conceptual issue has been the encoding of control information. This was developed in the context of framing and session identification. Although the emphasis here was on efficiency of representation, the most important issue is to focus on the information actually conveyed; for example, it is important to recognize that flags with bit stuffing, length count fields, and special communication control characters all convey the same information but in quite different ways.

From a more practical standpoint, discussions were given on how modems work, how CRCs work (and fail), how ARQ works and how it can be made to work more efficiently with carefully chosen time outs and control feedback, how various kinds of framing techniques work (and fail), how session identification can be accomplished, and how higher layer error recovery can be effected. Many existing networks have been used to illustrate these ideas.

Various standards have been discussed, but not in enough detail for one to actually implement them. Unfortunately, if one wishes to implement a protocol in conformance with some standard, one must read the documentation of the standard, which is long and tedious. The purpose here was to give some conceptual understanding of the standard so as to see what the standard accomplishes and how. There are many special-purpose networks in which standard protocols are inappropriate, and it is helpful to know why.

2.10 NOTES, SOURCES, AND SUGGESTED READINGS

Section 2.2. For more information on linear filters and their representation in the time and frequency domain, see any standard undergraduate text (*e.g.*, [Sie85]) on linear systems. For an extensive and up to date treatment of modulation and demodulation of digital signals, see [Pro83]. Also, [Qur85] provides a complete and beautifully organized treatment of adaptive equalization. For the information theoretic aspects of this chapter (*i.e.*, Shannon's theorem, entropy, error detection and correction coding, and source coding), see [Gal68]. Finally, for an elementary treatment of the topics in this section oriented toward current practice, see [Sta85].

Section 2.3. Treatments of parity check codes and cyclic codes (CRC) can be found in [Bla83], [ClC81], and [Gal68].

Sections 2.4 and 2.5. A classic early paper on ARQ and framing is [Gra72]. An entire subdiscipline has developed to prove the correctness of point-to-point protocols. Typically, (see *e.g.*, [BoS81]) those approaches use a combination of exhaustive computer search plus analytic tools to reduce the search space. More information on highly efficient ARQ and framing is given in [Gal81]. Selective repeat and the advantages of sending packets multiple times after errors is discussed in [Wel82]. A more complete analysis of choice of frame lengths is given in [Alt86].

Section 2.6. An excellent description of the standard DLCs is given in [Car80]. A careful discussion of the problems with the poll final alternation for unnumbered frames is in [BaS83].

Section 2.7.   TYMNET is discussed in [Rin76] and [Tym81]. The Codex networks are discussed in [HuS86].

Section 2.8.   See [Ryb81] for more discussion of the X25 standard.

PROBLEMS

2.1 Suppose the output in Fig. 2.3(a) is $1 - e^{-2t/T}$, for $0 \leq t \leq T$; $(e^2 - 1)e^{-2t/T}$, for $t > T$; and zero for $t < 0$. Find the output in Fig. 2.3(b) using the linearity and time invariance of the filter.

2.2 Let $s(t) = 1$, for $0 \leq t \leq T$, and $s(t) = 0$ elsewhere. Let $h(t) = \alpha e^{-\alpha t}$, for $t \geq 0$, and $h(t) = 0$, for $t < 0$. Use the convolution equation to find the output when $s(t)$ is passed through a filter of impulse response $h(t)$.

2.3 Integrate Eq. (2.1), for $s(\tau) = e^{j2\pi f\tau}$, to get Eqs. (2.2) and (2.3). *Hint:* Transform the variable of integration by $\tau' = t - \tau$.

2.4 Suppose a channel has the ideal low-pass frequency response $H(f) = 1$, for $-f_0 \leq f \leq f_0$, and $H(f) = 0$ elsewhere. Find the impulse response of the channel (use the inverse Fourier transform, Eq. (2.6)).

2.5 Let $s(t)$ be a given waveform and let $s_1(t) = s(\beta t)$ for some given positive β. Sketch the relationship between $s(t)$ and $s_1(t)$, for $\beta = 2$. Let $S(f)$ be the Fourier transform of $s(t)$. Find $S_1(f)$, the Fourier transform of $s_1(t)$, in terms of $S(f)$. Sketch the relationship for $\beta = 2$ (assume $S(f)$ real for your sketch).

2.6 Let $S(f)$ be the Fourier transform of $s(t)$.

   (a)   Show that the Fourier transform of $s(t) \cos(2\pi f_0 t)$ is $[S(f - f_0) + S(f + f_0)]/2$.

   (b)   Find the Fourier transform of $s(t) \cos^2(2\pi f_0 t)$ in terms of $S(f)$.

2.7 Suppose the expected frame length on a link is 1000 bits and the standard deviation is 500 bits.

   (a)   Find the expected time to transmit a frame on a 9600-bps link and on a 50,000-bps link.

   (b)   Find the expected time and standard deviation of the time required to transmit 10^6 frames on each of the above links (assume that all frame lengths are statistically independent of each other).

   (c)   The *rate* at which frames can be transmitted is generally defined as the reciprocal of the expected transmission time. Using the result in part (b), discuss whether this definition is reasonable.

2.8 Show that the final parity check in a horizontal and vertical parity check code, if taken as the modulo 2 sum of all the data bits, is equal to the modulo 2 sum of the horizontal parity checks and also equal to the modulo 2 sum of the vertical parity checks.

2.9 (a)   Find an example of a pattern of six errors that cannot be detected by the use of horizontal and vertical parity checks. *Hint*: Each row with errors and each column with errors will contain exactly two errors.

    (b)   Find the number of different patterns of four errors that will not be detected by a horizontal and vertical parity check code; assume the array is K bits per row and J bits per column.

2.10 Suppose a parity check code has minimum distance d. Define the distance between a code word and a received string (of the same length) as the number of bit positions in which the two are different. Show that if the distance between one code word and a given string is less than $d/2$, then the distance between any other code word and the given string must exceed $d/2$. Show that if a decoder maps a given received string into a code word at smallest distance from the string, then all combinations of fewer than $d/2$ errors will be corrected.

2.11 Consider a parity check code with three data bits and four parity checks. Suppose three of the code words are 1001011, 0101101, and 0011110. Find the rule for generating each of the parity checks and find the set of all eight code words. What is the minimum distance of this code?

2.12 Let $g(D) = D^4 + D^2 + D + 1$, and let $s(D) = D^3 + D + 1$. Find the remainder when $D^4 s(D)$ is divided by $g(D)$, using modulo 2 arithmetic.

2.13 Let $g(D) = D^L + g_{L-1}D^{L-1} + \cdots + g_1 D + 1$ (assume $L > 0$). Let $z(D)$ be a nonzero polynomial with highest and lowest order terms of degree j and i, respectively; that is, $z(D) = D^j + z_{j-1}D^{j-1} + \cdots + D^i$ (or $z(D) = D^j$, if $i = j$). Show that $g(D)z(D)$ has at least two nonzero terms. *Hint*: Look at the coefficient of D^{L+j} and of D^i.

2.14 Show that if $g(D)$ contains the factor $1 + D$, then all error sequences with an odd number of errors are detected. *Hint*: Recall that a nonzero error polynomial $e(D)$ is detected unless $e(D) = g(D)z(D)$, for some polynomial $z(D)$. Look at what happens if 1 is substituted for D in this equation.

2.15 For a given generator polynomial $g(D)$ of degree L and given data length K, let $c^{(i)}(D) = c_{L-1}^{(i)}D^{L-1} + \cdots + c_1^{(i)}D + c_0^{(i)}$ be the CRC resulting from the data string with a single 1 in position i (that is, $s(D) = D^i$), for $0 \leq i \leq K - 1$.

    (a)   For an arbitrary data polynomial $s(D)$, show that the CRC polynomial is $c(D) = \sum_{i=0}^{K-1} s_i c^{(i)}(D)$ (using modulo 2 arithmetic).

(b)   Letting $c(D) = c_{L-1}D^{L-1} + \cdots + c_1 D + c_0$, show that

$$c_j = \sum_{i=0}^{K-1} s_i c_j^{(i)}; \qquad 0 \le j < L$$

This shows that each c_j is a parity check and that a cyclic redundancy check code is a parity check code.

2.16 (a)   Consider a stop-and-wait ARQ strategy in which the sending DLC, rather than using a sequence number for successive packets, sends the number of times the given packet has been retransmitted. Thus, the format of the transmitted frames is $\boxed{j}\,\boxed{\text{packet}}\,\boxed{\text{CRC}}$, where j is 0 the first time a packet is transmitted, 1 on the first retransmission, etc. The receiving DLC returns an ack or nak (without any receive number) for each frame it receives. Show by example that this strategy does not work correctly, no matter what rule the receiving DLC uses for accepting packets (use the assumptions preceding subsection 2.4.1).

(b)   Redo part (a) with the following two changes: (1) the number j above is 0 on the initial transmission of a packet and 1 on *all* subsequent retransmissions of that packet, and, (2) frames have a fixed delay in each direction, are always recognized as frames, and the sending DLC never times out, simply waiting for an ack or either a nak or error.

2.17 (a)   Let T_t be the expected transmission time for sending a data frame. Let T_f be the feedback transmisson time for sending an ack or nak frame. Let T_d be the expected propagation and processing delay in one direction (the same in each direction). Find the expected time T between successive frame transmissions in a stop-and-wait system (assume there are no other delays and no frames get lost).

(b)   Let p_t be the probability of frame error in a data frame (independent of frame length), and p_f the probability of error in a feedback ack or nak frame. Find the probability q that a data packet is correctly received and acked on a given transmission. Show that $1/q$ is the expected number of times a packet must be transmitted for a stop-and-wait system (assume independent errors on all frames).

(c)   Combining parts (a) and (b), find the expected time required per packet. Evaluate for $T_t = 1$, $T_f = T_d = 0.1$, and $p_t = p_f = 10^{-3}$.

2.18 Redraw Figs. 2.21 and 2.22 with the same frame lengths and the same set of frames in error, but focusing on the packets from B to A. That is, show SN and $y_{\min}$ for node B and show RN and packets out for node A (assume all frames are carrying packets).

2.19 Give an example in which go back n will deadlock if receiving DLCs ignore the receive number RN in each frame not carrying the awaited packet. *Hint*: Construct a pattern of frame errors leading to a situation where y_{rec} at node B is n plus y_{min} at node A, and similarly for A and B reversed.

2.20 Give an example in which go back n ARQ fails if the modulus m is equal to n. For $m > n$, give an example where Eq. (2.28) is satisfied with equality and an example where Eq. (2.29) is satisfied with equality.

2.21 Assume that at time t, node A has a given y_{min} as the smallest packet number not yet acknowledged and $y_{max} - 1$ as the largest number yet sent. Let T_m be the minimum packet transmission time on a link and T_d be the propagation delay. Show that y_{rec} at node B must lie in the range from y_{min} to y_{max} for times in the range from $t - T_m - T_d$ to $t + T_m + T_d$.

2.22 (a) Let T_{min} be the minimum transmission time for data frames and T_d be the propagation and processing delay in each direction. Find the maximum allowable value T_{max} for frame transmission time such that a go back n ARQ system (of given n) will never have to go back or wait in the absence of tranmission errors or lost frames. *Hint*: Look at Fig. 2.24.

   (b) Redo part (a) with the added possibility that isolated errors can occur in the feedback direction.

2.23 Assume that frame transmission times τ are exponentially distributed with, for example, probability density $p(\tau) = e^{-\tau}$, for $\tau \geq 0$. Assume that a new frame always starts in each direction as soon as the previous one in that direction terminates. Assume that transmission times are all independent and that processing and propagation delays are negligible. Show that the probability q that a given frame is not acked before $n - 1$ additional frames have been sent (*i.e.*, the window is exhausted) is $q = (1 + n)2^{-n}$. *Hint*: Note that the set of times at which frame transmissions terminate at either node is a Poisson process and that a point in this process is equally likely to be a termination at A or B, with independence between successive terminations.

2.24 Show that if an isolated error in the feedback direction occurs on the ack of the given packet, then q in Prob. 2.23 becomes $q = [2 + n + (n+1)n/2]2^{-n-1}$.

2.25 Assume that frame transmission times τ have an Erlang distribution with probability density $p(\tau) = \tau e^{-\tau}$. Find the corresponding value of q in Prob. 2.23. *Hint*: The termination times at A can be regarded as alternate points in a Poisson process and the same is true for B.

2.26 Let γ be the expected number of transmitted frames from A to B per successfully accepted packet at B. Let β be the expected number of transmitted frames from A to B between the transmission of a given frame and the reception of feedback about that frame (including the frame in transmission when the feedback arrives). Let p be the probability that a frame arriving at B contains errors (with successive frames assumed independent). Assume that A is always busy transmitting frames, that n is large enough that A never goes back in the absence of feedback, and that A always goes back on the next frame after hearing that the awaited frame contained errors. Show that γ satisfies $\gamma = 1 + p(\beta + \gamma)$. Define the efficiency η as $1/\gamma$, and find η as a function of β and p.

2.27 Assume that a selective repeat system has the property that the sending DLC always finds out whether a given transmitted packet was successfully received during or before the βth frame transmission following the frame in which the given packet was transmitted. Give a careful demonstration that the sending DLC need never save more than $\beta + 1$ unacknowledged packets.

2.28 Find the efficiency of the ARPANET ARQ system under the assumptions that all eight virtual channels are always busy sending packets and that feedback always arrives about the fate of a given packet during or before the seventh frame transmission following the frame carrying the given packet.

2.29 Consider a generalized selective repeat ARQ system that operates in the following way: as in conventional go back n and selective repeat, let y_{rec} be the smallest numbered packet not yet correctly received, let y_{min} be the transmitter's estimate of y_{rec}, and let y_{max} be one greater than the largest numbered packet yet transmitted. Let y_{top} be the largest numbered packet correctly received and accepted (thus, for go back n, y_{top} would be $y_{\text{rec}} - 1$, whereas for conventional selective repeat, y_{top} could be as large as $y_{\text{rec}} + n - 1$). The rule at the transmitter is the same as for conventional go back n or selective repeat: The number z of the packet transmitted must satisfy

$$y_{\text{max}} - n \leq z \leq y_{\text{min}} + n - 1$$

As a consequence, $y_{\text{max}} \leq y_{\text{min}} + n$ is always satisfied. The rule at the receiver, for some given positive number k, is that a correctly received packet with number z is accepted if

$$y_{\text{rec}} \leq z \leq y_{\text{top}} + k \qquad (2.49)$$

(a) Assume initially that z (rather than $SN = z \bmod m$) is sent with each packet and that y_{rec} (rather than $RN = y_{\text{rec}} \bmod m$) is sent with each packet in the reverse direction. Show that for each received packet at the receiver,

$$z \leq y_{\text{rec}} + n - 1 \qquad (2.50)$$
$$z \geq y_{\text{top}} - n + 1$$

(b) Now assume that $SN = z \bmod m$ and $RN = y_{\text{rec}} \bmod m$. When z is received Eq. (2.50) is satisfied, but erroneous operation will result if $z - m$ or $z + m$ lie in the window specified by Eq. (2.49). How large need m be to guarantee that $z + m > y_{\text{top}} + k$ (that is, that $z + m$ is outside the window of Eq. (2.49))?

(c) Is the value of m determined in part (b) large enough to ensure that $z - m < y_{\text{rec}}$?

(d) How large need m be (as a function of n and k) to ensure correct operation?

(e) Interpret the special cases $k = 1$ and $k = n$.

2.30 (a) Apply the bit stuffing rules of subsection 2.5.2 to the following frame:
0 1 1 0 1 1 1 1 1 0 0 1 1 1 1 1 1 0 1 0 1 1 1 1 1 1 1 1 0 1 1 1 1 0 1 0

(b) Suppose the following string of bits is received:
0 1 1 1 1 1 1 0 1 1 1 1 1 0 1 1 0 0 1 1 1 1 1 0 0 1 1 1 1 1 0 1 1 1 1 1 0 1 1
0 0 0 1 1 1 1 1 1 0 1 0 1 1 1 1 1 0
Remove the stuffed bits and show where the actual flags are.

2.31 Suppose that the bit stuffing rule of subsection 2.5.2 is modified to stuff a 0 only after the appearance of 01^5 in the original data. Carefully describe how the destuffing rule at the receiver must be modified to work with this change. Show how your rule would destuff the following string:
0 1 1 0 1 1 1 1 1 0 1 1 1 1 1 0 1 1 1 1 1 0 1 0 1 1 1 1 1 0
If your destuffing rule is correct, you should remove only two 0's and find only one actual flag.

2.32 Bit stuffing must avoid the appearance of 01^6 within the transmitted frame, so we accept as given that an original string 01^6 will always be converted into 01^501. Use this, plus the necessity to destuff correctly at the receiver to show that a 0 must always be stuffed after 01^5. *Hint:* Consider the data string $01^501x_1x_2\ldots$. If a 0 is not stuffed after 01^5, the receiver cannot distinguish this from $01^6x_1x_2\ldots$ after stuffing, so stuffing is required in this case. Extend this argument to $01^50^k1x_1x_2\ldots$, for any $k > 1$.

2.33 Suppose the string 0101 is used as the bit string to indicate the end of a frame and the bit stuffing rule is to insert a 0 after each appearance of 010 in the original data; thus, 010101 would be modified by stuffing to 01001001. In addition, if the frame proper ends in 01, a 0 would be stuffed after the first 0 in the actual terminating string 0101. Show how the string 11011010010101011101 would be modified by this rule. Describe the destuffing rule required at the receiver. How would the string 11010001001001100101 be destuffed?

2.34 Let $A = E\{K\}2^{-j} + j + 1$ be the upper bound on overhead in Eq. (2.38) and let $j = \lfloor \log_2 E\{K\} \rfloor$. Show that A satisfies

$$1.914\ldots + \log_2 E\{K\} \leq A \leq 2 + \log_2 E\{K\}$$

Find the analytic expression for $1.914\ldots$. *Hint*: Define γ as $\log_2 E\{K\} - j$ and find the minimum and maximum of $A - log_2 E\{K\}$ as γ varies between 0 and 1.

2.35 Show that the probability that errors will cause a flag 01^60 to appear within a transmitted frame is approximately $(1/32)Kp$, where K is the number of bits in the frame proper before stuffing, and p is the probability of bit error. Assume that p is very small and the probability of multiple errors in a frame is negligible. Assume that the bits of the original frame are IID (independent, identically distributed) with equal probability of 0 and 1. *Hint*: This is trickier than it appears, since the bits after stuffing are no longer IID. First, find the probability that a stuffed bit in error causes a flag (not an abort) to appear and use the analysis of subsection 2.5.2 to approximate the expected number of stuffed bits as $K2^{-6}$. Then find the probability of a flag appearing due to errors in the original bits of the frame.

2.36 A certain virtual circuit network is designed for the case where all sessions carry heavy, almost steady, traffic. It is decided to serve the various sessions using each given link in round robin order, first sending one packet from the first session, then one from the second, and so forth up to the last, and then starting over with the first, etc., thus avoiding the necessity of sending a session number with each packet. To handle the unlikely possibility that a session has no packet to send on a link at its turn, we place a k-bit flag, 01^{k-1} in front of the information packet for the next session that has a packet. This flag is followed by a binary encoding of the number of sessions in order with nothing to send, 1 for one session, 01 for two, 001 for three, etc. Thus, for example, if a packet for the second session has just been sent, sessions three and four have no packets, and session five has the packet $\overline{x}_5$, we send $01^{k-1}01\overline{x}_5$ as the next packet. In addition, an insertion is used if an information packet happens to start with 01^{k-2}. Insertions are not required otherwise in information packets, and information packets carry their own length information.

(a) Assume that p is the probability that a session has no packet when it is that session's turn; this event is assumed independent of other sessions and of past history. Find the expected number of overhead bits per transmitted packet for flags, run length code, and insertions. Ignore, as negligible, any problems of what to do if no session has a packet to send.

(b) Suppose that the packets above, as modified by flags, run length code, and insertions, are the inputs to a data link control system using ARQ for error control and flags to indicate the end of packets. Explain if any problems arise due to the use of flags both on the DLC system and in the higher level scheme for identifying packets with sessions.

2.37 Consider a stop-and-wait data link control protocol. Each transmitted frame contains the sequence number, modulo 2, of the contained packet. When a frame arrives at the receiver, the sequence number of the packet is compared with the packet number awaited by the receiver; if the numbers are the same modulo 2 and the CRC is satisfied, the packet is accepted and the awaited packet number is incremented. An ack containing the new awaited packet number modulo 2 is sent back to the transmitter. If a frame is received with correct CRC but the wrong sequence number, an ack (containing the awaited packet number modulo 2) is also sent back to the transmitter. The new twist here is that frames can go out of order on the channel. More precisely, there is a known maximum delay T on the channel. If a packet is transmitted at some time t, it is either not received at all or received at an arbitrary time in the interval from t to $t + T$, independently of other transmissions. The return channel for the acks behaves the same way with the same maximum delay T. Assume that the receiver sends acks instantaneously upon receiving packets with valid CRCs.

(a) Describe rules for the transmitter to follow so as to ensure that each packet is eventually accepted, once and in order, by the receiver. You are not to put any extra protocol information in the packets or to change the receiver's operation. You should try to leave as much freedom as possible to the transmitter's operation subject to the restriction of correct operation.

(b) Explain why it is impossible to achieve correct operation if there is no bound on delay.

3

Delay Models

in Data Networks

3.1 INTRODUCTION

One of the most important performance measures of a data network is the average delay required to deliver a packet from origin to destination. Furthermore, delay considerations strongly influence the choice and performance of network algorithms, such as routing and flow control. For these reasons, it is important to understand the nature and mechanism of delay, and the manner in which it depends on the characteristics of the network.

Queueing theory is the primary methodological framework for analyzing network delay. Its use often requires simplifying assumptions since, unfortunately, more realistic assumptions make meaningful analysis extremely difficult. For this reason, it is sometimes impossible to obtain accurate quantitative delay predictions on the basis of queueing models. Nevertheless, these models often provide a basis for adequate delay approximations, as well as valuable qualitative results and worthwhile insights.

In what follows, we will focus on packet delay within the communication subnet (*i.e.*, the network layer). This delay is the sum of delays on each subnet link traversed by the packet. Each link delay in turn consists of four components.

1. The *processing* delay between the time the packet is correctly received at the head node of the link and the time the packet is assigned to an outgoing link

queue for transmission. (In some systems, we must add to this delay some additional processing time at the DLC and physical layers.)

2. The *queueing delay* between the time the packet is assigned to a queue for transmission and the time it starts being transmitted. During this time, the packet waits while other packets in the transmission queue are transmitted.

3. The *transmission delay* between the times that the first and last bits of the packet are transmitted.

4. The *propagation delay* from the time the last bit is transmitted at the head node of the link until the time it is received at the tail node. This is proportional to the physical distance between transmitter and receiver and is ordinarily small except in the case of a satellite link.

This accounting neglects the possibility that a packet may require retransmission on a link due to transmission errors or various other causes. For most links in practice, other than multiaccess links to be considered in Chapter 4, retransmissions are rare and will be neglected. The propagation delay depends on the physical characteristics of the link and is independent of the traffic carried by the link. The processing delay is also independent of the amount of traffic handled by the corresponding node if computation power is not a limiting resource. This will be assumed in our discussion. Otherwise, a separate processing queue must be introduced prior to the transmission queues. Most of our subsequent analysis focuses on the queueing and transmission delays. We first consider a single transmission line and analyze some classical queueing models. We then take up the network case and discuss the type of approximations involved in deriving analytical delay models.

While our primary emphasis is on packet-switched network models, some of the models developed are useful in a circuit-switched network context. Indeed, queueing theory was extensively developed in response to the need for performance models in telephony.

3.1.1 Multiplexing of Traffic on a Communication Link

The communication link considered is viewed as a bit pipe over which a given number of bits per second can be transmitted. This number is called the *transmission capacity* of the link. It depends both on the physical channel and the interface (*e.g.*, modems), and is simply the rate at which the interface accepts bits. The link capacity may serve several traffic streams (*e.g.*, virtual circuits or groups of virtual circuits) multiplexed on the link. The manner of allocation of capacity among these traffic streams has a profound effect on packet delay.

In the most common scheme, *statistical multiplexing*, the packets of all traffic streams are merged into a single queue and transmitted on a first-come first-serve basis. A variation of this scheme, which has roughly the same average delay per packet, maintains a separate queue for each traffic stream and serves the queues in sequence one packet at a time. However, if the queue of a traffic stream is empty, the next traffic stream is served and no communication resource is wasted. Since the entire transmission capacity C (bits/sec) is allocated to a single packet at a time, it takes L/C sec to transmit a packet that is L bits long.

In *time-division* (TDM) *and frequency-division multiplexing* (FDM) with m traffic streams, the link capacity is essentially subdivided into m portions—one per traffic stream. In FDM, the channel bandwidth W is subdivided into m channels each with bandwidth W/m (actually slightly less because of the need for guard bands between channels). The transmission capacity of each channel is roughly C/m, where C is the capacity that would be obtained if the entire bandwidth was allocated to a single channel. The transmission time of a packet that is L bits long is Lm/C, or m times longer than in the corresponding statistical multiplexing scheme. In TDM, allocation is done by dividing the time axis into slots of fixed length (*e.g.*, one bit or one byte long, or perhaps one packet long for fixed length packets). Again, conceptually, we may view the communication link as consisting of m separate links with capacity C/m. In the case where the slots are short relative to packet length, we may again regard the transmission time of a packet L bits long as Lm/C. In the case where the slots are of packet length, the transmission time of an L bit packet is L/C, but there is a wait of $(m-1)$ packet transmission times between packets of the same stream.

One of the themes that will emerge from our queueing analysis is that statistical multiplexing has smaller average delay per packet than either TDM or FDM. This is particularly true when the traffic streams multiplexed have a relatively low duty cycle. The main reason for the poor delay performance of TDM and FDM is that communication resources are wasted when allocated to a traffic stream with a momentarily empty queue, while other traffic streams have packets waiting in their queue. For a traffic analogy, consider an m-lane highway and two cases. In one case, cars are not allowed to cross over to other lanes (this corresponds to TDM or FDM), while in the other case, cars can change lanes (this corresponds roughly to statistical multiplexing). Restricting crossover increases travel time for the same reason that the delay characteristics of TDM or FDM are poor, namely some system resources (highway lanes or communication channels) may not be utilized while others are momentarily stressed.

Under certain circumstances, TDM or FDM may have an advantage. Suppose that each traffic stream has a "regular" character, *i.e.*, all packets arrive sufficiently apart so that no packet has to wait while the preceding packet is transmitted. If these traffic streams are merged into a single queue, it can be shown that the average delay per packet will decrease, but the variance of waiting time in queue will generally become positive (for an illustration see Prob. 3.7). Therefore, if maintaining small variability of delay is more important than decreasing delay, it may be preferable to use TDM or FDM. Another advantage of TDM and FDM is that there is no need to include identification of the traffic stream on each packet, thereby saving some overhead.

3.2 QUEUEING MODELS—LITTLE'S THEOREM

We consider queueing systems where customers arrive at random times to obtain service. The probability distribution of the time between two successive arrivals (the interarrival time), and the probability distribution of the customers' service time are given.

In the context of a data network, customers represent packets assigned to a communication link for transmission. Service time corresponds to the packet transmission time and is equal to L/C, where L is the packet length in bits and C is the link transmission capacity in bits/sec. In this chapter it is convenient to ignore the layer 2 distinction between packets and frames; thus packet lengths are taken to include frame headers and trailers. In a somewhat different context (which we will not dwell on very much), customers represent active conversations (or virtual circuits) between points in a network and service time corresponds to the duration of a conversation.

We shall be typically interested in estimating quantities such as:

1. The average number of customers in the system (*i.e.*, the "typical" number of customers either waiting in queue or undergoing service).
2. The average delay per customer (*i.e.*, the "typical" time a customer spends waiting in queue plus the service time).

We first need to clarify the meaning of the terms above. Let us denote

$$p_n(t) = \text{Probability of } n \text{ customers waiting in} \\ \text{queue or under service at time } t$$

The typical situation is one whereby we are given the initial probabilities $p_n(0)$ at time 0 and enough statistical information is provided to determine, at least in principle, the probabilities $p_n(t)$ for all times t. Then denoting

$$\overline{N}(t) = \text{Average number in the system at time } t$$

we have

$$\overline{N}(t) = \sum_{n=0}^{\infty} n\, p_n(t)$$

Note that both $\overline{N}(t)$ and $p_n(t)$ depend on t as well as the initial probability distribution $\{p_0(0),\ p_1(0),\ldots\}$. However, the queueing systems that we will consider typically *reach equilibrium* in the sense that for some p_n and N (independent of the initial distribution), we have

$$\lim_{t \to \infty} p_n(t) = p_n, \quad n = 0, 1, \ldots \tag{3.1}$$

and

$$N = \sum_{n=0}^{\infty} np_n = \lim_{t \to \infty} \overline{N}(t)$$

We will be interested primarily in the equilibrium probabilities and the average number in the system. Note that it is possible that $N = \infty$ and this will occur whenever the arrival rate exceeds the service capacity of the system. Individual sample functions of the number of customers in the system will be denoted by $N(t)$. The time average of such a sample function in the interval $[0, t]$ is defined by

$$N_t = \frac{1}{t} \int_0^t N(\tau)\, d\tau$$

Almost every system of interest to us is ⟨ergodic⟩ in the sense that   *conceguence*

$$\lim_{t \to \infty} N_t = \lim_{t \to \infty} \overline{N}(t) = N$$

holds with probability one. The equality of long term time average and ensemble average of various stochastic processes will often be accepted in this chapter on intuitive grounds since a rigorous mathematical justification requires technical arguments that are beyond the scope of this text.

Regarding average delay per customer, the situation is one whereby enough statistical information is available to determine in principle the probability distribution of delay of each individual customer (*i.e.*, the first, second, etc.). From this, we can determine the average delay of each customer. The average delay of the kth customer, denoted $\overline{T}_k$, typically converges as $k \to \infty$ to a steady-state value

$$T = \lim_{k \to \infty} \overline{T}_k$$

The limit above is what we will call average delay per customer. (Again, $T = \infty$ is possible.) For the systems of interest to us, the steady-state average delay T is also equal (with probability one) to the long-term time average of customer delay, *i.e.*,

$$T = \lim_{k \to \infty} \overline{T}_k = \lim_{k \to \infty} \frac{1}{k} \sum_{i=1}^{k} T_i$$

where T_i is the delay of the ith customer.

The average number in the system N and the average delay T are related by a simple formula that makes it possible to determine one given the other. This result, known as *Little's Theorem*, has the form

$$N = \lambda T$$

where

$$\lambda = \text{Average customer arrival rate}$$

and is given by

$$\lambda = \lim_{t \to \infty} \frac{\text{Expected number of arrivals in the interval } [0, t]}{t}$$

(We will be assuming that the limit above exists.) Phenomena reflecting Little's Theorem are familiar from everyday experience. For example, on a rainy day, traffic on a rush hour moves slower than average (large T) while the streets are more crowded (large N). Similarly, a fast-food restaurant (small T) needs a smaller waiting room (small N) than a regular restaurant for the same customer arrival rate.

Little's Theorem is really an accounting identity and its derivation is very simple. We will give a graphical proof, which assumes that customers are served in the order they arrive. A similar proof is possible for the case where the order of service is arbitrary (see Problems 3.31 and 3.32). For any sample system history let us denote:

$$\alpha(t) = \text{Number of arrivals in the interval } [0, t]$$
$$\beta(t) = \text{Number of departures in the interval } [0, t]$$

Assuming an empty system at time 0, the number in the system at time t is

$$N(t) = \alpha(t) - \beta(t)$$

Let t_i and T_i be the time of arrival and the time spent in the system, respectively, by the ith customer. Consider any time t and the shaded area in Fig. 3.1 which lies between the graphs of $\alpha(\tau)$ and $\beta(\tau)$ up to time t. This area can be expressed as

$$\int_0^t N(\tau)\, d\tau$$

but also as

$$\sum_{i=1}^{\beta(t)} T_i + \sum_{i=\beta(t)+1}^{\alpha(t)} (t - t_i)$$

Dividing both expressions above by t and equating them, we obtain

$$N_t = \lambda_t T_t \tag{3.2}$$

where

$$N_t = \frac{\int_0^t N(\tau)\, d\tau}{t} = \text{Time average of the number of customers in the system in the interval } [0, t]$$

$$\lambda_t = \frac{\alpha(t)}{t} = \text{Time average of the customer arrival rate in the interval } [0, t]$$

$$T_t = \frac{\displaystyle\sum_{i=1}^{\beta(t)} T_i + \sum_{i=\beta(t)+1}^{\alpha(t)} (t - t_i)}{\alpha(t)} = \text{Time average of the time a customer spends in the system in the interval } [0, t]$$

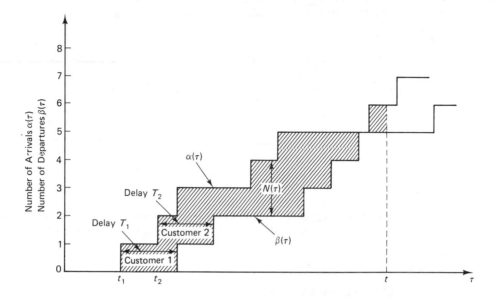

Figure 3.1   Proof of Little's Theorem. The shaded area can be expressed both as $\int_0^t N(\tau)\,d\tau$ and as $\displaystyle\sum_{i=1}^{\beta(t)} T_i + \sum_{i=\beta(t)+1}^{\alpha(t)} (t - t_i)$. Dividing both expressions by t, equating them, and taking the limit as $t \to \infty$ gives Little's Theorem.

Assuming that

$$N_t \to N, \ \lambda_t \to \lambda, \ T_t \to T$$

we obtain from Eq. (3.2) the desired formula.

Note that the expression T_t includes the total time spent in the system for all the arrivals from 1 to $\beta(t)$, but omits the time spent beyond t for the customers still in the system at time t. Assuming that $N_t \to N < \infty$, this end effect due to customers in the system at time t will be small relative to the accumulated time in the system of customers 1 to $\beta(t)$, and T_t for large t can be interpreted as the time average of the system time.

Strictly speaking, for the argument above to be correct, we must be assured that the time averages N_t, λ_t, T_t converge with probability one to the corresponding ensemble averages N, λ, and T. This is true in just about every case of interest to us, and in subsequent analysis, we will accept Little's Theorem without further scrutiny.

The significance of Little's Theorem is due in large measure to its generality. It holds for almost every queueing system that reaches statistical equilibrium in the limit. The system need not consist of just a single queue. Indeed, the theorem holds for many complex arrival-departure systems with appropriate interpretation of the terms N, λ, and T. The following examples illustrate its broad applicability.

Example 1

If λ is the arrival rate in a transmission line, N_Q is the average number of packets waiting in queue (but not under transmission), and W is the average time spent by a packet waiting in queue (not including the transmission time), Little's Theorem gives

$$N_Q = \lambda W$$

Furthermore if $\overline{X}$ is the average transmission time, then Little's Theorem gives the average number of packets under transmission as

$$\rho = \lambda \overline{X}$$

Since at most one packet can be under transmission, ρ is also the line's *utilization factor*, *i.e.*, the proportion of time that the line is busy transmitting a packet.

Example 2

Consider a network of transmission lines where packets arrive at n different nodes with corresponding rates $\lambda_1, \ldots, \lambda_n$. If N is the average total number of packets inside the network, then (regardless of the packet length distribution and method for routing packets) the average delay per packet is

$$T = \frac{N}{\sum_{i=1}^{n} \lambda_i}$$

Furthermore, Little's Theorem also yields $N_i = \lambda_i T_i$, where N_i and T_i are the average number in the system and average delay of packets arriving at node i, respectively.

Example 3

A packet arrives at a transmission line every K seconds with the first packet arriving at time 0. All packets have equal length and require αK seconds for transmission where $\alpha < 1$. The processing and propagation delay per packet is P seconds. The arrival rate here is $\lambda = 1/K$. Because packets arrive at a regular rate (equal interarrival times), there is no delay for queueing, so the time T a packet spends in the system (including the propagation delay) is

$$T = \alpha K + P$$

According to Little's Theorem, we have

$$N = \lambda T = \alpha + \frac{P}{K}$$

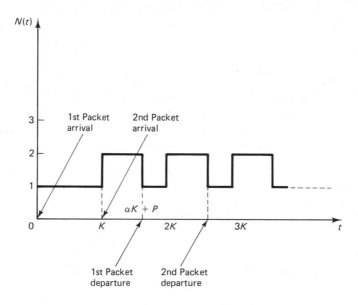

Figure 3.2   The number in the system in Example 3, $N(t)$, is deterministic and does not converge as $t \to \infty$. However, Little's Theorem holds if N, λ, and T are interpreted as time averages.

One should be careful about interpreting correctly the formula in this example. Here the number in the system $N(t)$ is a deterministic function of time. Its form is shown in Fig. 3.2 for the case where $K < \alpha K + P < 2K$, and it can be seen that $N(t)$ does not converge to any value (the system never reaches statistical equilibrium.) However, Little's Theorem is correct provided N is viewed as a long-term *time average* of $N(t)$, *i.e.*,

$$ N = \lim_{t \to \infty} \frac{\int_0^t N(\tau)\, d\tau}{t} $$

Example 4

Consider a window flow control system (as described in subsection 2.8.1) with a window of size N for each session. Suppose that a session always has packets to send and that acknowledgements take negligible time; then, when packet i arrives at the destination, packet $i + N$ is immediately introduced into the network. Since the number of packets in the system per session is always N, Little's Theorem asserts that the arrival rate λ of packets into the system for each session, and the average packet delay are related by $N = \lambda T$. Thus, if congestion builds up in the network and T increases, λ must decrease. Note also that if the network is congested and capable of delivering only λ packets per unit time for each session, then increasing the window size N for all sessions merely serves to increase the delay T.

Example 5

Consider a queueing system with K servers, and with room for at most $N \geq K$ customers (either in queue or in service). The system is always full; we assume that it starts with N customers and that a departing customer is immediately replaced by a new customer. (Queueing systems of this type are called *closed*.) Suppose that the average customer service time is $\overline{X}$. We want to find the average customer time in the system T. We apply Little's Theorem twice, first for the entire system, obtaining $N = \lambda T$, and then for the service portion of the system, obtaining $K = \lambda \overline{X}$ (since all servers are constantly busy). By eliminating λ in these two relations we have

$$T = \frac{N\overline{X}}{K}$$

Example 6: Estimating throughput in a time-sharing system

Little's Theorem can sometimes be used to provide bounds on the attainable system throughput λ. In particular, known bounds on N and T can be translated into throughput bounds via $\lambda = N/T$. As an example, consider a time-sharing computer system with N terminals. A user logs into the system through a terminal, and, after an initial reflection period of average length R, submits a job that requires an average processing time P at the computer. Jobs queue up inside the computer and are served by a single CPU according to some unspecified priority or time-sharing rule.

We would like to get estimates of the throughput sustainable by the system (in jobs per unit time), and corresponding estimates of the average delay of a user. Since we are interested in maximum attainable throughput, we assume that there is always a user ready to take the place of a departing user, so the number of users in the system is always N. For this reason, it is appropriate to adopt a model whereby a departing user immediately reenters the system as shown in Fig. 3.3.

Applying Little's Theorem to the portion of the system between the entry to the terminals and the exit of the system (points A and C in Fig. 3.3), we have

$$\lambda = \frac{N}{T} \tag{3.3}$$

where T is the average time a user spends in the system. We have

$$T = R + D \tag{3.4}$$

where D is the average delay between the time a job is submitted to the computer and the time its execution is completed. Since D can vary between P (case where the user's job does not have to wait for other jobs to be completed) and NP (case

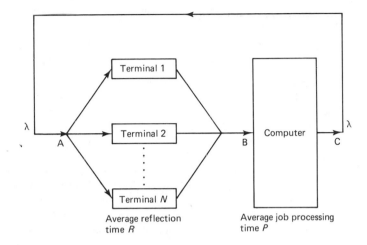

Figure 3.3 N terminals connected with a time-sharing computer system. To estimate maximum attainable throughput, we assume that a departing user immediately reenters the system or, equivalently, is immediately replaced by a new user.

where the user's job has to wait for the jobs of all the other users; compare with Ex. 5), we have

$$R + P \leq T \leq R + NP \tag{3.5}$$

Combining this relation with Eq. (3.3), we obtain

$$\frac{N}{R + NP} \leq \lambda \leq \frac{N}{R + P} \tag{3.6}$$

The throughput λ is also bounded above by the processing capacity of the computer. In particular, since the execution time of a job is P units on the average, it follows that the computer cannot process in the long run more than $1/P$ jobs per unit time, *i.e.*,

$$\lambda \leq \frac{1}{P} \tag{3.7}$$

(This conclusion can also be reached by applying Little's Theorem between the entry and exit points of the computer's CPU.)

By combining relations (3.6) and (3.7), we obtain the bounds

$$\frac{N}{R + NP} \leq \lambda \leq \min\left\{\frac{1}{P}, \frac{N}{R + P}\right\} \tag{3.8}$$

for the maximum attainable throughput. By using $T = N/\lambda$, we also obtain bounds for the average user delay when the system is fully loaded

$$\max \{NP, \ R + P\} \leq T \leq R + NP \tag{3.9}$$

These relations are illustrated in Fig. 3.4.

It can be seen that as the number of terminals N increases, the throughput approaches the maximum $1/P$, while the average user delay rises essentially in direct proportion with N. The number of terminals becomes a throughput bottleneck when $N < 1 + R/P$, in which case the computer resource stays idle for a substantial portion of the time while all users are engaged in reflection. In contrast, the limited processing power of the computer becomes the bottleneck when $N > 1 + R/P$. It is interesting to note that while the exact maximum attainable throughput depends on system parameters, such as the statistics of the reflection and processing times, and the manner in which jobs are served by the CPU, the bounds obtained are independent of these parameters. We owe this convenient situation to the generality of Little's Theorem.

3.3 THE M/M/1 QUEUEING SYSTEM

The $M/M/1$ queueing system consists of a single queueing station with a single server (in a communication context, a single transmission line). Customers arrive according to a Poisson process with rate λ, and the probability distribution of the service time is exponential with mean $1/\mu$ sec. We will explain the meaning of these terms shortly. The name $M/M/1$ reflects standard queueing theory nomenclature whereby:

1. The first letter indicates the nature of the arrival process (*e.g.*, M stands for memoryless, which here means a Poisson process (*i.e.*, exponentially distributed interarrival times), G stands for a general distribution of interarrival times, D stands for deterministic interarrival times).

2. The second letter indicates the nature of the probability distribution of the service times (*e.g.*, M, G, and D stand for exponential, general, and deterministic distributions, respectively). In all cases, successive interarrival times and service times are assumed to be statistically independent of each other.

3. The last number indicates the number of servers.

We have already established, via Little's Theorem, the relations

$$N = \lambda T, \qquad N_Q = \lambda W$$

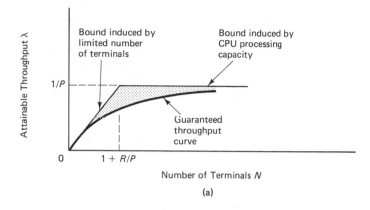

(a)

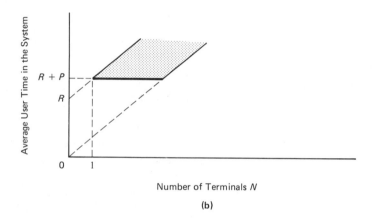

(b)

Figure 3.4   Bounds on throughput and average user delay in a time-sharing system. (a) Bounds on attainable throughput [Eq. (3.8)]. (b) Bounds on average user time in a fully loaded system [Eq. (3.9)]. The time increases essentially in proportion with the number of terminals N.

between the basic quantities,

N : Average number of customers in the system

T : Average customer time in the system

N_Q : Average number of customers waiting in queue

W : Average customer waiting time in queue

However, N, T, N_Q, and W cannot be specified further unless we know something more about the statistics of the system. Given these statistics, we will be able to derive the steady-state probabilities

$$p_n = \text{Probability of } n \text{ customers in the system, } n = 0, 1, \dots$$

From these probabilities, we can get

$$N = \sum_{n=0}^{\infty} n p_n$$

and, using Little's Theorem,

$$T = \frac{N}{\lambda}$$

Similar formulas exist for N_Q and W. Appendix B provides a summary of the results for the $M/M/1$ system and the other major systems analyzed later.

The analysis of the $M/M/1$ system as well as several other related systems, such as the $M/M/m$ or $M/M/\infty$ systems, is based on the theory of Markov chains summarized in Appendix A. An alternative approach is to use simple graphical arguments based on the concept of mean residual time introduced in section 3.5. This approach does not require that the service times are exponentially distributed, *i.e.*, it applies to the $M/G/1$ system. The price paid for this generality is that the characterization of the steady-state probabilities is less convenient and simple than for the $M/M/1$ system. The reader wishing to circumvent the Markov chain analysis may start directly with the $M/G/1$ system in section 3.5 after a reading of the preliminary facts on the Poisson process given in subsections 3.3.1 and 3.3.2.

3.3.1 Main Results

A stochastic process $\{A(t) \mid t \geq 0\}$ taking nonnegative integer values is said to be a *Poisson process* with rate λ if

1. $A(t)$ is a counting process that represents the total number of arrivals that have occurred from 0 to time t, *i.e.*, $A(0) = 0$, and for $s < t$, $A(t) - A(s)$ equals the number of arrivals in the interval $(s, t]$.
2. The numbers of arrivals that occur in disjoint time intervals are independent.

3. The number of arrivals in any interval of length τ is Poisson distributed with parameter $\lambda\tau$. That is, for all $t, \tau > 0$,

$$P\{A(t+\tau) - A(t) = n\} = e^{-\lambda\tau}\frac{(\lambda\tau)^n}{n!}, \quad n = 0, 1, \ldots \tag{3.10}$$

We list some of the properties of the Poisson process that will be of interest:

(a) Interarrival times are independent and exponentially distributed with parameter λ, i.e., if t_n denotes the time of the nth arrival, the intervals $\tau_n = t_{n+1} - l_n$ have the probability distribution

$$P\{\tau_n \le s\} = 1 - e^{-\lambda s}, \quad s \ge 0 \tag{3.11}$$

and are mutually independent. (The corresponding probability density function is $p(\tau_n) = \lambda e^{-\lambda\tau_n}$. The mean and variance of τ_n are $1/\lambda$ and $1/\lambda^2$, respectively.)

(b) For every $t \ge 0$ and $\delta \ge 0$

$$P\{A(t+\delta) - A(t) = 0\} = 1 - \lambda\delta + o(\delta) \tag{3.12}$$
$$P\{A(t+\delta) - A(t) = 1\} = \lambda\delta + o(\delta) \tag{3.13}$$
$$P\{A(t+\delta) - A(t) \ge 2\} = o(\delta) \tag{3.14}$$

where we generically denote by $o(\delta)$ a function of δ such that

$$\lim_{\delta \to 0}\frac{o(\delta)}{\delta} = 0$$

These equations can be verified using Eq. (3.10) (see Prob. 3.10).

Note that if the arrivals in n disjoint intervals are independent and Poisson distributed with parameters $\lambda\tau_1, \ldots, \lambda\tau_n$, then the number of arrivals in the union of the intervals is Poisson distributed with parameter $\lambda(\tau_1 + \cdots + \tau_n)$. This follows from properties of the Poisson distribution and guarantees that the requirement of Eq. (3.10) is consistent with the independence requirement in the definition of the Poisson process (see Prob. 3.10). Another fact that we will frequently use is that if two or more independent Poisson processes $A_1, \ldots, A_k$ are merged into a single process $A = A_1 + A_2 + \cdots + A_k$, then the latter process is Poisson with a rate equal to the sum of the rates of its components (see Prob. 3.10).

Our assumption regarding the service process is that *the customer service times have an exponential distribution with parameter μ*, i.e., if s_n is the service time of the nth customer,

$$P\{s_n \le s\} = 1 - e^{-\mu s}, \quad s \ge 0$$

(The probability density function of s_n is $p(s_n) = \mu e^{-\mu s_n}$, and its mean and variance are $1/\mu$ and $1/\mu^2$, respectively.) Furthermore, *the service times s_n are mutually independent and also independent of all interarrival times.* The parameter μ is called the *service rate*, and represents the rate (in customers served per unit time) at which the server operates when busy.

An important fact regarding the exponential distribution is its *memoryless*, character, which can be expressed as

$$P\{\tau_n > r + t \mid \tau_n > t\} = P\{\tau_n > r\}, \quad \text{for } r, t \geq 0$$

$$P\{s_n > r + t \mid s_n > t\} = P\{s_n > r\}, \quad \text{for } r, t \geq 0$$

for the interarrival and service times τ_n and s_n, respectively. This means that the additional time needed to complete a customer's service in progress is independent of when the service started. Similarly, the time up to the next arrival is independent of when the previous arrival occurred. Verification of the memoryless property follows from the calculation

$$P\{\tau_n > r + t \mid \tau_n > t\} = \frac{P\{\tau_n > r + t\}}{P\{\tau_n > t\}} = \frac{e^{-\lambda(r+t)}}{e^{-\lambda t}} = e^{-\lambda r} = P\{\tau_n > r\}$$

The memoryless property together with our earlier independence assumptions on interarrival and service times imply that once we know the number $N(t)$ of customers in the system at time t, the times at which customers will arrive or complete service in the future are independent of the arrival times of the customers presently in the system and of how much service the customer currently in service (if any) has already received. This means that $\{N(t) \mid t \geq 0\}$ *is a continuous-time Markov chain.*

We could analyze the process $N(t)$ in terms of continuous-time Markov chain methodology; most of the queueing literature follows this line of analysis. It is sufficient, however, for our purposes in this section to use the simpler theory of discrete-time Markov chains (briefly summarized in Appendix A).

Let us focus attention at the times

$$0, \ \delta, \ 2\delta, \ldots, k\delta, \ldots$$

where δ is a small positive number. We denote

$$N_k = \text{Number of customers in the system at time } k\delta$$

Since $N_k = N(k\delta)$ and, as discussed, $N(t)$ is a continuous-time Markov chain, we see that $\{N_k \mid k = 0, 1, \ldots\}$ is a discrete-time Markov chain. Let P_{ij} denote the corresponding transition probabilities

$$P_{ij} = P\{N_{k+1} = j \mid N_k = i\}$$

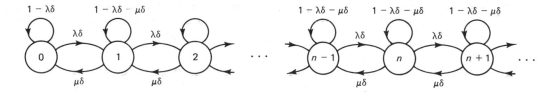

Figure 3.5   Discrete-time Markov chain for the $M/M/1$ system. The state n corresponds to n customers in the system. Transition probabilities shown are correct up to an $o(\delta)$ term.

Note that P_{ij} depends on δ, but to keep notation simple, we do not show this dependence. By using Eqs. (3.12) through (3.14), we have

$$P_{oo} = 1 - \lambda\delta + o(\delta) \tag{3.15}$$

$$P_{ii} = 1 - \lambda\delta - \mu\delta + o(\delta), \qquad\qquad i \geq 1 \tag{3.16}$$

$$P_{i,i+1} = \lambda\delta + o(\delta), \qquad\qquad i \geq 0 \tag{3.17}$$

$$P_{i,i-1} = \mu\delta + o(\delta), \qquad\qquad i \geq 1 \tag{3.18}$$

$$P_{ij} = o(\delta), \qquad\qquad i \text{ and } j \neq i,\, i+1,\, i-1$$

To see how these equations are verified, note that, when at a state $i \geq 1$, the probabilities of 0 arrivals and 0 departures in an interval $I_k = (k\delta, (k+1)\delta]$ is $(e^{-\lambda\delta})(e^{-\mu\delta})$; this is because the number of arrivals and the number of departures are Poisson distributed and independent of each other. Expanding this in a power series in δ,

$$P\{0 \text{ customers arrive and } 0 \text{ depart in } I_k\} = 1 - \lambda\delta - \mu\delta + o(\delta) \tag{3.19}$$

Similarly, we have that

$$P\{0 \text{ customers arrive and } 1 \text{ departs in } I_k\} = \mu\delta + o(\delta)$$

$$P\{1 \text{ customer arrives and } 0 \text{ depart in } I_k\} = \lambda\delta + o(\delta)$$

These probalities add up to one plus $o(\delta)$. Thus, the probability of more than one arrival or departure is negligible for δ small. This means that, for $i \geq 1$, p_{ii}, which is the probability of an equal number of arrivals and departures in I_k, is within $o(\delta)$ of the value in Eq. (3.19); this verifies Eq. (3.16). Equations (3.15), (3.17), and (3.18) are verified in the same way.

The state transition diagram for the Markov chain $\{N_k\}$ is shown in Fig. 3.5 where we have omitted the terms $o(\delta)$.

Consider now the steady-state probabilities

$$p_n = \lim_{k \to \infty} P\{N_k = n\}$$
$$= \lim_{t \to \infty} P\{N(t) = n\}$$

Note that for any $k \geq 1$, $n \geq 0$, during the time from δ to $k\delta$, the total number of transitions from state n to $n+1$ must differ from the total number of transitions from $n+1$ to n by at most 1. Thus, in steady state, the probability that the system is in state n and makes a transition to $n+1$ at the next transition instant is the same as the probability that the system is in state $n+1$ and makes a transition to n, i.e.,

$$p_n \lambda \delta + o(\delta) = p_{n+1} \mu \delta + o(\delta) \tag{3.20}$$

(These equations are called global balance equations corresponding to the set of states $\{0, 1, \ldots, n\}$ and $\{n+1, n+2, \ldots\}$. See Appendix A for a more general statement of these equations, and for an interpretation that parallels the argument given above to derive Eq. (3.20).) Since p_n is independent of δ, by taking the limit in Eq. (3.20) as $\delta \to 0$, we obtain

$$p_{n+1} = \rho p_n, \quad n = 0, 1, \ldots$$

where

$$\rho = \frac{\lambda}{\mu}$$

It follows that

$$p_{n+1} = \rho^{n+1} p_0, \quad n = 0, 1, \ldots \tag{3.21}$$

If $\rho < 1$ (service rate exceeds arrival rate), the probabilities p_n are all positive and add up to unity, so

$$1 = \sum_{n=0}^{\infty} p_n = \sum_{n=0}^{\infty} \rho^n \, p_0 = \frac{p_0}{1 - \rho} \tag{3.22}$$

This equation, together with Eq. (3.21), gives finally

$$p_n = \rho^n (1 - \rho), \quad n = 0, 1, \ldots \tag{3.23}$$

We can now calculate the average number of customers in the system in steady state:

$$N = \lim_{t \to \infty} E\{N(t)\} = \sum_{n=0}^{\infty} n \, p_n = \sum_{n=0}^{\infty} n \, \rho^n (1 - \rho)$$

$$= \rho(1 - \rho) \sum_{n=0}^{\infty} n \, \rho^{n-1} = \rho(1 - \rho) \frac{\partial}{\partial \rho} \left(\sum_{n=0}^{\infty} \rho^n \right)$$

$$= \rho(1 - \rho) \frac{\partial}{\partial \rho} \left(\frac{1}{1 - \rho} \right) = \rho(1 - \rho) \frac{1}{(1 - \rho)^2}$$

and, finally, using $\rho = \lambda/\mu$

$$N = \frac{\rho}{1 - \rho} = \frac{\lambda}{\mu - \lambda} \tag{3.24}$$

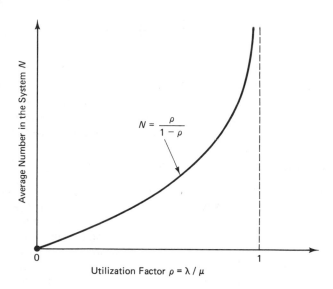

Figure 3.6   The average number in the system versus the utilization factor in the $M/M/1$ system. As $\rho \to 1$, $N \to \infty$.

This equation is shown in the diagram of Fig. 3.6. As ρ increases, so does N, and as $\rho \to 1$, we have $N \to \infty$. The diagram is valid for $\rho < 1$. If $\rho > 1$, the server cannot keep up with the arrival rate and the queue length increases without bound. In the context of a packet transmission system, $\rho > 1$ means that $\lambda L > C$, where λ is the arrival rate in packets/sec, L is the average packet length in bits, and C is the transmission capacity in bits/sec.

The average delay per customer (waiting time in queue plus service time) is given by Little's Theorem,

$$T = \frac{N}{\lambda} = \frac{\rho}{\lambda(1 - \rho)} \tag{3.25}$$

Using $\rho = \lambda/\mu$, this becomes

$$T = \frac{1}{\mu - \lambda} \tag{3.26}$$

The average waiting time in queue, W, is the average delay T less the average service time $1/\mu$, so

$$W = \frac{1}{\mu - \lambda} - \frac{1}{\mu} = \frac{\rho}{\mu - \lambda}$$

By Little's Theorem, the average number of customers in queue is

$$N_Q = \lambda W = \frac{\rho^2}{1 - \rho}$$

A very useful interpretation is to view the quantity ρ as the *utilization factor* of the queueing system, *i.e.*, the long-term proportion of time the server is busy. We showed this earlier in a broader context by using Little's Theorem (Ex. 1 in section 3.2). It follows that $\rho = 1 - p_0$, where p_0 is the probability of having no customers in the system, and we obtain an alternative verification of the formula derived for p_0 (Eq. (3.22)).

We illustrate these results by means of some examples from data networks:

Example 7: Increasing the arrival and transmission rates by the same factor

Consider a packet transmission system whose arrival rate (in packets/sec) is increased from λ to $K\lambda$, where $K > 1$ is some scalar factor. The packet length distribution remains the same but the transmission capacity is increased by a factor of K, so the average packet transmission time is now $1/(K\mu)$ instead of $1/\mu$. It follows that the utilization factor ρ and, therefore, the average number of packets in the system remain the same

$$N = \frac{\rho}{1 - \rho} = \frac{\lambda}{\mu - \lambda}$$

However, the average delay per packet is now $T = N/(K\lambda)$ and is therefore decreased by a factor of K. In other words, *a transmission line K times as fast will accommodate K times as many packets/sec at K times smaller average delay per packet*. This result is quite general, even applying to networks of queues. What is happening, as illustrated in Fig. 3.7, is that by increasing arrival rate and service rate by a factor K, the statistical characteristics of the queueing process are unaffected except for a change in time scale—the process is speeded up by a factor K. Thus, when a packet arrives, it will see ahead of it statistically the same number of packets as with a slower transmission line. However, the packets ahead of it will be moving K times faster.

Example 8: Statistical multiplexing compared with time- and frequency-division multiplexing

Assume that m statistically identical and independent Poisson packet streams each with an arrival rate of λ/m packets/sec are to be transmitted over a communication line. The packet lengths for all streams are independent and exponentially distributed. The average transmission time is $1/\mu$. If the streams are merged into a single Poisson stream, with rate λ, as in statistical multiplexing, the average delay per packet is

$$T = \frac{1}{\mu - \lambda}$$

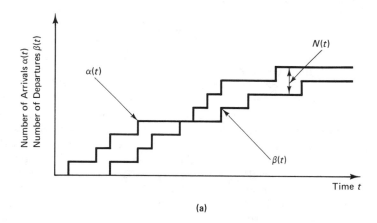

(a)

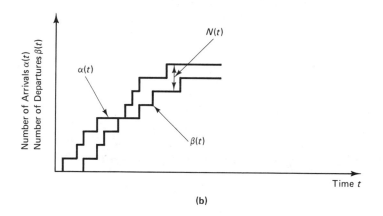

(b)

Figure 3.7   Increasing the arrival rate and the service rate by the same factor (see Ex. 7). (a) Sample paths of number of arrivals $\alpha(t)$ and departures $\beta(t)$ in the original system. (b) Corresponding sample paths of number of arrivals $\alpha(t)$ and departures $\beta(t)$ in the "speeded up" system, where the arrival rate and the service rate have been increased by a factor of two. The average number in the system is the same as before, but the average delay is reduced by a factor of two since customers are moving twice as fast.

If, instead, the transmission capacity is divided into m equal portions, one per packet stream as in time- and frequency-division multiplexing, each portion behaves like an $M/M/1$ queue with arrival rate λ/m and average service rate μ/m. Therefore, the average delay per packet is

$$T = \frac{m}{\mu - \lambda}$$

i.e., m times larger than for statistical multiplexing.

The preceding argument indicates that multiplexing a large number of traffic streams on separate channels in a transmission line performs very poorly in terms of delay. The performance is even poorer if the capacity of the channels is not allocated in direct proportion to the arrival rates of the corresponding streams—something that cannot be done (at least in the scheme considered here) if these arrival rates change over time. This is precisely why data networks that must contend with many low duty cycle traffic streams are organized on the basis of some form of statistical multiplexing. An argument in favor of time- and frequency-division multiplexing arises when each traffic stream is "regular" (as opposed to Poisson) in the sense that no packet arrives while another is transmitted, and thus there is no waiting in queue if that stream is transmitted on a dedicated transmission line. If several streams of this type are statistically multiplexed on a single transmission line, the average delay per packet will decrease, but the average waiting time in queue will become positive. For example in telephony each traffic stream is a voice conversation that is regular in the above sense, and time- and frequency-division multiplexing are still used widely.

3.3.2 Occupancy Distribution Upon Arrival

In our subsequent development, there are several situations where we will need a probabilistic characterization of a queueing system as seen by an arriving customer. In some systems, the times of customer arrivals are in some sense nontypical, so that the steady-state occupancy probabilities upon arrival

$$a_n = \lim_{t \to \infty} P\{N(t) = n| \text{ an arrival occurred just after time } t\} \qquad (3.27)$$

need not be equal to the corresponding unconditional steady-state probabilities

$$p_n = \lim_{t \to \infty} P\{N(t) = n\} \qquad (3.28)$$

It turns out, however, that for the $M/M/1$ system, we have

$$p_n = a_n, \quad n = 0, 1, \ldots \qquad (3.29)$$

Indeed *this equality holds under very general conditions for queueing systems with Poisson arrivals regardless of the distribution of the service times.* The only additional requirement we need is that future arrivals are independent of the current number in the system. More precisely, we assume that for every time t and interval $\delta > 0$, the number of arrivals in the interval $(t, t + \delta)$ is independent of the number in the system at time t. Given the Poisson hypothesis, essentially this amounts to assuming that, at any time, the service times of previously arrived customers, and the future interarrival times are independent—something that is very reasonable for packet transmission systems. In particular, the assumption holds if the arrival process is Poisson and interarrival times and service times are independent.

The basic reason why $a_n = p_n$ is that the events $\{N(t) = n\}$ and $\{$An arrival occurred just after $t\}$ are independent under our hypothesis. As a result, the conditional probability in Eq. (3.27) equals the unconditional probability in Eq. (3.28). For a more formal proof, let $A(t, t + \delta)$ be the event that an arrival occurs in the interval $(t, t + \delta)$. Let

$$p_n(t) = P\{N(t) = n\} \tag{3.30}$$

$$a_n(t) = P\{N(t) = n | \text{an arrival occurred just after time } t\} \tag{3.31}$$

We have, using Bayes' rule,

$$
\begin{aligned}
a_n(t) &= \lim_{\delta \to 0} P\{N(t) = n | A(t, t + \delta)\} \\
&= \lim_{\delta \to 0} \frac{P\{N(t) = n, \ A(t, t + \delta)\}}{P\{A(t, t + \delta)\}} \\
&= \lim_{\delta \to 0} \frac{P\{A(t, t + \delta) | N(t) = n\} \ P\{N(t) = n\}}{P\{A(t, t + \delta)\}}
\end{aligned} \tag{3.32}
$$

By assumption, the event $A(t, t + \delta)$ is independent of the number in the system at time t. Therefore,

$$P\{A(t, t + \delta) | N(t) = n\} = P\{A(t, t + \delta)\}$$

and we obtain from Eq. (3.32)

$$a_n(t) = P\{N(t) = n\} = p_n(t)$$

Taking the limit as $t \to \infty$, we obtain Eq. (3.29).

Thus, we have shown that the probability of an arrival finding n customers in the system equals the (unconditional) probability of n in the system. This is true at every time instant as well as in steady state regardless of the service time distribution. We can summarize this by saying that *when the arrival process is Poisson, an arriving customer finds the system in a "typical" state.*

As an example of what can happen if the arrival process is not Poisson, suppose that interarrival times are independent and uniformly distributed between two and four seconds, while customer service times are all equal to one second. Then an arriving customer always finds an empty system. On the other hand, the average number in the system as seen by an outside observer looking at a system at a random time is $1/3$.

For a similar example where the arrival process is Poisson but the service times of customers in the system and the future arrival times are correlated, consider a packet transmission system where packets arrive according to a Poisson process. The transmission time of the nth packet equals one half the interarrival time between packets n and $n + 1$. A packet upon arrival finds the system empty. However, the average number in the system, as seen by an outside observer looking at the system is easily seen to be 1/2.

3.3.3 Occupancy Distribution Upon Departure

Let us consider the distribution of the number of customers in the system just after a departure has occurred, *i.e.*, the probabilities

$$d_n(t) = P\{N(t) = n| \text{ a departure occurred just before time } t\}$$

The corresponding steady-state values are denoted

$$d_n = \lim_{t \to \infty} d_n(t), \quad n = 0, 1, \dots$$

It turns out that

$$d_n = a_n, \quad n = 0, 1, \dots$$

under very general assumptions—the only requirement essentially is that the system reaches a steady state with all n having positive steady-state probabilities, and that $N(t)$ changes in unit increments. (These assumptions certainly hold for a stable $M/M/1$ system ($\rho < 1$), but they also hold for most stable single-queue systems of interest.) For any sample path of the system and for every n, the number in the system will be n infinitely often (with probability one). This means that for each time the number in the system increases from n to $n+1$ due to an arrival, there will be a corresponding future decrease from $n + 1$ to n due to a departure. Therefore, in the long run, the proportion of transitions from n to $n + 1$ out of transitions from any k to $k + 1$ equals the proportion of transitions from $n + 1$ to n out of transitions from any $k + 1$ to k which implies $d_n = a_n$. Therefore, *in steady state, the system appears statistically identical to an arriving and a departing customer. When arrivals are Poisson,* we saw earlier that $a_n = p_n$; so, in this case, *both an arriving and a departing customer in steady state see a system that is statistically identical to the one seen by an observer looking at the system at a random time.*

3.4 THE M/M/m, M/M/∞, AND M/M/m/m SYSTEMS

We consider now a number of queueing systems that are similar to $M/M/1$ in that the arrival process is Poisson, the service times are independent, exponentially distributed, and independent of the interarrival times. Because of these assumptions, these systems can be modelled with continuous- or discrete-time Markov chains.

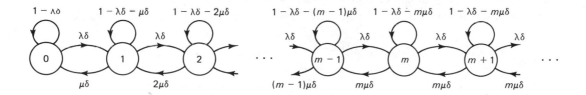

Figure 3.8   Discrete-time Markov chain for the $M/M/m$ system.

From the corresponding state transition diagram, we can derive a set of equations that can be solved for the steady-state occupancy probabilities. Application of Little's Theorem then yields the average delay per customer.

3.4.1 M/M/m: *The m-Server Case*

The $M/M/m$ queueing system is identical to the $M/M/1$ system except that there are m servers (or channels of a transmission line in a data communication context). A customer at the head of the queue is routed to any server that is available. The corresponding state transition diagram is shown in Fig. 3.8.

By writing down the equilibrium equations for the steady-state probabilities p_n and taking $\delta \to 0$, we obtain

$$\lambda p_{n-1} = n\,\mu\,p_n, \quad n \le m$$
$$\lambda p_{n-1} = m\,\mu\,p_n, \quad n > m$$

From these equations, we obtain

$$p_n = \begin{cases} p_0 \dfrac{(m\rho)^n}{n!}, & n \le m \\[3mm] p_0 \dfrac{m^m \rho^n}{m!}, & n > m \end{cases} \tag{3.33}$$

where ρ is given by

$$\rho = \frac{\lambda}{m\mu} < 1 \tag{3.34}$$

We can calculate p_0 using Eq. (3.33) and the condition $\sum_{n=0}^{\infty} p_n = 1$. We obtain

$$p_0 = \left[1 + \sum_{n=1}^{m-1} \frac{(m\rho)^n}{n!} + \sum_{n=m}^{\infty} \frac{(m\rho)^n}{m!} \frac{1}{m^{n-m}} \right]^{-1}$$

and, finally,

$$p_0 = \left[\sum_{n=0}^{m-1} \frac{(m\rho)^n}{n!} + \frac{(m\rho)^m}{m!(1-\rho)} \right]^{-1} \tag{3.35}$$

The probability that an arrival will find all servers busy and will be forced to wait in queue is

$$P\{\text{Queueing}\} = \sum_{n=m}^{\infty} p_n$$

$$= \sum_{n=m}^{\infty} \frac{p_0 m^m \rho^n}{m!} = \frac{p_0(m\rho)^m}{m!} \sum_{n=m}^{\infty} \rho^{n-m}$$

and, finally,

$$P_Q \triangleq P\{\text{Queueing}\} = \frac{p_0(m\rho)^m}{m!(1-\rho)} \tag{3.36}$$

where p_0 is given by Eq. (3.35). This equation is known as the *Erlang C formula* and is in wide use in telephony. (Denmark's A. K. Erlang is viewed as the foremost pioneer of queueing theory.)

The expected number of customers waiting in queue (not in service) is given by

$$N_Q = \sum_{n=0}^{\infty} n\, p_{m+n}$$

Using Eq. (3.33), we obtain

$$N_Q = \sum_{n=0}^{\infty} n\, p_0 \frac{m^m \rho^{m+n}}{m!} = \frac{p_0(m\rho)^m}{m!} \sum_{n=0}^{\infty} n\rho^n$$

Using Eq. (3.36) and the equation $(1-\rho)\sum_{n=0}^{\infty} n\rho^n = \rho/(1-\rho)$ encountered in the $M/M/1$ system analysis, we finally obtain

$$N_Q = P_Q \frac{\rho}{1-\rho} \tag{3.37}$$

Note that

$$\frac{N_Q}{P_Q} = \frac{\rho}{1-\rho}$$

represents the expected number found in queue by an arriving customer conditioned on the fact that he is forced to wait in queue, and is independent of the number of servers for a given $\rho = \lambda/m\mu$. This suggests in particular that, as long as there are customers waiting in queue, the queue size of the $M/M/m$ system behaves identically as in an $M/M/1$ system with service rate $m\mu$—the aggregate rate of the m servers. Some thought shows that indeed this is true in view of the memoryless property of the exponential distribution.

Using Little's Theorem and Eq. (3.37), we obtain the average time W a customer has to wait in queue:

$$W = \frac{N_Q}{\lambda} = \frac{\rho P_Q}{\lambda(1-\rho)} \tag{3.38}$$

The average delay per customer is, therefore,

$$T = \frac{1}{\mu} + W = \frac{1}{\mu} + \frac{\rho P_Q}{\lambda(1 - \rho)}$$

and, using $\rho = \lambda/m\mu$, we finally obtain

$$T = \frac{1}{\mu} + W = \frac{1}{\mu} + \frac{P_Q}{m\mu - \lambda} \tag{3.39}$$

Using Little's Theorem again, the average number of customers in the system is

$$N = \lambda T = \frac{\lambda}{\mu} + \frac{\lambda P_Q}{m\mu - \lambda}$$

and, using $\rho = \lambda/m\mu$, we obtain

$$N = m\rho + \frac{\rho P_Q}{1 - \rho}$$

Example 9: Using one vs. using multiple channels in statistical multiplexing

Consider a communication link serving m independent Poisson traffic streams with rate λ/m each. Suppose that the link is divided into m separate channels with one channel assigned to each traffic stream. However, if a traffic stream has no packet awaiting transmission, its corresponding channel is used to transmit a packet of another traffic stream. The transmission times of packets on each of the channels are exponentially distributed with mean $1/\mu$. The system can be modeled by the same Markov chain as the $M/M/m$ queue. Let us compare the average delays per packet of this system, and an $M/M/1$ system with the same arrival rate λ and service rate $m\mu$ (statistical multiplexing with one channel having m times larger capacity). In the former case, the average delay per packet is given by Eq. (3.39)

$$T = \frac{1}{\mu} + \frac{P_Q}{m\mu - \lambda}$$

while in the latter case, the average delay per packet is

$$\hat{T} = \frac{1}{m\mu} + \frac{\hat{P}_Q}{m\mu - \lambda}$$

where P_Q and $\hat{P}_Q$ denote the queueing probability in each case. When $\rho \ll 1$ (lightly loaded system) we have $P_Q \cong 0$, $\hat{P}_Q \cong 0$ and

$$\frac{T}{\hat{T}} \cong m$$

When ρ is only slightly less than 1, we have $P_Q \cong 1$, $\hat{P}_Q \cong 1$, $1/\mu \ll 1/(m\mu - \lambda)$ and

$$\frac{T}{\hat{T}} \cong 1$$

Therefore, for a light load, statistical multiplexing with m channels produces a delay almost m times larger than the delay of statistical multiplexing with the m channels combined in one (about the same as time- and frequency-division multiplexing). For a heavy load, the ratio of the two delays is close to one.

3.4.2 M/M/∞: *Infinite-Server Case*

In the limiting case where $m = \infty$ in the $M/M/m$ system, we obtain from Fig. 3.8

$$\lambda\, p_{n-1} = n\mu p_n\,, \quad n = 1, 2, \ldots$$

so

$$p_n = p_0 \left(\frac{\lambda}{\mu}\right)^n \frac{1}{n!}\,, \quad n = 1, 2, \ldots$$

From the condition $\sum_{n=0}^{\infty} p_n = 1$, we obtain

$$p_0 = \left[1 + \sum_{n=1}^{\infty} \left(\frac{\lambda}{\mu}\right)^n \frac{1}{n!}\right]^{-1}$$

$$= e^{-\lambda/\mu}$$

so, finally,

$$p_n = \left(\frac{\lambda}{\mu}\right)^n \frac{e^{-\lambda/\mu}}{n!}\,, \quad n = 0, 1, \ldots$$

Therefore, in steady state, *the number in the system is Poisson distributed with parameter λ/μ.* The average number in the system is

$$N = \frac{\lambda}{\mu}$$

By Little's Theorem, the average delay is N/λ or

$$T = \frac{1}{\mu}$$

This last equation can also be obtained by simply arguing that in an $M/M/\infty$ system, there is no waiting in queue, so T equals the average service time $1/\mu$. It can be shown that the number in the system is Poisson distributed even if the service time distribution is not exponential, *i.e.*, in the $M/G/\infty$ system (see Prob. 3.37).

Example 10: The quasistatic assumption

It is often convenient to assume that the external packet traffic entering a subnet node and destined for some other subnet node can be modeled by a stationary stochastic process that has a constant bit arrival rate (average bits/sec). This approximates a situation where the arrival rate changes slowly with time and constitutes what we refer to as the quasistatic assumption.

When there are only a few active sessions (*i.e.*, user pairs) for the given origin-destination pair, this assumption is seriously violated since the addition or termination of a single session can change the total bit arrival rate by a substantial factor. When, however, there are many active sessions, each with a bit arrival rate that is small relative to the total, it seems plausible that the quasistatic assumption is approximately valid. The reason is that session additions are statistically counterbalanced by session terminations, with variations in the total rate being relatively small. As analytical substantiation, let us assume that sessions are generated according to a Poisson process with rate λ, and terminate after a time which is exponentially distributed with mean $1/\mu$. Then the number of active sessions n evolves like the number of customers in an $M/M/\infty$ system, *i.e.*, is Poisson distributed with parameter λ/μ in steady-state. In particular, the mean and standard deviation of n are

$$N = E\{n\} = \lambda/\mu$$

$$\sigma_n = \left[E\left\{(n-N)^2\right\}\right]^{1/2} = (\lambda/\mu)^{1/2}$$

Suppose the ith active session generates traffic according to a stationary stochastic process having a bit arrival rate γ_i bits/sec. Assume that the rates γ_i are independent random variables with common mean $E\{\gamma_i\} = \Gamma$, and second moment $s_\gamma^2 = E\{\gamma_i^2\}$. Then the total bit arrival rate for n active sessions is the random variable $f = \sum_{i=1}^n \gamma_i$, which has mean

$$F = E\{f\} = (\lambda/\mu)\Gamma$$

The standard deviation of f, denoted σ_f, can be obtained by writing

$$\sigma_f^2 = E\left\{\left(\sum_{i=1}^n \gamma_i\right)^2\right\} - F^2$$

and carrying out the corresponding calculations (Prob. 3.21). The result is

$$\sigma_f = (\lambda/\mu)^{\frac{1}{2}} s_\gamma$$

Therefore, we have

$$\sigma_f/F = (s_\gamma/\Gamma)(\mu/\lambda)^{1/2} \tag{3.40}$$

Suppose now that the average bit rate Γ of a session is small relative to the total F, *i.e.*, a "many-small-sessions assumption" holds. Then, since $\Gamma/F = \mu/\lambda$, we have that μ/λ is small. If we reasonably assume that s_γ/Γ has a moderate value, it follows from Eq. (3.40) that σ_f/F is small. Therefore, the total arrival rate f is approximately constant thereby justifying the quasistatic assumption.

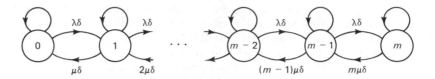

Figure 3.9   Discrete-time Markov chain for the $M/M/m/m$ system.

3.4.3 M/M/m/m: *The m-Server Loss System*

This system is identical to the $M/M/m$ system except that if an arrival finds all m servers busy, it does not enter the system and is lost—a model that is in wide use in telephony. (The last m in the $M/M/m/m$ notation indicates the limit on the number of customers in the system.) In data networks, it can be used as a model where arrivals correspond to requests for virtual circuit connections between two nodes and the number of virtual circuits allowed is m. The average service time $1/\mu$ is then the average duration of a virtual circuit conversation.

The corresponding state transition diagram is shown in Fig. 3.9. We have

$$\lambda p_{n-1} = n\mu p_n, \quad n = 1, 2, \ldots, m$$

so

$$p_n = p_0 \left(\frac{\lambda}{\mu}\right)^n \frac{1}{n!}, \quad n = 1, 2, \ldots, m$$

Solving for p_0 in the equation $\sum_{n=0}^{m} p_n = 1$, we obtain

$$p_0 = \left[\sum_{n=0}^{m} \left(\frac{\lambda}{\mu}\right)^n \frac{1}{n!}\right]^{-1}$$

The probability that an arrival will find all m servers busy and will therefore be lost is

$$p_m = \frac{(\lambda/\mu)^m/m!}{\sum_{n=0}^{m}(\lambda/\mu)^n/n!}$$

This equation is known as the *Erlang B formula*. It can be shown to hold even if the service time probability distribution is arbitrary, *i.e.*, for an $M/G/m/m$ system (see [Ros83], p. 170).

3.5 THE M/G/1 SYSTEM

Consider a single-server queueing system where customers arrive according to a Poisson process with rate λ, but the customer service times have a general distribution—not necessarily exponential as in the $M/M/1$ system. Suppose that customers are served in the order they arrive and that X_i is the service time of the ith arrival. We assume that the random variables $(X_1, X_2, \ldots)$ are identically distributed, mutually independent, and independent of the interarrival times.

Let

$$\overline{X} = E\{X\} = \frac{1}{\mu} = \text{ Average service time}$$

$$\overline{X^2} = E\{X^2\} = \text{ Second moment of service time}$$

Our objective is to derive and understand the *Pollaczek-Khinchin (P-K) formula:*

$$W = \frac{\lambda \overline{X^2}}{2(1 - \rho)} \tag{3.41}$$

where W is the expected customer waiting time in queue and $\rho = \lambda/\mu = \lambda \overline{X}$. Given Eq. (3.41), the total waiting time, in queue and in service, is

$$T = \overline{X} + \frac{\lambda \overline{X^2}}{2(1 - \rho)} \tag{3.42}$$

Applying Little's formula to W and T, we get the expected number of customers in the queue N_Q and the expected number in the system N

$$N_Q = \frac{\lambda^2 \overline{X^2}}{2(1 - \rho)} \tag{3.43}$$

$$N = \rho + \frac{\lambda^2 \overline{X^2}}{2(1 - \rho)} \tag{3.44}$$

For example, when service times are exponentially distributed, as in the $M/M/1$ system, we have $\overline{X^2} = 2/\mu^2$, and Eq. (3.41) reduces to the formula (see subsection 3.3.2)

$$W = \frac{\rho}{\mu(1 - \rho)} \qquad (M/M/1)$$

When service times are identical for all customers (the $M/D/1$ system, where D means deterministic), we have $\overline{X^2} = 1/\mu^2$, and

$$W = \frac{\rho}{2\mu(1 - \rho)} \qquad (M/D/1) \tag{3.45}$$

Since the $M/D/1$ case yields the minimum possible value of $\overline{X^2}$ for given μ, it follows that the values of W, T, N_Q, and N for an $M/D/1$ queue are lower bounds to the corresponding quantities for an $M/G/1$ queue of the same λ and μ. It is interesting to note that W and N_Q for the $M/D/1$ queue are exactly one half their values for the $M/M/1$ queue of the same λ and μ. The values of T and N for $M/D/1$, on the other hand, range from the same as $M/M/1$ for small ρ to one half of $M/M/1$ as ρ approaches 1. The reason is that the expected service time is the same in the two cases, and, for ρ small, most of the waiting occurs in service whereas, for ρ large, most of the waiting occurs in the queue.

We provide a proof of the Pollaczek-Khinchin formula based on the concept of the *mean residual service time*. This same concept will prove useful in a number of subsequent developments. For example, $M/G/1$ queues with priorities and reservation systems are analyzed later; then part of the service time is occupied with sending packets (*i.e.*, serving customers), and part with sending control information or making reservations for sending the packets.

Denote

W_i : The waiting time in queue of the ith customer.

R_i : The residual service time seen by the ith customer. By this we mean that if customer j is already being served when i arrives, R_i is the remaining time until customer j's service time is complete. If no customer is in service (*i.e.*, the system is empty when i arrives), then R_i is zero.

X_i : The service time of the ith customer.

N_i : The number of customers found waiting in queue by the ith customer upon arrival.

We have

$$W_i = R_i + \sum_{j=i-N_i}^{i-1} X_j$$

By taking expectations and using the fact that the random variables N_i and $X_{i-1}, \ldots, X_{i-N_i}$ are independent we have

$$E\{W_i\} = E\{R_i\} + E\left\{\sum_{j=i-N_i}^{i-1} E\{X_j|N_i\}\right\} = E\{R_i\} + \overline{X}E\{N_i\}$$

Taking the limit as $i \to \infty$ we obtain

$$W = R + \frac{1}{\mu}N_Q \tag{3.46}$$

where

R : Mean residual time, defined as $R = \lim_{i\to\infty} E\{R_i\}$.

In Eq. (3.46) (and throughout this section) all long-term average quantities should be viewed as limits when time or customer index increase to infinity. Thus, W, R, and N_Q are limits (as $i \to \infty$) of the average waiting time, residual time, and number found in queue, respectively, corresponding to the ith customer. We assume that these limits exist, and this is true of almost all systems of interest to us provided $\lambda < \mu$. Note that in Eq. (3.46) the average number in queue N_Q and the mean residual time R as seen by an arriving customer are also equal to the average number in queue and mean residual time seen by an outside observer at a random time. This is due to the Poisson character of the arrival process, which implies that the occupancy distribution upon arrival is typical (see subsection 3.3.2).

By Little's Theorem, we have

$$N_Q = \lambda W$$

and by substitution in Eq. (3.46), we obtain

$$W = R + \rho W \tag{3.47}$$

where $\rho = \lambda/\mu$ is the utilization factor; so, finally,

$$W = \frac{R}{1 - \rho} \tag{3.48}$$

We can calculate R by a graphical argument. In Fig. 3.10 the residual service time $r(\tau)$, (*i.e.*, the remaining time for completion of the customer in service at time τ) is plotted as a function of τ. Note that when a new service of duration X begins, $r(\tau)$ starts at X and decays linearly for X time units. Consider a time t for which $r(t) = 0$. The time average of $r(\tau)$ in the interval $[0, t]$ is

$$\frac{1}{t} \int_0^t r(\tau) \, d\tau = \frac{1}{t} \sum_{i=1}^{M(t)} \frac{1}{2} X_i^2 \tag{3.49}$$

where $M(t)$ is the number of service completions within $[0, t]$, and X_i is the service time of the ith customer. We can also write this equation as

$$\frac{1}{t} \int_0^t r(\tau) \, d\tau = \frac{1}{2} \frac{M(t)}{t} \frac{\sum_{i=1}^{M(t)} X_i^2}{M(t)} \tag{3.50}$$

and, assuming the limits below exist, we obtain

$$\lim_{t \to \infty} \frac{1}{t} \int_0^t r(\tau) \, d\tau = \frac{1}{2} \lim_{t \to \infty} \frac{M(t)}{t} \cdot \lim_{t \to \infty} \frac{\sum_{i=1}^{M(t)} X_i^2}{M(t)} \tag{3.51}$$

The two limits on the right are the time averages of the departure rate (which equals the arrival rate) and the second moment of the service time, respectively, while the limit on the left is the time average of the residual time. Assuming that time averages can be replaced by ensemble averages, we obtain

$$R = \frac{1}{2} \lambda \overline{X^2} \tag{3.52}$$

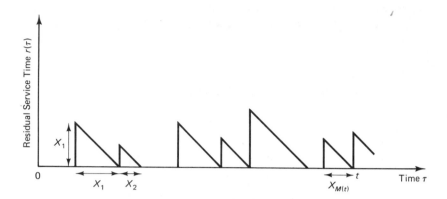

Figure 3.10   Derivation of the mean residual service time. During period $[0, t]$, the time average of the residual service time $r(\tau)$ is

$$\frac{1}{t} \int_0^t r(\tau)\, d\tau = \frac{1}{t} \sum_{i=1}^{M(t)} \frac{1}{2} X_i^2 = \frac{1}{2} \frac{M(t)}{t} \frac{\sum_{i=1}^{M(t)} X_i^2}{M(t)}$$

where X_i is the service time of the ith customer, and $M(t)$ is the number of service completions in $[0, t]$. Taking the limit as $t \to \infty$ and equating time and ensemble averages we obtain the mean residual time $R = (1/2)\lambda \overline{X^2}$

The Pollaczek-Khinchin formula,

$$W = \frac{\lambda \overline{X^2}}{2(1 - \rho)} \tag{3.53}$$

now follows by combining Eqs. (3.48) and (3.52). Our derivation was based on two assumptions: (a) the existence of the steady-state averages W, R, and N_Q; and (b) the equality (with probability one) of the long-term time averages appearing in Eq. (3.51) with the corresponding ensemble averages. These assumptions can be justified by careful applications of the law of large numbers, but the details are beyond the scope of this text. However, these are natural assumptions for the systems of interest to us, and we will base similar derivations on graphical arguments and interchange of time averages with ensemble averages without further discussion.

One curious feature of Eq. (3.53) is that an $M/G/1$ queue can have $\rho < 1$ but infinite W if the second moment of the service distribution is ∞. What is happening in this case is that a small fraction of customers have incredibly long service times. When one of these customers is served, an incredible number of arrivals are queued and delayed by a significant fraction of that service time. Thus, the contribution to W is proportional to the square of the service time, leading to an infinite W if $\overline{X^2}$ is infinite.

The above derivation of the P-K formula assumed that customers were served in order of arrival, *i.e.*, that the number of customers served between the ith arrival and service is just the number in queue at the ith arrival. It turns out, however, that this formula is valid for any order of servicing customers as long as the order is determined independently of the required service time. To see this, suppose that the ith and j^{th} customers are both in the queue and that they exchange places. The expected queueing time of customer i (over the service times of the customers in queue) will then be exchanged with that for customer j, but the average, over all customers, is unchanged. Since any service order can be considered as a sequence of reversals in queue position, the P-K formula remains valid (see also Problem 3.16).

To see why the P-K formula is invalid if the service order can depend on service time, consider a queue with two customers requiring 10 and 2 units of service time respectively. Assuming that the server becomes available at time 0, serving the first customer first results in one customer starting service at time 0 and the other at time 10. Serving the second customer first results in one customer starting at time 0 and the other at time 2. Thus, the average queueing time over the two customers is 5 in the first case and 1 in the second case. Clearly, queueing time is reduced by serving customers with small service time first. For this situation, the derivation of the P-K formula breaks down at Eq. (3.46) since the packets that will be transmitted before a newly arriving packet no longer have a mean service time equal to $1/\mu$.

Example 11: Delay Analysis of an ARQ System

Consider a goback n ARQ system such as the one discussed in section 2.4. Assume packets are transmitted in frames that are one time unit long, and there is a maximum wait for an acknowledgement of $n-1$ frames before a packet is retransmitted (see Fig. 3.11). In this system packets are retransmitted for two reasons:

1. A given packet transmitted in frame i might be rejected at the receiver due to errors, in which case the transmitter will transmit packets in frames $i + 1$, $i + 2, \ldots, i + n - 1$, (if any are available), and then go back to retransmit the packet in frame $i + n$.

2. A packet transmitted in frame i might be accepted at the receiver but the corresponding acknowledgement (in the form of the receive number) might not have arrived at the transmitter by the time the transmission of packet $i + n - 1$ is completed. This can happen due to errors in the return channel, large propagation delays, long return frames relative to the size of the goback number n, or a combination thereof.

We will assume (somewhat unrealistically) that retransmissions occur only due to #1 above, and that a packet is rejected at the receiver with probability p independently of other packets.

Consider the case where packets arrive at the transmitter according to a Poisson process with rate λ. It follows that the time interval between start of the first

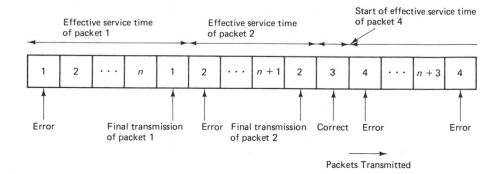

Figure 3.11 Illustration of the effective service times of packets in the ARQ system of Ex. 11. For example, packet 2 has an effective service time of $n + 1$ because there was an error in the first attempt to transmit it following the last transmission of packet 1, but no error in the second attempt.

transmission of a given packet after the last transmission of the previous packet, and end of the last transmission of the given packet is $1 + kn$ time units with probability $(1 - p)p^k$ (this corresponds to k retransmissions following the last transmission of the previous packet—see Fig. 3.11). Thus, the transmitter's queue behaves like an $M/G/1$ queue with service time distribution given by

$$P\{X = 1 + kn\} = (1 - p)p^k, \quad k = 0, 1, \ldots$$

The first two moments of the service time are

$$\overline{X} = \sum_{k=0}^{\infty}(1 + kn)(1 - p)p^k = (1 - p)\left(\sum_{k=0}^{\infty} p^k + n\sum_{k=0}^{\infty} kp^k\right)$$

$$\overline{X^2} = \sum_{k=0}^{\infty}(1 + kn)^2(1 - p)p^k$$

$$= (1 - p)\left(\sum_{k=0}^{\infty} p^k + 2n\sum_{k=0}^{\infty} kp^k + n^2\sum_{k=0}^{\infty} k^2 p^k\right)$$

We now note that $\sum_{k=0}^{\infty} p^k = 1/(1-p)$, $\sum_{k=0}^{\infty} kp^k = p/(1-p)^2$, and $\sum_{k=0}^{\infty} k^2 p^k = (p + p^2)/(1 - p)^3$. (The first sum is the usual geometric series sum, while the other two sums are obtained by differentiating the first sum twice.) Using these formulas in the equations for $\overline{X}$ and $\overline{X^2}$ above, we obtain

$$\overline{X} = 1 + \frac{np}{1 - p}$$

$$\overline{X^2} = 1 + \frac{2np}{1 - p} + \frac{n^2(p + p^2)}{(1 - p)^2}$$

The P-K formula gives the average packet time in queue and in the system (up to the end of the last transmission):

$$W = \frac{\lambda \overline{X^2}}{2(1 - \lambda \overline{X})}$$

$$T = \overline{X} + W$$

3.5.1 M/G/1 *Queues with Vacations*

Suppose that at the end of each busy period, the server goes on "vacation" for some random interval of time. Thus, a new arrival to an idle system, rather than going into service immediately, waits for the end of the vacation period (see Fig. 3.12). If the system is still idle at the completion of a vacation, a new vacation starts immediately. For data networks, vacations correspond to the transmission of various kinds of control and record-keeping packets when there is a lull in the data traffic; other applications will become apparent later.

Let $V_1, V_2, \ldots$ be the durations of the successive vacations taken by the server. We assume that $V_1, V_2, \ldots$ are independent and identically distributed (IID) random variables, also independent of the customer interarrival times and service times. As before, the arrivals are Poisson and the service times are IID with a general distribution. A new arrival to the system has to wait in the queue for the completion of the current service or vacation and then for the service of all the customers waiting before it. Thus, Eq. (3.48) is still valid (*i.e.*, $W = R/(1 - \rho)$), where now R is the mean residual time for completion of the service *or* vacation in process when the ith customer arrives.

The analysis of this new system is the same as that of the P-K formula except that vacations must be included in the graph of residual service times $r(\tau)$ (see Fig. 3.13). Let $M(t)$ be the number of services completed by time t and $L(t)$ be the number of vacations completed by time t. Then (as in Eq. (3.49)), for any t where a service or vacation is just completed, we have

$$\frac{1}{t} \int_0^t r(\tau) \, d\tau = \frac{1}{t} \sum_{i=1}^{M(t)} \frac{1}{2} X_i^2 + \frac{1}{t} \sum_{i=1}^{L(t)} \frac{1}{2} V_i^2 \tag{3.54}$$

As before, assuming that a steady state exists, $M(t)/t$ approaches λ with increasing t, and the first term on the right side of Eq. (3.54) approaches $\lambda \overline{X^2}/2$

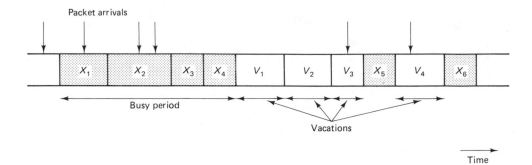

Figure 3.12   An $M/G/1$ system with vacations. At the end of a busy period, the server goes on vacation for time V with first and second moments $\overline{V}$ and $\overline{V^2}$, respectively. If the system is empty at the end of a vacation, the server takes a new vacation. An arriving customer to an empty system must wait until the end of the current vacation to get service.

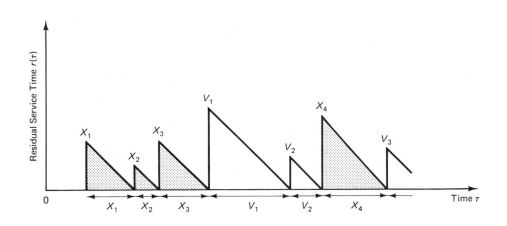

Figure 3.13   Residual service times for an $M/G/1$ system with vacations. Busy periods alternate with vacation periods.

as in the derivation of the P-K formula (cf. Eq. (3.52)). For the second term, note that as $t \to \infty$, the fraction of time spent serving customers approaches ρ, and thus the fraction of time occupied with vacations is $1 - \rho$. Assuming time averages can be replaced by ensemble averages we have $t(1 - \rho)/L(t) \to \overline{V}$ with increasing t, and thus the second term in Eq. (3.54) approaches $(1 - \rho)\overline{V^2}/(2\overline{V})$, where $\overline{V}$ and $\overline{V^2}$ are the first and second moments of the vacation interval, respectively. Combining this with $W = R/(1 - \rho)$, and assuming equality of the time and ensemble averages of R, we get

$$W = \frac{\lambda \overline{X^2}}{2(1 - \rho)} + \frac{\overline{V^2}}{2\overline{V}} \tag{3.55}$$

as the expected waiting time in queue for an $M/G/1$ system with vacations.

If we look carefully at the derivation of Eq. (3.55), we see that the mutual independence of the vacation intervals is not required (although the time and ensemble averages of the vacation intervals must still be equal) and the length of a vacation interval starting at time t need not be independent of the already completed service times or arrival times. Naturally, with this kind of dependence, it becomes more difficult to calculate $\overline{V}$ and $\overline{V^2}$, as these quantities might be functions of the underlying $M/G/1$ process.

Example 12: Frequency- and time-division multiplexing on a slot basis

We have m traffic streams of equal length packets arriving according to a Poisson process with rate λ/m each. If the traffic streams are frequency-division multiplexed on m subchannels of an available channel, the transmission time of each packet is m time units. Then, each subchannel can be represented by an $M/D/1$ queueing system and, by Eq. (3.45), with $\rho = \lambda$, $\mu = 1/m$, the average queueing delay per packet is

$$W_{\text{FDM}} = \frac{\lambda m}{2(1 - \lambda)} \tag{3.56}$$

Consider the same FDM scheme with the difference that packet transmissions can start only at times $m, 2m, 3m, \ldots$, i.e., at the beginning of a slot of m time units. We call this scheme *slotted frequency-division multiplexing* (SFDM), and note that it can be viewed as an $M/D/1$ queue with vacations. When there are no packets in the queue for a given stream at the beginning of a slot, the server takes a vacation for one slot, or m time units. Thus, $\overline{V} = m$, $\overline{V^2} = m^2$, and Eq. (3.55) becomes

$$W_{\text{SFDM}} = W_{\text{FDM}} + \frac{m}{2} \tag{3.57}$$

Finally, consider the case where the m traffic streams are time-division multiplexed in a scheme whereby the time axis is divided in m-slot frames with one slot dedicated to each traffic stream (see Fig. 3.14). Each slot is one time unit long and can carry a single packet. Then, if we compare this TDM scheme with the SFDM scheme, we see that the queue for a given stream in TDM is precisely the same as the queue for SFDM, and

$$W_{\text{TDM}} = W_{\text{SFDM}} = W_{\text{FDM}} + \frac{m}{2} = \frac{m}{2(1 - \lambda)} \tag{3.58}$$

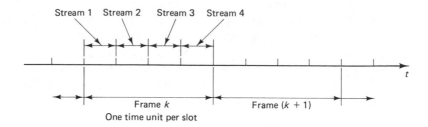

Figure 3.14   TDM with $m = 4$ traffic streams.

If we now look at the total delay for TDM, we get a different picture, since the service time is 1 unit of time rather than m units as in SFDM. By adding the service times to the queueing delays, we obtain

$$T_{\text{FDM}} = m + \frac{\lambda m}{2(1 - \lambda)}$$

$$T_{\text{SFDM}} = T_{\text{FDM}} + \frac{m}{2}$$

$$T_{\text{TDM}} = 1 + \frac{m}{2(1 - \lambda)} = T_{\text{FDM}} - \left(\frac{m}{2} - 1\right) \qquad (3.59)$$

Thus, the customer's average total delay is more favorable in TDM than in FDM (assuming $m > 2$). The longer average waiting time in queue for TDM is more than compensated by the faster service time. Note that the analysis above is generalized in Problem 3.22.

3.5.2 Reservations and Polling

Organizing transmissions from several packet streams into a statistical multiplexing system requires some form of scheduling. In some cases, this scheduling is naturally and easily accomplished; in other cases, however, some form of reservation or polling system is required.

A typical situation is one whereby there is a communication channel that can be accessed by several spatially separated users; however, only one user can transmit successfully on the channel at any one time. (This is called a *multiaccess channel*, and will be treated extensively in Chapter 4.) The communication resource of the channel can be divided over time into a portion used for packet transmissions and another portion used for reservation or polling messages that coordinate the packet transmissions. In other words, the time axis is divided into *data intervals*, where actual data is transmitted, and *reservation intervals*, used for scheduling future data. For uniform presentation, we use the term "reservation" even though "polling" may be more appropriate to the practical situation.

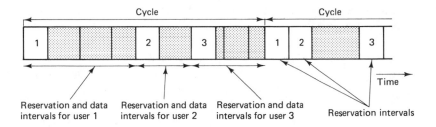

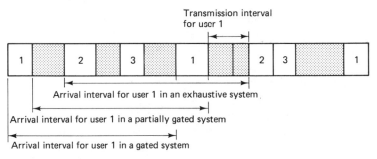

Packets arriving in the arrival interval shown are
transmitted in the transmission interval shown

Figure 3.15   A reservation or polling system with three users. In the
exhaustive version, a packet of a user that arrives during the user's reservation
or data interval is transmitted in the same data interval. In the partially gated
version, a packet of a user arriving during the user's data interval must wait
for an entire cycle and be transmitted during the next data interval of the
user. In the fully gated version, packets arriving during the user's reservation
interval must also wait for an entire cycle. The figure shows, for the three
systems, the association between the interval in which a packet arrives and
the interval in which the packet is transmitted.

We will consider m traffic streams (also called users), and assume that each
data interval contains packets of a *single* user. Reservations for these packets are
made in the immediately preceding reservation interval. All users are taken up in
cyclic order (see Fig. 3.15). There are several versions of this system differing in the
rule for deciding which packets are transmitted during the data interval of each user.
In the *gated* system, the rule is that only those packets that arrived prior to the
user's preceding reservation interval are transmitted. By contrast, in the *exhaustive*
system, the rule is that all available packets of a user are transmitted during the
corresponding data interval, including those that arrived in this data interval or the
preceding reservation interval. An intermediate version, which we call the *partially
gated* system, results when the packets transmitted in a user's data interval are

those that arrived up to the time this data interval began (and the corresponding reservation interval ended). A typical example of such reservation systems is one of the most common local area networks, the token ring. The users are connected by cable in a unidirectional loop. Each user transmits the current packet backlog, then gives the opportunity to a neighbor to transmit, and the process is repeated. (A more detailed description of the token ring is given in Chapter 4.)

We assume that the arrival processes of all users are independent Poisson with rate λ/m, and that the first and second moments of the packet transmission times are $\overline{X} = 1/\mu$ and $\overline{X^2}$, respectively. The utilization factor is $\rho = \lambda/\mu$. Interarrival times and transmission times are, as usual, assumed independent. While we assume that all users have identical arrival and service statistics, we allow the reservation intervals of different users to have different statistics.

Single-User System

Our general line of analysis of reservation systems can be better understood in terms of the special case where $m = 1$; so, we consider this case first. We may also view this as a system where all users share reservation and data intervals. Let V_ℓ be the duration of the ℓth reservation interval and assume that successive reservation intervals are independent and identically distributed random variables with first and second moments $\overline{V}$ and $\overline{V^2}$, respectively. We consider a gated system and assume that the reservation intervals are statistically independent of the arrival times and service durations. Finally, for convenience of exposition, we assume that packets are transmitted in the order of their arrival. As in our derivation of the P-K formula, expected delays and queue lengths are independent of service order as long as service order is independent of service requirement (*i.e.*, packet length).

Consider the ith data packet arriving at the system. This packet must wait in queue for the residual time R_i until the end of the current packet transmission or reservation interval. It must also wait for the transmission of the N_i packets currently in the queue (this includes both packets for which reservations were already made in the last reservation interval and earlier arrivals waiting to make a reservation). Finally, the packet must wait during the next reservation interval $V_{\ell(i)}$, say, in which its reservation will be made (see Fig. 3.16). Thus, the expected queueing delay for the ith packet is given by

$$E\{W_i\} = E\{R_i\} + E\{N_i\}/\mu + E\{V_{\ell(i)}\} \tag{3.60}$$

The similarity of this reservation system to the $M/G/1$ queue with vacations should be noted. The only difference is that in the gated reservation system, a reservation interval starts when all packets have been served from the previous interval, whereas in the vacation system, a vacation interval starts when *all* previous arrivals have been served. (In fact, the exhaustive version of this reservation system is equivalent to the vacation system.) The time-average mean residual time for the two systems is clearly the same (see Fig. 3.13), and is given by $\lambda\overline{X^2}/2 + (1-\rho)\overline{V^2}/2\overline{V}$.

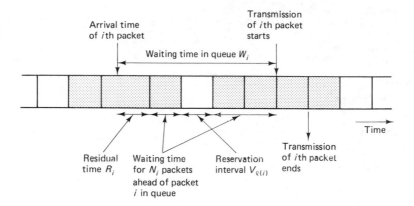

Figure 3.16   Calculation of the average waiting time in the single-user gated system. The expected waiting time $E\{W_i\}$ of the ith packet is

$$E\{W_i\} = E\{R_i\} + E\{N_i\}/\mu + E\{V_{\ell(i)}\}$$

The value of $\lim_{i \to \infty} E\{N_i\}/\mu$ is ρW in both systems, and finally the value of $\lim_{i \to \infty} E\{V_{\ell(i)}\}$ is just $\overline{V}$. Thus, from Eq. (3.60) the expected time in queue for the single-user reservation system is

$$W = \frac{\lambda \overline{X^2}}{2(1 - \rho)} + \frac{\overline{V^2}}{2\overline{V}} + \frac{\overline{V}}{1 - \rho} \quad \text{(single user, gated)} \qquad (3.61)$$

In the common situation where the reservation interval is a constant A, this simplifies to

$$W = \frac{\lambda \overline{X^2}}{2(1 - \rho)} + \frac{A}{2} \left(\frac{3 - \rho}{1 - \rho} \right) \qquad (3.62)$$

There is an interesting paradox associated with Eq. (3.61). We have seen that a fraction $1 - \rho$ of time is used on reservations. Since there is one reservation interval of mean duration $\overline{V}$ per cycle, we can conclude that the expected cycle length must be $\overline{V}/(1 - \rho)$ (Prob. 3.23 develops this result more carefully). The mean queueing delay in Eq. (3.61) can be an arbitrarily large multiple of this mean cycle length, which seems paradoxical since each packet is transmitted on the cycle following its arrival. The explanation of this is that more packets tend to arrive in long cycles than in short cycles, and thus mean cycle length is not representative of the cycle lengths seen by arriving packets; this is the same phenomenon that makes the mean residual service time used in the P-K formula derivation larger than one might think (see also Problem 3.15).

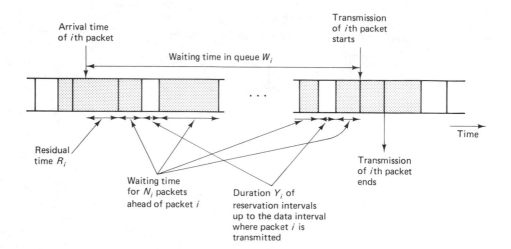

Figure 3.17   Calculation of the average waiting time in the multiuser system. The expected waiting time $E\{W_i\}$ of the ith packet is

$$E\{W_i\} = E\{R_i\} + E\{N_i\}/\mu + E\{Y_i\}$$

Multiuser System

Suppose that the system has m users, each with independent Poisson arrivals of rate λ/m. Again $\overline{X}$ and $\overline{X^2}$ are the first two moments of the service time for each user's packets. We denote by $\overline{V_i}$ and $\overline{V_i^2}$, respectively, the first two moments of the reservation intervals of user i. The service times and reservation intervals are all independent. We number the users $0, 1, \ldots, m - 1$ and assume that the ℓth reservation interval is used to make reservations for user $\ell \text{mod}(m)$ and the subsequent (ℓ^{th}) data interval is used to send the packets corresponding to those reservations.

Consider the ith packet arrival into the system (counting packets in order of arrival, regardless of user). As before, the expected delay for this packet consists of three terms: first, the mean residual time for the packet or reservation in progress; second, the expected time to transmit the number N_i of packets that must be transmitted before packet i; and third, the expected duration of reservation intervals (see Fig. 3.17). Thus,

$$E\{W_i\} = E\{R_i\} + E\{N_i\}/\mu + E\{Y_i\} \tag{3.63}$$

where Y_i is the duration of all the whole reservation intervals during which packet

i must wait before being transmitted. The time average mean residual time is calculated similarly as before, and is given by

$$R = \frac{\lambda \overline{X^2}}{2} + \frac{(1-\rho) \sum_{\ell=0}^{m-1} \overline{V_\ell^2}}{2 \sum_{\ell=0}^{m-1} \overline{V_\ell}} \tag{3.64}$$

The number of packets N_i that i must wait for is not equal to the number already in queue, but the order of serving packets is independent of packet service time; thus, each packet served before i still has a mean transmission time $1/\mu$ as indicated in Eq. (3.63) and by Little's formula, the value of $\lim_{i \to \infty} E\{N_i\}/\mu$ is ρW as before. Letting $Y = \lim_{i \to \infty} E\{Y_i\}$, we can thus write the steady state version of Eq. (3.63)

$$W = R + \rho W + Y$$

or, equivalently,

$$W = \frac{R+Y}{1-\rho} \tag{3.65}$$

We first calculate Y for an exhaustive system. Denote

$$\alpha_{\ell j} = E\{Y_i | \text{ packet } i \text{ arrives in user } \ell\text{'s reservation or data}$$
$$\text{interval and belongs to user } (\ell + j) \bmod(m)\}$$

We have

$$\alpha_{\ell j} = \begin{cases} 0, & j = 0 \\ \overline{V}_{(\ell+1)\bmod(m)} + \cdots + \overline{V}_{(\ell+j)\bmod(m)}, & j > 0 \end{cases}$$

Since packet i belongs to any user with equal probability $1/m$, we have

$$E\{Y_i | \text{ packet } i \text{ arrives in user } \ell\text{'s reservation or data interval}\}$$

$$= \frac{1}{m} \sum_{j=1}^{m-1} \alpha_{\ell j} = \sum_{j=1}^{m-1} \frac{m-j}{m} \overline{V}_{(\ell+j)\bmod(m)} \tag{3.66}$$

Since all users have equal data rate, the data intervals of all users have equal average length in steady state. Therefore, in steady state, a packet will arrive during user ℓ's data interval with probability ρ/m, and during user ℓ's reservation interval with probability $(1-\rho)\overline{V}_\ell \Big/ \left(\sum_{k=0}^{m-1} \overline{V}_k \right)$. Using this fact in Eq. (3.66) we obtain the following equation for $Y = \lim_{i \to \infty} E\{Y_i\}$

$$Y = \sum_{\ell=0}^{m-1} \left(\frac{\rho}{m} + \frac{(1-\rho)\overline{V}_\ell}{\sum_{k=0}^{m-1} \overline{V}_k} \right) \sum_{j=1}^{m-1} \frac{m-j}{m} \overline{V}_{(\ell+j)\bmod(m)}$$

$$= \frac{\rho}{m} \sum_{j=1}^{m-1} \frac{m-j}{m} \left(\sum_{\ell=0}^{m-1} \overline{V}_\ell \right) + \frac{(1-\rho)}{\sum_{k=0}^{m-1} \overline{V}_k} \sum_{\ell=0}^{m-1} \sum_{j=1}^{m-1} \frac{m-j}{m} \overline{V}_\ell \overline{V}_{(\ell+j)\bmod(m)} \tag{3.67}$$

The last sum above can be written

$$\sum_{\ell=0}^{m-1}\sum_{j=1}^{m-1}\frac{m-j}{m}\overline{V}_\ell\overline{V}_{(\ell+j)\bmod(m)} = \frac{1}{2}\left[\left(\sum_{\ell=0}^{m-1}\overline{V}_\ell\right)^2 - \sum_{\ell=0}^{m-1}\overline{V}_\ell^2\right]$$

(To see this, note that the right side above is the sum of all possible products $\overline{V}_\ell\overline{V}_{\ell'}$ for $\ell \neq \ell'$. The left side is the sum of all possible terms $(j/m)\overline{V}_\ell\overline{V}_{\ell'}$ and $[(m-j)/m]\overline{V}_\ell\overline{V}_{\ell'}$, where $j = |\ell - \ell'|$ and $\ell \neq \ell'$.) Using this expression, and denoting

$$\overline{V} = \frac{1}{m}\sum_{\ell=0}^{m-1}\overline{V}_\ell$$

as the reservation interval averaged over all users, we can write Eq. (3.67) as

$$Y = \frac{\rho\overline{V}(m-1)}{2} + \frac{(1-\rho)m\overline{V}}{2} - \frac{(1-\rho)\sum_{\ell=0}^{m-1}\overline{V}_\ell^2}{2m\overline{V}}$$
$$= \frac{(m-\rho)\overline{V}}{2} - \frac{(1-\rho)\sum_{\ell=0}^{m-1}\overline{V}_\ell^2}{2m\overline{V}}. \tag{3.68}$$

Combining Eq. (3.64), (3.65), and (3.68), we obtain

$$W = \frac{\lambda\overline{X^2}}{2(1-\rho)} + \frac{(m-\rho)\overline{V}}{2(1-\rho)} + \frac{\sum_{\ell=0}^{m-1}\left(\overline{V_\ell^2} - \overline{V}_\ell^2\right)}{2m\overline{V}}$$

Denoting

$$\sigma_V^2 = \frac{\sum_{\ell=0}^{m-1}\left(\overline{V_\ell^2} - \overline{V}_\ell^2\right)}{m}$$

as the variance of the reservation intervals averaged over all users, we finally obtain

$$W = \frac{\lambda\overline{X^2}}{2(1-\rho)} + \frac{(m-\rho)\overline{V}}{2(1-\rho)} + \frac{\sigma_V^2}{2\overline{V}} \qquad \text{(exhaustive)} \tag{3.69}$$

The partially gated system is the same as the exhaustive except that if a packet of a user arrives during a user's own data interval (an event of probability ρ/m in steady state), it is delayed by an additional $m\overline{V}$, the average sum of reservation intervals in a cycle. Thus, Y is increased by $\rho\overline{V}$ in the preceding calculation, and we obtain

$$W = \frac{\lambda\overline{X^2}}{2(1-\rho)} + \frac{(m+\rho)\overline{V}}{2(1-\rho)} + \frac{\sigma_V^2}{2\overline{V}} \qquad \text{(partially gated)} \tag{3.70}$$

Consider finally the fully gated system. This is the same as the partially gated system except that if a packet of a user arrives during a user's own reservation interval (an event of probability $(1 - \rho)/m$ in steady state), it is delayed by an additional $m\overline{V}$. This increases Y by an additional $(1 - \rho)\overline{V}$ and results in the equation

$$W = \frac{\lambda \overline{X^2}}{2(1 - \rho)} + \frac{(m + 2 - \rho)\overline{V}}{2(1 - \rho)} + \frac{\sigma_V^2}{2\overline{V}} \qquad \text{(gated)} \qquad (3.71)$$

In comparing these results with the single user system, consider the case where the reservation interval is a constant A/m. Thus, A is the overhead or reservation time for an entire cycle of reservations for each user, which is usually the appropriate parameter to compare with A in Eq. (3.62). We then have $(\overline{V} = A/m, \ \sigma_V^2 = 0)$

$$W = \frac{\lambda \overline{X^2}}{2(1 - \rho)} + \frac{A}{2}\left(\frac{1 - \rho/m}{1 - \rho}\right) \qquad \text{(exhaustive)} \qquad (3.72)$$

$$W = \frac{\lambda \overline{X^2}}{2(1 - \rho)} + \frac{A}{2}\left(\frac{1 + \rho/m}{1 - \rho}\right) \qquad \text{(partially gated)} \qquad (3.73)$$

$$W = \frac{\lambda \overline{X^2}}{2(1 - \rho)} + \frac{A}{2}\left(\frac{1 + (2 - \rho)/m}{1 - \rho}\right) \qquad \text{(gated)} \qquad (3.74)$$

It can be seen that delay is somewhat reduced in the multiuser case; essentially, packets are delayed by roughly the same amount until the reservation time in all cases but delay is quite small after the reservation in the multiuser case.

Limited Service Systems

We now consider a variation of the multiuser system whereby, in each user's data interval, *only the first* packet of the user waiting in queue (if any) is transmitted (rather than *all* waiting packets). We concentrate on the gated and partially gated versions of this system, since an exhaustive version does not make sense. As before, we have

$$E\{W_i\} = E\{R_i\} + E\{N_i\}/\mu + E\{Y_i\}$$

and by taking the limit as $i \to \infty$, we obtain

$$W = R + \rho W + Y \qquad (3.75)$$

Here R is given by Eq. (3.64) as before. To calculate the new formula for Y for the partially gated system, we argue as follows. A packet arriving during user ℓ's data or reservation interval will belong to any one of the users with equal probability $1/m$. Therefore, in steady state, the expected number of packets waiting in the individual queue of the user that owns the arriving packet, averaged over all users, is $\lim_{i \to \infty} E\{N_i\}/m = \lambda W/m$. Each of these packets causes an extra cycle of reservations $m\overline{V}$, so Y is increased by an amount $\lambda W \overline{V}$. Using this fact in Eq. (3.75), we see that

$$W = \frac{R + \widetilde{Y}}{1 - \rho - \lambda\overline{V}}$$

where $\widetilde{Y}$ is the value of Y obtained earlier for the partially gated system without the single-packet-per-data-interval restriction. Equivalently, we see from Eq. (3.65), that *the single-packet-per-data-interval restriction results in an increase of the average waiting time for the partially gated system by a factor*

$$\frac{1-\rho}{1-\rho-\lambda\overline{V}}$$

Using this fact in Eq. (3.70), we obtain

$$W = \frac{\lambda\overline{X^2}}{2(1-\rho-\lambda\overline{V})} + \frac{(m+\rho)\overline{V}}{2(1-\rho-\lambda\overline{V})} + \frac{\sigma_V^2(1-\rho)}{2\overline{V}(1-\rho-\lambda\overline{V})}$$

(limited service, partially gated)   (3.76)

Consider now the gated version. Y_i is the same as for the partially gated system except for an additional cycle of reservation intervals of average length $m\overline{V}$ associated with the event where packet i arrives during the reservation interval of its owner, and the subsequent data interval is empty. It is easily verified (Prob. 3.24) that the latter event occurs with steady-state probability $(1-\rho-\lambda\overline{V})/m$. Therefore, for the gated system Y equals the corresponding value for the partially gated system plus $(1-\rho-\lambda\overline{V})\overline{V}$. This adds $\overline{V}$ to the value of W for the partially gated system, and the average waiting time now is

$$W = \frac{\lambda\overline{X^2}}{2(1-\rho-\lambda\overline{V})} + \frac{(m+2-\rho-2\lambda\overline{V})\overline{V}}{2(1-\rho-\lambda\overline{V})} + \frac{\sigma_V^2(1-\rho)}{2\overline{V}(1-\rho-\lambda\overline{V})}$$

(limited service, gated)   (3.77)

Note that it is not enough that $\rho = \lambda/\mu < 1$ for W to be bounded; rather, $\rho + \lambda\overline{V} < 1$ is required or, equivalently,

$$\lambda\left(\frac{1}{\mu} + \overline{V}\right) < 1$$

This is due to the fact that each packet requires a separate reservation interval of average length $\overline{V}$, thereby effectively increasing the average transmission time from $1/\mu$ to $1/\mu + \overline{V}$.

As a final remark, consider the case of a very large number of users m and a very small average reservation interval $\overline{V}$. An examination of the equation given for the average waiting time W of every system considered so far shows that as $m \to \infty$, $\overline{V} \to 0$, $\sigma_V^2/\overline{V} \to 0$, and $m\overline{V} \to A$, where A is a constant, we have

$$W \to \frac{\lambda\overline{X^2}}{2(1-\rho)} + \frac{A}{2(1-\rho)}$$

It can be shown (Prob. 3.23) that $A/(1 - \rho)$ is the average length of a cycle (m successive reservation and data intervals). Thus, W approaches the $M/G/1$ average waiting time plus one half the average cycle length.

3.5.3 Priority Queueing

Consider the $M/G/1$ system with the difference that arriving customers are divided into n different priority classes. Class 1 has the highest priority, class 2 has the second highest, and so on. The arrival rate and the first two moments of service time of each class k are denoted λ_k, $\overline{X}_k = 1/\mu_k$, and $\overline{X_k^2}$, respectively. The arrival processes of all classes are assumed independent, Poisson, and independent of the service times.

Nonpreemptive Priority

We first consider the nonpreemptive priority rule whereby a customer undergoing service is allowed to complete service without interruption even if a customer of higher priority arrives in the meantime. A separate queue is maintained for each priority class. When the server becomes free, the first customer of the highest nonempty priority queue enters service. This priority rule is one of the most appropriate for modeling packet transmission systems.

   We will develop an equation for average delay for each priority class, which is similar to the P-K formula and admits a similar derivation. Denote

$$N_Q^k : \text{ Average number in queue for priority } k$$

$$W_k : \text{ Average queueing time for priority } k$$

$$\rho_k = \lambda_k/\mu_k : \text{ System utilization for priority } k$$

$$R : \text{ Mean residual service time}$$

We assume that the overall system utilization is less than one, $i.e.$,

$$\rho_1 + \rho_2 + \cdots + \rho_n < 1$$

When this assumption is not satisfied, there will be some priority class k such that the average delay of customers of priority k and lower will be infinite while the average delay of customers of priority higher than k will be finite. Problem 3.16 takes a closer look at this situation.

   Similarly, as in the derivation of the P-K formula given earlier, we have for the highest priority class

$$W_1 = R + \frac{1}{\mu_1} N_Q^1$$

Eliminating N_Q^1 from this equation using Little's Theorem

$$N_Q^1 = \lambda_1 W_1$$

we obtain

$$W_1 = R + \rho_1 W_1$$

and, finally,

$$W_1 = \frac{R}{1 - \rho_1} \qquad (3.78)$$

For the second priority class, we have a similar expression for the queueing delay W_2 except that we have to count the additional queueing delay due to customers of higher priority that arrive while a customer is waiting in queue. This is the meaning of the last term in the formula

$$W_2 = R + \frac{1}{\mu_1} N_Q^1 + \frac{1}{\mu_2} N_Q^2 + \frac{1}{\mu_1} \lambda_1 W_2$$

Using Little's Theorem $(N_Q^k = \lambda_k W_k)$ we obtain

$$W_2 = R + \rho_1 W_1 + \rho_2 W_2 + \rho_1 W_2$$

which yields

$$W_2 = \frac{R + \rho_1 W_1}{1 - \rho_1 - \rho_2}$$

Using the expression $W_1 = R/(1 - \rho_1)$ obtained earlier, we finally have

$$W_2 = \frac{R}{(1 - \rho_1)(1 - \rho_1 - \rho_2)}$$

The derivation is similar for all priority classes $k > 1$. The formula for the waiting time in queue is

$$W_k = \frac{R}{(1 - \rho_1 - \cdots - \rho_{k-1})(1 - \rho_1 - \cdots - \rho_k)} \qquad (3.79)$$

The average delay per customer of class k is

$$T_k = \frac{1}{\mu_k} + W_k \qquad (3.80)$$

The mean residual service time R must now be derived. As in the earlier derivation of the P-K formula (compare with Fig. 3.10) we have

$$R = \frac{1}{2} \left(\sum_{i=1}^{n} \lambda_i \right) \overline{X^2} \qquad (3.81)$$

where $\overline{X^2}$ denotes the second moment of service time averaged over all priority classes. In particular,

$$\overline{X^2} = \frac{\lambda_1}{\sum_{i=1}^{n} \lambda_i} \overline{X_1^2} + \cdots + \frac{\lambda_n}{\sum_{i=1}^{n} \lambda_i} \overline{X_n^2}$$

Substitution in Eq. (3.81) yields

$$R = \frac{1}{2} \sum_{i=1}^{n} \lambda_i \overline{X_i^2} \tag{3.82}$$

The average waiting time in queue and the average delay per customer for each class is obtained from Eqs. (3.79), (3.80), and (3.82)

$$W_k = \frac{\sum_{i=1}^{n} \lambda_i \overline{X_i^2}}{2(1 - \rho_1 - \cdots - \rho_{k-1})(1 - \rho_1 - \cdots - \rho_k)} \tag{3.83}$$

$$T_k = \frac{1}{\mu_k} + W_k$$

Note that it is possible to affect the average delay per customer by choosing the priority classes appropriately. It is generally true that average delay tends to be reduced when customers with short service times are given higher priority. (For an example from common experience, consider the supermarket practice of having special checkout counters for customers with few items. A similar situation can be seen in copying machine waiting lines, where people often give priority to others that need to make just a few copies.) An analytical substantiation can be obtained by considering a nonpreemptive system and two customer classes A and B with respective arrival and service rates λ_A, μ_A, and λ_B, μ_B. A straightforward calculation using the formulas above shows that if $\mu_A > \mu_B$, then the average delay per customer (averaged over both classes)

$$T = \frac{\lambda_A T_A + \lambda_B T_B}{\lambda_A + \lambda_B}$$

is smaller when A is given priority over B than when B is given priority over A. For related results, see Prob. 3.19.

The analysis given above does not extend easily to the case of multiple servers, primarily because there is no simple formula for the mean residual time. If, however, the service times of all priority classes are identically and exponentially distributed, there is a convenient characterization of R. Equation (3.79) then yields a closed-form expression for the average waiting times W_k (see Prob. 3.17).

Preemptive Resume Priority

One of the features of the nonpreemptive priority rule is that the average delay of a priority class depends on the arrival rate of lower priority classes. This is evident from Eq. (3.83) and is due to the fact that a high priority customer must wait for a lower priority customer already in service. This dependence is not present in the *preemptive resume priority discipline*, whereby service of a customer is interrupted when a higher priority customer arrives, and is resumed from the point of interruption once all customers of higher priority have been served.

As we consider the calculation of T_k, the average time in the system of priority k customers, we should keep in mind that the presence of customers of priorities $k+1$ through n does not affect this calculation. Therefore, we can treat each priority class as if it were the lowest in the system.

The system time T_k consists of three terms. The first is the customer's average service time $1/\mu_k$. The second is the average time required, upon arrival of a priority k customer, to service customers of priority 1 to k already in the system, i.e., the average unfinished work corresponding to priorities 1 through k. This term is equal to the average waiting time in the corresponding, ordinary $M/G/1$ system (without priorities), where the customers of priorities $k+1$ through n are neglected, i.e., (cf. Eq. (3.48))

$$\frac{R_k}{1 - \rho_1 - \cdots - \rho_k}$$

where R_k is the mean residual time

$$R_k = \frac{\sum\limits_{i=1}^{k} \lambda_i X_i^2}{2} \tag{3.84}$$

This follows since, at all times, the unfinished work (sum of remaining service times of all customers in the system) of an $M/G/1$-type system is independent of the priority discipline of the system. This is true of all queueing systems that are conservative in the sense that the server is always busy when the system is nonempty, and customers leave the system only after receiving their required service. The third term in the expression for T_k is the average waiting time for customers of priorities 1 through $k-1$ who arrive while the customer of class k is in the system. This term is

$$\sum_{i=1}^{k-1} \frac{1}{\mu_i} \lambda_i T_k = \sum_{i=1}^{k-1} \rho_i T_k$$

for $k > 1$, and is zero for $k = 1$. Collecting these terms, we obtain the equation

$$T_k = \frac{1}{\mu_k} + \frac{R_k}{1 - \rho_1 - \cdots - \rho_k} + \left(\sum_{i=1}^{k-1} \rho_i \right) T_k \tag{3.85}$$

The final result is, for $k = 1$,

$$T_1 = \frac{(1/\mu_1)(1 - \rho_1) + R_1}{1 - \rho_1} \tag{3.86}$$

and, for $k > 1$,

$$T_k = \frac{(1/\mu_k)(1 - \rho_1 - \cdots - \rho_k) + R_k}{(1 - \rho_1 - \cdots - \rho_{k-1})(1 - \rho_1 - \cdots - \rho_k)} \tag{3.87}$$

Figure 3.18   Two equal capacity transmission lines in tandem. If all packets have equal length, there is no queueing delay in the second queue.

where R_k is given by Eq. (3.84). As for the nonpreemptive system, there is no easy extension of this formula to the case of multiple servers unless the service times of all priority classes are identically and exponentially distributed (see Prob. 3.17).

3.6 NETWORKS OF TRANSMISSION LINES

In a data network, there are many transmission queues that interact in the sense that a traffic stream departing from one queue enters one or more other queues, perhaps after merging with portions of other traffic streams departing from yet other queues. Analytically, this has the unfortunate effect of complicating the character of the arrival processes at downstream queues. The difficulty is that the packet interarrival times become strongly correlated with packet lengths once packets have traveled beyond the first queue at their entry point in the network. As a result it is impossible to carry out a precise and effective analysis comparable to the one provided for queueing systems such as $M/M/1$, $M/G/1$, etc.

As an illustration of the phenomena that complicate the analysis, consider two transmission lines of equal capacity in tandem, as shown in Fig. 3.18. Assume that Poisson arrivals of rate λ packets/sec enter the first queue, and that all packets have *equal* length. Therefore, the first queue is $M/D/1$ and the average packet delay there is given by the Pollaczek-Khinchin formula. However, at the second queue, the interarrival times must be greater than or equal to $1/\mu$ (the packet transmission time). Furthermore, because the packet transmission times are equal at both queues, each packet arriving at the second queue will complete transmission at or before the time the next packet arrives, so there is *no waiting at the second queue.* Therefore, a delay model based on Poisson assumptions is totally inappropriate for the second queue.

Consider next the case of the two tandem transmission lines where packet lengths are exponentially distributed, and are independent of each other as well as of the interarrival times at the first queue. Then the first queue is $M/M/1$. The second queue, however, *cannot* be modeled as $M/M/1$. The reason is, again, that *the interarrival times at the second queue are strongly correlated with the packet lengths.* To see this, consider a busy period at the first queue where several packets are transmitted one after the other. The interarrival time at the second queue

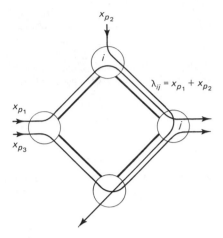

Figure 3.19   A network of transmission lines. The total arrival rate λ_{ij} at a link (i,j) is equal to the sum of arrival rates x_p of all packet streams p traversing the link.

between two such packets equals the transmission time of the second packet. As a result, long packets will typically wait less time at the second queue than short packets, since their transmission at the first queue takes longer, thereby giving the second queue more time to empty out. For a traffic analogy, consider a slow truck traveling on a busy narrow street together with several faster cars. The truck will typically see empty space ahead of it while being closely followed by the faster cars.

As an indication of the difficulty of analyzing queueing network problems involving dependent interarrival and service times, no analytical solution is known for even the simple tandem queueing problem of Fig. 3.18 involving Poisson arrivals and exponentially distributed service times. In the real situation where packet lengths and interarrival times are correlated, a simulation has shown that under heavy traffic conditions, average delay per packet is smaller than in the idealized situation where there is no such correlation. The reverse is true under light traffic conditions. It is not known whether and in what form this result can be extended to more general networks.

Consider now a network of communication links as shown in Fig. 3.19. Assume that there are several packet streams each following a path p that consists of a sequence of links through the network. Let x_p, in packets/sec, be the arrival rate of the packet stream associated with the path p. Then, the total arrival rate at link

(i, j) is

$$\lambda_{ij} = \sum_{\substack{\text{all } p \\ \text{traversing} \\ \text{link } (i,j)}} x_p \tag{3.88}$$

We have seen from the special case of two tandem queues that even if the packet streams are Poisson with independent packet lengths at their point of entry into the network, this property is lost after the first transmission line. To resolve the dilemma, it was suggested by Kleinrock [Kle64] that merging several packet streams on a transmission line has an effect akin to restoring the independence of interarrival times and packet lengths. It was concluded that it is often appropriate to adopt an $M/M/1$ queueing model for each communication link regardless of the interaction of traffic on this link with traffic on other links (see also the discussion preceding Jackson's theorem in section 3.8). This is known as the *Kleinrock independence approximation* and seems to be a reasonably good approximation for systems involving Poisson stream arrivals at the entry points, packet lengths that are nearly exponentially distributed, a densely connected network, and moderate to heavy traffic loads. Based on this $M/M/1$ model, the average number of packets in queue or service at (i, j) is

$$N_{ij} = \frac{\lambda_{ij}}{\mu_{ij} - \lambda_{ij}} \tag{3.89}$$

where $1/\mu_{ij}$ is the average packet transmission time on link (i, j). The average number of packets summed over all queues is

$$N = \sum_{(i,j)} \frac{\lambda_{ij}}{\mu_{ij} - \lambda_{ij}} \tag{3.90}$$

so by Little's Theorem, the average delay per packet (neglecting processing and propagation delays) is

$$T = \frac{1}{\gamma} \sum_{(i,j)} \frac{\lambda_{ij}}{\mu_{ij} - \lambda_{ij}} \tag{3.91}$$

where $\gamma = \sum_p x_p$ is the total arrival rate in the system. If the average processing and propagation delay d_{ij} at link (i, j) is not negligible, this formula should be adjusted to

$$T = \frac{1}{\gamma} \sum_{(i,j)} \left(\frac{\lambda_{ij}}{\mu_{ij} - \lambda_{ij}} + \lambda_{ij} d_{ij} \right) \tag{3.92}$$

Finally, the average delay per packet of a traffic stream traversing a path p is given by

$$T_p = \sum_{\substack{\text{all } (i,j) \\ \text{on path } p}} \left(\frac{\lambda_{ij}}{\mu_{ij}(\mu_{ij} - \lambda_{ij})} + \frac{1}{\mu_{ij}} + d_{ij} \right) \tag{3.93}$$

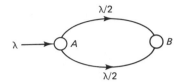

Figure 3.20　　　　A Poisson process with rate λ divided among two links. If division is done by randomization, each link behaves like an $M/M/1$ queue. If division is done by metering, the whole system behaves like an $M/M/2$ queueing system.

where the three terms in the sum above represent average waiting time in queue, average transmission time, and processing and propagation delay, respectively.

In many networks, the assumption of exponentially distributed packet lengths is not appropriate. Given a distribution function on packet lengths, one may keep the approximation of independence between queues but replace (3.89) with the P-K formula for average number in the system. Equations (3.90) to (3.93) would then be modified in an obvious way.

It should be mentioned that the main approximation involved in Eq. (3.90) is due to the correlation of the packet lengths and the packet interarrival times at the various queues in the network. If somehow this correlation was not present, *e.g.*, if a packet upon departure from a transmission line was assigned a new length drawn from an exponential distribution, then the average number of packets in the system would be given indeed by the formula

$$N = \sum_{(i,j)} \frac{\lambda_{ij}}{\mu_{ij} - \lambda_{ij}}$$

This fact (by no means obvious) is a consequence of Jackson's Theorem, which will be discussed in section 3.8.

In datagram networks that involve multiple path routing for some origin-destination pairs, the accuracy of the $M/M/1$ approximation deteriorates for another reason which is best illustrated by an example.

Example 13

Suppose node A sends traffic to node B along two equal capacity links in the simple network of Fig. 3.20. Packets arrive at A according to a Poisson process with rate λ packets/sec. Packet transmission times are exponentially distributed and independent of interarrival times similarly as in the $M/M/1$ system. Assume that the arriving traffic is to be divided equally among the two links. However, how should this division be implemented? Consider the following possibilities.

1. **Randomization**: Here each packet is assigned upon arrival at A to one of the two links based on the outcome of a fair coin flip. It is then possible to show that the arrival process on each of the two queues is

Poisson and independent of the packet lengths (see Prob. 3.11). There-fore, each of the two queues behaves like an $M/M/1$ queue with arrival rate $\lambda/2$ and average delay per packet

$$T_R = \frac{1}{\mu - \lambda/2} = \frac{2}{2\mu - \lambda} \tag{3.94}$$

which is consistent with the Kleinrock independence approximation.

2. **Metering**: Here each arriving packet is assigned to the queue that currently has the smallest total backlog in bits (equivalently to the queue that will empty its current backlog first). This scheme works like an $M/M/2$ system with arrival rate λ and with each link playing the role of a server. Using the result of subsection 3.4.1, the average delay per packet can be calculated to be

$$T_M = \frac{2}{(2\mu - \lambda)(1 + \rho)} \tag{3.95}$$

where $\rho = \lambda/2\mu$.

Comparing Eqs. (3.94) and (3.95), we see that metering performs better than randomization in terms of delay by a factor $1/(1+\rho)$. This is basically the same advantage that statistical multiplexing with multiple channels holds over time-division multiplexing as discussed in the Ex. 9 of subsection 3.4.1. Generally, it is preferable to use some form of metering rather than randomization when dividing traffic among alternate routes. However, in contrast with randomization, metering destroys the Poisson character of the arrival process at the point of division. In our example, when metering is used, the interarrival times at each link are neither exponentially distributed nor independent of preceding packet lengths. Therefore, the use of metering (which is recommended for performance reasons) tends to degrade the accuracy of the $M/M/1$ approximation.

3.7 TIME REVERSIBILITY—BURKE'S THEOREM

The analysis of the $M/M/1$, $M/M/m$, $M/M/\infty$, and $M/M/m/m$ systems was based on the relation that for any state j, the steady-state probability of j times the transition probability from j to $j+1$ is equal to the steady state probability of state $j+1$ times the transition probability from $j+1$ to j. These relations, called *detailed balance equations*, are valid for any Markov chain with integer states in which transitions can only occur between neighboring states, *i.e.*, from j to $j-1$, j, or $j+1$; these Markov chains are called *birth-death* processes. The detailed balance equations lead to an important property called time reversibility as we now explain.

Consider an irreducible, aperiodic, discrete-time Markov chain X_n, $X_{n+1}, \ldots$ having transition probabilities P_{ij} and stationary distribution $\{p_j | j \geq 0\}$. Suppose that the chain is in steady state, *i.e.*,

$$P\{X_n = j\} = p_j, \quad \text{for all } n$$

(this occurs if the initial state is chosen according to the stationary distribution, and is equivalent to imagining that the process began at time $-\infty$).

Suppose we trace the sequence of states going backwards in time. That is, starting at some n, consider the sequence of states $X_n, X_{n-1}, \ldots$. This sequence is itself a Markov chain as seen by the following calculation

$$P\{X_m = j | X_{m+1} = i, \ X_{m+2} = i_2, \ldots, X_{m+k} = i_k\}$$

$$= \frac{P\{X_m = j, X_{m+1} = i, \ X_{m+2} = i_2, \ldots, X_{m+k} = i_k\}}{P\{X_{m+1} = i, \ X_{m+2} = i_2, \ldots, X_{m+k} = i_k\}}$$

$$= \frac{P\{X_m = j\} P\{X_{m+1} = i | X_m = j\} P\{X_{m+2} = i_2, \ldots, X_{m+k} = i_k | X_m = j, X_{m+1} = i\}}{P\{X_{m+1} = i\} P\{X_{m+2} = i_2, \ldots, X_{m+k} = i_k | X_{m+1} = i\}}$$

$$= \frac{p_j P_{ji} P\{X_{m+2} = i_2, \ldots, X_{m+k} = i_k | X_{m+1} = i\}}{p_i P\{X_{m+2} = i_2, \ldots, X_{m+k} = i_k | X_{m+1} = i\}} = \frac{p_j P_{ji}}{p_i}$$

Thus, conditional on the state at time $m+1$, the state at time m is independent of that at times $m+2, m+3 \ldots$ The backward transition probabilities are given by

$$P_{ij}^* = P\{X_m = j | X_{m+1} = i\} = \frac{p_j P_{ji}}{p_i}, \qquad i, j \geq 0 \tag{3.96}$$

If $P_{ij}^* = P_{ij}$ for all i, j (i.e., the transition probabilities of the forward and reversed chain are identical), we say that the chain is *time reversible*.

We list some properties of the reversed chain:

1. The reversed chain is irreducible, aperiodic, and has the same stationary distribution as the forward chain. (This property can be shown either by elementary reasoning using the definition of the reversed chain, or by verifying the equality $p_j = \sum_{i=0}^{\infty} p_i P_{ij}^*$ using Eq. (3.96).) The intuitive idea here is that the reversed chain corresponds to the same process, looked at in the reversed time direction. Thus, if the steady state probabilities correspond to time averages (as they must for the concept of steady state to be meaningful), then the steady state is the same in both directions. Note that, in view of the equality of the stationary distribution of the forward and reverse chains, Eq. (3.96) can be intuitively explained. It expresses the fact that (with probability one) the proportion of transitions from j to i out of all transitions in the forward chain (which is $p_j P_{ji}$) equals the proportion of transitions from i to j out of all transitions in the reversed chain (which is $p_i P_{ij}^*$).

2. If we can find nonnegative numbers p_i, $i \geq 0$, summing to unity and find a transition probability matrix $P^* = [P_{ij}^*]$ such that

$$p_i P_{ij}^* = p_j P_{ji}, \quad i, j \geq 0 \tag{3.97}$$

then $\{p_i | i \geq 0\}$ is the stationary distribution and P_{ij}^* are the transition probabilities of the reversed chain. (To see this, add Eq. (3.97) over all j to obtain

$$\sum_{j=0}^{\infty} p_j P_{ji} = p_i \sum_{j=0}^{\infty} P_{ij}^* = p_i \tag{3.98}$$

and conclude that $\{p_i | i \geq 0\}$ is the stationary distribution.) This property, which holds regardless of whether the chain is time reversible, is useful if we can guess at the nature of the reversed chain and verify Eq. (3.97), thereby obtaining both the p_j and P_{ij}^*; see section 3.8.

3. A chain is time reversible if and only if the detailed balance equations hold:

$$p_i P_{ij} = p_j P_{ji}, \quad i, j \geq 0$$

This follows from Eq. (3.96), and the definition of time reversibility. Otherwise explained, a chain is time reversible if, for all i and j, the proportion of transitions from i to j out of all transitions equals the proportion of transitions from j to i. In particular, the chains corresponding to the queueing systems $M/M/1$, $M/M/m$, $M/M/\infty$, and $M/M/m/m$ discussed in sections 3.3 and 3.4 are time reversible (in the limit as $\delta \to 0$). More generally chains corresponding to birth-death processes ($P_{ij} = 0$ if $|i - j| > 1$) are time reversible.

The idea of time reversibility extends in a straightforward manner to continuous-time Markov chains. The corresponding analysis can be carried out either directly, or by discretizing time in intervals of length δ, considering the corresponding discrete-time chain, and passing back to the continuous chain by taking the limit as $\delta \to 0$. All results regarding the reversed chain carry over almost verbatim from their discrete-time counterparts by replacing transition probabilities with transition rates. In particular if the continuous-time chain has transition rates q_{ij}, is irreducible, and has a stationary distribution $\{p_j | j \geq 0\}$, then:

1. The reversed chain is a continuous-time Markov chain with the same stationary distribution as the forward chain and with transition rates

$$q_{ij}^* = \frac{p_j q_{ji}}{p_i}, \quad i, j \geq 0 \tag{3.99}$$

2. If a probability distribution $\{p_j | j \geq 0\}$ and nonnegative numbers q_{ij}^* (for $i, j = 0, 1, \ldots$) can be found such that

$$p_i q_{ij}^* = p_j q_{ji}, \quad i, j \geq 0 \tag{3.100}$$

and for all $i \geq 0$

$$\sum_{j=0}^{\infty} q_{ij} = \sum_{j=0}^{\infty} q_{ij}^* \tag{3.101}$$

then $\{p_j | j \geq 0\}$ is the stationary distribution of both the forward and the reversed chain, and q_{ij}^* are the transition rates of the reversed chain.

3. The forward chain is time reversible if and only if its stationary distribution and transition rates satisfy the detailed balanced equations

$$p_i q_{ij} = p_j q_{ji}, \quad i, j \geq 0$$

Consider now the $M/M/1$, $M/M/m$, and $M/M/\infty$ queueing systems. We assume that the initial state is chosen according to the stationary distribution so that the queueing systems are in steady state at all times. The reversed process can be represented by another queueing system where departures correspond to arrivals of the original system and arrivals correspond to departures of the original system (see Fig. 3.21). Because time reversibity holds for all these systems as discussed above, the forward and reversed systems are statistically indistinguishable in steady state. In particular by using the fact that the departure process of the forward system corresponds to the arrival process of the reversed system, we obtain the following result:

Burke's Theorem.   Consider an $M/M/1$, $M/M/m$, or $M/M/\infty$ system with arrival rate λ. Suppose the system starts in steady state. Then the following hold true:

(a)   The departure process is Poisson with rate λ.

(b)   At each time t, the number of customers in the system is independent of the sequence of departure times prior to t.

(c)   If customers are served in the order they arrive, then, given that a customer departs at time t, the arrival time of that customer is independent of the departure process prior to t.

Proof. (a)   This follows from the fact that the forward and reversed systems are statistically indistinguishable in steady state, and the departure process in the forward system is the arrival process in the reversed system. (b)   As shown in Fig. 3.22, for a fixed time t, the departures prior to t in the forward process are also the arrivals after t in the reversed process. The arrival process in the reversed system is independent Poisson, so the future arrival process does not depend on the current number in the system, which in forward system terms means that the past departure process does not depend on the current number in the system. (c) Consider a customer arriving at time t_1 and departing at time t_2 (see Fig. 3.23). In reversed system terms, the arrival process is independent Poisson, so the arrival process to the left of t_2 is independent of the times spent in the system of customers that arrived at or to the right of t_2. In particular $t_2 - t_1$ is independent of the (reversed system) arrival process to the left of t_2. In forward system terms, this means that $t_2 - t_1$ is independent of the departure process to the left of t_2. **QED**

Note that both parts (b) and (c) of Burke's Theorem are quite counterintuitive. One would expect that a recent stream of closely spaced departures suggests a busy system with an atypically large number of customers in queue. Yet Burke's Theorem shows that this is not so. Note carefully, however, that Burke's Theorem says nothing about the state of the system *before* a stream of closely spaced departures. Such a state would tend to have abnormally many customers in queue in

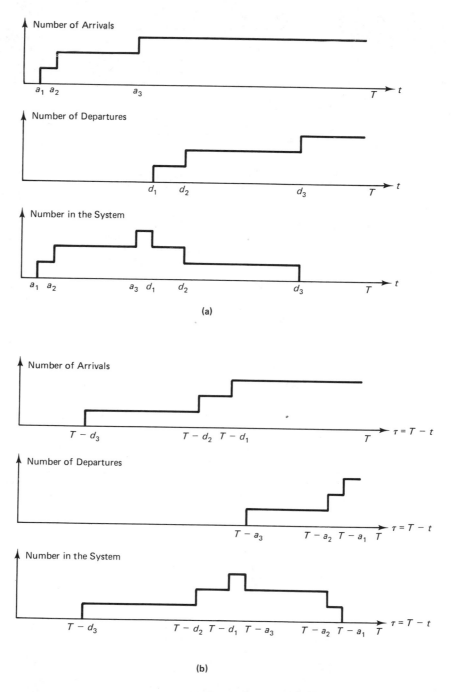

Figure 3.21   (a) Forward system number of arrivals, number of departures, and occupancy during $[0, T]$. (b) Reversed system number of arrivals, number of departures, and occupancy during $[0, T]$.

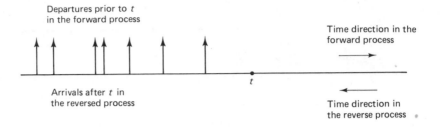

Departures prior to t
in the forward process

Time direction in the
forward process

Arrivals after t in
the reversed process

Time direction in
the reverse process

Figure 3.22   Customer departures *prior* to time t in the forward system, become customer arrivals *after* time t in the reversed system.

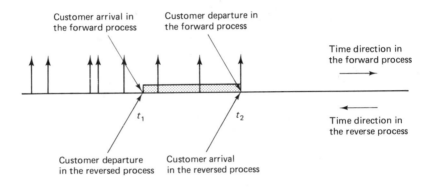

Customer arrival in
the forward process

Customer departure in
the forward process

Time direction in
the forward process

Time direction in
the reverse process

Customer departure
in the reversed process

Customer arrival
in the reversed process

Figure 3.23   Proof of part (c) of Burke's Theorem. In reversed system terms, customer arrivals after t_2 do not affect the time spent in the system of the customer that arrived at time t_2. In forward system terms, the time spent in the system by the customer $(t_2 - t_1)$ is independent of the departure process prior to the customer's departure.

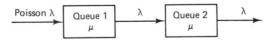

Figure 3.24   Two queues in tandem. The service times at the two queues are exponentially distributed and mutually independent. Using Burke's Theorem, we can show that the number of customers in queues 1 and 2 are independent at a given time and

$$P\{n \text{ at queue 1, } m \text{ at queue 2}\} = \rho_1^n (1 - \rho_1) \rho_2^m (1 - \rho_2),$$

i.e., the two queues behave as if they are independent $M/M/1$ queues in isolation.

accordance with intuition.

As an application of the theorem we analyze the simple queueing network involving Poisson arrivals and two queues in tandem with exponential service times (see Fig. 3.24). There is a major difference between this system and the one discussed in the previous section in that here we assume that the service times of a customer at the first and second queue are mutually independent as well as independent of the arrival process. This is what we called the Kleinrock independence approximation in the previous section. As a result of this assumption we will see that the occupancy distribution in the two queues is the same as if they were independent $M/M/1$ queues in isolation. This fact will also be shown in a more general context in the next section.

Let the rate of the Poisson arrival process be λ, and let the mean service times at queues 1 and 2 be $1/\mu_1$ and $1/\mu_2$ respectively. Let $\rho_1 = \lambda/\mu_1$ and $\rho_2 = \lambda/\mu_2$ be the corresponding utilization factors, and assume that $\rho_1 < 1$ and $\rho_2 < 1$. We will show that under steady-state conditions the following hold true:

(a)   The number of customers presently at queue 1 and at queue 2 are mutually independent, and independent of the sequence of past departure times from queue 2. Furthermore,

$$P\{n \text{ at queue } 1, m \text{ at queue } 2\} = \rho_1^n(1 - \rho_1)\rho_2^m(1 - \rho_2) \tag{3.102}$$

(b)   Assuming that customers are served at each queue in the order they arrive, the times (including service) spent by a customer in queue 1 and in queue 2 are mutually independent, and independent of the departure process from queue 2 prior to the customer's departure from the system.

To prove (a) above we first note that queue 1 is an $M/M/1$ queue so, by part (a) of Burke's Theorem, the departure process from queue 1 is Poisson and independent of the service times at queue 2. Therefore, queue 2, viewed in isolation, is an $M/M/1$ queue. Thus, from the results of section 3.1,

$$\begin{aligned} P\{n \text{ at queue } 1\} &= \rho_1^n(1 - \rho_1), \\ P\{m \text{ at queue } 2\} &= \rho_2^m(1 - \rho_2) \end{aligned} \tag{3.103}$$

From part (b) of Burke's theorem it follows that the number of customers presently in queue 1 is independent of the sequence of earlier arrivals at queue 2 and therefore also of the number of customers presently in queue 2. This implies that

$$P\{n \text{ at queue } 1, m \text{ at queue } 2\} = P\{n \text{ at queue } 1\} \cdot P\{m \text{ at queue } 2\}$$

and using Eq. (3.103) we obtain the desired product form (3.102).

To prove (b) above note that, by part (c) of Burke's Theorem, the time spent by a customer in queue 1 is independent of the sequence of arrival times at queue 2 prior to the customer's arrival at queue 2. However, these arrival times (together with the corresponding independent service times) determine the time the customer spends at queue 2 as well as the departure process from queue 2 prior to the customer's departure from the system. This proves the statement made in (b) above.

The assertion (b) above on the independence of the times spent by the same customer at queues 1 and 2 is quite counterintuitive, since one expects that a large number of customers found at queue 1 is likely to be reencountered at queue 2. As an illustration of how delicate this independence result is and how careful one should be about accepting such results without much thought, we note that the times a customer spends waiting *before entering service* at the two queues are *not* independent. To see this suppose $\mu_1 = \mu_2 = \mu$ and that λ is very small relative to μ. Then, almost all customers have zero waiting time at both queues. However, given that the wait of a customer at queue 1 is positive, the wait of the same customer at queue 2 will be positive with probability at least 1/2 (the probability that the customer will have a larger service time at queue 1 than the service time of the customer immediately ahead at queue 2). Therefore, for the same customer, the times spent waiting in queues 1 and 2 are not independent— they become independent when the corresponding service times are added.

Note that, by part (a) of Burke's Theorem, the arrival and the departure processes at both queues are Poisson. This fact together with facts (a) and (b) above can be similarly shown for a much broader class of queueing networks with Poisson arrivals and independent, exponentially distributed service times. We call such networks *acyclic* and define them as follows. We say that queue j is a *downstream neighbor* of queue i if there is a positive probability that a departing customer from queue i will next enter queue j. We say that queue j *lies downstream* of queue i if there is a sequence of queues starting from i and ending at j such that each queue after i in the sequence is a downstream neighbor of its predecessor. A queueing network is called acyclic if it is impossible to find two queues i and j such that j lies downstream of i, and i lies downstream of j. Having an acyclic network is essential for the Poisson character of the arrival and departure processes at each queue to be maintained (see the next section). However, the product form (3.102) of the occupancy distribution generalizes in a natural way to networks that are not acyclic as we show in the next section.

3.8 NETWORKS OF QUEUES—JACKSON'S THEOREM

As discussed in section 3.6, the main difficulty with analysis of networks of transmission lines is that the packet interarrival times after traversing the first queue are correlated with their lengths. It turns out that if somehow this correlation were eliminated (which is the premise of the Kleinrock independence approximation) and randomization is used to divide traffic among different routes, then the average number of packets in the system can be derived as if each queue in the network was $M/M/1$. This is an important result known as Jackson's Theorem. In this section we will derive a simple version of this theorem.

Consider a network of K single server queues in which customers arrive from outside the network at each queue i in accordance with independent Poisson processes at rate r_i. Once a customer is served at queue i, it proceeds to join each queue j with probability P_{ij} or to exit the network with probability $1 - \sum_{j=1}^{K} P_{ij}$. The total customer arrival rate at queue j, denoted λ_j, satisfies

$$\lambda_j = r_j + \sum_{i=1}^{K} \lambda_i P_{ij}, \quad j = 1, \ldots, K \tag{3.104}$$

These equations represent a linear system in which the total rates λ_j, $j = 1, \ldots, K$, constitute a set of K unknowns. We assume that they can be solved uniquely to yield λ_j, $j = 1, \ldots, K$ in terms of r_j, P_{ij}, i, $j = 1, \ldots, K$. It can be shown that this is guaranteed under very general assumptions—for instance, if all the departure probabilities $\left(1 - \sum_{j=1}^{K} P_{ij}\right)$ are positive, $i = 1, \ldots, K$, or, more generally, if for every queue i_1, there is a queue i with $\left(1 - \sum_{j=1}^{K} P_{ij}\right) > 0$ and a sequence $i_1, i_2, \ldots, i_k, i$ such that $P_{i_1 i_2} > 0, \ldots, P_{i_k i} > 0$.

The service times of customers at the ith queue are assumed exponentially distributed with mean $1/\mu_i$, and are assumed mutually independent and independent of the arrival process at the queue. The utilization factor of each queue is denoted

$$\rho_i = \frac{\lambda_i}{\mu_i}, \quad i = 1, \ldots, K, \tag{3.105}$$

and we assume $\rho_i < 1$ for all i.

In order to model a packet network such as the one considered in section 3.6 within the framework described above, it is necessary to accept several simplifying conditions in addition to assuming Poisson arrivals and exponentially distributed packet lengths. The first is the independence of packet lengths and interarrival times discussed earlier. The second is relevant to datagram networks, and has to do with the assumption that bifurcation of traffic at a network node can be modeled reasonably well by a randomization process whereby each departing packet from queue i joins queue j with probability P_{ij}—this need not be true, as discussed in section 3.6. Still a packet network differs from the model of this section because it involves several traffic streams which may have different routing probabilities at each node, and which maintain their identity as they travel along different routes. This difficulty can be partially addressed by using an extension of Jackson's Theorem that applies to a network with multiple classes of customers. Within this more general framework, we can model traffic streams corresponding to different origin-destination pairs as different classes of customers. If all traffic streams have the same average packet length, it turns out that Jackson's Theorem as stated below is valid assuming the simplifying conditions mentioned earlier.

Turning now to analysis, we view the system as a continuous-time Markov chain with states $n_1, n_2, \ldots, n_K$ where n_i denotes the number of customers at queue i. Let $P(n_1, \ldots, n_K)$ denote the stationary distribution of the chain. We have:

Jackson's Theorem.   Assuming $\rho_i < 1$, $i = 1, \ldots, K$, we have for all $n_1, \ldots, n_K \geq 0$

$$P(n_1, \ldots, n_K) = P_1(n_1)P_2(n_2) \cdots P_K(n_K) \tag{3.106}$$

where

$$P_i(n) = \rho_i^n (1 - \rho_i), \quad n \geq 0 \tag{3.107}$$

Proof. We use a technique outlined in the previous section whereby we guess at the transition rates of the reversed process and verify that, together with the stationary probabilities given by Eqs. (3.106) and (3.107), they satisfy the conditions for such rates given by Eqs. (3.100) and (3.101) of the previous section. (The Markov chain is not time reversible here. Nonetheless, the use of the reversed process is both analytically convenient and conceptually useful.)

More specifically denote state vectors as

$$n = (n_1, n_2, \ldots, n_K)$$

and denote (cf. Eq. (3.106))

$$P(n) = P_1(n_1)P_2(n_2) \cdots P_K(n_K) \tag{3.108}$$

For any two state vectors n and n', let $q_{nn'}$ be the corresponding transition rate. Jackson's Theorem will be proved if we can find rates $q_{nn'}^*$ such that for all n, n'

$$P(n)q_{nn'} = P(n')q_{n'n}^* \tag{3.109}$$

and

$$\sum_m q_{nm} = \sum_m q_{nm}^* \tag{3.110}$$

For state vectors n and n' of the form

$$n = (n_1, \ldots, n_i, \ldots, n_K)$$
$$n' = (n_1, \ldots, n_i + 1, \ldots, n_K)$$

we have

$$q_{nn'} = r_i \tag{3.111}$$

$$q_{n'n} = \mu_i \left(1 - \sum_j P_{ij}\right) \tag{3.112}$$

If we define

$$q^*_{nn'} = \lambda_i \left(1 - \sum_j P_{ij}\right) \tag{3.113}$$

$$q^*_{n'n} = \frac{\mu_i r_i}{\lambda_i}, \tag{3.114}$$

we see that Eq. (3.109) is satisfied.

Next consider state vectors n and n' of the form

$$n = (n_1, \ldots, n_i, \ldots, n_j, \ldots, n_K)$$
$$n' = (n_1, \ldots, n_i + 1, \ldots, n_j - 1, \ldots, n_K)$$

We have

$$q_{nn'} = \mu_j P_{ji} \tag{3.115}$$

If we define

$$q^*_{n'n} = \frac{\mu_i \lambda_j P_{ji}}{\lambda_i} \tag{3.116}$$

we see again that Eq. (3.109) is satisfied.

Since for all other types of pairs of state vectors n, n', we have

$$q_{nn'} = 0 \tag{3.117}$$

we can define

$$q^*_{n'n} = 0 \tag{3.118}$$

and be assured that Eq. (3.109) holds for all n and n'. Finally, a straightforward calculation using Eqs. (3.111) through (3.118) and Eq. (3.104) verifies that Eq. (3.110) holds. **QED**

Note that the transition rates $q^*_{nn'}$ defined by Eqs. (3.113), (3.114), (3.116), and (3.118), are those of the reversed process. It can be seen that the reversed process corresponds to a network of queues where traffic arrives at queue i from outside the network according to a Poisson process with rate $\lambda_i \left(1 - \sum_j P_{ij}\right)$ (cf. Eq. (3.113)). The routing probability from queue i to queue j in the reversed process is $\lambda_j P_{ji} / (r_i + \sum_k \lambda_k P_{ki})$ (cf. Eq. (3.114) and (3.116)).

There are several extensions of Jackson's theorem. For example, the product form (3.106) holds if each queue i has multiple servers, say m_i, rather than a single server. In that case, the formula corresponding to (3.107) is identical to the one of the $M/M/m_i$ system. Other extensions involve closed networks where there is a fixed number of customers circulating inside the network with no external arrivals or departures allowed (see Prob. 3.28).

We now turn to interpretation of Jackson's Theorem. First, from Eq. (3.106) we see that the numbers of customers at distinct queues at a given time are *independent*. The equation for the distribution of customers at each queue i is identical

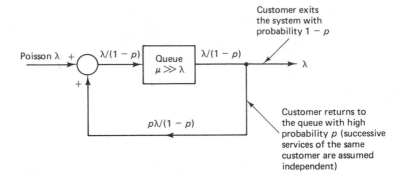

Figure 3.25   Example of a queue within a network where the external
arrival process is Poisson but the total arrival process at the queue is not
Poisson. An external arrival is typically processed fast (since μ is much larger
than λ), and with high probability returns to the queue through the feedback
loop. As a result, the total queue arrival process typically consists of bursts of
arrivals with each burst triggered by the arrival of a single customer from the
outside.

as for an $M/M/1$ queue (compare Eq. (3.107) and the corresponding equations in
section 3.3). This is a remarkable result particularly since one can show by example
that the arrival process at each queue need *not* be a Poisson process. In fact, if there
is a possibility that a customer may visit a queue more than once (a situation called
feedback), the arrival process will not be Poisson. As an example (see Fig. 3.25),
suppose that there is a single queue with a service rate which is very large relative
to the arrival rate from the outside. Suppose also that with probability p near
unity, a customer upon completion of service is fed back into the queue. Hence,
when an arrival occurs at the queue, there is a large probability of another arrival
at the queue in a short time (namely, the feedback arrival), whereas at an arbitrary
time point, there will be only a very slight chance of an arrival occurring shortly
since λ is small. In other words, queue arrivals tend to occur in bursts triggered by
the arrival of a single customer from the outside. Hence, the queue arrival process
does not have independent interarrival times and cannot be Poisson.

Unfortunately, our proof of Jackson's theorem is based on algebraic manipula-
tion, and gives little insight as to why this remarkable result holds. For this reason
we provide a heuristic explanation for the case of the feedback network of Fig. 3.25.
This explanation can be generalized and made rigorous albeit at the expense of a
great deal of technical complications (see [Wal83]).

Suppose that we introduce a delay Δ in the feedback loop of the single-queue

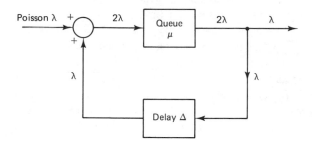

Figure 3.26   Heuristic explanation of Jackson's Theorem. Consider the introduction of an arbitrarily small positive delay Δ in the feedback loop of the network of Figure 3.25. An occupancy distribution of the queue that equals the $M/M/1$ equilibrium, and a content of the delay line that is an independent Δ segment of a Poisson process form an equilibrium distribution of the overall system. Therefore, the $M/M/1$ equilibrium distribution is an equilibrium for the queue as suggested by Jackson's Theorem even though the total arrival process to the queue is not Poisson.

network discussed above (see Fig. 3.26, where for convenience, we have chosen $p = 1/2$). Let us denote by $n(t)$ the number in the queue at time t, and by $f_\Delta(t)$ the content of the delay line at time t. The interpretation here is that $f_\Delta(t)$ is a function of time that specifies the customer output of the delay line in the subsequent Δ interval $(t, t + \Delta]$. Suppose that the initial distribution $n(0)$ of the queue state at time 0, is equal to the steady state distribution of an $M/M/1$ queue, *i.e.*,

$$P\{n(0) = n\} = \rho^n(1 - \rho) \tag{3.119}$$

where $\rho = 2\lambda/\mu$ is the utilization factor. Suppose also that $f_\Delta(0)$ is a portion of a Poisson arrival process with rate λ. The customers in $f_\Delta(0)$ have service times that are independent, exponentially distributed with parameter μ. We assume that $n(0)$ and $f_\Delta(0)$ are independent. Then, the input to the queue over the interval $[0, \Delta)$ will be the sum of two independent Poisson streams which are independent of the number in queue at time 0. It follows that the queue will behave in the interval $[0, \Delta)$ like an $M/M/1$ queue in equilibrium. Therefore, $n(\Delta)$ will be distributed according to the $M/M/1$ steady-state distribution of Eq. (3.119), and by part (b) of Burke's theorem, $n(\Delta)$ will be independent of the departure process from the queue in the interval $[0, \Delta)$, or, equivalently, of $f_\Delta(\Delta)$—the delay line content at time Δ. Furthermore, by part (a) of Burke's Theorem, $f_\Delta(\Delta)$ will be Poisson. Thus, to summarize, we started out with independent initial conditions $n(0)$ and $f_\Delta(0)$ which had the equilibrium distribution of an $M/M/1$ queue and the statistics of a Poisson process, respectively, and Δ seconds later we obtained corresponding quantities $n(\Delta)$ and $f_\Delta(\Delta)$ with the same properties. Using the same reasoning, we can show that for all t, $n(t)$ and $f_\Delta(t)$ have the same properties. It follows that the $M/M/1$ steady-state distribution of Eq. (3.119) is an equilibrium distribution for the queueing system for an arbitrary positive value of the feedback delay Δ, and this strongly suggests the validity of Jackson's Theorem. Note that this argument does not suggest that the feedback process and, therefore, also the total arrival process to the queue are Poisson. Indeed, it can be seen that successive Δ portions of the feedback arrival stream are correlated since, with probability 0.5, a departing customer from the queue appears as an arrival Δ seconds later. Therefore, over the interval $[0, \infty)$, the feedback process is not Poisson. This is consistent with our earlier observations regarding the example of Fig. 3.25.

3.9 SUMMARY

Queueing models provide qualitative insights on the performance of data networks, and quantitative predictions of average packet delay. An example of the former is the comparison of time-division and statistical multiplexing, while an example of the latter is the delay analysis of reservation systems.

To obtain tractable queueing models for data networks, it is frequently necessary to make simplifying assumptions. A prime example is the Kleinrock independence approximation discussed in section 3.6. Delay predictions based on this approximation are adequate for many uses. A more accurate alternative is simulation which, however, can be slow, expensive, and lacking in insight.

Little's Theorem is a simple but extremely useful result since it holds under very general conditions. To proceed beyond this theorem we assumed Poisson arrivals and independent interarrival and service times. This led to the $M/G/1$ system, and its extensions in reservation and priority queueing systems. We analyzed a surprisingly large number of important delay models using simple graphical arguments. An alternative analysis was based on the use of Markov chain models and led to the derivation of the occupancy probability distribution of the $M/M/1$, $M/M/m$, and related systems.

Reversibility is an important notion that helps to prove and understand Jackson's Theorem, and provides a taste of advanced queueing topics.

3.10 NOTES, SOURCES, AND SUGGESTED READING

Section 3.2. Little's Theorem was formalized in [Lit61]. Rigorous proofs under various assumptions are given in [Sti72] and [Sti74]. Several applications in finding performance bounds of computer systems are described in [StA85].

Section 3.3. For a general background on the Poisson process, Markov chains, and related topics, see [Ros80], [Ros83], and [KaT75]. Standard texts on queueing theory include [Coo81], [GrH85], [HeS82], and [Kle75]. A reference for the fact that Poisson arrivals see a typical occupancy distribution (subsection 3.3.2) is [Wol82a].

Section 3.4. Queueing systems that admit analysis via Markov chain theory include those where the service times have an Erlang distribution; see [Kle76], Chap. 4. For extensions to more general models and computational methods, see [Kei79], [Neu81], [Haj82], and [Twe82].

Section 3.5. The P-K formula is often derived by using z-transforms; see [Kle75]. This derivation is not very insightful, but gives the probability distribution of the system occupancy (not just the mean that we obtained via our much simpler analysis). For more on delay analysis of ARQ systems see [AnP86] and [ToW79].

The results on polling and reservation systems are of recent origin; see [Coo70], [Eis79], [FeA85], [FuC85], [IEE86], and [Kue79]. The original references that are closest to our analysis are [Has72] for unlimited service systems, [NoT78] for limited service systems, and [Hum78] for nonsymmetric polling systems. Reference [Tak86] is a monograph devoted to polling. There are two main reservation and polling systems considered in the literature: the symmetric case, where all users have identical arrival and reservation interval statistics, and the nonsymmetric case, where these statistics are user dependent. The former case admits simple expressions for the mean waiting times while the latter does not. We have considered the partially symmetric case, where all users have identical arrival statistics but different reservation interval statistics. The fact that simple expressions hold for this case has not been known earlier and, in this respect, our formulas are original. Our treatment in terms of simple graphical arguments is also original. The result of Prob. 3.25 on limited service systems with shared reservation and data intervals is new.

An extensive treatment of priority queueing systems is [Jai68]. A simpler, less comprehensive exposition is given in [Kle75].

Section 3.6. Delay analysis for data networks in terms of $M/M/1$ approximations was introduced in [Kle64]. References [Wol82b] and [PiW82] study via analysis and simulation the behavior of two queues in tandem when the service times of a customer at the two queues are dependent. The special issues [IEE86] provides a view of recent work on the subject.

Section 3.7. The notion of reversibility in queueing networks is explored in depth in [Kel79].

Section 3.8. There is an extensive literature on product form solutions of queueing networks following Jackson's original paper [Jac57]. The survey [DiK85] lists 314 references. Two books on the subject are [Kel79] and [BrB80]. The heuristic explanation of Jackson's theorem is due to [Wal83].

PROBLEMS

3.1 Customers arrive at a fast-food restaurant at a rate of five per minute, and wait to receive their order for an average of five minutes. Customers eat in the restaurant with probability 0.5, and carry out their order without eating with probability 0.5. A meal requires an average of 20 minutes. What is the average number of customers in the restaurant?

3.2 An absent-minded professor schedules two student appointments for the same time. The appointment durations are independent and exponentially distributed with mean thirty minutes. The first student arrives on time, but the second student arrives five minutes late. What is the expected time between the arrival of the first student and the departure of the second student?

3.3 A person enters a bank and finds all of the four clerks busy serving customers. There are no other customers in the bank, so the person will start service as soon as one of the customers in service leaves. Customers have independent, identical, exponential distribution of service time.

    (a) What is the probability that the person will be the last to leave the bank assuming no other customers arrive?

    (b) If the average service time is one minute, what is the average time the person will spend in the bank?

    (c) Will the answer in (a) change if there are some additional customers waiting in a common queue, and customers begin service in the order of their arrival?

3.4 Consider a packet stream whereby packets arrive according to a Poisson process with rate 10 packets/sec. If the interarrival time between any two successive packets is less than the transmission time of the first, the two packets are said to collide. (This notion will be made more meaningful in Chapter 4 when we talk about multiaccess schemes.) Find the probability that a packet collides with either its predecessor or its successor assuming:

    (a) All packets have a transmission time of 20 msec.

    (b) Packets have independent, exponentially distributed transmission times with mean 20 msec.

3.5 A communication line capable of transmitting at a rate of 50 Kbits/sec will be used to accommodate 10 sessions each generating Poisson traffic at a rate 150 packets/min. Packet lengths are exponentially distributed with mean 1000 bits.

(a) For each session, find the average number of packets in queue, the average number in the system, and the average delay per packet when the line is allocated to the sessions by using:

(1) 10 equal capacity time-division multiplexed channels

(2) statistical multiplexing.

(b) Repeat (a) for the case where 5 of the sessions transmit at a rate of 250 packets/min while the other 5 at a rate 50 packets/min.

3.6 Repeat part (a) of Prob. 3.5 for the case where packet lengths are not exponentially distributed, but 10% of the packets are 100 bits long and the rest are 1500 bits long. Repeat the problem for the case where the short packets are given nonpreemptive priority over the long packets.

3.7 A communication line is divided in two identical channels each of which will serve a packet traffic stream where all packets have equal transmission time T, and equal interarrival time $R > T$. Consider, alternatively, statistical multiplexing of the two traffic streams by combining the two channels into a single channel with transmission time $T/2$ for each packet. Show that the average system time of a packet will be decreased from T to something between $T/2$ and $3T/4$, while the variance of waiting time in queue will be increased from 0 to as much as $T^2/16$.

3.8 Persons arrive at a taxi stand with room for five taxis according to a Poisson process with rate one per minute. A person boards a taxi upon arrival if one is available and otherwise waits in a line. Taxis arrive at the stand according to a Poisson process with rate two per minute. An arriving taxi that finds the stand full departs immediately; otherwise, it picks up a customer if at least one is waiting, or else joins the queue of waiting taxis. What is the steady-state probability distribution of the taxi queue size?

3.9 A communication node A receives Poisson packet traffic from two other nodes 1 and 2 at rates λ_1 and λ_2, respectively, and transmits it on a link with capacity C bits/sec. The two input streams are assumed independent and their packet lengths are identically and exponentially distributed with mean L bits. A packet from node 1 is always accepted by A. A packet from node 2 is accepted only if the number of packets in A (in queue or under transmission) is less than a given number $K > 0$; otherwise, it is assumed lost.

(a) What is the range of values of λ_1 and λ_2 for which the expected number of packets in A will stay bounded as time increases?

(b) For λ_1 and λ_2 in the range of part (a) find the steady-state probability of having n packets in A ($0 \leq n < \infty$). Find the average time needed by a packet from source 1 to clear A once it enters A, and the average number of packets in A from source 1. Repeat for packets from source 2.

3.10 (a) Derive Eqs. (3.11) to (3.14).

   (b) Show that if the arrivals in two disjoint time intervals are independent and Poisson distributed with parameters $\lambda\tau_1$, $\lambda\tau_2$, then the number of arrivals in the union of the intervals is Poisson distributed with parameter $\lambda(\tau_1 + \tau_2)$.

   (c) Show that if k independent Poisson processes $A_1, \ldots, A_k$ are combined into a single process $A = A_1 + A_2 + \cdots + A_k$, then A is Poisson with rate λ equal to the sum of the rates $\lambda_1, \ldots \lambda_k$ of $A_1, \ldots, A_k$. Show also that the probability that the first arrival of the combined process comes from A_1 is λ_1/λ independently of the time of arrival.

   (d) Suppose we know that in an interval $[t_1, t_2]$ only one arrival of a Poisson process has occurred. Show that, conditional on this knowledge, the time of this arrival is uniformly distributed in $[t_1, t_2]$.

3.11 Packets arrive at a transmission facility according to a Poisson process with rate λ. Each packet is independently routed with probability p to one of two transmission lines and with probability $(1 - p)$ to the other. Show that the arrival processes at the two transmission lines are Poisson with rates λp and $\lambda(1 - p)$ respectively. Furthermore the two processes are independent.

3.12 Consider a system that is identical to $M/M/1$ except that when the system empties out, service does not begin again until k customers are present in the system (k is given). Once service begins it proceeds normally until the system becomes empty again. Find the steady state probabilities of the number in the system, the average number in the system, and the average delay per customer.

3.13 A telephone company establishes a direct connection between two cities expecting Poisson traffic with rate 30 calls/min. The durations of calls are independent and exponentially distributed with mean three minutes. Interarrival times are independent of call durations. How many circuits should the company provide to ensure that an attempted call is blocked (because all circuits are busy) with probability less than 0.01? It is assumed that blocked calls are lost, *i.e.*, a blocked call is not attempted again.

3.14 Consider an $M/M/\infty$ queue with servers numbered $1, 2, \ldots$ There is an additional restriction that upon arrival a customer will choose the lowest numbered server that is idle at the time. Find the fraction of time that each server is busy. Will the answer change if the number of servers is finite? *Hint:* Argue that in steady-state the probability that all of the first m servers are busy is given by the Erlang B formula of the $M/M/m/m$ system. Find the total arrival rate to servers $(m + 1)$ and higher, and from this the arrival rate to each server.

3.15 In the $M/G/1$ system, show that

$$P\{\text{the system is empty}\} = 1 - \lambda \overline{X}$$

Average length of time between busy periods $= 1/\lambda$

$$\text{Average length of busy period} \;=\; \frac{\overline{X}}{1 - \lambda \overline{X}}$$

$$\text{Average number of customers served in a busy period} \;=\; \frac{1}{1 - \lambda \overline{X}}$$

Consider the following argument: When a customer arrives the probability that another customer is being served is $\lambda \overline{X}$. Since the served customer has mean service time $\overline{X}$, the average time to complete the service is $\overline{X}/2$. Therefore the mean residual service time is $\lambda \overline{X^2}/2$. What is wrong with this argument?

3.16 *M/G/1 System with Arbitrary Order of Service.* Consider the $M/G/1$ system with the difference that customers are not served in the order they arrive. Instead, upon completion of a customer's service, one of the waiting customers in queue is chosen according to some rule, and is served next. Show that the P-K formula for the average waiting time in queue W remains valid provided the relative order of arrival of the customer chosen is independent of the service times of the customers waiting in queue. *Hint*: Argue that the independence hypothesis above implies that, at any time t, the number $N_Q(t)$ of customers waiting in queue is independent of the service times of these customers. Show that this in turn implies that $U = R + \rho W$ where R is the mean residual time, and U is the average steady-state unfinished work in the system (total remaining service time of the customers in the system). Argue that U and R are independent of the order of customer service.

3.17 *Priority Systems with Multiple Servers.* Consider the systems of subsection 3.5.3 where all priority classes have exponentially distributed service times with common mean $1/\mu$. Assume that there are m servers.

(a)   Consider the nonpreemptive system. Show that Eq. (3.79) yields the average queueing times with the mean residual time R given by

$$R = \frac{P_Q}{m\mu}$$

where P_Q is the steady-state probability of queueing given by the Erlang C formula of Eq. (3.36). (Here $\rho_i = \lambda_i/(m\mu)$ and $\rho = \sum_{i=1}^{n} \rho_i$.)

(b)   Consider the preemptive resume system. Write a formula for $W_{(k)}$— the average time in queue averaged over the first k priority classes. Use Little's Theorem to show that the average time in queue of a kth priority class customer can be obtained recursively from

$$W_1 = W_{(1)}$$

$$W_k = \frac{1}{\lambda_k} \left[W_{(k)} \sum_{i=1}^{k} \lambda_i - W_{(k-1)} \sum_{i=1}^{k-1} \lambda_i \right], \quad k = 2, 3, \ldots, n$$

3.18 Consider the nonpreemptive priority queueing system of subsection 3.5.3 for the case where the available capacity is sufficient to handle the highest priority traffic, but cannot handle the traffic of all priorities, *i.e.*,

$$\rho_1 < 1 < \rho_1 + \rho_2 + \cdots + \rho_n$$

Find the average delay per customer of each priority class. *Hint*: Determine the departure rate of the highest priority class that will experience infinite average delay, and the mean residual service time.

3.19 Consider an n-class, nonpreemptive priority system:

(a) Show that the sum $\sum_{k=1}^{n} \rho_k W_k$ is independent of the priority order of classes, and in fact

$$\sum_{k=1}^{n} \rho_k W_k = \frac{R\rho}{1 - \rho}$$

where $\rho = \rho_1 + \rho_2 + \cdots + \rho_n$. (This is known as the $M/G/1$ conservation law [Kle64].) *Hint*: Use Eq. (3.79). Alternatively argue that $U = R + \sum_{k=1}^{n} \rho_k W_k$, where U is the average steady-state unfinished work in the system (total remaining service time of customers in the system), and U and R are independent of the priority order of the classes.

(b) Suppose there is a cost c_k per unit time for each class k customer that waits in queue. Show that cost is minimized when classes are ordered so that

$$\frac{\overline{X_1}}{c_1} \leq \frac{\overline{X_2}}{c_2} \leq \cdots \leq \frac{\overline{X_n}}{c_n}$$

Hint: Express the cost as $\sum_{k=1}^{n} (c_k/\overline{X_k})(\rho_k W_k)$ and use part (a). Use also the fact that interchanging the order of any two adjacent classes leaves the waiting time of all other classes unchanged.

3.20 *M/M/1 Shared Service System.* Consider a system which is the same as $M/M/1$ except that whenever there are n customers in the system they are all served simultaneously at an equal rate $1/n$ per unit time. Argue that the steady-state occupancy distribution is the same as for the $M/M/1$ system. *Note*: It can be shown that the steady-state occupancy distribution is the same as for $M/M/1$ even if the service time distribution is not exponential, *i.e.*, for an $M/G/1$ type of system ([Ros83], p. 171).

3.21 In Ex. 10 of subsection 3.4.2, verify the formula $\sigma_f = (\lambda/\mu)^{1/2} s_\gamma$. *Hint*: Write

$$E\{f^2\} = E\{(\textstyle\sum_{i=1}^n \gamma_i)^2\} = E\{E\{(\textstyle\sum_{i=1}^n \gamma_i)^2 \,|n\}\},$$

and use the fact that n is Poisson distributed.

3.22 Show that Eq. (3.59) for the average delay of time-division multiplexing on a slot basis can be obtained as a special case of the results for the limited service reservation system. Generalize the expression (3.59) for the case where slot lengths are random and independent, and the traffic streams do not have equal rates and identical slot length distributions. *Hint*: Consider the gated system with zero packet length.

3.23 Show that the expected cycle lengths in the single-user and multiuser reservation systems are $\overline{V}/(1-\rho)$ and $m\overline{V}/(1-\rho)$, respectively. *Hint*: If L_k is the length of the kth cycle show that $E\{L_{k+1}|L_k\} = \overline{V} + \rho L_k$ for the single-user case.

3.24 Consider the limited service reservation system. Show that for both the gated and the partially gated versions:

(a) The steady-state probability of arrival of a packet during a reservation interval is $1 - \rho$.

(b) The steady-state probability of a reservation interval being followed by an empty data interval is $(1 - \rho - \lambda\overline{V})/(1 - \rho)$. *Hint*: If p is the required probability, argue that the ratio of the times used for data intervals and for reservation intervals is $(1 - p)\overline{X}/\overline{V}$.

3.25 *Limited Service Reservation System with Shared Reservation and Data Intervals.* Consider the gated version of the limited service reservation system with the difference that the m users share reservation and data intervals, *i.e.*, all users make reservations in the same interval and transmit at most one packet each in the subsequent data interval. Show that

$$W = \frac{\lambda\overline{X^2}}{2(1-\rho-\lambda\overline{V}/m)} + \frac{(1-\rho)\overline{V^2}}{2(1-\rho-\lambda\overline{V}/m)\overline{V}} + \frac{(1-\rho\alpha-\lambda\overline{V}/m)\overline{V}}{1-\rho-\lambda\overline{V}/m}$$

where $\overline{V}$ and $\overline{V^2}$ are the first two moments of the reservation interval, and α satisfies

$$\frac{\overline{K} + (\hat{K} - 1)(2\overline{K} - \hat{K})}{2m\overline{K}} - \frac{1}{2m} \le \alpha \le \frac{1}{2} - \frac{1}{2m}$$

where

$$\overline{K} = \frac{\lambda \overline{V}}{1 - \rho}$$

is the average number of packets per data interval, and $\hat{K}$ is the smallest integer which is larger than $\overline{K}$. Verify that the formula for W becomes exact as $\rho \to 0$ (light load), and as $\rho \to 1 - \lambda \overline{V}/m$ (heavy load). *Hint:* Verify that

$$W = R + \lambda W + \left(1 + \frac{\lambda W}{m} - S\right)\overline{V}$$

where $S = \lim_{i \to \infty} E\{S_i\}$ and S_i is the number (0 or 1) of packets of the owner of packet i that will start transmission between the time of arrival of packet i and the end of the cycle in which packet i arrives. Try to obtain bounds for S by considering separately the cases where packet i arrives in a reservation and in a data interval.

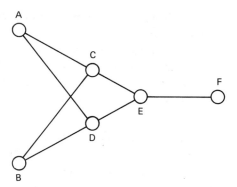

Figure 3.27

3.26 Consider the network in Fig. 3.27. There are four sessions: ACE, ADE, BCEF, and BDEF sending Poisson traffic at rates 100, 200, 500, and 600 packets/min., respectively. Packet lengths are exponentially distributed with mean 1000 bits. All transmission lines have capacity 50 kbits/sec, and there is a propagation delay of 2 msec on each line. Using the Kleinrock independence approximation, find the average number of packets in the system, the average delay per packet (regardless of session), and the average delay per packet of each session.

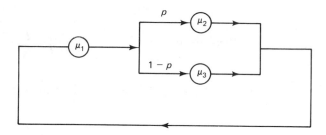

Figure 3.28

3.27 *Bounds on the Throughput of a Closed Queueing Network.* Packets enter the network of transmission lines shown in Fig. 3.28 at point A and exit at point B. A packet is first transmitted on one of the lines $L_1, \ldots, L_K$, where it requires on the average a transmission time $\overline{X}$, and is then transmitted in line L_{K+1}, where it requires on the average a transmission time $\overline{Y}$. To effect flow control, a maximum of $N \geq K$ packets are admitted into the system. Each time a packet exits the system at point B, an acknowledgement is sent back and reaches point A after a fixed time $\overline{Z}$. At that time, a new packet is allowed to enter the system. Use Little's Theorem to find upper and lower bounds for the system throughput under two circumstances:

(a)   The method of routing a packet to one of the lines $L_1, \ldots, L_K$ is unspecified.

(b)   The routing method is such that whenever one of the lines $L_1, \ldots, L_K$ is idle, there is no packet waiting at any of the other lines.

3.28 *Analysis of a Closed Queueing Network.* Certain systems are best modelled by *closed* queueing networks, where the number of customers in the system is fixed. Consider a closed queueing network with 3 customers shown in Fig. 3.29 together with the probabilities that a departing customer from a queue enters another.

(a)   How would you define the state of this system? Draw the state transition diagram and label the states and transition rates on your figure.

(b)   Show that the system is reversible and that occupancy probabilities have the product form

$$P(n_1, n_2, n_3) = \alpha \left(\frac{1}{\mu_1} \right)^{n_1} \left(\frac{p}{\mu_2} \right)^{n_2} \left(\frac{1-p}{\mu_3} \right)^{n_3}$$

where $n_1 + n_2 + n_3 = 3$, and α is a normalizing constant.

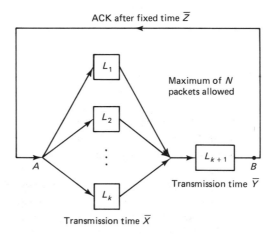

Figure 3.29

3.29 Consider two queues with independent Poisson arrivals and independent exponentially distributed service times. The arrival and service rates are denoted λ_i, μ_i, for $i = 1, 2$, respectively. The two queues share a waiting room with finite capacity B (including customers in service). Arriving customers that find the waiting room full are lost. Show that for $m + n \le B$, the steady-state probabilities are

$$P\{m \text{ in queue 1, } n \text{ in queue 2}\} = c\rho_1^m \rho_2^n$$

where $\rho_i = \lambda_i/\mu_i$, $i = 1, 2$, and c is a normalizing constant.

3.30 Consider the $M/M/1/m$ system which is the same as $M/M/1$ except that there can be no more than m customers in the system and customers arriving when the system is full are lost.

(a) Derive the steady-state occupancy probabilities.

(b) Show that the system is reversible, and characterize the departure process.

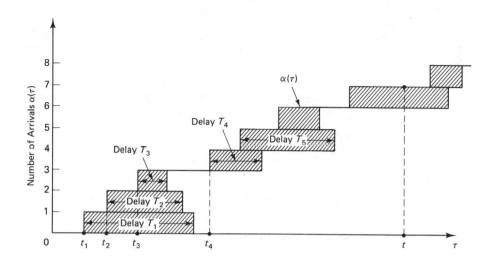

Figure 3.30

3.31 *Little's Theorem for Arbitrary Order of Service.* Use Fig. 3.30 to derive Little's Theorem for systems where the order of customer service is arbitrary, including cases where servers are shared by several customers, and customer service can be interrupted to serve customers of higher priority. In this figure t_i is the arrival time of the ith customer, and T_i is the customer's system time, *i.e.*, the time between the customer's arrival and departure from the system. *Hint*: Calculate the shaded area up to time t in two different ways.

3.32 *Little's Theorem for Arbitrary Order of Service; Analytical Proof.* Consider the analysis of Little's theorem in section 3.2 and the notation introduced there. Assume that the time average arrival and departure rates exist and are equal

$$\lambda = \lim_{k \to \infty} \alpha(t)/t = \lim_{t \to \infty} \beta(t)/t$$

and that the limit defining the time average system time

$$T = \lim_{k \to \infty} \frac{1}{k} \sum_{i=1}^{k} T_i$$

exists. Show that, regardless of the order customers are served, Little's Theorem $(N = \lambda T)$ holds with

$$N = \lim_{t \to \infty} \frac{1}{t} \int_0^t N(\tau) d\tau$$

Hint: Show that for all t, we have

$$\sum_{i=1}^{\beta(t)} T_i \le \int_0^t N(\tau)d\tau \le \sum_{i=1}^{\alpha(t)} T_i$$

3.33 *A Generalization of Little's Theorem.* Consider an arrival/departure system with arrival rate λ, where entering customers are forced to pay money to the system according to some rule.

(a) Argue that the following identity holds:

Average rate at which the system earns $=$

$\lambda \cdot$ (Average amount a customer pays)

(b) Show that Little's Theorem is a special case.

(c) Consider the $M/G/1$ system and the following cost rule: Each customer pays at a rate of y per unit time when its remaining service time is y, whether in queue or in service. Show that the formula in (a) can be written as

$$W = \lambda\left(\overline{X}W + \frac{\overline{X^2}}{2}\right)$$

which is the Pollaczek–Khinchin formula.

3.34 *M/G/1 Queue with Random Sized Batch Arrivals.* Consider the $M/G/1$ system with the difference that customers are arriving in batches according to a Poisson process with rate λ. Each batch has n customers, where n has a given distribution and is independent of customer service times. Adapt the proof of section 3.5 to show that the waiting time in queue is given by

$$W = \frac{\lambda \overline{n}\,\overline{X^2}}{2(1-\rho)} + \frac{\overline{X}(\overline{n^2} - \overline{n})}{2\overline{n}(1-\rho)}$$

Hint: Use the equation $W = R + \rho W + W_B$ where W_B is the average waiting time of a customer for other customers that arrived in the same batch.

3.35 *M/G/1 Queue with Overhead for Each Busy Period.* Consider the $M/G/1$ queue with the difference that the service of the first customer in each busy period requires an increment Δ over the ordinary service time of the customer. We assume that Δ has a given distribution and is independent of all other random variables in the model. Let $\rho = \lambda \overline{X}$ be the utilization factor. Show that

(a) $P_0 = P\{$ the system is empty$\} = (1 - \rho)/(1 + \lambda\overline{\Delta})$.

(b) Average length of busy period$= (\overline{X} + \overline{\Delta})/(1 - \rho)$

(c) The average waiting time in queue is

$$W = \frac{\lambda\overline{X^2}}{2(1 - \rho)} + \frac{\lambda[\overline{(X + \Delta)^2} - \overline{X^2}]}{2(1 + \lambda\overline{\Delta})}$$

3.36 *Single Vacation M/G/1 System.* Consider the $M/G/1$ system with the difference that each busy period is followed by a single vacation interval. Once this vacation is over, an arriving customer to an empty system starts service immediately. Assume that vacation intervals are independent, indentically distributed, and independent of the customer interarrival and service times. Derive the average waiting time in queue.

3.37 *The M/G/∞ System.* Consider a queueing system with Poisson arrivals at rate λ. There are an infinite number of servers, so that each arrival starts service at an idle server immediately on arrival. Each server has a general service time distribution and $F_X(x) = P\{X \leq x\}$ denotes the probability that a service starting at any given time τ is completed by time $\tau + x$ ($F_X(x) = 0$ for $x \leq 0$). The servers have independent and identical service time distributions.

(a) For x and δ ($0 < \delta < x$) very small, find the probability that there was an arrival in the interval $[\tau - x, \ \tau - x + \delta]$ *and* that this arrival is still being served at time τ.

(b) Show that the mean service time for any arrival is given by

$$\overline{X} = \int_0^\infty [1 - F_X(x)]\, dx$$

Hint: Use a graphical argument or integration by parts.

(c) Use (a) and (b) to verify that the number in the system is Poisson distributed with mean $\lambda\overline{X}$.

APPENDIX A: *Review of Markov Chain Theory*

The purpose of this appendix is to provide a brief summary of the results we need from discrete- and continuous-time Markov chain theory. We refer the reader to books on stochastic processes for detailed accounts.

3A.1 *Discrete-Time Markov Chains*

Consider a discrete-time stochastic process $\{X_n | n = 0, 1, 2, \ldots\}$ that takes values from the set of nonnegative integers, so the states that the process can be in are $i = 0, 1 \ldots$. The process is said to be a *Markov chain* if whenever it is in state i, there is a fixed probability P_{ij} that it will next be in state j regardless of the process history prior to arriving at i. That is, for all $n > 0, i_{n-1}, \ldots, i_0, i, j$

$$P_{ij} = P\{X_{n+1} = j | X_n = i, \ X_{n-1} = i_{n-1}, \ldots, X_0 = i_0\}$$
$$= P\{X_{n+1} = j | X_n = i\}$$

We refer to P_{ij} as the *transition probabilities*. They must satisfy

$$P_{ij} \geq 0, \ \sum_{j=0}^{\infty} P_{ij} = 1, \quad i = 0, 1, \ldots$$

The corresponding transition probability matrix is denoted

$$P = \begin{bmatrix} P_{00} & P_{01} & P_{02} & \cdots \\ P_{10} & P_{11} & P_{12} & \cdots \\ \cdot & \cdot & \cdot & \cdot & \cdot & \cdot \\ P_{i0} & P_{i1} & P_{i2} & \cdots \\ \cdot & \cdot & \cdot & \cdot & \cdot & \cdot \end{bmatrix}$$

Consider the n-step transition probabilities

$$P_{ij}^n = P\{X_{n+m} = j | X_m = i\}, \quad n \geq 0, i, j \geq 0 .$$

The *Chapman-Kolmogorov equations* provide a method for calculating P_{ij}^n. They are given by

$$P_{ij}^{n+m} = \sum_{k=0}^{\infty} P_{ik}^n P_{kj}^m, \quad n, m \geq 0, i, j \geq 0$$

From these equations, we see that P_{ij}^n are the elements of the matrix P^n (the transition probability matrix P raised to the nth power).

We say that two states i and j *communicate* if for some n and n', we have $P_{ij}^n > 0$, $P_{ji}^{n'} > 0$. If all states communicate, we say that the Markov chain is *irreducible.* We say that the Markov chain is *aperiodic* if for each state i there is no integer $d \geq 2$ such that $P_{ii}^n = 0$ except when n is a multiple of d. A probability distribution $\{p_j | j \geq 0\}$ is said to be a *stationary distribution* for the Markov chain if

$$p_j = \sum_{i=0}^{\infty} p_i P_{ij}, \quad j \geq 0. \tag{3A.1}$$

We will restrict attention to irreducible and aperiodic Markov chains, since this is the only type we will encounter. For such a chain, denote

$$p_j = \lim_{n \to \infty} P_{jj}^n, \quad j \geq 0$$

It can be shown that the limit above exists and when $p_j > 0$, then $1/p_j$ equals the *mean recurrence time of j*, i.e., the expected number of transitions between two successive visits to state j. If $p_j = 0$, the mean recurrence time is infinite. Another interpretation is that p_j represents the proportion of time the process visits j on the average. The following result will be of primary interest:

Theorem.   In an irreducible, aperiodic Markov chain, there are two possibilities:

1. $p_j = 0$ for all $j \geq 0$ in which case the chain has no stationary distribution.
2. $p_j > 0$ for all $j \geq 0$ in which case $\{p_j | j \geq 0\}$ is the unique stationary distribution of the chain.

A typical example of case 1 above is an $M/M/1$ queueing system where the arrival rate λ exceeds the service rate μ.

In case 2, there arises the issue of characterizing the stationary distribution $\{p_j | j \geq 0\}$. For queueing systems, the following technique is often useful. Multiplying the equation $P_{jj} + \sum_{\substack{i=0 \\ i \neq j}}^{\infty} P_{ji} = 1$ by p_j and using Eq. (3A.1), we have

$$p_j \sum_{\substack{i=0 \\ i \neq j}}^{\infty} P_{ji} = \sum_{\substack{i=0 \\ i \neq j}}^{\infty} p_i P_{ij} \tag{3A.2}$$

These equations are known as the *global balance equations*. They state that, at equilibrium, the probability of a transition out of j (left side of Eq. (3A.2)) equals the probability of a transition into j (right side of Eq. (3A.2)).

The global balance equations can be generalized to apply to an entire set of states. Consider a subset of states S. By adding Eq. (3A.2) over all $j \epsilon S$, we obtain

$$\sum_{j \epsilon S} p_j \sum_{i \notin S} P_{ji} = \sum_{i \notin S} p_i \sum_{j \epsilon S} P_{ij} \tag{3A.3}$$

which means that *the probability of a transition out of the set of states S equals the probability of a transition into S.*

An intuitive explanation of these equations is based on the fact that when the Markov chain is irreducible, the state (with probability one) will return to the set S infinitely many times. Therefore, for each transition out of S there must be (with probability one) a reverse transition into S at some later time. As a result, the proportion of transitions out of S (over all transitions) equals the proportion of transitions into S. This is precisely the meaning of the global balance equations (3A.3).

3A.2 Detailed Balance Equations

As an application of the global balance equations, consider a Markov chain typical of queueing systems and, more generally, birth-death systems where two successive states can only differ by unity as in Fig. 3A.1. We assume that $P_{i,i+1} > 0$ and $P_{i+1,i} > 0$ for all i. This is a necessary and sufficient condition for the chain to be irreducible. Consider the sets of states

$$S = \{0, 1, \ldots, n\}$$

Application of Eq. (3A.3) yields

$$p_n P_{n,n+1} = p_{n+1} P_{n+1,n}, \quad n = 0, 1, \ldots \tag{3A.4}$$

i.e., in steady state, the probability of a transition from n to $n+1$ equals the probability of a transition from $n+1$ to n. These equations can be very useful in computing the stationary distribution $\{p_j | j \geq 0\}$ (see sections 3.3 and 3.4).

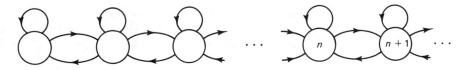

Figure 3A.1   Transition probability diagram for a birth-death process.

Equation (3A.4) is a special case of the equations

$$p_j P_{ji} = p_i P_{ij}, \quad i, j \geq 0 \tag{3A.5}$$

known as the *detailed balance equations*. These equations need not hold in any given Markov chain. However, in many important special cases, they do hold and greatly simplify the calculation of the stationary distribution. A common method of verifying the validity of the detailed balance equations for a given irreducible, aperiodic Markov chain is to hypothesize their validity and try to solve them for the steady-state probabilities p_j, $j \geq 0$. There are two possibilities; either the system (3A.5) together with $\sum_j p_j = 1$ is inconsistent or else a distribution $\{p_j | j \geq 0\}$ satisfying Eq. (3A.5) will be found. In the latter case, this distribution will clearly also satisfy the global balance equations (3A.2). These equations are equivalent to the condition

$$p_j = \sum_{i=0}^{\infty} p_i P_{ij}, \quad j = 0, 1, \ldots$$

so, by the theorem given earlier, $\{p_j | j \geq 0\}$ is the unique stationary distribution.

3A.3 Partial Balance Equations

Some Markov chains have the property that their stationary distribution $\{p_j | j \geq 0\}$ satisfies a set of equations which is intermediate between the global and the detailed balance equations. For every node j, consider a partition $S_j^1, \ldots, S_j^k$ of the complementary set of nodes $\{i | i \geq 0, i \neq j\}$ and the equations

$$p_j \sum_{i \in S_j^m} P_{ji} = \sum_{i \in S_j^m} p_i P_{ij}, \quad m = 1, 2, \ldots, k \tag{3A.6}$$

Equations of the form above are known as a set of *partial balance equations*. If a distribution $\{p_j | j \geq 0\}$ solves a set of partial balance equations, then it will also solve the global balance equations so it will be the unique stationary distribution of the chain. A technique that often proves useful is to guess the right set of partial balance equations satisfied by the stationary distribution and then proceed to solve them.

3A.4 Continuous-Time Markov Chains

A continuous-time Markov chain is a process $\{X(t) | t \geq 0\}$ taking values from the set of states $i = 0, 1, \ldots$ that has the property that each time it enters state i:

1. The time it spends in state i is exponentially distributed with parameter ν_i. We may view ν_i as the average rate (in transitions/sec) at which the process makes a transition when at state i.

2. When the process leaves state i, it will enter state j with probability P_{ij}, where $\sum_j P_{ij} = 1$.

   We will be interested in chains for which:

   1. The number of transitions in any finite length of time is finite with probability one (such chains are called *regular*).

   2. The discrete-time Markov chain with transition probabilities P_{ij} (called the *imbedded chain*) is irreducible.

Under the preceding conditions, it can be shown that the limit

$$p_j = \lim_{t \to \infty} P\{X(t) = j | X(0) = i\} \tag{3A.7}$$

exists and is independent of the initial state i. Furthermore if the imbedded chain has a stationary distribution $\{\pi_j | j \geq 0\}$, the steady-state probabilities p_j of the continuous chain are all positive and satisfy

$$p_j = \frac{\pi_j/\nu_j}{\sum_{i=0}^{\infty} \pi_i/\nu_i}, \quad j = 0, 1, \ldots \qquad (3A.8)$$

The interpretation here is that π_j represents the proportion of visits to state j, while p_j represents the proportion of time spent in state j in a typical system run. For every i and j, denote

$$q_{ij} = \nu_i P_{ij} \qquad (3A.9)$$

Since ν_i is the rate at which the process leaves i and P_{ij} is the probability that it then goes to j, it follows that q_{ij} is the rate at which the process makes a transition to j when at state i. Consequently, q_{ij} is called the *transition rate* from i to j.

Since we will often analyze continuous-time Markov chains in terms of their time-discretized versions, we describe the general method for doing this.

Consider any $\delta > 0$, and the discrete-time Markov chain $\{X_n | n \geq 0\}$, where

$$X_n = X(n\delta), \quad n = 0, 1, \ldots$$

The stationary distribution of $\{X_n\}$ is clearly $\{p_j | j \geq 0\}$, the stationary distribution of the continuous chain (cf. Eq. (3A.7)). The transition probabilities of $\{X_n | n \geq 0\}$ are

$$\overline{P_{ij}} = \delta q_{ij} + o(\delta), \quad i \neq j$$
$$\overline{P_{ii}} = 1 - \delta \sum_{j \neq i} q_{ij} + o(\delta)$$

Using these expressions in the global balance equations for the discrete chain (cf. Eq. (3A.2)) and taking the limit as $\delta \to 0$, we obtain

$$p_j \sum_{\substack{i=0 \\ i \neq j}}^{\infty} q_{ji} = \sum_{\substack{i=0 \\ i \neq j}}^{\infty} p_i q_{ij}, \quad j = 0, 1, \ldots \qquad (3A.10)$$

These are the global balance equations for the continuous chain. Similarly, the detailed balance equations take the form

$$p_j q_{ji} = p_i q_{ij}, \quad i, j = 0, 1, \ldots, \qquad (3A.11)$$

One can also write a set of partial balance equations and attempt to solve them for the distribution $\{p_j | j \geq 0\}$. If a solution is found, it provides the stationary distribution of the continuous chain.

A P P E N D I X B: *Summary of Results*

Notation

p_n: Steady-state probability of having n customers in the system

λ: Arrival rate (inverse of average interarrival time)

μ: Service rate (inverse of average service time)

N: Average number of customers in the system

N_Q: Average number of customers waiting in queue

T: Average customer time in the system

W: Average customer waiting time in queue (does not include service time)

$\overline{X}$: Average service time

$\overline{X^2}$: Second moment of service time

Little's Theorem

$$N = \lambda T$$
$$N_Q = \lambda W$$

Poisson distribution with parameter m

$$p_n = \frac{e^{-m}m^n}{n!}, \quad n = 0, 1, \ldots$$

$$\text{Mean} = \text{Variance} = m$$

Exponential distribution with parameter λ no

$$P\{\tau \le s\} = 1 - e^{-\lambda s}, \quad s \ge 0.$$
$$\text{Density: } p(\tau) = \lambda e^{-\lambda \tau}$$
$$\text{Mean} = 1/\lambda$$
$$\text{Variance} = 1/\lambda^2$$

Summary of $M/M/1$ System Results

(a) Utilization factor (proportion of time the server is busy)

$$\rho = \frac{\lambda}{\mu}$$

(b) Probability of n customers in the system

$$p_n = \rho^n(1 - \rho), \quad n = 0, 1, \ldots$$

(c) Average number of customers in the system

$$N = \frac{\rho}{1-\rho}$$

(d) Average customer time in the system

$$T = \frac{\rho}{\lambda(1-\rho)} = \frac{1}{\mu-\lambda}$$

(e) Average number of customers in queue

$$N_Q = \frac{\rho^2}{1-\rho}$$

(f) Average waiting time in queue of a customer

$$W = \frac{\rho}{\mu-\lambda}$$

Summary of $M/M/m$ System Results

(a) Ratio of arrival rate to maximal system service rate

$$\rho = \frac{\lambda}{m\mu}$$

(b) Probability of n customers in the system

$$p_0 = \left[\sum_{k=0}^{m-1} \frac{(m\rho)^k}{k!} + \frac{(m\rho)^m}{m!(1-\rho)} \right]^{-1}, \quad n = 0$$

$$p_n = \begin{cases} p_0 \dfrac{(m\rho)^n}{n!}, & n \le m \\ p_0 \dfrac{m^m \rho^n}{m!}, & n > m \end{cases}$$

(c) Probability that an arriving customer has to wait in queue (m customers or more in the system)

$$P_Q = \frac{p_0(m\rho)^m}{m!(1-\rho)} \qquad \text{(Erlang C Formula)}$$

(d) Average waiting time in queue of a customer

$$W = \frac{\rho P_Q}{\lambda(1-\rho)}$$

(e) Average number of customers in queue

$$N_Q = \frac{\rho P_Q}{1-\rho}$$

(f) Average customer time in the system

$$T = \frac{1}{\mu} + W$$

(g) Average number of customers in the system

$$N = m\rho + \frac{\rho P_Q}{1 - \rho}$$

Summary of $M/M/m/m$ System Results

(a) Probability of m customers in the system

$$p_0 = \left[\sum_{n=0}^{m} \left(\frac{\lambda}{\mu}\right)^n \frac{1}{n!}\right]^{-1}$$

$$p_n = p_0 \left(\frac{\lambda}{\mu}\right)^n \frac{1}{n!}, \quad n = 1, 2, \ldots, m$$

(b) Probability that an arriving customer is lost

$$p_m = \frac{(\lambda/\mu)^m / m!}{\sum_{n=0}^{m}(\lambda/\mu)^n/n!} \qquad \text{(Erlang B Formula)}$$

Summary of $M/G/1$ System Results

(a) Utilization factor

$$\rho = \frac{\lambda}{\mu}$$

(b) Mean residual service time

$$R = \frac{\lambda \overline{X^2}}{2}$$

(c) Pollaczek-Khinchin formula

$$W = \frac{R}{1 - \rho} = \frac{\lambda \overline{X^2}}{2(1 - \rho)}$$

$$T = \frac{1}{\mu} + W$$

$$N_Q = \frac{\lambda^2 \overline{X^2}}{2(1 - \rho)}$$

$$N = \rho + \frac{\lambda^2 \overline{X^2}}{2(1 - \rho)}$$

(d) Pollaczek-Khinchin formula for $M/G/1$ queue with vacations

$$W = \frac{\lambda \overline{X^2}}{2(1 - \rho)} + \frac{\overline{V^2}}{2\overline{V}}$$

$$T = \frac{1}{\mu} + W$$

where $\overline{V}$ and $\overline{V^2}$ are the first two moments of the vacation interval.

Summary of Reservation/Polling Results

(a) Average waiting time (m-user system, unlimited service)

$$W = \frac{\lambda \overline{X^2}}{2(1-\rho)} + \frac{(m-\rho)\overline{V}}{2(1-\rho)} + \frac{\sigma_V^2}{2\overline{V}} \qquad \text{(exhaustive)}$$

$$W = \frac{\lambda \overline{X^2}}{2(1-\rho)} + \frac{(m+\rho)\overline{V}}{2(1-\rho)} + \frac{\sigma_V^2}{2\overline{V}} \qquad \text{(partially gated)}$$

$$W = \frac{\lambda \overline{X^2}}{2(1-\rho)} + \frac{(m+2-\rho)\overline{V}}{2(1-\rho)} + \frac{\sigma_V^2}{2\overline{V}} \qquad \text{(gated)}$$

where $\rho = \lambda/\mu$, and $\overline{V}$ and σ_V^2 are the mean and variance of the reservation intervals, respectively, averaged over all users

$$\overline{V} = \frac{1}{m} \sum_{\ell=0}^{m-1} \overline{V}_\ell$$

$$\sigma_V^2 = \frac{1}{m} \sum_{\ell=0}^{m-1} \left(\overline{V_\ell^2} - \overline{V}_\ell^2 \right)$$

(b) Average waiting time (m-user system, limited service)

$$W = \frac{\lambda \overline{X^2}}{2(1-\rho-\lambda\overline{V})} + \frac{(m+\rho)\overline{V}}{2(1-\rho-\lambda\overline{V})} + \frac{\sigma_V^2(1-\rho)}{2\overline{V}(1-\rho-\lambda\overline{V})} \qquad \text{(partially gated)}$$

$$W = \frac{\lambda \overline{X^2}}{2(1-\rho-\lambda\overline{V})} + \frac{(m+2-\rho-2\lambda\overline{V})\overline{V}}{2(1-\rho-\lambda\overline{V})} + \frac{\sigma_V^2(1-\rho)}{2\overline{V}(1-\rho-\lambda\overline{V})} \qquad \text{(gated)}$$

(c) Average time in the system

$$T = \frac{1}{\mu} + W$$

Summary of Priority Queueing Results

(a) *Nonpreemptive Priority.* Average waiting time in queue for class k customers

$$W_k = \frac{\sum_{i=1}^{n} \lambda_i \overline{X_i^2}}{2(1 - \rho_1 - \cdots - \rho_{k-1})(1 - \rho_1 - \cdots - \rho_k)}$$

(b) *Nonpreemptive Priority.* Average time in the system for class k customers

$$T_k = \frac{1}{\mu_k} + W_k$$

(c) *Preemptive Resume Priority.* Average time in the system for class k customers

$$T_k = \frac{(1/\mu_k)(1 - \rho_1 - \cdots - \rho_k) + R_k}{(1 - \rho_1 - \cdots - \rho_{k-1})(1 - \rho_1 - \cdots - \rho_k)}$$

where

$$R_k = \frac{\sum_{i=1}^{k} \lambda_i \overline{X_i^2}}{2}$$

4

Multiaccess Communication

4.1 INTRODUCTION

The subnetworks considered thus far have consisted of nodes joined by point-to-point communication links. Each such link might consist physically of a pair of twisted wires, a coaxial cable, an optical fiber, a microwave radio link, etc. The implicit assumption about point-to-point links, however, is that the received signal on each link depends only on the transmitted signal and noise on that link.

There are many widely used communication media, such as satellite systems, radio broadcast, multidrop telephone lines, and multitap bus systems, for which the received signal at one node depends on the transmitted signal at two or more other nodes. Typically, such a received signal is the sum of attenuated transmitted signals from a set of other nodes, corrupted by distortion, delay, and noise. Such media, called *multiaccess media*, form the basis for local area networks (LANs), metropolitan area networks (MANs), satellite networks, and radio networks.

The layering discussed in Chapters 1 and 2 is not quite appropriate for multiaccess media. One needs an additional layer, often called the *medium access control* (MAC) layer, bewween the data link control (DLC) layer and the modem or physical layer. The purpose of this extra layer is to allocate the multiaccess medium among the various nodes. As we study this allocation issue, we shall see that the separation of functions between layers is not as clean as it is with point-to-point links. For example, feedback about transmission errors is part of the ARQ function of the DLC layer, but is often also central to the problem of allocation. Similarly, much of the function of routing is automatically implemented by the broadcast nature of multiaccess channels.

Conceptually, we can view multiaccess communication in queueing terms. Each node has a queue of packets to be transmitted and the multiaccess channel is a common server. Ideally, the server should view all the waiting packets as one combined queue to be served by the appropriate queueing discipline. Unfortunately, the server does not know which nodes contain packets; similarly, nodes are unaware of packets at other nodes. Thus, the interesting part of the problem is that knowledge about the state of the queue is distributed.

There are two extremes among the many strategies that have been developed for this generic problem. One is the "free-for-all" approach in which nodes normally send new packets immediately, hoping for no interference from other nodes. The interesting question here is when and how packets are retransmitted when collisions (*i.e.*, interference) occur. The other extreme is the "perfectly scheduled" approach in which there is some order (round robin for example) in which nodes receive reserved intervals for channel use. The interesting questions here are (1) what determines the scheduling order (it could be dynamic), (2) how long can a reserved interval last, and (3) how are nodes informed of their turns?

Sections 4.2 and 4.3 explore the free-for-all approach in a simple idealized environment that allows us to focus on strategies for retransmitting collided packets. Successively more sophisticated algorithms are developed that reduce delay, increase available throughput, and maintain stable operation. In later sections, these algorithms are adapted to take advantage of special channel characteristics so as to reduce delay and increase throughput even further. The more casual reader can omit subsection 4.2.3 and section 4.3.

Section 4.4 explores carrier sense multiple access (CSMA). Here the free-for-all approach is modified; a packet transmission is not allowed to start if the channel is sensed to be busy. We shall find that this set of strategies is a relatively straightforward extension of the ideas in sections 4.2 and 4.3. The value of these strategies is critically dependent on the ratio of propagation delay to packet transmission time, a parameter called β. If $\beta \ll 1$, CSMA can decrease delay and increase throughput significantly over the techniques of sections 4.2 and 4.3. The casual reader can omit subsections 4.4.2 and 4.4.4.

Section 4.5 deals with scheduling, or reserving, the channel in response to the dynamic requirements of the individual nodes. We start with satellite channels in subsection 4.5.1; here the interesting feature is dealing with $\beta \gg 1$. Next, subsections 4.5.2 to 4.5.4 treat the major approaches to LANs. These approaches can be viewed as reservation systems, and differ in whether the reservations are scheduled in a free-for-all manner or in a round robin manner. LANs are usually designed for the assumption that β is small, and subsection 4.5.5 explores systems with higher speed or greater geographical coverage for which β is large.

Finally, section 4.6 explores packet radio. Here the interesting issue is that each node interferes only with a limited subset of other nodes; thus, multiple nodes can transmit simultaneously without interference.

Before going into any of the above topics in detail, we briefly discuss some of the most widely used multiaccess media.

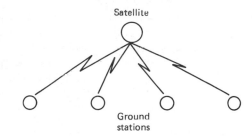

(a) Satellite multiaccess channel

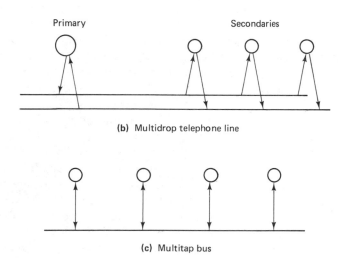

(b) Multidrop telephone line

(c) Multitap bus

Figure 4.1   Common multiaccess channels.

4.1.1 Satellite Channels

In a typical geosynchronous communication satellite system, many ground stations can transmit to a common satellite receiver, with the received messages being
relayed to the ground stations (see Fig. 4.1). Such satellites often have separate
antenna beams for different geographical areas, allowing independent reception and
relaying between areas. Also, FDM (or TDM) can be used, permitting different
earth stations within the region covered by a single antenna beam to be independently received.

It is thus possible to use a satellite channel as a collection of virtual point-
to-point links, with two virtual links being separated either by antenna beam or
multiplexing. The potential difficulty with this approach is the same as the difficulty
with using FDM or TDM for multiple sessions on a single point-to-point link,
namely increased delay and underutilization of the medium.

In subsection 4.5.1, we shall find that delay can be reduced and utilization increased by sharing the medium on a demand basis. This is more difficult than demand sharing (*i.e.*, statistical multiplexing) on a point-to-point link because the earth stations are not aware of the instantaneous traffic requirements of other earth stations. If several stations transmit at the same time (and in the same frequency band), then their signals are garbled and incorrectly received.

4.1.2 Multidrop Telephone Lines

Another example of a multiaccess channel is a multidrop telephone line. Such lines connect one primary node with a number of secondary nodes; the signal transmitted by the primary node goes over one pair of wires and is received by all the secondary nodes. Similarly, there is a return pair of wires which carries the sum of the transmitted signals from all the secondary nodes to the primary node. Conceptually, this is like a satellite channel. The secondary nodes, or earth stations, share the path to the primary node, or satellite, whereas the primary node, or satellite, broadcasts to all the secondary nodes, or earth stations. Most communication on a multidrop phone line is intended to go from primary to secondary or vice versa, whereas most communication on a satellite channel is relayed by the satellite from one earth station to another. Conceptually, this difference is not very important, since the major problem is that of sharing the channel from the secondary nodes to the primary, and it makes little difference whether the messages are removed at the primary node or broadcast back to all the secondary nodes.

The traditional mode of operation for multidrop telephone lines is for the primary node to poll (*i.e.*, request information from) each secondary node in some order. Each secondary node responds to its poll either by sending data back to the primary station or by indicating that it has no data to send. This strategy avoids interference between the secondary nodes, since nodes are polled one at a time, but there is a certain amount of inefficiency involved, both in the time to send a poll and the time to wait for a response from a node with no data.

4.1.3 Multitapped Bus

A third example of a multiaccess channel is a bus with multiple taps. In this case, each node can receive the signal sent by each other node, but again, if multiple nodes transmit at the same time, the received signal is garbled. We shall discuss this example later in the context of Ethernet, but for now, we observe that conceptually this channel is very similar to a satellite channel. Each node can communicate with each other node, but if nodes transmit simultaneously, the received signal cannot be correctly detected. The fact that nodes can hear each other directly here, as opposed to hearing each other via relay from the satellite, has some important practical consequences, but we will ignore this for now.

4.1.4 Packet Radio Networks

A fourth example of multiaccess communication is that of a packet radio network. Here each node is in reception range of some subset of other nodes. Thus, if only one node in the subset is transmitting, the given node can receive the transmission, whereas if multiple nodes are transmitting simultaneously in the same band, the reception will be garbled. Similarly, what one node transmits will be heard by a subset of the other nodes. In general, because of different noise conditions at the nodes, the subset of nodes from which a given node can receive is different from the subset to which the given node can transmit. The fact that each receiver hears a subset of transmitters rather than all transmitters makes packet radio far more complex than the other examples discussed. In the next four sections, we will study multiaccess channels in which a receiver can hear all transmitters, and then in section 4.6, we will discuss packet radio networks in more detail.

4.2 SLOTTED MULTIACCESS AND THE ALOHA SYSTEM

Satellite channels, multidrop telephone lines, and multitap bus systems all share the feature of a set of nodes sharing a communication channel. If two or more nodes transmit simultaneously, the reception is garbled, and if none transmit, the channel is unused. The problem is to somehow coordinate the use of the channel so that exactly one node is transmitting for an appreciable fraction of the time. We start by looking at a highly idealized model. We shall see later that multiaccess channels can often be used in practice with much higher utilization than is possible in this idealized model, but we shall also see that these practical extensions can be understood more clearly in terms of our idealization.

4.2.1 Idealized Slotted Multiaccess Model

The idealized model to be developed allows us to focus on the problem of dealing with the contention that occurs when multiple nodes attempt to use the channel simultaneously. Conceptually, we view the system as in Fig. 4.1(a), with m transmitting nodes and one receiver.

It will be observed that, aside from some questions of propagation delay, this same model can be applied with m nodes that can all hear each other (*i.e.*, the situation with a multitap bus). We first list the assumptions of the model and then discuss their implications.

1. *Slotted System*: Assume that all transmitted packets have the same length and that each packet requires one time unit (called a slot) for transmission. All transmitters are synchronized so that the reception of each packet starts at an integer time and ends before the next integer time.

2. *Poisson Arrivals*: Assume that packets arrive for transmission at each of the m transmitting nodes according to independent Poisson processes. Let λ

be the overall arrival rate to the system, and let λ/m be the arrival rate at each transmitting node.

3. *Collision or Perfect Reception*: Assume that if two or more nodes send a packet in a given time slot, then there is a *collision* and the receiver obtains no information about the contents or source of the transmitted packets. If just one node sends a packet in a given slot, then the packet is correctly received.

4. *0,1,e Immediate Feedback*: Assume that at the end of each slot, each node obtains feedback from the receiver specifying whether 0 packets, 1 packet, or more than one packet (e for error) were transmitted in that slot.

5. *Retransmission of Collisions*: Assume that each packet involved in a collision must be retransmitted in some later slot, with further such retransmissions until the packet is successfully received. A node with a packet that must be retransmitted is said to be *backlogged*.

6a. *No Buffering*: If one packet at a node is currently waiting for transmission or colliding with another packet during transmission, then new arrivals at that node are discarded and never transmitted. An alternative to this assumption is the following.

6b. *Infinite Set of Nodes* ($m = \infty$): The system has an infinite set of nodes and each newly arriving packet arrives at a new node.

Discussion of Assumptions

The slotted system assumption (1) has two effects. The first is to turn the system into a discrete-time system, thus simplifying analysis. The second is to preclude, for the moment, the possibility of carrier sensing or early collision detection. Carrier sensing is treated in section 4.4 and early collision detection is treated in section 4.5. Both allow much more efficient use of the multiaccess channel, but can be understood more clearly as an extension of the present model. Synchronizing the transmitters for slotted arrival at the receiver is not entirely trivial, but may be accomplished with relatively stable clocks, a small amount of feedback from the receiver, and some guard time between the end of a packet transmission and the beginning of the next slot.

The assumption of Poisson arrivals (2) is unrealistic for the case of multipacket messages. We discuss this issue in section 4.5 in terms of nodes making reservations for use of the channel.

The assumption of collision or perfect reception (3) ignores the possibility of errors due to noise and also ignores the possibility of "capture" techniques, by which a receiver can sometimes capture one transmission in the presence of multiple transmissions.

The assumption of immediate feedback (4) is quite unrealistic, particularly in the case of satellite channels. It is made to simplify the analysis, and we shall see later that delayed feedback complicates multiaccess algorithms but causes no fundamental problems. We also discuss the effects of more limited types of feedback later.

The assumption that colliding packets must be retransmitted (5) is certainly reasonable in providing reliable communication. In light of this assumption, the no-buffering assumption (6a) appears rather peculiar, since new arrivals to back-logged nodes are thrown away with impunity, but packets once transmitted must be retransmitted until successful. In practice, one generally provides some buffering along with some form of flow control to ensure that not too many packets back up at a node. Our interest in this section, however, is in multiaccess channels with a large number of nodes, a relatively small arrival rate λ, and small required delay (*i.e.*, the conditions under which TDM doesn't suffice). Under these conditions, the fraction of backlogged nodes is typically small, and new arrivals at backlogged nodes are almost negligible. Thus, the delay for a system without buffering should be relatively close to that with buffering. Also, the delay for the unbuffered system provides a lower bound to the delay for a wide variety of systems with buffering and flow control.

The alternative, infinite-node assumption (6b), similarly provides us with an upper bound to the delay that can be achieved with a finite number of nodes. In particular, given any multiaccess algorithm (*i.e.*, any rule that each node employs for selecting packet transmission times), each of a finite set of nodes can regard itself as a set of virtual nodes, one for each arriving packet. With the application of the given algorithm independently for each such packet, the situation is equivalent to that with an infinite set of nodes, *i.e.*, assumption 6b. In this approach, a node with several backlogged packets will sometimes send multiple packets in one slot, causing a sure collision. Thus, it appears that by avoiding such sure collisions and knowing the number of buffered packets at a node, a system with a finite number of nodes and buffering could achieve smaller delays than with $m = \infty$; in any case, however, the $m = \infty$ delay can always be achieved.

If the performance using assumption 6a is similar to that using 6b, then we are assured that we have a good approximation to the performance of a system with arbitrary assumptions about buffering. From a theoretical standpoint, assumption 6b captures the essence of multiaccess communication much better than 6a. We use 6a initially, however, because it is less abstract and also it provides some important insights about the relationship between TDM and other algorithms.

4.2.2 Slotted Aloha

The Aloha network [Abr70] was developed around 1970 to provide radio communication between the central computer and various data terminals at the campuses of the University of Hawaii. This multiaccess approach will be described in subsection 4.2.4, but first we discuss an improvement called slotted Aloha [Rob72]. The basic idea of this algorithm is that each unbacklogged node simply transmits a newly arriving packet in the first slot after the packet arrival, thus risking occasional collisions but achieving very small delay if collisions are rare. This approach should be contrasted with TDM, in which, with m nodes, an arriving packet would have to wait for an average of $m/2$ slots for its turn to transmit. Thus, slotted Aloha trans-

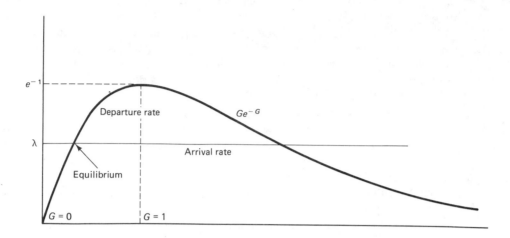

Figure 4.2   Departure rate as a function of attempted transmission rate G for slotted Aloha. Ignoring the dynamic behavior of G, departures (successful transmissions) occur a rate Ge^{-G}, and arrivals occur at a rate λ, leading to a hypothesized equilibrium point as shown.

mits packets almost immediately with occasional collisions, whereas TDM avoids collisions at the expense of large delays.

When a collision occurs in slotted Aloha, each node sending one of the colliding packets discovers the collision at the end of the slot and becomes backlogged. If each backlogged node were to simply retransmit in the next slot after being involved in a collision, then another collision would surely occur. Instead, such nodes wait for some random number of slots before retransmitting.

To gain some initial intuitive understanding of slotted Aloha, we start with an instructive but flawed analysis. With the infinite-node assumption (*i.e.*, 6b), the number of new arrivals transmitted in a slot is a Poisson random variable with parameter λ. If the retransmissions from backlogged nodes are sufficiently randomized, it is plausible to approximate the total number of retransmissions and new transmissions in a given slot as a Poisson random variable with some parameter $G > \lambda$. With this approximation, the probability of a successful transmission in a slot is Ge^{-G}. Finally, in equilibrium, the arrival rate, λ, to the system should be the same as the departure rate, Ge^{-G}. This relationship is illustrated in Fig. 4.2.

We see that the maximum possible departure rate (according to the above argument) occurs at $G = 1$ and is $1/e \approx 0.368$. We also note, somewhat suspiciously, that for any arrival rate less than $1/e$, there are two values of G for which the arrival rate equals the departure rate. The problem with this elementary approach is that it provides no insight into the dynamics of the system. As the number of backlogged packets changes, the parameter G will change; this leads to a feedback effect, generating further changes in the number of backlogged packets. To understand these dynamics, we will have to analyze the system somewhat more carefully.

The above simple picture, however, correctly identifies the maximum throughput rate of slotted Aloha as $1/e$ and also shows that G, the mean number of attempted transmissions per slot, should be on the order of 1 to achieve a throughput close to $1/e$. If $G < 1$, too many idle slots are generated, and if $G > 1$, too many collisions are generated.

To construct a more precise model, assume that each backlogged node retransmits with some fixed probability q_r in each successive slot until a successful transmission occurs. In other words, the number of slots from a collision until a given node involved in the collision retransmits is a geometric random variable having value $i \geq 1$ with probability $q_r(1 - q_r)^{i-1}$. The original version of slotted Aloha employed a uniform distribution for retransmission, but this is more difficult to analyze and has no identifiable advantages over the geometric distribution. We will use the no-buffering assumption (6a) and switch later to the infinite node assumption (6b).

The behavior of slotted Aloha can now be described as a discrete-time Markov chain. Let n be the number of backlogged nodes at the beginning of a given slot. Each of these nodes will transmit a packet in the given slot, independently of each other, with probability q_r. Each of the $m - n$ other nodes will transmit a packet in the given slot if one (or more) such packets arrived during the previous slot. Since such arrivals are Poisson distributed with mean λ/m, the probability of no arrivals is $e^{-\lambda/m}$; thus, the probability that an unbacklogged node transmits a packet in the given slot is $q_a = 1 - e^{-\lambda/m}$. Let $Q_a(i,n)$ be the probability that i unbacklogged nodes transmit packets in a given slot, and let $Q_r(i,n)$ be the probability that i backlogged nodes transmit,

$$Q_a(i,n) = \binom{m-n}{i}(1 - q_a)^{m-n-i}q_a^i \quad \text{not backlogged} \tag{4.1}$$

$$Q_r(i,n) = \binom{n}{i}(1 - q_r)^{n-i}q_r^i \quad \text{backlogged} \tag{4.2}$$

Note that from one slot to the next, the state (*i.e.*, the number of backlogged packets) increases by the number of new arrivals transmitted by unbacklogged nodes, less one if a packet is transmitted successfully. A packet is transmitted successfully, however, only if one new arrival and no backlogged packet, or no new arrival and one backlogged packet is transmitted. Thus, the state transition probability of going from state n to $n + i$ is given by

$$P_{n,n+i} = \begin{cases} Q_a(i,n), & 2 \leq i \leq (m-n) \\ Q_a(1,n)[1 - Q_r(0,n)], & i = 1 \\ Q_a(1,n)Q_r(0,n) + Q_a(0,n)[1 - Q_r(1,n)], & i = 0 \\ Q_a(0,n)Q_r(1,n), & i = -1 \end{cases} \tag{4.3}$$

Figure 4.3 illustrates this Markov chain. Note that the state can decrease by at most 1 in a single transition, and this makes it easy to calculate the steady-state

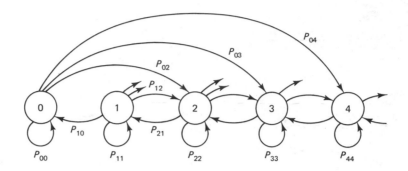

Figure 4.3 Markov chain for slotted Aloha. The state (*i.e.*, backlog) can decrease by at most one per transition, but can increase by an arbitrary amount.

probabilities iteratively, finding p_n for each successively larger n in terms of p_0 and finally finding p_0 as a normalizing constant (see Prob. 4.1). From this, the expected number of backlogged nodes can be found, and from Little's theorem, the average delay can be calculated.

Unfortunately, this system has some very strange properties for a large number of nodes, and the above steady-state results are very misleading. To get some intuitive understanding of this, note that we would like to choose the retransmission probability q_r to be moderately large to avoid large delays after collisions. If the arrival rate is small, and not many packets are involved in collisions, this works well and retransmissions are normally successful. On the other hand, if the system is afflicted with a run of bad luck and the number of backlogged packets n gets large enough to satisfy $q_r n \gg 1$, then collisions occur in almost all successive slots and the system remains heavily backlogged for a long time.

To understand this phenomenon quantitatively, define the *drift* in state n (D_n) as the expected change in backlog over one slot time, starting in state n. Thus, D_n is the expected number of new arrivals accepted into the system (*i.e.*, $(m-n)q_a$) less the expected number of successful transmissions in the slot; the expected number of successful transmissions is just the probability of a successful transmission, defined as P_{succ}. Thus,

$$D_n = (m-n)q_a - P_{\text{succ}} \qquad (4.4)$$

where

$$P_{\text{succ}} = Q_a(1,n)Q_r(0,n) + Q_a(0,n)Q_r(1,n) \qquad (4.5)$$

Define the attempt rate $G(n)$ as the expected number of attempted transmissions in a slot when the system is in state n, *i.e.*,

$$G(n) = (m-n)q_a + nq_r$$

If q_a and q_r are small, P_{succ} is closely approximated as the following function of

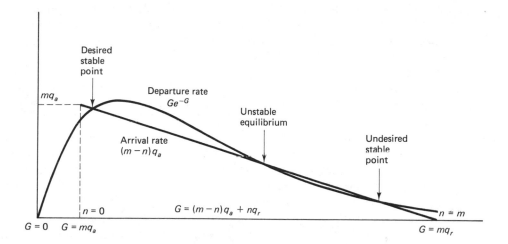

Figure 4.4   Instability of slotted Aloha. The horizontal axis corresponds to both the state n and the attempt rate G, which are related by the linear equation $G = (m - n)q_a + nq_r$ with $q_r > q_a$. For n to the left of the unstable point, D is negative and n drifts toward the desired stable point. For n to the right of the unstable point, D is positive and n drifts toward the undesired stable point.

the attempt rate:

$$P_{\text{succ}} \approx G(n)e^{-G(n)} \tag{4.6}$$

This approximation can be derived directly from Eq. (4.5), using the approximation $(1 - x)^y \approx e^{-xy}$ for small x in the expressions for Q_a and Q_r. Similarly, the probability of an idle slot is approximately $e^{-G(n)}$. Thus, the number of packets in a slot is well approximated as a Poisson random variable (as in the earlier intuitive analysis), but the parameter $G(n)$ varies with the state. Figure 4.4 illustrates Eqs. (4.4) and (4.6) for the case $q_r > q_a$ (This is the only case of interest, as discussed later). The drift is the difference between the curve and the straight line. Since the drift is the expected change in state from one slot to the next, the system, although perhaps fluctuating, tends to move in the direction of the drift and consequently tends to cluster around the two stable points with rare excursions between the two.

There are two important conclusions from this figure. First, the departure rate, *i.e.*, P_{succ}, is at most $1/e$ for large m. Second, the departure rate is almost zero for long periods whenever the system jumps to the undesirable stable point. Consider the effect of changing q_r. As q_r is increased, the delay in retransmitting a collided packet decreases, but also the linear relationship between n and the attempt rate $G(n) = (m - n)q_a + nq_r$ changes (*i.e.*, $G(n)$ increases with n faster when q_r is increased). If the horizontal scale for n is held fixed in Fig. 4.4, then this change in attempt rate corresponds to a contraction of the horizontal $G(n)$ scale, and thus to a horizontal contraction of the curve Ge^{-G}. This means that the number of backlogged packets required to exceed the unstable equilibrium point decreases. Alternatively, if q_r is decreased, retransmission delay increases, but it becomes more difficult to exceed the unstable equilibrium point. If q_r is decreased enough (while still larger than q_a), the curve Ge^{-g} will expand enough in Fig. 4.4 that only one stable state will remain. At this stable point, and similarly when $q_r = q_a$, the backlog is an appreciable fraction of m, and this means both that an appreciable number of arriving packets are discarded and that the delay is excessively large.

The question of what values of q_r and arrival rate lead to stable behavior, particularly when q_r and arrival rate vary from node to node and infinite buffering is provided at each node, has received considerable theoretical attention (e.g., [Tsy85]). These theoretical studies generally assume that nodes are considered backlogged immediately on arrival. Problem 4.8, however, illustrates that if q_r is small enough for stable operation, then the delay is considerably greater than that with TDM; thus these approaches are not of great practical importance.

If we replace the no-buffering assumption with the infinite-node assumption, then the attempt rate $G(n)$ becomes $\lambda + nq_r$ and the straight line representing arrivals in Fig. 4.4 becomes horizontal. In this case, the undesirable stable point disappears, and once the state of the system passes the unstable equilibrium, it tends to increase without bound. In this case, the corresponding infinite-state Markov chain has no steady-state distribution and the expected backlog increases without bound as the system continues to run. See [Pak69] and [Kap79] for mathematical analyses of such situations.

From a practical standpoint, if the arrival rate λ is very much smaller than $1/e$, and if q_r is moderate, then the system could be expected to remain in the desired stable state for very long periods. In the unlikely event of a move to the undesired stable point, the system could be restarted with backlogged packets lost. Rather than continuing to analyze this rather flawed system, however, we look at modifications of slotted Aloha that cure this stability issue.

4.2.3 Stabilized Slotted Aloha

One simple approach to achieving stability should be almost obvious now. P_{succ} is approximately $G(n)e^{-G(n)}$, which is maximized at $G(n) = 1$. Thus, it is desirable to dynamically change q_r to maintain the attempt rate $G(n)$ at 1. The difficulty here is that n is unknown to the nodes and can only be estimated from the feedback. There are many strategies for estimating n or the appropriate value of q_r (e.g., [HVL83] and [Riv85]). All of them, in essence, increase q_r when an idle slot occurs and decrease q_r when a collision occurs.

Stability and Maximum Throughput

The notion of stability must be clarified somewhat before proceeding. Slotted Aloha was called unstable in the last subsection on the basis of the representation in Fig. 4.4. Given the no-buffering assumption, however, the system has a well-defined steady-state behavior for all arrival rates. With the infinite-node assumption, on the other hand, there is no steady-state distribution and the expected delay grows without bound as the system continues to run. With the no-buffering assumption, the system discards large numbers of arriving packets and has a very large but finite delay, whereas with the infinite-node assumption, no arrivals are discarded but the delay becomes infinite.

In the following, we shall use the infinite-node assumption (6b), and define a multiaccess system as stable for a given arrival rate if the expected delay per packet (either as a time average or an ensemble average in the limit of increasing time) is finite. Ordinary slotted Aloha is unstable, in this sense, for any arrival rate greater than zero. Note that if a system is stable, then for a sufficiently large but finite number of nodes m, the system (regarding each arrival as corresponding to a new virtual node) has a smaller expected delay than TDM, since the delay of TDM, for a fixed overall arrival rate, increases linearly with m.

The maximum stable throughput of a multiaccess system is defined as the least upper bound of arrival rates for which the system is stable. For example, the maximum stable throughput of ordinary slotted Aloha is zero. Our purpose with these definitions is to study multiaccess algorithms that do not require knowledge of the number of nodes m and that maintain small delay (for given λ) independent of m. Some discussion will be given later to modifications that make explicit use of the number of nodes.

Returning to the stabilization of slotted Aloha, note that when the estimate of backlog is perfect, and $G(n)$ is maintained at the optimal value of 1, then (according to the Poisson approximation) idles occur with probability $1/e \approx 0.368$, successes occur with probability $1/e$, and collisions occur with probability $1 - 2/e \approx 0.264$. Thus, the rule for changing q_r should allow fewer collisions than idles. The maximum stable throughput of such a system is at most $1/e$. To see this, note that when the backlog is large, the Poisson approximation becomes more accurate, the success rate is then limited to $1/e$, and thus the drift is positive for $\lambda > 1/e$. It is important to observe that this argument depends on all backlogged nodes using the same retransmission probability. We shall see in section 4.3 that if nodes use both their own history of retransmissions and the feedback history in their decisions about transmitting, then maximum stable throughputs considerably higher than $1/e$ are possible.

P222

Pseudo-Bayesian algorithm

Rivest's pseudo-Bayesian algorithm [Riv85] is a particularly simple and effective way to stabilize Aloha. This algorithm is essentially the same as an earlier, independently derived, algorithm by Mikhailov [Mik79], but Rivest's Bayesian interpretation simplifies understanding. The algorithm differs from slotted Aloha in that new arrivals are regarded as backlogged immediately on arrival. Rather than being transmitted with certainty in the next slot, they are transmitted with probability q_r in the same way as packets involved in previous collisions. Thus, if there are n backlogged packets (including new arrivals) at the beginning of a slot, the attempt rate is $G(n) = nq_r$, and the probability of a successful transmission is $nq_r(1 - q_r)^{n-1}$. For unstabilized Aloha, this modification would not make much sense, since q_r has to be relatively small and new arrivals would be unnecessarily delayed. For stabilized Aloha, however, q_r can be as large as 1 when the estimated backlog is negligible, so that new arrivals are only held up when the system is already estimated to be congested. In Prob. 4.6, it is shown that this modification increases the probability of success if the backlog estimate is accurate.

The algorithm operates by maintaining an estimate $\hat{n}$ of the backlog n at the beginning of each slot. Each backlogged packet is then transmitted (independently) with probability $q_r(\hat{n}) = \min\{1, 1/\hat{n}\}$. The minimum operation limits q_r to at most 1, and, subject to this limitation, tries to achieve an attempt rate $G = nq_r$ of 1. For each k, the estimated backlog at the beginning of slot $k + 1$ is updated from the estimated backlog and feedback for slot k according to the rule:

$$\hat{n}_{k+1} = \begin{cases} \max\{\lambda, \hat{n}_k + \lambda - 1\}, & \text{for idle or success} \\ \hat{n}_k + \lambda + (e - 2)^{-1}, & \text{for collision} \end{cases} \qquad (4.7)$$

The addition of λ to the previous backlog accounts for new arrivals, and the max operation insures that the estimate is never less than the contribution from new arrivals. On successful transmissions, 1 is subtracted from the previous backlog to account for the successful departure. Finally, subtracting 1 from the previous backlog on idle slots and adding $(e - 2)^{-1}$ on collisions has the effect of decreasing $\hat{n}$ when too many idles occur and increasing $\hat{n}$ when too many collisions occur. For large backlogs, if $\hat{n} = n$, each of the n backlogged packets is independently transmitted in a slot with probability $q_r = 1/n$. Thus $G(n)$ is 1, and, by the Poisson approximation, idles occur with probability $1/e$ and collisions with probability $(e - 2)/e$, so that decreasing $\hat{n}$ by 1 on idles and increasing $\hat{n}$ by $(e - 2)^{-1}$ on collisions maintains the balance between n and $\hat{n}$ on the average.

It is shown in Prob. 4.9 that if the apriori probability distribution on n_k is Poisson with parameter $\hat{n}_k \geq 1$, then, given an idle or successful transmission in slot k, the probability distribution of n_{k+1} is Poisson with parameter $\hat{n}_k + \lambda - 1$. Given a collision, the resulting distribution of n_{k+1} is not quite Poisson, but is reasonably approximated as Poisson with parameter $\hat{n}_{k+1}$. For this reason, the algorithm is called pseudo-Bayesian.

Figure 4.5 provides some heuristic understanding of why the algorithm is stable for all $\lambda < 1/e$. The state of the system is characterized by n and $\hat{n}$, and the figure shows the expected drift in these variables from one slot to the next. If n and $\hat{n}$ are large and equal, then the expected drift of each is $\lambda - 1/e$, which is negative. On the other hand, if the absolute value of $n - \hat{n}$ is large, then the expected drift of n is positive, but the expected reduction in $|n - \hat{n}|$ is considerably larger. Thus, if the system starts at some arbitrary point in the $(n, \hat{n})$ plane, n might increase on the average for a number of slots, but eventually n and $\hat{n}$ will come closer together and then n will decrease on the average.

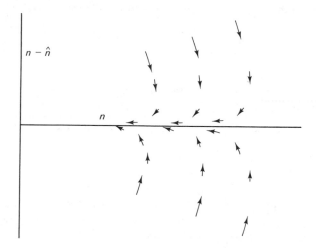

Figure 4.5   Drift of n and $n - \hat{n}$ for the pseudo-Bayesian stabilization algorithm. When the absolute value of $n - \hat{n}$ is large, it approaches 0 faster than n increases.

In applications, the arrival rate λ is typically unknown and slowly varying. Thus, the algorithm must either estimate λ from the time average rate of successful transmissions or set its value within the algorithm to some fixed value. It has been shown by Mikhailov (see [Kel85] and Tsitsiklis [Tsi86]) that if the fixed value $1/e$ is used within the algorithm, then stability is achieved for all actual $\lambda < 1/e$. Nothing has been proven about the behavior of the algorithm when a dynamic estimate of λ is used within the algorithm.

Approximate Delay Analysis

An exact analysis of expected delay for this algorithm, even with known λ, appears to be very difficult, but it is instructive to analyze an approximate model. Assume that λ is known and that the probability of successful transmission P_{succ} is $1/e$ whenever the backlog n is 2 or more, and that $P_{\text{succ}} = 1$ for $n = 1$. This is a reasonable model for very small λ, since very few collisions occur and q_r is typically 1. It is also reasonable for large $\lambda < 1/e$, since typically n is large and $\hat{n} \approx n$.

Let W_i be the delay from the arrival of the ith packet until the beginning of the ith successful transmission. Note that if the system were first-come first-serve, then W_i would be the queueing time of the ith arrival. By the same argument as in Section 3.5, however, the average of W_i over all i is equal to the expected queueing delay W. Let n_i be the number of backlogged packets at the instant before i's arrival; n_i does not include any packet currently being successfully transmitted, but does include current unsuccessful transmissions. W_i can be expressed as

$$W_i = R_i + \sum_{j=1}^{n_i} t_j + y_i \qquad (4.8)$$

R_i is the residual time to the beginning of the next slot, and t_1 (for $n_i > 0$) is the subsequent interval until the next successful transmission is completed. Similarly, t_j, $1 < j \le n_i$, is the interval from the end of the $(j-1)^{\text{th}}$ subsequent success to the end of the jth subsequent success. After those n_i successes, y_i is the remaining interval until the beginning of the next successful transmission, *i.e.*, the ith transmission overall.

Observe that for each interval t_j, the backlog is at least two, counting the new i^{th} arrival and the n_i packets already backlogged. Thus, each slot is successful with probability $1/e$, and the expected value of each t_j is e. Next, observe that Little's formula relates the expected values of W_i and n_i (*i.e.*, W_i is the wait not counting the successful transmission, and n_i is the number in the system not counting successful transmissions in process). Finally, the expected value of R_i is $1/2$ (counting time in slots). Thus, taking the expected value of Eq. (4.8) and averaging over i, we get

$$W = 1/2 + \lambda e W + E\{y\} \qquad (4.9)$$

Now consider the system at the first slot boundary at which both the $(i-1)^{\text{st}}$ departure has occurred and the ith arrival has occurred. If the backlog is 1 at that point (*i.e.*, only the ith packet is in the system), then y_i is 0. Alternatively, if $n > 1$, then $E\{y_i\} = e - 1$. Let p_n be the steady state probability that the backlog is n at a slot boundary. Then, since a packet is always successfully transmitted if the state is 1 at the beginning of the slot, we see that p_1 is the fraction of slots in which the state is 1 and a packet is successfully transmitted. Since λ is the total fraction of slots with successful transmissions, p_1/λ is the fraction of packets transmitted from state 1 and $1 - p_1/\lambda$ is the fraction transmitted from higher numbered states. It follows that

$$E\{y\} = \frac{(e-1)(\lambda - p_1)}{\lambda} \qquad (4.10)$$

Finally, we must determine p_1. From the argument above, we see that $\lambda = p_1 + (1 - p_0 - p_1)/e$. Also, state 0 can be entered at a slot boundary only if no arrivals occured in the previous slot and the previous state was 0 or 1. Thus, $p_0 = (p_0 + p_1)e^{-\lambda}$. Solving for p_1,

$$p_1 = \frac{(1 - \lambda e)(e^\lambda - 1)}{[1 - (e-1)(e^\lambda - 1)]} \qquad (4.11)$$

Combining Eqs. (4-9) to (4-11) yields

$$W = \frac{e - 1/2}{1 - \lambda e} - \frac{(e^\lambda - 1)(e - 1)}{\lambda[1 - (e-1)(e^\lambda - 1)]} \qquad (4.12)$$

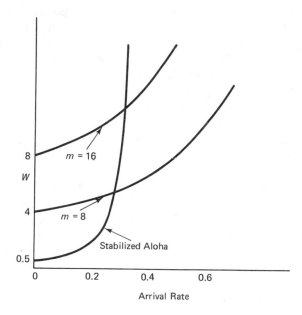

Figure 4.6   Comparison of expected waiting time W in slots, from arrival until beginning of successful transmission, for stabilized Aloha and for TDM with $m = 8$ and $m = 16$. For small arrival rates, the delay of stabilized Aloha is little more than waiting for the next slot, whereas as the arrival rate approaches $1/e$, the delay becomes unbounded.

This value of W is quite close to delay values for the Pseudo-Bayesian aloritdm obtained through simulation. Figure 4.6 plots $E\{W\}$ for this approximate model and compares it with the queueing delay for TDM with 8 and 16 nodes. It is quite surprising that the delay is so small even for arrival rates relatively close to $1/e$. It appears that the assumption of immediate feedback is unnecessary for stabilization strategies of this type to be stable; the argument is that feedback delay will make the estimate $\hat{n}$ less accurate, but $n/\hat{n}$ will still stay close to 1 for large n.

Binary Exponential Backoff

In the radio networks to be discussed in section 4.6, and in some other multiaccess situations, the assumption of $0,1,e$ feedback on all slots is unrealistic. In some systems, a node receives feedback only about whether or not its own packets were successfully transmitted; it receives no feedback about slots in which it doesn't transmit. Such limited feedback is sufficient for slotted Aloha, but is insufficient for the backlog estimation of the pseudo-Bayesian strategy. Binary exponential backoff [MeB76] is a stabilization strategy used in Ethernet that employs only this more limited form of feedback.

This strategy is very simple; if a packet has been transmitted unsuccessfully i

times, then the probability of transmission in successive slots is set at $q_r = 2^{-i}$ (or is uniformly distributed over the next 2^i slots after the ith failure). When a packet initially arrives in the system, it is transmitted immediately in the next slot.

Some rationale for this strategy can be seen by noting that when a packet first arrives (with this limited feedback), the node knows nothing of the backlog, so the immediate first transmission is reasonable. With successive collisions, any reasonable estimate of backlog would increase, motivating the decrease in the local q_r. To make matters worse, however, as q_r is reduced, the node gets less feedback per slot about the backlog, and thus, to play safe, it is reasonable to increase the backlog estimate by larger and larger amounts on each successive collision.

Unfortunately this strategy is unstable (*i.e.*, has infinite expected delay for $m = \infty$) for every arrival rate λ greater than 0 [Ald86]. It is unknown whether or not any strategy can achieve stability with this type of limited feedback. Problem 4.10, however, develops another strategy that can be used with this limited feedback and with a finite number of nodes with unlimited buffering to achieve finite expected delay for any λ less than 1. Unfortunately, the price of this high throughput is inordinately large delay.

4.2.4 Unslotted Aloha

Unslotted, or pure, Aloha [Abr70] was the precursor to slotted Aloha. In this strategy, each node, upon receiving a new packet, transmits it immediately rather than waiting for a slot boundary. Slots play no role in pure Aloha, so we temporarily omit the slotted system assumption. If a packet is involved in a collision, it is retransmitted after a random delay. Assume that if the transmission times for two packets overlap at all, then the CRCs on those packets will fail and retransmission will be required. We assume that the receiver rebroadcasts the composite received signal (or that all nodes receive the composite signal), so that each node, after a given propagation delay can determine whether its transmitted packets were correctly received or not. Thus, we have the same type of limited feedback discussed in the last subsection. Other types of feedback could be considered and Prob. 4.11 develops some of the peculiar effects of other feedback assumptions.

Figure 4.7 shows that if one packet starts transmission at time t, and all packets have unit length, then any other transmission starting between $t - 1$ and $t + 1$ will cause a collision. For simplicity, assume an infinite number of nodes (*i.e.*, assumption 6b) and let n be the number of backlogged nodes at a given time. For our present purposes, a node is considered backlogged from the time it has determined that its previously transmitted packet was involved in a collision until the time that it attempts retransmission. Assume that the period until attempted retransmission τ is an exponentially distributed random variable with probability density $xe^{-x\tau}$, where x is an arbitrary parameter interpreted as a node's retransmission attempt rate. Thus, with an overall Poisson arrival rate of λ to the system, the initiation times of attempted transmissions is a time-varying Poisson process of rate $G(n) = \lambda + nx$ in which n is the backlog at a given time.

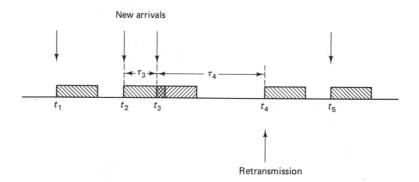

Figure 4.7   Unslotted Aloha. New arrivals are transmitted immediately
and unsuccessful transmissions are repeated after a random delay. Packet
transmission time is one unit, and two transmissions collide if their interde-
parture interval is less than one unit.

Consider the sequence of successive transmission attempts on the channel.
For some given i, let τ_i be the duration of the interval between the initiations of
the ith and $(i+1)^{\text{th}}$ transmission attempt. The ith attempt will be successful if
both τ_i and τ_{i-1} exceed 1 (assuming unit length packets). Given the backlog in
each intertransmission interval, these intervals are independent. Thus, assuming a
backlog of n for each interval, we have

$$P_{\text{succ}} = e^{-2G(n)} \tag{4.13}$$

Since attempted transmissions occur at rate $G(n)$, the throughput (*i.e.*, the
expected number of successful transmissions per unit time) as a function of n is

$$\text{Throughput}\,(n) = G(n)e^{-2G(n)} \tag{4.14}$$

Figure 4.8 illustrates this result. The situation is very similar to that of
slotted Aloha, except that the throughput has a maximum of $1/(2e)$, achieved when
$G(n) = 1/2$. The above analysis is approximate in the sense that Eq. (4.13) assumes
that the backlog is the same in the intervals surrounding a given transmission
attempt, whereas, according to our definition of backlog, the backlog decreases
by one whenever a backlogged packet initiates transmission and increases by one
whenever a collided packet is detected. For small x (*i.e.*, large mean time before
attempted retransmission), this effect is relatively small.

It can be seen from Fig. 4.8 that pure Aloha has the same type of stability
problem as slotted Aloha. For the limited feedback assumed here, stability is quite
difficult to achieve or analyze (as is the case with slotted Aloha). Very little is
known about stabilization for pure Aloha, but if λ is very small and the mean
retransmission time very large, then the system can be expected to run for long
periods without major backlog buildup.

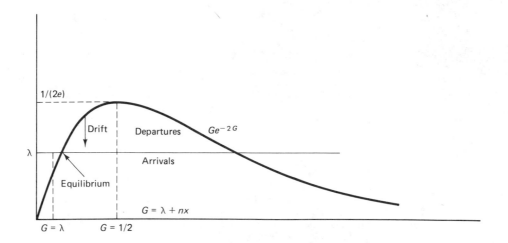

Figure 4.8   Pure Aloha as a function of the attempted transmission rate G. Successful departures leave the system at a rate Ge^{-2G}, and arrivals occur at a rate λ, leading to a hypothesized equilibrium at the point shown.

One of the major advantages of pure Aloha is that it can be used with variablelength packets, whereas with slotted Aloha, long packets must be broken up to fit into slots and short packets must be padded out to fill up slots. This compensates for some of the inherent throughput loss of pure Aloha and gives it an advantage in simplicity. Some analysis, with simplifying assumptions, of the effect of variable length packets appears in [Fer75] and [San80].

4.3 SPLITTING ALGORITHMS

We have seen that slotted Aloha requires some care for stabilization and is also essentially limited to throughputs of $1/e$. We now want to look at more sophisticated collision resolution techniques that both maintain stability without any complex estimation procedures and also increase the achievable throughput. To get an intuitive idea how this can be done, note that with relatively small attempt rates, when a collision occurs, it is most likely between only two packets. Thus, if new arrivals could be inhibited from transmission until the collision was resolved, each of the colliding packets could be independently retransmitted in the next slot with probability 1/2. This would lead to a successful transmission for one of the packets with probability 1/2, and the other could then be transmitted in the following slot. Alternatively, with probability 1/2, another collision or an idle slot occurs. In this case, each of the two packets would again be independently transmitted in the next slot with probability 1/2, and so forth until a successful transmission occurred, which would be followed by the transmission of the remaining packet.

With the above strategy, the two packets require two slots with probability

$1/2$, three slots with probability $1/4$, and i slots with probability $2^{-(i-1)}$. The expected number of slots for sending these two packets can thus be calculated to be three, yielding a throughput of $2/3$ for the period during which the collision is being resolved.

There are various ways in which the nodes involved in a collision could choose whether or not to transmit in successive slots. Each node could simply flip an unbiased coin for each choice. Alternatively (in a way to be described precisely later) each node could use the arrival time of its collided packet. Finally, assuming a finite set of nodes, each with a unique identifier represented by a string of bits, a node could use the successive bits of its identity to make the successive choices. This last alternative has the advantage of limiting the number of slots required to resolve a collision, since each pair of nodes must differ in at least one bit of their identifiers. All of these alternatives have the common property that the set of colliding nodes is split into subsets, one of which transmits in the next slot. If the collision is not resolved (*e.g.* if each colliding node is in the same subset), then a further splitting into subsets takes place. We call algorithms of this type *splitting algorithms*. In the subsequent development of these algorithms, we assume a slotted channel, Poisson arrivals, collisions or perfect reception, $(0, 1, e)$ immediate feedback, retransmission of collisions, and an infinite set of nodes, *i.e.*, the assumptions 1 to 6b of subsection 4.2.1.

4.3.1 Tree Algorithms

The first splitting algorithms were algorithms with a tree structure [Cap77], [TsM78], [Hay76]. When a collision occurs, say in the kth slot, all nodes not involved in the collision go into a waiting mode, and all those involved in the collision split into two subsets (*e.g.*, by each flipping a coin). The first subset transmits in slot $k + 1$, and if that slot is idle or successful, the second subset transmits in slot $k + 2$ (see Fig. 4.9). Alternatively, if another collision occurs in slot $k + 1$, then the first of the two subsets splits again, and the second subset waits for the resolution of that collision.

The rooted binary tree structure in Fig. 4.9 represents a particular pattern of idles, successes, and collisions resulting from such a sequence of splittings. S represents the set of packets in the original collision, and L (left) and R (right) represent the two subsets that S splits into. Similarly, LL and LR represent the two subsets that L splits into after L generates a collision. Each vertex in the tree corresponds to a subset (perhaps empty) of backlogged packets. Vertices whose subsets contain two or more packets have two upward branches corresponding to the splitting of the subset into two new subsets; vertices corresponding to subsets with 0 or 1 packet are leaf vertices of the tree.

The set of packets corresponding to the root vertex S is transmitted first, and after the transmission of the subset corresponding to any nonleaf vertex, the subset corresponding to the vertex on the left branch, and all of its descendant subsets, are transmitted before the subsets of the right branch. Given the immediate feedback

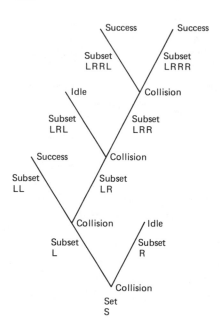

Slot	Xmit Set	Waiting Sets	Feedback
1	S	—	e
2	L	R	e
3	LL	LR, R	1
4	LR	R	e
5	LRL	LRR, R	0
6	LRR	R	e
7	LRRL	LRRR, R	1
8	LRRR	R	1
9	R	—	0

Figure 4.9   The tree algorithm. After a collision, all new arrivals wait and all nodes involved in the collision divide into subsets. Each successive collision in a subset causes that subset to again split into smaller subsets while other nodes wait.

we have assumed, it should be clear that each node, in principle, can construct this tree as the $0, 1, e$ feedback occurs; each node can keep track of its own subset in that tree, and thus each node can determine when to transmit its own backlogged packet.

The above transmission order corresponds to that of a stack. When a collision occurs, the subset involved is split, and each resulting subset is pushed on the stack (*i.e.*, each stack element is a subset of nodes); then the subset at the head of the stack (*i.e.*, the most recent subset pushed on the stack) is removed from the stack and transmitted. The list, from left to right, of waiting subsets in Fig. 4.9 corresponds to the stack elements starting at the head for the given slot. Note that a node with a backlogged packet can keep track of when to transmit by a counter determining the position of the packet's current subset on the stack. When the packet is involved in a collision, the counter is set to 0 or 1, corresponding to which subset the packet is placed in. When the counter is 0, the packet is transmitted, and if the counter is nonzero, it is incremented by 1 for each collision and decremented by 1 for each success or idle.

One problem with this tree algorithm is what to do with the new packet arrivals that come in while a collision is being resolved. A collision resolution period (CRP) is defined to be completed when a success or idle occurs and there are no remaining elements on the stack (*i.e.*, at the end of slot 9 in Fig. 4.9). At this time, a new CRP starts using the packets that arrived during the previous CRP. In the unlikely event that a great many slots are required in the previous CRP, there will be many new waiting arrivals, and these will collide and continue to collide until the subsets get small enough in this new CRP. The solution to this problem is as follows: at the end of a CRP, the set of nodes with new arrivals is immediately split into j subsets, where j is chosen so that the expected number of packets per subset is slightly greater than 1 (slightly greater because of the temporary high throughput available after a collision). These new subsets are then placed on the stack and the new CRP starts.

The tree algorithm is now essentially completely defined. Each node with a packet involved in the current CRP keeps track of its position in the stack as described above. All the nodes keep track of the number of elements on the stack and the number of slots since the end of the previous CRP. On the completion of that CRP, each node determines the expected number of waiting new arrivals, determines the new number j of subsets, and those nodes with waiting new arrivals randomly choose one of those j subsets and set their counter for the corresponding stack position.

The maximum throughput available with this algorithm, optimized over the choice of j as a function of expected number of waiting packets, is 0.43 packets per slot [Cap77]; we omit any analysis since we next show some simple ways of improving this throughput.

Improvements to the Tree Algorithm

First consider the situation in Fig. 4.10. Here, in slots 4 and 5, a collision is followed by an idle slot; this means that all the packets involved in the collision were assigned to the second subset. The tree algorithm would simply transmit this second subset, generating a guaranteed collision. An improvement results by omitting the transmission of this second subset, splitting it into two subsets, and transmitting the first subset. Similarly, if an idle again occurs, the second subset is again split before transmission and so forth.

This improvement can be visualized in terms of a stack and implemented by manipulating counters just like the original tree algorithm. Each node must now keep track of an additional binary state variable that takes the value 1 if, for some $i \geq 1$, the last i slots contained a collision followed by $i - 1$ idles; otherwise the state variable takes the value 0. If the feedback for the current slot is 0 and the state variable has the value 1, then the state variable maintains the value 1 and the subset on the top of the stack is split into two subsets that are pushed onto the stack in place of the original head element.

The maximum throughput with this improvement is 0.46 packets per slot [Mas80]. In practice, this improvement has a slight problem in that if an idle slot is incorrectly perceived by the receiver as a collision, then the algorithm continues splitting indefinitely, never making further successful transmissions. Thus, in practice, after some number h of idle slots followed by splits, the algorithm should

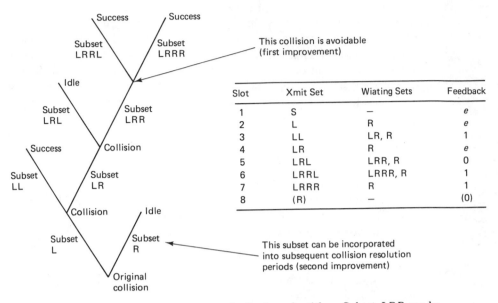

Slot	Xmit Set	Wiating Sets	Feedback
1	S	—	e
2	L	R	e
3	LL	LR, R	1
4	LR	R	e
5	LRL	LRR, R	0
6	LRRL	LRRR, R	1
7	LRRR	R	1
8	(R)	—	(0)

Figure 4.10   Improvements in the tree algorithm. Subset LRR can be split without first being transmitted since the feedback implies that it contains two or more packets. Also subset R is better combined with new arrivals since the number of packets in it is Poisson with an undesirably low rate.

be modified to simply transmit the next subset on the stack without first splitting it; if the feedback is very reliable, h can be moderately large, whereas otherwise h should be small.

The next improvement in the tree algorithm not only improves throughput but also greatly simplifies the analysis. Consider what happens when a collision is followed by another collision in the tree algorithm (see slots 1 and 2 of Fig. 4.10). Let x be the number of packets in the first collision and let x_L and x_R be the number of packets in the resultant subsets; thus, $x = x_L + x_R$. Assume that, apriori, before knowing that there is a collision, x is a Poisson random variable. Visualize splitting these x packets, by coin flip, say, into the two subsets with x_L and x_R packets, respectively, before knowing about the collision. Then apriori x_L and x_R are independent Poisson random variables each with half the mean value of x. Given the two collisions, then, x_L and x_R are independent Poisson random variables conditional on $x_L + x_R \geq 2$ and $x_L \geq 2$. The second condition implies the first, so the first can be omitted; this means that x_R, conditional on the feedback, is still Poisson with its original unconditional distribution. Problem 4.17 demonstrates this result in a more computational and less abstract way. Thus, rather than devoting a slot to this second subset, which has an undesirably small expected number of packets, it is better to regard the second subset as just another part of the waiting new arrivals that have never been involved in a collision.

When the above idea is incorporated into an actual algorithm, the first-come first-serve (FCFS) splitting algorithm, which is the subject of the next subsection, results. Before discussing this, we describe some variants of the tree algorithm.

Variants of the Tree Algorithm

The tree algorithm as described above requires all nodes to monitor the channel feedback and to keep track of when each collision resolution period ends. This is a disadvantage if the receivers at nodes are turned off when there are no packets to send. One way to avoid this disadvantage while maintaining the other features of the tree algorithm is to have new arrivals simply join the subset of nodes at the head of the stack. Thus, only currently backlogged nodes need to monitor the channel feedback. Algorithms of this type are called *unblocked stack algorithms*, indicating that new arrivals are not blocked until the end of the current collision resolution period. In contrast, the tree algorithm is often called a blocked stack algorithm.

With the tree algorithm, new arrivals are split into a variable number of subsets at the beginning of each collision resolution period, and then subsets are split into two subsets after each collision. With an unblocked stack algorithm, on the other hand, new arrivals are constantly being added to the subset at the head of the stack, and thus, collisions involve a somewhat larger number of packets on the average. Because of the relatively large likelihood of three or more packets in a collision, higher maximum throughputs can be achieved by splitting collision sets into three subsets rather than two. The maximum throughput thus available for unblocked stack algorithms is 0.40 [MaF85].

4.3.2 First-Come First-Serve Splitting Algorithms

In the second improvement to the tree algorithm described above, the second subset involved in a collision is treated as if it had never been transmitted if the first subset contains two or more packets. Recall also that a set of colliding packets can be split into two subsets in a variety of ways, *e.g.*, by coin flipping, by node identities, or by arrival time. For our present purposes, the simplest choice is splitting by arrival time. By using this approach, each subset will consist of all packets that arrived in some given interval, and when a collision occurs, that interval will be split into two smaller intervals. By always transmitting the earlier arriving interval first, the algorithm will always transmit successful packets in the order of their arrival, leading to the name first-come first-serve (FCFS).

At each integer time k, the algorithm specifies the packets to be transmitted in slot k (*i.e.*, from k to $k+1$) to be the set of all packets that arrived in some earlier interval, say from $T(k)$ to $T(k)+\alpha(k)$. This interval is called the *allocation interval* for slot k (see Fig. 4.11). We can visualize the packets arriving after $T(k) + \alpha(k)$ as being in a queue and those arriving between $T(k)$ and $T(k) + \alpha(k)$ as being in service. What is peculiar about this queue is that the number of packets in it is

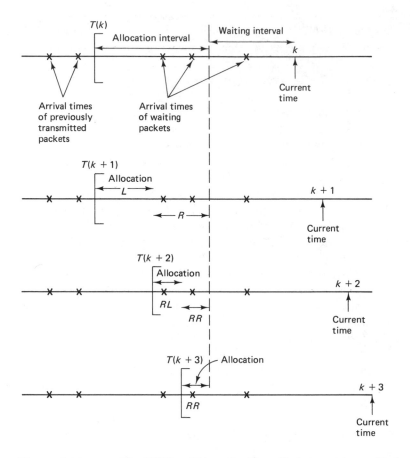

Figure 4.11   The FCFS splitting algorithm. Packets are transmitted in order of arrival. On collisions, the allocation interval generating a collision is split into two subintervals, with the left-most (earlier arrivals) transmitting first.

unknown, although the nodes all keep track of the allocation interval over which service (*i.e.*, transmission) is taking place.

The FCFS splitting algorithm is the set of rules by which the nodes calculate $T(k)$ and $\alpha(k)$ for each successive k on the basis of the feedback from the previous slot. These rules are simply the improved rules for the tree algorithm previously discussed, specialized to the case where sets of nodes are split in terms of packet arrival times.

Figure 4.11 illustrates these rules. When a collision occurs, as in slot k, the allocation interval is split into two equal subintervals and the left-most (*i.e.*, longest waiting) subinterval L is the allocation interval in slot $k+1$. Thus, $T(k+1) = T(k)$ (*i.e.*, the left boundary is unchanged) and $\alpha(k+1) = \alpha(k)/2$. When an idle, as in slot $k+1$, follows a collision, the first improvement to the tree algorithm is

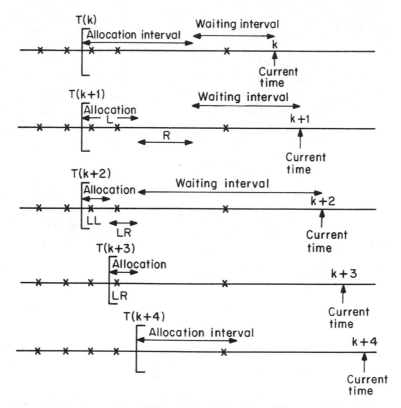

Figure 4.12   The FCFS splitting algorithm. When a collision follows another collision, the interval on the right side of the second collision is returned to the waiting interval. The CRP is completed in slot $k + 3$, and a new CRP is started with an allocation interval of fixed size.

employed. The previous right-most interval R is known to contain two or more packets and is immediately split, with RL forming the allocation interval for slot $k + 2$. Thus, $T(k + 2) = T(k + 1) + \alpha(k + 1)$ and $\alpha(k + 2) = \alpha(k + 1)/2$. Finally, successful transmissions occur in slots $k + 2$ and $k + 3$, completing the CRP.

Next consider the example of Fig. 4.12. Here a collision in slot k is followed by another collision in slot $k+1$. Here the second improvement to the tree algorithm is employed. Since interval L contains two or more packets, the collision in slot k tells us nothing about interval R, and we would like to regard R as if it had never been part of an allocation interval. As shown for slot k $+$ 2, this is simplicity itself. The interval L is split, with LL forming the next allocation interval and LR waiting; the algorithm simply forgets R. When LL and LR are successfully transmitted in slots $k + 2$ and $k + 3$, the CRP is complete.

In the tree algorithm, at the end of a CRP, all the waiting packets split into some number of subsets. Here, since the splitting is being done by allocation intervals in time, it is more appropriate to simply choose a new allocation interval of some given size, say α_0, to be discussed later. Note that this new interval, in slot $k+4$, includes the old interval R that previously lost its identity as a separate interval.

In terms of the tree of waiting subsets, the effect of having a right interval lose its identity whenever the corresponding left interval is split is to prune the tree so that it never has more than two leaves (correspondingly, the stack never remembers more than the top two elements). Whenever the allocation interval corresponds to the left subset of a split, there is a corresponding right subset that might have to be transmitted later. Conversely, when the allocation interval corresponds to a right subset, there are no more waiting intervals. Thus, the nodes in this algorithm need only remember the location of the allocation interval and whether it is a left or right interval. By convention, the initial interval of a CRP is regarded as a right interval. We can now state the algorithm followed by each node precisely. The algorithm gives the allocation interval (*i.e.*, $T(k)$ and $\alpha(k)$) and the status ($\sigma = L$ or R) for slot k in terms of the feedback, allocation interval, and status from slot $k-1$.

If feedback $= e$, then

$$
\begin{aligned}
T(k) &= T(k-1) \\
\alpha(k) &= \alpha(k-1)/2 \\
\sigma(k) &= L
\end{aligned}
\tag{4.15}
$$

If feedback $= 1$ and $\sigma(k-1) = L$, then

$$
\begin{aligned}
T(k) &= T(k-1) + \alpha(k-1) \\
\alpha(k) &= \alpha(k-1) \\
\sigma(k) &= R
\end{aligned}
\tag{4.16}
$$

If feedback $= 0$ and $\sigma(k-1) = L$, then

$$
\begin{aligned}
T(k) &= T(k-1) + \alpha(k-1) \\
\alpha(k) &= \alpha(k-1)/2 \\
\sigma(k) &= L
\end{aligned}
\tag{4.17}
$$

If feedback $= 0$ or 1 and $\sigma(k-1) = R$, then

$$
\begin{aligned}
T(k) &= T(k-1) + \alpha(k-1) \\
\alpha(k) &= \min[\alpha_0, k - T(k)] \\
\sigma(k) &= R
\end{aligned}
\tag{4.18}
$$

The final statement, Eq. (4.18) is used at the end of a collision resolution or when no collisions are being resolved. The size of the new allocation interval in

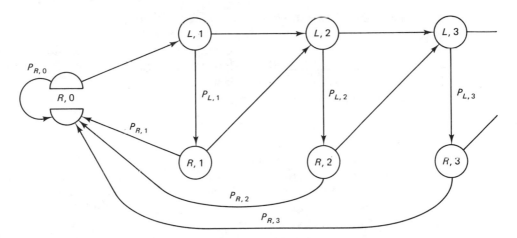

Figure 4.13   The Markov chain for FCFS splitting algorithm. The top states are entered after splitting an interval and correspond to the transmission of the left side of that inteval. The lower states are entered after success on the left side and correspond to transmission of the right side. Transitions from top to bottom and from bottom back to $R, 0$ correspond to successes.

this case is some constant value α_0 which could be chosen either to minimize delay for a given arrival rate or to maximize the stable throughput. Naturally, when the queue becomes depleted, the allocation interval cannot include packets that have not yet arrived, so the interval size is limited to $k - T(k)$, as indicated by the min operation in Eq. (4.18).

Analysis of FCFS Splitting Algorithm

Figure 4.13 is helpful in visualizing the evolution of a collision resolution period; we shall see later that the diagram can be interpreted as a Markov chain. The node at the left side of the diagram corresponds to the initial slot of a CRP; the node is split in two as an artifice to visualize the beginning and end of a CRP. If an idle or success occurs, the CRP ends immediately and a new CRP starts on the next slot. Alternatively, if a collision occurs, a transition occurs to node $(L, 1)$; L indicates the status and the 1 indicates that one split in the allocation interval has occurred.

Each subsequent idle or collision from a left allocation interval generates one additional split with a smaller left allocation interval, corresponding to a transition in the diagram from (L, i) to $(L, i + 1)$ where i is the number of times the original allocation interval has been split. A success from a left interval leads to a right interval with no additional split, corresponding to an (L, i) to (R, i) transition. A success from a right interval ends the CRP, with a transition back to $(R, 0)$, whereas a collision causes a new split, with a transition from (R, i) to $(L, i + 1)$.

We now analyze a single CRP. Assume that the size of the initial allocation interval is α_0. Each splitting of the allocation interval decreases this by a factor of

2, so that nodes (L, i) and (R, i) in the diagram correspond to allocation intervals of size $2^{-i}\alpha_0$. Given our assumption of a Poisson arrival process of rate λ, the number of packets in the original allocation interval is a Poisson random variable with mean $\lambda\alpha_0$. Similarly, the apriori distributions on the numbers of packets in disjoint subintervals are independent and Poisson. Define G_i as the expected number of packets, apriori, in an interval that has been split i times,

$$G_i = 2^{-i}\lambda\alpha_0 \qquad (4.19)$$

We next find the transition probabilities in Fig. 4.13 and show that they constitute a Markov chain, *i.e.*, that each transition is independent of the path used to reach the given node. Note that we are only interested (for now) in one period of collision resolution; we view the upper half of node $(R, 0)$ as the starting state and the lower half as the final state. We start from the left side and work to the right. $P_{R,0}$ is the probability of an idle or success (*i.e.*, 0 or 1 packet) in the first slot. Since the number of packets in the initial allocation interval is Poisson with mean G_0, the probability of 0 or 1 packets is

$$P_{R,0} = (1 + G_0)e^{-G_0} \qquad (4.20)$$

Next consider the state $(L, 1)$. This state is entered after a collision in state $(R, 0)$, which occurs with probability $1 - P_{R,0}$. Let x_L be the number of packets in the new allocation interval L (*i.e.*, the left half of the original interval), and let x_R be the number in R, the right half of the original interval. Apriori, x_L and x_R are independent Poisson random variables of mean G_1 each. The condition that $(L, 1)$ is entered is the condition that $x_L + x_R \geq 2$. The probability of success $P_{L,1}$ is thus the probability that $x_L = 1$ conditional on $x_L + x_R \geq 2$. Noting that both $x_L = 1$ and $x_L + x_R \geq 2$ occur if and only if $x_L = 1$ and $x_R \geq 1$, we have

$$P_{L,1} = \frac{P\{x_L = 1\}P\{x_R \geq 1\}}{P\{x_L + x_R \geq 2\}} = \frac{G_1 e^{-G_1}[1 - e^{-G_1}]}{1 - (1 + G_0)e^{-G_0}} \qquad (4.21)$$

State $(R, 1)$ is entered if and only if the above transition takes place, *i.e.*, if $x_L = 1$ and $x_R \geq 1$. Thus, the probability of success $P_{R,1}$ in state $(R, 1)$ is

$$P_{R,1} = \frac{P\{x_R = 1\}}{P\{x_R \geq 1\}} = \frac{G_1 e^{-G_1}}{1 - e^{-G_1}} \qquad (4.22)$$

We next show that Eqs. (4.21) and (4.22) generalize to $P_{L,i}$ and $P_{R,i}$ for all $i \geq 1$. That is,

$$P_{L,i} = \frac{G_i e^{-G_i}(1 - e^{-G_i})}{1 - (1 + G_{i-1})e^{-G_{i-1}}} \qquad (4.23)$$

$$P_{R,i} = \frac{G_i e^{-G_i}}{1 - e^{-G_i}} \qquad (4.24)$$

Consider state $(L, 2)$. This can be entered by a collision in state $(L, 1)$, an idle in $(L, 1)$, or a collision in $(R, 1)$. In the first case, interval L is split into LL and LR, and LL becomes the new allocation interval. In the second and third cases, R is split into RL and RR, with RL becoming the new allocation interval. For the first case, let x_{LL} and x_{LR} be the numbers of packets in LL and LR, respectively. Apriori, these are independent Poisson random variables of mean G_2 each. The collision from $(L, 1)$ means that $x_L + x_R \geq 2$ and $x_L \geq 2$, which is equivalent to the single condition $x_L \geq 2$. The situation is thus the same as in finding $P_{L,1}$ except that the intervals are half as large, so $P_{L,2}$ in Eq. (4.23) is correct in this case.

Next, consider the second case, that of an idle in $(L, 1)$. This means that $x_L + x_R \geq 2$ and $x_L = 0$, which is equivalent to $x_R \geq 2$ and $x_L = 0$. $P_{L,2}$ in this case is the probability that RL, the left half of R, contains one packet given that R contains at least two; again Eq. (4.23) is correct. Finally, for the case of a collision in $(R, 1)$, we have $x_L + x_R \geq 2$, $x_L = 1$, and $x_R \geq 2$, or equivalently $x_L = 1$, $x_R \geq 2$; Eq. (4.23) is again correct for $(L, 2)$. Thus, the Markov condition is satisfied for $(L, 2)$.

Generally, no matter how $(L, 2)$ is entered, the given interval L or R preceding $(L, 2)$ is an interval of size $\alpha_0/2$ of a Poisson process, conditional on the given interval containing two or more packets. If a success occurs on the left half, then the number of packets in the right half is Poisson, conditional on being one or more, yielding the expression for $P_{R,2}$ in Eq. (4.24). This argument repeats for $i = 3, 4, \ldots$ (or, more formally, induction can be applied). Thus, Fig. 4.13 is a Markov chain and Eqs. (4.20), (4.23), and (4.24) give the transition probabilities.

The analysis of this chain is particularly simple since no state can be entered more than once before the return to $(R, 0)$. The probabilities, $p(L, i)$ and $p(R, i)$, that (L, i) and (R, i) respectively are entered before returning to $(R, 0)$ can be calculated iteratively from the initial state $(R, 0)$:

$$p(L, 1) = 1 - P_{R,0} \tag{4.25}$$

$$p(R, i) = P_{L,i}\, p(L, i); \qquad i \geq 1 \tag{4.26}$$

$$p(L, i + 1) = (1 - P_{L,i})\, p(L, i) + (1 - P_{R,i}) p(R, i); \qquad i \geq 1 \tag{4.27}$$

Let K be the number of slots in a CRP; thus, K is the number of states visited in the chain, including the initial state $(R, 0)$, before the return to $(R, 0)$,

$$E\{K\} = 1 + \sum_{i=1}^{\infty} [p(L, i) + p(R, i)] \tag{4.28}$$

We also must evaluate the change in $T(k)$ from one CRP to the next. For the assumed initial interval of size α_0, this change is at most α_0, but, if left-hand intervals have collisions, then the corresponding right-hand intervals are returned to the waiting interval, and the change is less than α_0. Let f be the fraction of α_0 returned in this way over a CRP, so that $\alpha_0(1 - f)$ is the change in $T(k)$. The probability of a collision in state (L, i) is the probability that the left half interval in state (L, i) contains at least two packets given that the right and left intervals together contain at least two; *i.e.*,

$$P\{e \mid (L, i)\} = \frac{1 - (1 + G_i)e^{-G_i}}{1 - (1 + G_{i-1})e^{-G_{i-1}}} \tag{4.29}$$

The fraction of the original interval returned on such a collision is 2^{-i}, so the expected value of f is

$$E\{f\} = \sum_{i=1}^{\infty} p(L, i)P\{e \mid (L, i)\}2^{-i} \tag{4.30}$$

Note that $E\{f\}$ and $E\{K\}$ are functions only of $G_i = \lambda\alpha_0 2^{-i}$, for $i \geq 1$, and hence are functions only of the product $\lambda\alpha_0$. For large i, $P_{L,i}$ tends to $1/2$, and thus $p(L, i)$ and $p(R, i)$ tend to zero with increasing i as 2^{-i}. Thus, $E\{f\}$ and $E\{K\}$ can be easily evaluated numerically as functions of $\lambda\alpha_0$.

Finally, define the drift D to be the expected change in the time backlog, $k - T(k)$, over a CRP (again assuming an initial allocation of α_0). This is the expected number of slots in a CRP less the expected change in $T(k)$; so

$$D = E\{K\} - \alpha_0(1 - E\{f\}) \tag{4.31}$$

The drift is negative if $E\{K\} < \alpha_0(1 - E\{f\})$, or equivalently, if

$$\lambda < \frac{\lambda\alpha_0(1 - E\{f\})}{E\{K\}} \tag{4.32}$$

The right side of Eq. (4.32), as a function of $\lambda\alpha_0$, has a numerically evaluated maximum of 0.4871 at $\lambda\alpha_0 = 1.266$. $\lambda\alpha_0$ is the expected number of packets in the original allocation interval; as expected, it is somewhat larger than 1 (which would maximize the initial probability of success) because of the increased probability of success immediately after a collision. If α_0 is chosen to be 2.6 (*i.e.*, $1.266/0.4871$), then Eq. (4.32) is satisfied for all $\lambda < 0.4871$. Thus, the expected time backlog decreases (whenever it is initially larger than α_0), and we conclude* that the algorithm is stable for $\lambda < 0.4871$.

---

* For the mathematician, a more rigorous proof of stability is desirable. Define a busy period as a consecutive string of CRPs starting with a time backlog $k - T(k) < \alpha_0$ and continuing up to the beginning of the next CRP with $k - T(k) < \alpha_0$. The sequence of time backlogs at the beginnings of the CRPs in the busy period forms a random walk with the increments (except the first) having identical distributions with negative expectation for $\lambda < 0.4871$. Since $p(L, i)$ approaches 0 exponentially in i, the increments have a moment generating function, and from Wald's equality, the number N of CRPs in a busy period also has a moment generating function. Since the number of slots in a busy period is at most $N\alpha_0$, the number of slots also has a moment generating function, from which it follows that the expected delay per packet is finite.

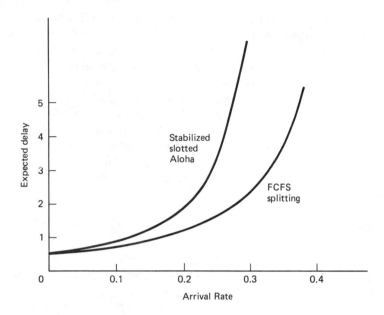

Figure 4.14   Comparison of expected delay for stabilized slotted Aloha and the FCFS splitting algorithm as a function of arrival rate. One becomes unbounded as the arrival rate approaches $1/e$, and the other as the arrival rate approaches 0.4871.

Expected delay is much harder to analyze than maximum stable throughput. Complex upper and lower bounds have been developed [HuB85, TsL80] and correspond closely to simulation results. Figure 4.14 plots this delay and compares it with stabilized slotted Aloha.

Improvements in the FCFS Splitting Algorithm

Splitting intervals into equal sized subintervals is slightly nonoptimal in achieving maximum stable throughput. When each interval is split into the optimally sized subintervals, the maximum stable throughput increases to 0.4878 [MoH79], [TsM80]. Another, even smaller, improvement of 3.6×10^{-7} results if, in state (R, i) for large i, some of the waiting interval is appended to the right side interval [VeP83]. While these improvements are not significant practically, they are of theoretical interest in determining optimality in terms of maximum stable throughput.

The maximum stable throughput, using assumptions 1 to 6b, is currently unknown. Considerable research has been devoted to finding upper bounds to throughput, and the tightest such bound is 0.587 [MiT81]. Thus, the maximum stable throughput achievable by any algorithm lies somewhere between 0.4878 and 0.587.

These questions of maximum throughput depend strongly on assumptions 1 to

6b. For any finite set of m nodes, we have seen that TDM can trivially achieve any throughput up to one packet per slot. This striking difference between finite and infinite m seems paradoxical until we recognize that with TDM, expected delay (for a given λ) increases linearly with m, whereas the algorithms that assume $m = \infty$ achieve a delay bounded independently of m.

We shall also see in the next two sections that much higher throughputs than 0.4878 are achievable if the slotted assumption is abandoned and early feedback is available when the channel is idle or experiencing a collision. Finally, rather surprisingly, if the feedback is expanded to specify the number of packets in each collision, then maximum stable throughput again increases to 1 [Pip81]. Unfortunately, this type of feedback is difficult to achieve in practice, and no algorithms are known for achieving these high throughputs even if the feedback were available.

Practical Details

The FCFS splitting algorithm is subject to the same deadlock problem as the first improvement on the tree algorithm if the feedback from an idle slot is mistaken as a collision. As before, this deadlock condition is eliminated by specifying a maximum number h of successive repetitions of Eq. (4.17) in the algorithm. On the $(h+1)^{\text{th}}$ successive idle after a collision, Eq. (4.16) is performed.

Also, the algorithm assumes that nodes can measure arrival times with infinite precision. In practice, if arrival times are measured with a finite number of bits, each node would generate extra bits, as needed for splitting, by a pseudo random number generator.

Last-Come First-Serve (LCFS) Splitting Algorithm

The FCFS splitting algorithm requires all nodes to monitor the channel feedback at all times. A recent modification allows nodes to monitor the feedback only after receiving a packet to transmit [Hum85], [MeP85]. The idea is to send packets in approximately last-come first-serve (LCFS) order; thus, the most recently arrived packets need not know the length of the waiting set since they have first priority in transmission.

Figure 4.15 illustrates this variation. New arrivals are in a "prewaiting mode" until they receive enough feedback to detect the end of a CRP; they then join the waiting set. The end of a CRP can be detected by feedback equal to 1 in one slot followed by either 0 or 1 in the next. Also, assuming the practical modification in which Eq. (4.17) can be repeated at most h successive times, feedback of h successive 0's followed by 1 or 0 also implies the end of a CRP.

After the waiting set has been extended on the right by the interval of time over which nodes can detect the end of the CRP, a new allocation set is chosen at the right end of the waiting set (thus, including part or all of the new interval). As shown in the figure, the waiting set, and consequently the allocation set, might consist of several disjoint intervals.

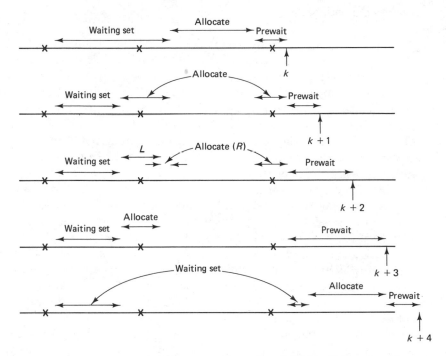

Figure 4.15   The last-come first-serve (LCFS) splitting algorithm. Arrivals wait for the beginning of a new CRP, but then are allocted in last-come first-serve fashion. Allocation sets and waiting sets can consist of more than one interval.

Backlogged nodes, after joining the waiting set keep track of their distance from the right end of the waiting set. This distance includes only unresolved intervals and unallocated (left or right) intervals. Nodes in the allocation set similarly track their distance from the right end of the allocation set. When a collision occurs, the allocated set splits as before, but here the right half is allocated next. Upon a right half collision, the corresponding left half is adjoined to the right end of the waiting set, increasing the distance of the right end from the previously waiting nodes. At the end of a CRP, the new arrival interval from which this event is detectable is first appended to the right end of the waiting set, and then the new allocation set is removed from the right end. Nodes do not know where the left end of the waiting set is, and thus the allocation set always has size α_0 (not counting gaps), with perhaps dummy space at the left.

When the backlog is large, the LCFS splitting algorithm has the same drift as the FCFS splitting algorithm, and thus it is stable for the same range of λ. With increasing h (where h is the allowable number of repetitions of Eq. (4.17) in the algorithm), the upper limit of this range approaches 0.4871 as before. The expected delay is somewhat larger than that for FCFS, primarily because of the time packets spend in the prewaiting mode.

Delayed Feedback

Assume that the feedback for the kth slot arrives sometime between the beginning of slot $k+j-1$ and $k+j$ for some fixed $j > 1$. Visualize time-division multiplexing the slots on the channel between j different versions of the FCFS splitting algorithm, with the exception of maintaining a common waiting set for all j algorithms. Each node monitors the progress of each of the j current CRPs and tracks the extent of the waiting set. At the end of a CRP for one of the j versions, an allocation set of size α_0 (or less if the waiting set is smaller) is removed from the left end of the waiting set to start the next CRP on that version. Since the j versions experience different delays, packets are no longer served in first-come first-serve order.

When a right subset is returned to the waiting set due to a collision in a left subset for one of the j versions, it is appended to the left end of the waiting set. These returns can fragment the waiting set into disjoint intervals, but nodes need only keep track of the size of the set not counting the gaps.

The same analysis as before justifies that the maximum stable throughput for any finite j is still 0.4871. The expected delay is larger than that of FCFS splitting because of the additional time required to resolve collisions. Note that the delay can essentially be considered as having two components—first, the delay in resolving collisions, which increases roughly with j, and, second, the delay in the waiting set, which is roughly independent of j. For large j and small λ, this suggests that α_0 should be reduced, thus reducing the frequency of collisions at some expense to the waiting set size.

Round Robin Splitting

A final variation of the FCFS splitting algorithm [HlG81] can be applied if there is an identifiable finite collection of nodes numbered 1 to m. Consider the nodes to be arranged conceptually in a circle with node $i+1$ following i, $1 \le i < m$, and node 1 following m. Rather than forming allocation sets in terms of packet arrival times, an allocation set consists of a contiguous set of nodes, say i to j around the circle. After completion of a CRP, the algorithm then allocates the next successive set of nodes around the circle. The size of allocation sets initiating CRPs varies with the time to pass around the circle, so that under light loading, an initial allocation set would contain all nodes, whereas under heavy loading, initial allocation sets would shrink to single nodes, which is equivalent to TDM.

4.4 CARRIER SENSING

In many multiaccess systems, such as local area networks, a node can hear whether other nodes are transmitting after a very small propagation and detection delay relative to a packet transmission time. The detection delay is the time required for a physical receiver to determine whether or not some other node is currently transmitting. This delay differs somewhat from the delay, first, in detecting the beginning of a new transmission, second, in synchronizing on the reception of a new transmission, and third, in detecting the end of an old transmission. We ignore these and other subtleties of the physical layer in what follows, and simply regard the medium as an intermittent synchronous multiaccess bit pipe on which idle periods can be distinguished (with delay) from packet transmission periods.

If nodes can detect idle periods quickly, it is reasonable to terminate idle periods quickly and to allow nodes to initiate packet transmissions after such idle detections. This type of strategy is called carrier sense multiple access (CSMA) [KlT75], and docs not necessarily imply the use of a carrier but simply the ability to quickly detect idle periods.

Let β be the propagation and detection delay (in packet transmission units) required for all sources to detect an idle channel after a transmission ends. Thus if τ is this time in seconds, C is the raw channel bit rate, and L is the expected number of bits in a data packet, then

$$\beta = \frac{\tau C}{L} \tag{4.33}$$

We shall see that the performance of CSMA degrades with increasing β and thus also degrades with increasing channel rate and with decreasing packet size.

Consider a slotted system in which, if nothing is being transmitted in a slot, then the slot terminates after β time units and a new slot begins. This assumption of dividing idle periods into slots of length β is not realistic, but it provides a simple model with good insight. We have thus eliminated our previous assumption that time is slotted into equal duration slots. We also eliminate our assumption that all data packets are of equal length, although we still assume a time normalization in which the expected packet transmission time is 1. In place of the instantaneous feedback assumption, we assume $0, 1, e$ feedback with a maximum delay β, as indicated above. For simplicity, we continue to assume an infinite set of nodes and Poisson arrivals of overall intensity λ. We first modify slotted Aloha for this new situation, then consider unslotted systems, and finally consider the FCFS splitting algorithm.

4.4.1 CSMA Slotted Aloha

The major difference between CSMA slotted Aloha and ordinary slotted Aloha is that idle slots in CSMA have a duration β. The other difference is that if a packet arrives at a node while a transmission is in progress, the packet is regarded as backlogged and begins transmission with probability q_r after each subsequent idle slot; packets arriving during an idle slot are transmitted in the next slot as usual. This technique was called nonpersistent CSMA in [KlT75] to distinguish it from two variations. In one variation, persistent CSMA, all arrivals during a busy slot simply postpone transmission to the end of that slot, thus causing a collision with relatively high probability. In the other, P-persistent CSMA, collided packets and new packets waiting for the end of a busy period use different probabilities for transmission. Aside from occasional comments, we will ignore these variations since they have no conceptual advantages over nonpersistent CSMA.

To analyze CSMA Aloha, we can use a Markov chain again, using the number n of backlogged packets as the state and the ends of idle slots as the state transition times. Note that each busy slot (success or collision) must be followed by an idle slot, since nodes are allowed to start transmission only after detecting an idle slot. For simplicity, we assume that all data packets have unit length. The extension to arbitrary length packets is not difficult, however, and is treated in Prob. 4.21. The time between successive state transitions is either β (in the case of an idle slot) or $1 + \beta$ (in the case of a busy slot followed by an idle). Rather than present the state transition equations, which are not particularly insightful, we simply modify the drift in Eq. (4.4) for this new model. At a transition into state n (i.e., at the end of an idle slot), the probability of no transmissions in the following slot (and hence the probability of an idle slot) is $e^{-\lambda\beta}(1 - q_r)^n$. The first term is the probability of no arrivals in the previous idle slot, and the second is the probability of no transmissions by the backlogged nodes. Thus, the expected time between state transitions in state n is $\beta + [1 - e^{-\lambda\beta}(1 - q_r)^n]$. Similarly, the expected number of arrivals between state transitions is

$$E\{\text{Arrivals}\} = \lambda[\beta + 1 - e^{-\lambda\beta}(1 - q_r)^n] \tag{4.34}$$

The expected number of departures between state transitions in state n is simply the probability of a successful transmission; assuming $q_r < 1$ this is given by

$$P_{\text{succ}} = [\lambda\beta + q_r n/(1 - q_r)]e^{-\lambda\beta}(1 - q_r)^n \tag{4.35}$$

The drift in state n is defined as the expected number of arrivals less the expected number of departures between state transitions,

$$D_n = \lambda[\beta + 1 - e^{-\lambda\beta}(1 - q_r)^n] - [\lambda\beta + q_r n/(1 - q_r)]e^{-\lambda\beta}(1 - q_r)^n \tag{4.36}$$

For small q_r, we can make the approximation $(1 - q_r)^{n-1} \approx (1 - q_r)^n \approx e^{-q_r n}$, and D_n can be expressed as

$$D_n \approx \lambda\left(\beta + 1 - e^{-g(n)}\right) - g(n)e^{-g(n)} \tag{4.37}$$

where

$$g(n) = \lambda\beta + q_r n \tag{4.38}$$

is the expected number of attempted transmissions following a transition to state n. From Eq. (4.37), the drift in state n is negative if

$$\lambda < \frac{g(n)e^{-g(n)}}{\beta + 1 - e^{-g(n)}} \tag{4.39}$$

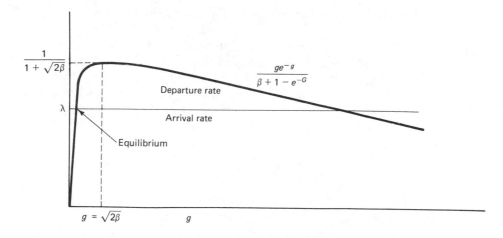

Figure 4.16   The departure rate, in packets per unit time, for CSMA slotted Aloha as a function of the attempted transmission rate g in packets per idle slot. If β, the duration of an idle slot as a fraction of a data slot, is small, the maximum departure rate is $1/(1 + \sqrt{2\beta})$.

The numerator in Eq. (4.39) is the expected number of departures per state transition, and the denominator is the expected duration of a state transition period; thus, the ratio can be interpreted as departure rate (*i.e.*, expected departures per unit time) in state n.   Figure 4.16 plots this ratio as a function of $g(n) = \lambda\beta + q_r n$.   For small β, this function has a maximum of approximately $1/(1 + \sqrt{2\beta})$ at $g(n) = \sqrt{2\beta}$.   This can be seen by approximating $e^{g(n)}$ by $1 + g(n) + g^2(n)/2$ for small $g(n)$.   To understand intuitively why the departure rate is maximized at $g = \sqrt{2\beta}$, note that for small β, very little time is wasted on a single idle slot, and significant time is wasted on a collision.   The point $g = \sqrt{2\beta}$ is where idles occur so much more frequently than collisions that the same expected overall time is wasted on each.

Figure 4.16 also shows that CSMA Aloha has the same stability problem as ordinary slotted Aloha.   For fixed q_r, $g(n)$ grows with the backlog n, and when n becomes too large, the departure rate is less than the arrival rate, leading to yet larger backlog.   From a practical standpoint, however, the stability problem is less serious for CSMA than for ordinary Aloha.   Note that β/q_r is the expected idle time that a backlogged node must wait to attempt transmission, and for small β and modest λ, q_r can be quite small without causing appreciable delay.   This means that the backlog must be very large before instability sets in, and one might choose to simply ignore the problem.

P-persistent CSMA, in which packets are transmitted after idle slots with probability p if they are new arrivals and transmitted with some much smaller probability q_r if they have had collisions, is a rudimentary way of obtaining a little extra protection against instability.   The next section explores stabilization in a more fundamental way.

4.4.2 Pseudo-Bayesian Stabilization for CSMA Aloha

Consider all packets as backlogged immediately after entering the system. At the end of each idle slot, each backlogged packet is independently transmitted with probability q_r, which will vary with the estimated channel backlog $\hat{n}$. In state n, the expected number of packets transmitted at the end of an idle slot is $g(n) = nq_r$. Since we have seen that the packet departure rate (in packets per unit time) is maximized (for small β and q_r) by $g(n) = \sqrt{2\beta}$, we choose q_r, for a given estimated backlog $\hat{n}$, as

$$q_r(\hat{n}) = \min\left[\frac{\sqrt{2\beta}}{\hat{n}}, \sqrt{2\beta}\right] \tag{4.40}$$

The min operation prevents $q_r(\hat{n})$ from getting too large when $\hat{n}$ is small; we cannot expect $n/\hat{n}$ to approach 1 when the backlog is small, and it is desirable to prevent too many collisions in this case. The appropriate rule for updating the estimated backlog (again assuming unit length packets) is

$$\hat{n}_{k+1} = \begin{cases} \hat{n}_k[1 - q_r(\hat{n}_k)] + \lambda\beta & \text{for idle} \\ \hat{n}_k[1 - q_r(\hat{n}_k)] + \lambda(1 + \beta) & \text{for success} \\ \hat{n}_k + 2 + \lambda(1 + \beta) & \text{for collision} \end{cases} \tag{4.41}$$

This rule is motivated by the fact that if the apriori distribution of n_k is Poisson with mean $\hat{n}_k$, then, given an idle, the aposteriori distribution of n_k is Poisson with mean $\hat{n}_k[1 - q_r(\hat{n}_k)]$ (see Prob. 4.20). Accounting for the Poisson arrivals in the idle slot of duration β, the resulting distribution of n_{k+1} is Poisson with mean $\hat{n}_{k+1}$ as shown above. Similarly, given a successful transmission, the aposteriori distribution on $n_k - 1$ (removing the successful packet) is Poisson with mean $\hat{n}_k[1 - q_r(\hat{n}_k)]$. Accounting for the Poisson arrivals in the successful slot and following idle slot, n_{k+1} is Poisson with mean $\hat{n}_{k+1}$ as shown. Finally, if a collision occurs, the aposteriori distribution of n_k is not quite Poisson, but is reasonably approximated as Poisson with mean $\hat{n}_k + 2$. Adding $\lambda(1 + \beta)$ for the new arrivals, we get the final expression in Eq. (4.41).

Note that when n_k and $\hat{n}_k$ are small, then q_r is large and new arrivals are scarcely delayed at all. When $\hat{n}_k \approx n_k$ and n_k is large, then the departure rate is approximately $1/(1+\sqrt{2\beta})$, so that for $\lambda < 1/(1+\sqrt{2\beta})$, the departure rate exceeds the arrival rate, and the backlog decreases on the average. Finally, if $|n_k - \hat{n}_k|$ is large, the expected change in backlog can be positive, but the expected change in $|n_k - \hat{n}_k|$ is negative; Fig. 4.5 again provides a qualitative picture of the expected changes in n_k and $n_k - \hat{n}_k$.

We now give a crude analysis of delay for this strategy (and other similar stabilized strategies) by using the same type of analysis as in subsection 4.2.3. Let W_i be the delay from the arrival of the ith packet until the beginning of the ith successful transmission. The average of W_i over all i is the expected queueing delay W. Let n_i be the number of backlogged packets at the instant before i's arrival, not counting any packet currently in successful transmission. Then

$$W_i = R_i + \sum_{j=1}^{n_i} t_j + y_i \qquad (4.42)$$

where R_i is the residual time to the next state transition, t_j $(1 \leq j \leq n_i)$ is the sequence of subsequent intervals until each of the next n_i successful transmissions are completed, and y_i is the remaining interval until the ith successful transmission starts.

The backlog is at least 1 in all of the state transition intervals in the period on the right-hand side of Eq. (4.42), and we make the simplifying approximation that the number of attempted transmissions in each of these intervals is Poisson with parameter g. We later choose $g = \sqrt{2\beta}$, but for the moment it can be arbitrary. This approximation is somewhat different from that in subsection 4.2.3, in which we assumed that a successful transmission always occurred with a backlog state of 1; the difference is motivated by Eq. (4.40) which keeps q_r small. The expected value for each t_j is given by

$$E\{t\} = e^{-g}(\beta + E\{t\}) + ge^{-g}(1 + \beta) + [1 - (1 + g)e^{-g}](1 + \beta + E\{t\}) \quad (4.43)$$

The first term corresponds to an idle transmission in the first state transition interval; this occurs with probability e^{-g}, uses time β, and requires subsequent time $E\{t\}$ to complete the successful transmission. The next two terms correspond similarly to a success and a collision, respectively. Solving for $E\{t\}$,

$$E\{t\} = \frac{\beta + 1 - e^{-g}}{ge^{-g}} \qquad (4.44)$$

Note that this is the reciprocal of the expected number of departures per unit time in Eq. (4.39), as we would expect. $E\{t\}$ is thus approximately minimized by $g = \sqrt{2\beta}$. Averaging over i and using Little's result in Eq. (4.42), we get

$$W(1 - \lambda E\{t\}) = E\{R\} + E\{y\} \qquad (4.45)$$

The expected residual time can be approximated by observing that the system spends a fraction $\lambda(1 + \beta)$ of the time in successful state transition intervals. The expected residual time for arrivals in these intervals is $(1 + \beta)/2$. The fraction of time spent in collision intervals is negligible (for small β) compared with that for success, and the residual time in idle intervals is negligible. Thus,

$$E\{R\} \approx \lambda(1 + \beta)^2/2 \qquad (4.46)$$

Finally, $E\{y\}$ is just $E\{t\}$ less the successful transmission interval, so $E\{y\} = E\{t\} - (1 + \beta)$. Substituting these expressions into Eq. (4.45) yields

$$W \approx \frac{\lambda(1 + \beta)^2 + 2[E\{t\} - (1 + \beta)]}{2[1 - \lambda E\{t\}]} \qquad (4.47)$$

This expression is minimized over g by minimizing $E\{t\}$, and we have already seen that this minimum (for small β) is $1 + \sqrt{2\beta}$, occuring at $g = \sqrt{2\beta}$. With this substitution, W is approximately

$$W \approx \frac{\lambda + 2\sqrt{2\beta}}{2[1 - \lambda(1 + \sqrt{2\beta})]} \qquad (4.48)$$

Note the similarity of this expression with the $M/D/1$ queueing delay given in Eq. (3.45) of Chapter 3. What we achieve by stabilizing CSMA Aloha is the ability to modify q_r with the backlog so as to maintain a departure rate close to $1/(1 + \sqrt{2\beta})$ whenever a backlog exists.

4.4.3 CSMA Unslotted Aloha

In CSMA slotted Aloha, we assumed that all nodes were synchronized to start transmissions only at time multiples of β in idle periods. Here we remove that restriction and assume that when a packet arrives, its transmission starts immediately if the channel is sensed to be idle. If the channel is sensed to be busy, or if the transmission results in a collision, the packet is regarded as backlogged. Each backlogged packet repeatedly attempts to retransmit at randomly selected times separated by independent, exponentially distributed random delays τ, with probability density $xe^{-x\tau}$. If the channel is idle at one of these times, the packet is transmitted, and this continues until such a transmission is successful. We again assume a propagation and detection delay of β, so that if one transmission starts at time t, another node will not detect that the channel is busy until $t + \beta$, thus causing the possibility of collisions.

Consider an idle period that starts with a backlog of n. The time until the first transmission starts (with the $m = \infty$ assumption) is an exponentially distributed random variable with rate

$$G(n) = \lambda + nx \qquad (4.49)$$

Note that $G(n)$ is the attempt rate in packets per unit time, whereas $g(n)$ in the last section was packets per idle slot. After the initiation of this first transmission, the backlog is either n (if a new arrival started transmission) or $n - 1$ (if a backlogged packet started). Thus the time, from this first initiation until the next new arrival or backlogged node senses the channel, is an exponentially distributed random variable of rate $G(n)$ or $G(n - 1)$. A collision occurs if this next sensing is done within time β. Thus, the probability that this busy period is a collision is $1 - e^{-\beta G(n)}$ or $1 - e^{-\beta G(n-1)}$. This difference is small if βx is small, and we neglect it in what follows. Thus, we approximate the probability of a successful transmission following an idle period by $e^{-\beta G(n)}$.

The expected time from the beginning of one idle period until the next is $1/G(n) + (1 + \beta)$; the first term is the expected time until the first transmission starts, and the second term $(1 + \beta)$ is the time until the first transmission ends and the channel is detected as being idle again. If a collision occurs, then there is a slight additional time, less than β, until the packets causing the collision are no longer detected; we neglect this contribution since it is negligible even with respect to β, which is already negligible. The departure rate during periods when the backlog is n is then given by

$$\text{Departure rate}(n) = \frac{e^{-\beta G(n)}}{1/G(n) + (1 + \beta)} \qquad (4.50)$$

For small β, the maximum value of this departure rate is approximately $1/(1+2\sqrt{\beta})$, occurring when $G(n) \approx \beta^{-1/2} - 1/2$. This maximum departure rate is slightly smaller than it is for the slotted case (see Eq. 4.39); the reason is the same as when CSMA is not being used—collisions are somewhat more likely for a given attempt rate in an unslotted system than a slotted system. For CSMA, with small β, however, this loss in departure rate is quite small. What is more, in a slotted system, β would have to be considerably larger than in an unslotted system to compensate for synchronization inaccuracies and worst-case propagation delays. Thus, unslotted Aloha appears to be the natural choice for CSMA.

CSMA unslotted Aloha has the same stability problems as all the Aloha systems, but it can be stabilized in the same way as CSMA slotted Aloha. The details are treated in Prob. 4.22.

4.4.4 FCFS Splitting Algorithm for CSMA

We next investigate whether higher throughputs or smaller delays can be achieved by the use of splitting algorithms with CSMA. We shall see that relatively little can be gained, but it is interesting to understand why. We return to the assumption of idle slots of duration β, and assume that $0, 1, e$ feedback is available. An idle slot occurs at the end of each success or collision to provide time for feedback. Thus, we regard successes and collisions as having a duration $1 + \beta$; the algorithm is exercised at the end of each such elongated success or collision slot, and also at the end of each normal idle slot.

The same algorithm as in Eqs. (4.15) to (4.18) can be used, although the size α_0 of the initial interval in a CRP should be changed. Furthermore, as we shall see shortly, intervals with collisions should not be split into equal subintervals. Since collisions waste much more time than idle slots, the basic allocation interval α_0 should be small. This means in turn that collisions with more than two packets are negligible, and thus the analysis is simpler than before.

We first find the expected time and the expected number of successes in a CRP. Let $g = \lambda\alpha_0$ be the expected number of arrivals in an initial allocation interval of size α_0. With probability e^{-g}, an original allocation interval is empty, yielding a collision resolution time of β with no successes. With probability ge^{-g}, there is an initial success, yielding a collision resolution time $1 + \beta$. Finally, with probability $(g^2/2)e^{-g}$, there is a collision, yielding a collision resolution time of $1 + \beta + T$ for some T to be calculated later; since collisions with more than two packets are negligible, we assume two successes for each CRP with collisions. Thus,

$$E\{\text{time/CRP}\} \approx \beta e^{-g} + (1+\beta)g e^{-g} + (1+\beta+T)(g^2/2)e^{-g} \quad (4.51)$$
$$E\{\text{packets/CRP}\} \approx g e^{-g} + 2\left(g^2/2\right)e^{-g} \quad\quad\quad (4.52)$$

As before, the maximum stable throughput for a given g is

$$\lambda_{\max} = \frac{E\{\text{packets/CRP}\}}{E\{\text{time/CRP}\}} \approx \frac{g+g^2}{\beta + g(1+\beta) + (g^2/2)(1+\beta+T)} \quad (4.53)$$

We can now maximize the right-hand side of Eq. (4.53) over g (*i.e.*, over α_0). In the limit of small β, we get the asymptotic expressions

$$g \approx \sqrt{2\beta/(T-1)} \quad (4.54)$$

$$\lambda_{\max} \approx \frac{1}{1+\sqrt{2\beta(T-1)}} \quad (4.55)$$

Finally, we must calculate T, the time to resolve a collision after it has occurred. Let x be the fraction of an interval used in the first subinterval when the interval is split; we choose x optimally later. The first slot after the collision is detected is idle, successful, or a collision with probabilities $(1-x)^2, 2x(1-x)$, or x^2, respectively. The expected time required for each of these three cases is $\beta + T$, $2(1+\beta)$, and $1+\beta+T$. Thus,

$$T \approx (1-x)^2(\beta+T) + 4x(1-x)(1+\beta) + x^2(1+\beta+T), \quad (4.56)$$

from which T can be expressed as a function of x.

By setting the derivative dT/dx to 0, we find after a straightforward calculation that T is minimized by

$$x = \sqrt{\beta+\beta^2} - \beta, \quad (4.57)$$

The resulting value of T, for small β, is $T \approx 2+\sqrt{\beta}$. Substituting this in Eq. (4.55), we see that

$$\lambda_{\max} \approx \frac{1}{(1+\sqrt{2\beta})} \quad (4.58)$$

For small β, then, the FCFS splitting algorithm has the same maximum throughput as slotted Aloha. This is not surprising, since without CSMA, the major advantage of the FCFS algorithm is its efficiency in resolving collisions, and with CSMA, collisions rarely occur. When collisions do occur, they are resolved in both strategies by retransmission with small probability. It is somewhat surprising at first that if we use the FCFS algorithm with equal subintervals (*i.e.*, $x = 1/2$), then we find that we are limited to a throughput of $1/(1+\sqrt{3\beta})$. This degradation is due to a substantial increase in the number of collisions.

4.5 *MULTIACCESS RESERVATIONS*

We now look at a very simple way of increasing the throughput of multiaccess channels that has probably become apparent. If the packets of data being transmitted are long, why waste these long slot times either sending nothing or sending colliding packets? It would be far more efficient to send very short packets either in a contention mode or a TDM mode, and to use those short packets to reserve longer noncontending slots for the actual data. Thus, the slots wasted by idles or collisions are all short, leading to a higher overall efficiency. There are many different systems that operate in this way, and our major objective is not so much to explore the minor differences between them, but to see that they are all in essence the same.

To start, we explore a somewhat "canonic" reservation system. Assume that data packets require one time unit each for transmission and that reservation packets require $v \ll 1$ time units each for transmission. The format of a reservation packet is unimportant; it simply has to contain enough information to establish the reservation. For example, with the instantaneous feedback indicating idle, success, or collision that we have been assuming, the reservation packet does not have to contain any information beyond its mere existence. After a successful reservation packet is transmitted, either the next full time unit or some predetermined future time can be automatically allocated for transmission of the corresponding data packet. The reservation packets can use any strategy, including time division multiplexing, slotted Aloha, or the splitting algorithm.

We can easily determine the maximum throughput S in data packets per time unit achievable in such a scheme. Let S_r be the maximum throughput, in successful reservation packets per reservation slot, of the algorithm used for the reservation packets (*i.e.*, $1/e$ for slotted Aloha, 0.478 for splitting, or 1 for TDM). Then, over a large number of reservations, the time required per reservation approaches v/S_r, and an additional one unit of time is required for each data packet. Thus, the total time per data packet approaches $1 + v/S_r$, and we see that

$$S = \frac{1}{(1 + v/S_r)} \tag{4.59}$$

This equation assumes that the reservation packet serves only to make the reservation and carries no data. As we shall see, in many systems, the reservation packet carries some of the data; thus for one time unit of data, it suffices to transmit the reservation packet of duration v followed by the rest of the data in time $1 - v$. In this case, the throughput becomes

$$S = \frac{1}{[1 + v(1/S_R - 1)]} \tag{4.60}$$

For example, with slotted Aloha, the throughput is $S = 1/[1 + v(e - 1)]$. It is apparent that if v is small, say on the order of 0.01, then the maximum throughput

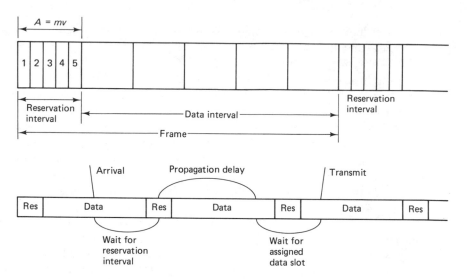

Figure 4.17　A satellite reservation system, using TDM to make reservations. Arrivals in one frame are transmitted in the second following frame.

approaches 1 and is not highly dependent on the collision resolution algorithm or on whether the reservation packet carries part of the data. We shall see later that Ethernet local area networks [MeB76] can be modeled almost in this way, and v about 0.01 is typical. Thus, such networks can achieve very high throughputs without requiring much sophistication for collision resolution.

4.5.1 Satellite Reservation Systems

One of the simplest reservation systems, with particular application to satellite networks [JBH78], has a frame structure as shown in Fig. 4.17. A number of data slots are preceded by a reservation period composed of m reservation slots, one reservation slot per node. Let v be the duration of a reservation slot, where, as usual, time is normalized to the average duration of a data packet; thus, v is the ratio of the number of bits used to make a reservation (including guard space and overhead) to the expected number of bits in a data packet. The reservation period in each frame has an overall duration of $A = mv$. The minimum duration of a frame is set to exceed the round trip delay 2β, so that the reservation slots at the beginning of one frame allocate the data slots for the next frame (see Fig. 4.17).

　　A frame is extended beyond the minimum length if need be to satisfy all the reservations. Note that the use of TDM for the reservation slots here makes a great deal more sense than it does for ordinary TDM applied to data slots. One reason is that the reservation slots are short, and, therefore, little time is wasted on a source with nothing to send. Another reason, for satellites, is that if collisions were allowed on the reservation slots, the channel propagation delay would make collision resolution rather slow. Equation (4.59) gives the maximum throughput of such a system as $1/(1 + v)$ under the assumption that each reservation packet can only make one data packet reservation. If we assume, alternatively, that a reservation packet can make multiple reservations for its source, it is not hard to see that the throughput can approach 1 arbitrarily closely, since under heavy loading, the frames get very long and negligible time is used by the infrequent reservation periods.

With the assumption that each reservation packet can make multiple data packet reservations, this system is very similar to the single-user reservation system analyzed in subsection 3.5.2, Chapter 3. The major difference is that, because of the propagation delay, the reservations requested in one reservation interval are for the data frame following the next reservation interval. Thus, if we assume Poisson packet arrivals, and if we neglect the minimum frame length requirement, the expected queueing delay for the ith packet becomes

$$E\{W_i\} = E\{R_i\} + E\{N_i\}/\mu + 2A \tag{4.61}$$

This expression is the same as Eq. (3.60) in Chapter 3, except that the last term is $2A$. Here $A = mv$ is the duration of the reservation interval, and it is multiplied by 2 since the packet has to wait for the next two reservation intervals before being transmitted. Using the same analysis as in Chapter 3, the expected queueing delay is

$$W = \frac{\lambda \overline{X^2}}{2(1 - \lambda)} + \frac{A}{2} + \frac{2A}{1 - \lambda} \tag{4.62}$$

This analysis allows the data packets to have a general length distribution with mean square $\overline{X^2}$ (which of course requires the reservations to contain length information), but we have normalized time to satisfy $\overline{X} = 1/\mu = 1$; thus, $\rho = \lambda$. Note that in the limit as v goes to 0, Eq. (4.62) goes to the queueing delay of an $M/G/1$ queue as we would expect. Also, W remains finite for $\lambda < 1$ as we predicted.

Unfortunately, this analysis has neglected the condition that the duration of each frame must be at least the round-trip delay 2β. Since 2β is typically many times larger than the reservation period A, we see that W in Eq. (4.62) is only larger than 2β for λ very close to 1. Since every packet must be delayed by at least 2β for the reservation to be made, we conclude that Eq. (4.62) is not a good approximation to delay except perhaps for λ very close to 1.

Rather than try to make this analysis more realistic, we observe that this variable frame length model has some undesirable features. First, if some nodes make errors in receiving the reservation information, then those nodes will lose track of the next reservation period; developing a distributed algorithm to keep the nodes synchronized on the reservation periods in the presence of errors is not easy. Second, the system is not very fair in the sense that very busy nodes can reserve many packets per frame, making the frames long and almost locking out more modest users.

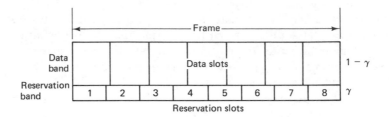

Figure 4.18   A reservation system with separate frequency band for reservations. Reservations are made by TDM in the reservation band.

For both these reasons, it is quite desirable to maintain a fixed frame length. Nodes can still make multiple reservations in one reservation slot, which is desirable if only a few nodes are active. With a fixed frame, however, it is sometimes necessary to postpone packets with reservations from one frame to the next.

Note that all nodes are aware of all reservations after the delay of 2β suffered by reservation packets. Thus, conceptually, we have a common queue of packets with reservations, and the nodes can jointly exercise any desired queueing discipline, such as first-come first-serve, round robin, or some priority scheme. So long as a packet is sent in every data slot for which the queue of packets with reservations is not empty, and so long as the discipline is independent of packet length, the expected delay is independent of queueing discipline.

It is quite messy to find the expected delay for this system, but with the slight modification in Fig. 4.18, a good approximate analysis is very simple. Suppose that a fraction γ of the available bandwidth is set aside for making reservations, and that TDM is used within this bandwidth, giving each node one reservation packet in each round-trip delay period 2β. With v as the ratio of reservation packet length to data packet length, $\gamma = mv/2\beta$. An arriving packet waits $2\beta/2$ time units on the average until the beginning of its reservation packet, then $2\beta/m$ units for the reservation packet transmission, and then 2β time units until the reservation is received. Thus, after $2\beta(3/2 + 1/m)$ time units, on the average, a packet joins the common queue.

The arrival process of packets with reservations to the common queue is approximately Poisson (*i.e.*, the number of arrivals in different reservation slots are independent and have a Poisson distribution). Once a packet is in the common queue, it has a service time of $X/(1 - \gamma)$ where X is the packet transmission time using the full bandwidth. The common queue is thus $M/G/1$ with $\rho = \lambda/(1 - \gamma)$. The total queueing delay, adding the expected time to enter the common queue (*i.e.*, $2\beta(3/2 + 1/m)$) to the $M/G/1$ delay in the common queue, is then

$$W = 3\beta + \frac{2\beta}{m} + \frac{\lambda\overline{X^2}}{2(1 - \gamma - \lambda)(1 - \gamma)} \tag{4.63}$$

We see that this strategy essentially achieves perfect scheduling at the expense of the delay for making reservations. For small λ, this delay seems excessive,

Slot 1	Slot 2	Slot 3	Slot 4	Slot 5	Slot 6	
15	idle	3	20	collision	2	Frame 1
15	7	3	idle	9	2	Frame 2
idle	7	3	collision	9	idle	Frame 3
18	7	3	collision	9	6	Frame 4
18	7	3	15	9	6	Frame 5

Figure 4.19   A reservation strategy with short packets and multiple packet messages. After a node captures a slot in a frame, it keeps that slot until finished.

since a number of data slots typically are wasted in each frame. This leads to the clever idea of using the unscheduled slots in a frame in a contention mode [WiE80]. Reservations are made in the following reservation interval for packets sent in these unscheduled slots. The convention is that if the packet gets through, its reservation is cancelled. This approach has the effect of achieving very small delay under light loading (because of no round-trip delay for reservations), and very high efficiency (as given by Eq. (4.63)) under heavy loading.

All the strategies above use TDM for making reservations, and this makes it somewhat difficult to add new sources or delete old sources from the system. In addition, as m increases, γ increases and more of the bandwidth is used up by reservations. This suggests using the reservation slots in a contention resolution mode [JBH78]. It is difficult to analyze such a system, but it is clear that for large m and small λ, the delay could be reduced—we would use many fewer than m minislots in the reservation part of the frame.

Another somewhat simpler reservation idea is to allow the first packet of a message to make a reservation for the subsequent packets. In the context of Eq. (4.60), we view the first packet as the reservation packet and the entire message as the data packet. Thus Eq. (4.60) yields the throughput of this scheme if we take v as the inverse of the expected number of packets in a message. The appropriate length for a packet in this scheme is a tradeoff between reservation inefficiency for long packets versus DLC inefficiency for short packets.

For satellite networks, these schemes are usually implemented with a frame structure (see Fig. 4.19), where a frame consists of a fixed number of packet slots [CRW73]. Enough packet slots are included in a frame so that the frame delay exceeds the round-trip delay.

When a source successfully transmits a packet in one of these slots, then it can automatically reserve the corresponding slot in the next frame and each following frame until its message is completed. This can be done either by using a field in the packet header saying that another packet is to follow or, more simply and less efficiently, by automatically reserving that slot in each subsequent frame until that slot is first empty. After the end of the reservation period, the given slot in the frame is open for contention. Note that some care must be used in the contention algorithm. It does not suffice for all waiting sources to simply pounce on the first idle slot after a reservation period, since that would yield an unacceptably high collision probability.

Another variation on this scheme is to have each source "own" a particular slot within the frame [Bin75]. When a source isn't using its own slot, other sources can capture it by contention, but when the source wants its own slot back, it simply transmits a packet in that slot and if a collision occurs, the other sources are forbidden to use that slot on the next frame, letting the owner capture it. This variation is somewhat more fair than the previous scheme, but the delays are larger, both because of the less efficient contention resolution and because of the large number of slots in a frame if the number of users is large. Also, there is the usual problem of deleting and adding new sources to the system.

4.5.2 Local Area Networks: CSMA/CD and Ethernet

The last subsection treated satellite networks where round-trip propagation delay was an important consideration in each reservation scheme. For local area networks, at least with today's technology, round-trip delay is a very small fraction of packet duration. Thus, instead of making a reservation for some slot far into the future, reservations can be made for the immediate future. Conceptually, this is not a big difference; it simply means that one must expect larger delays with satellite networks, since the feedback in any collision resolution strategy is always delayed by the round-trip propagation time. From a technological standpoint, however, the difference is more important since the physical properties of the media used for local area networks can simplify the implementation of reservation techniques.

Ethernet [MeB76] both illustrates this simplification and is a widely used technique for local area networks. A number of nodes are all connected onto a common cable so that when one node transmits a packet (and the others are silent), all the other nodes hear that packet. In addition, as in carrier sensing, a node can listen to the cable before transmitting (*i.e.*, conceptually, 0, 1, and idle can be distinguished on the bus). Finally, because of the physical properties of cable, it is possible for a node to listen to the cable while transmitting. Thus, if two nodes start to transmit almost simultaneously, they will shortly detect a collision in process and both cease transmitting. This technique is called CSMA/Collision Detection (CSMA/CD). On the other hand, if one node starts transmitting and no other node starts before the first node's signal has propagated throughout the cable, then the first node is guaranteed to finish its packet without collision. Thus, we can view the first portion of a packet as making a reservation for the rest.

Slotted CSMA/CD

For analytic purposes, it is easiest to visualize Ethernet in terms of slots and minislots. The minislots are of duration β, which denotes the time required for a signal to propagate from one end of the cable to the other and to be detected. If the nodes are all synchronized into minislots of this duration, and if only one node transmits in a minislot, all the other nodes will detect the transmission and not use subsequent minislots until the entire packet is completed. If more than one node transmits in a minislot, then each transmitting node will detect the condition by the end of the minislot and cease transmitting. Thus, the minislots are used in a contention mode, and when a successful transmission occurs in a minislot, it effectively reserves the channel for the completion of the packet.

CSMA/CD can be analyzed with a Markov chain in the same way as CSMA Aloha. We assume that each backlogged node transmits after each idle slot with probability q_r, and we assume at the outset that the number of nodes transmitting after an idle slot is Poisson with parameter $g(n) = \lambda + q_r n$. Consider state transitions at the ends of idle slots; thus, if no transmissions occur, the next idle slot ends after time β. If one transmission occurs, the next idle slot ends after $1 + \beta$. We can assume variable length packets here, but to correspond precisely to the model for idle slots, the packet durations should be multiples of the idle slot durations; we assume as before that the expected packet duration is 1. Finally, if a collision occurs, the next idle slot ends after 2β; in other words, nodes must hear an idle slot after the collision to know that it is safe to transmit.

The expected length of interval between state transitions is then β, plus an additional 1 times the success probability, plus an additional β times the collision probability;

$$E\{\text{Interval}\} = \beta + g(n)e^{-g(n)} + \beta[1 - (1 + g(n))e^{-g(n)}] \qquad (4.64)$$

The expected number of arrivals between state transitions is λ times this interval, so the drift in state n is $\lambda E\{\text{Interval}\} - P_{\text{succ}}$. The probability of success is simply $g(n)e^{-g(n)}$, so, as in Eq. (4.39), the drift in state n is negative if

$$\lambda < \frac{g(n)e^{-g(n)}}{\beta + g(n)e^{-g(n)} + \beta[1 - (1 + g(n))e^{-g(n)}]} \qquad (4.65)$$

The right-hand side of Eq. (4.65) is interpreted as the departure rate in state n. This quantity is maximized over $g(n)$ at $g(n) = 0.77$ and the resulting value of the right-hand side is $1/(1 + 3.31\beta)$. Thus, if CSMA/CD is stabilized (this can be done, *e.g.*, by the pseudo-Bayesian technique), the maximum λ at which the system is stable is

$$\lambda < \frac{1}{1 + 3.31\beta} \qquad (4.66)$$

The expected queueing delay for CSMA/CD, assuming the above slotted model and ideal stabilization, is calculated in the same way as for CSMA (see

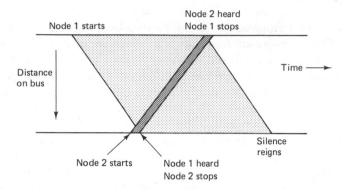

Figure 4.20   Collision detection. Node 2 starts to transmit almost β units after node 1; node 2 stops almost immediately, but node 1 continues for almost another β units before stopping.

Prob. 4.24). The result, for small β and mean-square packet duration $\overline{X^2}$, is

$$W \approx \frac{\lambda \overline{X^2} + \beta(4.62 + 2\lambda)}{2[1 - \lambda(1 + 3.31\beta)]} \tag{4.67}$$

The constant 3.31 in the maximum throughput in Eq. (4.66) is dependent on the detailed assumptions about the system. Different values are obtained by making different assumptions (see [Lam80], for example). If β is very small, as usual in Ethernet, then this value is not very important. More to the point, however, is that the unslotted version of CSMA/CD makes considerably more sense than the slotted version, both because of the difficulty of synchronizing on short minislots and the advantages of capitalizing on shorter than maximum propagation delays when possible.

Unslotted CSMA/CD

Figure 4.20 illustrates why the analysis of an unslotted system is somewhat messy. Suppose a node at one end of the cable starts to transmit and then, almost β time units later, a node at the other end starts. This second node ceases its transmission almost immediately upon hearing the first node, but nonetheless causes errors in the first packet and forces the first node to stop transmission another β time units later. Finally, another β time units goes by before the other end of the line is quiet. Another complication is that nodes closer together on the cable detect collisions faster than those more spread apart. As a result, the maximum throughput achievable with Ethernet depends on the arrangement of nodes on the cable and is very complex to calculate exactly.

To get a conservative bound on maximum throughput, however, we can find bounds on all the relevant parameters from the end of one transmission (either successful or aborted) to the end of the next. Assume that each node initiates transmissions according to an independent Poisson process whenever it senses the channel idle, and assume that G is the overall Poisson intensity. All nodes sense the beginning of an idle period at most β after the end of a transmission, and the expected time to the beginning of the next transmission is at most an additional $1/G$. This next packet will collide with some later starting packet with probability at most $1 - e^{-\beta G}$ and the colliding packets will cease transmission after at most 2β. On the other hand, the packet will be successful with probability at least $e^{-\beta G}$ and will occupy 1 time unit. The departure rate S for a given G is the success probability divided by the expected time of a success or collision; so

$$S > \frac{e^{-\beta G}}{\beta + 1/G + 2\beta(1 - e^{-\beta G}) + e^{-\beta G}} \qquad (4.68)$$

Optimizing the right-hand side of Eq. (4.68) over G, we find that the maximum occurs at $\beta G = (\sqrt{13} - 1)/6 = 0.43$; the corresponding maximum value is

$$S > \frac{1}{1 + 6.2\beta} \qquad (4.69)$$

This analysis is very conservative, but if β is small, then throughputs very close to 1 can be achieved and the difference between Eqs. (4.66) and (4.69) is not large. Note that maximum stable throughput approaches 1 with decreasing β as a constant times β for CSMA/CD, whereas the approach is as a constant times $\sqrt{\beta}$ for CSMA. The reason for this difference is that collisions are not very costly with CSMA/CD, and thus much higher attempt rates can be used. For the same reason, persistent CSMA (where new arrivals during a data slot are transmitted immediately at the end of the data slot) works reasonably for CSMA/CD but quite poorly for CSMA.

CSMA/CD (and CSMA) becomes increasingly inefficient with increasing bus length, with increasing data rate, and with decreasing data packet size. To see this, recall that β is in units of the data packet duration. Thus if τ is propagation delay (and detection time) in seconds, C is the raw data rate on the bus, and L is the average packet length, then $\beta = \tau C/L$. Neither CSMA nor CSMA/CD are reasonable system choices if β is more than a few tenths.

The IEEE 802 Standards

The Institute of Electrical and Electronic Engineers (IEEE) has developed a set of standards, denoted 802, for LANs. The standards are divided into five parts, 802.1 to 802.5. The 802.1 standard deals with interfacing the LAN protocols to higher layers. 802.2 is a data link control standard very similar to HDLC as discussed in chapter 2. Finally, 802.3 to 802.5 are medium access control (MAC) standards referring to CSMA/CD, token bus, and token ring systems, respectively. The 802.3 standard is essentially the same as Ethernet, using unslotted persistent CSMA/CD

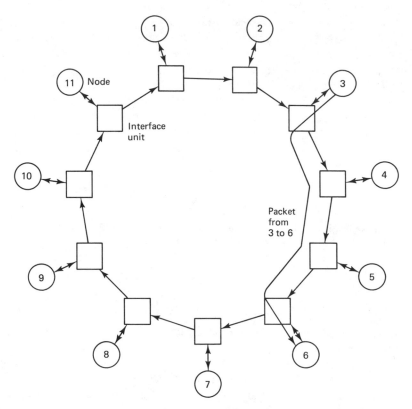

Figure 4.21   A ring network. Travel of data around the ring is uni-directional. Each node either relays the received bit stream to the next node with a one bit delay or transmits its own packet, discarding the incoming bit stream.

with binary exponential backoff. We will discuss the 802.5 and 802.4 standards briefly in the next two subsections.

4.5.3 Local Area Networks: Token Rings

Token ring networks ([FaN69] and [FaL72]) constitute another popular approach to local area networks. In such networks, the nodes are arranged logically in a ring with each node transmitting to the next node around the ring (see Fig. 4.21). Normally, each node simply relays the received bit stream from the previous node on to the next. It does this with at least a one bit delay, allowing the node to read and regenerate the incoming binary digit before sending it on to the next node. Naturally, when a node transmits its own packet to the next node, it must discard what is being received. For the system to work correctly, we must ensure that what is being received and discarded is not a packet that has not yet reached its destination. Conceptually, we visualize a "token" which exists in the net and which is passed from node to node. Whatever node has the token is allowed to transmit a packet, and when the packet is finished, the token is passed on to the next node. Nodes with nothing to send are obligated to pass the token on rather than saving it.

When we look at the properties that a token must have, we see that they are essentially the properties of the flags we studied for DLC, and that the same flag could be used as a token and to indicate the end of a packet. That is, whenever the node that is currently transmitting a packet finishes the transmission, it places the token or flag, for example 01111110, at the end of the packet as usual. When the next node reads this token, it simply passes the token on if it has no packet to send, but if it does have a packet to send, it inverts the last token bit, turning the token into 01111111. This modified token, 01111111, is usually called a *busy token*, and the original, 01111110, is called a *free token*. The node then follows this busy token with its own packet. Bit stuffing by inserting a 0 after 011111 is used within the data packets to avoid having either type of token appear in the data. Thus, every node can split the received stream into packets by recognizing the free and busy tokens, and the free token constitutes the passing of permission to send from one node to the next.

Let us look closely at how packets travel around the ring. Suppose for example that at time 0, node 1 receives a free token, inverts the last bit to form a busy token, and then starts to transmit a packet (see Fig. 4.22a). Each subsequent node around the ring simply delays this bit stream by one bit per node and relays it on to the next node. The intended recipient of the packet both reads the packet into the node and also relays it around the ring.

After a round trip delay, the bit stream gets back to the originator, node 1 for our example. A round trip delay is defined as the propagation delay of the ring plus m bits, where m is the number of nodes. Assuming that the packet length is longer than the round trip delay (in bits), the first part of the incoming packet is automatically removed by node 1, since node 1 is still transmitting a subsequent portion of the packet. When node 1 completes sending the packet, it appends a free token and then sends idle fill while the remainder of the just transmitted packet is returning to node 1 on the ring. After the last bit of the packet has returned, node 1 starts to relay what is coming in with a one bit delay. If some other node had a packet to send, then the first thing relayed through node 1 is a busy token followed by that packet; if no other node had a packet to send, then the free token is relayed through node 1, and continues to circulate until some node has a packet to send.

Since all nodes follow this same strategy, when the idle token arrives at node 1 in the received bit stream, it must be followed by idle fill. This idle fill persists until the node sending that idle fill relays the busy token sent by node 1 (see Fig. 4.22). Thus, busy tokens are always followed by packets and idle tokens are always followed by enough idle fill to make up the round trip delay on the ring.

Note that the round trip delay must be at least as large as the token length; otherwise a node, on completing a packet transmission and sending a free token,

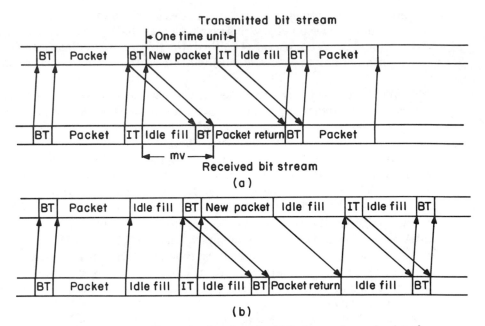

Figure 4.22   Transmitted and received bit stream at one ring interface unit of a token ring network. The interface unit transmits what is received with a one bit delay until seeing an idle token (IT). It converts the idle token into a busy token (BT) and then transmits its own packet. In part (a), this is followed by an idle token, whereas in part (b), the interface unit waits for the packet to return around the ring before transmitting the idle token. In each case, idle fill is transmitted after the idle token until the token (either busy or idle) returns around the ring, and then the unit reverts to relaying what is received with a one bit delay.

will discard the first part of the token as it returns to the node through the ring. One way to look at this is that the storage around the ring (*i.e.*, the propagation length in bits plus number of nodes) must be sufficient to store the token. Since the node transmitting a packet also reads it before removing it from the network, it is possible, either by checking bit by bit or by checking a CRC, for the transmitting node to verify that the packet was correctly received. It is also possible for the receiving node to set a bit in a given position at the end of the packet if the CRC checks. Actually, neither of these techniques is foolproof, since an error could occur between the receiving node and its ring interface or an error could occur on the given bit set by the receiving node.

      There are many variations in the detailed operation of a ring net. Each node could be restricted to sending a single packet each time it acquires the token, or a node could empty its queue of waiting packets before releasing the token to the next node. Also, priorities can be introduced fairly easily in a ring net by having a field for priorities in a fixed position after the free or busy token; any node could alter the bits in this field to indicate a high priority packet. Other nodes, with lower priority traffic, would relay free tokens rather than using them, so as to allow nodes with high priority packets to transmit first. Obviously, when a node transmits its high priority packets, it would then reduce the value in the priority field.

Another variation is in the handling of ARQ. If a node transmits a free token immediately at the end of a packet transmission, then that node will no longer have control of the channel if the packet was not delivered error free. An alternative is for a node to send idle fill after completing a packet transmission until verifying whether or not the packet was correctly received (see Fig. 4.22b). If correct reception occurs, then a free token is transmitted; otherwise, a busy token is sent followed by a retransmission. As seen in the figure, each busy or idle token is preceded by a round trip delay of idle fill. Idle tokens also have idle fill following them. This alternative makes it somewhat easier to see what is happening on a ring (since at most one packet is active at a time), but it lowers efficiency and increases delay, particularly for a large ring.

Yet another variation is in the physical layout of the ring. If the cable making up the ring is put into a star configuration, as shown in Fig. 4.23, then a number of benefits accrue. First, a disadvantage of a ring net is that each node requires an active interface in which each bit is read and retransmitted. If an interface malfunctions, the entire ring fails. By physically connecting each interface at a common location, it is easier to find a failed interface and bypass it at the central site. If the interface is also located at the central site (which is not usually done), then the propagation delay around the ring is materially reduced.

The most important variation in a ring network is the treatment of free and busy token failures. If a free token is destroyed by noise, or if multiple free tokens are created, or if a busy token is created and circulates indefinitely, then the system fails. One obvious solution to this problem is to give a special node responsibility for recreating a lost free token or destroying spurious tokens; this is rather complex because of the possibility of the special node failing or leaving the network.

IEEE 802.5 Token Ring Standard

The more common solution to token failure, which is used in the IEEE 802.5 standard, is for each node to recognize the loss of a token or existence of multiple tokens after a time-out. If a node has a packet to transmit after a time-out occurs, it simply transmits a busy token followed by the packet followed by a free token, simultaneously purging the ring of all other tokens. If successful, the ring is again functional; if unsuccessful, due to two or more nodes trying to correct the situation at the same time, then the colliding nodes try again after random delays.

The IEEE 802.5 standard also uses the star configuration and postpones releasing the token until the current packet is acknowledged. This standard uses a 24-bit token in place of the 8-bit token and contains elaborate procedures to recover from many possible malfunctions. The standard has been implemented in VLSI chips to implement a token ring running at 4 megabits per second; the

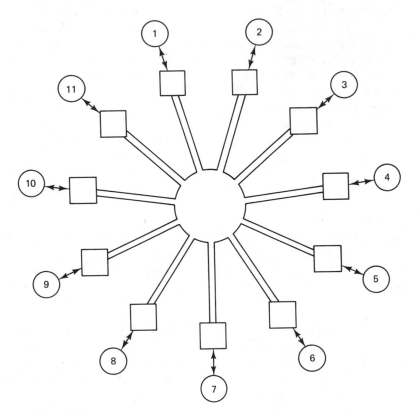

Figure 4.23   A ring network in a star configuration. Nodes can be
bypassed or added from the central site.

complexity of these chips, given the simplicity of the token ring concept, is truly
astonishing.

Expected Delay for Token Rings

Let us analyze the expected delay on a token ring. Assume first that each node,
upon receiving a free token, empties its queue before passing the free token to the
next node. Assume that there are m nodes, each with independent Poisson input
streams of rate λ/m. Let v be the average propagation delay from one node to the
next plus the relaying delay (usually one or a few bits) at a node. View the system
conceptually from a central site, observing the free token passing around the ring.
Let $\overline{X} = 1$ be the mean transmission time for a packet (including its busy token).
Thus, $\rho = \lambda$. The mean queueing delay W is that of an exhaustive, multi-user

system; the delay is given by Eq. (3.69) in Chapter 3 as

$$W = \frac{\lambda \overline{X^2}}{2(1-\lambda)} + \frac{(m-\lambda)v}{2(1-\lambda)} \tag{4.70}$$

Note that the first term is the usual $M/G/1$ queueing delay. The second term gives us the delay under no loading, $mv/2$. Observe that mv is the propagation delay around the entire ring, β, plus m times the one or few bits delay within each interface to a node. If β is small relative to a packet transmission time and if λ is relatively large, then W is very close to the $M/G/1$ delay.

Next we look at the situation in which a node can transmit at most one packet with each free token. The system is then the partially gated, limited service system of subsection 3.5.2. The delay is given by Eq. (3.76) as

$$W = \frac{\lambda \overline{X^2} + (m+\lambda)v}{2(1-\lambda-\lambda v)} \tag{4.71}$$

In this case, we note that the maximum stable throughput has been reduced somewhat to $1/(1+v)$. In the analysis above, we have included the token length as part of the packet overhead and included in v only the propagation delay plus bit delay at a node interface. This is not a terminological issue, but instead necessary to use the queueing results in Chapter 3. According to that analysis, v is the delay inserted at a node even when the node has nothing to send, and that delay does not include the entire token, but only the one or few bits of transit delay within the node. Problem 4.27 modifies Eq. (4.71) for the case in which a transmitting node waits for the packet to return (as in the IEEE 802.5 standard) before passing on the free token. In essence, this adds one round trip delay (*i.e.*, mv) to the transmission time of each packet, and the maximum throughput is reduced to $1/(1+mv)$. This can be a significant loss if mv is large.

In comparing the token ring with CSMA/CD, note that if the propagation and detection delay is small relative to the packet transmission time, then both systems have maximum throughputs very close to 1 packet per unit time. The token ring avoids stability problems, whereas CSMA/CD avoids the complexities of lost tokens and has slightly smaller delay under very light loads. Both are well established technologies, and one chooses between them on the basis of cost, perceived reliability, and personal preference. If the propagation delay is large ($\beta > 1$), then CSMA/CD loses its advantage over pure collision resolution and the IEEE 802.5 version of the token ring degrades similarly (since $mv > \beta$). On the other hand a token ring in which nodes pass the free token on immediately after completing a packet transmission does not suffer this degradation (*i.e.*, the maximum throughput is $1/(1+v)$ and v can be very much less than β if m is large).

Slotted Rings and Register Insertion Rings

Assuming that traffic on a ring is uniformly distributed between different source-destination pairs, a packet need be transmitted on only half of a ring's links on the

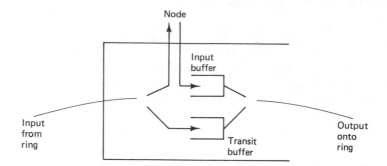

Figure 4.24   Interface to a register insertion ring. The output onto the ring comes from either the input buffer or the transit buffer. The input from the ring goes to the transit buffer or directly to the node, if addressed there.

average. Since in the token ring, a packet travels on every one of the links, we see that half the system's transmission capability is potentially wasted. It is therefore conceivable that a different control strategy could achieve twice the throughput.

Slotted rings and register insertion rings allow this higher potential throughput, at least in principle. A slotted ring is best viewed as a conveyor belt of packet slots; the ring is extended by shift registers within the nodes to provide the desired number of slots. When a node has a packet to send, it looks for an empty slot in the conveyor belt and places the packet in that slot, marking the slot as full. When the destination node sees the packet, it removes it and marks the slot as empty again.

One disadvantage of a slotted ring is that all packets must have equal length (as contrasted with token rings and CSMA/CD). Another disadvantage is significant delay (due to the conveyor belt length) even under light load. This can be compensated for by making the packets very short, but the added DLC overhead caused by short packets loses much of the potential throughput gain. Finally, to accomplish ARQ, it is common to leave packets in their slots until they return to the sending node; this automatically throws away the potential doubling of throughput.

The register insertion ring provides true store and forward buffering of ring traffic within the nodes. Each node has a buffer for transit traffic and a buffer for new arrivals (see Fig. 4.24). When a new arrival is being transmitted, incoming ring traffic that must be forwarded is saved in the transit buffer. When the transit traffic is being transmitted, the buffer gradually empties as either idle fill or packets destined for the given node arrive at the ring input. New arrivals are inhibited from transmission whenever the transit buffer does not have enough space to store the input from the ring while the new packet is being inserted on the ring.

The register insertion ring is capable of higher throughputs and has only a slightly greater delay for light loading than the token ring. Its greatest disadvantage is that it loses the fair allocation and guaranteed access provided by the token ring's round robin packet service. The token ring is much more popular for applications, probably because maximum throughput is not the dominant consideration for most local area networks.

4.5.4 Local Area Networks: Token Buses and Polling

The general idea of the token ring is used in a wide variety of communication situations. The idea is that there are m nodes with ordered identities and the nodes are offered service one at a time in round robin order. The differences between these systems lie in the question of how one node knows when the previous node has finished service (or refused the offer of service). In other words, what mechanism performs the role of the token, and what is the delay, v, in passing this virtual token from one node to the next?

Polling, as discussed briefly in section 4.1.2, is a common example of such a system. The polls sent by the central node to each of the secondary nodes act as tokens. The token passing delay in a polling system is quite large, involving first a communication from a polled node back to the central node, and then a new polling request from the central node to the next secondary node.

Hub polling is a way of avoiding the above double delays. The central station polls (*i.e.*, passes the token to) the first secondary node; each secondary node, after using the channel, passes the token on to the next secondary node. If the nodes are ordered in terms of distance on the multi-drop telephone line or bus, then, of course, token passing delay is reduced even further.

A token bus can be implemented on the same type of physical bus as a CSMA/CD system. The nodes are ordered in a round robin fashion, and when a node finishes sending its packet or packets, it sends a token to the next node in order, giving it permission to send next. A node that has nothing to send simply sends the token to the next node. Conceptually, it can be seen that a token bus is essentially the same as a hub polling system. Polling is the more common terminology with a central node, and token bus is more common for a fully distributed system. Equations (4.70) and (4.71) give the delay associated with these systems under the assumptions of sending all queued packets per poll and one packet per poll, respectively. Both equations assume equal average traffic for all nodes. The parameter v in these equations can be interpreted in general as the delay, in an empty system, from token arrival at one node to the next, averaged over the nodes.

Recall that for the token ring, v included only propagation delay from node to node plus one or a few bits delay through the node; the initiation of token transmission from a node starts before the token is completely received from the previous node. Here, the token length (which can be considerable) is included in v, since one token must be fully received and decoded before the next node starts. Thus, the expected delay in the limit of zero load is inherently larger for the token bus than the token ring.

The performance of token buses and polling systems depends critically on the parameter v (*i.e.*, from Eq. (4.71)), the maximum throughput is $1/(1 + v)$ and the expected delay in the limit $\lambda \to 0$ is $mv/2$). Assuming for the moment that the nodes are numbered independently of position on the bus, it is reasonable to take the average propagation delay as $\beta/3$ (see Prob. 4.29), where $\beta = \tau C/L$ is the normalized propagation time from one end of the bus to the other (*i.e.*, the time measured as a fraction of the average packet length). Here τ is propagation time in seconds, C is the channel bit rate, and L is expected packet length. Similarly, the normalized token transmission time is k/L, where k is the length of the token. Thus,

$$v = \frac{\tau C}{3L} + \frac{k}{L} + \delta \tag{4.72}$$

where δ is the normalized time for the receiver to detect a token. In our previous discussions, we included δ as part of the propagation delay β, but here we count this time separately.

The quantity τC is the number of bits that can travel along the bus at one time. If $\tau C/3$ is small relative to k then improving the performance of the algorithm depends on decreasing the length of the token. Conversely, if $\tau C/3$ is large, then k is relatively unimportant and improvements depend on reducing the effects of propagation delay. One obvious way to reduce the effect of propagation delay is to number the nodes sequentially from one end of the bus to the other. If this is done, then the sum of the propagation delays over all nodes is 2β; that is, there is a cumulative propagation delay of β moving down the bus to poll all nodes, and then another β to return. Thus, the average value of v is

$$v = \frac{2\tau C}{mL} + \frac{k}{L} + \delta \tag{4.73}$$

This is a major reduction in propagation delay, but it makes it somewhat more difficult to add new nodes to the bus. Note that the propagation delays are much smaller than the average as reservation opportunities move down the bus, but then there is a long reservation interval of duration β to return from the end of the bus to the beginning. We recall from subsection 5.2 of Chapter 3 that Eqs. (4.70) and (4.71) are valid using the average value of v.

IEEE 802.4 Token Bus Standard

The IEEE 802.4 standard corresponds essentially to the system we have just described. We will briefly describe some of its features. To allow new nodes to enter the round robin token structure, each node already in the strcture periodically sends a special control packet inviting waiting nodes to join. All waiting nodes respond, and if more than one, a splitting algorithm is used to select one. The new node enters the round robin after the inviting node, and the new node subsequently addresses the token to the node formerly following the inviting node. An old node can drop out of the round robin simply by sending a control packet to its predecessor directing the predecessor to send subsequent tokens to the successor of the node that is dropping out. Finally, failure recovery is essentially accomplished by all nodes dropping out, then one starting by contention, and finally the starting node adding new nodes by the procedure above.

Implicit Tokens: CSMA/CA

Consider how to reduce the token size. One common approach is to replace the token with an implicit token represented by the channel becoming idle. Two of the better known acronyms for this are BRAM [CFL79] and MSAP [KlS80]. In these schemes, when a node completes a packet transmission, it simply goes idle. The next node in sequence, upon detecting the idle channel, starts transmission if it has a packet or otherwise remains idle. Successive nodes in the sequence wait for successively longer times, after hearing an idle, before starting transmission, thus giving each of the earlier stations an opportunity to transmit if it has packets. These schemes are often called CSMA/Collision Avoidance (CSMA/CA) schemes.

To see how long a node must hear an idle channel before starting to transmit, consider the worst case in which the node that finishes a packet is at one end of the bus, the next node is at the opposite end, and the second node is at the first end again. Then the second node will detect the idle channel almost immediately at the end of the transmission, but the first node will not detect the event until $\beta + \delta$ units later, and the second node will not know whether the first node is going to transmit until an additional delay of $\beta + \delta$. Thus, the second node must wait for $2(\beta + \delta)$ before starting to transmit. By the same argument, we see that each successive node must wait an additional increment of $2(\beta + \delta)$. Thus, this scheme replaces an explicit token of duration k/L with an implicit token of duration $2(\beta + \delta) = 2(\tau C/L + \delta)$. The scheme is promising, therefore, in situations where τC and δ are small.

If the nodes are ordered on the bus, and the delays are known and built into the algorithm, then the durations of the implicit tokens are greatly reduced, as in Eq. (4.73), but the complexity is greatly increased. There are many variations on this scheme dealing with the problems of maintaining synchronization after long idle periods and recovering from errors (see [FiT84] for an excellent critical summary).

4.5.5 Higher-Speed Local Area Networks

Increasing requirements for data communications, as well as the availability of high data rate communication media, such as optical fiber, coaxial cable, and CATV systems, motivate the use of higher and higher speed local area networks. For our purposes, we define a higher-speed local area network as one in which β exceeds 1. Recall that β is the ratio of propagation delay to average packet transmission time, so $\beta > 1$ means that a transmitter will have finished sending a packet before a distant receiver starts to hear it. Since $\beta = \tau C/L$, we see that increasing propagation delay τ, increasing data rate C, and decreasing expected packet length L all contribute to making the net higher speed. There has also been great interest in extending local area techniques to wider area coverages, such as metropolitan

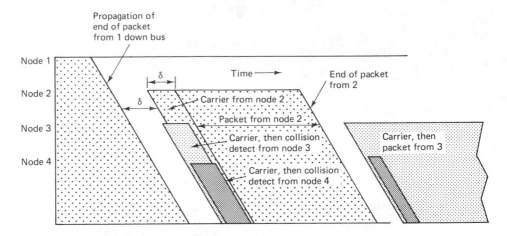

Figure 4.25   Implicit tokens on a unidirectional bus. Each node with traffic transmits carrier on hearing silence; then defers to upstream nodes on hearing carrier.

areas; the larger areas here can cause a network to become higher speed even at modest data rates.

We have already seen the effect of β on the performance of local area networks. CSMA/CD degrades rapidly with increasing β and becomes pointless for $\beta > 1$. If β is a small fraction of the number of nodes m, then, from Eq. (4.71), the token ring maintains high maximum throughput and small delay for small λ. Note that Eq. (4.71) assumes that each node transmits the free token immediately after completing its transmission. If the node waits for its packet to propagate around the ring before releasing the token (as is done in the IEEE 802.5 standard), then at most one packet can be transmitted each $1 + \beta$ time units, and the maximum throughput degrades as $1/\beta$.

The token bus, with implicit or explicit tokens, also degrades as $1/\beta$ if the nodes are numbered arbitrarily. If the nodes are numbered sequentially with respect to physical bus location, then, as seen by Eq. (4.73), the maximum throughput is degraded substantially only when β is a substantial fraction of the number of nodes m. If an ack is awaited after each packet, however, this throughput advantage is lost.

One of the most attractive possibilities for higher-speed local networks lies in the use of buses that propagate signals in only one direction. Optical fibers have this property naturally and cable technology is well developed for unidirectional transmission.

With a unidirectional bus, it is possible to combine the features of implicit tokens with those of collision detection so as to almost eliminate token delay. To see how this is done, consider Fig. 4.25, and for now ignore the problem of how packets on the bus get to their destinations. Assume that a node on the left end of

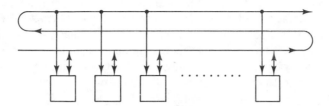

Figure 4.26   The bus structure for Expressnet. Each node transmits on the lower portion of the bus and listens on both lower and upper portions. Contention is resolved on the lower portion with the left-most node taking priority. Reception and detection of the end of a cycle takes place from the upper portion.

the bus has just finished transmission. Each subsequent node that has a packet to send starts to transmit carrier as soon as it detects the channel to be idle.

If δ is the time required for a node to detect idle and to start transmitting carrier, then we see from the figure that if two nodes have packets to send at the completion of a given packet, then the second node will start to send carrier at a delay δ after the end of the previous packet passes that node. The carrier sent by the first node will reach the second node at essentially the same time as the second node starts to send carrier. Since the second node can detect whether or not the first node is sending carrier after another delay of δ, the second node (and all further nodes) can terminate the transmission of carrier after this delay δ. Thus, if each node starts to transmit its packet after sending carrier for δ, the node is assured that no earlier node can be transmitting, and that all subsequent nodes will cease transmitting before any of the packet information arrives.

We see that the implicit token is simply the termination of transmission on the line. The time v for this token to travel from one node to the next is simply the propagation time from one node to the next. We view the length of the packet as containing δ units of time for detection at the end and δ units of time for carrier at the beginning. In a sense, this is the ideal system with TDM reservations. The time for making a reservation consists only of propagation delay (essentially the implicit token has zero length), and the packets follow immediately after the reservations.

Expressnet

The above discussion ignored the questions of how to receive the transmitted packets and how to return to the beginning of the bus and restart the process after all nodes have their turns. We first illustrate how these problems are solved in the Expressnet system [TBF83], and then briefly describe several alternative approaches.

Expressnet uses a unidirectional bus with two folds as shown in Fig. 4.26. Packets are transmitted on the first portion of the bus, as explained above, and nodes read the packets from the third portion of the bus. When a silence interval longer than δ is detected on the third portion of the bus, it is clear that all nodes have had a chance to transmit and it is time to start a new cycle. Thus, all nodes with packets to send again start to send carrier. Because of the double fold in the bus, however, nodes on the left end of the bus hear the idle signal before those on the right, and the carrier signals will again overlap for the next cycle as in Fig. 4.25.

The system is still not quite complete, since there is a problem if no node has a packet to send in a cycle. This is solved by having all nodes, busy or not, transmit carrier for a duration δ when they hear the onset of a silent interval longer than δ on the third portion of the bus. All nodes with packets must then extend their burst of carrier to a duration 2δ. This extra period of δ is necessary to detect silence on the first portion of the bus if none of the earlier nodes have packets to send. These extra bursts of carrier from all nodes keep the system synchronized during idle periods.

Since the propagation delay from when a node starts to transmit until the signal arrives at the corresponding point on the third portion of the bus is 2β, and since the transmission of the burst of carrier and its detection take time 2δ, we see that the average reservation interval is

$$v = 2(\beta + \delta)/m \tag{4.74}$$

Equations (4.70) and (4.71) again give the expected queueing delay for multiple packets per reservation and a single packet per reservation, respectively.

There are many possible variations on how to use this unidirectional bus. One could replace the double folded structure with a single fold, reading packets on the return trip on the bus, and then using a special node at the left end of the bus to start new cycles. One could also use two buses, one in each direction. A node could then send traffic to nodes on its right on the right going bus and traffic to nodes on its left on the left going bus. Special nodes on each end of the two buses would then interchange information for starting new cycles in each direction. Other possibilities include using a separate control wire, or a separate frequency band, to take the place of the implicit reservation tokens. [FiT84] contrasts a large set of these possible approaches.

Homenets

The previous approaches to higher-speed local networks were based on the use of a unidirectional bus. CATV systems, on the other hand, typically have a tree structure with transmissions from the root of the tree being broadcast throughout the tree. To use such networks for data, there is usually a separate frequency band for communication from the leaves of the tree in toward the root. When packets are sent inward toward the root from different leaves, there is the usual problem of collisions, but the use of implicit reservation tokens based on bus position no longer works.

Homenets [MaN85] provide an interesting approach to coping with the prob-

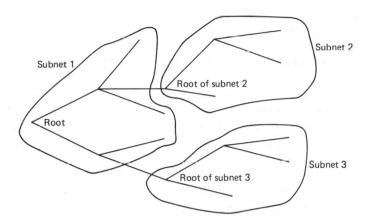

Figure 4.27   A CATV network divided into subnets in the Homenet strategy. Each subnet has one incoming and one outgoing frequency band and uses CSMA/CD to resolve collisions with a subnet.

lem of large β on such a net. The idea is to break up the CATV net into subnets called homenets. Each homenet forms its own subtree in the overall network tree, as shown in Fig. 4.27, and each homenet has its own frequency bands, one for propagation inward toward the root and the other for propagation outward. This strategy cures the problem of large β in two ways. First, the propagation delay within a homenet is greatly reduced from its value in the entire net, and second, by using a restricted bandwidth, the data rate within the homenet is reduced. With this two-fold decrease in β, it becomes reasonable to use CSMA/CD within the homenet.

  This leaves us with two unanswered questions. First, since the nodes transmit their packets inward toward the root, how do other outlying nodes in the same homenet hear collisions? Second, how are the packets received by nodes outside the homenet? The solution to the first question is for the node at the root of a given homenet to receive the signal on the homenet's incoming frequency band and to both forward it toward the root of the entire net, and also to convert it to the homenet's outgoing frequency band and broadcast it back out to the homenet. This allows the nodes to detect collisions within the propagation delay of the homenet. The solution to the second question is for all of the incoming frequency bands to be forwarded to the root of the entire net, which then converts these bands to the outgoing frequency bands and rebroadcasts all the signals back through the entire network. The root node for each homenet then filters out the signal from the overall root on its own outgoing frequency (since that signal is just a delayed replica of what it has already transmitted outward) and forwards the other bands over its own homenet.

  One additional advantage of this strategy is that the nodes need only transmit and receive within these restricted frequency bands. When a session is set up between two nodes, the receiver at each node must know of the outgoing frequency band for the sender's homenet, and then it simply receives the desired packets out of the signal in that band.

4.5.6 Generalized Polling and Splitting Algorithms

The last subsection treated multiaccess systems in the presence of large propagation delays. Here, we look at the opposite case in which $\beta \ll 1$. One example of this arises with very short buses, such as in the back plane of a multimicroprocessor system. Another example occurs for polling on multidrop telephone lines; here the data rates are small, leading to packet transmission times much greater than the propagation delay.

In these situations, we see from Eqs. (4.72) and (4.73) that the reservation time per node v is linearly increasing with the detection delay δ and with the (implicit or explicit) token delay. From the queueing delay formulas, Eqs. (4.70) and (4.71), the queueing delay is $mv/2$ in the limit of light load; furthermore, if mv is large relative to the packet transmission time, delay increases at least linearly with mv at all stable loads. Thus, we want to reduce mv, the reservation overhead per cycle.

For simplicity, we now model the multiaccess channel, at least for the purpose of reservations, as a bit synchronous binary "or" channel. That is, at each bit time, the output of the channel is 1 if the input for one or more nodes is 1; otherwise, the output is 0. This is a reasonable model if a separate control wire is used for reservations; it is also reasonable if nodes use short bursts of carrier to request reservations (*i.e.*, the existence of carrier can be detected, but not the number of nodes sending carrier).

This model is very similar to our original slotted multiaccess model in section 4.2. One difference is that the slot time is reduced to a single bit time; the other difference is that the feedback, instead of being 0,1,e, is now 0 or positive. We regard the slots as reservation slots and recognize (as in the examples above), that packets can be transmitted at higher rates than one bit per reservation slot. The question of interest is how many reservation slots are required to make a reservation?

The simplest strategy within this model is to make reservations by TDM within the reservation slots. Under heavy loading, most nodes will have a packet to send at each turn, and almost each reservation slot successfully establishes a reservation. In the light loading limit, an arriving packet has to wait $m/2$ reservation slots on the average; this is the situation we would like to avoid.

A better strategy, under light loading, is to use a logarithmic search for a node with a packet (see [NiS74], [Hay76]). Suppose the nodes are numbered 0 to $m - 1$ and let $n_1, \ldots, n_k$ be the binary representation of any given node number where

$$k = \lceil \log_2 m \rceil$$

The algorithm proceeds in successive collision resolution periods (CRP) to find the lowest numbered node that has a packet to send. In the first slot of a CRP, all active nodes (*i.e.*, all nodes with waiting packets) send a 1 and all other nodes

				Nodes				Output	
000	001	010	011	100	101	110	111	y	
0	0	1	1	0	0	1	0	1	Slot 1
0	0	1	1	0	0	0	0	1	Slot 2
0	0	0	0	0	0	0	0	0	Slot 3
0	0	1	0	0	0	0	0	1	Slot 4

Figure 4.28   A logarithmic search for the lowest numbered active node. Nodes 010, 011, and 110 have packets. At the end of slot 2, node 110 becomes inactive; at the end of slot 4, node 011 becomes inactive. Outputs from slot 2 to 4, complemented, are 010.

send 0 (*i.e.*, nothing). If the channel output, say y_0, is 0, then the CRP is over and a new CRP starts on the next slot to make reservations for any packets that may have arrived in the interim. If $y_0 = 1$ on the other hand, then one or more nodes have packets and the logarithmic search starts.

Assuming $y_0 = 1$, all active nodes with $n_1 = 0$ send a 1 in the next slot. If y_1, the output in this slot, is 1, it means that the lowest numbered node's binary representation starts with 0; otherwise it starts with 1. In the former case, all active nodes with $n_1 = 1$ become inactive and wait for the end of the CRP to become active again. In the latter case, all active nodes have $n_1 = 1$ and all remain active.

The general rule on the $(i+1)^{\text{st}}$ slot of the CRP, $1 \le i \le k$, (assuming $y_0 = 1$) is that all active nodes with $n_i = 0$ send a 1; at the end of the slot, if the channel output y_i is 1, then all nodes with $n_i = 1$ become inactive. Figure 4.28 shows an example of this strategy. It should be clear that at the end of the $(k+1)^{\text{st}}$ slot, only the lowest numbered node is active and the binary representation of that node's number is the bit-wise complement of $y_1, \ldots, y_k$.

To maintain fairness and to serve the nodes in round robin order, the nodes should be renumbered after each reservation is made. If the reservation is for node n, say, then each node subtracts $n + 1$ modulo m from its current number. Thus, a node's number is one less than its round robin distance from the last node that transmitted; obviously, this rule could be modified by priorities in any desired way.

Assuming that a packet is sent immediately after a reservation is made and that the next CRP starts after that transmission, it is easy to find the expected delay of this algorithm. Each CRP that starts when the system is busy lasts for $k + 1$ reservation slots. Thus, we regard the packet transmission time as simply being extended by these $k + 1$ slots. If the system is empty at the beginning of a CRP, then the CRP lasts for one reservation slot and this can be regarded as the server going on vacation for one reservation slot. Equation (3.55) in Chapter 3 gives the queueing delay for this system.

In contrasting this logarithmic search reservation strategy with TDM reservations, we see that logarithmic search reduces delay from $m/2$ to $k+1$ reservation slots per packet for light loads but increases delay from 1 to $k+1$ reservation slots per packet at heavy loads. The obvious question is how to combine these strategies to have the best of both worlds? The answer to this question comes from viewing this problem as a source coding problem, much like the framing issue in Chapter 2. The TDM strategy here corresponds to the use of a unary code there to encode frame lengths. The logarithmic search here corresponds to the use of ordinary binary representation. We noticed the advantage there of going to a combined unary-binary representation. In the current context, this means that each CRP should test only a limited number of nodes, say the 2^j lowest numbered nodes, at a time. If the output is 1, then the lowest numbered node in that set is resolved as above in j additional slots. If the output is 0, then 2^j is subtracted from each node's number and the next CRP starts. Problem 4.30 finds the expected number of reservation slots per packet and the optimal choice of j under several different assumptions.

Note the similarity of these algorithms to the splitting algorithms of section 4.3. The ideas are the same, and the only difference is that "success" cannot be distinguished from collision here; thus, even though only one node in an active subset contains a packet, the subset must be split until only one node remains.

4.6 PACKET RADIO NETWORKS

Subsection 4.1.4 briefly described packet radio networks as multiaccess networks in which not all nodes could hear the transmissions of all other nodes. This feature is characteristic both of line-of-sight radio communication in the UHF band (300–3,000 megahertz) and also of non-line-of-sight communication at HF (3–30 megahertz). Our interest here is in the effect of partial connectivity on multiaccess techniques rather than the physical characteristics of the radio broadcast medium.

The topology of a radio network can be described by a graph as in Fig. 4.29. The graph, $G = (N, L)$, contains a set of nodes N and a set of links L. Each link in L corresponds to an ordered pair of nodes, say (i, j), and indicates that transmissions from i can be heard at j. In some situations, node j might be able to hear i, but i is unable to hear j. In such a case $(i, j) \in L$ but $(j, i) \notin L$. This asymmetry does not occur in Fig. 4.29 where each edge denotes two links, one in each direction.

Our assumption about communication in this multiaccess medium is that if node i transmits a packet, that packet will be correctly received by node j if and only if

1. there is a link from i to j, i.e., $(i, j) \in L$ and

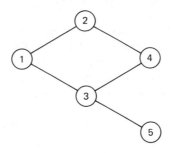

Figure 4.29   A packet radio network; each edge indicates that two nodes at the ends of the edge can hear each other's transmission.

2. no other node k for which $(k, j) \in L$ is transmitting while i is transmitting, and

3. j itself is not transmitting while i is transmitting.

Thus, for Fig. 4.29, we see that if nodes 1 and 3 are transmitting simultaneously, node 2 will correctly receive the packet from 1 and node 4 will correctly receive the packet from 3. On the other hand, if nodes 2 and 3 are transmitting simultaneously, nodes 1 and 4 will each see a collision, but node 5 will correctly receive the packet from 3.

It can be seen from this example that having a large number of links in a graph is not necessarily desirable. A large number of links increases the number of pairs of nodes that can communicate directly, but also increases the likelihood of collisions. This tradeoff is further explored in subsection 4.6.3.

One interesting question that can now be posed is how much traffic can be carried in such a network. Define a *collision-free set* as a set of links that can carry packets simultaneously with no collisions at the receiving ends of the links. For example, ((1,2), (3,4)) and ((2,1), (5,3)) are both collision-free sets; also, the empty set and each set consisting of a single link are collision-free sets. It is convenient to order the links in some arbitrary order and represent each collision-free set as a vector of 0's and 1's called a *collision-free vector* (CFV). The ℓth component of a CFV is 1 if and only if the ℓth link is in the corresponding collision-free set. For example, some CFV's are listed below for the graph of Fig. 4.29.

(1,2)	(2,1)	(1,3)	(3,1)	(2,4)	(4,2)	(3,4)	(4,3)	(3,5)	(5,3)
1	0	0	0	0	0	1	0	0	0
1	0	0	0	0	0	0	0	1	0
0	1	0	0	0	0	0	1	0	0
0	1	0	0	0	0	0	0	0	1

4.6.1 TDM for Packet Radio Nets

One simple way to use a packet radio net is to choose a given collection of collision-free sets and to cycle between them by TDM. That is, in the ith slot of a TDM cycle, all links in the ith collision-free set can carry packets. With such a TDM strategy, there are no collisions, and the fraction of time that a given link can carry packets is simply the fraction of the collection of collision-free sets that contain that link.

More compactly, if $x_1, \ldots, x_J$ are the CFV's corresponding to a collection of J collision free sets, then the vector $f = \left(\sum_j x_j \right) / J$ gives the fraction of time that each link can be used. As a slight generalization, the TDM frame could be extended and each collision-free set could be used some arbitrary number of times in the frame. If α_j is the fraction of frame slots using the jth collision-free set, then

$$ f = \sum_j \alpha_j x_j \tag{4.75} $$

gives the fractional utilization of each link. A vector of the form $\sum_j \alpha_j x_j$, in which $\sum_j \alpha_j = 1$ and $\alpha_j \geq 0$ for $1 \leq j \leq J$, is called a convex combination of the vectors $x_1, \ldots, x_J$. What we have just seen is that any convex combination of CFVs can be approached arbitrarily closely as a fractional link utilization vector through the use of TDM.

Suppose that instead of using TDM as above, we use some sort of collision resolution approach in the network. At any given time, the vector of links that are successfully transmitting packets is a CFV. Averaging this vector of successful link transmissions over time, we get a vector whose ℓ^{th} component is the fraction of time that the ℓth link is carrying packets successfully. This is also a convex combination of CFVs. Thus, we see that any link utilization that is achievable with collision resolution is also achievable by TDM.

One difficulty with TDM is that delays are longer than necessary for a lightly loaded network. This is not as serious as when all nodes are connected to a common receiver, since if all nodes have only a small number of incoming links, many links can transmit simultaneously and the waiting for a TDM slot is reduced.

A more serious problem with the TDM approach is that the nodes in a packet radio network are usually mobile, and thus the topology of the network is constantly changing. This means that the collision-free sets keep changing, requiring frequent updates of the TDM schedule. This is a difficult problem since even for a static network, the problem of determining whether a potential vector of link utilizations is a convex combination of CFVs falls into a class of difficult problems known as *NP complete* [Ari84]. See [PaS82] for an introduction to the theory of NP complete problems; for our purposes, this simply indicates that the worst-case computational effort to solve the problem increases very rapidly with the number of links in the network. The essential reason for this difficulty is that the number of different collision-free sets typically increases exponentially with the number of links in the network.

Frequency-division multiplexing (FDM) can also be used for packet radio networks in a way very similar to TDM. All links in a collision-free set can use the same frequency band simultaneously, so in principle the links can carry the same amount of traffic as in TDM. This approach is used in cellular radio networks for mobile voice communication. Here the area covered by the network is divided into a large number of local areas called cells, with each cell having a set of frequency bands for use within the cell. The set of frequency bands used by one cell can be reused by other cells that are sufficiently separated from one another to avoid interference. This provides a simple and practical way to choose a collection of collision-free sets. This same cellular separation principle could be used for TDM.

The discussion so far has ignored the question of how to route packets from source to destination. With the use of a given TDM or FDM structure, each link in the net has a given rate at which it can send packets, and the resource-sharing interaction between links has been removed. Thus, the problem of routing is essentially the same as in conventional networks with dedicated links between nodes; this problem is treated in Chapter 5. When collision resolution strategies are used, however, we shall see that routing is considerably more complicated than in the conventional network case.

4.6.2 Collision Resolution for Packet Radio Nets

Collision resolution is quite a bit trickier for packet radio nets than for the single receiver systems studied before. The first complication is obtaining feedback information. For the example of Fig. 4.29, suppose that links (2,4) and (3,5) contain packets in a given slot. Then node 4 perceives a collision and node 5 correctly receives a packet. If nodes 5 and 4 send feedback information, node 3 will experience a feedback collision. A second problem is that if a node perceives a collision, it does not know how many packets were addressed to it. For both reasons, we cannot assume the perfect $0,1,e$ feedback that we assumed previously. It follows that the splitting algorithms of section 4.3 cannot be used and the stabilization techniques of subsection 4.2.3 require substantial revisions.

Fortunately, slotted and unslotted Aloha are still applicable, and, to a certain extent, some of the ideas of carrier sensing and reservation can still be used. We start by analyzing how slotted Aloha can work in this environment. When an unbacklogged node receives a packet to transmit (either a new packet entering the network, or a packet in transit that has to be forwarded to another node), it sends the packet in the next slot. If no acknowledgement (ack) of correct reception arrives within some time-out period, then the node becomes backlogged and the packet is retransmitted after a random delay. Finally, a backlogged node becomes unbacklogged when all of its packets have been successfully transmitted and acked.

There are a number of ways in which acks can be returned to the transmitting node. The simplest is that if node i sends a packet to j that must be forwarded on to some other node k, then if i hears j's transmission to k, that serves as an ack of the (i,j) transmission. This technique is somewhat defective in two ways.

First, some other technique is required to ack packets whose final destination is j. Second, suppose that j successfully relays the packet to k, but i fails to hear the transmission because of a collision. This causes an unnecessary retransmission from i to j, and also requires some way for j to ack, since j has already forwarded the packet to k. Another approach, which can be used in conjunction with the implicit acks above, is for each node to include explicit acks for the last few packets it has received in each outgoing packet. This approach requires a node to send a dummy packet carrying ack information if the node has no data to send for some period. A third approach, which seems somewhat inferior to the approach above, is to provide time at the end of each slot for explicit acks of packets received within the slot.

Let us now analyze what happens in slotted Aloha for a very heavily loaded network. In particular, assume that all nodes are backlogged all the time and have packets to send on all outgoing links at all times. We can assume that the nodes have infinite buffers to store the backlogged packets, but for the time being, we are not interested in the question of delay. This assumption of constant backlogging is very different from our assumptions in section 4.2, but the reasons for this will be discussed later. For all nodes i and j, let q_{ij} be the probability that node i transmits a packet to node j in any given slot, and let Q_i be the probability that node i transmits to any node. Thus,

$$Q_i = \sum_j q_{ij} \qquad (4.76)$$

To simplify notation, we simply assume that q_{ij} is zero if (i, j) is not in the set of links L. Let p_{ij} be the probability that a transmission on (i, j) is successful. Under our assumption of heavy loading, each node transmits or not in a slot independently of all other nodes. Since p_{ij} is the probability that none of the other nodes in range of j, including j itself, is transmitting, we have

$$p_{ij} = (1 - Q_j) \prod_{\substack{k:(k,j)\in L \\ k \neq i}} (1 - Q_k) \qquad (4.77)$$

Finally, the rate f_{ij} of successful packet transmissions per slot, *i.e.*, the throughput, on link (i, j) is

$$f_{ij} = q_{ij}\, p_{ij} \qquad (4.78)$$

Equations (4.76) to (4.78) give us the link throughputs in terms of the attempt rates q_{ij} under the heavy loading assumption. The question of greater interest, however, is to find the attempt rates q_{ij} that will yield a desired set of throughputs (if that set of throughputs is feasible).

This problem can be solved through an iterative approach. To simplify notation, let q denote a vector whose components are the attempt rates q_{ij}, let p and f be vectors whose components are p_{ij} and f_{ij}, respectively, and let Q be a vector with components Q_i. Given a desired throughput vector f, we start with an initial

q^0 which is a vector of 0's. We then use Eq. (4.76) and (4.77) to find Q^0 and p^0 (Q^0 is thus a vector of 0's and p^0 a vector of 1's). Equation (4.78) is then used to obtain the next iteration for q; that is, the components of q^1 are given by

$$q^1_{ij} = \frac{f_{ij}}{p^0_{ij}} \tag{4.79}$$

For each successive iteration, Q^n is found from Eq. (4.76) using q^n, and p^n is found from Eq. (4.77) using Q^n; then q^{n+1} is found from Eq. (4.78) using p^n. Note that $q^1 \geq q^0$ (*i.e.*, each component of q^1 is greater than or equal to the corresponding component of q^0). Thus, $Q^1 \geq Q^0$, and $p^1 \leq p^0$. From Eq. (4.78) it can then be seen that $q^2 \geq q^1$. Continuing this argument, it is seen that, so long as none of the components of Q exceed 1, q is nondecreasing with successive iterations and p is nonincreasing. It follows that either some component of Q must exceed 1 at some iteration or else q approaches a limit, say q^*, and in this limit Eqs. (4.76) to (4.78) are simultaneously satisfied with the resulting Q^* and p^*.

We now want to show that if (4.76) to (4.78) have any other solution, say q', Q', p', (subject, of course, to $q' \geq 0, Q' \leq 1$) then $q' \geq q^*, Q' \geq Q^*$, and $p' \leq p^*$. To see this, we simply observe that $q^0 \leq q', Q^0 \leq Q', p^0 \geq p'$. From (4.78) then, $q^1 \leq q'$. Continuing this argument over successive iterations, $q^n \leq q', Q^n \leq Q'$, and $p^n \geq p'$ for all n, so the result holds in the limit. This argument also shows that if some component of Q^n exceeds 1 for some n, then Eq. (4.76) to (4.78) have no solution, *i.e.*, that the given f is infeasible.

Next, assume we know the input rates to the network and know the routes over which the sessions will flow, so that in principle we can determine the steady-state rates f'_{ij} at which the links must handle traffic. We would like to choose the throughputs of each link under heavy load to exceed these steady-state rates so that the backlogs do not build up indefinitely. One approach then is to find the largest number $\beta > 1$ for which $f = \beta f'$ is feasible under the heavy load assumption. Given this largest f, and the corresponding attempt rates q, we can then empty out the backlog as it develops.

There is one difficulty here, and that is, if some nodes are backlogged and others are not, then the unbacklogged nodes no longer choose their transmission times independently. Thus, it is conceivable in bizarre cases that some backlogged nodes fare more poorly when other nodes are unbacklogged than they do when all nodes are backlogged. Problem 4.32 gives an example of this phenomenon. One way to avoid this difficulty is for new packets at a node to join the backlog immediately rather than being able to transmit in the next slot. This, of course, increases delay under light loading conditions. The other approach is to live dangerously and hope for the best. To a certain extent, one has to do this anyway with packet radio, since with a changing topology, one cannot maintain carefully controlled attempt rates.

Our reason for focusing on the heavily loaded case is that the number of links entering each node is usually small for a packet radio net, and thus, the attempt rates can be moderately high even under the heavy loading assumption. For the single-receiver case, on the other hand, the number of nodes tends to be much larger, and thus the attempt rates appropriate for heavy loading tend to create large delays. The other reason is that stabilization is a much harder problem here than in the single-receiver case; a node cannot help itself too much by adjusting its own attempt rates, since other nodes might be causing congestion but not experiencing any congestion themselves (see Prob. 4.32).

4.6.3 Transmission Radii for Packet Radio

In the previous subsections, we viewed the set of links in a packet radio net as given. It can be seen, however, that if a node increases its transmitter power, then its transmission will be heard by a larger set of nodes. The following qualitative argument shows that it is desirable to keep the power level relatively small so that each node has a moderately small set of incoming and outgoing links. Assume for simplicity that we have a symmetric net in which each node has exactly n incoming links and n outgoing links. Suppose further that each link has an identical traffic carrying requirement. It is not hard to convince oneself that Eqs. (4.76) to (4.78) are satisfied by an identical attempt rate q on each link. Each Q_i is then nq, each p_{ij} is given by $(1 - nq)^n$, and finally,

$$f = q(1 - nq)^n \qquad (4.80)$$

It is easy to verify that f is maximized by choosing $q = 1/[n(n + 1)]$, and the resulting value of f is approximately $1/(en^2)$. Each node then sends packets successfully at a rate of $1/en$. If there are m nodes in the network and the average number of links on the path from source to destination is J, then the rate at which the network can deliver packets is $m/(Jen)$ packets per slot.

Now let us look at what happens when the transmission radius R over which a node can be heard varies. The number of nodes within radius R of a given node will vary roughly as R^2; so the rate at which an individual node sends packets successfully will decrease as $1/R^2$. On the other hand, as R increases, the routing will presumably be changed to send the packets as far as possible toward the destination on each link of the path. Thus, we expect the number of links on a path to decrease as $1/R$. Thus, if J is proportional to $1/R$ and n is proportional to R^2, the rate at which the network can deliver packets is proportional to $1/R$, leading us to believe that R should be kept very small.

The above very crude analysis leaves out two important factors. First, when R and n are large, a packet can move almost a distance R toward its destination on each link of a well chosen path, so that J is essentially proportional to $1/R$ in that region. When R gets small, however, the paths become very circuitous and thus, J decreases with R much faster than $1/R$ for small R. Second, when R is too small, the network is not very well connected, and some links might have to carry very large amounts of traffic. This leads us to the conclusion that R should be small, but not too small, so that n is considerably larger than 1. Takagi and

Kleinrock [TaK85] have done a much more careful analysis (although still with some questionable assumptions) and have concluded that the radius should be set so that n is on the order of 8.

4.6.4 Carrier Sensing and Busy Tones

We saw in section 4.4 that carrier sensing yielded a considerable improvement over slotted Aloha in the situation where all nodes could hear all other nodes and the propagation delay is small. For line-of-sight radio, the propagation delay is typically small relative to packet transmission times, so it is reasonable to explore how well carrier sensing will work here. Unfortunately, if node i is transmitting to node j, and node k wants to transmit to j, there is no assurance that k can hear i. There might be an obstruction between i and k, or they might simply be out of range of each other. Thus, carrier sensing will serve to prevent some collisions from occurring, but cannot prevent others. To make matters worse, with carrier sensing, there is no uniform slotting structure, and thus, carrier sensing loses some of the advantage that slotted Aloha has over pure Aloha. Finally, radio transmission is subject to fading and variable noise, so that the existence of another transmitting node, even within range, is hard to detect in a short time. For these reasons, carrier sensing is not very effective for packet radio.

A busy tone [ToK75], [SiS81] is one approach to improving the performance of carrier sensing in a packet radio network. Whenever any node detects a packet being transmitted, it starts to send a signal, called a busy tone, in a separate frequency band. Thus, when node i starts to send a packet to node j, node j (along with all other nodes that can hear i) will start to send a busy tone. All the nodes that can hear j will thus avoid transmitting; thus, assuming reciprocity (*i.e.*, the nodes that can hear j are the same as the nodes that j can hear), it follows that j will experience no collision.

A problem with the use of busy tones is that when node i starts to send a packet, *all* the nodes in range of i will start to send busy tones, and thus every node within range of any node in range of i will be inhibited from transmitting. Using the very crude type of analysis in the last subsection, and assuming a transmission radius of R, we see that when node i starts to transmit, most of the nodes within radius $2R$ of i will be inhibited. This number will typically be about four times the number of nodes within radius R of the receiving node, which is the set of nodes that should be inhibited. Thus, from a throughput standpoint, this is not a very promising approach.

Another variation on the busy tone approach is for a node to send a busy tone only after it receives the address part of the packet and recognizes itself as the intended recipient. Aside from the complexity, this greatly increases β, the time over which another node could start to transmit before hearing the busy tone.

It can be seen that packet radio is an area in which many more questions than answers exist, both in terms of desirable structure and in terms of analysis. Questions of modulation and detection of packets make the situation even more complex. In military applications, it is often desirable to use spread spectrum techniques for sending packets. One of the consequences of this is that if two packets are being received at once, the receiver can often lock on to one, with the other acting only as wide-band noise. If a different spread spectrum code is used for each receiver, then the situation is even better, since the receiver can look for only its own sequence and thus reject simultaneous packets sent to other receivers. Unfortunately, attenuation is often quite severe in line-of-sight communication, so that unwanted packets can arrive at a node with much higher power levels than the desired packets, and still cause a collision.

4.7 SUMMARY

The central problem of multiaccess communication is that of sharing a communication channel between a multiplicity of nodes where each node has sporadic service requirements. This problem arises in local area networks, metropolitan area networks, satellite networks, and various types of radio networks.

Collision resolution is one approach to such sharing. Inherently, collision resolution algorithms can achieve small delay with a large number of lightly loaded nodes, but stability is a major concern. The joint issues of stability, throughput, and delay are studied most cleanly with the infinite node assumption. This assumption lets one study collision resolution without the added complication of individual queues at each node. Under this assumption, we found that throughputs up to $1/e$ packets per slot were possible with stabilized slotted Aloha, and throughputs up to 0.487 packets per slot were possible with splitting algorithms.

Reservations provide the other major approach to multiaccess sharing. The channel can be reserved by a prearranged fixed allocation (*e.g.*, TDM or FDM) or can be reserved dynamically. Dynamic reservations further divide into the use of collision resolution and the use of TDM (or round robin ordering) to make the reservations for channel use. CSMA/CD (*i.e.*, Ethernet) is a popular example of the use of collision resolution to make (implicit) reservations. Token rings, token buses, and their elaborations, are examples of the use of round robin ordering to make reservations.

There are an amazing variety of ways to use the special characteristics of particular multiaccess media to make reservations in round robin order. Some of these variations require a time proportional to β (the propagation delay) to make a reservation, and some require a time proportional to β/m where m is the number of nodes. These latter variations are particularly suitable for higher speed systems with $\beta > 1$.

Packet radio systems lie at an intermediate point between pure multiaccess systems where all nodes share the same medium (and thus no explicit routing is required) and point to point networks (where routing but no multiaccess sharing is required). Radio networks are still in a formative and fragmentary stage of research.

4.8 NOTES, SOURCES, AND SUGGESTED READING

Section 4.2.   The Aloha network is first described in [Abr70] and the slotted improvement in [Rob72]. The problem of stability was discussed in [Met73], [LaK75], and [CaH75]. Binary exponential backoff was developed in [MeB76]. Modern approaches to stability are treated in [HVL83] and [Riv85].

Section 4.3.   The first tree algorithms are due to [Cap77], [TsM78], and [Hay76]. [Mas80] provided improvements and simple analysis techniques. The FCFS splitting algorithm is due to [Gal78] and, independently, [TsM80]. Upper bounds on maximum throughput (with assumptions 1 to 6b of subsection 4.2.1) are in [Pip81] and [MiT81]. The March 1985 issue of the IEEE Transactions on Information Theory is a special issue on Random-Access Communications; the articles provide an excellent snapshot of the current status of work related to splitting algorithms.

Section 4.4.   The classic works on CSMA are [KlT75] and [Tob74]

Section 4.5.   The literature on local area networks and satellite networks is somewhat overwhelming. [Sta85] provides a wealth of practical details. Good source references in the satellite area are [JBH78], [CRW73], [Bin75], and [WiE80]. For local area networks, [MeB76] is the source work on Ethernet, and [FaN69] and [FaL72] are source works on ring nets. [CPR78] and [KuR82] are good overview articles. [FiT84] does an excellent job of comparing and contrasting the many approaches to implicit and explicit tokens and polling on buses.

Section 4.6.   [KGB78] provides a good overview of packet radio. Busy tones are described in [ToK75] and [SiS81]. Transmission Radii are discussed in [TaK85].

P R O B L E M S

4.1 (a) Verify that the steady-state probabilities p_n for the Markov chain in Fig. 4.3 are given by the solution to the equations:

$$p_n = \sum_{i=0}^{n+1} p_i P_{in}$$

$$\sum_{n=0}^{m} p_n = 1$$

(b) For $n < m$, use (a) to express p_{n+1} in terms of $p_0, p_1, \ldots, p_n$.

(c) Express p_1 in terms of p_0 and then p_2 in terms of p_0.

(d) For $m = 2$, solve for p_0 in terms of the transition probabilities.

4.2 (a) Show that P_{succ} in Eq. (4.5) can be expressed as

$$P_{\text{succ}} = \left[\frac{(m-n)q_a}{1-q_a} + \frac{nq_r}{1-q_r} \right] (1-q_a)^{m-n}(1-q_r)^n$$

(b) Use the approximation $(1-x)^y \approx e^{-xy}$ for small x to show that for small q_a and q_r,

$$P_{\text{succ}} \approx G(n)e^{-G(n)}$$

where $G(n) = (m-n)q_a + nq_r$

(c) Note that $(1-x)^y = e^{y \ln(1-x)}$. Expand $\ln(1-x)$ in a power series and show that

$$\frac{(1-x)^y}{e^{-xy}} = \exp\left(-\frac{x^2 y}{2} - \frac{x^3 y}{3} \cdots \right)$$

Show that this ratio is close to 1 if $x \ll 1$ and $x^2 y \ll 1$.

4.3 (a) Redraw Fig. 4.4 for the case in which $q_r = 1/m$ and $q_a = 1/me$.

(b) Find the departure rate (*i.e.*, P_{succ}) in the fully backlogged case $n = m$.

(c) Note that there is no unstable equilibrium or undesired stable point in this case and show (graphically) that this holds true for any value of q_a.

(d) Solve numerically (using $q_a = 1/me$) for the value of G at which the stable point occurs.

(e) Find n/m at the stable point. Note that this is the fraction of the arriving packets that are not accepted by the system at this typical point.

4.4 Consider the idealized slotted multiaccess model of subsection 4.2.1 with the no-buffering assumption. Let n_k be the number of backlogged nodes at the beginning of the kth slot and let $\bar{n}$ be the expected value of n_k over all k. Note that $\bar{n}$ will depend on the particular way in which collisions are resolved, but we regard $\bar{n}$ as given here.

(a) Find the expected number of *accepted* arrivals per slot, $\bar{N}_a$, as a function of $\bar{n}, m$, and q_a, where m is the number of nodes and q_a is the arrival rate per node.

(b) Find the expected departure rate per slot, $\overline{P}_{\mathrm{succ}}$, as a function of $\overline{n}, m$, and q_a. *Hint:* How is N_a related to $\overline{P}_{\mathrm{succ}}$? Recall that both are averages over time.

(c) Find the expected number of packets in the system, $\overline{N}_{\mathrm{sys}}$, immediately after the beginning of a slot (the number in the system is the backlog plus the accepted new arrivals).

(d) Find the expected delay T of an accepted packet from its arrival at the beginning of a slot until the completion of its successful transmission at the end of a slot. *Hint:* Use Little's Theorem; it may be useful to redraw the diagram used to prove Little's Theorem.

(e) Suppose that the strategy for resolving collisions is now modified and the expected backlog $\overline{n}$ is reduced to $\overline{n}' < \overline{n}$. Show that N_a increases, $\overline{P}_{\mathrm{succ}}$ increases, $\overline{N}_{\mathrm{sys}}$ decreases, and T decreases. Note that this means that improving the system with respect to one of these parameters improves it with respect to all.

4.5 Assume for simplicity that each transmitted packet in a slotted Aloha system is successful with some fixed probability p. New packets are assumed to arrive at the beginning of a slot and are transmitted immediately. If a packet is unsuccessful, it is retransmitted with probability q_r in each successive slot until successfully received.

(a) Find the expected delay T from the arrival of a packet until the completion of its successful transmission. *Hint:* Given a packet has not been successfully transmitted before, what is the probability that it is both transmitted and successful in the ith slot $(i > 1)$ after arrival?

(b) Suppose that the number of nodes m is large, and that q_a and q_r are small. Show that in state n, the probability p that a given packet transmission is successful is approximately $p = e^{-G(n)}$, where $G(n) = (m - n)q_a + nq_r$.

(c) Now consider the stable equilibrium state n^* of the system where $G = G(n^*)$; $Ge^{-G} = (m - n^*)q_a$. Substitute (b) into your expression for T for (a), using $n = n^*$, and show that

$$T = 1 + \frac{n^*}{q_a(m - n^*)}$$

(Note that if n^* is assumed to be equal to $\overline{n}$ in Prob. 4.4, this is the same as the value of T found there).

(d) Solve numerically for T in the case where $q_a m = 0.3$ and $q_r m = 1$; show that $n^* \approx m/8$, corresponding to 1/8 loss of incoming traffic, and $T \approx m/2$, giving roughly the same delay as TDM.

4.6 (a) Consider P_{succ} as given exactly in Eq. (4.5). For given q_a, m, n, show that the value of q_r that maximizes P_{succ} satisfies

$$\frac{1}{1 - q_r} - \frac{q_a(m - n)}{1 - q_a} - \frac{q_r n}{1 - q_r} = 0$$

(b) Consider the value of q_r that satisfies the above equation as a function of q_a, say $q_r(q_a)$. Show that $q_r(q_a) > q_a$ (assume that $q_a < 1/m$).

(c) Take the total derivative of P_{succ} with respect to q_a, using $q_r(q_a)$ for q_r, and show that this derivative is negative. *Hint*: Recall that $\partial P_{\text{succ}}/\partial q_r$ is 0 at $q_r(q_a)$ and compare $\partial P_{\text{succ}}/\partial q_a$ with $\partial P_{\text{succ}}/\partial q_r$.

(d) Show that if q_r is chosen to maximize P_{succ} and $q_r < 1$, then P_{succ} is greater if new arrivals are treated immediately as backlogged than if new arrivals are immediately transmitted. *Hint:* In the backlog case, a previously unbacklogged node transmits with probability $q_a q_r < q_a$.

4.7 Consider a slotted Aloha system with "perfect capture". That is, if more than one packet is transmitted in a slot, the receiver "locks onto" one of the transmissions and receives it correctly; feedback immediately informs each transmitting node about which node was successful and the unsuccessful packets are retransmitted later.

(a) Give a convincing argument why expected delay is minimized if all waiting packets attempt transmission in each slot.

(b) Find the expected system delay assuming Poisson arrivals with overall rate λ. *Hint*: Review the example in subsection 3.5.1.

(c) Now assume that the feedback is delayed, and that if a packet is unsuccessful in the slot, it is retransmitted on the kth subsequent slot rather than the first subsequent slot. Find the new expected delay as a function of k. *Hint:* Consider the system as k subsystems, the ith subsystem handling arrivals in slots j such that $j \bmod k = i$.

4.8 Consider a slotted system in which all nodes have infinitely large buffers and all new arrivals (at Poisson rate λ/m per node) are allowed into the system, but are considered as backlogged immediately rather than transmitted in the next slot. While a node contains one or more packets, it independently transmits one packet in each slot, with probability q_r. Assume that any given transmission is successful with probability p.

(a) Show that the expected time from the beginning of a backlogged slot until the completion of the first success at a given node is $1/pq_r$. Show that the second moment of this time is $(2 - pq_r)/(pq_r)^2$.

(b) Note that the assumption of a constant success probability allows each node to be considered independently. Assume that λ/m is the Poisson arrival rate at a node, and use the service time results of (a) to show that the expected delay is

$$T = \frac{1}{q_r p(1-\rho)} + \frac{1-2\rho}{2(1-\rho)}$$

$$\rho = \frac{\lambda}{mpq_r}$$

(c) Assume $p = 1$ (this yields a smaller T than any other value of p, and corresponds to very light loading). Find T for $q_r = 1/m$; observe that this is roughly twice the delay for TDM if m is large.

4.9 Assume that the number of packets n in a slotted Aloha system at a given time is a Poisson random variable with mean $\hat{n} \geq 1$. Suppose each packet is independently transmitted in the next slot with probability $1/\hat{n}$.

(a) Find the probability that the slot is idle.
(b) Show that the aposteriori probability that there were n packets in the system, given an idle slot, is Poisson with mean $\hat{n} - 1$.
(c) Find the probability that the slot is successful.
(d) Show that the aposteriori probability that there were $n + 1$ packets in the system, given a success, is $e^{-(\hat{n}-1)}(\hat{n} - 1)^n/n!$ (*i.e.*, the number of remaining packets is Poisson with mean $\hat{n} - 1$).

4.10 Consider a slotted Aloha system satisfying assumptions 1 to 6a of subsection 4.2.1 *except* that each of the nodes has a limitless buffer to store all arriving packets until transmission *and* that nodes receive immediate feedback only about whether or not their own packets were successfully transmitted. Each node is in one of two different modes. In mode 1, a node transmits (with probability 1) in each slot, repeating unsuccessful packets, until its buffer of waiting packets is exhausted; at that point the node goes into mode 2. In mode 2, a node transmits a "dummy packet" in each slot with probability q_r until a successful transmission occurs, at which point it enters mode 1 (dummy packets are used only to simplify the mathematics). Assume that the system starts with all nodes in mode 2. Each node has Poisson arrivals of rate λ/m.

(a) Explain why at most one node at a time can be in mode 1.
(b) Given that a node is in mode 1, find its probability, p_1, of successful transmission. Find the mean time $\bar{x}$ between successful transmissions

and the second moment $\overline{x^2}$ of this time. *Hint:* Review the ARQ example in subsection 3.5.1, Chapter 3, with $N = 1$.

(c)   Given that all nodes are in mode 2, find the probability p_2 that some dummy packet is successfully transmitted in a given slot. Find the mean time $\overline{v}$ until the completion of such a successful transmission and its second moment $\overline{v^2}$.

(d)   Regard the intervals of time when all nodes are in mode 2 as reservation intervals. Show that the mean time a packet must wait in queue before first attempting transmission is

$$ W = \frac{R + E\{S\}\overline{v}}{1 - \rho}, \quad \rho = \lambda \overline{X} $$

where R is the mean residual time until completion of a service in mode 1 or completion of a reservation interval, and S is the number of whole reservation intervals until the node at which the packet arrived is in mode 1.

(e)   Show that

$$ W = \frac{\lambda(2 - p_1)}{2p_1^2(1 - \rho)} + \frac{2 - p_2}{2p_2} + \frac{m - 1}{p_2(1 - \rho)} $$

Show that W is finite if $q_r < (1 - \lambda)/(m - 1)$.

4.11 Consider the somewhat unrealistic feedback assumption for unslotted Aloha in which all nodes are informed, precisely τ time units after the beginning of each transmission whether or not that transmission was successful. Thus, in the event of a collision, each node knows how many packets were involved in the collision, and each node involved in the collision knows how many other nodes started transmission before itself. Assume each transmission lasts one time unit and assume $m = \infty$. Consider a retransmission strategy in which the first node involved in a collision waits one time unit after receiving feedback on its collision and then transmits its packet. Successive nodes in the collision retransmit in order spaced one time unit apart. All new arrivals to the system while these retransmissions are taking place wait until the retransmissions are finished. At the completion of the retransmissions, each backlogged node chooses a time to start its transmission uniformly distributed over the next time unit. All new arrivals after the end of the above retransmissions start transmission immediately.

(a)   Approximate the above system as a reservation system with reservation intervals of duration $1+\tau$ (note that this is an approximation in the sense that successful transmissions will sometimes occur in the reservation intervals, but the approximation becomes more accurate as the loading becomes higher). Find the expected packet delay for this approximation (assume Poisson arrivals at rate λ).

(b)   Show that the delay above remains finite for all $\lambda < 1$.

4.12 This problem illustrates that the maximum throughput of unslotted Aloha can be increased up to e^{-1} at an enormous cost in delay. Consider a finite but large set m of nodes with unlimited buffering at each node. Each node waits until it has accumulated k packets and then transmits them one after the other in the next k time units. Those packets involved in collisions, plus new packets, are then retransmitted a random time later, again k at a time. Assume that the starting time of transmissions from all nodes collectively is a Poisson process with parameter G (*i.e.*, ignore stability issues).

(a)   Show that the probability of success on the jth of the k packets in a sequence is $e^{-G(k+1)}$. *Hint:* Consider the intervals between the initiation of the given sequence and the previous sequence and subsequent sequence.

(b)   Show that the thoughput is $kGe^{-G(k+1)}$, and find the maximum throughput by optimizing over G.

4.13 (a)   Consider a CRP that results in the feedback pattern $e, 0, e, e, 1, 1, 0$ when using the tree algorithm as illustrated in Fig. 4.9. Redraw this figure for this feedback pattern.

(b)   Which collision or collisions would have been avoided if the first improvement to the tree algorithm had been used.

(c)   What would the feedback pattern have been for the CRP if both improvements to the tree algorithms had been used.

4.14 Consider the tree algorithm in Fig. 4.9. Given that k collisions occur in a CRP, determine the number of slots required for the CRP. Check your answer with the particular example of Fig. 4.9. *Hint 1:* Note that each collision corresponds to a nonleaf node of the rooted tree. Consider "building" any given tree from the root up, successively replacing leaf nodes by internal nodes with two upward going edges. *Hint 2:* For another approach, consider what happens in the stack for each collision, idle or success.

4.15 Consider the tree algorithm in Fig. 4.9. Assume that after each collision, each packet involved in the collision flips an unbiased coin to determine whether to go into the left or right subset.

(a)   Given a collision of k packets, find the probability that i packets go into the left subset.

(b) Let A_r be the expected number of slots required in a CRP involving k packets. Note that $A_0 = A_1 = 1$. Show that for $k \geq 2$,

$$A_k = 1 + \sum_{i=0}^{k} \binom{k}{i} 2^{-k}(A_i + A_{k-i})$$

(c) Simplify your answer in (b) to the form

$$A_k = c_{kk} + \sum_{i=0}^{k-1} c_{ik} A_i$$

and find the coefficients c_{ik}. Evaluate A_2 and A_3 numerically. For more results on A_k for large k, and the use of A_k in evaluating maximum throughput, see [Mas80].

4.16 (a) Consider the first improvement to the tree algorithm as shown in Fig. 4.10. Assume that each packet involved in a collision flips an unbiased coin to join either the left or right subset. Let B_k be the expected number of slots required in a CRP involving k packets; note that $B_0 = B_1 = 1$. Show that for $k \geq 2$,

$$B_k = 1 + \sum_{i=1}^{k} \binom{k}{i} 2^{-k}(B_i + B_{k-i}) + 2^{-k} B_k$$

(b) Simplify your answer to the form

$$B_k = C'_{kk} + \sum_{i=1}^{k-1} C'_{ik} B_i$$

and evaluate the constants C'_{ik}. Evaluate B_2 and B_3 numerically. (See [Mas80].)

4.17 Let X_L and X_R be independent Poisson distributed random variables, each with mean G. Use the definition of conditional probabilities to evaluate the following:

(a) $P\{X_L = 0 \mid X_L + X_R \geq 2\}$
(b) $P\{X_L = 1 \mid X_L + X_R \geq 2\}$
(c) $P\{X_L \geq 2 \mid X_L + X_R \geq 2\}$
(d) $P\{X_R = 1 \mid X_L = 1, X_L + X_R \geq 2\}$

(e) $P\{X_R = i \mid X_L = 0, X_L + X_R \geq 2\}$ $(i \geq 2)$

(f) $P\{X_R = i \mid X_L \geq 2, X_L + X_R \geq 2\}$

4.18 Suppose that at time k, the FCFS splitting algorithm allocates a new interval from $T(k)$ to $T(k) + \alpha_0$. Suppose that this interval contains a set of packets with arrival times $T(k) + 0.1\alpha_0, T(k) + 0.6\alpha_0, T(k) + 0.7\alpha_0$, and $T(k) + 0.8\alpha_0$.

(a) Find the allocation intervals for each of the subsequent times until the CRP is completed.

(b) Indicate which of the rules of Eqs. (4.15) – (4.18) are used in determining each of these allocation intervals.

(c) Indicate the path through the Markov chain in Fig. 4.13 for this sequence of events.

4.19 (a) Show that $\overline{n}$, the expected number of packets successfully transmitted in a CRP of the FCFS splitting algorithm is given by

$$\overline{n} = 1 - e^{-G_0} + \sum_{i=1}^{\infty} p(R, i)$$

(Assume the initial allocation interval is α_0, with $G_0 = \alpha_0 \lambda$.)

(b) Show that
$$\overline{n} = \lambda \alpha_0 (1 - E\{f\})$$

where $E\{f\}$ is the expected fraction of α_0 returned to the waiting interval in a CRP. (This provides an alternative way to calculate $E\{f\}$.)

4.20 Show, for Eq. (4.41), that if n_k is a Poisson random variable with mean $\hat{n}_k$, then the aposteriori distribution of n_k, given an idle, is Poisson with mean $\hat{n}_k[1 - q_r(\hat{n}_k)]$ Show that the aposteriori distribution of $n_k - 1$, given a success, is Poisson with mean $\hat{n}_k[1 - q_r(\hat{n}_k)]$.

4.21 *Slotted CSMA with variable packet lengths.* Assume that the time to transmit a packet is a random variable X; for consistency with the slotted assumption, assume X is discrete, taking values that are integer multiples of β. Assume all transmissions are independent and identically distributed (IID) with mean $\overline{X} = 1$.

(a) Let Y be the longer of two IID transmissions X_1 and X_2 (*i.e.*, $Y = \max(X_1, X_2)$). Show that the expected value of Y satisfies $\overline{Y} \leq 2\overline{X}$. Show that if X takes the value of β with large probability and $k\beta$ (for a large k) with small probability, then this bound is close to equality.

(b)   Show that the expected time between state transitions, given a collision of two packets, is at most $2 + \beta$.

(c)   Let $g(n) = \lambda\beta + q_r n$ be the expected number of attempted transmissions following a state transition to state n, and assume that this number of attempts is Poisson with mean $g(n)$. Show that the expected time between state transitions in state n is at most

$$\beta e^{-g(n)} + (1 + \beta)g(n)e^{-g(n)} + (1 + \beta/2)g^2(n)e^{-g(n)}$$

Ignore collisions of more than two packets as negligible.

(d)   Find a lower bound to the expected number of departures per unit time in state n (see Eq. (4.39)).

(e)   Show that this lower bound is maximized (for small β) by

$$g(n) \approx \sqrt{\beta}$$

with a corresponding throughput of approximately $1 - 2\sqrt{\beta}$.

4.22 *Pseudo-Bayesian stabilization for unslotted CSMA.* Assume that at the end of a transmission, the number n of backlogged packets in the system is a Poisson random variable with mean $\hat{n}$. Assume that, in the idle period until the next transmission starts, each backlogged packet attempts transmission at rate x and each new arrival starts transmission immediately. Thus, given n, the time τ until the next transmission starts has probability density $p(\tau \mid n) = (\lambda + xn)e^{-(\lambda + xn)\tau}$.

(a)   Find the unconditional probability density $p(\tau)$.

(b)   Find the aposteriori probability $p(n, b \mid \tau)$ that there were n backlogged packets and one of them started transmission first, given that the transmission starts at τ.

(c)   Find the aposteriori probability $p(n, a \mid \tau)$ that there were n backlogged packets and a new arrival started transmission first, given that this transmission starts at τ.

(d)   Let n' be the number of backlogged packets immediately after the next transmission starts (not counting the packet being transmitted); *i.e.*, $n' = n - 1$ if a backlogged packet starts and $n' = n$ if a new arrival starts. Show that, given τ, n' is Poisson with mean $\hat{n}' = \hat{n}e^{-\tau x}$.

This means that the pseudo-Bayesian rule for updating estimated backlog (assuming unit time transmission) is to estimate the backlog at the end of the $(k + 1)^{\text{st}}$ transmission in terms of the estimate at the end of the kth

transmission and the idle period τ_k between the transmissions by

$$\hat{n}_{k+1} = \begin{cases} \hat{n}_k e^{-\tau_k x_k} + \lambda(1+\beta); & \text{success} \\ \hat{n}_k e^{-\tau_k x_k} + 2 + \lambda(1+\beta); & \text{collision} \end{cases}$$

$$x_k = \beta^{-\frac{1}{2}} \min\left(\frac{1}{\hat{n}_k}, 1\right)$$

4.23 Give an intuitive explanation of why the maximum throughput, for small β, is approximately the same for CSMA slotted Aloha and FCFS splitting with CSMA. Show that the optimal expected number of packets transmitted after a state transition in Aloha is the same as that at the beginning of a CRP for FCFS splitting. Note that after a collision, the expected numbers are slightly different in the two systems, but the difference is unimportant since collisions are rare.

4.24 *Delay of ideal slotted CSMA/CD.* Assume that for all positive backlogs, the number of packets attempting transmission in an interval is Poisson with mean g.

(a) Start with Eq. (4.42), which is valid for CSMA/CD as well as CSMA. Show that for CSMA/CD,

$$E\{t\} = \frac{\beta e^{-g} + (1+\beta)ge^{-g} + 2\beta[1 - (1+g)e^{-g}]}{ge^{-g}}$$

Show that $E\{t\}$ is minimized over $g > 0$ by $g = 0.77$, and

$$\min_g E\{t\} = 1 + 3.31\beta$$

(b) Show that for this g and mean packet length 1,

$$W = \frac{\bar{R} + \bar{y}}{1 - \lambda(1 + 3.31\beta)}$$

(c) Evaluate $\bar{R}$ and $\bar{y}$ to verify Eq. (4.67) for small β.

(d) Discuss the assumption of a Poisson distributed number of packets attempting transmission in each interval, particularly for a backlog of 1.

4.25 Show that for unslotted CSMA/CD, the maximum interval of time over which a transmitting node can hear a collision is 2β (note in Fig. 4.20 that the time when a collision event starts at one node until it ends at another node can be as large as 3β).

4.26 Consider an unslotted CSMA/CD system in which the propagation delay is negligible compared to the time β required for a node to detect that the channel is idle or busy. Assume that each packet requires one time unit for transmission. Assume that β time units after either a successful transmission or a collision ends, all backlogged nodes attempt transmission after a random delay and that the composite process of initiation times is Poisson of rate G (up to time β after the first initiation). For simplicity, assume that each collision lasts for β time units.

  (a) Find the probability that the first transmission initiation after a given idle detection is successful.
  (b) Find the expected time from one idle detection to the next.
  (c) Find the throughput (for the given assumptions).
  (d) Optimize the throughput numerically over G.

4.27 Modify Eq. (4.71) for the case in which a node, after transmitting a packet, waits for the packet to return before transmitting the free token. *Hint:* View the added delay as an increase in the packet transmission time.

4.28 Show by example that a node in a register insertion ring might have to wait an arbitrarily long time to transmit a packet once its transit buffer is full.

4.29 Suppose two nodes are randomly placed on a bus; that is, each is placed independently, and the position of each is chosen from a uniform distribution over the length of the bus. Assuming that the length of the bus is 1 unit, show that the expected distance between the nodes is 1/3.

4.30 Assume, for the analysis of generalized polling in subsection 4.5.6, that each node has a packet to send with probability q.

  (a) Find the probability $P\{i\}$ that node i, $i \geq 0$, is the lowest numbered node with a packet to send.
  (b) Assume that the CRP tests only the first 2^j lowest numbered nodes at a time for some j. Represent the lowest numbered node with a packet as $i = k2^j + r$, where k is an integer, and $0 \leq r < 2^j$. Show that, given i, the number of reservation slots needed to find i is $k + 1 + j$.
  (c) Assume that the total number of nodes is infinite and approximate k above by $i2^{-j}$. Find the expected number of reservation slots to find the lowest numbered node i containing a packet.
  (d) Find the integer value of j that minimizes your answer in (c). *Hint:* Find the largest value of j for which the expected number of reservation slots is less than the expected number for $j + 1$.

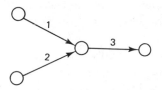

Figure 4.30

4.31 Consider the simple packet radio network shown in Fig. 4.30 and let f_ℓ be the throughput on link ℓ ($\ell = 1, 2, 3$); the links are used only in the direction shown.

(a) Note that at most one link can be in any collision-free set. Using generalized TDM (as in Eq. (4.75)), show that any set of throughputs satisfying $f_1 + f_2 + f_3 \leq 1, f_\ell \geq 0$ ($\ell = 1, 2, 3$) can be achieved.

(b) Suppose that $f_1 = f_2 = f$ and $f_3 = 2f$ for some f. Use Eqs. (4.77) and (4.78) to relate f_1, f_2, f_3 to the attempt rates q_1, q_2, q_3 for slotted Aloha. Show that $q_1 = q_2$ and $q_3 = 2f$.

(c) Find the maximum achievable value of f for (b).

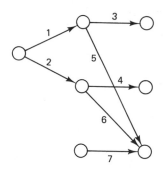

Figure 4.31

4.32 Consider the packet radio network shown in Fig. 4.31 in which the links are only used in the direction shown. Links 5 and 6 carry no traffic but serve to cause collisions for link 7 when packets are transmitted on links 3 and 4 respectively.

(a) Show that throughputs $f_1 = f_2 = f_3 = f_4 = 1/3, f_7 = 4/9$ are feasible for the assumption of heavy loading and independent attempts on each link. Find the corresponding attempt rates and success rates from Eqs. (4.77) and (4.78).

(b) Now assume that links 3 and 4 are used to forward incoming traffic and always transmit in the slot following a successful incoming packet. Show that with $f_1 = f_2 = f_3 = f_4 = 1/3, f_7$ is restricted to be no more than $1/3$.

(c) Assume finally that packet attempts on links 1 and 2 are in alternating order and links 3 and 4 operate as in (b). Show that $f_1 = f_2 = f_3 = f_4 = 1/2$ is feasible, but that f_7 must then be 0.

5

Routing

in

Data Networks

5.1 INTRODUCTION

We have frequently referred to the routing algorithm as the network layer protocol that guides packets through the communication subnet to their correct destination. The times at which routing decisions are made depend on whether the network uses datagrams or virtual circuits. In a datagram network, two successive packets of the same user pair may travel along different routes, and a routing decision is necessary for each individual packet (see Fig. 5.1). In a virtual circuit network, a routing decision is made when each virtual circuit is set up. The routing algorithm is used to choose the communication path for the virtual circuit. All packets of the virtual circuit subsequently use this path up to the time that the virtual circuit is either terminated or rerouted for some reason (see Fig. 5.2).

Routing in a network typically involves a rather complex collection of algorithms that work more or less independently and yet support each other by exchanging services or information. The complexity is due to a number of reasons. First, routing requires coordination between all the nodes of the subnet rather than just a pair of modules as, for example, in data link and transport layer protocols. Second, the routing system must cope with link and node failures, requiring redirection of traffic and an update of the databases maintained by the system. Third, to achieve high performance, the routing algorithm may need to modify its routes when some areas within the network become congested.

The main emphasis will be on two aspects of the routing problem. The first has to do with selecting routes to achieve high performance. In subsections 5.2.3–5.2.5, we discuss algorithms based on shortest paths that are commonly used in

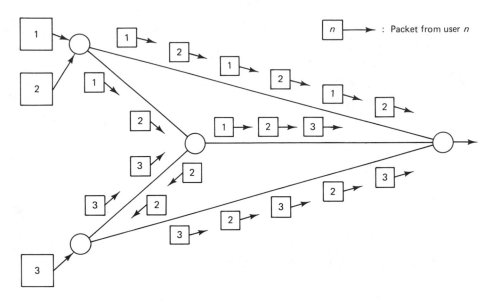

Figure 5.1   Routing in a datagram network. Two packets of the same user pair can travel along different routes. A routing decision is required for each individual packet.

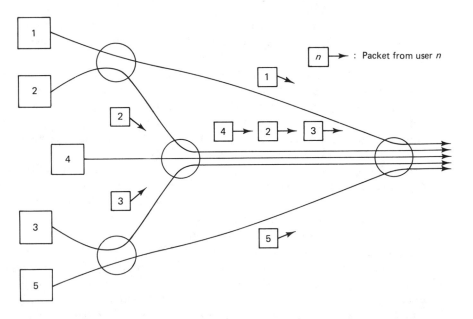

Figure 5.2   Routing in a virtual circuit network. All packets of each virtual circuit use the same path. A routing decision is required only when a virtual circuit is set up.

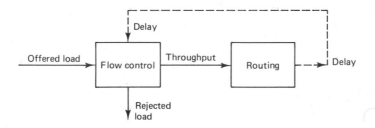

Figure 5.3   Interaction of routing and flow control. As good routing
keeps delay low, flow control allows more traffic into the network.

practice. In sections 5.5, 5.6, and 5.7 we describe sophisticated routing algorithms
that try to achieve near optimal performance. The second aspect of routing that
we will emphasize is broadcasting routing related information (including link and
node failures and repairs) to all network nodes. This issue, examined in section 5.3,
involves subtleties that are not fully appreciated within the field.

The introductory sections set the stage for the main development. The remainder of this section explains in nonmathematical terms the main objectives in
the routing problem and provides an overview of current routing practice. Subsections 5.2.1–5.2.3 present some of the main notions and results of graph theory,
principally in connection with shortest paths and minimum weight spanning trees.
Section 5.4 uses the material on graph theory to describe methods for topological
design of networks. Finally, section 5.8 reviews the routing system of the Codex
network, and its relation with the optimal routing algorithm of section 5.7.

5.1.1 Main Issues in Routing

The two main functions performed by a routing algorithm are the selection of routes
for various origin-destination pairs and the delivery of messages to their correct
destination once the routes are selected. The second function is straightforward to
accomplish through a variety of protocols and data structures (known as routing
tables), some of which will be described in the context of practical networks in
subsection 5.1.2. The focus will be on the first function (selection of routes) and
how it affects network performance.

There are two main performance measures that are substantially affected by
the routing algorithm—*throughput* (quantity of service), and *average packet delay*
(quantity of service). Routing interacts with flow control in determining these
performance measures by means of a feedback mechanism shown in Fig. 5.3. When
the traffic load offered by the external sites to the subnet is relatively low, it will
be fully accepted into the network, *i.e.*,

$$\text{Throughput} \; = \; \text{Offered load}$$

When the offered load is excessive, a portion will be rejected by the flow control

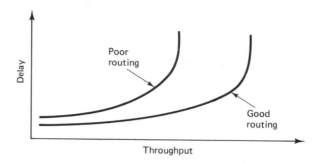

Figure 5.4   Delay-throughput operating curves for good and bad routing.

algorithm and

$$\text{Throughput} \ = \ \text{Offered load} - \text{Rejected load}$$

The traffic accepted into the network will experience an average delay per packet that will depend on the routes chosen by the routing algorithm. However, throughput will also be greatly affected (if only indirectly) by the routing algorithm because typical flow control schemes operate on the basis of striking a balance between throughput and delay, *i.e.*, they start rejecting offered load when delay starts getting excessive. Therefore, *as the routing algorithm is more successful in keeping delay low, the flow control algorithm allows more traffic into the network*. While the precise balance between delay and throughput will be determined by flow control, the effect of good routing under high offered load conditions is to realize a more favorable delay-throughput curve along which flow control operates, as shown in Fig. 5.4.

The following examples illustrate the discussion above:

Example 1

In the network of Fig. 5.5, all links have capacity 10 units. (The units by which link capacity and traffic load is measured is immaterial and is left unspecified.) There is a single destination (node 6) and two origins (nodes 1 and 2). The offered load from each of nodes 1 and 2 to node 6 is 5 units. Here, the offered load is light and can be easily accommodated with small delay by routing along the left-most and right-most paths, $1 \rightarrow 3 \rightarrow 6$ and $2 \rightarrow 5 \rightarrow 6$, respectively. If instead, however, the routes $1 \rightarrow 4 \rightarrow 6$ and $2 \rightarrow 4 \rightarrow 6$ are used, the flow on link (4,6) will equal capacity, resulting in very large delays.

Example 2

For the same network, assume that the offered loads at nodes 1 and 2 are 5 and 15 units, respectively (see Fig. 5.6). If routing from node 2 to the destination is done along a single path, then at least 5 units of offered load will have to be rejected since all path capacities equal 10. Thus, the total throughput can be no more than 15

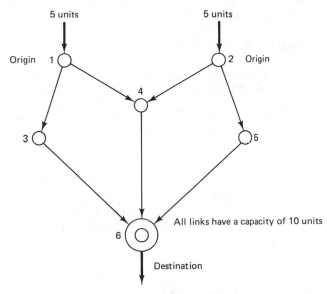

Figure 5.5   Network for Example 1. All links have a capacity of 10 units. If all traffic is routed through the middle link (4,6), congestion occurs. If instead paths $(1 \to 3 \to 6)$ and $(2 \to 5 \to 6)$ are used, the average delay is small.

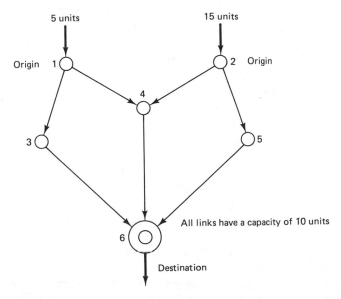

Figure 5.6   Network for Example 2. All links have a capacity of 10 units. The input traffic can be accommodated with multiple-path routing, but at least 5 units of traffic must be rejected if a single-path routing is used.

units. On the other hand, suppose that the traffic originating at node 2 is evenly split between the two paths $2 \rightarrow 4 \rightarrow 6$ and $2 \rightarrow 5 \rightarrow 6$, while the traffic originating at node 1 is routed along $1 \rightarrow 3 \rightarrow 6$. Then, the traffic arrival rate on each link will not exceed 75% of capacity, the delay per packet will be reasonably small, and (given a good flow control scheme) no portion of the offered load will be rejected. Arguing similarly, it is seen that when the offered loads at nodes 1 and 2 are both large, the maximum total throughput that this network can accommodate is between 10 and 30 units, depending on the routing scheme. This example also illustrates that to achieve high throughput, the traffic of some origin-destination pairs may have to be divided among more than one route.

In conclusion, *the effect of good routing is to increase throughput for the same value of average delay per packet under high offered load conditions and to decrease average delay per packet under low offered load conditions.* Furthermore, it is evident that the routing algorithm should be operated in a way that keeps average delay per packet as low as possible for any given level of throughput. While this is easier said than done, it provides a clearcut objective that can be expressed mathematically and dealt with analytically.

5.1.2 An Overview of Routing in Practice

The purpose of this section is to survey current routing practice, to introduce classifications of different schemes, and to provide a context for the analysis presented later.

There are a number of ways to classify routing algorithms. One way is to divide them into *centralized* and *distributed*. In centralized algorithms, all route choices are made at a central node, while in distributed algorithms, the computation of routes is shared among the network nodes with information exchanged between them as necessary. We note, however, that this classification sometimes relates to the implementation rather than the mathematical description of an algorithm. It is possible that a centralized and a distributed routing algorithm are equivalent at some level of mathematical abstraction.

Another classification of routing algorithms relates to whether they change routes in response to the traffic input patterns. In *static* routing algorithms, the path used by the sessions of each origin-destination pair is fixed regardless of traffic conditions. It can only change in response to a link or node failure. This type of algorithm cannot achieve a high throughput under a broad variety of traffic input patterns. It is recommended for either very simple networks or for networks where efficiency is not essential. Most major packet networks use some form of *adaptive* routing where the paths used to route new traffic between origins and destinations change occasionally in response to congestion. The idea here is that congestion can build up in some part of the network due to changes in the statistics of the input traffic load. Then, the routing algorithm should try to change its routes and guide traffic around the point of congestion.

There are many routing algorithms in use with different levels of sophistication and efficiency. This variety is partly due to historical reasons and partly due to the diversity of needs in different networks. In this section we will describe the routing algorithms of three networks (ARPANET, TYMNET, and SNA), which together constitute a representative sample of current practice. The routing algorithm of the Codex network will be described in section 5.8 because this algorithm is better understood after studying optimal routing in sections 5.5 through 5.7.

Routing in the ARPANET

The routing algorithm of the ARPANET, first implemented in 1969, has played an important historical role in the development of the subject. On one hand, this was an ambitious, distributed, adaptive algorithm that stimulated considerable research on routing and distributed computation in general. On the other hand, the algorithm had some fundamental flaws that were finally corrected in 1979 when the algorithm was replaced by a new version. Unfortunately, by that time the original algorithm had been adopted by several other networks.

Both ARPANET algorithms are based on the notion of a *shortest path* between two nodes. Here, each communication link is assigned a positive number called its *length*. A link can have a different length in each direction. Each path (*i.e.*, a sequence of links) between two nodes has a length equal to the sum of the lengths of its links (see section 5.2 for more details). The ARPANET algorithms try to route a packet along a minimum length (or shortest) path between the origin and destination nodes of the packet. The idea here is that, if the length of each link is representative of the level of congestion on the link, then a shortest path contains relatively few and uncongested links, and is therefore desirable for routing.

In both ARPANET algorithms, the length of each link is dependent on some measure of traffic congestion of the link, and is periodically updated. Thus, the ARPANET algorithms are adaptive and, since the ARPANET uses datagrams, two successive packets of the same session may follow different routes. This has two undesirable effects. First, packets can arrive at their destination out of order and must, therefore, be put back in order upon arrival. (This can also happen because of the data link protocol of the ARPANET, which uses eight logical channels; see the discussion in Chapter 2.) Second, the ARPANET algorithms are prone to oscillations. This phenomenon is explained in some detail in subsection 5.2.5, but basically the idea is that selecting routes through one area of the network increases the lengths of the corresponding links. As a result, at the next routing update the algorithm tends to select routes through different areas. This makes the first area desirable at the subsequent routing update with an oscillation resulting. The feedback effect between link lengths and routing updates was a primary flaw of the original ARPANET algorithm that caused difficulties over several years and eventually led to its replacement. The latest algorithm is also prone to oscillations, but not nearly as much as the first (see subsection 5.2.5).

In the original ARPANET algorithm, neighboring nodes exchanged their estimated shortest distances to each destination every 625 msecs. The algorithm for updating a node's shortest distance to each destination is based on the Bellman-Ford method discussed in subsections 5.2.3 and 5.2.4. Each link length was made dependent on the number of packets waiting in the link queue at the time of the update. Thus, link lengths were changing very rapidly, reflecting statistical traffic fluctuations as well as the effect of routing updates. To stabilize oscillations, a large positive constant was added to the link lengths. Unfortunately, this reduced the sensitivity of the algorithm to traffic congestion.

In the latest ARPANET algorithm [MRR80], the length of each link is calculated by keeping track of the delay of each packet in crossing the link. Each link length is updated periodically every 10 seconds, and is taken to be the average packet delay on the link during the preceding 10 second period. The delay of a packet on a link is defined as the time between the packet's arrival at the link's start node and the time the packet is correctly delivered to the link's end node (propagation delay is also included). Each node monitors the lengths of its outgoing links and broadcasts these lengths throughout the network at least once every 60 seconds by using a flooding algorithm (see subsection 5.3.1). Each node upon reception of a new link length, recalculates a shortest path from itself to each destination, using an incremental form of Dijkstra's algorithm (see subsection 5.2.3). The algorithm is asynchronous in nature in that link length update messages are neither transmitted nor received simultaneously at all nodes. It turns out that this tends to improve the stability properties of the algorithm (see subsection 5.2.5).

Note that a node is not concerned with calculating routing paths that originate at other nodes even though the information available at each node (network topology plus lengths of all links) is sufficient to compute a shortest path from every origin to every destination. In fact, the routing tables of an ARPANET node contain only the first outgoing link of the shortest path from the node to each destination (see Fig. 5.7). When the node receives a new packet, it checks the packet's destination, it consults its routing table, and it places the packet in the corresponding outgoing link queue. If all nodes visited by a packet have calculated their routing tables on the basis of the same link length information, it is easily seen that the packet will travel along a shortest path. It is actually possible that a packet will occasionally travel in a loop because of changes in routing tables as the packet is in transit. However, looping of this type is rare, and when it happens, it is unlikely to persist.

A replacement of the existing ARPANET routing algorithm is being planned for 1987. The details of the algorithm are not yet finalized, and are subject to change. A key feature of this algorithm is that it uses multiple paths for the same origin-destination node pair. Furthermore traffic is divided in several service classes, each routed independently of the others. The paths corresponding to an origin-destination pair, and service class are updated over fairly long time intervals (say 5 to 15 minutes). This is done by a shortest path computation where the length of each link depends on the service class, the link characteristics, and the traffic carried by the link in the preceding time interval. The paths are also updated as quickly as possible in response to a link or node failure. For each service class and

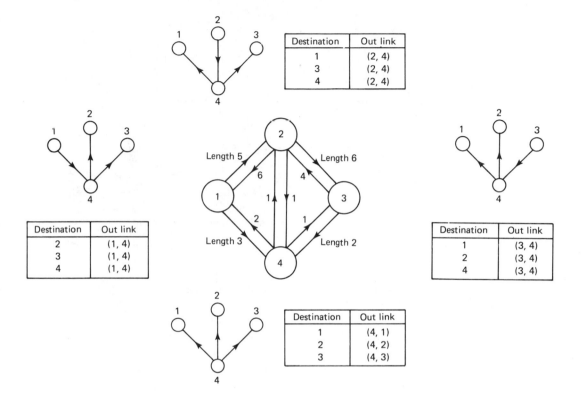

Figure 5.7   Routing tables maintained by the nodes in the ARPANET algorithm. Each node calculates a shortest path from itself to each destination, and enters the first link on that path in the routing table.

origin-destination pair, the fraction of the input traffic that travels along each path is adjusted over a short time interval (say 10 to 30 seconds) on the basis of congestion information along the paths during the preceding time interval. Because of the use of multiple paths, this type of algorithm is capable of higher throughput than the existing one, and can make use of the optimal routing methodology developed in sections 5.5 through 5.7.

Routing in the TYMNET

The TYMNET routing algorithm, originally implemented in 1971, is based on the shortest path method, and is adaptive like the ARPANET algorithms. However,

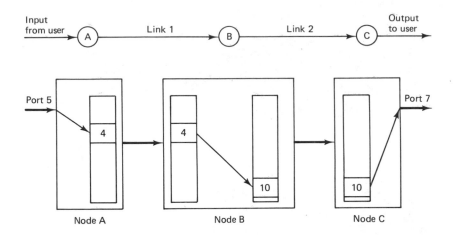

Figure 5.8   Structure of TYMNET routing tables. For the virtual circuit on the path ABC, the routing table at node A maps input port 5 onto channel 4 on link 1. At node B, incoming channel 4 is mapped into outgoing channel 10 on link 2. At node C, incoming channel 10 is mapped into output port 7.

the implementation of the adaptive shortest path idea is very different in the two networks.

In the TYMNET, the routing algorithm is centralized and is operated at a special node called the supervisor. TYMNET uses virtual circuits, so a routing decision is needed only at the time a virtual circuit is set up. A virtual circuit request received by the supervisor is assigned to a shortest path connecting the origin and destination nodes of the virtual circuit. The supervisor maintains a list of current link lengths and does all the shortest path calculations. The length of each link depends on the load carried by the link as well as other factors, such as the type of the link and the type of virtual circuit being routed [Tym81]. While the algorithm can be classified as adaptive, it does not have the potential for oscillations of the ARPANET algorithms. This is due primarily to the use of virtual circuits rather than datagrams as explained in subsection 5.2.5.

Once the supervisor has decided upon the path to be used by a virtual circuit, it informs the nodes on the path and the necessary information is entered in each node's routing tables. These tables are structured as shown in Fig. 5.8. Basically, a virtual circuit is assigned a channel (or port) number on each link it crosses. The routing table at each node matches each virtual circuit's channel number on the incoming link with a channel number on the outgoing link. In the original version of TYMNET (now called TYMNET I), the supervisor maintains an image of the routing tables of all nodes and explicitly reads and writes the tables in the nodes. In the current version (TYMNET II), the nodes maintain their own tables. The supervisor establishes a new virtual circuit by sending a "needle" packet to the origin node. The needle contains routing information and threads its way through the network, building the circuit as it goes, with the user data following behind it. The routing information includes the node sequence of the routing path, and some flags indicating circuit class. When a needle enters a TYMNET II node, its contents are checked. If the circuit terminates at this node, it is assigned to the port connected with the appropriate external site. Otherwise, the next node on the route is checked. If it is unknown (because of a recent link failure or some other error), the circuit is zapped back to its origin. Otherwise, the routing tables are updated and the needle is passed to the next node.

The TYMNET algorithm is well thought out and has performed well over the years. Several of its ideas were implemented in the Codex network, which is a similarly structured network (see section 5.8). The Codex algorithm, however, is distributed and more sophisticated. A potential concern with the TYMNET algorithm is its vulnerability to failure of the supervisor node. In TYMNET, this is handled by using backup supervisor nodes. A distributed alternative, used in the Codex network, is to broadcast all link lengths to all nodes (as in the ARPANET), and to give each node the responsibility of routing the circuits originating or terminating at that node.

Routing in SNA

Routing in IBM's SNA is somewhat unusual in that the method for choosing routes is partially left to the user. SNA provides instead a framework within which a number of routing algorithm choices can be made. Specifically, for every origin-destination pair, SNA provides several paths along which virtual circuits can be built. The rule for assignment of virtual circuits to paths is subject to certain restrictions but is otherwise left unspecified. The preceding oversimplified description is couched in the general terminology of paths and virtual circuits used in this text. SNA uses a different terminology which we now review.

The architecture of SNA does not fully conform to the OSI seven layer architecture used as our primary model. The closest counterpart in SNA of the OSI network layer is called the path control layer, and provides virtual circuit service to the immediately higher layer called the transmission control layer. The path control layer has three functions: transmission group control, explicit route control, and virtual route control. The first fits most appropriately in the data link control layer of the OSI model, whereas the second and third correspond to the routing and flow control functions, respectively, of the network layer in the OSI model.

A transmission group in SNA terminology is a set of one or more physical communication lines between two neighboring nodes of the network. The transmission group control function makes the transmission group appear to higher layers as a single physical link. There may be more than one transmission group connecting a pair of nodes. The protocol places incoming packets on a queue, sends them out on the next available physical link, and sequences them if they arrive out of order. Resequencing of packets is done at every node, unlike the ARPANET which resequences only at the destination node.

An explicit route in SNA terminology is what we have been referring to as a path within a subnet. Thus, an explicit route is simply a sequence of transmission groups providing a physical path between an origin and a destination node. There are several explicit routes provided (up to eight in SNA 4.2) for each origin-destination pair which can be modified only under supervisory control. The method for choosing these explicit routes is left to the network manager. Each node stores the next node for each explicit route in its routing tables, and each packet carries an explicit route number. Therefore, when a packet arrives at a node, the next node on the packet's path (if any) is determined by a simple table lookup.

A virtual route in SNA terminology is essentially what we have been calling a virtual circuit. A user pair conversation (or session) uses only one virtual route. However, a virtual route can carry multiple sessions. Each virtual route belongs to a priority (or service) class. Each transmission group can serve up to three service classes, each with up to eight virtual routes, for a maximum of 24 virtual routes. When a user requests a session through a subnet entry node, a service class is specified on the basis of which the entry node will attempt to establish the session over one of its virtual routes. If all the communication lines of a transmission group fail, then every session using that transmission group must be rerouted. If no alternate virtual route can be found, the session is aborted. When new transmission groups are established, all nodes are notified via special control packets, so each node has a copy of the network topology and knows which explicit routes are available and which are not.

5.2 NETWORK ALGORITHMS AND SHORTEST PATH ROUTING

Routing methods involve the use of a number of simple graph theoretic algorithms. Consider, for example, the shortest path problem whereby we are given a length for every link in the network, and the objective is to find a path joining two given nodes that has minimum total length. If the length of each link is defined to reflect congestion of the link in some way, then finding the shortest path is equivalent to finding the "least congested" path between the two nodes, which is a problem relevant to routing (see also the earlier descriptions of the ARPANET and TYMNET algorithms). In this section we consider in detail the shortest path problem and its role in routing, together with other related problems of interest. We start by introducing some basic graph theoretic notions.

5.2.1 Undirected Graphs

We define a *graph*, $G = (\mathcal{N}, \mathcal{A})$, to be a finite nonempty set $\mathcal{N}$ of *nodes* and a collection $\mathcal{A}$ of pairs of distinct nodes from $\mathcal{N}$. Each pair of nodes in $\mathcal{A}$ is called an *arc*.

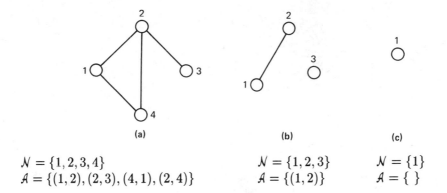

$\mathcal{N} = \{1, 2, 3, 4\}$
$\mathcal{A} = \{(1, 2), (2, 3), (4, 1), (2, 4)\}$

$\mathcal{N} = \{1, 2, 3\}$
$\mathcal{A} = \{(1, 2)\}$

$\mathcal{N} = \{1\}$
$\mathcal{A} = \{ \ \}$

Figure 5.9   Three examples of graphs with a set of nodes $\mathcal{N}$ and a set or arcs $\mathcal{A}$.

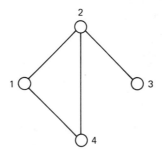

Figure 5.10   Illustration of walks, paths, and cycles. The sequences (1,4,2,3), (1,4,2,1), (1,4,2,1,4,1), (2,3,2), and (2) are all walks. The sequences (1,4,2,3) and (2) are each paths; and (1,4,2,1) is a cycle. Note that (2) and (2,3,2) are not considered cycles.

Several examples of graphs are given in Fig. 5.9. Nodes are often called vertices, and arcs are often called edges, branches, or links. The major purpose of the formal definition $G = (\mathcal{N}, \mathcal{A})$ is to stress that the location of the nodes and the shapes of the arcs in a pictorial representation are totally irrelevant. If n_1 and n_2 are nodes in a graph and (n_1, n_2) is an arc, then this arc is said to be *incident* on n_1 and n_2. Some authors define graphs so as to allow arcs to have both ends incident on the same node, but we have intentionally disallowed such loops. We have also disallowed multiple arcs between the same pair of nodes.

A *walk* in a graph G is a sequence of nodes $(n_1, n_2, \ldots, n_\ell)$ of nodes such that $(n_1, n_2), (n_2, n_3), \ldots, (n_{\ell-1}, n_\ell)$ each are arcs of G. A walk with no repeated nodes is a *path*. A walk $(n_1, \ldots, n_\ell)$ with $n_1 = n_\ell$, $\ell > 3$, and no repeated nodes other than $n_1 = n_\ell$ is called a *cycle*. These definitions are illustrated in Fig. 5.10.

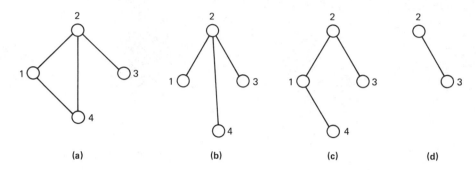

Figure 5.11   A graph (a) and three subgraphs (b), (c), and (d). Subgraphs (b) and (c) are spanning trees.

We say that a graph is *connected* if for each node i there is a path $(i = n_1, n_2, \ldots, n_\ell = j)$ to each other node j. Note that the graphs in Fig. 5.9(a) and (c) are connected whereas the graph in Fig. 5.9(b) is not connected. We spot an absence of connectivity in a graph by seeing two sets of nodes with no arcs between them. The following lemma captures this insight. The proof is almost immediate and is left as an exercise.

Lemma.   Let G be a connected graph and let S be any nonempty strict subset of the set of nodes N. Then, at least one arc (i, j) exists with $i \in S$ and $j \notin S$.

We say that $G' = (\mathcal{N}', \mathcal{A}')$ is a *subgraph* of $G = (\mathcal{N}, \mathcal{A})$ if G' is a graph, $\mathcal{N}' \subset \mathcal{N}$, and $\mathcal{A}' \subset \mathcal{A}$. For example, the last three graphs in Fig. 5.11 are subgraphs of the first.

A *tree* is a connected graph that contains no cycles. A *spanning tree* of a graph G is a subgraph of G that is a tree and that includes all the nodes of G. For example, the subgraphs in Fig. 5.11 (b) and (c) are spanning trees of the graph in Fig. 5.11(a). The following simple algorithm constructs a spanning tree of an arbitrary connected graph $G = (\mathcal{N}, \mathcal{A})$:

1. Let n be an arbitrary node in $\mathcal{N}$. Let $\mathcal{N}' = \{n\}$, $\mathcal{A}' = \{\ \}$.
2. If $\mathcal{N}' = \mathcal{N}$ then stop $(G' = (\mathcal{N}', \mathcal{A}')$ is a spanning tree); else go to Step 3.
3. Let $(i, j) \in \mathcal{A}$ be an arc with $i \in \mathcal{N}'$, $j \in \mathcal{N} - \mathcal{N}'$. Update $\mathcal{N}'$ and $\mathcal{A}'$ by

$$\mathcal{N}' := \mathcal{N}' \cup \{j\}$$
$$\mathcal{A}' := \mathcal{A}' \cup \{(i, j)\}$$

Go to Step 2.

To see why the algorithm works, note that Step 3 is only entered when $\mathcal{N}'$ is a proper subset of $\mathcal{N}$, so that the earlier Lemma guarantees the existence of the arc (i, j). We use induction on successive executions of Step 3 to see that

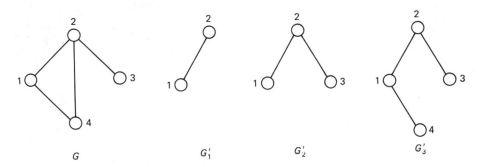

Figure 5.12   Algorithm for constructing a spanning tree of a given graph G.

$G' = (\mathcal{N}', \mathcal{A}')$ is always a tree. Initially, $G' = (\{n\}, \{\})$ is trivially a tree, so assume that $G' = (\mathcal{N}', \mathcal{A}')$ is a tree before the update of Step 3. This ensures that there is a path between each pair of nodes in $\mathcal{N}'$ using arcs of $\mathcal{A}'$. After adding node j and arc (i, j), each node has a path to j simply by adding j to the path to i, and similarly j has a path to each other node. Finally, node j cannot be in any cycles since (i, j) is the only arc of G' incident to j, and there are no cycles not including j by the inductive hypothesis. Figure 5.12 shows G' after each execution of Step 3 for one possible choice of arcs.

Observe that the algorithm starts with a subgraph of one node and zero arcs and adds one node and one arc on each execution of Step 3. This means that the spanning tree, G', resulting from the algorithm always has N nodes, where N is the number of nodes in G, and $N-1$ arcs. Since G' is a subgraph of G, the number of arcs, A, in G must satisfy $A \geq N - 1$; this is true for every connected graph G. Next, assume that $A = N - 1$. This means that the algorithm uses all arcs of G in the spanning tree G', so that $G = G'$, and G must be a tree itself. Finally, if $A \geq N$, then G contains at least one arc (i, j) not in the spanning tree G' generated by the algorithm. Letting $(j, \ldots, i)$ be the path from j to i in G', it is seen that $(i, j, \ldots, i)$ is a cycle in G and G cannot be a tree. The following proposition summarizes these results:

Proposition.   Let G be a connected graph with N nodes and A arcs. Then,
1. G contains a spanning tree.
2. $A \geq N - 1$.
3. G is a tree if and only if $A = N - 1$.

Figure 5.13 shows why connectedness is a neccesary assumption for the last part of the proposition.

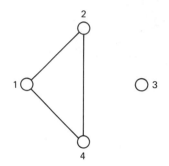

Figure 5.13   A graph with $A = N - 1$, which is both disconnected and
contains a cycle.

5.2.2 Minimum Weight Spanning Trees

Let us consider a problem of interest in data networks that lends itself to distributed
algorithmic solution. Given a connected graph $G = (\mathcal{N}, \mathcal{A})$ with N nodes and A
arcs, and a weight w_{ij} for each arc $(i, j) \in \mathcal{A}$, the problem is to construct a spanning
tree with minimum sum of arc weights. Such a tree is called a *minimum weight
spanning tree* (MST for short). An MST may be useful for disseminating messages
destined for every node in a data network–for example, control messages from a
supervisor node. In this context, an arc weight represents the communication cost
of a message along the arc in either direction, and the total spanning tree weight
represents the cost of broadcasting a message to all nodes along the spanning tree.

Any subtree (*i.e.*, a subgraph which is a tree) of an MST will be called a
fragment. Note that a node by itself is considered a fragment. An arc having one
node in a fragment and the other node not in this fragment is called an *outgoing
arc* from the fragment. The following proposition is of central importance for MST
algorithms.

Proposition 1.   Given a fragment F, let $\alpha = (i, j)$ be a minimum weight
outgoing arc from F, where the node j is not in F. Then F, extended by arc α and
node j, is a fragment.

Proof. Denote by M the MST of which F is a subtree. If arc α belongs to
M we are done, so assume otherwise. Then there is a cycle formed by α and the
arcs of M. Since node j does not belong to F, there must be some arc $\beta \neq \alpha$
that belongs to the cycle and to M, and which is outgoing from F (see Fig. 5.14).
Deleting β from M and adding α results in a subgraph M' with $(N - 1)$ arcs and
no cycles which, therefore, must be a spanning tree. Since α has smaller or equal
weight than β, M' must be an MST, so F extended by α and j forms a fragment.
QED.

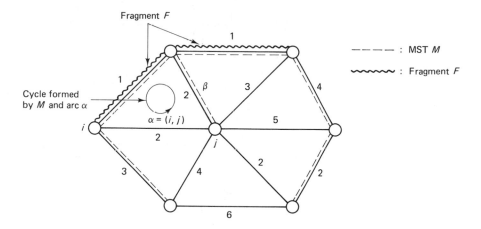

Figure 5.14   Proof of Proposition 1. The numbers next to the arcs are the arc weights. F is a fragment which is a subtree of an MST M. Let α be a minimum weight outgoing arc from F not belonging to M. Let $\beta \neq \alpha$ be an arc that is outgoing from F and simultaneously belongs to M and to the cycle formed by α and M. Deleting β from M and adding α in its place forms another MST M'. When F is extended by α, it forms a fragment.

Proposition 1 can be used as the basis for MST construction algorithms. The idea is to start with one or more disjoint fragments and enlarge or combine them by adding minimum weight outgoing arcs. One method (the Prim-Dijkstra algorithm) starts with an arbitrarily selected single node as a fragment and enlarges the fragment by successively adding a minimum weight outgoing arc. Another method (Kruskal's algorithm) starts with each node being a single node fragment; it then successively combines two of the fragments by using the arc that has minimum weight over all arcs that when added to the current set of fragments do not form a cycle (see Fig. 5.15). Both of these algorithms terminate in $N - 1$ iterations.

Kruskal's algorithm proceeds by building up simultaneously several fragments that eventually join into an MST; however, only one arc at a time is added to the current set of fragments. Proposition 1 suggests the possibility of adding simultaneously to each fragment a minimum weight outgoing arc in a distributed algorithmic manner. This is possible if there is a unique MST.

A distributed algorithm for constructing the MST in a graph with a unique MST is as follows. Start with a set of fragments (these can be the nodes by themselves, for example). Each fragment determines its minimum weight outgoing arc, adds it to itself, and informs the fragment that lies at the other end of this arc. It can be seen that as long as the arc along which two fragments join is indeed a minimum weight outgoing arc for some fragment, the algorithm maintains a set of fragments of the MST at all times, and no cycle is ever formed. Furthermore, new arcs will be added until there are no further outgoing arcs and there is only one fragment (by necessity the MST). Therefore, the algorithm cannot stop short of

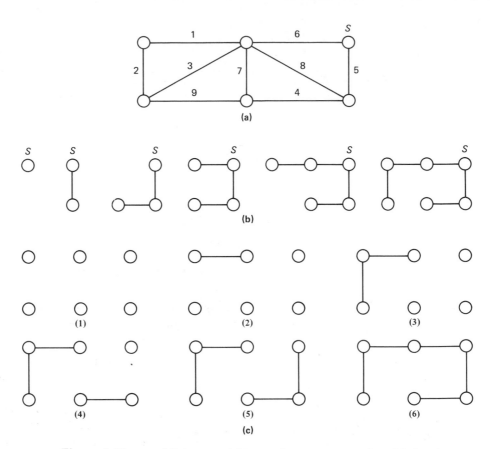

Figure 5.15   Minimum weight spanning tree construction. (a) Graph with arc weights as indicated. (b) Successive iterations of the Prim-Dijkstra algorithm. The starting fragment consists of the single node marked S. the fragment is successively extended by adding a minimum weight outgoing arc. (c) Successive iterations of the Kruskal algorithm. The algorithm starts with all nodes as fragments. At each iteration, we add the arc that has minimum weight out of all arcs that are outgoing from one of the fragments.

finding the MST. Indeed, for the algorithm to work correctly, it is not necessary that the procedure for arc addition be synchronized for all fragments. What is needed, however, is a scheme for the nodes and arcs of a fragment to determine the minimum weight outgoing arc. There are a number of possibilities along these lines, but it is of interest to construct schemes that accomplish this with low communication overhead. This subject is addressed in [GHS83] to which we refer for further details. Reference [Hum83] considers the case where the arc weights are different in each direction.

To see what can go wrong in the case of multiple MSTs, consider the triangular network of Fig. 5.16 where all arc lengths are unity. If we start with the three

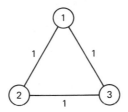

Figure 5.16   Counterexample for distributed MST construction with nondistinct arc weights. Nodes 1,2, and 3 can add simultaneously to their fragments arcs (1,2), (2,3), and (3,1), respectively, with a cycle resulting.

nodes as fragments and allow each fragment to add to itself an arbitrary, minimum weight outgoing arc, there is the possibility that the arcs (1,2), (2,3), and (3,1) will be simultaneously added by nodes 1, 2, and 3, respectively, with a cycle resulting.

The following proposition points the way on how to handle the case of multiple MSTs.

Proposition 2.   If all arc weights are distinct, there exists a unique MST.

Proof. Suppose that there exist two distinct MSTs denoted M and M'. Let α be the minimum weight arc that belongs to either M or M' but not to both. Assume for concreteness that α belongs to M. Consider the graph formed by the union of M' and α. It must contain a cycle (since $\alpha \notin M'$), and at least one arc of this cycle, call it β, does not belong to M (otherwise M would contain a cycle). Since the weight of α is strictly smaller than that of β, it follows that deleting β from M' and adding α in its place results in a spanning tree of strictly smaller weight than M'. This is a contradiction since M' is optimal.   QED.

Consider now an MST problem where the arc weights are not distinct. The ties between arcs with the same weight can be broken by using the identities of their end nodes, *i.e.*, in the case of equal weight, prefer the arc with a minimum identity end node, and, if these nodes are the same, break the tie in favor of the arc whose other node has a smaller identity. Thus, by implementing, if necessary, the scheme just described one can assume without loss of generality that arc weights are distinct, and that the MST is unique.

5.2.3 Shortest Path Algorithms

In what follows, we shall be interested in traffic flowing over the arcs of a network. This makes it necessary to distinguish the direction of the flow, and thus to give a reference direction to the arcs themselves.

A *directed graph* or *digraph* $G = (\mathcal{N}, \mathcal{A})$ is a finite nonempty set $\mathcal{N}$ of nodes and a collection $\mathcal{A}$ of *ordered* pairs of distinct nodes from $\mathcal{N}$; each ordered pair of nodes

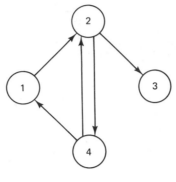

$$\mathcal{N} = \{1, 2, 3, 4\}$$
$$\mathcal{A} = \{(1, 2), (2, 3), (2, 4), (4, 2), (4, 1)\}$$

Figure 5.17   Representation of a directed graph.

in $\mathcal{A}$ is called a *directed arc* (or simply arc). Pictorially, a digraph is represented in the same way as a graph, but an arrow is placed on the representation of the arc, going from the first node of the ordered pair to the second (see Fig. 5.17). Note in Fig. 5.17 that (2,4) and (4,2) are different arcs.

Given any digraph $G = (\mathcal{N}, \mathcal{A})$, there is an associated (undirected) graph $G' = (\mathcal{N}', \mathcal{A}')$ where $\mathcal{N}' = \mathcal{N}$ and $(i, j) \in \mathcal{A}'$ if either $(i, j) \in \mathcal{A}$, or $(j, i) \in \mathcal{A}$, or both. We say that $(n_1, n_2, ..., n_\ell)$ is a walk, path, or cycle in a digraph if it is a walk, path, or cycle in the associated graph. In addition, $(n_1, n_2, ..., n_\ell)$ is a *directed walk* in a digraph G if (n_i, n_{i+1}) is a directed arc in G for $1 \leq i \leq \ell - 1$. A *directed path* is a directed walk with no repeated nodes, and a *directed cycle* is a directed walk $(n_1, ..., n_\ell)$, for $\ell > 2$ with $n_1 = n_\ell$ and no repeated nodes. Note that (n_1, n_2, n_1) is a directed cycle if (n_1, n_2) and (n_2, n_1) are both directed arcs, whereas (n_1, n_2, n_1) cannot be an undirected cycle if (n_1, n_2) is an undirected arc.

A digraph is *strongly connected* if for each pair of nodes i and j there is a directed path $(i = n_1, n_2, ..., n_\ell = j)$ from i to j. A digraph is *connected* if the associated graph is connected. The first graph in Fig. 5.18 is connected but not strongly connected since there is no directed path from 3 to 2. The second graph is strongly connected.

Consider a directed graph $G = (\mathcal{N}, \mathcal{A})$ with number of nodes N and number of arcs A, in which each arc (i, j) is assigned some real number d_{ij} as the length or distance of the arc. Given any directed path $p = (i, j, k, ..., \ell, m)$, the *length* of p is defined as $d_{ij} + d_{jk} + \cdots + d_{\ell m}$. The length of a directed walk or cycle is defined analogously. Given any two nodes i, m of the graph, the shortest path problem is to find a minimum length (*i.e.*, shortest) path from i to m.

The shortest path problem appears in a surprisingly large number of contexts.

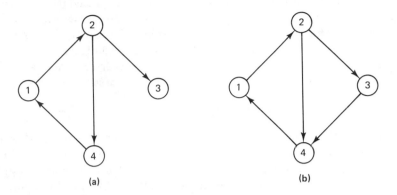

(a)   (b)

Figure 5.18   Both digraphs (a) and (b) are connected, (b) is strongly connected, but (a) is not strongly connected since there is no directed path from 3 to 2.

If d_{ij} is the cost of using a given link (i, j) in a data network, then the shortest path from i to m is the minimum cost route over which to send data. Thus, if the cost of a link equals the average packet delay to cross the link, the minimum cost route is also a minimum delay route. Unfortunately, in a data network, the average link delay depends on the traffic load carried by the link, which in turn depends on the routes selected by the routing algorithm. Because of this feedback effect, the routing problem is more complex than just solving a shortest path problem; however, the shortest path problem is still an integral part of all the formulations of the routing problem to be considered. As another example, if p_{ij} is the probability that a given arc (i, j) in a network is usable, and each arc is usable independently of all the other arcs, then finding the shortest path between i and m with arc distances $-\ln p_{ij}$ is equivalent to finding the most reliable path from i to j.

Another application of shortest paths is in the PERT networks used by organizations to monitor the progress of large projects. The nodes of the network correspond to subtasks, and an arc from subtask i to j indicates that the completion of task j is dependent on the completion of i. If t_{ij} is the time required to complete j after i is completed, the distance for (i, j) is taken as $d_{ij} = -t_{ij}$. The shortest path from project start to finish is then the most time consuming path required for the completion of the project, and the shortest path indicates the critical subtasks for which delays would delay the entire project. Yet another example is that of discrete dynamic programming problems, which can be viewed as shortest path problems [Ber87]. Finally, many more complex graph theoretic problems require the solution of shortest path problems as subproblems.

In the following, three standard algorithms for the shortest path problem are developed—the Bellman-Ford algorithm, the Dijkstra algorithm, and the Floyd-Warshall algorithm. The first two algorithms find the shortest paths from a given source node to all other nodes (or, equivalently, from all nodes to a given destination node), and the third algorithm finds the shortest paths from all nodes to all other nodes. It turns out that if one simply wants to find the shortest path from a single node i to another single node j, there is no known way of doing this without essentially finding the shortest paths from all nodes to j or finding the shortest paths from i to all other nodes. Later, distributed algorithms for the shortest path problem will be discussed, but these will be easier to understand if the centralized algorithms for solving the problem are learned first.

The Bellman-Ford Algorithm

Suppose that node 1 is the "source" node, and the shortest path lengths from node 1 to each other node in the graph are to be found. The arc distances can be negative or positive for this algorithm, but we assume that there are no cycles of negative length; this assumption will be discussed more fully later. To simplify the notation, let $d_{ij} = \infty$ if (i,j) is not an arc of the graph. The trick in the Bellman-Ford algorithm is to first find the shortest path lengths subject to the constraint that the paths contain at most one arc, then to find the shortest path lengths with a constraint of paths of at most two arcs, and so forth. The shortest path, subject to the constraint that the path contain at most h arcs, is referred to as the shortest $(\leq h)$ path.

Let $D_i^{(h)}$ be the shortest $(\leq h)$ path length from node 1 to node i. By convention, we take $D_1^{(h)} = 0$ for all h. The Bellman-Ford algorithm is then as follows:

Initially,

$$D_i^{(0)} = \infty, \quad \text{for all } i \neq 1 \tag{5.1}$$

For each successive $h \geq 0$,

$$D_i^{(h+1)} = \min_j [D_j^{(h)} + d_{ji}], \quad \text{for all } i \neq 1 \tag{5.2}$$

The algorithm is illustrated in Fig. 5.19. To prove its validity, first note that Eqs. (5.1) and (5.2) give $D_i^{(1)} = d_{1i}$ for all $i \neq 1$ which are the correct shortest (≤ 1) path lengths. We now use induction on h, assuming, for a given h, that $D_i^{(h)}$ is the shortest $(\leq h)$ path length for all $i \neq 1$, and proving that Eq. (5.2) gives the shortest $(\leq h+1)$ path length from node 1 to each node $i \neq 1$. We first show that the left side of Eq. (5.2) is greater than or equal to the right side, and then demonstrate the opposite inequality. Suppose that $(1, \ldots, m, k, i)$ is a shortest $(\leq h+1)$ path from 1 to i. Then, its path length is the path length of $(1, \ldots, m, k)$ plus d_{ki}. Since $(1, \ldots, m, k)$ contains at most h arcs,

$$D_i^{(h+1)} \geq D_k^{(h)} + d_{ki} \geq \min_j [D_j^{(h)} + d_{ji}]$$

For the opposite inequality, suppose that a given k minimizes the right-hand side of Eq. (5.2), and that $(1, \ldots, m, k)$ is the shortest $(\leq h)$ path, which by assumption has length $D_k^{(h)}$. Then the length of $(1, \ldots, m, k, i)$ is equal to the right

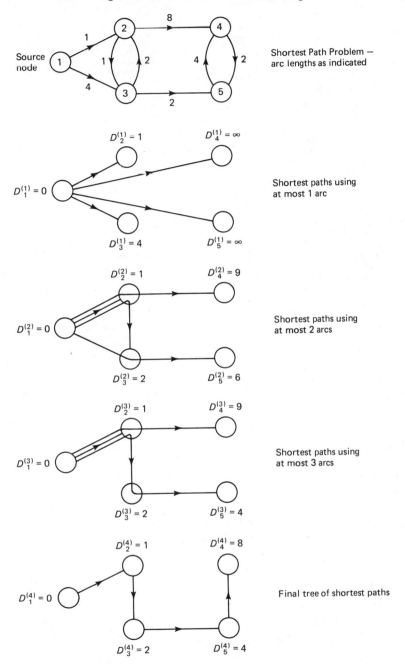

Figure 5.19   Successive iterations of the Bellman-Ford method.

Figure 5.20   Graph with a negative cycle. The shortest path length from 1 to 2 is 1. The Bellman-Ford algorithm gives $D_2^{(2)} = 1$ and $D_2^{(3)} = -1$, indicating the existence of a negative cycle.

hand side of Eq. (5.2). Therefore, if $(1, \ldots, m, k, i)$ is a path,

$$D_i^{(h+1)} \leq D_k^{(h)} + d_{ki} = \min_j [D_j^{(h)} + d_{ji}]$$

Finally, if $(1, \ldots, m, k, i)$ is not a path (*i.e.*, if it contains a cycle), then i must lie on the path $(1, \ldots, m, k)$, and since cycles by hypothesis all have nonnegative length, the inequality above is maintained and Eq. (5.2) is established.

A path can contain at most $N - 1$ arcs (where N is the number of nodes), so if there are no negative length cycles, $D_i^{(N-1)}$ is the shortest path length from node 1 to i. It is also easy to see that if $D_i^{(h+1)} = D_i^{(h)}$ for all i, then no further iterations with larger h will change the shortest path lengths, and $D_i^{(h)}$ is the shortest path length for each i.

In the worst case, the algorithm must be iterated $N - 1$ times, each iteration must be done for $N - 1$ nodes, and, for each node, the minimization must be taken over no more than $N - 1$ alternatives. Thus, the amount of computation grows at worst as N^3, which is written as $O(N^3)$. Generally the notation $O(p(N))$, where $p(N)$ is a polynomial in N, is used to indicate a number depending on N that is smaller than $cp(N)$ for all N, where c is some constant independent of N. Actually, a more careful accounting shows that the amount of computation is $O(mA)$ where A is the number of arcs, and m is the number of iterations required for termination (m is also the maximum number of arcs contained in a shortest path).

Now let us look more carefully at the effect of negative length cycles. Consider the graph in Fig. 5.20. The shortest walk length from node 1 to 2, for walks of three or fewer arcs, is -1, and corresponds to the walk (1,2,3,2); the shortest path length, however, is +1 for the path (1,2). What the Bellman-Ford algorithm is really doing is finding the shortest $(\leq h + 1)$ walk length from 1 to i subject to the constraint that node 1 is not repeated in the walk. If there are negative length cycles not including node 1, then successively longer walks acquire smaller and smaller lengths, and the Bellman-Ford algorithm never converges. One can test for negative cycles (not involving node 1) simply by comparing $D_i^{(N)}$ with $D_i^{(N-1)}$ for each i. If equality is maintained, it follows that $D_i^{(h)} = D_i^{(N-1)}$, for all i and $h \geq N$, thereby implying that the shortest path lengths have been found and there are no negative cycles (except perhaps ones including node 1). If inequality holds for any i, then this means that there is a walk from 1 to i with N arcs, passing through node 1 only once, and having smaller length than every walk from 1 to i

with $(N-1)$ arcs or less. Therefore, this walk must contain a negative length cycle. In the example of Figure 5.20, it can be verified that $D_2^{(2)} = 1$ and $D_2^{(3)} = -1$, indicating the existence of a negative length cycle.

Let D_i be the shortest path length from node 1 to i, with $D_1 = 0$. Assuming no negative length cycles, then when Eq. (5.2) converges with $h = N - 1$, it can be written

$$D_i = \min_j [D_j + d_{ji}], \quad \text{for all } i \neq 1 \tag{5.3a}$$

$$D_1 = 0 \tag{5.3b}$$

This is called *Bellman's equation* and expresses that the shortest path length from node 1 to i is the sum of the path length to the node before i (on the shortest path) plus the distance on the final arc of the path. From the solution of this equation (which we get from the Bellman-Ford algorithm), it is easy to find the shortest paths (as opposed to the shortest path lengths), assuming that all cycles not including node 1 have a positive length. To do this, select, for each $i \neq 1$, one arc (j, i) that attains the minimum in Eq. (5.3a) and consider the subgraph consisting of these $N - 1$ arcs. To find the shortest path to any node i, start from i and follow the corresponding arcs of the subgraph backwards until node 1 is reached. Note that the same node cannot be reached twice before reaching node 1, since a cycle would be formed that (on the basis of Eq. (5.3)) would have zero length. Since the subgraph connects every node to node 1, and has $N - 1$ arcs, it must be a spanning tree. We call this subgraph the *shortest path spanning tree*, and note that it has the special structure of having a root (node 1), with every arc of the tree directed away from the root. Problem 5.7 addresses the issue of how such a spanning tree can be obtained when there are cycles of zero length. Problem 5.4 explores the difference between a shortest path spanning tree and a minimum weight spanning tree.

Using the preceding construction, it can be shown that *if there are no zero (or negative) length cycles, then Bellman's equation (5.3) has a unique solution.* To see this, suppose that $\tilde{D}_i, i = 1, \ldots, n$, solve Eq. (5.3) with $\tilde{D}_1 = 0$. Then, from the construction above, $\tilde{D}_i$ is the length of the corresponding path from node 1 to node i. Therefore, $\tilde{D}_i \geq D_i$, where D_i is the true shortest distance for all i. To show the reverse inequality, consider the Bellman-Ford algorithm with two different initial conditions. The first initial condition is $D_i^{(0)} = \infty$, for $i \neq 1$, and $D_1^{(0)} = 0$, in which case the true shortest distances D_i are obtained after $N - 1$ iterations. The second initial condition is $D_i^{(0)} = \tilde{D}_i$, for all i, in which case $\tilde{D}_i$ is obtained after every iteration (since $\tilde{D}_i$ solve Bellman's equation). Since the second initial condition is, for every i, less than or equal to the first, it is seen from Eq. (5.2) that $\tilde{D}_i \leq D_i$, for all i. Therefore, $\tilde{D}_i = D_i$, and the only solution of Bellman's equation are the true shortest distances D_i. Conversely, with a little thought, it can be seen that *if there are zero length cycles not involving node 1, then Bellman's equation always has a nonunique solution* (although the Bellman-Ford algorithm still converges to the correct shortest distances). This fact is considered in Problem 5.8.

Part of the popularity of the Bellman-Ford algorithm, particularly for distributed applications, is that when arc lengths are positive, the initial conditions $D_i^{(0)}$ for $i \neq 1$ can be arbitrary nonnegative numbers, and the iterations (5.2) can be done in parallel for different nodes in virtually any order. An analysis of this type of algorithm will be given in the next section.

Dijkstra's Algorithm

This algorithm requires that all arc lengths are positive (fortunately, the case for data network applications). Its worst-case computational requirements are considerably less than those of the Bellman-Ford algorithm. The general idea is to find the shortest paths in order of increasing path length. The shortest of the shortest paths from node 1 must be the single-arc path to the closest neighbor of node 1, since any multiple-arc path must be longer than the first arc length because of the positive length assumption. The next shortest of the shortest paths must either be the single-arc path to the next closest neighbor of 1 or the shortest two-arc path through the previously chosen node, etc. To formalize this procedure into an algorithm, we view each node i as being labeled with an estimate D_i of the shortest path length from node 1. When the estimate becomes certain, we regard the node as being *permanently labeled*, and keep track of this with a set P of permanently labeled nodes. The node added to P at each step will be the closest to node 1 out of those that are not yet in P. Fig. 5.21 illustrates the main idea. The detailed algorithm is as follows:

Initially $P = \{1\}$, $D_1 = 0$, and $D_j = d_{1j}$ for $j \neq 1$.

Step 1. (Find the next closest node.) Find $i \notin P$ such that

$$D_i = \min_{j \notin P} D_j$$

Set $P := P \cup \{i\}$. If P contains all nodes then stop; the algorithm is complete.

Step 2. (Updating of labels.) For all $j \notin P$ set

$$D_j := \min[D_j, D_i + d_{ij}]$$

Go to Step 1.

The operation of this algorithm and of the Bellman-Ford algorithm is illustrated in Fig. 5.22. To see why the algorithm works, one must interpret the path length estimates D_i for i not in P. We claim that D_i (at the beginning of each iteration of Step 1) is the shortest distance from node 1 to i for which all nodes on the path except i lie in the set P. This is satisfied initially, and Step 2 of the algorithm can be seen to maintain the condition for each new node added to P. By induction, now, it is seen that if each node in P is at least as close to node 1

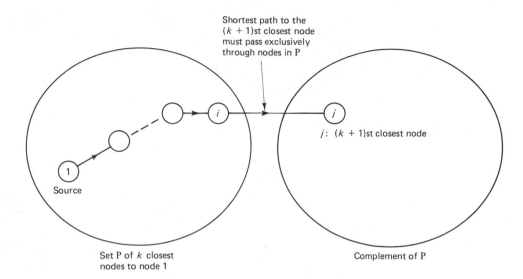

Figure 5.21   Basic idea of Dijkstra's algorithm. At the kth step we have the set P of the k closest nodes to node 1 as well as the shortest distance D_i from node 1 to each node i in P. Of all paths connecting node 1 to some node not in P, the shortest one must pass exclusively through nodes in P (since $d_{ij} > 0$). Therefore, the $(k+1)^{\text{st}}$ closest node and the corresponding shortest distance are obtained by minimizing over $j \notin P$ the quantity $\min_{i \in P}\{D_i + d_{ij}\}$. This calculation can be organized efficiently as discussed in the text resulting in an $O(N^2)$ computational complexity.

as each node not in P, then the next closest node beyond P must have a shortest path for which all but the final node lie in P; thus, Step 1 chooses this node.

Since each step in Dijkstra's algorithm requires a number of operations proportional to N, and the steps are iterated $N-1$ times, it is seen that in the worst case the computation is $O(N^2)$ rather than $O(N^3)$ as in the Bellman-Ford algorithm. However, there are many problems where $A \ll N^2$, and the Bellman-Ford algorithm terminates in very few iterations (say $m \ll N$), in which case its required computation $O(mA)$ can be less than the $O(N^2)$ requirement of Dijkstra's algorithm.

The Floyd-Warshall Algorithm

This algorithm, unlike the previous two, finds the shortest paths between all pairs of nodes together. Like the Bellman-Ford algorithm, the arc distances can be positive or negative, but again there can be no negative length cycles. All three algorithms iterate to find the final solution, but each iterates on something different. The Bellman-Ford algorithm iterates on the number of arcs in a path, the Dijkstra algorithm iterates on the length of the path, and, finally, the Floyd-Warshall algorithm iterates on the set of nodes that are allowed as intermediate nodes on the paths.

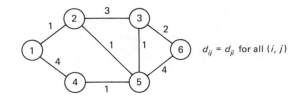

Bellman–Ford

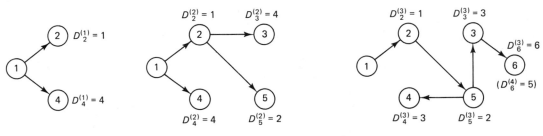

Dijkstra

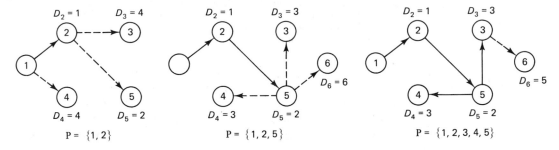

Figure 5.22   Example using the Bellman-Ford and Dijkstra algorithms.

The Floyd-Warshall algorithm starts like both other algorithms with single arc distances (*i.e.*, no intermediate nodes) as starting estimates of shortest path lengths. It then calculates shortest paths under the constraint that only node 1 can be used as an intermediate node, and then with the constraint that only nodes 1 and 2 can be used, and so forth.

To state the algorithm more precisely, let $D_{ij}^{(n)}$ be the shortest path length from node i to j with the constraint that only nodes $1, 2, \ldots, n$ can be used as intermediate nodes on paths. The algorithm then is as follows:

Initially,

$$D_{ij}^{(0)} = d_{ij}, \text{ for all } i, j \quad i \neq j \tag{5.4}$$

For $n = 0, 1, \ldots, N - 1$,

$$D_{ij}^{(n+1)} = \min[D_{ij}^{(n)}, D_{i(n+1)}^{(n)} + D_{(n+1)j}^{(n)}], \text{ for all } i \neq j \tag{5.5}$$

To see why this works, we use induction again. For $n = 0$, the initialization clearly gives the shortest path lengths subject to the constraint of no intermediate nodes on paths. Now, suppose for a given n, $D_{ij}^{(n)}$ in the above algorithm gives the shortest path lengths using nodes 1 to n as intermediate nodes. Then the shortest path length from i to j, allowing nodes 1 to $n + 1$ as intermediate nodes, either contains node $n + 1$ on the shortest path, or doesn't contain node $n + 1$. For the first case, the constrained shortest path from i to j goes first from i to $n + 1$ and then from $n + 1$ to j, giving the length in the final term of Eq. (5.5). For the second case, the constrained shortest path is the same as the one using nodes 1 to n as intermediate nodes, yielding the length of the first term in the minimization of Eq. (5.5).

Since each of the N steps above must be executed for each pair of nodes, the computation involved in the Floyd-Warshall algorithm is $O(N^3)$, the same as if the Dijkstra algorithm was repeated for each possible choice of source node.

5.2.4 Distributed Asynchronous Bellman-Ford Algorithm

Consider a routing algorithm that routes each packet along a shortest path from the packet's origin to its destination. The link lengths may change either due to link failures and repairs, or due to changing traffic conditions in the network. It is therefore neccesary to update shortest paths in response to these changes. We described several such algorithms in subsection 5.1.2 in connection with the ARPANET and the TYMNET.

In this subsection, we consider an algorithm similar to the one originally implemented in the ARPANET in 1969. It is closely related to the one currently used in DNA (DEC's Digital Network Architecture) [Wec80]. The idea is to compute the shortest distances from every node to every other node by means of a distributed version of the Bellman-Ford algorithm. An interesting aspect of this algorithm is that it requires very little information to be stored at the network nodes. Indeed, a node need not know the detailed network topology. It suffices for a node to know the length of its outgoing links and the identity of every node in the network.

We assume that each link (i, j) has a positive length d_{ij}. We also assume that the network stays always strongly connected, and that if (i, j) is a link then (j, i) is also a link. We envision a practical situation where the lengths d_{ij} can change with time. In the analysis, however, it is assumed that the lengths d_{ij} are fixed while the initial conditions for the algorithm are allowed to be essentially arbitrary. These assumptions provide an adequate model for a situation where the link lengths stay fixed after some time t_0 following a number of changes that occurred before t_0.

We focus on the shortest distance D_i from each node i to a generic destination node taken for concreteness to be node 1. (In reality, a separate version of the algorithm must be executed for each destination node.) From Bellman's equation,

$$D_i = \min_{j \in N(i)} [d_{ij} + D_j], \quad i \neq 1 \tag{5.6}$$

$$D_1 = 0 \tag{5.7}$$

where $N(i)$ denotes the set of current neighbors of node i, *i.e.*, the nodes connected with i via an up link. These equations are equivalent but slightly different than the ones given in the previous subsection. There the problem was to find the shortest distances *from* a given node 1 to all other nodes, while here the problem is to find the shortest distances *to* a given node 1 from all other nodes. One version of the problem can be obtained from the other simply by reversing the direction of each link while keeping its length unchanged.

The Bellman-Ford algorithm is given by

$$D_i^{(h+1)} = \min_{j \in N(i)} [d_{ij} + D_j^{(h)}], \quad i \neq 1 \tag{5.8}$$

$$D_1^{(h+1)} = 0 \tag{5.9}$$

In the previous subsection, convergence to the correct shortest distances was shown for the initial conditions

$$D_i^{(0)} = \infty, \quad i \neq 1 \tag{5.10}$$

$$D_1^{(0)} = 0 \tag{5.11}$$

The algorithm is well suited for distributed computation since the iteration (5.8) can be executed at each node i in parallel with every other node. One possibility is for all nodes i to execute (5.8) simultaneously, exchange the results of the computation with their neighbors, and execute (5.8) again with the index h incremented by one. When the initial conditions are those of Eqs. (5.10) and (5.11), the algorithm will terminate after at most $N - 1$ iterations (where N is the number of nodes) with each node i knowing both the shortest distance D_i, and the outgoing link on the shortest path to node 1.

Unfortunately, implementing the algorithm in such a synchronous manner is not as easy as it appears. There is a twofold difficulty here. First, a mechanism is needed for getting all nodes to agree to start the algorithm. Second, a mechanism is needed to abort the algorithm and start a new version if a link status or length changes as the algorithm is running. While it is possible to cope successfully with these difficulties [Seg81], the resulting algorithm is far more complex than the pure Bellman-Ford method given by Eqs. (5.8) and (5.9).

A simpler alternative is to use a version of the Bellman-Ford algorithm that does not insist on maintaining synchronism between nodes, and on starting with the particular initial conditions (5.10) and (5.11). This eliminates the need for either an algorithm initiation or an algorithm restart protocol. The algorithm simply operates indefinitely by executing from time to time at each node $i \neq 1$ the iteration

$$D_i := \min_{j \in N(i)} [d_{ij} + D_j], \qquad (5.12)$$

using the latest estimates D_j received from the neighbors $j \in N(i)$, and the latest status and lengths of the outgoing links from node i. The algorithm also requires that each node i transmit from time to time its latest estimate D_i to all its neighbors. However, there is no need for either the iterations (5.12) or the message transmissions to be synchronized at all nodes. Furthermore, no assumptions are made on the initial values $D_j, \ j \in N(i)$ available at each node i. The only requirement is that a node i will eventually execute the iteration (5.12) if this changes D_i, and will eventually transmit the result to the neighbors. Thus, a totally asynchronous mode of operation is envisioned.

It turns out that the algorithm is still valid when executed asynchronously as described above. It will be shown that if a number of link length changes occur up to some time t_0, and no other changes occur subsequently, then within finite time from t_0 the asynchronous algorithm finds the correct shortest distance of every node i. The shortest distance estimates available at time t_0 can be arbitrary nonnegative numbers, so it is not necessary to reinitialize the algorithm after each link status or link length change.

The original 1969 ARPANET algorithm was based on iteration (5.12), and was implemented asynchronously much like the scheme described above. Neighboring nodes exchanged their current shortest distance estimates D_j needed in Eq. (5.12) every 625 msec, but this exchange was not synchronized across the network. Furthermore, the algorithm was not restarted following a link length change or a link failure. The major difference between the ARPANET algorithm and the one analyzed in the present subsection is that the link lengths d_{ij} were changing very frequently in the ARPANET algorithm, and the eventual steady state assumed in our analysis was seldom reached.

We now state formally the distributed, asynchronous Bellman-Ford algorithm and proceed to establish its validity. At each time t, a node $i \neq 1$ has available:

$D_j^i(t)$: The estimate of the shortest distance of each neighbor node $j \in N(i)$ which was latest communicated to node i.

$D_i(t)$: The estimate of the shortest distance of node i which was latest computed at node i according to the Bellman-Ford iteration.

The distance estimates for the destination node 1 are defined to be zero, so

$$D_1(t) = 0, \quad \text{for all } t \geq t_0$$

$$D_1^i(t) = 0, \quad \text{for all } t \geq t_0, \text{ and } i \text{ with } 1 \in N(i)$$

Each node i also has available the link lengths d_{ij}, for all $j \in N(i)$, which are assumed positive and constant after the initial time t_0. We assume that the distance estimates do not change except at some times $t_0, t_1, t_2, \ldots$, with $t_{m+1} > t_m$, for all m, and $t_m \to \infty$ as $m \to \infty$, when at each processor $i \neq 1$, one of three events happens:

1. Node i updates $D_i(t)$ according to

$$D_i(t) := \min_{j \in N(i)} [d_{ij} + D_j^i(t)]$$

   and leaves the estimates $D_j^i(t)$, $j \in N(i)$, unchanged.

2. Node i receives from one or more neighbors $j \in N(i)$ the value of D_j which was computed at node j at some earlier time, updates the estimate D_j^i, and leaves all other estimates unchanged.

3. Node i is idle in which case all estimates available at i are left unchanged.

Let T^i be the set of times for which an update by node i as in #1 above occurs, and T_j^i the set of times when a message is received at i from node j as in #2 above. We assume the following:

Assumption 1.   Nodes never stop updating their own estimates and receiving messages from all their neighbors, $i.e.$, T^i and T_j^i have an infinite number of elements for all $i \neq 1$ and $j \in N(i)$.

Assumption 2.   All the initial node estimates $D_i(t_0)$ and $D_j^i(t_0)$, $j \in N(i)$, are nonnegative. Furthermore, all estimates communicated to nodes by neighbors before the initial time t_0 and received after time t_0 are nonnegative.

Assumption 3.   Old distance information is eventually purged from the system, $i.e.$, given any time $\bar{t} \geq t_0$, there exists a time $\tilde{t} > \bar{t}$ such that estimates D_j computed at a node j prior to time $\bar{t}$ are not received at any neighbor node i ($j \in N(i)$) after time $\tilde{t}$.

The following proposition shows that the estimates $D_i(t)$ converge to the correct shortest distances within finite time. The proof (which can be skipped without loss of continuity) is interesting in that it serves as a model for proofs of validity of several other asynchronous distributed algorithms (see the convergence proof of the algorithm of subsection 5.3.3, and references [Ber82a] and [Ber83]).

Proposition.   There is a time t_m such that

$$D_i(t) = D_i, \quad \text{for all } t \geq t_m, \ i = 1, \ldots, N$$

where D_i is the correct shortest distance from node i to the destination node 1.

Proof. The idea of the proof is to define for every node i two sequences $\{\underline{D}_i^k\}$ and $\{\overline{D}_i^k\}$ with

$$\underline{D}_i^k \leq \underline{D}_i^{k+1} \leq D_i \leq \overline{D}_i^{k+1} \leq \overline{D}_i^k \tag{5.13}$$

and

$$\underline{D}_i^k = D_i = \overline{D}_i^k, \quad \text{for k sufficiently large} \tag{5.14}$$

These sequences are obtained from the Bellman-Ford algorithm by starting at two different initial conditions. It is then shown that for every k and i, all estimates $D_i(t)$ satisfy

$$\underline{D}_i^k \le D_i(t) \le \overline{D}_i^k, \quad \text{for all } t \text{ sufficiently large} \tag{5.15}$$

A key role in the proof is played by the monotonicity property of the Bellman-Ford iteration. This property states that if for some scalars $\overline{D}_j$ and $\tilde{D}_j$,

$$\overline{D}_j \ge \tilde{D}_j, \quad \text{for all } j \in N(i)$$

then the direction of the inequality is preserved by the iteration, *i.e.*,

$$\min_{j \in N(i)} [d_{ij} + \overline{D}_j] \ge \min_{j \in N(i)} [d_{ij} + \tilde{D}_j]$$

A consequence of this property is that if D_i^k are sequences generated by the Bellman-Ford iteration (5.8) and (5.9) starting from some initial condition $D_i^0, i = 1, \ldots, N$, and we have $D_i^1 \ge D_i^0$ for each i, then $D_i^{k+1} \ge D_i^k$, for each i and k. Similarly, if $D_i^1 \le D_i^0$, for each i, then $D_i^{k+1} \le D_i^k$, for each i and k.

Consider the Bellman-Ford algorithm given by Eqs. (5.8) and (5.9). Let $\overline{D}_i^k, i = 1, \ldots, N$ be the kth iterate of this algorithm when the initial condition is

$$D_i^{(0)} = \infty, \quad i \ne 1 \tag{5.16}$$

$$D_1^{(0)} = 0 \tag{5.17}$$

and let $\underline{D}_i^k, i = 1, \ldots, N$ be the kth iterate when the initial condition is

$$D_i^{(0)} = 0, \quad i = 1, 2, \ldots, N$$

Lemma.   The sequences $\{\underline{D}_i^k\}$ and $\{\overline{D}_i^k\}$ defined above satisfy Eqs. (5.13) and (5.14).

Proof. Relation (5.13) is shown by induction using the monotonicity property of the Bellman-Ford iteration, and the choice of initial conditions above. To show Eq. (5.14), first note that from the convergence analysis of the Bellman-Ford algorithm of the previous section, for all i,

$$\overline{D}_i^k = D_i, \quad k \ge N - 1 \tag{5.18}$$

so only $\underline{D}_i^k = D_i$, for sufficiently large k, remains to be established. To this end, we first use an induction argument to show that $\underline{D}_i^k$ is, for every k, the sum of no more than k link lengths. Then, using the relation $\underline{D}_i^k \leq D_i$, we see that, for every k, $\underline{D}_i^k$ cannot be the sum of more than

$$\frac{\max_i D_i}{\min_{(i,j)} d_{ij}} \tag{5.19}$$

link lengths. Therefore, the number of all possible values of $\underline{D}_i^k$, for $i = 1, \ldots, N$, and $k = 0, 1, \ldots$ is finite. Since $\underline{D}_i^k$ is monotonically nondecreasing in k for all i, it follows that for some $\overline{k}$

$$\underline{D}_i^{\overline{k}} = \underline{D}_i^{\overline{k}+1}, \quad \text{for all } i = 1, \ldots, N$$

Therefore, the scalars $\underline{D}_i^{\overline{k}}$ satisfy Bellman's equation, which has as its unique solution the shortest distances D_i. It follows that

$$\underline{D}_i^k = D_i, \quad \text{for all } i = 1, \ldots, N, \quad k \geq \overline{k} \tag{5.20}$$

Equations (5.18) and (5.20) show Eq. (5.14). QED.

We now complete the proof of the proposition by showing by induction that for every k there exists a time $t(k)$ such that for all $t \geq t(k)$

$$\underline{D}_i^k \leq D_i(t) \leq \overline{D}_i^k, \quad i = 1, 2, \ldots, N \tag{5.21}$$

$$\underline{D}_j^k \leq D_j^i(t) \leq \overline{D}_j^k, \quad j \in N(i), \quad i = 1, 2, \ldots, N \tag{5.22}$$

and for all $t \in T_j^i, t \geq t(k)$,

$$\underline{D}_j^k \leq D_j[\tau_j^i(t)] \leq \overline{D}_j^k, \quad j \in N(i), \quad i = 1, 2, \ldots, N \tag{5.23}$$

where $\tau_j^i(t) \leq t$ is the largest time at which the estimate $D_j^i(t)$ available at node i at time t was computed using Eq. (5.12) at node j. (Formally, $\tau_j^i(t)$ is defined as the largest time in T^j that is less than t, and is such that $D_j[\tau_j^i(t)] = D_j^i(t)$.)

Indeed, the induction hypothesis is true for $k = 0$ (for $t(0) = t_0$) by virtue of the nonnegativity assumption on the initial estimates residing at the nodes or in the process of being communicated to the nodes (Assumption 2). Assuming the induction hypothesis is true for a given k, it will be shown that there exists a time $t(k + 1)$ with the required properties. Indeed from relation (5.22) and the monotonicity of the Bellman-Ford iteration, we have that for every $t \in T^i, t \geq t(k)$ (i.e., a time t for which $D_i(t)$ is updated via the Bellman-Ford iteration),

$$\underline{D}_i^{k+1} \leq D_i(t) \leq \overline{D}_i^{k+1}$$

Therefore, if $t'(k)$ is the smallest time $t \in T^i$, with $t \geq t(k)$, then

$$\underline{D}_i^{k+1} \leq D_i(t) \leq \overline{D}_i^{k+1}, \quad \text{for all } t \geq t'(k), \quad i = 1, \ldots, N \tag{5.24}$$

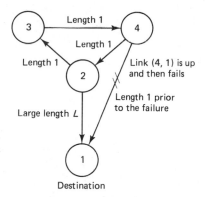

Figure 5.23   Example where the number of iterations of the (synchronous) Bellman-Ford algorithm is excessive. Suppose the initial conditions are the shortest distances from nodes 2, 3, and 4 to node 1 before link (4,1) fails ($D_2 = 3$, $D_3 = 2$, $D_4 = 1$). Then, after link (4,1) fails, nearly L iterations will be required before node 2 realizes that its shortest path to node 1 is the direct link (2,1). This is an example of the so called "bad news phenonenon", whereby the algorithm reacts slowly to a sudden increase in one or more link lengths.

Since $\tau_j^i(t) \rightarrow \infty$ as $t \rightarrow \infty$ (by Assumptions 1 and 3) we can choose a time $t(k+1) \geq t'(k)$ so that $\tau_j^i(t) \geq t'(k)$, for all $i, j \in N(i)$, and $t \geq t(k+1)$. Then, in view of Eq. (5.24), for all $t \geq t(k+1)$,

$$\underline{D}_j^{k+1} \leq D_j^i(t) \leq \overline{D}_j^{k+1}, \quad j \in N(i), \quad i = 1, 2, \ldots, N \tag{5.25}$$

and for all $t \in T_j^i$, $t \geq t(k+1)$,

$$\underline{D}_j^{k+1} \leq D_j[\tau_j^i(t)] \leq \overline{D}_j^{k+1}, \quad j \in N(i), \quad i = 1, 2, \ldots, N \tag{5.26}$$

This completes the induction proof.   QED.

The preceding analysis assumes that the network is connected. If not, then the analysis applies to the portion of the network that is connected with node 1. For a node i that belongs to a different network component than node 1 and has at least one neighbor (so that it can execute the algorithm), it can be seen that $D_i(t) \rightarrow \infty$ as $t \rightarrow \infty$. This property can be used by a node to identify the destinations to which it is not connected.

We close this section with a discussion of two weaknesses of the asynchronous Bellman-Ford method. The first is that in the worst case, the algorithm may require an excessive number of iterations to terminate (see the example of Fig. 5.23). This is not due to the asynchronous nature of the algorithm, but rather to the arbitrary choice of initial conditions (an indication is provided by the argument preceding expression (5.19)). The second, demonstrated in the example of Fig. 5.24,

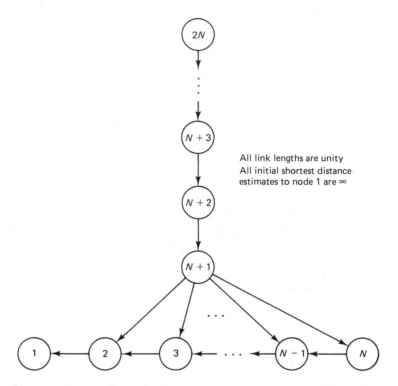

All link lengths are unity
All initial shortest distance
estimates to node 1 are ∞

Figure 5.24   Example where the asynchronous version of the Bellman-
Ford algorithm requires many more message transmissions than the synchronous version. The initial estimates of shortest distance of all nodes is ∞. Consider the following sequence of events where all communications are received
with zero delay:

1. Node 2 updates its shortest distance and communicates the result to 3.
Node 3 updates and communicates the result to 4.... Node $N - 1$ updates
and communicates the result to N. Node N updates and communicates the
result to $N + 1$. (These are $N - 1$ messages.)
2. Node $N + 1$ updates and communicates the result to $N + 2$.... Node $2N - 1$
updates and communicates the result to $2N$. Node $2N$ updates. (These are
$N - 1$ messages.)
3. For $i = N - 1, N - 2, \ldots, 2$, in that order, node i communicates its update
to $N + 1$ and sequence #2 above is repeated. (These are $N(N - 2)$ messages.)

The total number of messages is $N^2 - 2$. If the algorithm were executed
synchronously, only $3(N - 1) - 1$ messages would be needed. The difficulty
in the asynchronous version is that a lot of unimportant information arrives
at node $N + 1$ early and triggers a lot of unnecessary messages starting from
$N + 1$ and proceeding all the way to $2N$.

is that in the worst case, the algorithm requires an excessive number of message transmissions. It is not presently known to what extent these weaknesses affect the "average" performance of the algorithm—the example of Fig. 5.24 requires an unlikely sequence of events.

5.2.5 Adaptive Routing Based on Shortest Paths

The possibility of using link lengths that reflect the traffic conditions on the links in the recent past was discussed in earlier sections. The idea is to assign a large length to a congested link so that the shortest path algorithm will tend not to use it as part of a routing path. This sounds attractive at first, but on second thought one gets alerted to the possibility of oscillations. We will see that this possibility is particularly dangerous in datagram networks.

Stability Issues in Datagram Networks

For a simple example of oscillation, consider a datagram network, and suppose that there are two paths along which an origin can send traffic to a destination. Routing along a path during some time period will increase its length, so the other path will tend to be chosen for routing in the next time period, resulting in an oscillation between the two paths. It turns out that a far worse type of oscillation is possible, as illustrated in the following example:

Example 1

Consider the 16-node network shown in Fig. 5.25, where node 16 is the only destination. Let the traffic input (in data units/sec) at each node $i = 1, \ldots, 7, 9, \ldots, 15$ be one unit and let the traffic input of node 8 be $\epsilon > 0$, where ϵ is very small. Assume that the length of link (i, j) is

$$d_{ij} = F_{ij}$$

where F_{ij} is the arrival rate at the link counting input and relayed traffic. Suppose that all nodes compute their shortest path to the destination every T seconds using as link lengths the arrival rates F_{ij} during the preceding T seconds, and route all their traffic along that path for the next T seconds. Assume that we start with nodes 1 through 7 routing clockwise and nodes 8 through 15 routing counterclockwise. This is a rather good routing, balancing the traffic input between the two directions. Figure 5.26 shows the link rates corresponding to the initial and subsequent shortest path routings. Thus, after three shortest path updates, the algorithm is locked into an oscillatory pattern whereby all traffic swings from the clockwise to the counterclockwise direction and back at alternate updates. This is certainly the worst type of routing performance that could occur.

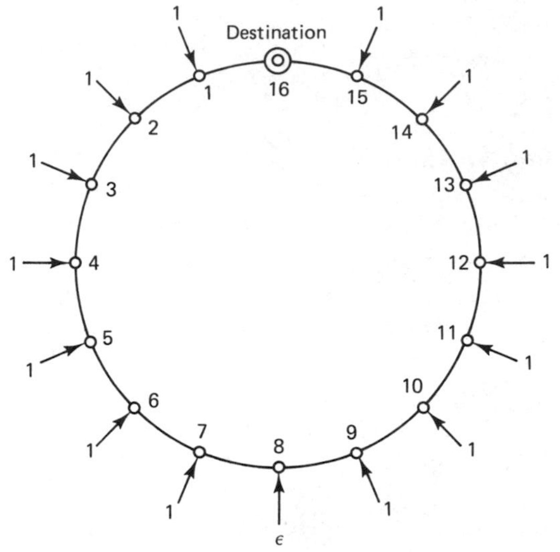

Figure 5.25   Sixteen-node ring network of Example 1. Node 16 is the only destination.

The difficulty in the preceding example is due to the fact that link arrival rates depend on routing, which in turn depends on arrival rates via the shortest path calculation, with a feedback effect resulting. This is similar to the stability issue in feedback control theory, and can be analyzed using a related methodology [Ber82b]. Actually, it can be shown that the type of instability illustrated above will occur generically if the length d_{ij} of link (i, j) increases continuously and monotonically with the link arrival rate F_{ij}, and $d_{ij} = 0$ when $F_{ij} = 0$. It is possible to damp the oscillations by adding a positive constant to the link length so that $d_{ij} = \alpha > 0$ when $F_{ij} = 0$. The scalar α (link length at zero load) is known as a *bias* factor. Oscillations in the original ARPANET algorithm discussed in subsection 5.1.2 were damped by using a substantial bias factor. Indeed, if α is large enough, it can

---

Figure 5.26   Oscillations in a ring network for link lengths d_{ij} equal to the link arrival rates F_{ij}. Each node sends one unit of input traffic to the destination except for the middle node 8, which sends $\epsilon > 0$, where ϵ is very small. The numbers next to the links are the link rates in each of the two directions. As an example of the shortest path calculations, at the first iteration the middle node 8 computes the length of the clockwise path as $28(= 0 + 1 + 2 + \cdots + 7)$, and the length of the counterclockwise path as $28 + 8\varepsilon(= \varepsilon + 1 + \varepsilon + 2 + \varepsilon + \ldots + 7 + \varepsilon)$, and switches its traffic to the shortest (clockwise) path at the 2nd routing. The corresponding numbers for node 9 are 28 and $28 + 7\varepsilon$, so node 9 also switches its traffic to the clockwise path. All other nodes find that the path used at the first routing is shortest, and therefore they do not switch their traffic to the other path.

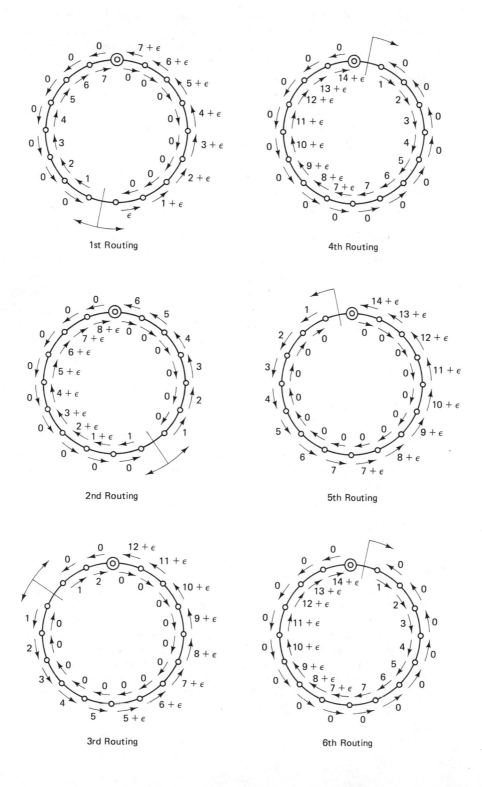

1st Routing

2nd Routing

3rd Routing

4th Routing

5th Routing

6th Routing

be seen that the corresponding shortest paths will be the ones associated with the minimum number of links to the destination. This is static routing, which cannot exhibit any oscillation of the type seen earlier, but is also totally insensitive to traffic congestion. In the current ARPANET algorithm described in subsection 5.1.2, the bias α in effect equals the sum of the average packet transmission time, the processing delay, and the propagation delay along a link. This value is apparently adequate in view of the light load typically carried by the ARPANET. The second possibility to damp oscillations is to introduce a mechanism for averaging the lengths of links over a time period spanning more than one shortest path updates. This tends to improve the stability of the algorithm albeit at the expense of reducing its speed of response to congestion. It turns out that asynchronous shortest path updating by the network nodes results in a form of length averaging that is beneficial for stability purposes. (See [Ber79b] and [Ber82b] for further discussion.)

Stability Issues in Virtual Circuit Networks

The oscillatory behavior exhibited above is associated principally with datagram networks. It will be shown that oscillations are less severe in virtual circuit networks. A key feature of a datagram network in this regard is that each packet of a user pair is not required to travel on the same path as the preceding packet. Therefore, the time that an origin-destination pair will continue to use a shortest path after it is changed due to a routing update is very small. As a result, a datagram network reacts very fast to a shortest path update, with all traffic switching to the new shortest paths almost instantaneously.

The situation is quite different in a virtual circuit network where every session is assigned a fixed communication path at the time it is first established. There the average duration of a virtual circuit is often large relative to the shortest path updating period. As a result, the network reaction to a shortest path update is much more gradual since old sessions continue to use their established communication paths and only new sessions are assigned to the most recently calculated shortest paths.

The following example demonstrates these phenomena:

Example 2

Consider the simple two-link network with one origin and one destination shown in Fig. 5.27(a). Suppose the arrival rate is r bits/sec. Assuming the two links have equal capacity C, an "optimal" routing algorithm should somehow divide the input r equally between the two links, thereby allowing a throughput up to $2C$.

Consider the performance of a typical adaptive algorithm based on shortest paths, to see how it performs on this example network. The algorithm divides the time axis into T-second intervals. It measures the average arrival rate (bits/second) on both links during each T-second interval, and directs all traffic (datagrams or virtual circuits) generated during every T-second interval along the link that had the smallest rate during the preceding T-second interval.

If the network uses datagrams then, assuming T is much larger than the time required to empty the queue of waiting packets at the time of an update, each link

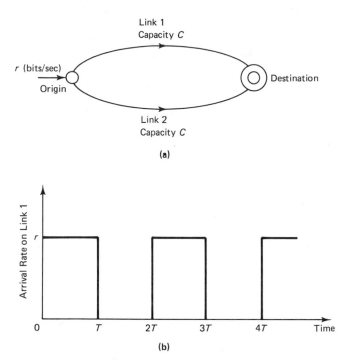

Figure 5.27   (a) Two-link network of Example 2. (b) Arrival rate on link 1 in Example 2 using the shortest path rule in the datagram case. Essentially, only one path is used for routing at any one time if the shortest path update period is much larger than the time required to empty the queue of waiting packets at the time of an update.

will essentially carry either no traffic or all the input traffic $\overset{\bullet}{r}$ at alternate time intervals as shown in Fig. 5.27(b).

Next consider the case where the network uses virtual circuits which are generated according to a Poisson process at a rate λ per second. Each virtual circuit uses the link on which it was assigned by the routing algorithm for its entire duration, assumed exponentially distributed with mean $1/\mu$ seconds. Therefore, according to the $M/M/\infty$ queueing results (cf. subsection 3.4.2), the number of active virtual circuits is Poisson distributed with mean λ/μ. If γ is the average communication rate (bits/sec) of a virtual circuit, we must have $r = (\lambda/\mu)\gamma$, or

$$\gamma = \frac{r\mu}{\lambda} \tag{5.27}$$

Suppose that the shortest path updating interval T is small relative to the average duration of the virtual circuits $1/\mu$. Then, approximately a fraction μT of the virtual circuits that were carried on each link at the beginning of a T-second interval will be terminated at the end of the interval. There will be λT virtual circuits on the average added on the link that carried the least traffic during the preceding interval.

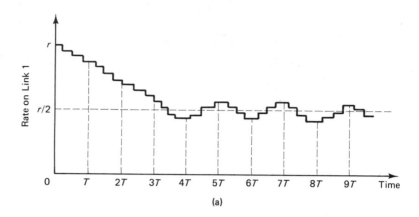

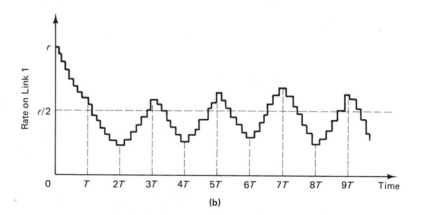

Figure 5.28a,b   Arrival rate on link 1 in Example 2 when virtual circuits are used. (a) Virtual circuits last a long time, and the shortest paths are updated frequently (μT is small). (b) Virtual circuits last a short time, and the shortest paths are updated frequently (μT is moderate).

This amounts to an added arrival rate of $\gamma \lambda T$ bits/sec or, using Eq. (5.27), $r\mu T$ bits/sec. Therefore, the average rates x_1^k and x_2^k (bits/sec) on the two links at the kth interval will evolve approximately according to

$$x_i^{k+1} = \begin{cases} (1 - \mu T)x_i^k + r\mu T, & \text{if } i \text{ is shortest, } i.e., \ x_i^k = \min\{x_1^k, x_2^k\} \\ (1 - \mu T)x_i^k, & \text{otherwise} \end{cases} \qquad (5.28)$$

Figure 5.28 provides examples of the evolution of the average rate on link 1. From Eq. (5.28) it can be seen that as $k \to \infty$, the average rates x_1 and x_2 will tend to oscillate around $r/2$ with a magnitude of oscillation roughly equal to $r\mu T$.

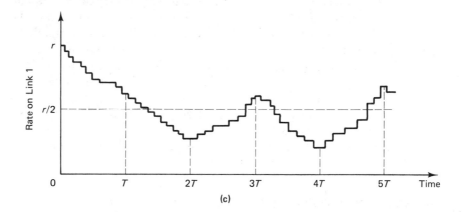

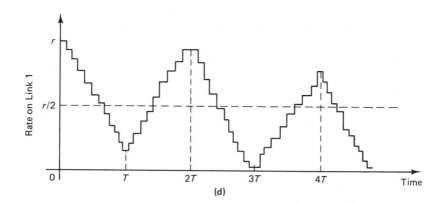

Figure 5.28c,d   Arrival rate on link 1 in Example 2 when virtual circuits are used. (c) Virtual circuits last a long time, and the shortest paths are updated infrequently (μT is moderate). (d) Virtual circuits last a short time, and shortest paths are updated infrequently (μT is large). In the limit as $\mu \to \infty$, the datagram case is obtained.

Therefore, if the average duration of a virtual circuit is large relative to the shortest path updating interval ($\mu T \ll 1$), the routing algorithm performs almost optimally, keeping traffic divided in nearly equal proportions among the two links. Conversely, if the product μT is large, the analysis above indicates considerable oscillation of the link rates. Figure 5.28 demonstrates the relation between μ, T, and the magnitude of oscillation.

The preceding example illustrates behavior that has been demonstrated analytically for general virtual circuit networks [GaB83]. It is also shown in [GaB83] that the average duration of a virtual circuit is a critical parameter for the performance of adaptive shortest path routing. If it is very large, the rate of convergence of the algorithm will be slow, essentially because virtual circuits that are misplaced on congested paths persist for a long time. If it is very small, the shortest path update interval must be accordingly small for the oscillation around optimality to be small (cf. Fig. 5.28). Unfortunately, there is a practical limit on how small the update interval can be, because frequent updates require more overhead and because sufficient time between updates is needed to measure accurately the current link lengths. The problem with a large duration of virtual circuits would not arise if virtual circuits could be rerouted during their lifetime. In the Codex network, described in section 5.8, such rerouting is allowed, thereby resulting in an algorithm that is more efficient than the one of this section.

5.3 BROADCASTING ROUTING INFORMATION— COPING WITH LINK FAILURES

A problem that often arises in routing is the transfer of control information from points in the network where it is collected to other points where it is needed. This problem is surprisingly challenging when links are subject to failure. In this section, the nature of the difficulties is explained, and ways to address the difficulties are considered. This section provides also the opportunity to look at several instructive examples of distributed algorithms.

One practical example of broadcasting routing information has already been discussed in subsection 5.1.2 in connection with the current ARPANET algorithm. Here, all link lengths are periodically broadcast to all nodes, which then proceed to update their routing tables through a shortest path computation. Other cases include situations where it is desired to alert higher layers about topological changes, or to update data structures that might be affected by changes in the network topology, such as a spanning tree used for broadcasting messages to all nodes. (The term *network topology* will be used extensively in this section. It is synonymous with the list of nodes and links of the network together with the status (up or down) of each link.)

Getting routing information reliably to the places where it is needed in the presence of potential link failures involves subtleties that are generally not fully appreciated. Here are some of the difficulties:

1. Topological update information must be communicated over links that are themselves subject to failure. Indeed in some networks, one must provide for the event where portions of the network get disconnected from each other. As an example consider a *centralized* algorithm where all information regarding topological changes is communicated to a special node called the network control center (NCC). The NCC maintains in its memory the routing tables of the entire system, and updates them upon receipt of new topological information by using some algorithm that is of no concern here. It then proceeds to communicate all information needed for local routing operations to the nodes affected. Aside from the generic issue of collecting and disseminating

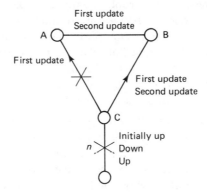

Figure 5.29   Example where the flooding algorithm in its pure form
fails. Link n is initially up, then it goes down, then up again. Suppose that
the two updates travel on the path CBA faster than the first update travels
on the link CA. Suppose also that link CA fails after the first update, but
before the second update travels on it. Then, the last message received by A
asserts that link n is down, while the link is actually up. The difficulty here is
that outdated information is mistakenly taken to be new.

information over failure-prone links, a special problem that such an algorithm
must contend with is the possibility of the NCC failing, or becoming disconnected from a portion of the network. In some cases, it is possible to provide
redundancy and ensure that such difficulties will occur very rarely. In other
cases, however, the resolution of these difficulties may be neither simple nor
foolproof, so that it may be advisable to abandon the centralized approach
altogether and to adopt a distributed algorithm.

2. One has to deal with multiple topological changes (such as a link going down
   and up again within a short time), so the problem arises of distinguishing
   between old and new update information. As an example, consider a popular method for broadcasting topological change information called *flooding*.
   Here a node monitors the status of all its outgoing links, and upon detecting a change, sends a packet to all its neighbors reporting that change. The
   neighbors send this packet to their neighbors, and so on. Some measures
   are needed to prevent update packets from circulating indefinitely in the network, but this question is discussed later. Flooding works when there is a
   single topological change, but can fail in its pure form when there are multiple changes as shown in the example of Fig. 5.29. Methods for overcoming
   this difficulty will be discussed later in this section where it will be shown
   that apparently simple solutions sometimes involve subtle failure modes.

3. Topological update information will be processed by some algorithm that
   computes new routing paths (for example, a shortest path algorithm). It is
   possible, however, that new topological update information arrives as this
   algorithm is running. Then, either the algorithm must be capable of coping

with changes in the problem data as it executes, or else it must be aborted and a new version must be started upon receipt of new data. Achieving either of these may be nontrivial, particularly when the algorithm is distributed.

4. The repair of a single link can cause two parts of the network which were disconnected to reconnect. Each part may have out of date topology information about the other part. The algorithm must ensure that eventually the two parts agree and adopt the correct network topology.

The difficulties discussed above arise also in the context of broadcasting information related to the congestion status of each link. An important difference, however, is that incorrect congestion information typically has less serious consequences than incorrect topological information; the former can result at worst in choice of inferior routes, while the latter can result in choice of nonexistent routes. Thus, one can afford to allow for a small margin of error in an algorithm that broadcasts routing information other than topological updates, if that leads to substantial algorithmic simplification or reduction in communication overhead. Note, however, that in some schemes, such as the ARPANET flooding algorithm to be discussed shortly, topological update information is embedded within congestion information, and the same algorithm is used to broadcast both.

As we approach the subject of broadcasting topological update information, we must first recognize that it is impossible for every node to know the correct network topology at all times. Therefore, the best that we can expect from an algorithm is that it can cope successfully with any finite number of topological changes within finite time. By this we mean that if a finite number of changes occur up to some time and no other changes occur subsequently, then all nodes within each connected portion of the network should know the correct status of each link in that portion within finite time.

In the discussion of validity of various schemes in the sense described above, we will assume the following:

1. Network links preserve the order and correctness of transmissions. Furthermore, nodes maintain the integrity of messages that are stored in their memory.

2. A link failure is detected by both end nodes of the link, although not necessarily simultaneously. By this we mean that any link declared down by one end node will also eventually be declared down by the other, before the first end node declares it up again.

3. There is a data link protocol for recognizing, at the ends of a failed link, when the link is again operational. If one of the end nodes declares the link to be up, then within finite time, either the opposite end node also declares the link up or the first declares it down again.

4. A node can crash in which case each of its adjacent links is, within finite time, declared down by the node at the opposite end of the link.

The preceding assumptions provide a basis for discussion and analysis of specific schemes, but are not always satisfied in practice. For example, on rare occasions, Assumption 1 is violated because damaged data frames may pass the error detection test of Data Link Control, or because a packet may be altered inside a node's memory due to hardware malfunction. Thus, in addition to analysis of the normal case where these assumptions are satisfied, one must also weigh the consequences of the exceptional case where they are not. Keep in mind here that topology updating is a low level algorithm on which other algorithms rely for correct operation.

Note that it is not assumed that the network will always remain connected. In fact, the topology update algorithm together with some protocol for bringing up links should be capable of starting up the network from a state where all links are down.

5.3.1 Flooding–The ARPANET Algorithm

Flooding was previously described as an algorithm whereby a node broadcasts a topological update message to all nodes by sending the message to its neighbors, which in turn send the message to their neighbors, etc. Actually, the update messages may include other routing-related information in addition to link status. For example, in the ARPANET, each message originating at a node includes a time average of packet delay on each outgoing link from the node. The time average is taken over 10 second intervals. The time interval between update broadcasts by the node varies in the ARPANET from 10 to 60 seconds depending on whether there has been a substantial change in any single-link average delay or not. In addition, a message is broadcast once a status change in one of the node's outgoing links is detected.

A serious difficulty with certain forms of flooding is that they may require a large number of message transmissions. The example of Fig. 5.30 demonstrates the difficulty, and shows that it is necessary to store enough information in update messages and network nodes to ensure that each message is transmitted by each node only a finite number of times (and preferably only once). In the ARPANET, update messages from each node are marked by a *sequence number*. When a node j receives a message that originated at some node i, it checks to see if its sequence number is greater than the sequence number of the message last received from i. If so, the message together with its sequence number is stored in memory, and its contents are transmitted to all neighbors of j except the one from which the message was received. Otherwise, the message is discarded. Assuming the sequence number field is large enough, one can be sure that wraparound of the sequence numbers will never occur under normal circumstances. (With a 48-bit field and one update per millisecond it would take more than 5,000 years for wraparound to occur.)

The use of sequence numbers guarantees that each topological update message will be transmitted at most once by each node to its neighbors. Also, it resolves the difficulty of distinguishing between new and old information, which was discussed earlier and illustrated in the example of Fig. 5.29. Nonetheless, there are subtle difficulties with sequence numbers relating to exceptional situations, such as when

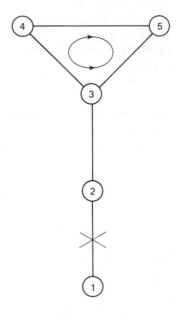

Figure 5.30   Example of a form of flooding where the transmission of messages never terminates. The rule is that a node that receives a message relays it to all of its neighbor nodes except the one from which the message was received. A failure of link (1,2) is communicated to node 3 which triggers an indefinite circulation of the failure message along the loop (3,4,5) in both directions. This form of flooding works only if the network has no cycles.

portions of the network become disconnected, or when equipment malfunctions. For example, when a complete or partial network reinitialization takes place (perhaps following a crash of one or more nodes), it may be necessary to reset some sequence numbers to zero, since a node may not remember the sequence number it was using in the past. Consider a time period when two portions of the network are disconnected. During this period, each portion cannot learn about topological changes occurring in the other portion. If sequence numbers are reset in one of the two portions while they are disconnected, there may be no way for the two portions to figure out the correct topology after they connect again by relying on the sequence number scheme alone. Another concern is that a sequence number could be altered either inside a node's memory due to a malfunction, or due to an undetected error in transmission. Suppose, for example, that an update message originating at node i reaches another node j, has its sequence number changed accidentally to a high number, and is flooded throughout the network. Then, the erroneous sequence number will take over, and, in the absence of a correcting mechanism, node i will not be listened to until its own (correct) sequence number catches up with the wrong one. Similarly, the sequence number of a node that is accidentally set to a high number inside the node itself can wraparound, at which time all subsequent update messages from the node will be ignored by the network.

The ARPANET resolves the problems associated with sequence numbers by using two devices:

1. Each update message includes an *age field*, which indicates the amount of time that the message has been circulating inside the network. Each node visited by a message keeps track of the message's arrival time and increments its age field (taking into account the transmission and propagation time) before transmitting it to its neighbors. (The age field is incremented slightly differently in the ARPANET; see [Per83].) Thus, a node can calculate the age of all messages in its memory at any time. A message whose age exceeds a prespecified limit is not transmitted further. Otherwise, the message is transmitted to all neighbor nodes except the one from which the message was received.

2. Each node is required to transmit update messages *periodically* in addition to the messages transmitted when a link status change is detected (there is at least one of these from every node every 60 seconds).

The rule used regarding the age field is that an "aged" message is superceded by a message that has not "aged" yet regardless of sequence numbers. (A message that has not "aged" yet is superceded only if the new message has a higher sequence number.) This rule guarantees that damaged or incorrect information with a high sequence number will not be relied upon for too long. The use of periodic update messages guarantees that up-to-date information will become available within some fixed time following reconnection of two portions of the network. Of course, the use of periodic updates implies a substantial communication overhead penalty and is a major drawback of the ARPANET scheme. The effect of this, however, is lessened by the fact that the update packets include additional routing-related information, namely the average packet delay on the node's outgoing links since the preceding update.

5.3.2 Flooding without Periodic Updates

It is possible to operate the flooding scheme with sequence numbers correctly without using an age field or periodic updates. The following simple scheme (suggested by P. Humblet) improves on the reliability of the basic sequence number idea by providing a mechanism for coping with node crashes and some transmission errors. It requires, however, that the sequence number field be so large that wraparound never occurs. The idea is to modify the flooding rules so that the difficulties with reconnecting disconnected network components are adequately dealt with. We briefly describe the necessary modifications leaving some of the details for the reader to work out. We concentrate on the case of broadcasting topological information but a similar scheme can be constructed to broadcast other routing information.

As before, we assume that when the status of an outgoing link from a node changes, that node broadcasts an update message containing the status of all its outgoing links to all its current neighbors. The message is stamped by a sequence number which is either zero or is larger by one than the last sequence number used by the node in the past. There is a restriction here, namely that a zero sequence number is allowed only when the node is recovering from a crash (defined as a situation where all of the node's adjacent links are down and the node is in the process of bringing one or more of these links up). As before, there is a separate sequence number associated with each origin node.

The first flooding rule modification has to do with bringing up links that have been down. When this happens, the end nodes of the link, in addition to broadcasting a regular update message on all of their outgoing links, should exchange their current views of the network topology. By this we mean that they should send to each other all the update messages stored in their memory that originated at other nodes together with the corresponding sequence numbers. These messages are then propagated through the network using the modified flooding rules described below. This modification guarantees that the latest update information will reach nodes in disconnected network portions upon reconnection. It also copes with a situation where, after a crash, a node does not remember the sequence number it used in the past. Such a node must use a zero sequence number following the crash, and then, through the topology exchange with its neighbors that takes place when its adjacent links are brought up, become aware of the highest sequence number present in the other nodes' memories. The node can then increment that highest sequence number and flood the network with a new update message.

In order for the scheme to work correctly we modify the flooding rule regarding the circumstances under which an update message is discarded. To this end we order, for each node i, the topological update messages originated at i. For two such messages A and B, we say that $A > B$ if A has a greater sequence number than B, or if A and B have identical sequence numbers and the content of A is greater than the content of B according to some lexicographic rule (for example, if the content of A interpreted as a binary number is greater than the similarly interpreted content of B). Any two messages A and B originating at the same node can thus be compared in the sense that $A > B$, or $B > A$, or $A = B$, the last case occurring only if the sequence numbers and contents of A and B are identical.

Suppose that node j receives an update message A that has originated at node i, and let B be the message originated at node i and currently stored in node j's memory. The message is discarded if $A < B$ or $A = B$. If $A > B$, the flooding rule is now as follows:

1. If $j \neq i$ then node j stores A in its memory in place of B, and sends a copy of A on all its adjacent links except the one on which A was received.

2. If $j = i$ (*i.e.*, node i receives a message it issued some time in the past), then node i sends to all its neighbors a new update message carrying the current status of all its outgoing links together with a sequence number that is 1 plus the sequence number of A.

To see why it is necessary to compare the contents of A and B in the case of equal sequence numbers, consider the following example. There are three nodes, 1,2, and 3, connected in tandem with two (undirected) links (1,2) and (2,3). Suppose, initially, that both links are up, and the messages stored in all the nodes' memories carry the correct link status information and have a sequence number of zero. Consider a scenario whereby link (2,3) goes down, then link (1,2) goes down, and then link (2,3) comes up while node 2 resets its sequence number to zero. Then, nodes 2 and 3 exchange their (conflicting) view of the status of the directed links (1,2) and (2,1), but, if the earlier flooding rules are used, both nodes discard each other's update message since it carries a sequence number zero which is equal to the one stored in their respective memories. By contrast, if the steps of the modified flooding algorithm described above are traced, it is seen that (depending on the lexicographic rule used) either the (correct) view of node 2 regarding link (2,1) will prevail right away, or else node 2 will issue a new update message with sequence number 1 and its view will again prevail. Note that node 3 may end up with an incorrect view of the status of link (1,2). This happens because nodes 1 and 3 are not connected with a path of up links. For the same reason, however, the incorrect information stored by node 3 regarding the outgoing link of node 1 is immaterial.

The algorithm of this section suffers from a difficulty that seems generic to all event-driven algorithms that do not employ periodic updates: it is vulnerable to memory and transmission errors. If, for example, a message's sequence number, is altered to a very high number either during a transmission or while residing inside a node's memory, then it may happen that the message's originating node will not be listened to until its sequence number catches up with the high numbers that are unintentionally stored in some nodes' memories. It turns out that this particular difficulty can be corrected by modifying the flooding rule discussed earlier. Specifically, if node j receives A and has B with $A < B$ in its memory, then message A is discarded as in the earlier rule, but in addition message B is sent back to the neighbor from which A was received. (The neighbor will then propagate B further.) Suppose now that a node issues an update message carrying a sequence number which is less than the sequence number stored in some other node's memory. Then, because of the modification just described, if the two nodes are connected by a path of up links, the higher sequence number (call it k), will be propagated back to the originator node which can then issue a new update message with sequence number $k + 1$ according to Rule 2 above. Unfortunately, there is still a problem associated with a possible sequence number wraparound (for example, when k above is the highest number possible within the field of possible sequence numbers). There is also still the problem of update messages themselves being corrupted by memory or transmission errors (rather than just their sequence numbers being corrupted). It seems that there is no clean way to address these difficulties other than the use of ad hoc error recovery schemes using an age field, and periodic updates (see Problem 5.13).

5.3.3 Topology Broadcast without Sequence Numbers

In this subsection, we discuss a flooding-like algorithm called the *Shortest Path Topology Algorithm* (SPTA) which, unlike the previous schemes, does not use se-

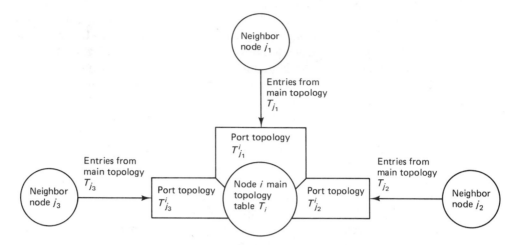

Figure 5.31   Data structures of SPTA at node i are the main topology table T_i and the port topology tables $T_{j_1}^i$, $T_{j_2}^i$, and $T_{j_3}^i$. Changes in the main topology tables of the neighbor nodes j_1, j_2, and j_3 are transferred with some delay to the corresponding port topology tables of node i, except if the change corresponds to a link that is adjacent to i. Such a change is entered directly in its main and port topology tables. Also, when an adjacent failed link comes up, node i transmits its entire main topology table over that link. Finally, when an entry of a port topology changes, the entire main topology table is recalculated using the main topology update algorithm.

quence numbers and avoids the attendant reset and wraparound problems. SPTA resolves the problem of distinguishing old from new information in an interesting way. Whenever a node has conflicting information about the status of a particular link from two different neighbors, it resolves the conflict in favor of what it considers the most "reliable" information. The "reliability" of existing information is reevaluated when new information comes in, and existing information is discarded once it is either superceded by new information or is proven "unreliable". This informal description will be made precise shortly, but essentially "reliability" of information is measured in number of links from the point of its origin, and is calculated by means of a shortest path type of calculation. Throughout this subsection, we will make the same assumptions as with flooding about links preserving the order and correctness of transmissions, and nodes being able to detect adjacent link status changes.

The data structures that each node i maintains in the SPTA are (see Fig. 5.31):

1. The *main topology table* T_i where node i stores the believed status of every link. This is the "official" table used by the routing algorithm at the node. The main topology tables of different nodes may have different entries at different times. The goal of the SPTA is to get these tables to agree after a finite amount of time from the last topological change.

2. The *port topology tables* T_j^i. There is one such table for each neighbor node j.

Node i stores the status of every link in the network, as latest communicated by neighbor node j, in T_j^i.

The algorithm consists of five simple rules:

Communication Rules

1. When a link status entry of a node's main topology table changes, the new entry is transmitted on each of the node's operating adjacent links.

2. When a failed link comes up, each of its end nodes transmits its entire main topology table to the opposite end node over that link. Upon reception of this table the opposite end node enters the new link status in its main and port topology tables.

Topology Table Update Rules

3. When an adjacent link of a node fails, the failed status is entered into the node's main and port topology tables.

4. When a node receives a link status message from a neighbor, it enters the message into the port topology table associated with that neighbor.

5. When an entry of a main topology T_i changes due to a status change of an adjacent link, or an entry of a port topology T_j^i changes due to a communication from neighbor node j, then node i updates its main topology table by using the following algorithm. (It is assumed that the algorithm is restarted if an adjacent link changes status, or a new message is received from a neighbor node while the algorithm executes.) The idea in the algorithm is for node i to believe, for each link ℓ, the status communicated by a neighbor that lies on a shortest path from node i to link ℓ. A shortest path is calculated on the basis of a length of unity for each up link, and a length of infinity for each down link.

Main Topology Update Algorithm at Node i

The algorithm proceeds in iterations that are similar to those of Dijkstra's shortest path algorithm when all links have a unit length (subsection 5.2.3). At the start of the kth iteration, there is a set of nodes P_k. Each node in P_k carries a label which is just the ID number of some neighbor node of i. The nodes in P_k are those that can be reached from i via a path of k links or less that are up according to node i's main topology table at the start of the kth iteration. The label of a node $m \in P_k$ is the ID number of the neighbor of i that lies on a path from i to m that has a minimum number of (up) links. In particular, P_1 consists of the nodes connected with i via an up link, and each node in P_1 is labeled with its own ID number. During the kth iteration, P_k is either augmented by some new nodes to form P_{k+1} or else the algorithm terminates. Simultaneously, the status of the links with at least one end node in P_k but no end node in P_{k-1}, *i.e.*, the set of links

$$L_k = \{(m,n) \mid m \notin P_{k-1}, n \notin P_{k-1}, \ m \text{ or } n \text{ (or both) belongs to } P_k\}$$

is entered in the main topology table T_i. (For notational completeness, we define $P_0 = \{i\}$ in the equation for L_1.) The kth iteration is as follows:

Step 1. For each link $(m, n) \in L_k$, do the following: Let (without loss of generality) m be an end node belonging to P_k, and let "j" be the label of m. Copy the status of (m, n) from the port topology T_j^i into the main topology table T_i. If this status is up and $n \notin P_k$, give to node n the label "j".

Step 2. Let M_k be the set of nodes that were labeled in Step 1. If M_k is empty, terminate. Otherwise, set $P_{k+1} = P_k \cup M_k$, and go to the $(k+1)^{\text{st}}$ iteration.

The algorithm is illustrated in Fig. 5.32. Since each link is processed only once in Step 1 of the algorithm, it is clear that the computational requirements are proportional to the number of links. It is straightforward to verify the following properties of the main topology update algorithm:

1. The set P_k, for $k \geq 1$, is the set of nodes m with the property that, in the finally obtained topology T_i, there is a path of k or less up links connecting m with i.

2. The set L_k, $k \geq 1$, is the set of links ℓ with the property that, in the finally obtained topology T_i, all paths of up links connecting one of the end nodes of ℓ with node i has no less than k links, and there is exactly one such path with k links.

3. The final entry of T_i for a link $\ell \in L_k$, is the entry from the port topology of a neighbor that is on a path of k up links from i to one of the end nodes of ℓ. If there are two such neighbors with conflicting entries, the algorithm arbitrarily chooses the entry of one of the two.

4. When the main topology update algorithm executes at node i in response to failure of an adjacent link (i, j), the information in the port topology T_j^i is in effect disregarded. This is due to the fact that node j is not included in the set P_1, and, therefore, no node is subsequently given the label "j" during execution of the algorithm.

The operation of the SPTA for the case of a single-link status change is shown in Fig. 5.33. The algorithm works roughly like flooding in this case, but there is no need for numbering the update messages to bound the number of message transmissions. Figure 5.34 illustrates the operation of the SPTA for the case of multiple-link status changes, and illustrates how the SPTA handles the problem of distinguishing old from new information (cf. Fig. 5.29). A key idea here is that when a link (i, j) fails, all information that came over that link is effectively disregarded as discussed above.

We now provide a proof of correctness of the SPTA. At any given time the correct topology table (as seen by an omniscient observer) is denoted by T^*. We say that at that time *link ℓ is connected with node i* if there is a path connecting i with one of the end nodes of ℓ, and consisting of links that are up according to T^*. We say that at that time, node j is an *active neighbor* of node i if link (i, j) is

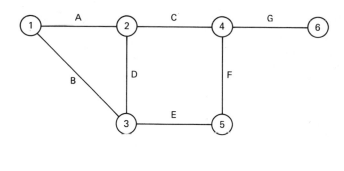

(a)

$$P_1 = \{2,3\}, \quad P_2 = \{2,3,5\}, \quad P_3 = \{2,3,5,4\}, \quad P_4 = \{2,3,5,4,6\}$$
$$L_1 = \{D,C,E\}, \quad L_2 = \{F\}, \quad L_3 = \{G\}$$

(b)

Link	Port Topology T_2^1	Port Topology T_3^1	Distance	Believes Neighbor	Final Main Topology of Node 1
A	—	—	0	—	U
B	—	—	0	—	U
C	D	U	1	2	D
D	U	U	1	2,3	U
E	U	U	1	3	U
F	U	U	2	3	U
G	D	U	3	3	U

(c)

Figure 5.32   Illustration of the main topology update algorithm for node 1 in the network (a). The node sets P_k and the link sets L_k are given in (b). The contents of the port topologies T_2^1 and T_3^1 at node 1 are given in the table in (c) (where D means down, U means up). There is conflicting information on the status of links C and G. Node 1 believes node 2 on the status of link C since node 2 is closer to this link. Node 1 believes node 3 on the status of link G since node 3 is closer to this link (given that link C was declared down by node 1).

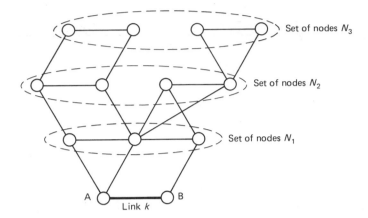

Figure 5.33   Operation of the SPTA for a single link status change.
The status change information propagates to nodes in the set N_1 (one link
away from A or B or both), then to nodes in N_2 (two links away from A or
B or both), then to N_3, and so on. Specifically, when link k changes status,
the change is entered in the topology tables of A and B and is broadcast to
the nodes in N_1. It is entered in the port topology tables T_A^i and/or T_B^i of
nodes i in N_1. Since the distance to link k through nodes $j \neq A, B$ is greater
than zero, the new status of link k will be eventually entered in the main
topology tables of each node in N_1. It will then be broadcast to nodes in N_2,
and entered in the corresponding port topology tables, etc. The number of
required message transmissions does not exceed $2L$, where L is the number of
undirected network links.

up according to T^*. We say that at that time, *node i knows the correct topology* if
the main topology table T_i agrees with T^* on the status of all links connected with
i. We assume that at some initial time t_s, each node knows the correct topology
(for example, at network reset time when all links are down), and all active port
topologies T_j^i agree on all entries with the corresponding main topologies T_j. After that time, several links change status. However, there is a time t_0 after which no

Figure 5.34   (See figure on following page.) Operation of the SPTA for
the topology change scenario of Fig. 5.29. The example demonstrates how the
SPTA copes with a situation where pure flooding fails. (a) Example network
with four links and four nodes. Initially, all links are up. Three changes occur:
(1) link (3,4) goes down, (2) link (3,4) goes up, and (3) link (1,3) goes down.
(b) Assumed sequence of events, message transmissions, and receptions of the
SPTA. All topology table updating is assumed to take place instantaneously
following an event. (c) Main and port topology table contents at each node
following each event. U and D mean up and down, respectively. For example,
a table entry UUUD means that links (1,2), (2,3), and (1,3) are up, and link
(3,4) is down. Tables that change after an event are in bold. Note that the
last event changes not only the entry for link (1,3) in T_1, but also the entry for
link (3,4). Also, after the last event, the port topology table T_3^1 is incorrect,
but this is inconsequential since the connecting link (1,3) is down.

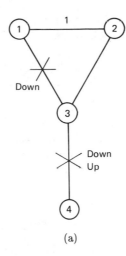

(a)

Event Number	1	2	3
Event	Link (3,4) goes down. Message is transmitted from 3 to 1 and 2. Message is received at 2.	Message is transmitted from 2 to 1. Message is received at 1.	Link (3,4) goes up. Message is transmitted from 3 to 1 and 2. Message is received at 2.
Event Number	4	5	6
Event	Message is transmitted from 2 to 1. Message is received at 1.	Message from 3 to 1 sent during Event 1 is received.	Link (1,3) goes down. Messages from 1 and 3 are sent to 2 and 4. Messages received at 2 and 4.

(b)

Event Number		1	2	3	4	5	6
	T_1	UUUU	UUUU	UUUU	UUUU	**UUUD**	**UUDU**
Tables at Node 1	T_1^2	UUUU	**UUUD**	UUUD	**UUUU**	UUUU	**UUDU**
	T_1^3	UUUU	UUUU	UUUU	UUUU	**UUUD**	**UUDD**
	T_2	**UUUD**	UUUD	**UUUU**	UUUU	UUUU	**UUDU**
Tables at Node 2	T_2^1	UUUU	UUUU	UUUU	UUUU	UUUU	**UUDU**
	T_2^3	**UUUD**	UUUD	**UUUU**	UUUU	UUUU	**UUDU**
	T_3	**UUUD**	UUUD	**UUUU**	UUUU	UUUU	**UUDU**
Tables at Node 3	T_3^1	**UUUD**	UUUD	**UUUU**	UUUU	UUUU	**UUDU**
	T_1^2	**UUUD**	UUUD	**UUUU**	UUUU	UUUU	**UUDU**
	T_1^4	**UUUD**	UUUD	**UUUU**	UUUU	UUUU	**UUDU**
Tables at Node 4	T_4	**UUUD**	UUUD	**UUUU**	UUUU	UUUU	**UUDU**
	T_4^3	**UUUD**	UUUD	**UUUU**	UUUU	UUUU	**UUDU**

(c)

link changes status, and the end nodes of each link are aware of the correct link status. We will show the following:

Proposition.   The SPTA works correctly in the sense that, under the preceding assumptions, there is a time $t_f \geq t_0$ such that each node knows the correct topology for all $t \geq t_f$.

Proof. In what follows, we say that a link ℓ is at distance n away from i if in the graph defined by T^*, the shortest path from i to the closest end node of ℓ is n links long. We will show by induction that for each integer $n \geq 0$, there is a time $t_n \geq t_0$ after which, for each node i, T_i agrees with T^* for all links that are at a distance n or less from i. The induction hypothesis is clearly true for $n = 0$, since each node i knows the correct status of its adjacent links and records them in its main topology table T_i. We first establish the following lemma.

Lemma.   Assume that the induction hypothesis is true for time t_n. Then, there is a time $t'_{n+1} \geq t_n$ after which the port topology table T_j^i, for each active neighbor j of node i, agrees with T^* for each link at a distance n or less from j.

Proof. Consider waiting a sufficient amount of time after t_n for all messages which were sent from j to i before t_n to arrive. By Rules 1, 2, and 4 of the algorithm, T_j^i agrees with T_j for all links which are not adjacent to i. Therefore, by the induction hypothesis, T_j^i agrees with T^* for each link at a distance of n or less from j. This proves the lemma.

To complete the proof of the proposition, one must show that there is a time $t_{n+1} \geq t'_{n+1}$ such that for all $t \geq t_{n+1}$ and nodes i, T_i agrees with T^* for each link ℓ which is at a distance $n + 1$ from i. Consider the first time link ℓ is processed by the topology update algorithm after all port topologies T_j^i and T^* agree on all links at distance n or less from j as per the preceding lemma. Then, link ℓ will belong to the set L_{n+1}. Also, the closest end node(s) of ℓ to node i will belong to the set P_{n+1}, and will have a label which is one of the active neighbors of i (say j) that is at distance n from ℓ. By the lemma, the port topology T_j^i agrees with T^* on all links at distance n from j. Therefore, the entry of T_j^i for link ℓ, which will be copied into T_i when link ℓ is processed, will agree with the corresponding entry of T^*. Because the conclusion of the lemma holds for all t after t'_{n+1}, the entry for link ℓ in T_i will also be correct in all subsequent times at which link ℓ will be processed by the main topology update algorithm.   QED.

Note that the lemma above establishes that the active port topology tables also eventually agree with the corresponding main topology tables. This shows that the initial conditions for which validity of the algorithm was shown, reestablish themselves following a sufficiently long period for which no topological changes occur.

The main advantage of the SPTA over the ARPANET flooding algorithm is that it does not require the use of sequence numbers with the attendant reset difficulties, and the use of an age field, the proper size of which is network dependent and changes as the network expands. Furthermore, the SPTA is entirely event driven, and does not require the substantial overhead associated with the regular periodic updates of the ARPANET algorithm.

Consider now the behavior of SPTA when we cannot rely on the assumption that errors in transmission or in nodes' memories are always detected and corrected. Like all event-driven algorithms, SPTA has no ability to correct such errors. Without periodic retransmission, an undetected error can persist for an arbitrary length of time. Thus, in situations where extraordinary reliability is needed, a node should periodically retransmit its main table to each of its neighbors. This would destroy the event-driven property of SPTA, but would maintain its other desirable characteristics, and allow recovery from undetected database errors.

We finally note that the SPTA can be used to broadcast information other than link status throughout the network. For example, in the context of an adaptive routing algorithm, one might be interested in broadcasting average delay, or traffic arrival rate information for each link. What is needed for the SPTA is to allow for additional, perhaps nonbinary, information entry in the main and port topology tables in addition to the up-down status of links. When this additional information depends on the link direction, it is necessary to make a minor modification to the SPTA so that there are separate entries in the topology tables for each link direction. This matter is considered in Problem 5.14.

5.4 FLOW MODELS, OPTIMAL ROUTING, AND TOPOLOGICAL DESIGN

In order to evaluate the performance of a routing algorithm, we need to quantify the notion of traffic congestion. In this section, we formulate performance models (referred to as *flow models*) based on the traffic arrival rates at the network links. We use these models to formulate problems of optimal routing that will be the subject of sections 5.5-5.7. We also use flow models in discussing the design of various parts of the network topology in subsections 5.4.1 to 5.4.3.

Traffic congestion in a data network can be quantified in terms of the statistics of the arrival processes of the network queues. These statistics determine the distributions of queue length and packet waiting time at each link. It is evident that desirable routing is associated with a small mean and variance of packet delay at each queue. Unfortunately, it is generally difficult to express this objective in a single figure of merit suitable for optimization. A principal reason is that, as seen in Chapter 3, there is usually no accurate analytical expression for the means or variances of the queue lengths in a data network.

A convenient but somewhat imperfect alternative is to measure congestion at a link in terms of the *average* traffic carried by the link. More precisely, we assume that the statistics of the arrival process at each link (i, j) change only due to routing updates, and that we measure congestion on (i, j) via the traffic arrival rate F_{ij}. We call F_{ij} the *flow* of link (i, j), and we express it in data units/sec where the data units can be bits, packets, messages, etc. Sometimes, it is meaningful to express flow in units that are assumed directly proportional to data units/sec such as virtual circuits traversing the link.

Implicit in flow models is the assumption that the statistics of the traffic entering the network do not change over time. This is a reasonable hypothesis when these statistics change very slowly relative to the average time required to empty the queues in the network, and when link flows are measured experimentally using time averages. A typical network where such conditions hold is one accommodating a large number of users for each origin-destination pair, with the traffic rate of each of these users being small relative to the total rate (see subsection 3.4.2).

An expression of the form

$$\sum_{(i,j)} D_{ij}(F_{ij}) \tag{5.29}$$

where each function D_{ij} is monotonically increasing, is often appropriate as a cost function for optimization. A frequently used formula is

$$D_{ij}(F_{ij}) = \frac{F_{ij}}{C_{ij} - F_{ij}} + d_{ij}F_{ij} \tag{5.30}$$

where C_{ij} is the transmission capacity of link (i, j) measured in the same units as F_{ij}, and d_{ij} is the processing and propagation delay. With this formula the expression (5.29) becomes the average number of packets in the system based on the hypothesis that each queue behaves as an M/M/1 queue of packets—a consequence of the Kleinrock independence approximation and Jackson's Theorem discussed in sections 3.6 and 3.8. While this hypothesis is typically violated in practice, the expression of Eqs. (5.29) and (5.30) represents a useful measure of performance in practice, principally because it expresses qualitatively the fact that congestion sets in when a flow F_{ij} approaches the corresponding link capacity C_{ij}. Another cost function with similar qualitative properties is given by

$$\max_{(i,j)} \left\{ \frac{F_{ij}}{C_{ij}} \right\} \tag{5.31}$$

i.e., maximum link utilization. A computational study [Vas79] has shown that it typically makes little difference whether the cost function of Eqs. (5.29) and (5.30), or Eq. (5.31) is used for routing optimization. This indicates that one should employ the cost function that is easiest to optimize. In what follows we concentrate on cost functions of the form (5.29). The analysis and computational methods of sections 5.5 through 5.7 extend to more general cost functions (see Problem 5.27).

We now formulate a problem of optimal routing. For each pair $w = (i, j)$ of distinct nodes i and j (also referred to as an origin-destination (or OD) pair), the input traffic arrival process is assumed stationary with rate r_w.[1] Thus r_w (measured in data units/sec) is the arrival rate of traffic entering the network at node i and destined for node j. The routing objective is to divide each r_w among the many paths from origin to destination in a way that the resulting total link flow pattern minimizes the cost function (5.29). More precisely, denote

W: The set of all OD pairs.

P_w: The set of all directed paths connecting the origin and destination nodes of OD pair w. (In a variation of the problem, P_w is a given subset of the set of all directed paths connecting origin and destination of w. The optimality conditions and algorithms to be given later apply nearly verbatim in this case.)

x_p: The flow (data units/sec) of path p.

Then, the collection of all path flows $\{x_p | w\epsilon W, p\epsilon P_w\}$ must satisfy the constraints

$$\sum_{p\epsilon P_w} x_p = r_w, \qquad \text{for all } w\epsilon W,$$

$$x_p \geq 0, \qquad \text{for all } p\epsilon P_w, w\epsilon W$$

as shown in Figure 5.35. The total flow F_{ij} of link (i,j) is the sum of all path flows traversing the link

$$F_{ij} = \sum_{\substack{\text{all paths } p \\ \text{containing } (i,j)}} x_p$$

Consider a cost function of the form

$$\sum_{(i,j)} D_{ij}(F_{ij}) \tag{5.32}$$

and the problem of finding the set of path flows $\{x_p\}$ that minimize this cost function subject to the constraints above.

By expressing the total flows F_{ij} in terms of the path flows in the cost function (5.32) the problem can be written as

$$\text{minimize} \sum_{(i,j)} D_{ij}\left[\sum_{\substack{\text{all paths } p \\ \text{containing } (i,j)}} x_p \right]$$

$$\text{subject to} \sum_{p\epsilon P_w} x_p = r_w, \text{ for all } w\epsilon W \tag{5.33}$$

$$x_p \geq 0, \text{ for all } p\epsilon P_w, w\epsilon W$$

---

[1] Sometimes it is useful to adopt a broader view of an OD pair and consider it simply as a class of users that shares the same set of paths. This allows modelling of multiple priority classes of users. In this context we would allow several OD pairs to have the same origin and destination nodes. The subsequent analysis and algorithms extend to this broader context almost verbatim. To simplify the following exposition, however, we assume that there is at most one OD pair associated with each pair of nodes.

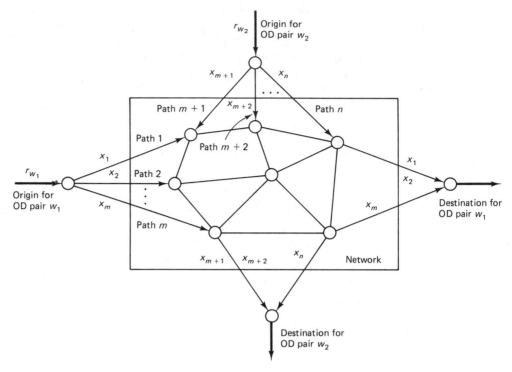

Figure 5.35   Schematic representation of a network with two OD pairs
w_1 and w_2. The paths of the OD pairs are $P_{w_1} = \{1, 2, \ldots, m\}$ $P_{w_2} = \{m + 1, m + 2, \ldots, n\}$. The traffic inputs r_{w_1} and r_{w_2} are to be divided into
the path flows $x_1, \ldots, x_m$ and $x_{m+1}, \ldots, x_n$, respectively.

Thus, the problem is formulated in terms of the unknown path flows $\{x_p | p \epsilon P_w, w \epsilon W\}$.
This is the main optimal routing problem that will be considered. A characteriza-
tion of its optimal solution will be given in section 5.5, and, interestingly, it will be
expressed in terms of shortest paths. Algorithms for its solution will be given in
sections 5.6 and 5.7.

The optimal routing problem just formulated is amenable to analytical inves-
tigation, and distributed computational solution. However, it has some limitations
that are worth explaining. The main limitation has to do with the choice of the
cost function (5.29) as a figure of merit. The underlying hypothesis here is that
one achieves reasonably good routing by optimizing the average levels of link traffic without paying attention to other aspects of the traffic statistics. Thus, the
cost function (5.29) is insensitive to undesirable behavior associated with high variance, and with correlations of packet interarrival times and transmission times. To
illustrate this fact, consider the example given in section 3.6 where we had a node A

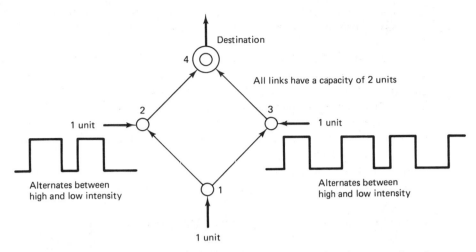

Figure 5.36   Network of Example 1 where routing based on queue length information is beneficial. The traffic originating at nodes 2 and 3 alternates in intensity between 2 units and 0 units over large time intervals. A good form of routing gets information on the queue sizes at links (2,4) and (3,4) and routes the traffic originating at node 1 on the path of least queue size.

sending Poisson traffic to a node B along two equal capacity links. We compared splitting of the traffic between the two links by using randomization and by using metering. It was concluded that metering is preferable to randomization in terms of average packet delay. Yet, randomization and metering are rated equally by the cost function (5.29), since they result in the same flow on each link. The problem here is that delay on each link depends on second and higher moments of the arrival process, yet the cost function (5.29) reflects a dependence on just the first moment.

Since metering is based on keeping track of current queue lengths, the preceding example shows that routing can be improved by using queue length information. Here is another example that illustrates the same point.

Example 1

Consider the network shown in Figure 5.36. Here there are three origin-destination pairs, each with an arrival rate of 1 unit. The OD pairs (2,4) and (3,4) route their traffic exclusively along links (2,4) and (3,4) respectively. Since all links have a capacity of 2 units the two paths (1,2,4) and (1,3,4) are equally attractive for the traffic of OD pair (1,4). An optimal routing algorithm based on time average link rates would alternate sending packets of OD pair (1,4) along the two paths, thereby resulting in total rate of 1.5 units on each of the bottleneck links (2,4) and (3,4). This would work reasonably well if the traffic of the OD pairs (2,4) and (3,4) had a Poisson character. Consider, however, the situation where, instead, this traffic alternates in intensity between 2 units and 0 units over large time intervals. Then, the queues in link (2,4) and (3,4) would build up (not necessarily simultaneously) over some large time intervals and empty out during others. Suppose now that a more dynamic form of routing is adopted, whereby node 1 is kept informed about queue sizes at links (2,4) and (3,4), and routes packets on the path of least queue size. Queueing delay would then be greatly reduced.

Unfortunately, it is impractical to keep nodes informed of all queue lengths in a large network. Even if the overhead for doing so was not prohibitive, the delays involved in transferring the queue length information to the nodes could make this information largely obsolete. It is not known at present how to implement effective and practical routing based on queue length information, so we will not consider the subject further. For an interesting but untested alternative see Problem 5.36.

The remainder of this section considers the use of network algorithms, flow models, and the optimal routing problem in the context of topological design of a network. The reader may skip this material without loss of continuity.

5.4.1 An Overview of Topological Design Problems

In this subsection we discuss algorithms for designing the topology of a data network. Basically we are given a set of traffic demands, and we want to put together a network that will service these demands at minimum cost while meeting some performance requirements. A common, broadly stated formulation of the problem is as follows:

We assume that we are given:
   1. The geographical location of a collection of devices that need to communicate with each other. For simplicity, these devices are called *terminals*.
   2. A traffic matrix giving the input traffic flow from each terminal to every other terminal.

We want to design (cf. Fig. 5.37):
   1. The *topology of a communication subnet* to service the traffic demands of the terminals. This includes the location of the nodes, the choice of links, and the capacity of each link.
   2. The *local access network*, *i.e.*, the collection of communication lines that will connect the terminals to entry nodes of the subnet.

The design objectives are:
   1. Keep the average delay per packet or message below a given level (for the given nominal traffic demands and assuming some type of routing algorithm).
   2. Satisfy some reliability constraint to guarantee the integrity of network service in the face of a number of link and node failures.
   3. Minimize a combination of capital investment and operating costs while meeting 1 and 2 above.

It is evident that this is, in general, a very broad problem that may be difficult to formulate precisely, let alone solve. However, in many cases, the situation simplifies somewhat. For example, part of the problem may be already solved because portions of the local access network and/or the subnet might be already in place. There may be also a natural decomposition of the problem—for example, the

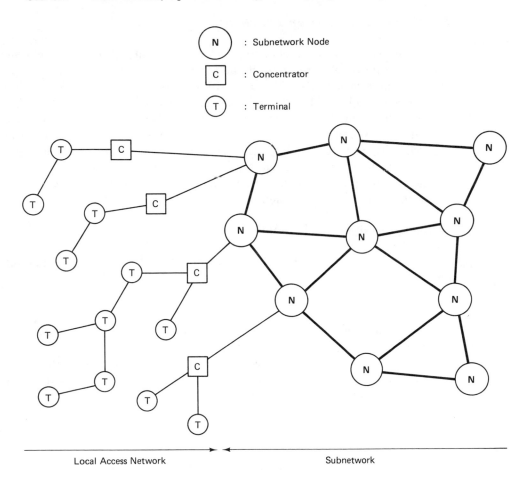

Figure 5.37   The main aspects of the topology design problem are the design of the local access network and the communication subnet.

subnet topology design problem may be naturally decoupled from the local access network design problem. In fact, this will be assumed in the presentation. Still, one seldom ends up with a clean problem that can be solved exactly in reasonable time. One typically has to be satisfied with an approximate solution obtained through heuristic methods that combine theory, trial and error, and common sense.

The next subsection considers the subnet design problem, assuming that the local access network has been designed and therefore, the matrix of input traffic flow for every pair of subnet nodes is known. Subsequently, in subsection 5.4.3, the local access network design problem is considered.

5.4.2 The Subnet Design Problem

Given the location of the subnet nodes and an input traffic flow for each pair of these nodes, we want to select the capacity and flow of each link so as to meet some delay and reliability constraints while minimizing costs. Except in very simple cases, this turns out to be a difficult combinatorial problem. To illustrate the difficulties, we consider a simplified version of the problem where we want to choose the link capacities so as to minimize a linear cost. We impose a delay constraint but neglect any reliability constraints. Note that by assigning zero capacity to a link we, in effect, eliminate the link. Therefore the capacity assignment problem includes as a special case the problem of choosing the pairs of subnet nodes that will be directly connected with a communication line.

Capacity Assignment Problem

The problem is to choose the capacity C_{ij} of each link (i, j) so as to minimize the linear cost

$$\sum_{(i,j)} p_{ij} C_{ij} \qquad (5.34)$$

where p_{ij} is a known positive price per unit capacity, subject to the constraint that the average delay per packet should not exceed a given constant T.

The flow on each link (i, j) is denoted F_{ij} and is expressed in the same units as capacity. We adopt the M/M/1 model based on the Kleinrock independence approximation, so we can express the average delay constraint as

$$\frac{1}{\gamma} \sum_{(i,j)} \frac{F_{ij}}{C_{ij} - F_{ij}} \leq T \qquad (5.35)$$

where γ is the total arrival rate into the network. We assume that there is a given input flow for each origin-destination pair and γ is the sum of these. The link flows F_{ij} depend on the known input flows and the scheme used for routing. We will first assume that routing and therefore also the flows F_{ij} are known, and later see what happens when this assumption is relaxed.

When the flows F_{ij} are known, the problem is to minimize the linear cost (5.34) over the capacities C_{ij} subject to the constraint (5.35), and it is intuitively clear that the constraint will be satisfied as an equality at the optimum. We introduce a Lagrange multiplier β and form the Lagrangian function

$$L = \sum_{(i,j)} \left(p_{ij} C_{ij} + \frac{\beta}{\gamma} \frac{F_{ij}}{C_{ij} - F_{ij}} \right)$$

In accordance with the Lagrange multiplier technique, we set the partial derivatives $\partial L / \partial C_{ij}$ to zero

$$\frac{\partial L}{\partial C_{ij}} = p_{ij} - \frac{\beta F_{ij}}{\gamma (C_{ij} - F_{ij})^2} = 0$$

Solving for C_{ij},

$$C_{ij} = F_{ij} + \sqrt{\frac{\beta F_{ij}}{\gamma p_{ij}}} \qquad (5.36)$$

and substituting in the constraint equation, we obtain

$$T = \frac{1}{\gamma} \sum_{(i,j)} \frac{F_{ij}}{C_{ij} - F_{ij}} = \sum_{(i,j)} \sqrt{\frac{p_{ij} F_{ij}}{\beta \gamma}}$$

From the last equation,

$$\sqrt{\beta} = \frac{1}{T} \sum_{(i,j)} \sqrt{\frac{p_{ij} F_{ij}}{\gamma}} \qquad (5.37)$$

which when substituted in Eq. (5.36) yields the optimal solution:[2]

$$C_{ij} = F_{ij} + \frac{1}{T} \sqrt{\frac{F_{ij}}{\gamma p_{ij}}} \sum_{(m,n)} \sqrt{\frac{p_{mn} F_{mn}}{\gamma}}$$

The solution, after rearranging, can also be written as

$$C_{ij} = F_{ij} \left(1 + \frac{1}{\gamma T} \frac{\sum_{(m,n)} \sqrt{p_{mn} F_{mn}}}{\sqrt{p_{ij} F_{ij}}} \right) \qquad (5.38)$$

Finally, by substitution in (5.34), the optimal cost is

$$\text{Optimal cost} = \sum_{(i,j)} p_{ij} F_{ij} + \frac{1}{\gamma T} \left(\sum_{(i,j)} \sqrt{p_{ij} F_{ij}} \right)^2 \qquad (5.39)$$

Consider now the problem of optimizing the network cost with respect to both the capacities C_{ij} and the flows F_{ij} (equivalently the routing). This problem can be solved by minimizing the cost (5.39) with respect to F_{ij} and then obtaining the optimal capacities from the closed form expression (5.38). Unfortunately, it turns out that the cost (5.39) has many local minima and is very difficult to minimize. Furthermore, in these local minima, there is a tendency for many of the flows

---

[2] It is rigorous to argue at this point that the capacities C_{ij} of Eq. (5.38) are optimal. The advanced reader can verify this by first showing that the average delay expression of (5.35) is convex and differentiable over the set of all C_{ij} with $C_{ij} > F_{ij}$, and by arguing that the equation $\partial L / \partial C_{ij} = 0$ is a sufficient condition for optimality that is satisfied by the positive Lagrange multiplier β of (5.37) and the capacities C_{ij} of (5.38) (see [Las70], p.84, or [Roc70], p. 283).

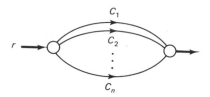

Figure 5.38   Minimizing the total capacity $C_1 + \cdots + C_n$ while meeting an average delay contraint results in a minimum connectivity network (all links are eliminated except one).

F_{ij} and corresponding capacities C_{ij} to be zero. The resulting networks tend to have low connectivity (few links with large capacity) and may violate reliability constraints. The nature of this phenomenon can be understood by considering the simple network of Fig. 5.38 involving two nodes and n links. Suppose we want to choose the capacities $C_1 \ldots C_n$ so as to minimize the sum $C_1 + \cdots + C_n$ while dividing the input rate λ among the n links so as to meet an average delay constraint. From our comparison of statistical and time-division multiplexing (sections 3.1 and 3.3), we know that delay increases if a transmission line is divided into smaller lines, each serving a fraction of the total traffic. It is therefore evident that the optimal solution is the minimal connectivity topology whereby all links are eliminated, except one which has just enough capacity to meet the delay constraint. It makes no difference which lines are eliminated so this problem has n local minima. Each of these happens to be also a global minimum, but this is a coincidence due to the extreme simplicity of the example.

The conclusion from the preceding discussion is that the simultaneous optimization of link flows and capacities is a hard combinatorial problem. Furthermore, even if this problem is solved, the network topology obtained will tend to concentrate capacity in a few large links, and possibly violate reliability constraints. The preceding formulation is also unrealistic because, in practice, capacity costs are not linear. Furthermore, the capacity of a leased communication line usually must be selected from a finite number of choices. In addition, the capacity of a line is typically equal in both directions, while this is not necessarily true for the choice of Eq. (5.38). These practical constraints enhance further the combinatorial character of the problem, and make an exact solution virtually impossible. As a result, the only real option for addressing the problem subject to these contraints is to use heuristic schemes that are described next.

Heuristic Methods for Capacity Assignment

Typically, these methods start with some network topology, and then successively perturb this topology by changing one or more link capacities at a time. Thus, these methods search "locally" around an existing topology for another topology that satisfies the constraints and has lower cost. Note that the term topology here means the set of capacities of all potential links of the network. In particular, a link with zero capacity represents a link that in effect does not exist. Usually, the following are assumed:

1. The nodes of the network and the input traffic flow for each pair of nodes are known.

2. A routing model has been adopted that determines the flows F_{ij} of all links (i, j) given all link capacities C_{ij}. The most common possibility here is to assume that link flows are determined via an optimal routing model of the form (5.33). In particular, F_{ij} can be determined by minimizing the average packet delay

$$D = \frac{1}{\gamma} \sum_{(i,j)} \left(\frac{F_{ij}}{C_{ij} - F_{ij}} + d_{ij} F_{ij} \right) \qquad (5.40)$$

based on M/M/1 approximations (cf. Eq.(5.30)), where γ is the known total input flow into the network, and C_{ij} and d_{ij} are the known capacity and the processing and propagation delay, respectively, of link (i, j). Several algorithms described in sections 5.6 and 5.7 can be used for this purpose.

3. There is a delay constraint that must be met. Typically, it is required that the chosen capacities C_{ij} and link flows F_{ij} (determined by the routing algorithm as in 2 above) result in a delay D given by Eq. (5.40) (or a similar formula) that is below a certain threshold.

4. There is a reliability constraint that must be met. As an example, it is common to require that the network be 2-connected, *i.e.*, after a single node failure, all other nodes remain connected. More generally, it may be required that after $k - 1$ nodes fail, all other nodes remain connected—such a network is said to be k-connected. We postpone a discussion of how to evaluate the reliability of a network for later.

5. There is a cost criterion according to which different topologies are ranked.

The objective is to find a topology that meets the delay and reliability constraints as per 3 and 4 above, and has as small a cost as possible as per 5 above. We describe a prototype iterative heuristic method for addressing the problem. At the start of each iteration, there is available a *current best topology* and a *trial topology*. The former topology satisfies the delay and reliability constraints and is the best one in terms of cost that we have found so far, while the latter topology is the one that will be evaluated in the current iteration. We assume that these topologies are chosen initially by some ad hoc method—for example, by establishing an ample number of links to meet the delay and reliability constraints. The steps of the iteration are as follows:

Step 1 (Assign Flows). Calculate the link flows F_{ij} for the trial topology by means of some routing algorithm as per assumption 2 above.

Step 2 (Check Delay). Evaluate the average delay per packet D [as given, for example, by Eq. (5.40)] for the trial topology. If

$$D \le T$$

where T is a given threshold, go to Step 3; else go to Step 5.

Step 3 (Check Reliability). Test whether the trial topology meets the reliability constraints. (Methods for carrying out this step will be discussed shortly.) If the constraints are not met go to Step 5; else go to Step 4.

Step 4 (Check Cost Improvement). If the cost of the trial topology is less than the cost of the current best topology, replace the current best topology with the trial topology.

Step 5 (Generate a New Trial Topology). Use some heuristic to change one or more capacities of the current best topology, thereby obtaining a trial topology that has not been considered before. Go to Step 1.

Note that a trial topology is adopted as the current best topology in Step 4 only if it satisfies the delay and reliability constraints in Steps 2 and 3, and improves the cost (Step 4). The algorithm terminates when no new trial topology can be generated, or when substantial further improvement is deemed unlikely. Naturally, there is no guarantee that the final solution is optimal. One possibility to attempt further improvement is to repeat the algorithm with a different starting topology. Another possibility is to modify Step 4 so that on occasion a trial topology is accepted as a replacement of the current best topology even if its cost is larger than the best found so far. A scheme of this type, known as *simulated annealing*, has become popular recently [KGV83]. It can be shown under mild assumptions that a globally optimal solution can be found by simulated annealing [Haj85], [Tsi85]. The amount of computing time required, however, may be excessive. This approach has not been tried yet in the topology design context.

There are a number of heuristic rules proposed in the literature for generating new trial topologies (Step 5). One possibility is simply to lower the capacity of a link that seems underutilized (low F_{ij}/C_{ij} and F_{ji}/C_{ji}) or to eliminate the link altogether. Another possibility is to increase the capacity of some overutilized link when the delay constraint is not met. A combination of these possibilities is the *branch exchange heuristic*, whereby one link is deleted and another link is added. A useful way to choose the links to be deleted and added is the so called *saturated cut method*. The idea here is to identify a partition (or cut) of the nodes into two sets N_1 and N_2 such that the links joining N_1 and N_2 are highly utilized. It then seems plausible that adding a link between a node in N_1 and a node in N_2 will help reduce the high level of utilization across the cut. The method works as follows (see Fig. 5.39):

1. Prepare a list of all undirected links (i, j), sorted in order of decreasing utilization as measured by max $\{F_{ij}/C_{ij}, F_{ji}/C_{ji}\}$.

2. Find a link k such that (a) if all links above k on the list are eliminated the network remains connected, and (b) if k is eliminated together with all links above it on the list, the network separates in two disconnected components N_1 and N_2.

3. Remove the most underutilized link in the network, and replace it with a new link that connects a node in the component N_1, and a node in the component N_2.

There are a number of variations of the scheme described above. For example,

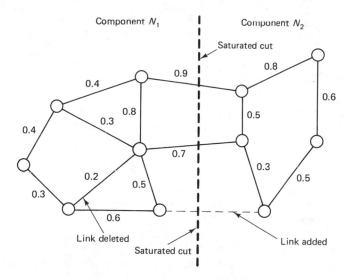

Figure 5.39   Illustration of the cut saturation method for performing a branch exchange heuristic. The number next to each arc is the link utilization. Links of high utilization are temporarily removed until the network separates into two components N_1 and N_2. A link is then added that connects a node in N_1 with a node in N_2 while a link of low utilization is deleted.

in selecting the link to remove, one may take into account the cost of capacity for the link. Needless to say that prior knowledge about the network and the cost structure for link capacity can be effectively incorporated into the heuristics. In addition, the design process can be enhanced by using an interactive program that can be appropriately guided by the designer. We now turn our attention to methods for evaluating reliability of a network.

Network Reliability Issues

We have already mentioned that a common reliability requirement for a network is that it must be k-connected. We now define k-connectivity more formally.

We say that *two nodes i and j* in an undirected graph are *k-connected* if there is a path connecting i and j in every subgraph obtained by deleting $(k-1)$ nodes other than i and j together with their adjacent arcs from the graph. It is easily seen that this is equivalent to requiring that either i and j are connected with an arc or that there are at least k paths connecting i and j which are node-disjoint in the sense that any two of them share no nodes other than i and j. We say that *the graph is k-connected* if every pair of nodes is k-connected. These definitions are illustrated in Fig. 5.40. Another notion of interest is that of *arc connectivity*, which is defined as the minimum number of arcs that must be deleted before the graph becomes disconnected. A lower bound k on arc connectivity can be established by checking for k-(node) connectivity in an expanded graph where each arc (i, j) is

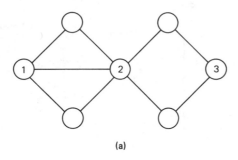

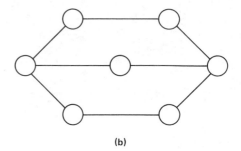

(a)   (b)

Figure 5.40   Illustration of the definition of k-connectivity. In graph
(a), nodes 1 and 2 are 6-connected, nodes 2 and 3 are 2-connected, and nodes
1 and 3 are 1-connected. Graph (a) is 1-connected. Graph (b) is 2-connected.

replaced by two arcs (i, n) and (n, j), where n is a new node. This is evident by
noting that failure of node n in the expanded graph can be associated with failure
of the arc (i, j) in the original graph.

It is possible to calculate the number of node-disjoint paths connecting two
nodes by setting up and solving a max-flow problem. This is a classical combinatorial problem treated in detail in many sources [Law76] and [PaS82]. It is not
discussed here, since the subject is somewhat tangential to the purposes of this section. The reader who is already familiar with this problem can see its connection
with the problem of k-connectivity of two nodes from Fig. 5.41.

One way to check k-connectivity of a graph is to check k-connectivity of every
pair of nodes. There are, however, more efficient methods. One particular method,
due to Kleitman [Kle69] operates as follows:

Choose an arbitrary node n_0 and check k-connectivity between that node and
every other node. Delete n_0 and its adjacent arcs from the graph, choose another
node n_1, and check $(k - 1)$-connectivity between that node and every other node.
Continue in this manner until either node n_{k-1} is checked to be 1-connected to
every remaining node, or $(k - i)$-connectivity of some node $n_i, i = 0, 1, \ldots, k - 1$,
to every remaining node cannot be verified. In the latter case, it is evident that
the graph is not k-connected: if node n_i is not $(k - i)$-connected to some other
remaining node, then $(k - i - 1)$ nodes can be found such that their deletion along
with nodes $n_0, \ldots, n_{i-1}$ disconnects the graph. The process is demonstrated in
Fig. 5.42.

To establish the validity of Kleitman's algorithm, it must be shown that when
nodes $n_0, \ldots, n_{k-1}$ can be found as described above, then the graph is k-connected.
The argument is by contradiction. If the graph is not k-connected there must exist
nodes i and j, and a set of $(k - 1)$ nodes $\mathcal{F}_0$ $(i \notin \mathcal{F}_0, j \notin \mathcal{F}_0)$, such that deletion of $\mathcal{F}_0$
leaves no path connecting i and j. Then n_0 must belong to $\mathcal{F}_0$ because if $n_0 \notin \mathcal{F}_0$,
then, since n_0 is k-connected to every other node, it follows that there are paths P_i
and P_j connecting n_0, i, and j even after the set $\mathcal{F}_0$ is deleted. It follows that a path

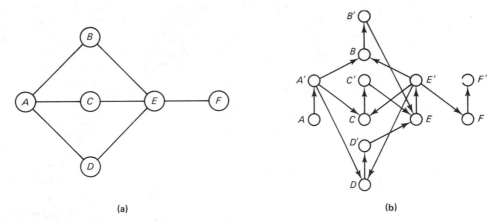

(a)   (b)

Figure 5.41   Illustration of test of k-connectivity for those familiar with the max-flow problem. To find the number of node-disjoint paths from node A to node F in graph (a), do the following: (1) Replace each node i with two nodes i and i' and a directed arc (i, i'). (2) Replace each arc (i, j) of graph (a) with two directed arcs (i', j) and (j', i). (3) Delete all arcs incoming to A and outgoing from F', thereby obtaining graph (b). (4) Assign infinite capacity to arcs (A, A') and (F, F'), and unit capacity to all other arcs. Then, the maximum flow that can be sent from node A to node F' in graph (b) equals the number of node-disjoint paths connecting nodes A and F in graph (a).

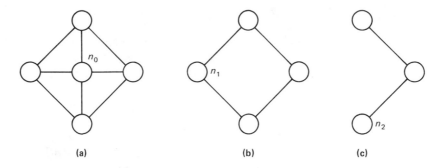

(a)   (b)   (c)

Figure 5.42   Verifying 3-connectivity of graph (a) by Kleitman's algorithm. An arbitrary node n_0 is chosen, and 3-connectivity between n_0 and every other node is verified. Then, node n_0 and its adjacent arcs are deleted, thereby obtaining graph (b). An arbitrary node n_1 of (b) is chosen, and 2-connectivity between n_1 and every other node in (b) is verified. Then, node n_1 and its adjacent arcs are deleted, thereby obtaining graph (c). Since graph (c) is connected, it follows that the original graph (a) is 3-connected.

from i to j can be constructed by first using P_i to go from i to n_0, and then using P_j to go from n_0 to j. Next, consider the sets $\mathcal{F}_1 = \mathcal{F}_0 - \{n_0\}$, $\mathcal{F}_2 = \mathcal{F}_1 - \{n_1\}, \ldots$. Similarly, n_1 must belong to $\mathcal{F}_1$ and n_2 must belong to $\mathcal{F}_2$, etc. After this argument is used $(k-1)$ times, it is seen that $\mathcal{F}_0 = \{n_0, n_1, \ldots, n_{k-2}\}$. Therefore, after $\mathcal{F}_0$ is deleted from the graph, node n_{k-1} is still intact, and, by definition of n_{k-1}, so are the paths from n_{k-1} to i and j. These paths can be used to connect i and j, contradicting the hypothesis that deletion of $\mathcal{F}_0$ leaves i and j disconnected.

Kleitman's algorithm requires a total of $\sum_{i=1}^{k}(N-i) = kN - k(k+1)/2$ connectivity tests of node pairs, where N is the number of nodes. There is another algorithm due to Even [Eve75] which requires roughly N connectivity tests. The reader is referred to [Eve75] for details.

The preceding formulation of the reliability problem addresses the worst case where the most unfavorable combination of k node failures occurs. An alternative formulation is to assign failure probabilities to all network elements (nodes and links), and evaluate the probability that a given pair of nodes becomes disconnected. To get an appreciation of the difficulties involved in this approach, suppose that there are n failure-prone elements in the network. Then, the number of all distinct combinations of surviving elements is 2^n. Let s_k denote the kth combination, and p_k denote the probability of its occurrence. The probability that the network remains connected is

$$P_C = \sum_{s_k \in C} p_k \tag{5.41}$$

where C is the set of combinations of surviving elements for which the network remains connected. Thus, evaluation of P_C involves some form of implicit or explicit enumeration of the set C. This is in general a very time consuming procedure. However, shortcuts and approximations have been found making the evaluation of the survival probability P_C feasible for some realistic networks ([BaP83], [Ben86]). An alternative approach evaluates a lower bound for P_C by ordering the possible combinations of surviving elements according to their likelihood, and then adding p_k over a subset of most likely combinations from C ([LaL86] and [LiS84]). A similar approach using the complement of C gives an upper bound to P_C.

Spanning Tree Topology Design

For some networks, where reliability is not a serious issue, a spanning tree topology may be appropriate. Using such a topology is consistent with the idea of concentrating capacity on just a few links to reduce the average delay per packet (cf. the earlier discussion on capacity assignment).

It is possible to design a spanning tree topology by assigning a weight w_{ij} to each possible link (i, j) and by using the minimum weight spanning tree (MST) algorithms of subsection 5.2.2. A potential difficulty arises when there is a constraint on the amount of traffic that can be carried by any one link. This gives rise to the *constrained MST problem*, where a matrix of input traffic from every node to every other node is given, and an MST is to be designed subject to the constraint that the flow on each link will not exceed a given upper bound. Because of this constraint, the problem has a combinatorial character, and is usually addressed using heuristic methods.

One possibility is to modify the Kruskal or Prim-Dijkstra algorithms, described in subsection 5.2.2, so that at each iteration, when a new link is added to the current fragments, a check is made to see if the flow constraints on the links of the fragments are satisfied. If not, the link is not added, and another link is considered. This type of heuristic can be combined also with some version of the branch exchange heuristic discussed earlier in connection with the general subnet design problem.

A special case of the constrained MST problem can be addressed using the *Essau-Williams algorithm* [EsW66]. In this case, there is a central node denoted 0, and N other nodes. All traffic must go through the central node, so it can be assumed that there is input traffic only from the noncentral nodes to the central node and the reverse. Problems of this type arise also in the context of the local access design problem, with the central node playing the role of a traffic concentrator.

The Essau-Williams algorithm is, in effect, a branch exchange heuristic. One starts with the spanning tree where the central node is directly connected with each of the N other nodes. (It is assumed that this is a feasible solution.) At each successive iteration, a link $(i,0)$ connecting some node i with the central node 0 is deleted from the current spanning tree, and a link (i,j) is added. These links are chosen so that:

1. No cycle is formed.
2. The capacity constraints of all the links of the new spanning tree are satisfied.
3. The saving $w_{i0} - w_{ij}$ in link weight obtained by exchanging $(i,0)$ with (i,j) is positive, and is maximized over all nodes i and j for which 1 and 2 are satisfied.

The algorithm terminates when there are no nodes i and j for which requirements 1–3 are satisfied when $(i,0)$ is exchanged with (i,j). The operation of the algorithm is illustrated in Figure 5.43.

5.4.3 The Local Access Network Design Problem

Here we assume that a communication subnet is available, and we want to design a network that connects a collection of terminals with known demands to the subnet. This problem is often addressed in the context of a hierarchical strategy, whereby groups of terminals are connected, perhaps through local area networks, to various types of concentrators, which are in turn connected to higher levels of concentrators, etc. It is difficult to recommend a global design strategy without knowledge of the given practical situation. However, there are a few subproblems that arise frequently. We will discuss one such problem known as the *concentrator location problem*.

In this problem, there are n sources located at known geographical points. For example, a source may be a gateway of a local area network that connects several terminals within a customer's facility; or it could be a host computer through which several time-sharing terminals access some network. The nature of the sources is not material to the discussion. The problem is to connect the n sources to

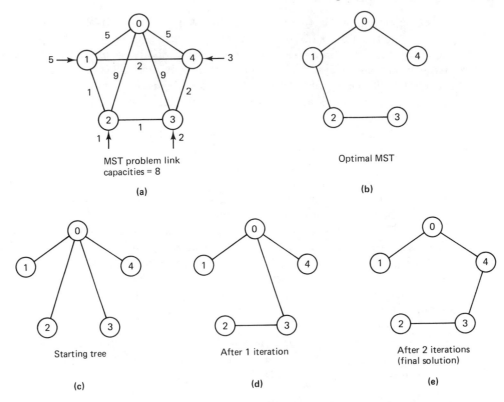

Figure 5.43   Illustration of the Essau–Williams, constrained MST heuristic algorithm. The problem data is given in (a). Node 0 is the central node. The link weights are shown next to the links. The input flows from nodes 1,2,3, and 4 to the central node are shown next to the arrows. The flow on each link is constrained to be no more than 8. The algorithm terminates after two iterations with the tree (e) having a total weight of 13. Termination occurs because when link (1,0) or (4,0) is removed and a link that is not adjacent to node 0 is added, then some link capacity constraint (link flow ≤ 8) will be violated. The optimal tree, shown in (b), has a total weight of 12.

m concentrators that are themselves connected to a communication subnet (see Fig. 5.44). We denote

a_{ij}: The cost of connecting source i to concentrator j.

Consider the variables x_{ij} where

$$x_{ij} = \begin{cases} 1, & \text{if source } i \text{ is connected to concentrator } j \\ 0, & \text{otherwise} \end{cases}$$

Then, the total cost of a source assignment specified by a set of variables $\{x_{ij}\}$ is

$$\text{Cost} = \sum_{i=1}^{n} \sum_{j=1}^{m} a_{ij} x_{ij} . \tag{5.42}$$

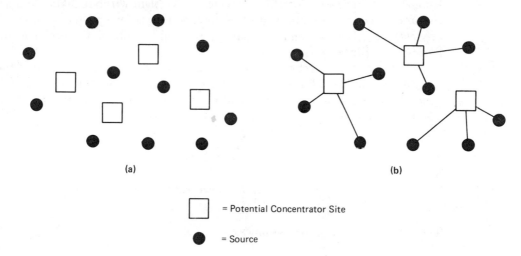

(a)   (b)

☐ = Potential Concentrator Site

● = Source

Figure 5.44   (a) A collection of sources and potential concentrator locations. (b) A possible assignment of sources to concentrators.

We assume that each source is connected to only one concentrator so that there is the constraint

$$\sum_{j=1}^{m} x_{ij} = 1, \qquad \text{for all sources } i \tag{5.43}$$

Also, there is a maximum number of sources K_j that can be handled by concentrator j. This is expressed by the constraint

$$\sum_{i=1}^{n} x_{ij} \leq K_j, \qquad \text{for all concentrators } j \tag{5.44}$$

The problem is to select the variables x_{ij} so as to minimize the cost (5.42) subject to the constraints (5.43) and (5.44).

Even though the variables x_{ij} are constrained to be 0 or 1, the problem above is not really a difficult combinatorial problem. If the integer constraint

$$x_{ij} = 0 \text{ or } 1$$

is replaced by the noninteger constraint

$$0 \leq x_{ij} \leq 1 \tag{5.45}$$

the problem becomes a linear transportation problem that can be solved by very efficient algorithms such as the simplex method. It can be shown that the solution obtained from the simplex method will be integer, *i.e.*, x_{ij} will be either 0 or 1 (see

[Dan63] and [PaS82]). Therefore, solving the problem without taking into account the integer constraints automatically obtains an integer optimal solution. There are methods other than simplex that can be used for solving the problem ([Ber85], [FoF62] and [Roc84]).

Next, consider a more complicated problem whereby the location of the concentrators is not fixed but instead is subject to optimization. There are m potential concentrator sites, and there is a cost b_j for locating a concentrator at site j. The cost then becomes

$$\text{Cost} = \sum_{i=1}^{n}\sum_{j=1}^{m} a_{ij}x_{ij} + \sum_{j=1}^{m} b_j y_j \tag{5.46}$$

where

$$y_j = \begin{cases} 1, & \text{if a concentrator is located at site } j \\ 0, & \text{otherwise} \end{cases}$$

The constraint (5.44) now becomes

$$\sum_{i=1}^{n} x_{ij} \leq K_j y_j, \qquad \text{for all concentrators } j \tag{5.47}$$

Thus, the problem is to minimize the cost (5.46) subject to the constraints (5.43) and (5.47), and the requirement that x_{ij} and y_j are either zero or one.

This problem has been treated extensively in the operations research literature where it is known as the warehouse location problem. It is considered to be a difficult combinatorial problem that can usually be solved only approximately. A number of exact and heuristic methods have been proposed for its solution. We refer to the literature for further details [AkK77], [AlM76], [CFN77], [KeH63], [Khu72], [RaW83].

5.5 CHARACTERIZATION OF OPTIMAL ROUTING

We now return to the optimal routing problem formulated in the beginning of section 5.4. The main objective in this section is to provide an interesting characterization of optimal routing. It will be shown that optimal routing directs traffic exclusively along paths which are shortest with respect to some link lengths that depend on the flows carried by the links. This characterization motivates algorithms that are the subject of sections 5.6 and 5.7.

Recall the form of the cost function

$$\sum_{(i,j)} D_{ij}(F_{ij}) \tag{5.48}$$

Here F_{ij} is the total flow (in data units/sec) carried by link (i,j) given by

$$F_{ij} = \sum_{\substack{\text{all paths } p \\ \text{containing } (i,j)}} x_p \tag{5.49}$$

where x_p is the flow (in data units/sec) of path p. For every OD pair w, there are the constraints

$$\sum_{p \in P_w} x_p = r_w \tag{5.50}$$

$$x_p \geq 0, \quad \text{for all } p \in P_w \tag{5.51}$$

where r_w is the given traffic input of the OD pair w (in data units/sec), and P_w is the set of directed paths of w. The problem expressed in terms of the unknown path flow vector $x = \{x_p \mid p \in P_w, w \in W\}$ is written as

$$\text{minimize} \sum_{(i,j)} D_{ij} \left[\sum_{\substack{\text{all paths } p \\ \text{containing } (i,j)}} x_p \right],$$

$$\text{subject to} \sum_{p \in P_w} x_p = r_w, \quad \text{for all } w \in W \tag{5.52}$$

$$x_p \geq 0, \quad \text{for all } p \in P_w, w \in W$$

In what follows we will characterize an optimal routing in terms of derivatives of the functions D_{ij}. We assume that each D_{ij} is a twice differentiable function of F_{ij} and is defined in an interval $[0, C_{ij})$, where C_{ij} is either a positive number (typically representing the capacity of the link) or else infinity. The first and second derivatives of D_{ij} are denoted D'_{ij} and D''_{ij}, respectively, and are assumed strictly positive for all F_{ij} in $[0, C_{ij})$. This implies in particular that D_{ij} is a convex[3] monotonically increasing function of F_{ij} in the interval $[0, C_{ij})$ (see Fig. 5.45). We further assume that $D_{ij}(F_{ij}) \to \infty$ as $F_{ij} \to C_{ij}$. It is straightforward to verify that, since link flows are linear functions of path flows, the problem of Eq. (5.52), viewed as a problem in the path flow variables $\{x_p\}$, has a convex, twice differentiable cost function and a convex constraint set.

A characterization of the optimal solutions of the routing problem of Eq. (5.52) is obtained by specializing the following general necessary and sufficient condition for optimality:

Lemma.   Let f be a differentiable convex function of the n-dimensional vector $x = (x_1, \ldots, x_n)$, and let X be a convex set of vectors. Then $x^* \in X$ is an optimal solution of the problem

$$\text{minimize } f(x)$$

$$\text{subject to } x \in X \tag{5.53}$$

---

[3] A set of vectors X is said to be convex if the line segment connecting any two vectors in X is also contained in X. Algebraically, $[\alpha x_1 + (1 - \alpha)x_2] \in X$, for all $x_1, x_2 \in X$ and $\alpha \in [0, 1]$. A function f of the vector x is said to be convex over a convex set X if $f[\alpha x_1 + (1 - \alpha)x_2] \leq \alpha f(x_1) + (1 - \alpha)f(x_2)$, for all $x_1, x_2 \in X$ and $\alpha \in [0, 1]$. Figure 5.45 demonstrates these definitions.

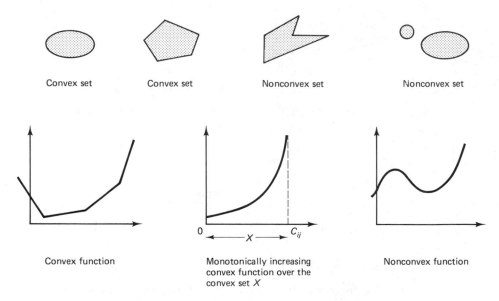

Figure 5.45   Convex and nonconvex sets and functions.

if and only if

$$\sum_{i=1}^{n} \frac{\partial f(x^*)}{\partial x_i}(x_i - x_i^*) \geq 0, \quad \text{for all } x \in X \tag{5.54}$$

where $\partial f(x^*)/\partial x_i$ is the first derivative of f with respect to the ith coordinate x_i evaluated at x^*.

Proof. Assume x^* is an optimal solution and for every $x \in X$, consider the function $g(\alpha) = f[x^* + \alpha(x - x^*)]$ of the scalar variable α. Then, $g(\alpha)$ attains a minimum at $\alpha = 0$ over the interval $[0,1]$, so $dg(0)/d\alpha \geq 0$. But

$$\frac{dg(0)}{d\alpha} = \sum_{i=1}^{n} \frac{\partial f(x^*)}{\partial x_i}(x_i - x_i^*)$$

(using the chain rule), so Eq. (5.54) is proved.

Conversely, assume that Eq. (5.54) holds and x^* is not an optimal solution. We will arrive at a contradiction. Indeed let $\tilde{x} \in X$ be such that $f(\tilde{x}) < f(x^*)$ and consider the function $g(\alpha) = f[x^* + \alpha(\tilde{x} - x^*)]$. Then, $dg(0)/d\alpha \geq 0$ (by Eq. (5.54)) while $f(x^*) = g(0) > g(1) = f(\tilde{x})$. Some thought shows (see Problem 5.24) that these conditions contradict the convexity of $g(\alpha)$ over $[0,1]$ and hence also the convexity of f.   QED.

A geometric interpretation of the lemma is given in Fig. 5.46. Since both the cost function and the constraint set of the minimization problem of Eq. (5.52)

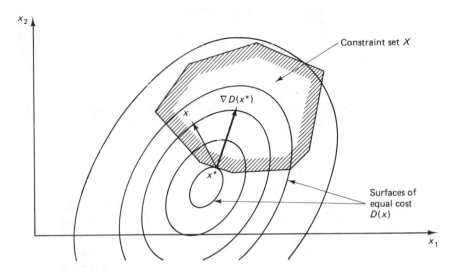

Figure 5.46   Geometric interpretation of the optimality condition of Eq. (5.54). The gradient vector of the first partial derivatives

$$\nabla D(x^*) = \begin{bmatrix} \dfrac{\partial D(x^*)}{\partial x_1} \\ \cdot \\ \dfrac{\partial D(x^*)}{\partial x_n} \end{bmatrix}$$

at the optimum x^* makes an angle 90° or less with all vectors $x - x^*$ as x ranges over the constraint set X.

are convex, the lemma can be applied. Let x be the vector of path flows x_p. For concreteness, assume that the paths p are numbered sequentially. Thus, if $W = \{w_1, w_2, \ldots, w_m\}$ is the set of OD pairs, the corresponding sets of paths are

$$P_{w_1} = \{1, 2, \ldots, n_1\}$$
$$P_{w_2} = \{(n_1 + 1), \ldots, n_2\}$$
$$\cdots$$
$$P_{w_m} = \{(n_{m-1} + 1), \ldots, n_m\}$$

where $n_1, n_2, \ldots, n_m$ are some integers with $n_1 < n_2 < \cdots < n_m$. The coordinates of the path flow vector x are the path flows $x_1, x_2, \ldots, x_{n_m}$, *i.e.*,

$$x = \begin{bmatrix} x_1 \\ x_2 \\ \vdots \\ x_{n_m} \end{bmatrix}$$

Denote $D(x)$ as the cost function of the problem of Eq. (5.52)

$$D(x) = \sum_{(i,j)} D_{ij} \left[\sum_{\substack{\text{all paths } p \\ \text{containing } (i,j)}} x_p \right]$$

and $\partial D(x)/\partial x_p$ as the partial derivative of D with respect to x_p. Then

$$\frac{\partial D(x)}{\partial x_p} = \sum_{\substack{\text{all links } (i,j) \\ \text{on path } p}} D'_{ij}, \tag{5.55}$$

where the first derivatives D'_{ij} are evaluated at the total flows corresponding to x. From Eq. (5.55) it is seen that $\partial D/\partial x_p$ is the *length of path p when the length of each link* (i,j) *is taken to be the first derivative* D'_{ij} *evaluated at* x. Consequently, $\partial D/\partial x_p$ is called in what follows the *first derivative length of path p*.

According to the lemma, $x^* = \{x_p^*\}$ is an optimal path flow vector if it satisfies the constraints of the routing problem and the condition (5.54). This condition can be written as

$$\sum_{w \in W} \sum_{p \in P_w} \frac{\partial D(x^*)}{\partial x_p}(x_p - x_p^*) \geq 0 \tag{5.56}$$

for all x_p satisfying the constraints

$$\sum_{p \in P_w} x_p = r_w, \quad x_p \geq 0, \quad \text{for all } p \in P_w, w \in W \tag{5.57}$$

The conditions (5.56) and (5.57) can be decoupled with respect to OD pair and written for each $w \in W$ as

$$\sum_{p \in P_w} \frac{\partial D(x^*)}{\partial x_p}(x_p - x_p^*) \geq 0, \quad \text{for all } x_p \geq 0, \tag{5.58}$$

$$\text{and } p \in P_w \text{ with } \sum_{p \in P_w} x_p = r_w$$

(To see this, fix an OD pair w and set $x_p = x_p^*$ in Eq. (5.56) for all $w' \neq w$ and $p \in P_{w'}$). The condition (5.58) is equivalent to having, for all $w \in W$

$$x_p^* > 0 \quad \text{only if} \quad \frac{\partial D(x^*)}{\partial x_{p'}} \geq \frac{\partial D(x^*)}{\partial x_p}, \quad \text{for all } p' \in P_w \tag{5.59}$$

To see this, consider a path p with $x_p^* > 0$ and some other path p', and for a small $\epsilon > 0$, apply Eq. (5.58) with $x_p = x_p^* - \epsilon$, $x_{p'} = x_{p'}^* + \epsilon$, and $x_{p''} = x_{p''}^*$ for all other

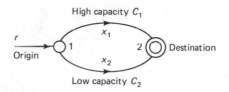

Figure 5.47   Example routing problem involving a single OD pair and two paths.

paths $p'' \neq p, p'$. In words condition (5.59) says that *a set of path flows is optimal if and only if path flow is positive only on paths with a minimum first derivative length.* Condition (5.59) also implies that at an optimum, the paths along which the input flow r_w of OD pair w is split must have *equal* length (and less or equal length to that of all other paths of w).

Example

Consider the two link network shown in Fig. 5.47, where nodes 1 and 2 are the only origin and destination, respectively. The given input r is to be divided into the two path flows x_1 and x_2 so as to minimize a cost function based on the $M/M/1$ approximation

$$D(x) = D_1(x_1) + D_2(x_2)$$

where for $i = 1, 2, D_i(x_i) = x_i/(C_i - x_i)$, and C_i is the capacity of link i. For the problem to make sense, we must assume that r is less than the maximum throughput $C_1 + C_2$ that the network can sustain.

At the optimum, the shortest path condition (5.59) must be satisfied as well as the constraints

$$x_1^* + x_2^* = r, \quad x_1^* \geq 0, \quad x_2^* \geq 0$$

Assume that $C_1 \geq C_2$. Then, from elementary reasoning, the optimal flow x_1 cannot be less than x_2 (it makes no sense to send more traffic on the slower link). The only possibilities are:

1. $x_1^* = r$ and $x_2^* = 0$. According to Eq. (5.59) this can happen only if

$$\frac{dD_1(r)}{dx_1} \leq \frac{dD_2(0)}{dx_2}$$

Equivalently (since the derivative of $x/(C - x)$ is $C/(C - x)^2$),

$$\frac{C_1}{(C_1 - r)^2} \leq \frac{1}{C_2}$$

or

$$r \leq C_1 - \sqrt{C_1 C_2} \tag{5.60}$$

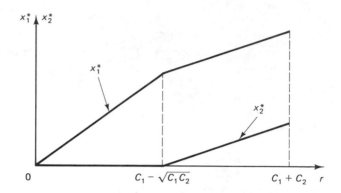

Figure 5.48   Optimal path flows for the routing example. When the traffic input is low, only the high-capacity link is used. As the input increases beyond the threshold $C_1 - \sqrt{C_1 C_2}$, some traffic is routed on the low-capacity link.

2. $x_1^* > 0$ and $x_2^* > 0$. In this case, Eq. (5.59) implies that the lengths of paths 1 and 2 are equal, *i.e.*,

$$\frac{dD_1(x_1^*)}{dx_1} = \frac{dD_2(x_2^*)}{dx_2}$$

or, equivalently,

$$\frac{C_1}{(C_1 - x_1^*)^2} = \frac{C_2}{(C_2 - x_2^*)^2} \tag{5.61}$$

This equation together with the constraint $x_1^* + x_2^* = r$ determine the values of x_1^* and x_2^*. A straightforward calculation shows that the solution is

$$x_1^* = \frac{\sqrt{C_1}\left[r - (C_2 - \sqrt{C_1 C_2})\right]}{\sqrt{C_1} + \sqrt{C_2}}$$

$$x_2^* = \frac{\sqrt{C_2}\left[r - (C_1 - \sqrt{C_1 C_2})\right]}{\sqrt{C_1} + \sqrt{C_2}}$$

The optimal solution is shown in Fig. 5.48 for r in the range $[0, C_1 + C_2)$ of possible inputs. It can be seen that for values of r low enough so that Eq. (5.60) holds, the faster link 1 is used exclusively. When r exceeds the threshold value

$$C_1 - \sqrt{C_1 C_2}$$

for which the first derivative lengths of the two links are equalized and relation (5.60) holds as an equation, the slower link 2 is also utilized. As r increases, the flows on both links increase while the equality of the first derivative lengths, as in Eq. (5.61), is maintained. This behavior is typical of optimal routing when the cost function is based on the M/M/1 approximation; *for low input traffic, each OD pair tends to use only one path for routing (the fastest in terms of packet transmission time), and as traffic input increases, additional paths are used to avoid overloading the fastest path.* More generally this type of behavior is associated with link cost functions D_{ij} with the property that the derivative $D'_{ij}(0)$ at zero flow depends only on the link capacity and decreases as the link capacity increases (see Problem 5.25).

We were able to solve the preceding example analytically only because of its extreme simplicity. Unfortunately in more complex problems we typically have to resort to a computational solution–either centralized or distributed. The following sections deal with some of the possibilities.

Finally, note that while the optimal routing problem was formulated in terms of a fixed set of input rates, the optimal solution $\{x_p^*\}$ can be implemented naturally even when the input rates are time varying. This can be done by working with the *fractions* of flow

$$\xi_p = \frac{x_p^*}{r_w}, \quad \text{for all } p \in P_w$$

and by requiring each OD pair w to divide traffic (packets or virtual circuits) among the available paths according to these fractions. In virtual circuit networks, where the origin nodes are typically aware of the detailed description of the paths used for routing, it is easy to implement the routing process in terms of the fractions ξ_p. The origins can estimate the data rate of virtual circuits and can route new virtual circuits in such a way as to bring about a close match between actual and desired fractions of traffic on each path. In some datagram networks or in networks where the detailed path descriptions are not known at the origin nodes, it may be necessary to maintain in a routing table at each node i a routing variable $\phi_{ik}(j)$ for each link (i, k) and destination j. This routing variable is defined as the fraction of all flow arriving at node i, destined for node j, and routed along link (i, k). Mathematically,

$$\phi_{ik}(j) = \frac{f_{ik}(j)}{\sum_m f_{im}(j)}, \quad \text{for all } (i, k) \text{ and } j \tag{5.62}$$

where $f_{ik}(j)$ is the flow that travels on link (i, k) and is destined for node j. Given an optimal solution of the routing problem in terms of the path flow variables $\{x_p^*\}$, it is possible to determine the corresponding link flow variables $f_{ik}(j)$ and, by Eq. (5.62), the corresponding optimal routing variables $\phi_{ik}(j)$. A direct formulation and distributed computational solution of the optimal routing problem in terms of the variables $\phi_{ik}(j)$ is given in references [Gal77], [Ber79a], [Gaf79] and [BGG84].

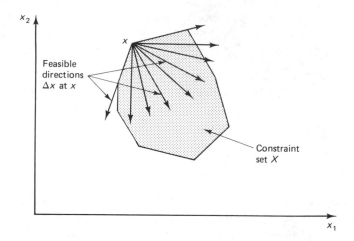

Figure 5.49   Feasible directions Δx at a feasible point x. Δx is a feasible direction if changing x by a small amount along the direction Δx still maintains feasibility.

5.6 FEASIBLE DIRECTION METHODS FOR OPTIMAL ROUTING

In the previous section it was shown that optimal routing results only if flow travels along minimum first derivative length (MFDL) paths for each OD pair. Equivalently, a set of path flows is strictly suboptimal only if there is a positive amount of flow that travels on a non-MFDL path. This suggests that suboptimal routing can be improved by shifting flow to an MFDL path from other paths for each OD pair. The adaptive shortest path method for datagram networks of subsection 5.2.5 does that in a sense, but shifts *all* flow of each OD pair to the shortest path with oscillatory behavior resulting. It is more appropriate to shift only *part* of the flow of other paths to the shortest path. This section considers methods based on this idea. Generally, these methods solve computationally the optimal routing problem by decreasing the cost function through incremental changes in path flows.

Given a feasible path flow vector $x = \{x_p\}$ (*i.e.*, a vector x satisfying the constraints of the problem), consider changing x along a direction $\Delta x = \{\Delta x_p\}$. There are two main requirements imposed on the direction Δx:

1. The first requirement is that Δx should be a *feasible direction* in the sense that small changes along Δx maintain the feasibility of the path flow vector x (see Fig. 5.49). Mathematically, it is required that for some $\overline{\alpha} > 0$ and all $\alpha \in [0, \overline{\alpha}]$, the vector $x + \alpha \Delta x$ is feasible, or, equivalently,

$$\sum_{p \in P_w} \Delta x_p = 0, \quad \text{for all } w \in W \tag{5.63}$$

$$x_p + \alpha \Delta x_p \geq 0, \quad \text{for all } \alpha \in [0, \bar{\alpha}], \ p \in P_w, \ w \in W \tag{5.64}$$

Equation (5.63) follows from the feasibility requirement

$$\sum_{p \in P_w} (x_p + \alpha \Delta x_p) = r_w$$

and the fact that x is feasible, which implies

$$\sum_{p \in P_w} x_p = r_w$$

It simply expresses the fact that to maintain feasibility, all increases of flow along some paths must be compensated by corresponding decreases along other paths of the same OD pair. One way to obtain feasible directions is to select another feasible vector $\bar{x}$ and take

$$\Delta x = \bar{x} - x$$

In fact, a little thought reveals that all possible feasible directions can be obtained in this way up to scalar multiplication.

2. The second requirement is that Δx should be a *descent direction* in the sense that the cost function can be decreased by making small movements along the direction Δx starting from x (see Fig. 5.50). Since the gradient $\nabla D(x)$ is normal to the equal cost surfaces of the cost function D, it is clear from Fig. 5.50 that the descent condition translates to the condition that the inner product of $\nabla D(x)$ and Δx is negative, *i.e.*,

$$\sum_{w \in W} \sum_{p \in P_w} \frac{\partial D(x)}{\partial x_p} \Delta x_p < 0 \tag{5.65}$$

This condition can be verified mathematically by observing that the first derivative of the function $G(\alpha) = D(x + \alpha \Delta x)$ at $\alpha = 0$ is equal to the inner product in Eq. (5.65). Note that the partial derivative $\partial D(x)/\partial x_p$ is given by

$$\frac{\partial D(x)}{\partial x_p} = \sum_{\substack{\text{all links } (i,j) \\ \text{on path } p}} D'_{ij}(F_{ij}),$$

and can be viewed as the first derivative length of path p (the length of link (i,j) is $D'_{ij}(F_{ij})$, cf. section 5.5). One way to satisfy the condition of Eq. (5.65), which is in fact commonly used in algorithms, is to require that Δx satisfies the conservation of flow condition (5.63) and that

$$\Delta x_p \leq 0, \quad \text{for all paths } p \text{ that are nonshortest}$$
$$\text{in the sense } \partial D(x)/\partial x_p > \partial D(x)/\partial x_{\bar{p}} \text{ for some}$$
$$\text{path } \bar{p} \text{ of the same OD pair}$$
$$\Delta x_p < 0, \quad \text{for at least one nonshortest path p.} \tag{5.66}$$

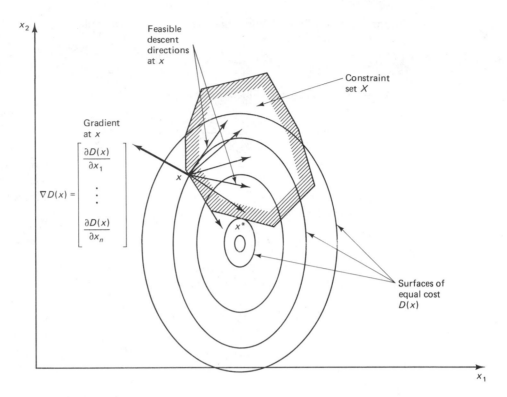

Figure 5.50   Descent directions at a feasible point x form an angle greater than 90° with the gradient $\nabla D(x)$. At the optimal point x^*, there are no feasible descent directions.

In words, conditions (5.63) and (5.66) state that some positive flow is shifted from nonshortest paths to the shortest paths (with respect to the lengths $D'_{ij}(F_{ij})$), and no flow is shifted from shortest paths to nonshortest ones. Since $\partial D(x)/\partial x_p$ is minimal for those (shortest) paths $\bar{p}$ for which $\Delta x_{\bar{p}} > 0$, and, according to Eq. (5.63), the sum of Δx_p over $p \in P_w$ is zero, it is seen that Eqs. (5.63) and (5.66) imply the descent condition (5.65).

This leads to a broad class of iterative algorithms for solving the optimal routing problem. Their basic iteration is given by

$$x := x + \alpha \Delta x$$

where Δx is a feasible descent direction (*i.e.*, satisfies conditions (5.63) to (5.65) or (5.63), (5.64), and (5.66)), and α is a positive stepsize chosen so that the cost function is decreased, *i.e.*,

$$D(x + \alpha \Delta x) < D(x)$$

and the vector $x + \alpha \Delta x$ is feasible. The stepsize α could be different in each iteration. It is seen using the optimality condition of section 5.5, that a feasible

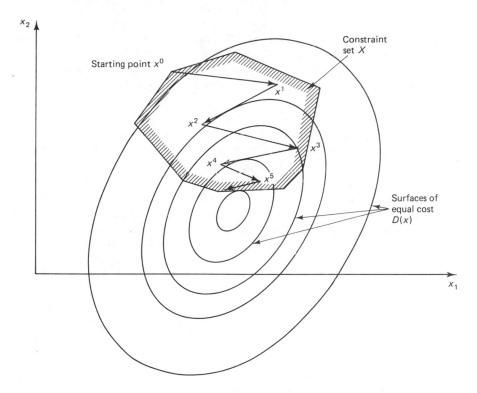

Figure 5.51   Sample path of an iterative descent method based on feasible descent directions. At each iteration, a feasible point of lower cost is obtained.

descent direction can be found at x if and only if x is not optimal. Figure 5.51 illustrates the operation of such an algorithm.

5.6.1 The Frank-Wolfe (Flow Deviation) Method

Here is one way to implement the philosophy of incremental changes along feasible descent directions:

Given a feasible path flow vector $x = \{x_p\}$, find a minimum first derivative length (MFDL) path for each OD pair. (The first derivatives D'_{ij} are evaluated, of course, at the current vector x.) Let $\bar{x} = \{\bar{x}_p\}$ be the vector of path flows that would result if all input r_w for each OD pair $w \in W$ is routed along the corresponding MFDL path. Let α^* be the stepsize that minimizes $D[x + \alpha(\bar{x} - x)]$ over all $\alpha \in [0,1]$, $i.e.$,

$$D[x + \alpha^*(\bar{x} - x)] = \min_{\alpha \in [0,1]} D[x + \alpha(\bar{x} - x)] \qquad (5.67)$$

The new set of path flows is obtained by

$$x_p := x_p + \alpha^*(\bar{x}_p - x_p), \quad \text{for all } p \in P_w, w \in W \qquad (5.68)$$

and the process is repeated.

The algorithm above is a special case of the so called *Frank-Wolfe method* for solving general, nonlinear programming problems with convex constraint sets (see [Zan69]). It has been called the *flow deviation method* (see [FGK73]), and can be shown to reduce the value of the cost function to its minimum in the limit (see Problem 5.31) although its convergence rate near the optimum tends to be very slow.

Note that the feasible direction used in iteration (5.68) is of the form (5.66), *i.e.*, a proportion α^* of the flow of all the nonshortest paths (those paths for which $x_p = 0$) is shifted to the shortest path (the one for which $\bar{x}_p = r_w$) for each OD pair w. The characteristic property here is that flow is shifted from the nonshortest paths in *equal* proportions. This distinguishes the Frank-Wolfe method from the gradient projection methods to be discussed in the next section. The latter methods also shift flow from the nonshortest paths to the shortest paths, however, they do so in generally unequal proportions.

Here is a simple example illustrating the Frank-Wolfe method:

Example

Consider the three-link network with one origin and one destination shown in Fig. 5.52. There are three paths with corresponding flows x_1, x_2, and x_3 which must satisfy the constraints

$$x_1 + x_2 + x_3 = 1, \quad x_1 \geq 0, x_2 \geq 0, x_3 \geq 0$$

The cost function is

$$D(x) = \frac{1}{2}(x_1^2 + x_2^2 + 0.1x_3^2) + 0.55x_3$$

(The linear term $0.55x_3$ can be attributed to a large processing and propagation delay on link 3.)

This is an easy problem that can be solved analytically. It can be argued (or shown using the optimality condition of section 5.5) that at an optimal solution $x^* = (x_1^*, x_2^*, x_3^*)$, we must have by symmetry $x_1^* = x_2^*$, so there are two possibilities: either (a) $x_3^* = 0$ and $x_1^* = x_2^* = 1/2$, or (b) $x_3^* = \beta > 0$ and $x_1^* = x_2^* = (1 - \beta)/2$. Case (b) is not possible because, according to the optimality condition of section 5.5, if $x_3^* > 0$, the length of path 3 $(= \partial D(x^*)/\partial x_3 = 0.1\beta + 0.55)$ must be less or equal to the lengths of paths 1 and 2$(= \partial D(x^*)/\partial x_1 = (1 - \beta)/2)$, which is clearly false. Therefore, the optimal solution is $x^* = (1/2, 1/2, 0)$.

Consider now application of the Frank-Wolfe iteration (5.68) at a feasible path flow vector $x = (x_1, x_2, x_3)$. The three paths have first derivative lengths

$$\frac{\partial D(x)}{\partial x_1} = x_1, \quad \frac{\partial D(x)}{\partial x_2} = x_2, \quad \frac{\partial D(x)}{\partial x_3} = 0.1x_3 + 0.55$$

It is seen, using essentially the same argument as above, that the shortest path is either 1 or 2, depending on whether $x_1 \leq x_2$ or $x_2 < x_1$, and the corresponding

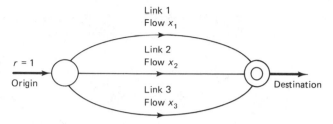

Iteration # k	0	10	20	40	80	160	320
x_1	0.4	0.4593	0.4702	0.4795	0.4866	0.4917	0.4950
x_2	0.3	0.4345	0.4562	0.4717	0.4823	0.4893	0.4938
x_3	0.3	0.1061	0.0735	0.0490	0.0310	0.0189	0.0110
Cost	0.2945	0.2588	0.2553	0.2532	0.2518	0.2510	0.2506
Error Ratio $\dfrac{D(x^{k+1}) - D(x^*)}{D(x^k) - D(x^*)}$	0.7164	0.9231	0.9576	0.9774	0.9882	0.9939	0.9969

Figure 5.52   Example problem and successive iterates of the Frank-Wolfe method. The cost function is

$$D(x) = \frac{1}{2}(x_1^2 + x_2^2 + x_3^2) + 0.55x_3$$

The optimal solution is $x^* = \left(\frac{1}{2}, \frac{1}{2}, 0\right)$. As the optimal solution is approached, the method becomes slower. In the limit, the ratio of successive errors $D(x^{k+1}) - D(x^*)/D(x^k) - D(x^*)$ tends to unity.

shortest path flows are $\bar{x} = (1, 0, 0)$ and $\bar{x} = (0, 1, 0)$, respectively. (The tie is broken arbitrarily in favor of path 1 in case $x_1 = x_2$.) Therefore, the Frank-Wolfe iteration takes the form

$$\begin{bmatrix} x_1 \\ x_2 \\ x_3 \end{bmatrix} := \begin{bmatrix} x_1 \\ x_2 \\ x_3 \end{bmatrix} + \alpha^* \begin{bmatrix} 1 - x_1 \\ -x_2 \\ -x_3 \end{bmatrix} = \begin{bmatrix} x_1 + \alpha^*(x_2 + x_3) \\ (1 - \alpha^*)x_2 \\ (1 - \alpha^*)x_3 \end{bmatrix}, \quad \text{if } x_1 \le x_2$$

$$\begin{bmatrix} x_1 \\ x_2 \\ x_3 \end{bmatrix} := \begin{bmatrix} x_1 \\ x_2 \\ x_3 \end{bmatrix} + \alpha^* \begin{bmatrix} -x_1 \\ 1 - x_2 \\ -x_3 \end{bmatrix} = \begin{bmatrix} (1 - \alpha^*)x_1 \\ x_2 + \alpha^*(x_1 + x_3) \\ (1 - \alpha^*)x_3 \end{bmatrix}, \quad \text{if } x_2 < x_1$$

Thus, at each iteration, a proportion α^* of the flows of the nonshortest paths is shifted to the shortest path.

The stepsize α^* is obtained by line minimization over $[0,1]$ (cf. Eq. (5.67)). Because $D(x)$ is quadratic, this minimization can be done analytically. We have

$$D[x + \alpha(\overline{x} - x)] = \frac{1}{2}([x_1 + \alpha(\overline{x}_1 - x_1)]^2 + [x_2 + \alpha(\overline{x}_2 - x_2)]^2$$
$$+ 0.1[x_3 + \alpha(\overline{x}_3 - x_3)]^2) + 0.55[x_3 + \alpha(\overline{x}_3 - x_3)]$$

Differentiating with respect to α and setting the derivative to zero we obtain the unconstrained minimum $\overline{\alpha}$ of $D[x + \alpha(\overline{x} - x)]$ over α. This is given by

$$\overline{\alpha} = -\frac{x_1(\overline{x}_1 - x_1) + x_2(\overline{x}_2 - x_2) + (0.1x_3 + 0.55)(\overline{x}_3 - x_3)}{(\overline{x}_1 - x_1)^2 + (\overline{x}_2 - x_2)^2 + 0.1(\overline{x}_3 - x_3)^2}$$

where $\overline{x} = (\overline{x}_1, \overline{x}_2, \overline{x}_3)$ is the current shortest path flow vector $[(1,0,0)$ or $(0,1,0)$, depending on whether $x_1 \leq x_2$ or $x_2 < x_1]$. Since $(\overline{x} - x)$ is a descent direction, we have $\overline{\alpha} \geq 0$. Therefore, the stepsize α^*, which is the constrained minimum over $[0,1]$ (cf. Eq. (5.67)), is given by

$$\alpha^* = \min[1, \overline{\alpha}]$$

(In this example, it can be verified that $\overline{\alpha} < 1$, implying that $\alpha^* = \overline{\alpha}$.)

Figures 5.52 and 5.53 show successive iterates of the method. It can be seen that the rate of convergence becomes slow near the optimal solution. The reason is that as x^* is approached, the directions of search tend to become orthogonal to the direction leading from the current iterate x^k to x^*. In fact, it can be seen from Fig. 5.52 that the ratio of successive cost errors

$$\frac{D(x^{k+1}) - D(x^*)}{D(x^k) - D(x^*)}$$

while always less than one, actually converges to one as $k \to \infty$. This is known as *sublinear* convergence rate [Ber82d], and is typical of the Frank-Wolfe method ([CaC70] and [Dun79]).

The determination of an optimal stepsize α^* satisfying Eq. (5.67) requires a one-dimensional minimization over $[0,1]$ which can be carried out through any one of several existing methods (see [Lue84]). A simpler method is to choose the stepsize α^* in Eq. (5.68) by means of

$$\alpha^* = \min\left[1, -\frac{\sum_{(i,j)}(\overline{F}_{ij} - F_{ij})D'_{ij}}{\sum_{(i,j)}(\overline{F}_{ij} - F_{ij})^2 D''_{ij}}\right] \tag{5.69}$$

Here, $\{F_{ij}\}$ and $\{\overline{F}_{ij}\}$ are the sets of total link flows corresponding to $\{x_p\}$, and $\{\overline{x}_p\}$, respectively, *i.e.*, F_{ij} (or $\overline{F}_{ij}$) is obtained by adding all flows x_p (or $\overline{x}_p$) of paths p traversing the link (i,j). The first and second derivatives, D'_{ij} and D''_{ij}, respectively, are evaluated at F_{ij}. The formula for α^* in Eq. (5.69) is obtained

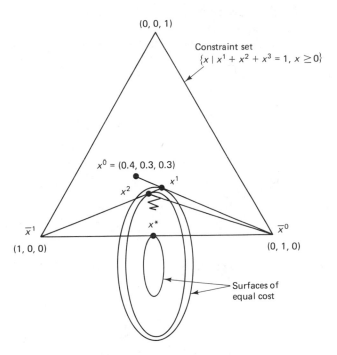

Figure 5.53   Successive iterates of the Frank-Wolfe method in the two-node, three-link example. Slow convergence is due to the fact that as the optimal solution x^* is approached, the directions of search tend to become orthogonal to the direction leading to the optimum.

by making a second order Taylor approximation $\tilde{G}(\alpha)$ of $G(\alpha) = D[x + \alpha(\bar{x} - x)]$ around $\alpha = 0$

$$\tilde{G}(\alpha) = \sum_{(i,j)} \{D_{ij}(F_{ij}) + \alpha D'_{ij}(F_{ij})(\overline{F}_{ij} - F_{ij})$$
$$+ \left(\alpha^2/2\right) D''_{ij}(F_{ij})(\overline{F}_{ij} - F_{ij})^2\}$$

and by minimizing $\tilde{G}(\alpha)$ with respect to α over the interval $[0,1]$ as in the earlier example.

It can be shown that the algorithm with the choice of Eq. (5.69) for the stepsize converges to the optimal set of total link flows provided the starting set of total link flows is sufficiently close to the optimal. For the type of cost functions used in routing problems (*e.g.*, Eq. (5.30) in section 5.4), it appears that the stepsize choice of Eq. (5.69) typically leads to convergence even when the starting total link flows are far from optimal. The stepsize rule of Eq. (5.69) is also more suitable for distributed implementation than the stepsize rule of Eq. (5.67) (see Problem 5.26). However, even with this rule, the method appears inferior for distributed application to the projection method of the next section primarily because it is essential for the network nodes to synchronize their calculations in order to obtain the stepsize of Eq. (5.69).

The Frank-Wolfe method has an insightful geometrical interpretation. Suppose that we have a feasible path flow vector $x = \{x_p\}$, and we try to find a path flow variation $\Delta x = \{\Delta x_p\}$ which is feasible in the sense of Eqs. (5.63) and (5.64), *i.e.*,

$$\sum_{p \in P_w} \Delta x_p = 0, \quad \text{for all } w \in W$$

$$x_p + \Delta x_p \geq 0, \quad \text{for all } p \in P_w, w \in W \tag{5.70}$$

and along which the initial rate of change (cf. Eq. (5.65))

$$\sum_{w \in W} \sum_{p \in P_w} \frac{\partial D(x)}{\partial x_p} \Delta x_p$$

of the cost function D is most negative. Such a variation Δx is obtained by solving the optimization problem

$$\text{minimize} \sum_{w \in W} \sum_{p \in P_w} \frac{\partial D(x)}{\partial x_p} \Delta x_p$$

subject to the constraints (5.70)

and it is easily seen that $\Delta x = \overline{x} - x$ is an optimal solution where $\overline{x}$ is the shortest path flow vector generated by the Frank-Wolfe method. The process of finding Δx can be visualized as in Fig. 5.54. It can be seen that $\overline{x}$ is a vertex of the polyhedron of feasible path flow vectors that lies furthest out along the negative gradient direction $-\nabla D(x)$ thereby minimizing the inner product of $\nabla D(x)$ and Δx subject to the constraints (5.70).

Successive iterations of the Frank-Wolfe method are shown in Fig. 5.55. At each iteration, a vertex of the feasible set (*i.e.*, the shortest path flow $\overline{x}$) is obtained by solving a shortest path problem; then the next path flow vector is obtained by a search along the line joining the current path flow vector with the vertex. The search ensures that the new path flow vector has lower cost than the previous one.

We finally mention an important situation where the Frank-Wolfe method has an advantage over other methods. Suppose that one is not interested in obtaining optimal path flows, but that the only quantities of interest are the optimal total link flows F_{ij} or just the value of optimal cost. (This arises in topological design studies; see subsection 5.4.2.) Then, the Frank-Wolfe method can be implemented in a way that only the current total link flows together with the current shortest paths for all OD pairs are maintained in memory at each iteration. This can be done by computing the total link flows corresponding to the shortest path flow vector $\overline{x}$ and executing the line search indicated in Eq. (5.67) in the space of total link flows. The amount of storage required in this implementation is relatively small, thereby

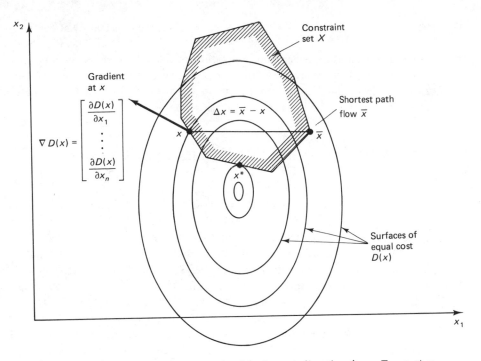

Figure 5.54 Finding the feasible descent direction $\Delta x = \bar{x} - x$ at a point x in the Frank-Wolfe method. $\bar{x}$ is the shortest path flow (or extreme point of the feasible set X) that lies furthest out along the negative gradient direction $-\nabla D(x)$.

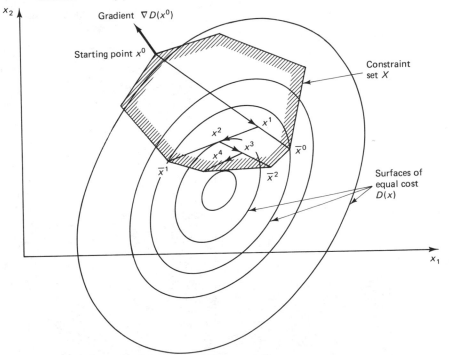

Figure 5.55 Successive iterations of the Frank-Wolfe method. At each iteration, a vertex of the feasible set (a shortest path flow) is found. The next path flow vector is obtained by a search on the line segment connecting the current path flow vector with the vertex.

allowing the solution of very large network problems. If, however, one is interested in optimal path flows as well as total link flows, the storage requirements of the Frank-Wolfe method are about the same as those of other methods, including the projection methods to be discussed in the next section.

5.7 PROJECTION METHODS FOR OPTIMAL ROUTING

We now consider a class of feasible direction algorithms for solving the optimal routing problem that are faster than the Frank-Wolfe method, and lend themselves more readily to distributed implementation. These methods are also based on shortest paths, and determine a minimum first derivative length (MFDL) path for every OD pair at each iteration. An increment of flow change is calculated for each path on the basis of the relative magnitudes of the path lengths and, sometimes, the second derivatives of the cost function. If the increment is so large that the path flow becomes negative, then the path flow is simply set to zero, *i.e.*, it is "projected" back onto the positive orthant. There are several methods of this type that are of interest in connection with the routing problem. They may all be viewed as constrained versions of common, unconstrained optimization methods, such as steepest descent and Newton's method, which are described in detail in nonlinear programming texts, (*e.g.*, [Zan69], [Pol71], [Ber82d], [Lue84]). We first present these methods briefly in a general, nonlinear optimization setting and subsequently specialize them to the routing problem.

Unconstrained Nonlinear Optimization

Let f be a twice differentiable function of the n-dimensional vector $x = (x_1, \ldots, x_n)$, with a gradient and Hessian matrix at any x denoted $\nabla f(x)$ and $\nabla^2 f(x)$

$$\nabla f(x) = \begin{bmatrix} \dfrac{\partial f(x)}{\partial x_1} \\ \ldots \\ \dfrac{\partial f(x)}{\partial x_n} \end{bmatrix}$$

$$\nabla^2 f(x) = \begin{bmatrix} \dfrac{\partial^2 f(x)}{(\partial x_1)^2} & \cdots & \dfrac{\partial^2 f(x)}{\partial x_1 \partial x_n} \\ & \ldots & \\ \dfrac{\partial^2 f(x)}{\partial x_n \partial x_1} & \cdots & \dfrac{\partial^2 f(x)}{(\partial x_n)^2} \end{bmatrix}$$

We assume that for all x, $\nabla^2 f(x)$ is a positive semidefinite matrix that depends continuously on x.[4] It can be shown that this guarantees that f is a convex function (see [Lue84], p. 180). The *method of steepest descent* for finding an unconstrained minimum of f starts with some initial guess x^0 and proceeds according to the iteration

$$x^{k+1} = x^k - \alpha^k \nabla f(x^k), \quad k = 0, 1, \ldots \tag{5.71}$$

where α^k is a positive scalar stepsize determined according to some rule. The idea here is similar to the one discussed in the previous section, namely changing x^k along a descent direction. In Eq. (5.71), the change is made along the negative gradient, which is a descent direction since it makes a negative inner product with the gradient vector (unless $\nabla f(x^k) = 0$, in which case the vector x^k is optimal). Common choices for α^k are the minimizing stepsize determined by

$$f[x^k - \alpha^k \nabla f(x^k)] = \min_{\alpha > 0} f[x^k - \alpha \nabla f(x^k)] \tag{5.72}$$

and a constant positive stepsize $\overline{\alpha}$

$$\alpha^k \equiv \overline{\alpha}, \quad \text{for all } k \tag{5.73}$$

There are a number of convergence results relating to iteration (5.71) with the stepsize choices of Eqs. (5.72) or (5.73). For example, if f has a unique unconstrained minimizing point it may be shown that the sequence $\{x^k\}$ generated by Eqs. (5.71) and (5.72) converges to this minimizing point for every starting x^0 (see [Ber82d], [Lue84]). Also, given any starting vector x^0, the sequence generated by Eqs. (5.71) and (5.73) converges to the minimizing point provided $\overline{\alpha}$ is chosen sufficiently small. Unfortunately, however, the speed of convergence of $\{x^k\}$ can be quite slow. It can be shown ([Lue84], p. 218) that for the case of the line minimization rule of Eq. (5.72), if f is a positive definite quadratic function then there holds

$$\frac{f(x^{k+1}) - f^*}{f(x^k) - f^*} \leq \left(\frac{M - m}{M + m} \right)^2 \tag{5.74}$$

where $f^* = \min_x f(x)$, and M and m are the largest and smallest eigenvalues of $\nabla^2 f(x)$, respectively. Furthermore, there exist starting points x^0 such that

---

[4] A symmetric $n \times n$ matrix A with elements A_{ij} is said to be *positive semidefinite* if the quadratic form

$$\sum_{i=1}^{n} \sum_{j=1}^{n} A_{ij} z_i z_j$$

is nonnegative for all vectors $z = (z_1, \ldots, z_n)$. The matrix A is said to be *positive definite* if this quadratic form is positive for all vectors $z \neq 0$.

Eq. (5.74) holds with equality for every k. So, if the ratio M/m is large (this corresponds to the equal-cost surfaces of f being very elongated ellipses), the rate of convergence is slow. Similar results can be shown for the method of Eqs. (5.71) and (5.73) and these results also hold in a qualitatively similar form for functions f with an everywhere continuous and positive definite Hessian matrix.

The rate of convergence of the steepest descent method can be improved by premultiplying the gradient by a suitable positive definite scaling matrix B^k, thereby obtaining the iteration

$$x^{k+1} = x^k - \alpha^k B^k \nabla f(x^k), \quad k = 0, 1, \ldots \tag{5.75}$$

This method is also based on the idea of changing x^k along a descent direction. (The direction of change $-B^k \nabla f(x^k)$ makes a negative inner product with $\nabla f(x^k)$, since B^k is a positive definite matrix.) From the point of view of rate of convergence, the best method is obtained with the choice

$$B^k = [\nabla^2 f(x^k)]^{-1} \tag{5.76}$$

(assuming $\nabla^2 f(x^k)$ is invertible). This is *Newton's method*, which can be shown to have a very fast (quadratic) rate of convergence near the minimizing point when the stepsize α^k is taken as unity. Unfortunately, this excellent convergence rate is achieved at the expense of the potentially substantial overhead associated with the inversion operation in Eq. (5.76). It is often useful to consider other choices of B^k which approximate the "optimal" choice $[\nabla^2 f(x^k)]^{-1}$ but do not require as much overhead. A simple choice that often works well is to take B^k as a diagonal approximation to the inverse Hessian, *i.e.*,

$$B^k = \begin{bmatrix} \left[\dfrac{\partial^2 f(x^k)}{(\partial x_1)^2}\right]^{-1} & & & \\ & \left[\dfrac{\partial^2 f(x^k)}{(\partial x_2)^2}\right]^{-1} & & 0 \\ & & \cdot \quad \cdot \quad \cdot & \\ 0 & & & \left[\dfrac{\partial^2 f(x^k)}{(\partial x_n)^2}\right]^{-1} \end{bmatrix} \tag{5.77}$$

With this choice, iteration (5.75) can be written in the simple form

$$x_i^{k+1} = x_i^k - \alpha^k \left[\frac{\partial^2 f(x^k)}{(\partial x_i)^2}\right]^{-1} \frac{\partial f(x^k)}{\partial x_i}, \quad i = 1, \ldots, n \tag{5.78}$$

Nonlinear Optimization Over the Positive Orthant

Next consider the problem of minimizing the function f subject to the nonnegativity constraints $x_i \geq 0$, for $i = 1, \ldots, n$, *i.e.*, the problem

$$\begin{aligned} &\text{minimize } f(x) \\ &\text{subject to } x \geq 0 \end{aligned} \tag{5.79}$$

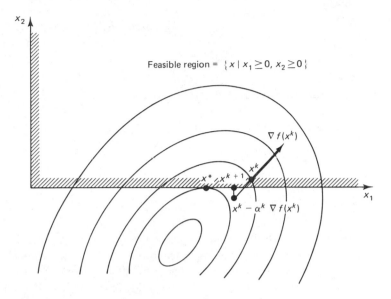

Figure 5.56   Operation of the gradient projection method. A step is made in the direction of the negative gradient and the result is orthogonally projected on the positive orthant. It can be shown that the step $(x^{k+1} - x^k)$ is a descent direction (makes a negative inner product with $\nabla f(x^k)$), and if the stepsize α is sufficiently small, the iteration improves the cost, *i.e.*, $f(x^{k+1}) < f(x^k)$.

A straightforward analog of the steepest descent method is given by

$$x^{k+1} = [x^k - \alpha^k \nabla f(x^k)]^+, \quad k = 0, 1, \dots \tag{5.80}$$

where for any vector z, we denote by $[z]^+$ the projection of z onto the positive orthant

$$[z]^+ = \begin{bmatrix} \max\{0, z_1\} \\ \max\{0, z_2\} \\ \vdots \\ \max\{0, z_n\} \end{bmatrix}. \tag{5.81}$$

An illustration of how this method operates is given in Fig. 5.56. It can be shown that the convergence results mentioned earlier in connection with the unconstrained steepest descent method of Eq. (5.71) also hold true for the constrained analog of Eq. (5.80) (see Problem 5.32 and [Ber76]). The same is true for the method

$$x^{k+1} = [x^k - \alpha^k B^k \nabla f(x^k)]^+$$

where B^k is a *diagonal*, positive definite scaling matrix (see Problem 5.33). When B^k above is given by Eq. (5.77), the following iteration is obtained (cf. Eqs. (5.78) and (5.81)):

$$x_i^{k+1} = \max\left\{0, x_i^k - \alpha^k \left[\frac{\partial^2 f(x^k)}{(\partial x_i)^2}\right]^{-1} \frac{\partial f(x^k)}{\partial x_i}\right\}, \quad i = 1, \ldots, n \quad (5.82)$$

Application to Optimal Routing

Consider now the optimal routing problem

$$\text{minimize } D(x) \overset{\Delta}{=} \sum_{(i,j)} D_{ij}(F_{ij})$$

$$\text{subject to } \sum_{p \in P_w} x_p = r_w, \quad x_p \geq 0, \quad \text{for all } p \in P_w, w \in W \quad (5.83)$$

where each total link flow F_{ij} is expressed in terms of the path flow vector $x = \{x_p\}$ as the sum of path flows traversing the link (i, j). Assume that after k iterations, a feasible path flow vector $x^k = \{x_p^k\}$ is obtained, and let $\{F_{ij}^k\}$ be the corresponding set of total link flows. For each OD pair w, let $\overline{p}_w$ be an MFDL path (with respect to the current link lengths $D_{ij}'(F_{ij}^k)$). The problem of Eq. (5.83) can be converted (for the purpose of the next iteration) to a problem involving only positivity constraints by expressing the flows of the MFDL paths $\overline{p}_w$ in terms of the other path flows while eliminating the equality constraints

$$\sum_{p \in P_w} x_p = r_w$$

in the process. For each w, $x_{\overline{p}_w}$ is substituted in the cost function $D(x)$ using the equation

$$x_{\overline{p}_w} = r_w - \sum_{\substack{p \in P_w \\ p \neq \overline{p}_w}} x_p \quad (5.84)$$

thereby obtaining a problem of the form

$$\text{minimize } \tilde{D}(\tilde{x})$$

$$\text{subject to } \quad x_p \geq 0, \quad \text{for all } w \in W, p \in P_w, p \neq \overline{p}_w \quad (5.85)$$

where $\tilde{x}$ is the vector of all path flows which are *not* MFDL paths.

We now calculate the derivatives that will be needed to apply iteration (5.82) to the problem of Eq. (5.85). Using Eq. (5.84) and the definition of $\tilde{D}(\tilde{x})$ we obtain

$$\frac{\partial \tilde{D}(\tilde{x}^k)}{\partial x_p} = \frac{\partial D(x^k)}{\partial x_p} - \frac{\partial D(x^k)}{\partial x_{\overline{p}_w}}, \quad \text{for all } p \in P_w, p \neq \overline{p}_w \quad (5.86)$$

for all $w \in W$. In section 5.5 it was shown that $\partial D(x)/\partial x_p$ is the first derivative length of path p, i.e.,

$$\frac{\partial D(x^k)}{\partial x_p} = \sum_{\substack{\text{all links} \\ (i,j) \text{ on path } p}} D'_{ij}(F^k_{ij}), \tag{5.87}$$

Regarding second derivatives, a straightforward differentiation of the expressions (5.86) and (5.87) for the first derivative shows that

$$\frac{\partial^2 \tilde{D}(\tilde{x}^k)}{(\partial x_p)^2} = \sum_{(i,j) \in L_p} D''_{ij}(F^k_{ij}), \qquad \text{for all } w \in W, p \in P_w, \ p \neq \bar{p}_w \tag{5.88}$$

where, for each p,

L_p: Set of links belonging to either p, or the corresponding MFDL path $\bar{p}_w$, but not both.

Expressions for both the first and second derivatives of the "reduced" cost $\tilde{D}(\tilde{x})$, are now available and thus the projection method of Eq. (5.82) can be applied. The iteration takes the form (cf. Eqs. (5.82), (5.86), and (5.88))

$$x_p^{k+1} = \max\{0, x_p^k - \alpha^k H_p^{-1}(d_p - d_{\bar{p}_w})\},$$
$$\text{for all } w \in W, \ p \in P_w, \ p \neq \bar{p}_w \tag{5.89}$$

where d_p and $d_{\bar{p}_w}$ are the first derivative lengths of the paths p and $\bar{p}_w$ given by (cf. Eq. (5.87))

$$d_p = \sum_{\substack{\text{all links } (i,j) \\ \text{on path } p}} D'_{ij}(F^k_{ij}), \qquad d_{\bar{p}_w} = \sum_{\substack{\text{all links } (i,j) \\ \text{on path } \bar{p}_w}} D'_{ij}(F^k_{ij}), \tag{5.90}$$

and H_p is the "second derivative length"

$$H_p = \sum_{(i,j) \in L_p} D''_{ij}(F^k_{ij}) \tag{5.91}$$

given by Eq. (5.88). The stepsize α^k is some positive scalar which may be chosen by a variety of methods. For example, α^k can be constant or can be chosen by some form of line minimization. Stepsize selection will be discussed later.

The following observations can be made regarding iteration (5.89):

1. Since for each OD pair $w \in W$, we have $d_p \geq d_{\bar{p}_w}$ for all $p \neq \bar{p}_w$, it follows that all the nonshortest path flows $x_p(p \neq \bar{p}_w)$ that are positive will be reduced with the corresponding increment of flow being shifted to the MFDL path $\bar{p}_w$. If the stepsize α^k is large enough, then all flow from the nonshortest paths will be shifted to the shortest path. Therefore, iteration (5.89) may also be

viewed as a generalization of the adaptive routing method based on shortest paths discussed in subsection 5.2.5, with α^k, H_p, and $(d_p - d_{\bar{p}_w})$ determining the amounts of flow shifted to the shortest path.

2. Those nonshortest path flows $x_p, p \neq \bar{p}_w$ that are zero will stay at zero. Therefore, the calculation indicated in Eq. (5.89) should only be carried out for paths that carry positive flow.

3. Only paths that carried positive flow at the starting flow pattern or were MFDL paths at some previous iteration can carry positive flow at the beginning of an iteration. This is important in that it tends to keep the number of flow carrying paths small with a corresponding reduction in the amount of calculation and bookkeeping needed at each iteration.

Regarding the choice of the stepsize α^k, there are several possibilities. It is possible to select α^k to be constant ($\alpha^k \equiv \alpha$, for all k). With this choice, it can be shown that given any starting set of path flows, there exists $\bar{\alpha} > 0$ such that, if $\alpha \in (0, \bar{\alpha}]$, then a sequence generated by iteration (5.89) to (5.91) converges to the optimal cost of the problem (see Problem 5.32). A crucial question has to do with the magnitude of the constant stepsize. It is known from nonlinear programming experience and analysis that a stepsize equal to unity usually works well with Newton's method as well as diagonal approximations to Newton's method (cf. Eq. (5.77)) that employ scaling based on second derivatives ([Lue84] and [Ber82d]). Experience has verified that a choice of α^k in Eq. (5.89) near unity typically works quite well regardless of the values of the input flows r_w [BGV79]. Even better performance is usually obtained if iteration (5.89) is carried out *one OD pair (or one origin) at a time*, i.e., first carry out (5.89) with $\alpha^k = 1$ for a single OD pair (or origin), adjust the corresponding total link flows to account for the effected change in the path flows of this OD pair (or origin), and continue with the next OD pair until all OD pairs are taken up cyclically. The rationale for this is based on the fact that dropping the off-diagonal terms of the Hessian matrix (cf. Eqs. (5.75) and (5.77)), in effect, neglects the interaction between the flows of different OD pairs. In other words, iteration (5.89) is based to some extent on the premise that each OD pair will adjust its own path flows while the other OD pairs will keep theirs unchanged. Carrying out iteration (5.89) one OD pair at a time reduces the potentially detrimental effect of the neglected off-diagonal terms of the Hessian, and increases the likelihood that the unity stepsize is appropriate and effective. Under these circumstances, experience shows that iteration (5.89) typically works well with a unity stepsize.

Using a constant stepsize is well suited for distributed implementation. For centralized computation, it is possible to choose α^k by a simple form of line search. For example, start with a unity stepsize, evaluate the corresponding cost, and if no reduction is obtained over $D(x^k)$, successively reduce the stepsize until a cost reduction $D(x^{k+1}) < D(x^k)$ is obtained. (It is noted for the theoretically minded, that this scheme cannot be shown to converge to the optimal solution. However, it typically works well in practice. Similar schemes with better theoretical convergence properties are described in [Ber76] and [Ber82c].) Still another possibility for a line search is discussed in Problem 5.32.

The projection algorithm typically yields rapid convergence to a neighborhood of an optimal solution. Once it comes near a solution (how "near" depends on the problem), it tends to slow down. Its progress is often satisfactory near a solution and usually far better than that of the Frank-Wolfe method. Figure 5.57 provides a comparison of the projection method and the Frank-Wolfe method for the example of the previous section.

For a projection algorithm to converge fast after it approaches an optimal solution, it is necessary that the off-diagonal terms of the Hessian matrix are taken into account. Surprisingly, it is possible to implement sophisticated methods of this type (see [BeG83]), but we will not go into this further. Suffice to say that these methods are based on a more accurate approximation of a constrained version of Newton's method (using the conjugate gradient method) near an optimal solution. However, when far from a solution, their speed of convergence is usually only slightly superior to that of iteration (5.89). So, if one is only interested in getting fast near an optimal solution in few iterations, but the subsequent rate of progress is of little importance (as is often the case in practical routing problems), the simple iteration (5.89) is usually satisfactory.

We finally note that iteration (5.89) is well suited for distributed implementation. The most straightforward possibility is for all nodes i to broadcast to all other nodes the current total flows F_{ij}^k of their outgoing links (i, j), using, for example, a flooding algorithm or the SPTA of subsection 5.3.3. Each node then computes the MFDL paths of OD pairs for which it is the origin and executes iteration (5.89) for some fixed stepsize. This corresponds to an "all OD pairs at once" mode of implementation. The method can also be implemented in an asynchronous, distributed format, whereby the computation and information reception are not synchronized at each node. The validity of the method under these conditions is shown in [TsB86].

We close this section with an example of application of the algorithm of Eqs. (5.89) to (5.91):

Example

Consider the network shown in Fig. 5.58. There are only two OD pairs $(1,5)$ and $(2,5)$ with corresponding inputs $r_1 = 4$ and $r_2 = 8$. Consider the following two paths for each OD pair:

Paths of OD Pair $(1, 5)$

$$p_1(1) = \{(1, 4), (4, 5)\}$$
$$p_2(1) = \{(1, 3), (3, 4), (4, 5)\}$$

Paths of OD Pair $(2, 5)$

$$p_1(2) = \{(2, 4), (4, 5)\}$$
$$p_2(2) = \{(2, 3), (3, 4), (4, 5)\}$$

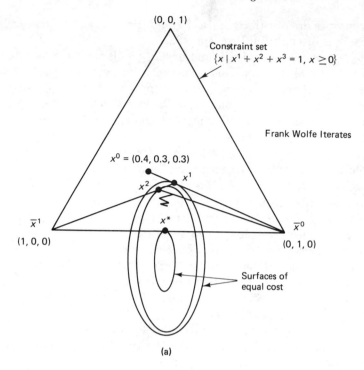

(a)

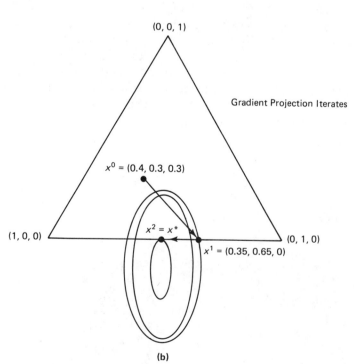

(b)

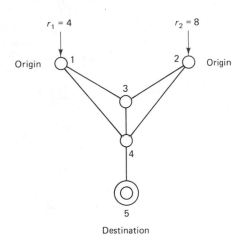

Figure 5.58   The network, for the example, where node 5 is the only destination and there are two origins, nodes 1 and 2.

Consider the instance of the routing problem where the link cost functions are all identical and are given by

$$D_{ij}(F_{ij}) = (\tfrac{1}{2})(F_{ij})^2, \quad \text{for all } (i,j)$$

Consider an initial path flow pattern whereby each OD pair input is routed through the middle link (3,4). This results in a flow distribution given in Tables 7.1 and 7.2.

Table 7.1 Initial path flows for the routing example

OD Pair	Path	Path Flow
(1,5)	$p_1(1)$	0
	$p_2(1)$	4
(2,5)	$p_1(2)$	0
	$p_2(2)$	8

Table 7.2 Initial total link flows for the routing example

Link	Total Link Flow
(1,3)	4
(1,4)	0
(2,3)	8
(2,4)	0
(3,4)	12
(4,5)	12
others	0

Figure 5.57   Iterates of (a) the Frank-Wolfe and (b) the gradient projection method for the example of the previous section. The gradient projection method converges much faster. It sets the flow x_3 to the correct value 0 in one iteration, and (because the Hessian matrix here is diagonal and the cost is quadratic) requires one more iteration to converge.

The first derivative length of each link is given by

$$D'_{ij}(F_{ij}) = F_{ij}$$

so the total link flows given in Table 7.2 are also the link lengths for the current iteration. The corresponding first derivative lengths of paths are given in the following table:

Table 7.3 Initial first derivative lengths for the routing example.

OD Pair	Path	1st Derivative Length
(1,5)	$p_1(1)$	12
	$p_2(1)$	28
(2,5)	$p_1(2)$	12
	$p_2(2)$	32

Therefore, the shortest paths for the current iteration are $p_1(1)$ and $p_1(2)$ for OD pairs (1,5) and (2,5), respectively.

The form of iteration (5.89) to (5.91) is illustrated for the first OD pair. Here, for the nonshortest path $p = p_2(1)$ and the shortest path $\bar{p} = p_1(1)$ we have $d_p = 28$ and $d_{\bar{p}} = 12$. Also, $H_p = 3$ (each link has a second derivative length $D''_{ij} = 1$, and there are three links that belong to either $p_1(1)$ or $p_2(1)$, but not to both, cf. Eqs. (5.88) and (5.91)). Therefore, iteration (5.89) takes the form

$$x_p := \max\{0, 4 - \alpha^k(1/3)(28 - 12)\}$$
$$= \max\{0, 4 - 16\alpha^k/3\} = 4 - \min\{4, 16\alpha^k/3\}$$

and

$$x_{\bar{p}} := r_1 - x_p$$

More generally, let $x_1(1), x_2(1), x_1(2)$, and $x_2(2)$ denote the flows along the paths $p_1(1), p_2(1), p_1(2)$, and $p_2(2)$, respectively, at the beginning of an iteration. The corresponding path lengths are

$$d_{p_1(1)} = x_1(1) + r_1 + r_2$$
$$d_{p_2(1)} = 2x_2(1) + x_2(2) + r_1 + r_2$$
$$d_{p_1(2)} = x_1(2) + r_1 + r_2$$
$$d_{p_2(2)} = 2x_2(2) + x_2(1) + r_1 + r_2$$

The second derivative length H_p of Eq. (5.91) equals 3. The algorithm (5.89) to (5.91) takes the following form. For $i = 1, 2$,

$$x_1(i) := \begin{cases} x_1(i) - \min\left[x_1(i), (\alpha^k/3)[d_{p_1(i)} - d_{p_2(i)}]\right], & \text{if } d_{p_1(i)} > d_{p_2(i)} \\ x_1(i) + \min\left[x_2(i), (\alpha^k/3)[d_{p_2(i)} - d_{p_1(i)}]\right], & \text{otherwise} \end{cases}$$
$$x_2(i) := r_i - x_1(i)$$

Table 7.4 Sequence of costs generated by the gradient projection method for the routing example, and for a variety of stepsizes

Iteration	All-at-Once Mode			One-at-a-Time Mode		
k	$\alpha^k \equiv 0.5$	$\alpha^k \equiv 1.0$	$\alpha^k \equiv 1.8$	$\alpha^k \equiv 0.5$	$\alpha^k \equiv 1.0$	$\alpha^k \equiv 1.8$
0	184.00	184.00	184.00	184.00	184.00	184.00
1	110.88	104.00	112.00	114.44	101.33	112.00
2	102.39	101.33	118.72	103.54	101.00	109.15
3	101.28	101.03	112.00	101.63		101.79
4	101.09	101.00	118.72	101.29		101.56
5	101.03		112.00	101.08		101.33
6	101.01		118.72	101.03		101.18
7	101.00		112.00	101.01		101.12
8			118.72	101.00		101.09
9			112.00			101.06
10			118.72			101.03

Notice that the presence of link (4,5) does not affect the form of the iteration, and indeed this should be so since the total flow of link (4,5) is always equal to $r_1 + r_2$ independent of the routing.

Table 7.4 gives sequences of successive cost function values obtained by the algorithm for different stepsize values, and the "all OD pairs at once" and "one OD pair at a time" modes of implementation. The difference between these two implementation modes is that in the all-at-once mode, the OD pairs are processed simultaneously during an iteration using the link and path flows obtained at the end of the previous iteration. In the one-at-a-time mode the OD pairs are processed sequentially, and, following the iteration of one OD pair, the link flows are adjusted to reflect the results of the iteration, before carrying out an iteration for the other OD pair. The stepsize is chosen to be constant at one of three possible values ($\alpha^k \equiv 0.5$, $\alpha^k \equiv 1$, and $\alpha^k \equiv 1.8$). It can be seen that for a unity stepsize, the convergence to a neighborhood of a solution is very fast in both the one-at-a-time and the all-at-once modes. As the stepsize is increased, the danger of divergence increases with divergence typically occurring first for the all-at-once mode. This can be seen from the table, where for $\alpha^k \equiv 1.8$, the algorithm converges (slowly) in the one-at-a-time mode but diverges in the all-at-once mode.

5.8 ROUTING IN THE CODEX NETWORK

In this section, the routing system of the network marketed by Codex, Inc. will be discussed. References [HuS86] and [HSS86] further describe the system in detail. The Codex network uses virtual circuits internally for user traffic, and datagrams for system traffic (accounting, control, routing information, etc.). It was decided to use datagrams for system traffic because the alternative, namely establishing a virtual circuit for each pair of nodes, was deemed too expensive in terms of network resources. Note that for each user session, there are two separate virtual circuits carrying traffic in opposite directions, but not necessarily over the same set of links. Routing decisions are done separately in each direction.

There are two algorithms for route selection. The first, used for datagram routing of internal system traffic, is a simple shortest path algorithm of the type discussed in section 5.2. The shortest path calculations are done as part of the second algorithm, which is used for selecting routes for new virtual circuits and for rerouting old ones. We will focus on the second algorithm, which is more important and far more sophisticated than the first.

The virtual circuit routing algorithm has much in common with the gradient projection method for optimal routing of the previous section. There is a cost function D_{ij} for each link (i,j) that depends on the link flow, but also on additional parameters, such as the link capacity, the processing and propagation delay, and a priority factor for the virtual circuits currently on the link. Each node monitors the parameters of its adjacent links, and periodically broadcasts them to all other nodes. If all virtual circuits have the same priority, the link cost function has the form

$$D_{ij}(F_{ij}) = \frac{F_{ij}}{C_{ij} - F_{ij}} + d_{ij}F_{ij}$$

where F_{ij} is the total data rate on the link, d_{ij} is the processing and propagation delay, and C_{ij} is the link capacity. This formula is based on the $M/M/1$ delay approximation–see the discussion of sections 3.6 and 5.4. When there are more than one, say M, priority levels for virtual circuits, the link cost function has the form

$$D_{ij}(F_{ij}^1, \ldots, F_{ij}^M) = \left(\sum_{k=1}^{M} p_k F_{ij}^k\right)\left(\frac{1}{C_{ij} - \sum_{k=1}^{M} F_{ij}^k} + d_{ij}\right)$$

where F_{ij}^k is the total link flow for virtual circuits of priority k, and p_k is a positive weighting factor. The form of this expression is motivated by the preceding formula, but otherwise has no meaningful interpretation based on a queueing analysis.

Routing of a new virtual circuit is done by assignment on a path that is shortest for the corresponding OD pair. This path is calculated at the destination node of the virtual circuit on the basis of the network topology, and the flow and other parameters latest received for each network link. The choice of link length is motivated by the fact that the communication rate of a virtual circuit may not be negligible compared with the total flow of the links on its path. The length used is the link cost difference between when the virtual circuit is routed through the link and when it is not. Thus, if the new virtual circuit has an estimated data rate Δ and priority class k, the length of link (i,j) is

$$D_{ij}\left(F_{ij}^1, \ldots, F_{ij}^k + \Delta, \ldots, F_{ij}^M\right) - D_{ij}(F_{ij}^1, \ldots, F_{ij}^M) \qquad (5.92)$$

As a result, routing of a new virtual circuit on a shortest path with respect to the link length (5.92) results in a minimum increase in total cost. When all virtual circuits have the same priority, the link length (5.92) becomes

$$D_{ij}(F_{ij} + \Delta) - D_{ij}(F_{ij}) \qquad\qquad (5.93)$$

If Δ is very small then the link lengths (5.93) are nearly equal to $\Delta D'_{ij}(F_{ij})$. Otherwise (by the mean value theorem of calculus), they are proportional to the corresponding derivatives of D_{ij} at some intermediate point between the current flow and the flow resulting when the virtual circuit is routed through (i, j). Thus, the link lengths (5.93) are approximations to the first derivatives of link costs that are used in the gradient projection method. The link lengths (5.92) also admit a similar interpretation (see Problem 5.27).

Rerouting of old virtual circuits is done in a similar manner. If there is a link failure, virtual circuits crossing the link are rerouted as if they are new. Rerouting with the intent of alleviating congestion is done by all nodes gradually once new link flow information is received. Each node scans the virtual circuits terminating at itself. It selects one of the virtual circuits as a candidate for rerouting, and calculates the length of each link as the difference of link cost with and without that virtual circuit on the link. The virtual circuit is then rerouted on the shortest path if it does not lie already on the shortest path. An important parameter here is the number of virtual circuits chosen for rerouting between successive link flow broadcasts. This corresponds to the stepsize parameter in the gradient projection method, which determines how much flow is shifted on a shortest path at each iteration. The problem, of course, is that too many virtual circuits may be rerouted simultaneously by several nodes acting without coordination, thereby resulting in oscillatory behavior similar to the one discussed in subsection 5.2.5. The Codex network uses a heuristic rule whereby only a fraction of the existing virtual circuits are (pseudorandomly) considered for rerouting between successive link flow broadcasts.

5.9 SUMMARY

Routing is a sophisticated data network function that requires coordination between the network nodes through distributed protocols. It affects the average packet delay, and the network throughput.

Our main focus was on methods for route selection. The most common approach, shortest path routing, can be implemented in a variety of ways as exemplified by the ARPANET and TYMNET algorithms. Depending on its implementation, shortest path routing may cause low throughput, poor response to traffic congestion, and oscillatory behavior. These drawbacks are more evident in datagram than in virtual circuit networks. A more sophisticated alternative is optimal routing based on flow models. Several algorithms were given for computation of an optimal routing, both centralized and distributed. As the statistics of the input arrival processes change more rapidly, the appropriateness of the type of optimal routing we focused on diminishes. In such cases it is difficult to recommend routing methods that are simultaneously efficient and practical.

Another interesting aspect of the routing problem relates to the dissemination of routing-related information over failure-prone links. We described several alternative algorithms based on flooding ideas.

Finally, routing must be taken into account when designing a network's topology, since the routing method determines how effectively the link capacities are utilized. We described exact and heuristic methods for addressing the difficulties of topological design.

5.10 NOTES, SOURCES, AND SUGGESTED READING

Section 5.1.   Surveys of routing, including descriptions of some practical routing algorithms can be found in [Eph86], and [ScS80]. Routing in the ARPANET is described in [McW77], [MRR78], and [MRR80]. The TYMNET system is described in [Tym81]. Routing in SNA is described in [Ahu79] and [Atk80]. A route selection method for SNA networks is described in [GaH83]. Descriptions of other routing systems may be found in [Wec80] and [SpM81].

Section 5.2.   There are many sources for the material on graphs, spanning trees and shortest paths–for example, [PaS82], [Law76]. Particularly fast, shortest path algorithms are described in [Pap74], [DGK79].

The material on asynchronous shortest path algorithms is taken from [Ber82a]. For further work on general asynchronous distributed algorithms, see [Ber83] and [BTA84].

For more on stability issues of shortest path routing algorithms, see [Ber79], [Ber82b] and [GaB83].

Section 5.3.   The difficulties with the ARPANET flooding algorithm and some remedies are described in [Ros81], and [Per83]. The SPTA appeared in the thesis [Spi85]. For related work, see [EpB81], [Fin79], [GaB81], [Seg83], and [SoH86].

Section 5.4.   There is considerable literature on routing based on queue state information. These works consider data networks but also relate to routing and control problems in other contexts. See [EVW80], [FoS78], [HaO84], [MoS82], [Ros86], [SaH86], [SaO82], [Sar82], [StK85], [Yum81].

Surveys on topological design of data networks are provided in [BoF77], [GeK77], [KeB83], [McS77], and [MoS86]. For further material on network reliability, see [BaP73], [Bal79], [Ben86], [LaL86], [LiS84], [PrB84] and the references quoted therein.

Section 5.5.   The optimal routing problem considered is a special case of a multicommodity network flow problem. The problem arises also in the context of transportation networks in a form that is very similar to the one discussed here—see [AaM81], [Daf71], [Daf80], [DeK81], [FlN74], [LaH84].

Section 5.6.   The Frank-Wolfe method [FrW56] has been proposed in the context of the routing problem in [FGK73]. Problems 5.31 and 5.32 give a self-contained presentation of the convergence properties of this method as well as those of the gradient projection method.

Section 5.7.   The gradient projection method was applied to multicommodity flow problems based on a path flow formulation in [Ber80]. Extensions were described in [BeG82], [BeG83], and [GaB84a]. A public domain FORTRAN implementation of the gradient projection method is given in [BGT83]. The optimal routing algorithm of [Gal77], which adjusts link flow fractions (see the end of section 5.5), bears a relationship with the gradient projection method (see [BGG84]). Extensions of the algorithm are given in [Ber79a], [Gaf79], and [BGG84]. Computational and simulation results relating to this algorithm and its extensions may be found in [BGV79] and [ThC86].

Section 5.8.   The comments of P. Humblet, one of the principal designers of the Codex network, were very helpful in preparing this section. Additional material can be found in [HuS86] and [HSS86].

PROBLEMS

5.1 Find a minimum weight spanning tree of the graph in Fig. 5.59 using the Prim-Dijkstra and the Kruskal algorithms.

5.2 Find the shortest path tree from node 1 to every other node for the graph of Fig. 5.60 using the Bellman-Ford and Dijkstra algorithms.

5.3 The number shown next to each link of the network in Fig. 5.61 is the probability of the link failing during the lifetime of a virtual circuit from node A to node B. It is assumed that links fail independently of each other. Find the most reliable path from A to B, $i.e.$, the path for which the probability that all its links stay intact during the virtual circuit's lifetime is maximal. What is this probability?

5.4 A shortest path spanning tree (subsection 5.2.3) differs from a minimum weight spanning tree in that the arc lengths refer to directed arcs, while in the minimum weight spanning tree problem, the arcs weights refer to undirected arcs or, equivalently, the arc weights are assumed equal in both directions. However, even if all arcs have equal length in both directions, a minimum weight spanning tree (for arc weights equal to the corresponding lengths)

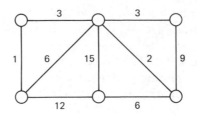

Figure 5.59

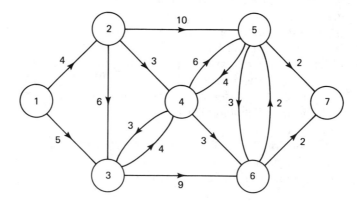

Figure 5.60

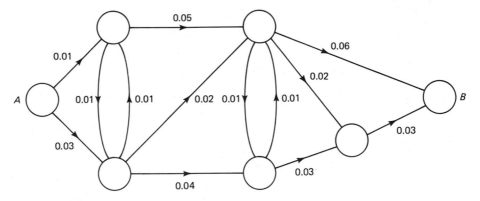

Figure 5.61

need not be a shortest path spanning tree. To see this, consider a network with three nodes A, B, and C, and three bidirectional arcs AB, BC, CA. Choose a weight for each arc so that the minimum weight spanning tree is not a shortest path tree with root node C (the length of an arc in each of its two directions is equal to the arc weight).

5.5 Consider Example 1 in subsection 5.2.5.

(a) Repeat the example with $N = 6$ instead of $N = 16$. (Nodes $1, 2, 4$, and 5 send 1 unit to node 6, while node 3 sends ϵ with $0 < \epsilon \ll 1$.)

(b) Repeat (a) with the difference that the length d_{ij} of link (i, j) is $\alpha + F_{ij}$ for $\alpha = 1$ (instead of F_{ij}). Consider all possible choices of initial routing.

(c) What is the minimum value of α for which the shortest paths of all nodes except node 3 eventually stay constant regardless of the choice of initial routing?

(d) Repeat (a) with the difference that at each iteration after the first, the length of each link is the average of the link arrival rates corresponding to the current and the preceding routings (instead of the arrival rates at just the current routing).

5.6 Show that (even in the presence of negative length cycles) the value of $D_i^{(h)}$ generated by the Bellman-Ford algorithm is the length of the shortest $(\leq h)$ walk from node 1 to node i subject to the constraint that node 1 is not repeated in the walk.

5.7 Consider the Bellman-Ford algorithm assuming there are no cycles of negative length. For each node $i \neq 1$, let (j_i, i) be an arc such that j_i attains the minimum in the equation

$$D_i^{(h_i)} = \min_j \left[D_j^{(h_i-1)} + d_{ji} \right]$$

where h_i is the largest h such that $D_i^{(h)} \neq D_i^{(h-1)}$. Consider the subgraph consisting of the arcs (j_i, i), for $i \neq 1$, and show that (even if there are zero length cycles) it is a spanning tree consisting of shortest paths. *Hint*: Show that $h_i > h_{j_i}$.

5.8 Consider the shortest path problem assuming there are no negative length cycles. Show that if there is a cycle of zero length not containing node 1, then Bellman's equation has more than one solution.

5.9 Suppose we have a directed graph which has no directed cycles. We are given a length d_{ij} for each directed arc (i, j) and we want to compute a shortest path from node 1 to all other nodes. Assume that there is at least one directed path from node 1 to every other node. Show that nodes $2, 3, \ldots, N$ can be renumbered so that there is an arc from i to j only if $i < j$. Show that once the nodes are renumbered, Bellman's equation can be solved with $O(N^2)$ operations at worst.

5.10 Consider the shortest path problem from node 1 to every other node. Assume that a positive lower bound is known for all arc lengths. Modify Dijkstra's algorithm by allowing more than one node to enter the set of permanently labeled nodes at each iteration. Show that the modified algorithm is correct.

5.11 Consider a network in which each node knows the network topology and a positive length for each directed arc. Each node has already calculated the shortest path from itself to every other node of the network (assume the graph is strongly connected). Assume that one arc, (i, k), *increases* in length. Show how to modify Dijkstra's algorithm for a given origin node, to recalculate as efficiently as possible the shortest paths from itself to all other nodes.

5.12 *Verifying the termination of the distributed Bellman-Ford algorithm [ChM82].* The objective of the following algorithm (based on the Bellman-Ford method) is to compute in a distributed way a shortest path from a single origin (node 1) to all other nodes *and* to notify node 1 that the computation has terminated. Assume that all links (i, j) are bidirectional, have nonnegative length d_{ij}, maintain the order of messages sent on them, and operate with no errors or failures. Each node i maintains an estimate D_i of the shortest distance from node 1 to itself. Initially $D_i = \infty$, for all nodes $i \neq 1$, and $D_1 = 0$. Node 1 initiates the computation by sending the estimate $D_1 + d_{1j}$ to all neighbor nodes j. The algorithmic rules for each node $j \neq 1$ are as follows:

(1) When node j receives an estimate $D_i + d_{ij}$ from some other node i, after some unspecified finite delay (but before processing a subsequently received estimate), it does the following:

If $D_j \leq D_i + d_{ij}$, node j sends an ACK to node i.

If $D_j > D_i + d_{ij}$, node j sets $D_j = D_i + d_{ij}$, marks node i as its best current predecessor on a shortest path, sends an ACK to its previous best predecessor (if any), and sends the estimate $D_j + d_{jk}$ to each neighbor k.

(2) Node j sends an ACK to its best current predecessor once it receives an ACK for each of the latest estimates sent to its neighbors.

We assume that each ACK is uniquely associated with a previously sent estimate, and that node 1 responds with an ACK to any length estimate it receives.

(a) Show that eventually node 1 will receive an ACK from each of its neighbors, and at that time D_i will be the correct shortest distance for each node i.

(b) What are the advantages and disadvantages of this algorithm compared with the distributed, asynchronous Bellman-Ford algorithm of subsection 5.2.4?

5.13 Consider the second flooding algorithm of subsection 5.3.2. Suppose there is a known upper bound on the time an update message requires to reach every node connected with the originating node. Devise a scheme based on an age field to supplement the algorithm so that it works correctly even if the sequence numbers can wraparound due to a memory or communication error. *Note*: Packets carrying an age field should be used only in exceptional circumstances after the originating node detects an error.

5.14 Modify the SPTA so that it can be used to broadcast one-directional link information other than status throughout the network (cf. the remarks at the end of subsection 5.3.3). The link information is collected by the start node of the link. Justify the modified algorithm.

Hint: Add to the existing algorithm additional main and port tables to hold the directional link information. Formulate update rules for these tables using the node labels provided by the main topology update algorithm of section 5.3.3.

5.15

    (a) Give an example where the following algorithm for broadcasting topological update information fails. Initially, all nodes know the correct status of all links.

        Update Rules:

    (1) When an adjacent link changes status, the node sends the new status in a message on all operating adjacent links.

    (2) When a node receives a message about a nonadjacent link which differs from its view of the status of the link, it changes the status of the link in its topology table. It also sends the new status in a message on all operating adjacent links *except* the one on which it received the message.

    (3) When a node receives a message about an adjacent link which differs from its view of the status of the link, it sends the correct status on the link on which it received the message.

        Hint: Failure occurs with simple network topologies, such as the one shown in Fig. 5.29.

    (b) Give an example of failure when the word "except" in rule 2 is changed to "including".

5.16 Describe what, if anything, can go wrong in the topology broadcast algorithms of section 5.3 if the assumption that messages are received across links in the order transmitted is relaxed. Consider the ARPANET flooding algorithm, the two algorithms of subsection 5.3.2, and the SPTA of subsection 5.3.3.

5.17 *Distributed computation of the number of nodes in a network.* Consider a strongly connected communication network with N nodes and A (bidirectional) links. Each node knows its identity and the set of its immediate neighbors but not the network topology. Node 1 wishes to determine the number of nodes in the network. As a first step, it initiates an algorithm for finding a *directed, rooted spanning tree with node 1 as the root*. By this we mean a tree each link (i, k) of which is directed and oriented towards node 1 along the unique path on the tree leading from i to 1 (see the example tree shown in Fig. 5.62).

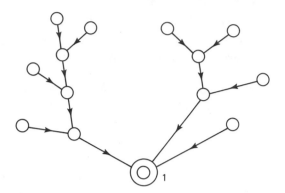

Figure 5.62

(a) Devise a distributed algorithm involving exchange of messages between nodes that constructs such a tree. The algorithm is initiated by node 1 and should involve no more than $O(A)$ message transmissions. Communication along any link is assumed error free. At the end of the algorithm, the end nodes of each link should know whether the link is part of the tree, and, if so, they should know its direction.

(b) Supplement the algorithm derived in (a) by another algorithm involving no more than $O(N)$ message transmissions by means of which node 1 gets to know N.

(c) Assuming each message transmission takes an equal amount of time T, derive an upper bound for the time needed to complete the algorithms in (a) and (b).

5.18 Consider the minimum weight spanning tree problem. Show that the following procedure implements the Prim-Dijkstra algorithm and that it requires $O(N^2)$ arithmetic operations. Let node 1 be the starting node, and set initially $P = \{1\}$, $T = \{\ \}$, $D_1 = 0$, and $D_j = w_{1j}$, $a_j = 1$ for $j \neq 1$.

Step 1: Find $i \notin P$ such that
$$D_i = \min_{j \notin P} D_j$$
and set $T := T \cup \{(j, a_i)\}$, $P := P \cup \{i\}$. If P contains all nodes then stop.

Step 2: For all $j \notin P$, if $w_{ij} < D_j$ set $D_j := w_{ij}$, $a_j := i$. Go to Step 1.

Note: Observe the similarity with Dijkstra's algorithm for shortest paths.

5.19 Use Kleitman's algorithm to prove or disprove that the network shown in Fig. 5.63 is 3-connected. What is the maximum k for which the network is k-connected?

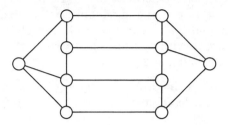

Figure 5.63

5.20 Suppose you had an algorithm that would find the maximum k for which two nodes in a graph are k-connected (for example the max-flow algorithm test illustrated in Fig. 5.41). How would you modify Kleitman's algorithm to find the maximum k for which the graph is k-connected? Apply your modified algorithm to the graph of Problem 5.19 (Fig. 5.63).

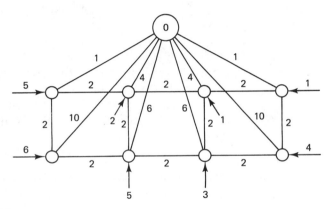

Figure 5.64

5.21 Use the Essau-Williams heuristic algorithm to find a constrained MST for the network shown in Fig. 5.64. Node 0 is the central node. The link weights are shown next to the links. The input flows from each node to the concentrator are shown next to the arrows. All link capacities are 10.

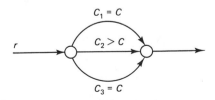

Figure 5.65

5.22 Consider the network shown in Fig. 5.65 involving one OD pair with a given input rate r and three links with capacities C_1, C_2, and C_3 respectively. Assume that $C_1 = C_3 = C$, and $C_2 > C$, and solve the optimal routing problem with cost function based on the $M/M/1$ delay approximation, and r between 0 and $2C + C_2$.

5.23 Consider the problem of finding the optimal routing of one unit of input flow in a single OD pair, three-link network for the cost function

$$D(x) = \frac{1}{2}\left[(x_1^2) + 2(x_2^2) + (x_3^2)\right] + 0.7x_3$$

Mathematically, the problem is

$$\text{minimize } D(x)$$
$$\text{subject to } x_1 + x_2 + x_3 = 1$$
$$x_1, x_2, x_3 \geq 0$$

(a) Show that $x_1^* = 2/3$, $x_2^* = 1/3$, and $x_3^* = 0$ is the optimal solution.

(b) Carry out several iterations of the Frank-Wolfe method and the projection method starting from the point $(1/3,\ 1/3,\ 1/3)$. Do enough iterations to demonstrate a clear trend in rate of convergence. (Use a computer for this if you wish.) Plot the successive iterates on the simplex of feasible flows.

5.24 Let g be a convex differentiable funtion of a single variable α. Suppose that $dg(0)/(d\alpha) \geq 0$. Show that $g(\alpha) \geq g(0)$ for all $\alpha \geq 0$. *Hint*: Show that for every two scalars α_1 and α_2 we have

$$g(\alpha_2) \geq g(\alpha_1) + \frac{dg(\alpha_1)}{d\alpha}(\alpha_2 - \alpha_1)$$

by using the inequality

$$(1 - \mu)g(\alpha_1) + \mu g(\alpha_2) \geq g[\alpha_1 + \mu(\alpha_2 - \alpha_1)], \quad \mu \epsilon [0, 1]$$

5.25 Consider the optimal routing problem of Section 5.5. Assume that each link cost is chosen to be the same convex function $D(F)$ of the link flow F, where the first link cost derivative at zero flow $D'(0)$ is positive.

(a) For sufficiently small values of origin-destination pair input rates r_w show that optimal routings use only minimum-hop paths from origins to destinations.

(b)   Construct an example showing that optimal routings do not necessarily have the minimum-hop property for larger values of r_w.

5.26 Consider the Frank-Wolfe method with the stepsize of Eq. (5.69) in section 5.6. Describe an implementation as a distributed synchronous algorithm involving communication from origins to links and the reverse. At each iteration of this algorithm, each origin should calculate the stepsize of Eq. (5.69), and update accordingly the path flows that originate at itself.

5.27 *Extensions of the gradient projection method.*

(a)   Show how the optimality condition of section 5.5 and the gradient projection method can be extended to handle the situation where the cost function is a general convex, twice differentiable function of the path flow vector x.

(b)   Discuss the special case where the cost of link (i, j) is $D_{ij}(\tilde{F}_{ij}, F_{ij})$ where

$$\tilde{F}_{ij} = \sum_{k=1}^{M} p_k F_{ij}^k, \qquad F_{ij} = \sum_{k=1}^{M} F_{ij}^k$$

p_k is a positive scalar weighting factor for priority class k, and F_{ij}^k is the total flow of priority class k crossing link (i, j) (cf. the Codex algorithm cost function).

5.28 *Optimal broadcast routing along spanning trees.* Consider the optimal routing problem of section 5.4. Suppose that in addition to the regular OD pair input rates r_w that are to be routed along directed paths, there is additional traffic R to be broadcast from a single node, say 1, to all other nodes along one or more directed spanning trees rooted at node 1. The spanning trees to be used for routing are to be selected from a given collection T, and the portion of R to be broadcast along each is subject to optimization.

(a)   Characterize the path flow rates and the portions of R broadcast along spanning trees in T that minimize a total link cost, such as the one given by Eq. (5.29) in section 5.4.

(b)   Extend the gradient projection method to solve this problem.

(c)   Extend your analysis to the case where there are several root nodes and there is traffic to be broadcast from each of these nodes to all other nodes.

Hint: Consider the first derivative total weights of spanning trees in addition to the first derivative lengths of paths.

5.29 *Optimal routing with VCs using the same links in both directions.* Consider the optimal routing problem of section 5.4 with the additional restriction that the traffic originating at node i and destined for node i' must use the same path (in the reverse direction) as the traffic originating at i' and destined for i. In particular assume that if w and w' are the OD pairs (i, i') and (i', i), respectively, there is a proportionality constant $c_{ww'}$ such that if $p \in P_w$ is a path and $p' \in P_{w'}$ is the reverse path, and x_p and $x_{p'}$ are the corresponding path flows, then $x_p = c_{ww'} x_{p'}$. Derive the conditions characterizing an optimal routing, and appropriately extend the gradient projection method.

5.30 *Use of the M/M/1-based cost function with the gradient projection method.* When the cost function

$$\sum_{(i,j)} D_{ij}(F_{ij}) = \sum_{(i,j)} \frac{F_{ij}}{C_{ij} - F_{ij}}$$

is minimized using the gradient projection method, there is potential difficulty due to the fact that some link flow F_{ij} may exceed the capacity C_{ij}. One way to get around this is to replace D_{ij} with a function $\tilde{D}_{ij}$ that is identical with D_{ij} for F_{ij} in the interval $[0, \rho C_{ij}]$, where ρ is some number less than one (say $\rho = 0.99$), and is quadratic for $F_{ij} > \rho C_{ij}$. The quadratic function is chosen so that D_{ij} and $\tilde{D}_{ij}$ have equal values and first two derivatives at the point $F_{ij} = \rho C_{ij}$. Derive the formula for $\tilde{D}_{ij}$. Show that if the link flows F_{ij}^* that minimize

$$\sum_{(i,j)} D_{ij}(F_{ij})$$

result in link utilizations not exceeding ρ (*i.e.*, $F_{ij}^* \le \rho C_{ij}$ for all (i, j)), then F_{ij}^* also minimize

$$\sum_{(i,j)} \tilde{D}_{ij}(F_{ij})$$

5.31 *Convergence of the Frank-Wolfe algorithm.* The purpose of this problem and the next one is to guide the advanced reader through convergence proofs of the Frank-Wolfe and the gradient projection methods. Consider the problem

$$\text{minimize } f(x)$$
$$\text{subject to } x \in X$$

where f is a differentiable function of the n-dimensional vector x, and X is a closed, bounded, convex set. Assume that the gradient of f satisfies

$$|\nabla f(x) - \nabla f(y)| \le L|x - y|, \quad \text{for all } x, y \in X$$

where L is a positive constant and $|z|$ denotes the Euclidean norm of a vector z, *i.e.*,

$$|z| = \sqrt{\sum_{i=1}^{n}(z_i)^2}$$

(This assumption can be shown to hold if $\nabla^2 f$ exists and is continuous over X.)

(a) Show that for all vectors x, Δx, and scalars α, such that $x \in X$, $x + \Delta x \in X$, $\alpha \in [0, 1]$,

$$f(x + \alpha \Delta x) \leq f(x) + \alpha \nabla f(x)^T \Delta x + \frac{\alpha^2 L}{2}|\Delta x|^2$$

where superscript T denotes transpose. *Hint*: Use the Taylor formula

$$f(x + y) = f(x) + \nabla f(x)^T y + \int_0^1 [\nabla f(x + ty) - \nabla f(x)]^T y \, dt$$

(b) Use part (a) to show that if Δx is a descent direction at x (*i.e.*, $\nabla f(x)^T \Delta x < 0$), then

$$\min_{\alpha \in [0,1]} f(x + \alpha \Delta x) \leq f(x) + \delta$$

where

$$\delta = \begin{cases} \dfrac{1}{2}\nabla f(x)^T \Delta x, & \text{if} \quad \nabla f(x)^T \Delta x + L|\Delta x|^2 < 0 \\[2mm] -\dfrac{|\nabla f(x)^T \Delta x|^2}{2LR^2}, & \text{otherwise} \end{cases}$$

where R is the diameter of X, *i.e.*,

$$R = \max_{x,y \in X} |x - y|$$

Hint: Minimize over $\alpha \in [0, 1]$ in both sides of the inequality of part (a).

(c) Consider the Frank-Wolfe method

$$x^{k+1} = x^k + \alpha^k \Delta x^k$$

where $x^0 \in X$ is the starting vector, Δx^k solves the problem

$$\text{minimize } \nabla f(x^k)^T \Delta x$$
$$\text{subject to } x^k + \Delta x \in X$$

and α^k is a minimizing stepsize

$$f(x^k + \alpha^k \Delta x^k) = \min_{\alpha \in [0,1]} f(x^k + \alpha \Delta x^k)$$

Show that every limit x^* of the sequence $\{x^k\}$ satisfies the optimality condition

$$\nabla f(x^*)^T (x - x^*) \geq 0 \quad \text{for all } x \in X$$

Hint: Argue that, if $\{x^k\}$ has a limit point and δ^k corresponds to x^k as in part (b), then $\delta^k \to 0$, and, therefore, also $\nabla f(x^k)^T \Delta x^k \to 0$. Taking the limit in the relation $\nabla f(x^k)^T \Delta x \leq \nabla f(x^k)^T (x - x^k)$ for all $x \in X$, argue that a limit point x^* must satisfy $0 \leq \nabla f(x^*)^T (x - x^*)$ for all $x \in X$.

5.32 *Convergence of the gradient projection method.* Consider the minimization problem and the assumptions of Problem 5.31. Consider also the iteration

$$x^{k+1} = x^k + \alpha^k (\bar{x}^k - x^k)$$

where x^k is the projection of $x^k - s\nabla f(x^k)$ on X where s is some fixed positive scalar, *i.e.*, x^k solves

$$\text{minimize } |x - x^k + s\nabla f(x^k)|^2$$
$$\text{subject to } x \in X$$

(a)   Assume that a^k is a minimizing stepsize

$$f[x^k + \alpha^k (\bar{x}^k - x^k)] = \min_{\alpha \in [0,1]} f[x^k + \alpha(\bar{x}^k - x^k)]$$

and show that every limit point x^* of $\{x^k\}$ satisfies the optimality condition

$$\nabla f(x^*)^T (x - x^*) \geq 0, \qquad \text{for all } x \in X$$

Hint: Follow the hints of Problem 5.31. Use the following necessary condition satisfied by the projection (cf. the Lemma of section 5.5)

$$[x^k - s\nabla f(x^k) - x^k]^T (x - \bar{x}^k) \leq 0, \qquad \text{for all } x \in X$$

to show that $s\nabla f(x^k)^T(\bar{x}^k - x^k) \leq -|\bar{x}^k - x^k|^2$.

(b)   Assume that $a^k = 1$ for all k. Show that if $s < 2/L$ then the conclusion of (a) holds.

5.33 *Gradient projection method with a diagonal scaling matrix.* Consider the problem

$$\text{minimize } f(x)$$
$$\text{subject to } x \geq 0$$

of section 5.7. Show that the iteration

$$x_i^{k+1} = \max\{0, x_i^k - \alpha^k b_i \frac{\partial f(x^k)}{\partial x_i}\}, \quad i = 1, \ldots, n$$

with b_i some positive scalars, is equivalent to the gradient projection iteration

$$y_i^{k+1} = \max\{0, y_i^k - \alpha^k \frac{\partial h(y^k)}{\partial y_i}\}, \quad i = 1, \ldots, n$$

where the variables x_i and y_i are related by $x_i = \sqrt{b_i}y_i$, and $h(y) = f(Ty)$, and T is the diagonal matrix with the ith diagonal element equal to $\sqrt{b_i}$.

5.34 *Routing in networks with frequently changing topology [GaB81].* In some situations (for example, mobile packet radio networks) topological changes are so frequent that topology broadcast algorithms are somewhat impractical. The algorithms of this problem are designed to cope with situations of this type. Consider a connected undirected graph with a special node referred to as the *destination.* Consider the collection C of directed acyclic graphs obtained by assigning a unique direction to each of the undirected links. A graph G in C is said to be *rooted at the destination* if, for every node, there is a directed path in G starting at the node and ending at the destination. Show that the following two distributed asynchronous algorithms will yield a graph in C that is rooted at the destination starting from any other graph in C.
Algorithm A. A node other than the destination with no outgoing links reverses the direction of all its adjacent links. (This is done repeatedly until every node other than the destination has an outgoing link.)
Algorithm B. Every node i other than the destination keeps a list of its neighboring nodes j that have reversed the direction of the corresponding links (i, j). At each iteration, each node i that has no outgoing link reverses the directions of the links (i, j), for all j that do not appear on its list, and empties the list. If no such j exists (*i.e.*, the list is full), node i reverses the directions of all incoming links and empties the list. Initially all lists are empty.
Hint: For algorithm A, assign to each node a distinct number. With each set of node numbers, associate the graph in C where each link is directed from a

higher to a lower number. Consider an algorithm where each node reverses
link directions by changing its number. Use a similar idea for algorithm B.

5.35 *Virtual circuit routing by flooding.* In some networks where it may be hard
to keep track of the topology as it changes (*e.g.*, packet radio networks),
it is possible to use flooding to set up virtual circuits. The main idea is
that a node m, which wants to set up a virtual circuit to node n, should
flood an "exploratory" packet through the network. A node that rebroadcasts
this packet stamps its ID number on it so that when the destination node n
receives an exploratory packet, it knows the route along which it came. The
destination node can then choose one of the potentially many routes carried by
the copies of the exploratory packet received and proceed to set up the virtual
circuit. Describe one or more flooding protocols that will make this process
workable. Address the issues of indefinite or excessive message circulation
in the network, appropriate numbering of exploratory packets, unpredictable
link failures and delays, potential confusion between the two end nodes of
virtual circuits, etc.

5.36 *Optimal dynamic routing based on window ratio strategies.* Consider the optimal routing problem of section 5.4 in a datagram network. Suppose we want
to implement a set of path flows $\{x_p\}$ calculated on the basis of a nominal
set of traffic inputs $\{r_w\}$. The usual solution, discussed in section 5.5, is to
route the traffic of each OD pair w in a way that matches closely the actual
fractions of packets routed on the paths $p \in P_w$ with the desired fractions
x_p/r_w. With this type of implementation each OD pair w takes into account
changes in its own input traffic r_w, but makes no effort to adapt to changes
in the input traffic of other OD pairs, or to queue lengths inside the network.
This problem considers the following more dynamic alternative.

Suppose that each OD pair w calculates the average number of packets N_p
travelling on each path $p \in P_w$ by means of Little's theorem

$$N_p = x_p T_p, \qquad \text{for all } p \in P_w, w \in W$$

where T_p is the estimated average round trip packet delay on path p (time
between introduction of the packet into the network and return of an end-to-
end acknowledgement for the packet). The origin of each OD pair w monitors
the *actual* number of routed but unacknowledged packets $\tilde{N}_p$ on path p and
routes packets in a way that roughly equalizes the ratios $\tilde{N}_p/N_p$ for all paths
$p \in P_w$. Note that this scheme is sensitive to changes in delay on the paths
of an OD pair due to statistical fluctuations of the input traffic and/or the
routing policies of other OD pairs. The difficulty with this scheme is that the
delays T_p are unknown when the numbers N_p are calculated, and therefore T_p
must be estimated somehow. The simplest possibility is to use the measured
value of average delay during a preceding time period. You are asked to
complete the argument in the following analysis of this scheme for a simple
special case.

Suppose that there is a single OD pair and only two paths with flows and path delays denoted x_1, x_2, and $T_1(x)$, $T_2(x)$ respectively where $x = (x_1, x_2)$. The form of the path delay functions $T_1(x)$, $T_2(x)$ is unknown. We assume that $x_1 + x_2 = r$ for some constant r. Suppose that we measure x_1, x_2, $T_1(x)$, $T_2(x)$, then calculate new nominal path flows $\bar{x}_1$, $\bar{x}_2$ using some unspecified algorithm, and then implement them according to the ratio scheme described above.

(a) Argue that the actual path flow vector $\tilde{x} = (\tilde{x}_1, \tilde{x}_2)$ is determined from $\tilde{x}_1 + \tilde{x}_2 = r$ and the relation

$$\frac{\tilde{x}_1 T_1(\tilde{x})}{\bar{x}_1 T_1(x)} = \frac{\tilde{x}_2 T_2(\tilde{x})}{\bar{x}_2 T_2(x)}$$

(b) Assume that T_1 and T_2 are monotonically increasing in the sense that if $z = (z_1, z_2)$, and $z' = (z_1', z_2')$ are such that $z_1 > z_1'$, $z_2 < z_2'$ and $z_1 + z_2 = z_1' + z_2'$ then $T_1(z) > T_1(z')$ and $T_2(z) < T_2(z')$. Show that the path flows $\tilde{x}_1$, $\tilde{x}_2$ of part (a) lie in the interval between x_1 and $\bar{x}_1$, and x_2 and $\bar{x}_2$ respectively.

(c) Consider a convex cost function of the form $\sum_{(i,j)} D_{ij}(F_{ij})$. Under the assumption in (b) show that, if $\bar{x}$ gives a lower cost than x, the same is true for $\tilde{x}$.

6

Flow Control

6.1 INTRODUCTION

In most networks, there are circumstances where the externally offered load is larger than can be handled even with optimal routing. Then, if no measures are taken to restrict the entrance of traffic into the network, queue sizes at bottleneck links will grow indefinitely and eventually exceed the buffer space at the corresponding nodes. When this happens, packets arriving at nodes with no available buffer space will have to be discarded and later retransmitted, thereby wasting communication resources. As a result, a phenomenon similar to a highway traffic jam occurs whereby, as the offered load increases, the actual network throughput decreases while packet delay becomes excessive. It is thus necessary at times to prevent some of the offered traffic from entering the network in order to avoid this type of congestion. This is the function of flow control algorithms.

In this chapter we describe schemes currently used for flow control, explain their advantages and limitations, and discuss potential approaches for their improvement. In the remainder of the section we identify the main objectives of flow control. In section 6.2 we describe window strategies, which are the most popular flow control methods at present. In section 6.3 we describe flow control in some representative networks (ARPANET, TYMNET, SNA, and the Codex network). Section 6.4 is devoted to advanced schemes which aim to improve the performance of window strategies.

Throughout the chapter we emphasize flow control at the network layer. Issues of flow control at the transport layer are discussed in section 6.2.4.

423

6.1.1 Main Objectives of Flow Control

Generally, a flow control issue arises whenever there is a constraint on the communication rate between two points due to limited capacity of the communication lines or the processing hardware. Thus, a flow control scheme may be needed between two users at the transport layer, between a user and an entry point of the subnet (network layer), or between two nodes of the subnet (network layer). We will emphasize flow control issues within the subnet, since flow control in other contexts is in most respects similar and often less complicated than within the subnet.

Our focus will be on two flow control objectives. First, *strike a good compromise between throttling users and keeping average delay per message at a reasonable level.* Second, *maintain fairness for all users in the offered traffic that is prevented from entering the network.* Another objective, dominant in the early days of networking when buffer space was expensive, is the prevention of throughput degradation and deadlock due to buffer overflow. We also consider this objective important and discuss the mechanism of throughput degradation and the means for avoiding deadlock later. However, this objective will be indirectly accomplished by maintaining the average delay per packet (and, therefore, the average queue sizes) at a low level. The primary reason for concentrating on delay rather than buffer overflow is to facilitate analysis and conceptual understanding.

Keeping Delay Small within the Subnet

A small average delay per packet is certainly desirable from a user's point of view. However, it is important to realize that network level flow control does *not necessarily* reduce delay for network users; it simply shifts delay from the network layer to higher layers. That is, by restricting entrance to the subnet, flow control keeps packets waiting outside the subnet rather than in queues inside it. Thus, flow control may not be of much help to the user whose packets are getting through at an excruciatingly slow pace, and, indeed, at times flow control actually increases the delay. Flow control is helpful primarily in that it can prevent a disastrous traffic jam inside the subnet that would make matters worse for many users. The only way to reduce the user's dissatisfaction caused by large delays is to ensure that the need for flow control does not arise often, either by increasing the network's communication resources (line capacities, etc.), or by improving the routing algorithm. Another possibility is, of course, to prevent new users from logging into a nearly congested network, but this is sometimes difficult to implement and causes a different type of dissatisfaction.

The main reason why it is important to keep delay small within the subnet rather than outside it, is to avoid wasting subnet resources in packet retransmissions. These can occur in two ways: first, when queue sizes build up to the point where node buffers become full and incoming packets are discarded; second, when acknowledgements are so slow in returning that the source node mistakenly thinks that some packets have been lost and proceeds to retransmit them. Retransmis-

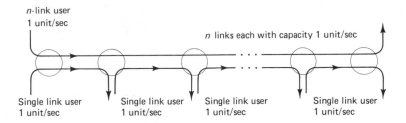

Figure 6.1   Example showing that maximizing throughput may be incompatible with fairness. A maximum throughput of n units/sec can be achieved if the n-link user is shut off completely. Giving equal rates of 1/2 unit/sec to all users achieves a throughput of only $(n+1)/2$ units/sec.

sions waste network resources, effectively reduce network throughput, and cause congestion to spread.

Note, however, that keeping network delay low when offered load is large can only be achieved by lowering network throughput. Thus, there is a natural trade-off between allowing free user access to the network and keeping delay at a level low enough so that retransmissions or other inefficiencies do not degrade network performance. A somewhat oversimplified guideline is that, ideally, flow control should not be exercised at all when network delay is below some critical level, and, under heavy load conditions, should reject as much offered traffic as necessary to keep delay at the critical level. This is, unfortunately, easier said than done, since neither delay nor throughput can be meaningfully represented by single numbers in a flow control context.

Fairness

When offered traffic must be cut back, it is important to do so fairly. This is by no means trivial, since maximizing total network throughput is often incompatible with fairness. For example, consider the situation shown in Fig. 6.1. There are $n+1$ users each offering 1 unit/sec of traffic along a sequence of n links with capacity of 1 unit/sec. One user's traffic goes over all n links while the rest of the traffic goes over only one link. A maximum throughput of n units/sec can be achieved by accepting all the traffic of the single-link users while shutting off the n-link user. However, the egalitarian solution requiring an equal rate of acceptance for all users results in a maximum throughput of $(n+1)/2$ units/sec.

Generally, a compromise is required between fairness and throttling those users that are most responsible for congestion. Note also that there may be several priority classes of users, in which case fairness is meaningful only within a priority class. Finally, it should be mentioned that some of the flow control proposals in the literature are quite defective with respect to fairness. For example, there are schemes that essentially reject traffic from sources at a node if the buffers in that node are too close to being full, but continue to accept traffic sent from other nodes.

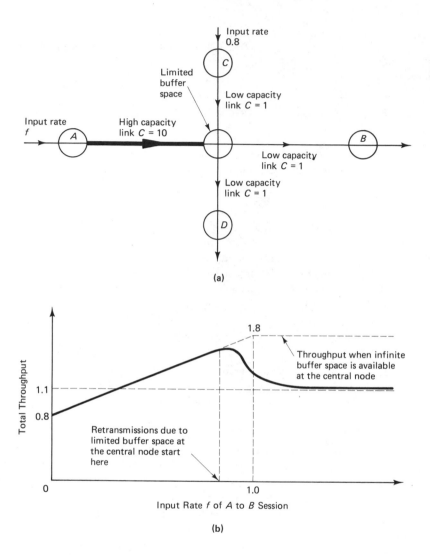

Figure 6.2   Example demonstrating throughput degradation due to
retransmissions caused by buffer overflow. (a) For f approaching unity, the
central node buffer is almost always full, thereby causing retransmissions. Because the A-to-B session uses a line 10 times faster than the C-to-D session,
it has 10 times greater chance of capturing a free buffer and getting a packet
accepted at the central node. As a result, the throughput of the A-to-B session
approaches unity, while the throughput of the C-to-D session approaches 0.1.
(b) Total throughput as a function of the input rate of the A-to-B session.

The trouble here is that if one node is heavily loaded due to traffic coming from some other nodes, then the offending through traffic is not inhibited at all, while the sources connected to the heavily loaded node are shut out entirely.

Buffer Overflow

The term *congestion* is often used to refer to a phenomenon whereby a higher offered load to the network leads to lower throughput and higher delay. Congestion, in this sense, is familiar to everyone from the behavior of highway networks, where traffic jams occur when there are too many cars on the highways. Not only does delay go up, but also the throughput of the highway goes down. This behavior is in marked contrast to the type of queueing model considered in the context of routing, where lower throughput is associated with lower delay. It has already been mentioned that congestion can be caused by buffer overflow. The following example (from [GeK80]) illustrates how this can happen.

Example 1

Consider the five-node network shown in Fig. 6.2(a) with two sessions: one from top to bottom with a Poisson input rate of 0.8, and the other from left to right with a Poisson input rate f. Assume that the central node has a large but finite buffer pool that is shared by the two sessions. If the buffer pool is full, an incoming packet is rejected and then retransmitted by the sending node. For small f, the buffer rarely fills up and the total throughput of the system is $0.8 + f$. When f is close to unity (which is the capacity of the right-most link), the buffer of the central node is almost always full, while the top and left nodes are busy most of the time retransmitting packets trying to capture a buffer space at the central node. Since the left node is transmitting 10 times faster than the top node, the left-to-right throughput will be roughly 10 times larger than the top-to-bottom throughput. The left-to-right throughput will be roughly unity (the capacity of the right-most link), so that the total throughput will be roughly 1.1. This is illustrated in more detail in Fig. 6.2(b), where it can be seen that the total throughput decreases towards 1.1 as the offered load f increases.

This example also illustrates how limited buffer space can lead to unfairness. It is possible for some of the sessions to capture almost all the buffers, and, in effect, prevent other sessions from using the network.

Another difficulty associated with buffer overflow is that a deadlock can occur when two or more nodes are unable to move packets due to unavailable space at all potential receivers. The simplest example of this is two nodes A and B routing packets directly to each other as shown in Fig. 6.3(a). If all the buffers of both A and B are full of packets destined for B and A, respectively, then the nodes are deadlocked into continuously retransmitting the same packets with no success, as there is no space to store the packets at the receiver. This problem can also occur in a more complex manner whereby more than two nodes arranged in a cycle are deadlocked because their buffers are full of packets destined for other nodes in the cycle (see Fig. 6.3(b)). There are simple ways to preclude this type of deadlock

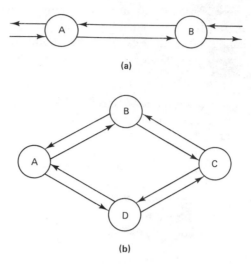

Figure 6.3   Deadlock due to buffer overflow. In (a), all buffers of A and B are full of packets destined for B and A, respectively. As a result, no packet can be accepted at either node. In (b), all buffers of A, B, C, and D are full of packets destined for C, D, A, and B, respectively.

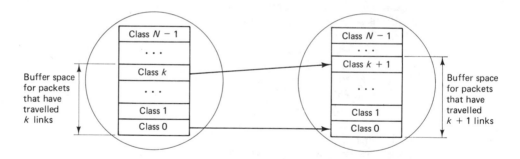

Figure 6.4   Organization of node memory in buffer classes to avoid deadlock due to buffer overflow. A packet that has traveled k links is accepted at a node only if there is an available buffer of class k or lower, where k ranges from 0 to $N - 1$ (where N is the number of nodes). Assuming that packets that travel more than $N - 1$ links are discarded as having traveled in a loop, no deadlock occurs. The proof consists of showing by induction (starting with $k = N - 1$) that at each node the buffers of class k cannot fill up permanently.

by organizing packets in priority levels and allocating extra buffers for packets of higher priority [RaH76] [Gop85]. A typical choice is to assign a level of priority to a packet equal to the number of links it has traversed in the network, as described in Fig. 6.4. If packets are not allowed to loop, it is then possible to show that a deadlock of the type just described cannot occur.

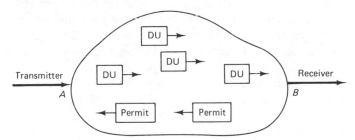

Total number of data units and permits $\leq$ window size W_{AB}

Figure 6.5   Window flow control between a transmitter and a receiver consists of an upper bound W_{AB} on the number of data units and permits in transit inside the network.

Despite the examples above, congestion and buffer overflow are not as fundamental an issue in flow control as delay. With current technology, buffers are inexpensive and networks should be designed so that buffer overflows are rare. To put it in another way, buffers should be large enough that delay becomes objectionable before buffers start to overflow. This point of view is not widely appreciated in the network field, primarily because of the influence of the ARPANET, which was built before buffers became so inexpensive.

6.2 WINDOW FLOW CONTROL

In this section we describe the most frequently used class of flow control methods. In subsections 6.2.1 to 6.2.3, the main emphasis is on flow control within the communication subnet. Flow control outside the subnet is briefly discussed in subsection 6.2.4.

A communication process between a transmitter A and a receiver B is said to be *window flow controlled* if there is an upper bound on the number of data units that have been transmitted by A and are not yet known by A to have been disposed of by B (see Fig. 6.5). The upper bound (a positive integer) is called the *window size* or, simply, the *window*. The receiver B notifies the transmitter A that it has disposed of a data unit by sending a special message to A, which is called a *permit* (other names in the literature are *acknowledgement, allocate message,* etc.). Upon receiving a permit, A is free to send one more data unit to B. Thus, a permit may be viewed as a form of passport that a data unit must obtain before entering the logical communication channel between A and B. The number of permits in use should not exceed the window size.

Permits are either contained in special control packets, or are piggybacked on regular data packets. They can be implemented in a number of ways—see the practical examples of section 6.3, and the following discussion. The communication process being flow controlled can be a single virtual circuit, a group of virtual circuits (for example all virtual circuits using the same path), or the entire packet stream originating at one node and destined for another node. The transmitter and receiver can be for example two nodes of the communication subnet, or a user's machine and the entry node of the communication subnet. Finally, the data units in a window can be messages, packets, or bytes for example.

The general idea in the window strategy is that the input rate of the transmitter is reduced when permits return slowly. Therefore, if there is congestion along the communication path of the process, the attendant large delays of the permits cause a natural slowdown of the transmitter's data rate. However, the window strategy has an additional dimension, whereby the receiver may intentionally delay permits to restrict the transmission rate of the process. For example, the receiver may do that to avoid buffer overflow.

In the subsequent discussion, we consider two strategies, end-to-end and node-by-node windowing. The first strategy refers to flow control between the entry and exit subnet nodes of a communication process, while the second strategy refers to flow control between every pair of successive nodes along a virtual circuit's path.

6.2.1 End-to-End Windows

In the most common version of end-to-end window flow control, the window size is $W \cdot A$, where W and A are some positive numbers. Each time a new batch of A data units is received at the destination node, a permit is sent back to the source allocating a new batch of A data units. In a variation of this scheme, the destination node will send a new A-data unit permit upon reception of just the first of an A-data unit batch (see the SNA pacing scheme description in the next section). To simplify the following exposition, we will henceforth assume that $A = 1$, but our conclusions are valid regardless of the value of A. Also, for concreteness, we talk in terms of packets but the window maintained may consist of other data units such as bytes.

Usually, a numbering scheme for packets and permits is used so that permits can be associated with packets previously transmitted. One possibility is to use a sliding window protocol similar to those used for data link control, whereby a packet contains a sequence number and a "next expected" number. The latter number can serve as one or more permits for flow control purposes (see also the discussion in subsection 2.8.1 in Chapter 2). For example, suppose that node A receives from node B a packet with "next expected" number k. Then, A knows that B has disposed of all packets sent by A and numbered less than k, and, therefore, A is free to send those packets up to number $k + W - 1$ that it has not sent yet, where W is the window size. In such a scheme, both the sequence number and the "next expected" number are represented modulo m, where $m \geq W + 1$, similarly as for the goback n ARQ system (Problem 6.12). In some networks (*e.g.*, the ARPANET and the Codex network—see section 6.3), this scheme is combined with an end-to-end acknowledgement protocol.

To simplify the subsequent presentation, the particular manner in which per-

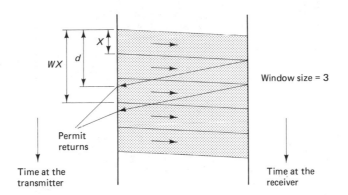

Figure 6.6   Example of full-speed transmission with a window size $W = 3$. The round-trip delay d is less than the time WX required to transmit the full window of W packets.

mits are implemented will be ignored. It will be assumed that the source node simply counts the number x of packets it has transmitted but for which it has not yet received back a permit, and transmits new packets only as long as $x < W$.

Figure 6.6 shows the flow of packets for the case where the round-trip packet/ permit delay d is smaller than the time required to transmit the full window of W packets, *i.e.*,

$$d \leq WX$$

where X is the transmission time of a single packet. (To simplify the following exposition, assume that all packets have equal transmission time and equal round-trip delay.) Then the source is capable of transmitting at the full speed of $1/X$ packets/sec, and flow control is not active.

The case where flow control is active is shown in Fig. 6.7. Here,

$$d > WX$$

and the round-trip delay d is so large that the full allocation of W packets can be transmitted before the first permit returns. Assuming the source always has a packet waiting in queue, the rate of transmission is W/d packets/sec.

If the results of Figs. 6.6 and 6.7 are combined, it is seen that the maximum rate of transmission corresponding to a round-trip delay d is given by

$$r = \min \left\{ \frac{1}{X}, \frac{W}{d} \right\} \tag{6.1}$$

Figure 6.8 illustrates the flow control mechanism; the source transmission rate is reduced in response to congestion and the attendant large delay. Furthermore, the window scheme reacts very fast to congestion—within at most W packets' transmission time. This fast reaction, coupled with low overhead, is the major advantage of window strategies over other (nonwindow) schemes.

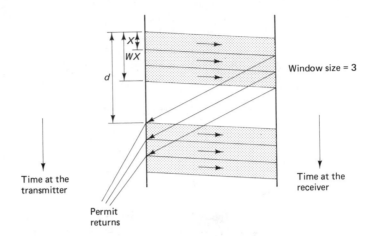

Figure 6.7   Example of delayed transmission with a window size $W = 3$. The round-trip delay d is more than the time WX required to transmit the full window of W packets. As a result, window flow control becomes active, restricting the input rate to W/d.

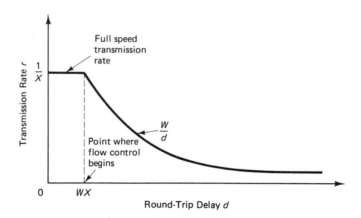

Figure 6.8   Transmission rate vs round-trip delay in a window flow control system. This oversimplified relationship assumes that all packets require equal transmission time at the source, and have equal round trip packet/permit delay.

Limitations of End-to-End Windows

End-to-end windows have some drawbacks that we now discuss. We recall that the two main objectives of flow control were identified as striking a reasonable compromise between low delay and large throughput, and maintaining fairness for all users. It turns out that the end-to-end window strategy (with fixed window size) is not fully satisfactory in either respect.

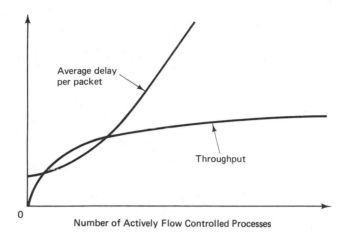

Figure 6.9   Average delay per packet and throughput as a function of the number of actively window flow controlled processes in the network. When the network is heavily loaded, the average delay per packet increases approximately linearly with the number of active processes, while the total throughput stays approximately constant. (This assumes that there are no retransmissions due to buffer overflow and/or large permit delays. In the presence of retransmissions, throughput may decrease as the number of active processes increases.)

Consider first the issue of delay. Suppose that there are n actively flow controlled processes in the network with window sizes $W_1, \ldots, W_n$. Then, the total number of packets in the network is $\sum_{i=1}^{n} \beta_i W_i$, where β_i is a factor between 0 and 1 that depends on the relative magnitude of return delay for the permit. By Little's Theorem, the average delay per packet is given by

$$T = \frac{\sum_{i=1}^{n} \beta_i W_i}{\lambda}$$

where λ is the throughput (total accepted input rate of processes). As the number of actively flow controlled processes increases, the throughput λ is limited by the link capacities and will, therefore, approach a constant. (This constant will depend on the network, the location of sources and destinations, and the routing algorithm.) Therefore, the delay T will roughly increase proportionately to the number of actively flow controlled processes (more accurately their total window size) as shown in Fig. 6.9. Thus, if the maximum number of processes is very large, the end-to-end window scheme may not be able to keep delay at a reasonable level and prevent congestion. The difficulty is that windows throttle users when delays are large, but not quite as much as necessary.

One may consider using small window sizes as a remedy to the problem of very large delays under high load conditions. Unfortunately, there is a limit below which window sizes cannot be reduced without unnecessarily throttling users under light load conditions. Indeed, if a process is using an n-link path with a packet

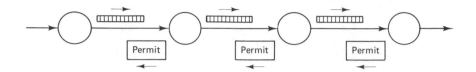

Figure 6.10   The window size must be at least equal to the number of links on the path to achieve full-speed transmission. (Assuming equal transmission time on each link, a packet should be simultaneously transmitted at each link along the path to achieve nonstop transmission.) If permit delay, is comparable to the forward delay the window size should be doubled. If the propagation delay is not negligible, an even larger window size is needed.

transmission time X on each link, the round-trip packet permit delay will be at least nX and considerably more if permits are not given high priority on the return channel. For example, if permits are piggybacked on return packets travelling on the same path in the opposite direction, the return time will be at least nX also. So from Fig. 6.8, we see that full-speed transmission will not be possible for that process even under light load conditions, unless the window size exceeds the number of links n on the path (see Fig. 6.10). For this reason, typically recommended window sizes are between n and $3n$. This recommendation assumes that the transmission time on each link is much larger than the processing and propagation delay. When the propagation delay is much larger than the transmission time, as in satellite links, the appropriate window size is much larger.

What is really needed in end-to-end window flow control to achieve a good delay-throughput trade-off is dynamic adjustment of window sizes. Under light load conditions, windows should be large and allow unimpeded transmission, while under heavy load conditions, windows should shrink somewhat, thereby not allowing delay to become excessive. This is not easy to do systematically, but some possibilities will be examined in section 6.4.

End-to-end windows can also perform poorly with respect to fairness. It was argued earlier that the proper window size of a process should be proportional to the number of links on its path. This means that at a heavily loaded link, long-path processes can have many more packets awaiting transmission than short-path processes, thereby obtaining a proportionately larger throughput. A typical situation is illustrated in Fig. 6.11. Here the windows of all processes accumulate at the heavily loaded link. If packets are transmitted in the order of their arrival, the rate of transmission obtained by each process is roughly proportional to its window size, and this favors the long-path processes.

The fairness properties of end-to-end windows can be improved if flow controlled processes of the same priority class are served via a round robin scheme at each transmission queue. This is typically easy to do when each process is a virtual circuit. In a datagram network, the effectiveness of the round robin scheme depends on whether each packet carries enough indentifying information to allow its association at each node with a particular flow controlled process.

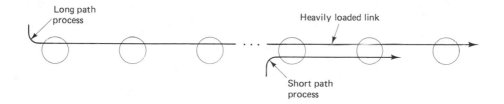

Figure 6.11   End-to-end windows discriminate in favor of long-path processes. It is necessary to give a large window to a long-path process to achieve full-speed transmission. Therefore, a long-path process will typically have more packets waiting at a heavily loaded link than a short-path process, and will receive proportionally larger service (assuming packets are transmitted on a first-come first-serve basis).

6.2.2 Node-by-Node Windows for Virtual Circuits

In this strategy, there is a separate window for every virtual circuit and pair of adjacent nodes along the path of the virtual circuit. Much of the discussion on end-to-end windows applies to this strategy as well. Since here the path along which flow control is exercised is effectively one link long, the size of a window measured in packets is typically two or three for terrestrial links.

Let us focus on a pair of successive nodes along a virtual circuit's path referred to as the transmitter and the receiver. The main idea in the node-by-node scheme is that the receiver can avoid the accumulation of a large number of packets into its memory by slowing down the rate at which it returns permits to the transmitter. In the most common strategy, the receiver maintains a W-packet buffer for each virtual circuit and returns a permit to the transmitter only if it has space to store an extra packet within its W-packet buffer. A packet is considered to have been cleared from the W-packet buffer once it is either delivered to a user outside the subnet or it is entered in the data link control (DLC) unit leading to the subsequent node on the virtual circuit's path.

Consider now the interaction of the windows along three successive nodes ($i - 1$, i, and $i + 1$) on a virtual circuit's path. Suppose that the W-packet buffer of node i is full. Then, node i will send a permit to node $i - 1$ once it delivers an extra packet to the DLC of the $(i, i + 1)$ link, which in turn will occur once a permit sent by node $(i + 1)$ is received at node i. Thus, there is coupling of successive windows along the path of a virtual circuit. In particular, suppose that congestion develops at some link. Then, the W-packet window at the start node of the congested link will fill up for each virtual circuit crossing the link. As a result, the W-packet windows of nodes lying upstream of the congested link will progressively fill up, including the windows of the origin nodes of the virtual circuits crossing the congested link. At that time, these virtual circuits will be actively flow controlled. The phenomenon whereby windows progressively fill up from the point

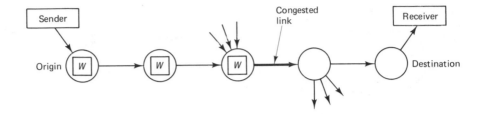

Figure 6.12   Backpressure effect in node-by-node flow control. Each node along a virtual circuit's path can store no more than W packets for that virtual circuit. The window storage space of each successive node lying upstream of the congested link fills up. Eventually the window of the origin node fills at which time transmission stops.

of congestion towards the virtual circuit origins is known as *backpressure* and is illustrated in Fig. 6.12.

One attractive aspect of node-by-node windows can be seen from Fig. 6.12. In the worst case, where congestion develops on the last link (say the nth) of a virtual circuit's path, the total number of packets inside the network for the virtual circuit will be approximately nW. If the virtual circuit were flow controlled via an end-to-end window, the total number of packets inside the network would be roughly comparable. (This assumes a window size of $W = 2$ in the node-by-node case, and of $W \simeq 2n$ in the end-to-end case based on the rule of thumb of using a window size that is twice the number of links of the path between transmitter and receiver.) The important point, however, is that these packets will be uniformly distributed along the virtual circuit's path in the node-by-node case, but will be concentrated at the congested link in the end-to-end case. Because of this the amount of memory required at each node to prevent buffer overflow may be much smaller for node-by-node windows than for end-to-end windows.

Distributing the packets of a virtual circuit uniformly along its path alleviates also the fairness problem, whereby large window processes monopolize a congested link at the expense of small window processes (cf. Fig. 6.11). This is particularly true when the window sizes of all virtual circuits are roughly equal, as, for example, when the circuits involve only terrestial links. A fairness problem, however, may still arise when satellite links are involved. It is necessary to choose a large window size for such links to achieve unimpeded transmission when traffic is light because of the large propagation delay. The difficulty arises at a node serving both virtual circuits with large window size that come over a satellite link and virtual circuits with small window size that come over a terrestrial link (see Fig. 6.13). If these circuits leave the node along the same transmission line, a fairness problem may develop when this line gets heavily loaded. A reasonable way to address this difficulty is to schedule transmissions of packets from different virtual circuits on a round robin basis (with adjustments made to account for different priority classes).

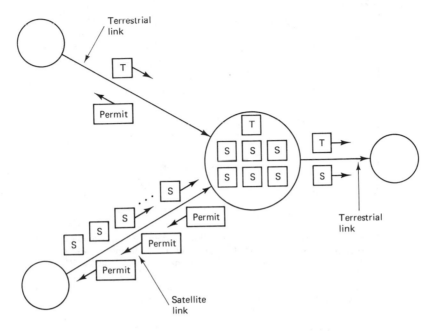

Figure 6.13   A potential fairness problem at a node serving virtual circuits that come over a satellite link (large window) and virtual circuits that come over a terrestrial link (small window). If virtual circuits are served on a first-come first-serve basis, the virtual circuits with large windows will receive better service on a subsequent transmission line. This problem can be alleviated by serving virtual circuits via a round robin scheme.

6.2.3 The Isarithmic Method

The isarithmic method may be viewed as a version of window flow control, whereby there is a single global window for the entire network. The idea here is to limit the total number of packets in the network by having a fixed number of permits circulating in the subnet. A packet enters the subnet, after capturing one of these permits. It then releases the permit at its destination node. The total number of packets in the network is thus limited by the number of permits. This has the desirable effect of placing an upper bound on average packet delay that is independent of the number of sessions in the network. Unfortunately, the issues of fairness and congestion within the network depend on how the permits are distributed which is not addressed by the isarithmic approach. There are no known sensible algorithms to control the location of the permits, and this is the main difficulty in making the scheme practical. There is also another difficulty, namely that permits can be destroyed through various malfunctions and there may be no easy way to keep track of how many permits are circulating in the network.

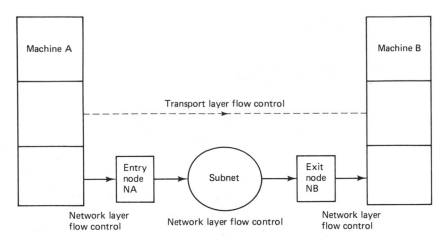

Figure 6.14   User-to-user flow control. A user sends data from machine
A to a user in machine B via the subnet using the entry and exit nodes NA and
NB. There is a conceptual node-by-node network layer flow control system
along the connection A–NA–NB–B. There may also be direct user-to-user
flow control at the transport layer, particularly if several users with different
flow control needs are collectively flow controlled at the network layer.

6.2.4 Window Flow Control at the User Level

Much of what has been described so far about window strategies is applicable to
flow control of a session between two users, either at the network layer or the
transport layer.

Figure 6.14 illustrates a typical situation. A user sends data out of machine
A to an entry node NA of the subnet, which is forwarded to the exit node NB
and is then delivered to machine B. There is (network layer) flow control between
the entry and exit nodes NA and NB (either end-to-end or node-by-node involving
a sequence of nodes). There is also (network layer) window flow control between
machine A and entry node NA, which keeps machine A from swamping node NA
with more data than the latter can handle. Similarly, there is window flow control
between exit node NB and machine B, which keeps NB from overwhelming B
with too much data. Putting the pieces together we see that there is a network
layer flow control system extending from machine A to machine B, which operates
much like the node-by-node window flow control system of subsection 6.2.2. In
essence, we have a three-link path where the subnet between nodes NA and NB is
viewed conceptually as the middle link. A similar situation occurs when two users
communicate across several networks connected through gateways.

It would appear that the system just described would be sufficient for flow
control purposes, and, in many cases, it is. For example, it is the only one provided
in the TYMNET and the Codex network on a virtual circuit basis. There may be a
need, however, for additional flow control at the transport layer, whereby the input

traffic rate of a user at machine A is controlled directly by the receiver at machine B. The reason is that the network layer window flow control from machine A to node NA may apply collectively to multiple user pair sessions. These sessions may, for a variety of reasons, be multiplexed into a single traffic stream, but may have different individual flow control needs. For example, in SNA there is a transport layer flow control algorithm which is the same as the one used in the network layer except that it is applied separately for each session rather than to a group of sessions (see the description given in the next section).

6.3 OVERVIEW OF FLOW CONTROL IN PRACTICE

In this section, the flow control systems of several existing networks are described, including the $X.25$ standard. All of these systems use window strategies of one form or another.

Flow Control in the ARPANET

Flow control in the ARPANET is based on end-to-end windows. The entire packet stream of each pair of machines connected to the subnet (known as *hosts*) is viewed as flowing on a logical pipe. For each such pipe there is a window of eight messages between the corresponding origin and destination subnet nodes. Each message consists of one or more packets up to a maximum of eight. A transmitted message carries a number indicating its position in the corresponding window. The destination node, upon disposing of a message, sends back a special control packet (permit) to the origin, which in the ARPANET is called RFNM (ready for next message). The RFNM is also used as an end-to-end acknowledgement for error control purposes. Upon reception of an RFNM, the origin node frees up a space in the corresponding window and is allowed to transmit an extra message. If an RFNM is not received after a specified time-out, the origin node sends a control packet asking the destination node whether the corresponding message was received. This protects against loss of an RFNM, and provides a mechanism for retransmission of lost messages.

There is an additional mechanism within the subnet for multipacket messages that ensures that there is enough memory space to reassemble these messages at their destination. (Packets in the ARPANET may arrive out of order at their destination.) Each multipacket message must reserve enough buffer space for reassembly at the receiver before it gets transmitted. This is done via a reservation message called REQALL (request for allocation) that is sent by the origin to the destination node. The reservation is granted when the destination node sends an ALL (allocate) message to the origin. When a long file is sent through the network, there is a long sequence of multipacket messages that must be transmitted. It would then be wasteful to obtain a separate reservation for each message. To resolve this problem, ALL messages are piggybacked on the returning RFNMs of multipacket messages, so that there is no reservation delay for messages after the first one in a file. If the reserved buffer space is not used by the origin node within a given time-out, it is returned to the destination via a special message. Single-packet messages do not need a reservation before getting transmitted. If, however, such a message finds the destination's buffers full, it is discarded and a copy is eventually retransmitted by the origin node after obtaining an explicit buffer reservation.

A number of improvements to the ARPANET scheme are scheduled for implementation in late 1986 [Mal86]. First, the window size can be configured up to a maximum of 127; this allows efficient operation in the case where satellite links are used. Second, there can be multiple independent connections (up to 256) between two hosts, each with an independent window; this provides some flexibility in accomodating classes of traffic with different priorities and/or throughput needs. Third, an effort is made to improve the fairness properties of the current algorithm through a scheme that tries to allocate fairly the buffer space available at each node to all hosts. Finally the reservation scheme for multipacket messages described above has been eliminated. Instead the destination node simply reserves space for a multipacket message upon receiving the first packet of the message. If space is not available the packet is discarded and is retransmitted after a time-out by the origin node.

Flow Control in the TYMNET

Flow control in the TYMNET is exercised separately for each virtual circuit via a sequence of node-by-node windows. There is one such window per virtual circuit and link on the path of the virtual circuit. Each window is measured in bytes, and its size varies with the expected peak data rate (or throughput class) of the virtual circuit. Flow control is activated via the backpressure effect discussed in section 6.2.2. Fairness is enhanced by serving virtual circuits on a link via a round robin scheme. This is accomplished by combining groups of bytes from several virtual circuits into data link control frames. The maximum number of bytes for each virtual circuit in a frame depends on the level of congestion on the link and the priority class of the virtual circuit. Flow control permits are piggybacked on data frames, and are highly encoded so that they don't require much bandwidth.

Flow Control in SNA

We recall from section 5.1.2 that the counterpart in SNA of the OSI architecture network layer is called the path control layer, and that it includes a flow control function called virtual route control. The corresponding algorithm, known as the virtual route pacing scheme, is based on an end-to-end window for each virtual circuit (or virtual route in SNA terminology). An interesting aspect of this scheme is that the window size (measured in packets) is dynamically adjusted depending on traffic conditions. The minimum window size is usually equal to the number of links on the path, and the maximum window size is three times as large. Each packet header contains two bits that are set to zero at the source. An intermediate node on the path that is "moderately congested" sets the first bit to 1. If the node is "badly congested", it sets both bits to 1. Otherwise, it does not change the bits. Upon arrival of the packet, the destination looks at the bits and increments the window size for no congestion, decrements the window size for moderate congestion, or sets the window size to the minimum for bad congestion.

Actually, the SNA scheme is a little different than the end-to-end window scheme focused on so far. In the main scheme discussed in subsection 6.2.1, the window size is $W \cdot A$, and returning permits result in allocations of A packets each. We concentrated on the case where $A = 1$. In SNA, however $W = 1$ and A (rather than W) is adjusted between the minimum and maximum window size referred to earlier. Furthermore, the destination node can send a new A-packet allocation message (permit) upon reception of the first packet in an A-packet batch. Thus, full-speed transmission under light load conditions can be maintained even though $W = 1$.

In addition to virtual route control, SNA provides transport layer flow control on a session by session basis, which is known as session level pacing. This becomes necessary because a virtual route in SNA may contain several sessions that may have different flow control needs. The main idea here is to prevent the transmitting end of a session from sending data more quickly than the receiving end can process. Session level pacing is basically a window scheme, whereby the transmitting end can introduce a new packet into the subnet upon receiving a permit (called a pacing response in SNA) from the other end. An interesting twist is that pacing responses can be delayed at the node through which the transmitting end of the session accesses the subnet. This provides the subnet with the means to control the rate at which it accepts data from external users.

Flow Control in the Codex Network

In the Codex network, there is an end-to-end window associated with each virtual circuit. The window size is measured in bytes, and is proportional to the number of links on the virtual circuit path and a nominal data rate for the virtual circuit. Returning permits are combined with end-to-end acknowledgements used for error control purposes so the window scheme does not require additional communication overhead. Data link control (DLC) frames on each link are formed by concatenating groups of bytes from several virtual circuits that have traffic in queue. There is a maximum group size for each virtual circuit. Virtual circuits are served on a round robin basis and this provides a natural mechanism for maintaining fairness.

There is also an additional flow control mechanism in the Codex network that is unrelated to the window scheme but plays a complementary role. The idea is to match the transmission rate of a virtual circuit along its incoming and outgoing links at each node on its path under heavy load conditions. Without going into details (see [HSS86]), this is accomplished by adjusting the maximum number of bytes that a virtual circuit can insert in a DLC frame. As an example, suppose that a virtual circuit is slowed down on a given link due to heavy load. Then, the start node of the link sends a special message to the preceding node along the virtual circuit's path, which proceeds to reduce the maximum number of bytes that a DLC frame can carry for this virtual circuit. One effect of this scheme is that, when congestion develops downstream, the end-to-end window of a virtual circuit will not pile up entirely at the point of congestion, but rather will be spread more or less evenly along the virtual circuit path starting from the source node and ending at the point of congestion. This, combined with large memory space at the nodes, tends to make buffer overflow unlikely.

Flow Control in X.25

As discussed also in subsection 2.8.3, flow control at the X.25 packet level is implemented by means of a separate window for each virtual circuit. The default window size is 2, but it may be set as high as 7 or 127. Flow control is exercised in both directions, *i.e.*, from the user's machine (DTE) to the entry point of the network (DCE), and, reversely, from DCE to DTE. The implementation of the window strategy is reminiscent of DLC protocols. Each data packet contains a three-bit sequence number and a three-bit piggyback number. (If the window size is 127, then these numbers are seven bits long.) The sequence number gives the position of the packet within the sender's window, while the piggyback number is the number of the next packet expected to be received by the sender. Thus, the piggyback number plays the role of a permit allowing the receiver to advance the corresponding window.

There is also a provision in X.25 for flow control between two DTEs communicating through the subnet. The X.25 packet format contains a special bit (called the D bit) that determines whether the piggyback number of a packet received by a DTE relates to the directly attached DCE ($D = 0$), or the remote DTE ($D = 1$). In the latter case, the piggyback number serves as a permit for the advancement of a window maintained for flow control purposes between the two DTEs.

6.4 FLOW CONTROL SCHEMES BASED ON INPUT RATE ADJUSTMENT

We have seen that one of the basic difficulties with window flow control with fixed window sizes is that the average delay per packet increases proportionately to the number of actively flow controlled processes. A remedy would be to reduce window sizes as the number of these processes increases. Unfortunately, it is not easy to find good ways to do this in practice. For this reason, we look at more systematic formulations of the flow control problem, whereby the input rates of flow controlled processes are adjusted directly in response to traffic conditions inside the network.

In the first approach considered (subsection 6.4.1), we formulate an optimization problem that mathematically expresses the first objective of flow control—striking a proper balance between maintaining high throughput and keeping average delay per packet at a reasonable level. In the second approach (subsection 6.4.2), we emphasize fairness while maintaining average delay per packet at an acceptable level.

The algorithms to be developed provide an appropriate level of input rate for each process. The practical implementation of these input rates is not always easy, particularly when dealing with rapid variations in offered load. In subsection 6.4.3, we will discuss how to implement input rates using window schemes. The window sizes will be adjustable, depending on level of congestion inside the network, thereby alleviating the major limitation of fixed window size flow control.

6.4.1 Combined Optimal Routing and Flow Control

We consider the possibility of combining routing and end-to-end flow control within the subnet by adjusting optimally *both* the routing variables and the origin-destination (OD) pair input rates. A special case arises when routing is fixed and the only variables to be adjusted are the input rates—a problem of pure flow control.

We adopt a flow model similar to the one discussed in the context of optimal routing in section 5.4. We denote by r_w the input rate of an OD pair w. In some cases, r_w may be measured in bits/sec, and then its optimal value may be viewed as a target value for rate averaged over a reasonably long interval of time, *e.g.*, transmit no more than $r_w T$ bits over a time interval of length T. If r_w is measured in terms of virtual circuits, then its optimal value can be viewed as a target that the origin node strives to achieve by blocking or allowing new requests generated from external sites. Similarly, in integrated voice and data networks, r_w can be related to the rate of encoding of digitized voice, and can be directly adjusted at the origin nodes. In what follows we first concentrate on formulating a problem of adjusting routing variables together with the inputs r_w so as to minimize some "reasonable" cost function. We subsequently show that *this problem is mathematically equivalent to the optimal routing problem examined in the previous chapter (r_w is fixed)*, and, therefore, the optimality conditions and algorithms given there are applicable.

If we minimize the cost function $\sum_{(i,j)} D_{ij}(F_{ij})$ of the routing problem with respect to both the path flows $\{x_p\}$ and the inputs $\{r_w\}$, we unhappily find that the optimal solution is $x_p = 0$ and $r_w = 0$ for all p and w. This indicates that the cost function should include a penalty for inputs r_w becoming too small and leads to the problem

$$\text{minimize} \sum_{(i,j)} D_{ij}(F_{ij}) + \sum_{w \in W} e_w(r_w)$$

$$\text{subject to} \sum_{p \in P_w} x_p = r_w, \quad \text{for all } w \epsilon W$$

$$x_p \geq 0, \quad \text{for all } p \epsilon P_w, \ w \epsilon W$$

$$0 \leq r_w \leq \bar{r}_w, \quad \text{for all } w \epsilon W$$

(6.2)

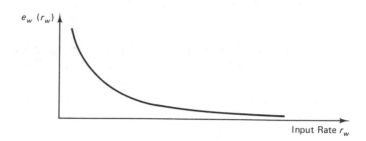

Figure 6.15   Typical form of penalty function for throttling the input rate r_w.

Here the minimization is to be carried out jointly with respect to $\{x_p\}$ and $\{r_w\}$. The given values $\bar{r}_w$ represent the desired input by OD pair w, *i.e.*, the offered load for w, defined as the input for w that would result if no flow control was exercised. As before, F_{ij} is the total flow on link (i,j), *i.e.*, the sum of all path flows traversing the link. The functions e_w are of the form shown in Fig. 6.15 and provide a penalty for throttling the inputs r_w. They are convex, monotonically decreasing on the set of positive numbers $(0,\infty)$, and tend to ∞ as r_w tends to zero. We assume that their first and second derivatives, e'_w and e''_w, exist on $(0,\infty)$ and are strictly negative and positive, respectively. An interesting class of functions e_w is specified by the following formula for their first derivative

$$e'_w(r_w) = -\left(\frac{a_w}{r_w}\right)^{b_w}, \qquad \text{for } a_w \text{ and } b_w \text{ given positive constants} \qquad (6.3)$$

As will be explained later in this section, the parameters a_w and b_w influence the optimal magnitude of input r_w and the priority of OD pair w, respectively.

The value of the preceding formulation is enhanced if we adopt a broader view of w and consider it as *a class of users sharing the same set of paths P_w*. This allows different priorities (*i.e.*, different functions e_w) for different classes of users even if they share the same paths. A problem where P_w consists of a single path for each w, can also be considered. This is a problem of pure flow control, namely choosing the optimal fraction of the desired input flow of each user class that should be allowed into the network.

We now show that the combined routing and flow control problem of Eq. (6.2) is mathematically equivalent to a routing problem of the type considered in section 5.4. Let us introduce a new variable y_w for each $w \in W$ via the equation

$$y_w = \bar{r}_w - r_w \qquad (6.4)$$

We may view y_w as the *overflow* (the portion of $\bar{r}_w$ blocked out of the network), and consider it as a flow on an *overflow link* directly connecting the origin and destination nodes of w as shown in Fig. 6.16. If we define a new function E_w by

$$E_w(y_w) = e_w(\bar{r}_w - y_w) \qquad (6.5)$$

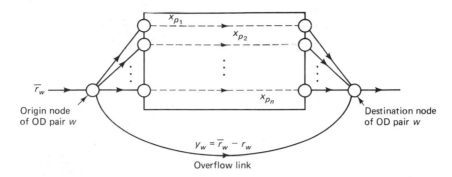

Figure 6.16   Mathematical equivalence of the flow control problem with an optimal routing problem based on the introduction of an artificial overflow link for each OD pair w. The overflow link carries the rejected traffic, *i.e.*, the difference between desired and accepted input flow, $\bar{r}_w - r_w$. The cost of the overflow link is obtained from the cost e_w for throttling the input by a change of variable.

the problem of Eq. (6.2) becomes, in view of Eq. (6.4),

$$\text{minimize} \sum_{(i,j)} D_{ij}(F_{ij}) + \sum_{w \in W} E_w(y_w) \tag{6.6}$$

$$\text{subject to} \sum_{p \in P_w} x_p + y_w = \bar{r}_w, \quad \text{for all } w \in W$$

$$x_p \geq 0, \quad \text{for all } p \in P_w, \, w \in W$$

$$y_w \geq 0, \quad \text{for all } w \in W$$

The form of the function E_w of Eq. (6.4) is shown in Fig. 6.17. If $e_w(r_w) \to \infty$ as $r_w \to 0$ (*i.e.*, there is "infinite penalty" for completely shutting off the class of users w), then $E_w(y_w) \to \infty$ as the overflow y_w approaches its maximum value— the maximum input $\bar{r}_w$. *E_w may be viewed as a "delay" function for the overflow link, and $\bar{r}_w$ may be viewed as the "capacity" of the link.*

It is now clear that the problem of Eq. (6.6) is of the type considered in section 5.4, and that the algorithms and optimality conditions given in sections 5.5 through 5.7 apply. In particular, the application of the shortest path optimality condition of section 5.5 yields the following result:

A feasible set of path flows $\{x_p^*\}$ and inputs $\{r_w^*\}$ is optimal for the problem of Eq. (6.2) if and only if the following conditions hold for each $p \in P_w$ and $w \in W$:

$$x_p^* > 0 \quad \text{only if} \quad d_p^* \leq d_{p'}^*, \text{ for all } p' \in P_w, \text{ and } d_p^* \leq -e_w'(r_w^*) \tag{6.7a}$$

$$r_w^* < \bar{r}_w \quad \text{only if} \quad -e_w'(r_w^*) \leq d_p^*, \text{ for all } p \in P_w \tag{6.7b}$$

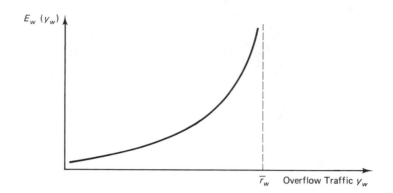

Figure 6.17   Cost function for the overflow link. The cost $E_w(y_w)$ for overflow traffic y_w equals the cost $e_w(r_w)$ for input traffic $r_w = \bar{r}_w - y_w$.

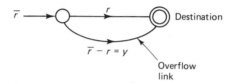

Figure 6.18   Example problem involving an origin and a destination connected by a single link.

where d_p^* is the first derivative length of path p $[d_p^* = \sum_{(i,j)\epsilon p} D_{ij}'(F_{ij}^*)$, and F_{ij}^* is the total flow of link (i,j) corresponding to $\{x_p^*\}]$.

Note that the optimality conditions (6.7) depend only on the derivatives of the functions D_{ij} and e_w. This means that arbitrary constants could be added to D_{ij} and e_w without affecting the optimum. Note also from Eq. (6.7b) that the optimum point r_w^* is independent of $\bar{r}_w$ as long as $\bar{r}_w > r_w^*$. This is a desirable feature for a flow control strategy, preventing users who are being actively flow controlled from attempting to increase their share of the resources by increasing their demands. A simple example illustrates the optimality conditions (6.7).

Example 2

Consider the situation in Fig. 6.18 involving a single link connecting origin and destination. The cost function is

$$\frac{r}{C-r} + \frac{a}{r}$$

where the first term represents a penalty due to large delay [cf. the term $D_{ij}(F_{ij})$ in Eq. (6.2)], and the second term represents a penalty for small throughput [cf. the term $e_w(r_w)$ in *Eq.* (6.2)]. The constant C is the capacity of the link, while the parameter a is a positive weighting factor. The equivalent routing problem [cf. problem of Eq. (6.6)] is

$$\text{minimize } \frac{r}{C-r} + \frac{a}{\bar{r}-y}$$

$$\text{subject to } r + y = \bar{r}, \qquad r \geq 0, \ y \geq 0$$

where $y = \bar{r} - r$ represents the amount of offered load rejected by flow control (equivalently, the flow on the fictitious overflow link). The conditions (6.7) show that there will be no flow control $(y = 0, r = \bar{r})$ if

$$\frac{C}{(C-\bar{r})^2} < \frac{a}{\bar{r}^2}$$

i.e., if the first derivative length of the overflow link exceeds the first derivative length of the regular link. Equivalently, there will be no flow control if

$$\bar{r} < C \frac{\sqrt{a}}{\sqrt{a} + \sqrt{C}}$$

According to Eq. (6.7), when there is flow control $(y > 0, \ r < \bar{r})$, the two first derivative lengths must be equal, *i.e.*,

$$\frac{C}{(C-r)^2} = \frac{a}{(\bar{r}-y)^2}$$

Substituting $y = \bar{r} - r$ and working out the result,

$$r = C \frac{\sqrt{a}}{\sqrt{a} + \sqrt{C}}$$

The solution as a function of offered load is shown in Fig. 6.19. Note that the throughput is independent of the offered load beyond a certain point as discussed earlier. The maximum throughput $C\sqrt{a}/(\sqrt{a} + \sqrt{C})$ can be regulated by adjustment of the parameter a and tends to the capacity C as $a \to \infty$.

The meaning of the parameters a_w and b_w in the cost function specified by the formula [cf. Eq. (6.3)]

$$e'_w(r_w) = -(a_w/r_w)^{b_w}$$

can now be clarified in the light of the optimality conditions (6.7b). Consider two distinct classes of users, w_1 and w_2, sharing the same paths $(P_{w_1} = P_{w_2})$. Then, the conditions (6.7b) imply that at an optimal solution in which both classes of users are throttled $(r^*_{w_1} < \bar{r}_{w_1}, \ r^*_{w_2} < \bar{r}_{w_2})$

$$-e'_{w_1}(r^*_{w_1}) = -e'_{w_2}(r^*_{w_2}) = \min_{p \in P_{w_1}} \{d^*_p\} = \min_{p \in P_{w_2}} \{d^*_p\} \qquad (6.8)$$

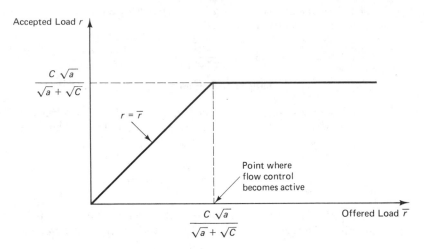

Figure 6.19   Optimal accepted load as a function of offered load in the flow control example. Flow control becomes active when the offered load exceeds a threshold level that depends on the weighting factor a.

If e'_{w_1} and e'_{w_2} are specified by parameters a_{w_1}, b_{w_1} and a_{w_2}, b_{w_2} as in Eq. (6.3), it can be seen that:

a) If $b_{w_1} = b_{w_2}$ then

$$\frac{r^*_{w_1}}{r^*_{w_2}} = \frac{a_{w_1}}{a_{w_2}}$$

and it follows that the parameter a_w influences the optimal, relative input rate of the user class w.

b) If $a_{w_1} = a_{w_2} = a$ and $b_{w_1} < b_{w_2}$ (see Fig. 6.20), then the condition (6.8) specifies that when the input flows must be made small ($r^*_{w_1}, r^*_{w_2} < a$), the user class w_2 (the one with higher parameter b_w) will be allowed a larger input. It follows that the parameter b_w influences the relative priority of the user class w under heavy load conditions.

6.4.2 Max-Min Flow Control

One of the most difficult aspects of flow control is that of treating all users fairly when it is necessary to turn traffic away from the network. Fairness can be defined in a number of different ways, but our intuitive notion of fairness, is that any user is entitled to as much network use as any other user. Figure 6.21 clarifies some of the ambiguities in this notion. One session flows through the tandem connection of all arcs, and each other session goes through only one arc. It is plausible to limit sessions 0,1, and 2 to a rate of 1/2 each, since this gives each of these sessions as much rate as the others. It would be rather pointless, however, to restrict session 3 to a rate of 1/2. Session 3 might better be limited to 5/2, since any lower limit

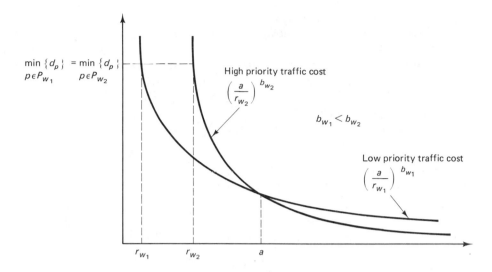

Figure 6.20   Incorporating priorities of user classes in the cost function of the flow control formulation. The user class with larger b_w will be throttled less under heavy load conditions.

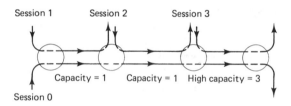

Figure 6.21   The fair solution is to give to sessions 0, 1, and 2 a rate of $1/2$ each and to give session 3 a rate of $5/2$ to avoid wasting the extra capacity available at the right-most link.

would waste some of the capacity of the right-most link, and any higher limit would be unfair because it would further restrict session 0.

This example leads to the idea of maximizing the network use allocated to the users with the minimum allocation, thus giving rise to the term *max-min flow control*. After these most poorly treated users are given the greatest possible allocation, there might be considerable latitude left for choosing allocations for the other users. Again, it is reasonable to maximize the allocation for the most poorly treated of these users, and so forth, until all allocations are specified. An alternative way to express this intuition, which turns out to be equivalent to the above, is to maximize the allocation of each user i subject to the constraint that an incremental increase in i's allocation does not cause a decrease of some other user's allocation that is already as small as i's or smaller.

Before defining these max-min allocations more precisely, we specify our model

more carefully. We assume a directed graph $G = (\mathcal{N}, \mathcal{A})$ for the network and a set
of sessions P using the network. Each session p has a fixed path in the network
associated with it, and p is used both to refer to the session and to its path (if
several sessions use the same path, then several indices p refer to the same path).
Thus, in our model we assume a fixed, single-path routing method.

The allocated rate for session p is denoted by r_p, and the allocated flow on
arc a of the network is then

$$F_a = \sum_{p \in P} \delta_p(a) r_p \qquad (6.9)$$

where $\delta_p(a)$ is 1 if a is on path p and is 0 otherwise. Letting C_a be the capacity of
arc a, we have the following constraints on the vector r of allocated rates:

$$r_p \geq 0, \quad \text{for all } p \in P \qquad (6.10a)$$

$$F_a \leq C_a, \quad \text{for all } a \in \mathcal{A} \qquad (6.10b)$$

The problem then is to find a vector of allocated rates that is feasible (*i.e.*,
satisfies Eq. (6.10)) and that is fair in the max-min sense above. Max-min fairness
can now be defined:

A vector of rates r is *max-min fair* if it satisfies Eq. (6.10) and, for each $p \in P$,
r_p cannot be increased (while maintaining Eq. (6.10))without decreasing $r_{p'}$
for some session p' for which $r_{p'} \leq r_p$. More formally still, r is max-min fair if
r satisfies (6.10) and for each $\bar{r}$ satisfying (6.10) and for each $p \in P$, if $r_p < \bar{r}_p$,
then for some p', $r_p \geq r_{p'}$ and $r_{p'} > \bar{r}_{p'}$.

An important property of any max-min fair rate vector is the following: for
each session p, there is some arc a on path p (called p's *bottleneck arc*) such that,
first, $F_a = C_a$, and, second, r_p is at least as large as the rate of any other session
using that bottleneck arc. To see this, note that if there were no such arc, then r_p
could be incrementally increased without decreasing the rate of any other session
p' with $r_{p'} \leq r_p$, thus contradicting the assumption that r was max-min fair. Also
note that if the above property is satisfied for all sessions for some rate vector r,
then r must be max-min fair. To see this, observe that if any r_p is increased, then
at least one session on p's bottleneck arc must have its flow decreased. Figure 6.22
provides an example of a max-min fair rate vector and illustrates the concept of a
bottleneck arc.

Next, a simple algorithm for computing max-min fair rate vectors is given.
The idea of the algorithm is to start with an all-zero rate vector and to increase
the rates on all paths together until $F_a = C_a$ for one or more arcs a. At this point,
each session using a saturated arc (*i.e.*, an arc with $F_a = C_a$) has the same rate at
every other session using that arc. Thus, these saturated arcs serve as bottleneck
arcs for all sessions using them.

At the next step of the algorithm, all sessions not using these saturated arcs
are incremented equally in rate until one or more new arcs become saturated. Note
that some sessions using the previously saturated arcs might also be using these
newly saturated arcs, but all other sessions using these newly saturated arcs will

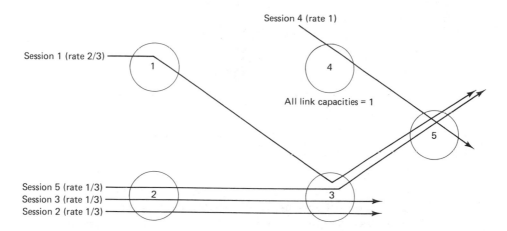

Figure 6.22   Max-min fair solution for an example network. The
bottleneck arcs of sessions 1, 2, 3, 4, and 5 are (3,5), (2,3), (2,3), (4,5), and
(2,3), respectively. Arc (3,5) is not a bottleneck arc for session 5 since sessions
1 and 5 share this arc and session 1 has a larger rate than session 5. Arc (1,3)
is not a bottleneck arc of any session since it has an excess capacity of 1/3 in
the fair solution.

have the same rate; these newly saturated arcs thus serve as bottleneck arcs for
those sessions not using the previously saturated arcs. The algorithm continues
from step to step, always equally incrementing all sessions not passing through
any saturated arc; when all sessions pass through at least one saturated arc, the
algorithm stops.

In the algorithm, as stated more precisely below, A^k denotes the set of arcs
not saturated at the beginning of step k. Similarly, P^k denotes the set of sessions
not passing through any saturated arc at the beginning of step k. Also n_a^k denotes
the number of sessions using arc a that are in P^k. Note that this is the number of
sessions that will share arc a's yet unused capacity. Finally $\tilde{r}^k$ is the increment of
rate added to all of the sessions in P^k during the kth step.

Initial conditions: $k = 1, F_a^0 = 0,\ r_p^0 = 0, P^1 = P$, and $A^1 = A$.

1. $\quad n_a^k := $ number of paths $p \epsilon P^k$ with $\delta_p(a) = 1$

2. $\quad \tilde{r}^k := \min_{a \epsilon A^k}(C_a - F_a^{k-1})/n_a^k$

3. $\quad r_p^k := \begin{cases} r_p^{k-1} + \tilde{r}^k, & \text{for } p \epsilon P^k \\ r_p^{k-1} & \text{otherwise} \end{cases}$

4. $F_a^k := \sum_{a \in A} \delta_p(a) r_p^k$

5. $A^{k+1} := \{a | C_a - F_a^k > 0\}$

6. $P^{k+1} := \{p | \delta_p(a) = 0, \text{ for all } a \notin A^{k+1}\}$

7. $k := k + 1$

8.   If P^k is empty, then stop; else go to 1.

At each step k, an equal increment of rate is added to all sessions not yet passing through a saturated arc, and, thus, at each step k, all sessions in P^k have the same rate. All sessions in P^k passing through an arc that saturates in step k have at least as great a rate as any other session on that arc, and, hence, are bottlenecked by that arc. Thus, it should be clear that a max-min fair rate vector results.

Example 3

Consider the problem of max-min fair allocation for the five sessions and the network shown in Fig. 6.22. All arcs have a capacity of one.

Step 1: All sessions get a rate of $1/3$. Arc (2,3) is saturated at this step, and the rate of the three sessions (2, 3, and 5) that go through it is fixed at $1/3$.

Step 2: Sessions 1 and 4 get an additional rate increment of $1/3$ for a total of $2/3$. Arc (3,5) is saturated, and the rate of session 1 is fixed at $2/3$.

Step 3: Session 4 gets an additional rate increment of $1/3$ for a total of 1. Arc (4,5) is saturated, and the rate of session 4 is fixed at 1. Since now all sessions go through at least one saturated arc, the algorithm terminates with the max-min fair solution shown in Fig. 6.22.

Several generalizations can be made to the basic approach described above. First, to keep the flow on each arc strictly below capacity, we can replace C_a in the algorithm with some fixed fraction of C_a. Next, consider ways to assign different priorities to different kinds of traffic and to make these priorities sensitive to traffic levels. If $b_p(r_p)$ is an increasing function representing the priority of p at rate r_p, then the max-min fairness criterion can be modified as follows: for each p, maximize r_p subject to the constraint that any increase in r_p would cause a decrease of r_p, for some p' satisfying $b_{p'}(r_{p'}) \leq b_p(r_p)$. It is easy to modify the algorithm above to calculate fair rates with such priorities. Another twist on the same theme is to require that each r_p be upper bounded by $C_a - F_a$ on each arc used by path p. The rationale here is to maintain enough spare capacity on each arc to be able to add an extra session. The problem here, however, is that as the number of sessions on an arc grow, the reserve capacity shrinks to zero and the buffer requirement grows with the number of sessions, just like the corresponding growth using windows. This difficulty can be bypassed by replacing the constraint $r_p \leq C_a - F_a$ by a constraint of the form $r_p \leq (C_a - F_a)q_a$, where q_a is a positive scalar factor depending on the number of sessions crossing arc a (see Problem 6.16).

There has been a great deal of work on distributed algorithms that dynamically adjust the session rates to maintain max-min fairness as the sessions change. A representative algorithm [Hay81] will help in understanding the situation. In this algorithm, v_a^k represents an estimate of the maximum allowable session rate on arc a at the kth iteration, F_a^k is the allocated flow on arc a corresponding to the rates r_p^k, and n_a is the number of sessions using arc a. The typical iteration of the algorithm is:

$$v_a^{k+1} = v_a^k + \left(C_a - F_a^k\right)/n_a$$
$$r_p^{k+1} = \min_{\substack{\text{arcs } a \text{ on} \\ \text{path } p}} v_a^{k+1}$$

Each iteration can be implemented in a distributed way by first passing the values v_a^{k+1} from the arcs a to the sessions using those arcs, and then passing the values r_p^{k+1} from the sessions p to the arcs used by these sessions. The major problem is that the allocated rates can wander considerably before converging, and arc flows can exceed capacity temporarily. There are other algorithms that do not suffer from this latter difficulty ([GaB84b] and [Mos84]).

Recently, another approach to implementing max-min fair rates has been explored that avoids both the problem of communication in a distributed algorithm and also the problem of the ambiguity in the meaning of rate for interactive traffic [HaG86]. The idea is very simple: serve different sessions on each arc in the network on a round robin basis. This means that *if* a session always has a packet waiting at a node when its turn comes up on the outgoing arc, then that session gets as much service as any other session using that arc. Thus, to achieve max-min fairness, it is only necessary that each session always has a packet waiting at its bottleneck arc. It can be shown, in fact, that by using node-by-node windowing with a large enough window, a session that always has something to send will always have a packet waiting at its bottleneck arc (see [HaG86] and [Hah86]).

6.4.3 Implementation of Input Rates in a Dynamic Environment

The major difficulty with flow control approaches based on input rate adjustment is that they cannot cope well with rapid changes of the offered load of various sessions. A strict implementation of a session rate of r packets/sec would be to admit 1 packet each $1/r$ seconds. This, however, amounts to a form of time-division multiplexing and tends to introduce intolerable delays when the offered load of the sessions is bursty. A more appropriate implementation is to admit as many as N packets ($N > 1$) every N/r seconds. This allows a burst of as many as N packets into the network without delay, and is better suited for a dynamically changing load. There are several variations of this scheme, including the following that is patterned after window flow control.

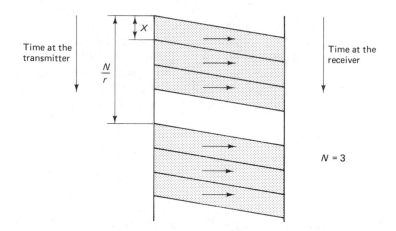

Figure 6.23   Time window flow control with $N = 3$. The count of packet allocation is decremented when a packet is transmitted and incremented N/r seconds later.

An allocation of N packets (a window) is given to each session, and a count x of the unused portion of this allocation is kept at the session origin. Packets from the session are admitted into the network as long as $x > 0$. Each time a packet is admitted, the count is decremented by 1, and N/r secs later (r is the rate assigned to the session), the count is incremented by 1 as shown in Fig. 6.23. This scheme, called *time window flow control*, is very similar to window flow control with window size N except that the count is restored N/r secs after admitting a packet instead of after a round-trip delay when the corresponding permit returns. (Another possibility is to allocate N packets initially to a session, and subsequently restore the count back to N every $1/r$ secs, whether the session used any part of the allocation or not.) Thus, this scheme relies on some flow control algorithm to determine the rate r and, implicitly, the interval at which the count is restored after admission of a packet, while in ordinary window flow control, this interval is determined by the prevailing traffic conditions along the session path. It is evident that ordinary window flow control reacts faster to congestion and, therefore, is better suited for an environment where offered load changes rapidly. In other cases, direct rate adjustment with a scheme such as the one described above offers the advantage of more accurate control of delay and/or fairness with respect to throughput.

An alternative to trying to adjust a session input rate directly is to try to *determine an end-to-end window size that will lead to the desired rate*. In such a scheme, desired input rates are calculated through some algorithm (such as the ones given earlier), and they are implemented via end-to-end windows with appropriate size. The simplest possibility is to calculate a window size W for a session by means of the relation (cf. Little's Theorem)

$$W = rd \qquad (6.11)$$

where
  r: The desired input rate (in packets/sec) for the session (as calculated by some algorithm).

  d: The estimated, average round-trip delay per packet for the session.

One difficulty with this scheme is that the round-trip delay d in Eq. (6.11) is not known at the time the new window size W is calculated. Therefore, one must estimate d in some way—for example, through historical measurements, analysis, or both. Despite this difficulty, schemes of this type are likely to work well in practice as evidenced by simulations reported in [ThC86].

6.5 SUMMARY

In this chapter we identified the major flow control objectives as keeping average delay relatively low within the subnet, and treating users fairly. We reviewed the major flow control methods, and we saw that the dominant strategies in practice are based on windows. There are good reasons for this since window strategies combine low overhead with fast reaction to congestion. However window strategies can also have major limitations, particularly when implemented with fixed window size. We described two input rate adjustment schemes that attempt to rectify these limitations. The first scheme extends the optimal routing methodology of Chapter 5 to the flow control context, and combines routing and flow control into a single algorithm. The second scheme assumes fixed, single-path routing for each session, and focuses on maintaining flow control fairness.

6.6 NOTES, SOURCES, AND SUGGESTED READING

Section 6.1.   Extensive discussions of flow control can be found in the April 1981 special issue of the *IEEE Transactions on Communications*. An informative survey is [GeK80].

Section 6.2.   The special difficulties of window flow control along satellite links are discussed in [GrB83].

Section 6.3.   Flow control in the ARPANET is described in several sources, *e.g.* [Kle76] and [KlO77]. The TYMNET flow control system is discussed in [Tym81].

For further discussion on SNA, see [Ahu79] and [GeY82], and for more on the Codex network, see [HSS86].

Section 6.4. The combined optimal routing and flow control was formulated in [GaG80] and [Gol80]. For additional material on this subject, see [Ibe81] and [Gaf82]. A simulation together with a discussion of practical implementation schemes is given in [ThC86]. Flow control based on adjusting the rate of encoding of digitized voice has been considered in [BGS80]. The material on fair flow control is based on [Hay81]. For related work, see [Jaf81], [GaB84b], [Mos84], [Hah86], and [HaG86].

PROBLEMS

6.1 Consider a window flow controlled virtual circuit going over a satellite link. All packets have a transmission time of 5 msecs. The round-trip processing and propagation delay is 0.5 secs. Find a lower bound on the window size for the virtual circuit to be able to achieve maximum speed transmission when there is no other traffic on the link.

6.2 Suppose that the virtual circuit in Problem 6.1 goes through a terrestrial link in addition to the satellite link. The transmission time on the terrestrial link is 20 msecs, and the processing and propagation delay is negligible. What is the maximum transmission rate in packets/sec that can be attained for this virtual circuit assuming no flow control? Find a lower bound to an end-to-end window size that will allow maximum transmission rate assuming no other traffic on the links. Does it make a difference whether the terrestrial link is before or after the satellite link?

6.3 Suppose that node-by-node windows are used in the two-link system of Problem 6.2. Find lower bounds on the window size required along each link in order to achieve maximum speed transmission, assuming no other traffic on the links.

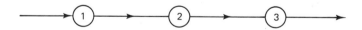

Figure 6.24

6.4 The three-node network of Fig. 6.24 contains only one virtual circuit from node 1 to 3, and uses node-by-node windows. Each packet transmission on link (1,2) takes one sec, and on link (2,3) takes two secs; processing and propagation delay is negligible. Permits require one sec to travel on each link. There is an inexhaustible supply of packets at node 1. The system starts at time 0 with W permits at node 1, W permits at node 2, and no packets stored at nodes 2 and 3. For $W = 1$, find the times, from 0 to 10 secs at which a packet transmission starts at node 1 and node 2. Repeat for $W = 2$.

6.5 In the discussion of node-by-node window flow control, it was assumed that node i can send a permit back to its predecessor $(i - 1)$ once it releases a packet to the DLC of link $(i, i + 1)$. The alternative is for node i to send the permit when it receives the DLC acknowledgement that the packet has been correctly received at node $i + 1$. Discuss the relative merits of the two schemes. Which scheme requires more memory? What happens when link $(i, i + 1)$ is a satellite link?

6.6 A recently proposed alternative approach to flow control operates as follows. For each origin-destination pair (i, j) in the network, there is an associated Poisson process of rate λ_{ij} that delivers permits for pair (i, j) to node i. These permits are queued in a limited size queue for the (i, j) pair (say, with room for W permits). When a packet for j arrives from outside the network at i, a permit is removed from the queue and the packet enters the network; if the queue of permits is empty, the packet is not accepted into the network. If a permit for (i, j) arrives and the queue is full, the permit is thrown away. Discuss the drawbacks of this scheme.

6.7 Consider a combined optimal routing and flow control problem involving the network of Fig. 6.25 (cf. subsection 6.4.1).

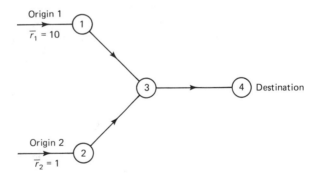

Figure 6.25

The cost function is

$$(F_{13})^2 + (F_{23})^2 + (F_{34})^2 + a/r_1 + a/r_2$$

where a is a positive scalar parameter. Find the optimal values of the rates r_1 and r_2 for each value of a.

6.8 Consider six nodes arranged in a ring and connected with unit capacity bidirectional links $(i, i + 1)$, $i = 1, 2, 3, 4, 5$, and $(6,1)$. There are two sessions from nodes 1, 2, 3, 4, and 5 to node 6, one in the clockwise, and one in the counterclockwise direction. Similarly, there are two sessions form nodes 2, 3, and 4 to node 5, and two sessions from node 3 to node 4. Find the max-min fair rates for these sessions.

6.9 Suppose the definition of a fair rate vector of subsection 6.4.2 is modified so that, in addition to Eq. (6.10), there is an additional constraint $r_p \leq b_p$ that the rate of a session p must satisfy. Here, b_p is the maximum rate at which session p is capable of transmitting. Modify the algorithm given in subsection 6.4.2 to solve this problem. Find the fair rates for the example given in this section when $b_p = 1$, for $p = 2, 4, 5$ and $b_p = 1/4$, for $p = 1, 3$. *Hint:* Add a new link for each session.

6.10 The purpose of this problem is to illustrate how the relative throughputs of competing sessions can be affected by the priority rule used to serve them. Consider two sessions A and B sharing the first link L of their paths as shown in Fig. 6.26. Each session has an end-to-end window of two packets. Permits for packets of A and B arrive d_A and d_B secs, respectively, after the end of transmission on link L. We assume that d_A is exponentially distributed with mean of unity, while (somewhat unrealistically) we assume that $d_B = 0$. Packets require a transmission time on L which is exponentially distributed with mean of unity. Packet transmission times, and permit delays are all independent. We assume that a new packet for A (B) enters the transmission queue of L immediately upon receipt of a permit for A (B).

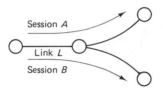

Figure 6.26

a) Suppose that packets are transmitted on L on a first-come first-serve basis. Argue that the queue of L can be represented by a Markov chain with the 10 queue states BB, BBA, BAB, ABB, BBAA, BABA, BAAB, ABBA, ABAB, AABB (each letter stands for a packet of the corresponding session). Show that all states have equal steady-state probability and that the steady-state throughputs of sessions A and B in packets/sec are 0.4 and 0.6, respectively.

b) Now suppose that transmissions on link L are scheduled on a round robin basis. Between successive packet transmissions for session B, session A transmits one packet, if it has one waiting. Draw the state transition diagram of a five-state Markov chain which models the queue of L. Solve for the equilibrium state probabilities. What are the steady-state throughputs of sessions A and B?

c) Finally, suppose that session A has nonpreemptive priority over session B at link L. Between successive packet transmissions for session B, session A transmits as many packets as it can. Session B only regains control of the link when A has nothing to send. Draw the state transition diagram of a five-state Markov chain which models L and its queue. Solve for the equilibrium state probabilities. What are the steady-state throughputs of sessions A and B?

6.11 Consider a window between an external source and the node by which that source is connected to the subnet. The source generates packets according to a Poisson process of rate λ. Each generated packet is accepted by the node if a permit is available. If no permit is available, the packet is discarded, never to return. When a packet from the given source enters the DLC unit of an outgoing link at the node, a new permit is instantaneously sent back to the source. The source initially has two permits and the window size is 2. Assume that the other traffic at the node imposes a random delay from the time a packet is accepted at the node to the time it enters the DLC unit. Specifically, assume that in any arbitrarily small interval δ, there is a probability $\mu\delta$ that a waiting packet from the source (or the first of two waiting packets) will enter the DLC; this event is independent of everything else.

a) Construct a Markov chain for the number of permits at the source.

b) Find the probability that a packet generated by the source is discarded.

c) Explain whether the probability in (b) would increase or decrease if the propagation and transmission delay from source to node and the reverse were taken into account.

d) Suppose that a buffer of size k is provided at the source to save packets for which no permit is available; when a permit is received, one of the buffered packets is instantly sent to the network node. Find the new Markov chain describing the system, and find the probability that a generated packet finds the buffer full.

6.12 Consider a network with end-to-end window flow control applied to each virtual circuit. Assume that the data link control operates perfectly, and that packets are never thrown away inside the network; thus, packets always arrive at the destination in the order sent, and all packets eventually arrive.

a) Suppose the destination sends permits in packets returning to the source; if no return packet is available for some time-out period, a special permit packet is sent back to the source. These permits consist of the number modulo m of the next packet awaited by the destination. What is the restriction on the window size W in terms of the modulus m? Why?

b) Suppose next that the permits contain the number modulo m of *each* of the packets in the order received since the last acknowledgement was sent. Does this change your answer to part (a)? Explain.

c) Is it permissible for the source to change the window size W without prior agreement from the destination? Explain.

d) How can the destination reduce the effective window size below the window size used by the source without prior agreement from the source (by effective window size we mean the maximum number of packets for the source-destination pair that can be in the network at one time)?

6.13 Consider a node-by-node window scheme. In an effort to reduce the required buffering, the designers associated the windows with destinations rather than with virtual circuits. Assume that all virtual circuit paths to a given destination j use a directed spanning tree so that each node $i \neq j$ has only one outgoing arc for traffic to that destination. Assume that each node $i \neq j$ originally has permits for two packets for j that can be sent over the outgoing arc to j. Each time that node i releases a packet for j into its DLC unit on the outgoing link, it sends a new permit for one packet back over the incoming link over which that packet arrived. If the packet arrived from a source connected to i, the permit is sent back to the source (each source also originally has two permits for the given destination).

a) How many packet buffers does node i have to reserve for packets going to destination j to guarantee that every arriving packet for j can be placed in a buffer?

b) What are the pros and cons of this scheme compared with the conventional node-by-node window scheme on a virtual circuit basis?

6.14 Consider a network using node-by-node windows for each virtual circuit. Describe a strategy for sending and reclaiming permits so that buffer overflow never occurs regardless of how much memory is available for packet storage at each node, and of how many virtual circuits are using each link. *Hint:* You need to worry about too many permits becoming available to the transmitting node of each link.

6.15 Describe how the gradient projection method for optimal routing can be used to solve in distributed fashion the combined optimal routing and flow control problem of subsection 6.4.1.

6.16 *Alternative formulation of max-min fair flow control ([Jaf81] and [GaB84]).* Consider the max-min flow control problem where the rate vector r is required, in addition, to satisfy $r_p \leq (C_a - F_a)q_a$, for each session p, and arc a crossed by session p. Here, q_a are given positive scalars.

(a) Show that a max-min fair rate vector exists and is unique, and give an algorithm for calculating it.

(b) Show that for a max-min fair rate vector, the utilization factor $\rho_a =$

F_a/C_a of each arc a satisfies

$$\rho_a \leq \frac{n_a q_a}{1 + n_a q_a}$$

where n_a is the number of sessions crossing arc a.

REFERENCES

[AaM81] Aashtiani, H. Z., and Magnanti, T. L. 1981. Equilibria on a Congested Transportation Network. *SIAM J. Algeb Disc Math.* 2:213–226.

[Abr70] Abramson, N. 1970. The Aloha System—Another Alternative for Computer Communications. *Proc. Fall Joint Comput Conf, AFIPS Conf.* 37.

[Ahu79] Ahuja V. 1979. Routing and Flow Control in Systems Network Architecture. *IBM Syst J.* 18:298–314.

[AkK77] Akinc, U., and Khumawala, B. 1977. An Efficient Branch and Bound Algorithm for the Capacitated Warehouse Location Problem. *Manage Sci.* 23:585–594.

[Ald86] Aldous, D. 1986. *Ultimate Instability of Exponential Back-off Protocol for Acknowledgement-Based Transmission Control of Random Access Communication Channels.* Berkeley, CA: University of California, Dept. of Statistics.

[AlM76] Alcouffe, A., and Muratet, G. 1976. Optimum Location of Plants. *Manage Sci.* 23:267–274.

[Alt86] Altes, T. 1986. *Minimum Delay Packet Length* (Report LIDS-TH-1602). Cambridge, MA: MIT Laboratory for Information and Decision Systems.

[AnP86] Anagnostou, M., and Protonotarios, E. 1986. Performance Analysis of the Selective Repeat ARQ Protocol. *IEEE Trans Commun.* COM-34, 2:127–135.

[Ari84] Arikan, E. 1984. Some Complexity Results About Packet Radio Networks. *IEEE Trans Inf Theory.* 681–685.

[Atk80] Atkins, J. D. 1980. Path Control: The Transport Network of SNA. *IEEE Trans Commun.* COM-28:527–538.

[Bal79] Ball, M. O. 1979. Computing Network Reliability. *Oper Res.* 27:823–838.

[BaP83] Ball, M. O., and Provan, J. S. 1983. Calculating Bounds on Reachability and Connectedness in Stochastic Networks. *Networks.* 13:253–278.

[BaS83] Baratz, L., and Segall, A. 1983. *Reliable Link Initialization Procedures* (Report RC10032). IBM Thomas J. Watson Research Center.

[BCM75] Basket, F., Chandy, K. M., Muntz, R. R., and Palacios, F. G. 1975. Open, Closed, and Mixed Networks of Queues with Different Classes of Customers. *J Assoc Comput Mach.* 22:248–260.

[BeG82] Bertsekas, D.P., and Gafni, E. 1982. Projection Methods for Variational Inequalities with Application to the Traffic Assignment Problem. In D. C. Sorensen and R. J.-B. Wets (Eds.), *Math Prog Study* (Vol. 17, pp. 139–159). Amsterdam: North-Holland.

[BeG83] Bertsekas, D. P., and Gafni, E. M. 1983. Projected Newton Methods and Optimization of Multicommodity Flows. *IEEE Trans Auto Contr.* AC-28, 12:1090–1096.

[Ben86] Benjamin, R. 1986. Analysis of Connection Survivability in Complex Strategic Communications Networks. *IEEE J Select Areas Commun.* SAC-4:243–253.

[Ber76] Bertsekas, D. P. 1976. On the Goldstein-Levitin-Polyak Gradient Projection Method. *IEEE Trans Auto Contr.* AC-21:174–184.

[Ber79a] Bertsekas, D. P. 1979. Algorithms for Nonlinear Multicommodity Network Flow Problems. In A. Bensoussan and J. L. Lions (Eds.), *International Symposium on Systems Optimization and Analysis* (pp. 210–224). New York: Springer-Verlag.

[Ber79b] Bertsekas, D. P. 1979. Dynamic Models of Shortest Path Routing Algorithms for Communication Networks with Multiple Destinations. *Proc 1979 IEEE Conf Dec Contr* (Ft. Lauderdale, FL): 127–133.

[Ber80] Bertsekas, D. P. 1980, October. A Class of Optimal Routing Algorithms for Communication Networks. *Proc 5th Int Conf Comput Commun* (Atlanta, GA). 71–76.

[Ber82a] Bertsekas, D. P. 1982. Distributed Dynamic Programming. *IEEE Trans Auto Contr.* AC-27:610–616.

[Ber82b] Bertsekas, D. P. 1982. Dynamic Behavior of Shortest Path Routing Algorithms for Communication Networks. *IEEE Trans Auto Contr.* AC-27:60–74.

[Ber82c] Bertsekas, D. P. 1982. Projected Newton Methods for Optimization Problems with Simple Constraints. *SIAM J Contr Optim.* 20:221–246.

[Ber82d] Bertsekas, D. P. 1982. *Constrained Optimization and Lagrange Multiplier Methods.* New York: Academic Press.

[Ber83] Bertsekas, D. P. 1983. Distributed Asynchronous Computation of Fixed Points. *Math Prog.* 27:107–120.

[Ber85] Bertsekas, D. P. 1985. A Unified Framework for Primal-Dual Methods in Minimum Cost Network Flow Problems. *Math Prog.* 32:125–145.

[Ber87] Bertsekas, D. P. 1987. *Dynamic Programming: Deterministic and Stochastic Models.* Englewood Cliffs, NJ: Prentice-Hall.

[BGG84] Bertsekas, D. P., Gafni, E. M., and Gallager, R. G. 1984. Second Derivative Algorithms for Minimum Delay Distributed Routing in Networks. *IEEE Trans Commun.* COM-32:911–919.

[BGS80] Bially, T., Gold, B., Seneff, S. 1980. A Technique for Adaptive Voice Flow Control in Integrated Packet Networks. *IEEE Trans Commun.* COM-28:325–333.

[BGT84] Bertsekas, D. P., Gendron, R., and Tsai, W. K. 1984. *Implementation of an Optimal Multicommodity Network Flow Algorithm Based on Gradient Projection and a Path Flow Formulation* (Report LIDS-P-1364. Cambridge, MA: MIT Laboratory for Information and Decision Systems.

[BGV79] Bertsekas D. P., Gafni, E. M., and Vastola, K. S. 1979. Validation of Algorithms for Optimal Routing of Flow in Networks. *Proc 1978 IEEE Conf Dec Contr* (San Diego).

[Bin75] Binder, R. 1975. A Dynamic Packet Switching System for Satellite Broadcast Channels. *Proc ICC.* 41.1–41.5.

[Bla83] Blahut, R. E. 1983. *Theory and Practice of Error Control Codes.* Reading, MA: Addison-Wesley.

[BoF77] Boorstyn, R. R., and Frank, H. 1977. Large-Scale Network Topological Optimization. *IEEE Trans Commun.* COM-25:29–47.

[BoS82] Bochmann, G. V., and Sunshine, C. A. 1982. A Survey of Formal Methods. In P. Green (Ed.), *Computer Network Architecture.* New York: Plenum.

[BrB80] Bruell, S. C., and Balbo, G., 1980. *Computational Algorithms for Closed Queueing Networks.* New York: Elsevier North Holland.

[BTA84] Bertsekas, D. P., Tsitsiklis, J. N., and Athans, M. 1984. *Convergence Theories of Distributed Iterative Processes* (Report LIDS-P1412). Cambridge, MA: MIT Laboratory for Information and Decision Systems.

[Bux81] Bux, W. 1981, October. Local Area Networks: A Performance Comparison. *IEEE Trans Commun.* Com. 29: 1465–1473.

[CaC68] Cannon, M. D., and Cullum, C. D. 1968. A Tight Upper Bound on the Rate of Convergence of the Frank-Wolfe Algorithm. *SIAM J Contr Optim.* 6:509–516.

[CaH75] Carleial, A. B., and Hellman, M. E. 1975. Bistable Behavior of Slotted Aloha-Type Systems. *IEEE Trans Commun.* Com. 23: 401–410.

[Cap77] Capetanakis, J. I. 1977. *The Multiple Access Broadcast Channel: Protocol and Capacity Considerations.* PhD Diss., MIT, Dept. of Electrical Engineering and Computer Science. Also in *IEEE Trans Info Theory.* September 1979, IT-25:505–515.

[Car80] Carlson, D. E. 1980. Bit-Oriented Data Link Control Procedures. *IEEE Trans Commun.* 455–467. (Also in [Gre82].)

[CFL79] Chlamtac, Franta, W., and Levin, K. D. 1979. BRAM: The Broadcast Recognizing Access Method. *IEEE Trans Commun.* COM-27:1183–1190.

[CFN77] Cornuejols, G., Fisher, M. L., and Nemhauser, G. L. 1977. Location of Bank Accounts to Optimize Float: An Analytic Study of Exact and Approximate Algorithms. *Manage Sci.* 23:789–810.

[CHM82] Chandy, K. M., and Misra, J. 1982. Distributed Computation on Graphs. *Commun ACM.* 25:833–837.

[ClC81] Clark, G. C., and Cain, J. B. 1981. *Error Correction Coding for Digital Communication.* New York: Plenum.

[Coo70] Cooper, R. B. 1970. Queues Served in Cyclic Order: Waiting Times. *Bell Syst Tech J.* 49:399–413.

[Coo81] Cooper, R. B. 1981. *Introduction to Queueing Theory* (2d ed.). New York: Elsevier North Holland.

[CPR78] Clark, D. D., Pogran, K. T., and Reed, D. P. 1978. An Introduction to Local Area Networks, *Proc IEEE.* 1497–1517.

[CRW73] Crowther, W., Rettburg, R., Walden, D., Ornstein, S., and Heart, F. 1973. A System for Broadcast Communication: Reservation Aloha. *Proc 6th Hawaii Int Conf Syst Sc.* 371–374.

[Daf71] Dafermos, S. C. 1971. An Extended Traffic Assignment Model with Applications to Two-Way Traffic. *Trans Sci.* 5:366–389.

[Daf80] Dafermos, S. C. 1980. Traffic Equilibrium and Variational Inequalities. *Trans Sci.* 14:42–54.

[Dan63] Dantzig, G. B. 1963. *Linear Programming and Extensions.* Princeton, NJ: Princeton University Press.

[DeK81] Dembo, R. S., and Klincewicz, J. G. 1981. A Scaled Reduced Gradient Algorithm for Network Flow Problems with Convex Separable Costs. *Math Prog Studies.* 15:125–147.

[DGK79] Dial, R., Glover, F., Karney, D., and Klingman, D. 1979. A Computational Analysis of Alternative Algorithms and Labeling Techniques for Finding Shortest Path Trees. *Networks.* 9:215–248.

[DiK85] Disney, R. L., and Konig, D. 1985. Queueing Networks: A Survey of Their Random Processes. *SIAM Rev.* 27:335–403.

[Dun79] Dunn, J. C. 1979. Rates of Convergence of Conditional Gradient Algorithms Near Singular and Nonsingular Extremals. *SIAM J Contr Optim.* 17:187–211.

[Eis79] Eisenberg, M. 1979. Two Queues with Alternating Service. *SIAM J Appl Math.* 20:287–303.

[EpB81] Ephremides, A., and Baker, D. J. 1981. The Architectural Organization of a Mobile Radio Network Via a Distributed Algorithm. *IEEE Trans Commun.* COM-29:1694–1701.

[Eph86] Ephremides, A. 1986. The Routing Problem in Computer Networks. In I. F. Blake and H. V. Poor (Eds.), *Communication and Networks* (pp. 299–324). New York: Springer-Verlag.

[Erl78] Erlenkotter, D. 1978. A Dual-Based Procedure for Uncapacitated Facility Location. *Oper Res.* 26:992–1009.

[EsW66] Essau, L. R., and Williams, K. C. 1966. On Teleprocessing System Design. *IBM Syst J.* 5:142–147.

[Eve75] Even S. 1975. An Algorithm for Determining Whether the Connectivity of a Graph is at Least k. *SIAM J Comput.* 4:393–396.

[EVW80] Ephremides, A., Varaiya, P., and Walrand, J. 1980. A Simple Dynamic Routing Problem. *IEEE Trans Auto Contr.* AC-25,4:690–693.

[FaL72] Farber, D. J., and Larson, K. C. 1972. *The System Architecture of the Distributed Computer System—The Communications System*. Paper presented at the Symposium on Computer Networks, Polytechnic Institute of Brooklyn, New York.

[FaN69] Farmer, W. D., and Newhall, E. E. 1969. An Experimental Distributed Switching System to Handle Bursty Computer Traffic. *Proc ACM Symp Probl Opt Data Commun Syst.* 1–33.

[FeA85] Ferguson, M. J., and Aminetzah, Y. J. 1985. Exact Results for Nonsymmetric Token Ring Systems. *IEEE Trans Commun.* COM-33:223–231.

[Fer75] Ferguson, M. J. 1975. A Study of Unslotted Aloha with Arbitrary Message Lengths. *Proc. 4th Data Commun Symp* (Quebec, PQ, Canada). 5.20–5.25

[FGK73] Fratta, L., Gerla, M., and Kleinrock, L. 1973. The Flow Deviation Method: An Approach to Store-and-Forward Communication Network Design. *Networks.* 3:97–133.

[FiT84] Fine, M., and Tobagi, F. A. 1984. Demand Assignment Multiple Access Schemes in Broadcast Bus Local Area Networks. *IEEE Trans. Comput.* 1130–1159.

[Fin79] Finn, S. G. 1979. Resynch Procedures and a Fail-Safe Network Protocol. *IEEE Trans Commun.* COM-27:840–845.

[FlN74] Florian, M., and Nguyen, S. 1974. A Method for Computing Network Equilibrium with Elastic Demand. *Transport Sci.* 8:321–332.

[FoF62] Ford, L. R., Jr., and Fulkerson, D. R. 1962. *Flows in Networks*. Princeton, NJ: Princeton University Press.

[FoS78] Foschini, G. J., and Salz, J. 1978. A Basic Dynamic Routing Problem and Diffusion. *IEEE Trans Commun.* COM-26, 3:320–327.

[FrW56] Frank, M., and Wolfe, P. 1956. An Algorithm for Quadratic Programming. *Naval Res Logist Quart.* 3:149–154.

[FuC85] Fuhrmann, S. W., and Cooper, R. B. 1985. Stochastic Decompositions in the M/G/1 Queue with Generalized Vacations. *Oper Res.* 33:1117–1129.

[GaB81] Gafni, E. M., and Bertsekas, D. P. 1981. Distributed Routing Algorithms for Networks with Frequently Changing Topology. *IEEE Trans Commun.* COM-29:11–18.

[GaB83] Gafni, E. M., and Bertsekas, D. P. 1983. Asymptotic Optimality of Shortest Path Routing (Report LIDS-P-1307).Cambridge, MA: MIT Laboratory for Information and Decision Systems. (Forthcoming in *IEEE Trans Inf Theory*.)

[GaB84a] Gafni, E. M., and Bertsekas, D. P. 1984. Two-Metric Projection Methods for Constrained Optimization. *SIAM J Contr Optim.* 22, 6:936–964.

[GaB84b] Gafni, E. M., and Bertsekas, D. P. 1984. Dynamic Control of Session Input Rates in Communication Networks. *IEEE Trans Auto Contr.* AC-29:1009–1016.

[Gaf79] Gafni, E. M. 1979. *Convergence of a Routing Algorithm.* MS thesis, University of Illinois, Dept. of Electrical Engineering, Urbana, IL.

[Gaf82] Gafni, E. M. 1982. *The Integration of Routing and Flow Control for Voice and Data in Integrated Packet Networks.* PhD thesis, MIT, Dept. of Electrical Engineering and Computer Science, Cambridge, MA.

[GaG80] Gallager, R. G., and Golestaani, S. J. 1980. Flow Control and Routing Algorithms for Data Networks. *Proc 5th Intern Conf Commun.* 779–784.

[GaH83] Gavish, B., and Hantler, S. 1983. An Algorithm for Optimal Route Selection in SNA Networks. *IEEE Trans Commun.* COM-31:1154–1161.

[Gal68] Gallager, R. G. 1968. *Information Theory and Reliable Communications.* New York: John Wiley & Sons.

[Gal77] Gallager, R. G. 1977. A Minimum Delay Routing Algorithm Using Distributed Computation. *IEEE Trans Commun.* COM-23:73–85.

[Gal78] Gallager, R. G. 1978. Conflict Resolution in Random Access Broadcast Networks. *Proc. AFOSR Workshop Commun Theory Appl* (Provincetown, MA). 74–76.

[Gal81] Gallager, R. G. 1981. Applications of Information Theory for Data Communication Networks. In J. Skwirzynski (Ed.), *New Concepts in Multi-user Communication.* (Series E, No. 43), NATO Advanced Study Institutes (Sijthoff and Noordhoff).

[Gav85] Gavish, B. 1985. Augmented Lagrangean Based Algorithms for Centralized Network Design. *IEEE Trans Commun.* COM-33:1247–1257.

[GeK77] Gerla, M., and Kleinrock L. 1977. On the Topological Design of Distributed Computer Networks. *IEEE Trans Commun.* COM-25:48–60.

[GeK80] Gerla, M., and Kleinrock, L. 1980. Flow Control: A Comparative Survey. *IEEE Trans Commun.* COM-28:553–574.

[GeP85] Georgiadis, L., and Papantoni-Kazakos, P. 1985. *A 0.487 Throughput Limited Sensing Algorithm.* Storrs, Ct: University of Connecticut.

[GeY82] George, F. D., and Young, G. E. 1982. SNA Flow Control: Architecture and Implementation. *IBM Syst J.* 21:179–210.

[GGM85] Goodman, J., Greenberg, A. G., Madras, N., and March, P. 1985. On the Stability of Ethernet. *Proc. 17th Ann HCM Symp Theory Comput.*

[GHS83] Gallager, R. G., Humblet, P. A., and Spira, P. M. 1983. A Distributed Algorithm for Minimum-Weight Spanning Trees. *ACM Trans Prog Lang Syst.* 5:66–77.

[Go180] Golestaani, S.J.1980. *A Unified Theory of Flow Control and Routing on Data Communication Networks.* PhD thesis, MIT, Dept. of Electrical Engineering and Computer Science, Cambridge, MA.

[Gop85] Gopal, I. S., 1985. Prevention of Store-and-Forward Deadlock in Computer Networks. *IEEE Trans Commun*. COM-33:1258–1264.

[Gra72] Gray, J. P. 1972. Line Control Procedures. *Proc IEEE*. 1301–1312.

[GrB83] Grover, G. A., and Bharath-Kumar, K. 1983. Windows in the Sky—Flow Control in SNA Networks with Satellite Links. *IBM Syst J*. 22:451–463.

[Gre82] Green, P. E. 1982. *Computer Network Architectures and Protocols*. New York: Plenum.

[Gre84] Green, P. E. 1984. Computer Communications: Milestones and Prophecies. *IEEE Commun*. 49–63.

[Gre86] Green, P. E. 1986. Protocol Conversion. *IEEE Trans Commun*. 257–268.

[GrH85] Gross, D., and Harris, C. M. 1985. *Fundamentals of Queueing Theory* (2d ed.). New York: John Wiley & Sons.

[Gun81] Gunther, K. D. 1981. Prevention of Deadlocks in Packet-Switched Data Transport Systems. *IEEE Trans Commun*. COM-29:512–524.

[HaG86] Hahne, E. L., an Gallager, R. G. 1986. *Round Robin Scheduling for Fair Flow Control in Data Communication Networks* (Report LIDS-P-1537). Cambridge, MA: MIT Laboratory for Information and Decisions Systems.

[Hah86] Hahne, E. 1986, forthcoming. PhD thesis, MIT, Dept. of Electrical Engineering and Computer Science, Cambridge, MA.

[Haj82] Hajek, B. 1982. Birth-and-Death Processes with Phases and General Boundaries. *J Appl Prob*. 19:488–499.

[Haj85] Hajek, B. 1985. *Cooling Schedules for Optimal Annealing* (preprint). Urbana-Champaign, IL: University of Illinois, Dept. of Electrical Engineering.

[HaL82] Hajek, B., and van Loon, T. 1982. Decentralized Dynamic Control of a Multiaccess Broadcast Channel. *IEEE Trans Auto Contr*. AC-27:559–569.

[HaO84] Hajek, B., and Ogier, R. G. 1984. Optimal Dynamic Routing in Communication Networks with Continuous Traffic. *Networks*. 14:457–487.

[Has72] Hashida, O. 1972. Analysis of Multiqueue. *Rev. Elect Commun. Lab*. 20:189–199.

[Hay76] Hayes, J. 1976. An Adaptive Technique for Local Distribution (Bell Telephone Laboratory Technical Memo TM-76-3116-1. (Also in *IEEE Trans Commun* (1978). COM-26:1178–1186.)

[Hay81] Hayden, H. 1981. *Voice Flow Control in Integrated Packet Networks* (Report LIDS-TH-1152). Cambridge, MA: MIT Laboratory for Information and Decision Systems.

[Hay84] Hayes, J. F. 1984. *Modeling and Analysis of Computer Communications Networks*. New York: Plenum.

[HeS82] Heyman, D. P., and Sobel, M. J. 1982. *Stochastic Models in Operations Research, Vol. 1*. New York: McGraw-Hill.

[HlG81] Hluchyj, M. G., and Gallager, R. G. 1981. Multiaccess of a Slotted Channel by Finitely

Many Users. *Proc Nat Telecommun Conf* (New Orleans, LA). (Also LIDS Report P-1131, MIT, Cambridge, MA, August 1981.)

[HSS86] Humblet, P. A., Soloway, S. R., and Steinka, B. 1986. *Algorithms for Data Communication Networks—Part 2*. Codex Corp.

[HuB85] Huang, J.-C., and Berger, T. 1985. Delay Analysis of the Modified 0.487 Contention Resolution Algorithm. *IEEE Trans Inf Theory*. IT-31:264–273.

[HuM80] Humblet, P. A., and Mosely, J. 1980. Efficient Accessing of a Multiaccess Channel. *Proc 19th Conf Dec Contr* (Albuquerque, NM).

[Hum78] Humblet, P. A. 1978. *Source Coding for Communication Concentrators* (Report ESL-R-798). Cambridge, MA: MIT.

[Hum83] Humblet, P. A. 1983. A Distributed Algorithm for Minimum Weight Directed Spanning Trees. *IEEE Trans Commun*. COM-31:756–762.

[Hum86] Humblet, P. A. 1986. On the Throughput of Channel Access Algorithms with Limited Sensing. *IEEE Trans Commun*. COM-34:345–347.

[HuS86] Humblet, P. A., and Soloway, S. R. 1986. *Algorithms for Data Communication Networks—Part I*. Codex Corp.

[Ibe81] Ibe, O. C. 1981. *Flow Control and Routing in an Integrated Voice and Data Communication Network*. PhD thesis, MIT, Dept. of Electrical Engineering and Computer Science, Cambridge, MA.

[IEE86] *IEEE Journal on Selected Areas in Communications, Special Issue on Network Performance Evaluation*. 1986, September. SAC-4, 6.

[Jac57] Jackson, J. R. 1957. Networks of Waiting Lines. *Oper Res*. 5:518–521.

[Jaf81] Jaffe, J. M. 1981. A Decentralized "Optimal" Multiple-User Flow Control Algorithm. *IEEE Trans Commun*. COM-29:954–962.

[Jai68] Jaiswal, N. K. 1968. *Priority Queues*. New York: Academic Press.

[JBH78] Jacobs, I. M., Binder, R., and Hoversten, E. V. 1978. General Purpose Packet Satellite Networks, *Proc. IEEE*. 1448–1468.

[Kap79] Kaplan, M. 1979. A Sufficient Condition for Nonergodicity of a Markov Chain. *IEEE Trans Inf Theory*. IT-25:470–471.

[KaT75] Karlin, S., and Taylor, H. M. 1975. *A First Course in Stochastic Processes*. New York: Academic Press.

[KeB83] Kershenbaum, A., and Boorstyn, R. R. 1983. Centralized Teleprocessing Network Design. *Networks*. 13:279–293.

[KeH63] Keuhn, A. A., and Hamburger, M. J. 1963. A Heuristic Program for Locating Warehouses. *Manage Sci*. 9:643–666.

[Kei79] Keilson, J. 1979. *Markov-Chain Models—Rarity and Exponentiality*. New York; Springer-Verlag.

[Kel79] Kelly, F. P. 1979. *Reversibility and Stochastic Networks*. New York: John Wiley & Sons.

[Kel85] Kelly, F. P. 1985. Stochastic Models of Computer Communication Systems. *J Royal Stat Soc.* B, 47, 1

[KGB78] Kahn, R. E., Gronemeyer, S. A., Burchfiel, J., and Kungelman, R. C. 1978. Advances in Packet Radio Technology. *Proc IEEE.* 1468–1496.

[KGV83] Kirkpatrick, S., Gelatt, C. D., Jr., and Vecchi, M. P. 1983. Optimization by Simulated Annealing. *Science.* 220:671–680.

[Khu72] Khumawala, B. M. 1972. An Efficient Branch and Bound Algorithm for the Warehouse Location Problem. *Manage Sci.* 18:B 718–B731.

[Kle64] Kleinrock, L. 1964. *Communication Nets: Stochastic Message Flow and Delay.* New York; McGraw-Hill.

[Kle69] Kleitman, D. 1969. Methods for Investigating the Connectivity of Large Graphs. *IEEE Trans Circ. Theory.* CT-16:232-233

[Kle75] Kleinrock, L. 1975. *Queueing Systems, Vol. 1.* New York: John Wiley & Sons.

[Kle76] Kleinrock, L. 1976. *Queueing Systems, Vol. 2.* New York: John Wiley & Sons.

[Kle86] Klessig, R. W. 1986. Overview of Metropolitan Area Networks. *IEEE Commun.* 9–15.

[KlL75] Kleinrock, L., and Lam, S. 1975. Packet Switching in Multiaccess Broadcast Channel: Performance Evaluation. *IEEE Trans Commun.* 410–423.

[KlO77] Kleinrock, L., and Opterbeck, H. 1977. Throughput in the ARPANET—Protocols and Measurements. *IEEE Trans Commun.* COM-25:95–104.

[KlS80] Kleinrock, L., and Scholl. 1980. Packet Switching in Radio Channels: New Conflict Free Multiple Access Schemes. *IEEE Trans Commun.* 1015–1029.

[KlT75] Kleinrock, L., and Tobagi, F. A. 1975. Packet Switching in Radio Channels: Part 1: CSMA Modes and Their Throughput-Delay Characteristics. *IEEE Trans Commun.* COM-23:1400–1416.

[KoM74] Konheim, A. G., and Meister, B. 1974. Waiting Lines and Times in a System with Polling. *J ACM.* 21:470–490.

[KSK76] Kemeny, J. G., Snell, J. L., and Knapp, A. W. 1976. *Denumerable Markov Chains.* New York: Springer-Verlag.

[Kue79] Kuehn, P. J. 1979. Multiqueue Systems with Nonexhaustive Cyclic Service. *Bell Syst Tech J.* 58:671–698.

[KuR82] Kummerle, K., and Reiser, M. 1982. Local Area Networks—An Overview. *J. Telecommun Netw.* 1, 4.

[LaH84] Lanphongpanich, S., and Hearn, D. 1984. Simplicial Decomposition of the Asymmetric Traffic Assignment Problems. *Trans Res.* 18B:123–133.

[LaK75] Lam, S., and Kleinrock, L. 1975. Packet Switching in a Multiaccess Broadcast Channel: Dynamic Control Procedures. *IEEE Trans Commun.* COM-23:891–904.

[LaL86] Lam, Y. F., and Li, V. O. K. 1986. An Improved Algorithm for Performance Analysis of Networks with Unreliable Components. *IEEE Trans Commun.* COM-34:496–497.

[Lam80] Lam, S. 1980. A Carrier Sense Multiple Access Protocol for Local Networks. *Computer Networks.* 4:21–32.

[Las70] Lasdon, L. S. 1970. *Optimization Theory for Large Systems*. New York: Macmillan.

[Law76] Lawler, E. L. 1976. *Combinatorial Optimization: Networks and Matroids*. New York: Holt, Rinehart and Winston.

[Lei80] Leiner, B. M. 1980. A Simple Model for Computation of Packet Radio Network Communication Performance. *IEEE Trans Commun*. COM-28:2020–2023.

[LiF82] Limb, J. O., and Flores, C. 1982. Description of Fasnet, Or Unidirectional Local Area Communications Network. *Bell Syst Tech J*.

[Lim84] Limb, J. O. 1984. Performance of Local Area Networks at High Speed. *IEEE Commun*. 41–45.

[LiS84] Li, V. O. K., and Silvester, J. A. 1984. Performance Analysis of Networks with Unreliable Components. *IEEE Trans Commun*.COM-32:1105–1110.

[Lit61] Little, J. 1961. A Proof of the Queueing Formula L = W. *Oper Res. J*. 18:172–174.

[Lue84] Luenberger, D. G. 1984. *Linear and Nonlinear Programming*. Reading MA: Addison-Wesley.

[MaF85] Mathys, P., and Flajolet, P. 1985. Q-ary Collision Resolution Algorithms in Random-Access Systems with Free or Blocked Channel Access. *IEEE Trans Inf Theory*. IT-31:217–243.

[Mal86] Malis, A. G. 1986. *PSN End-to-End Functional Specification* (RFC 979). BBN Communications Corp., Network Working Group.

[MaN85] Maxemchuck, N. F., and Netravali, A. N. 1985. Voices and Data on a CATV Network. *IEEE J Select Areas Commun*. SAC-3:300–311.

[Mas80] Massey, J. L. 1980. *Collision-Resolution Algorithms and Random Access Communications*. (Report UCLA-ENG-8016). Los Angeles: University of California.

[McS77] McGregor, P. V., and Shen, D. 1977. Network Design: An Algorithm for the Access Facility Location Problem. *IEEE Trans Commun*. COM-25:61–73.

[McW77] McQuillan, J. M., and Walden, D. C. 1977. The ARPANET Design Decisions. *Networks*. 1.

[MeB76] Metcalf, R. M., Boggs, D. R. 1976. Ethernet: Distributed Packet Switching for Local Computer Networks. *Commun ACN*. 395–404.

[Met73] Metcalfe, R. 1973. *Steady State Analysis of a Slotted and Controlled Aloha System with Blocking*. Paper presented at 6th Hawaii Conference on System Science (Honolulu).

[Mik79] Mikhailov, V. A. 1979. *Methods of Random Multiple Access*. Candidate Engineering thesis, Moscow Institute of Physics and Technology.

[MiT81] Mikhailov, V. A., and Tsybakov, B. S. 1981. Upper Bound for the Capacity of a Random Multiple Access System. *Prob. Peredachi Inf* (USSR). 17:90–95.

[MoH85] Mosely, J., and Humblet, P. A. 1985. A Class of Efficient Contention Resolution Algorithms for Multiple Access Channels. *IEEE Trans Commun*.COM-33:145–151.

[MoS82] Moss, F. H., and Segall, A. 1982. An Optimal Control Approach to Dynamic Routing in Networks. *IEEE Trans Auto Contr*. AC-27:329–339.

[MoS86] Monma, C. L., and Sheng, D. D. 1986. Backbone Network Design and Performance Analysis: A Methodology for Packet Switching Networks. *IEEE J Select Areas Commun*. SAC-4:946–965.

[Mos84] Mosely, J. 1984. *Asynchronous Distributed Flow Control Algorithms*. PhD thesis, MIT, Dept. of Electrical Engineering and Computer Science.

[MRR78] ,McQuillan, J. M., Richer, I., Rosen, E. C., and Bertsekas, D. P. 1978. *ARPANET Routing Algorithm Improvements, Second Semiannual Report* (Prepared for ARPA and DCA). Bolt, Beranek, and Newman, Inc.

[MRR80] McQuillan, J. M., Richer, I., and Rosen, E. C. 1980. The New Routing Algorithm for the ARPANET. *IEEE Trans Commun*. COM-28:711–719.

[Neu81] Neuts, M. F. 1981. *Matrix-Geometric Solutions in Stochastic Models—An Algorithmic Approach*. Baltimore, MD: The Johns Hopkins University Press.

[NiS74] Nisnevitch, L., and Strasbourger, E. 1974. Decentralized Priority in Data Communication. *Proc 2nd Ann Symp Comput Arch*.

[NoT78] Nomura, M., and Tsukamoto, K. 1978. Traffic Analysis of Polling Systems. *Trans Inst Elect Commun Eng* (Japan). J61-B:600–607.

[Nyq28] Nyquist, H. 1928. Certain Topics in Telegraph Transmission Theory. *Trans AIEE*. 47:617–644.

[Pak69] Pakes, A. G. 1969. Some Conditions for Ergodicity and Recurrence of Markov Chains. *Op Res*. 17:1059–1061.

[Pap74] Pape, U. 1974. Implementation and Efficiency of Moore-Algorithms for the Shortest Route Problem. *Math Prog*. 7:212–222.

[PaS82] Papadimitriou, C. H., and Steiglitz, K. 1982. *Combinatorial Optimization: Algorithms and Complexity*. Englewood Cliffs, NJ: Prentice-Hall.

[Per83] Perlman, R. 1983. Fault-Tolerant Broadcast of Routing Information. *Computer Networks*. 7:395–405. (Also *Proc IEEE Infocom '83*, San Diego.)

[Pip81] Pippenger, N. 1981. Bounds on the Performance of Protocols for a Multiple Access Broadcast Channel. *IEEE Trans Inf Theory*. IT-27.

[PiW82] Pinedo, M., and Wolff, R. W. 1982. A Comparison Between Tandem Queues with Dependent and Independent Service Times. *Oper Res*. 30:464–479.

[Pol71] Polak, E. 1971. *Computational Methods in Optimization*. New York: Academic Press.

[PrB84] Provan, J. S., and Ball, M. O. 1984. Computing Network Reliability in Time Polynomial in the Number of Cuts. *Oper Res*. 32:516–526.

[Pro83] Proakis, J. G. 1983. *Digital Communications*. New York: McGraw-Hill.

[Qur85] Qureshi, S. 1985. Adaptive Equalization. *Proc IEEE*. 1349–1387.

[RaH76] Raubold, E., and Haenle, J. 1976. A Method of Deadlock-Free Resource Allocation and Flow Control in Packet Networks. *Proc Int Conf Comput Commun* (Toronto).

[RaW83] Ramamoorthy, C. V., and Wah, B. W. 1983. The Isomorphism of Simple File Allocation. *IEEE Trans Comput.* C-32:221–231.

[Rin76] Rinde, J. 1976. TYMNET I: An Alternative to Packet Switching. *Proc 3rd Int Conf Comput Commun.*

[Riv85] Rivest, R. L. 1985. *Network Control by Bayessian Broadcast* (Report MIT/LCS/TM-285). Cambridge, MA: MIT, Laboratory for Computer Science.

[Rob72] Roberts, L. G. 1972. *Aloha Packet System With and Without Slots and Capture.* (ASS Note 8). Stanford, CA: Stanford Research Institute, Advanced Research Projects Agency, Network Information Center.

[Roc70] Rockafellar, R. T. 1970. *Convex Analysis.* Princeton, NJ: Princeton University Press.

[Roc84] Rockafellar, R. T. 1984. *Network Flows and Monotropic Programming.* New York: John Wiley & Sons.

[Ros80] Ross, S. M. 1980. *Introduction to Probability Models.* New York: Academic Press.

[Ros83] Ross, S. M. 1983. *Stochastic Processes.* New York: John Wiley & Sons.

[Ros86] Rosberg, Z. 1986. Deterministic Routing to Buffered Channels. *IEEE Trans Commun.* COM-34:504–507.

[Ros81] Rosen, E. C. 1981. Vulnerabilities of Network Control Protocols: An Example. *Comput Commun Rev.*

[Ryb80] Rybczynski, A. 1980. X.25 Interface and End-to-End Virtual Circuit Service Characteristics. *IEEE Trans Commun.* 500-509. (Also in [Gre82].)

[SaH86] Sasaki, G., and Hajek, B. 1986 (forthcoming). Optimal Dynamic Routing in Single Commodity Networks by Iterative Methods. *IEEE Trans Commun.*

[San80] Sant, D. 1980. Throughout of Unslotted Aloha Channels with Arbitrary Packet Interarrival Time Distribution. *IEEE Trans Commun.* COM-28:1422–1425.

[SaO82] Sarachik, P. E., and Ozguner, U. 1982. On Decentralized Dynamic Routing for Congested Traffic Networks. *IEEE Trans Auto Contr.* AC-27:1233–1238.

[Sar82] Sarachik, P. E. 1982. An Effective Local Dynamic Strategy to Clear Congested Multi-destination Networks. *IEEE Trans Auto Contr.* AC-27:510–513.

[ScS80] Schwartz, M., and Stern, T. E. 1980. Routing Techniques Used in Computer Communication Networks. *IEEE Trans Commun.* COM-28:539–552.

[Seg81] Segall, A. 1981. Advances in Verifiable Fail-Safe Routing Procedures. *IEEE Trans Commun.* COM-29:491–497.

[Seg83] Segall, A. 1983. Distributed Network Protocols. *IEEE Trans Inf Theory.* IT-29:23–34.

[Sha48] Shannon, C. E. 1948. A Mathematical Theory of Communication. *Bell Syst Tech J.*

27:379–423 (Part 1), 623–656 (Part 2). (Reprinted in book form by the University of Illinois Press, Urbana, 1949.)

[Sie86] Siebert, W. M. 1986. *Circuits, Signals, and Systems*. Cambridge, MA: MIT Press; and New York: McGraw-Hill.

[SiS81] Sidi, M., and Segall, A. 1981. A Busy-Tone-Multiple-Access-Type Scheme for Packet-Radio Networks. In G. Payolk (Ed.), *Performance of Data Communication Systems and Time Applications*. (pp. 1–10). New York: North Holland.

[SoH86] Soloway, S. R., and Humblet, P. A. 1986. *On Distributed Network Protcols for Changing Topologies*. Codex Corp.

[SpM81] Sproule, D. E., and Mellor, F. 1981. Routing, Flow and Congestion Control and the Datapac Network. *IEEE Trans Commun*. COM-29:386–391.

[Sta85] Stallings, W. 1985. *Data Computer Communications*. New York: Macmillan.

[StA85] Stuck, B. W., and Arthurs, E. 1985. *A Computer Communications Network Performance Analysis Primer*. Englewood Cliffs, NJ: Prentice-Hall.

[Sti72] Stidham, S., 1972. L = W: A Discounted Analogue and a New Proof. *Oper Res*. 20:1115–1125.

[Sti74] Stidham, S., Jr. 1974. A Last Word on L = W. *Oper Res*. 22:417–421.

[StK85] Stassinopoulos, G. I., and Konstantopoulos, P. 1985. Optimal Congestion Control in Single Destination Networks. *IEEE Trans Commun*. COM-33:792–800.

[TaK85] Takagi, H., and Kleinrock, L. 1985. Throughput Delay Characteristics of Some Slotted-Aloha Packet Radio Networks. *IEEE Trans Commun*. COM-33:1200–1207.

[Tak86] Takagi, H., 1986. *Analysis of Polling Systems*. Cambridge, MA: MIT Press.

[Tan81] Tanenbaum, A. S. 1981. *Computer Networks*. Englewood Cliffs, NJ: Prentice-Hall.

[TBF83] Tobagi, F., Borgonovo, F., and Fratta, L. 1983. Express-Net: A High Performance Integrated-Services Local Area Network. *IEEE J Select Areas Commun*. SAC-1.

[ThC86] Thaker, G. H., and Cain, J. B. 1986. Interactions Between Routing and Flow Control Algorithms. *IEEE Trans Commun*. COM-34:269–277.

[Tob74] Tobagi, F. A. 1974. *Random Access Techniques for Data Transmission Over Packet Switched Radio Networks*. PhD thesis, UCLA, Computer Science Dept.

[ToK75] Tobagi, F. A., and Kleinrock, L. 1975. Packet Switching in Radio Channels: Part II—The Hidden Terminal Problem in CSMA and Busy-Tone Solution. *IEEE Trans Commun*. COM-23:1417–1433.

[ToW79] Towsley, D., and Wolf, J. K. 1979. On the Statistical Analysis of Queue Lengths and Waiting Times for Statistical Multiplexors with ARQ Retransmission Schemes. *IEEE Trans Commun* COM-27:693–702.

[TsB86] Tsitsiklis, J. N., and Bertsekas, D. P. 1986. Distributed Asynchronous Optimal Routing in Data Networks. *IEEE Trans Auto Contr*. AC-31:325–331.

[Tsi85] Tsitsiklis, J. N. 1985. *Markov Chains with Rare Transitions and Simulated Annealing* (Report LIDS-1497). Cambridge, MA: MIT Laboratory for Information and Decision Systems.

[Tsi86] Tsitsiklis, J. N. 1986. *Analysis of a Multiaccess Control Scheme* (Report LIDS-P-1534). Cambridge, MA: MIT Laboratory for Information and Decision Systems.

[TsM78] Tsybakov, B. S., and Mikhailov, V. A. 1978. Free Synchronous Packet Access in a Broadcast Channel with Feedback. *Prob Peredachi Infor* (USSR). 14, 4:32–59.

[TsM80] Tsybakov, B. S., and Mikhailov, V. A. 1980. Random Multiple Access of Packets: Part and Try Algorithm. *Prob Peredachi Infor* (USSR). 16:65–79.

[Tsy85] Tsybakov, B. S. 1985. Survey of USSR Contributions to Random Multiple-Access Communications. *IEEE Trans Inf Theory*. 143–165.

[Twe82] Tweedie, R. L. 1982. Operator-Geometric Stationary Distributions for Markov Chains with Application to Queueing Models. *Adv Appl Prob*. 14:368–391.

[Tym81] Tymes, L. 1981. Routing and Flow Control in TYMNET. *IEEE Trans Commun*. COM-29:392–398.

[Vas79] Vastola, K. S. 1979. *A Numerical Study of Two Measures of Delay for Network Routing*. MS thesis, University of Illinois, Dept. of Electrical Engineering. Urbana.

[VvP83] Vvedenskaya, N. D., and Pinsker, M. S. 1983. Non-Optimality of the Part-and-Try Algorithm. In *Abstracts of the International Workshop of Convolutional Codes, Multiuser Communication*, Sochi, USSR. 141–148.

[Wal83] Walrand, J. 1983. Probabilistic Look at Networks of Quasi-Reversible Queues. *IEEE Trans Inf Theory*. IT-29:825–831

[WaV80] Walrand, J., and Varaiya, P. 1980. Interconnections of Markov Chains and Quasi-Reversible Queueing Networks. *Stoc Proc Appl*. 10:209–219.

[Wec80] Wecker, S. 1980. The Digital Network Architecture. *IEEE Trans Commun*. COM-28:510–526.

[Wel82] Weldon, E. J. 1982. An Improved Selective Repeat ARQ Strategy. *IEEE Trans Commun*. COM-30:480–486.

[WiE80] Wieselthier, J. E., and Ephremides, A. 1980. A New Class of Protocols for Multiple Access in Satellite Networks. *IEEE Trans Auto Contr*. AC-25:865–880.

[Wol82a] Wolff, R. W. 1982. Poisson Arrivals See Time Averages. *Oper Res*. 30:223–231

[Wol82b] Wolff, R. W. 1982. Tandem Queues with Dependent Service Times in Light Traffic. *Oper Res*. 82:619–635.

[Yum81] Yum, T. P. 1981. The Design and Analysis of a Semidynamic Deterministic Routing Rule. *IEEE Trans Commun*. COM-29, 4:498–504.

[Zan69] Zangwill, W. 1969. *Nonlinear Programming: A Unified Approach*. Englewood Cliffs, NJ: Prentice-Hall.

INDEX

A

Voice network, 6
Voice-grade. *See* Communication
    channels

W

Walk in a graph, 309

Wide-area networks, 5, 25
Window flow control, 97, 119, 429–39

X

X.25 standard, 85, 99–102, 442
X.21 interface, 19–20, 99

NOTES

NOTES

NOTES

NOTES

NOTES

NOTES

NOTES

NOTES